PARLIAMENT
FUNCTIONS, PRACTICE AND PROCEDURES

AUSTRALIA
The Law Book Company
Sydney

CANADA
The Carswell Company Ltd
Toronto, Ontario

INDIA
N. M. Tripathi (Private) Ltd
Bombay

Eastern Law House (Private) Ltd
Calcutta

M.P.P. House
Bangalore

Universal Book Traders
New Dehli

ISRAEL
Steimatzky's Agency Ltd
Tel Aviv

PAKISTAN
Pakistan Law House
Karachi

PARLIAMENT
FUNCTIONS, PRACTICE AND PROCEDURES

BY

J.A.G. GRIFFITH

Emeritus Professor of Public Law
(University of London)

AND

MICHAEL RYLE

Clerk of Committees in the House of Commons

WITH

M.A.J. WHEELER-BOOTH
Clerk Assistant of the House of Lords

LONDON
SWEET & MAXWELL
1989

Published by
Sweet & Maxwell Ltd. of
100 Avenue Road, London NW3 3PF
Computerset by
M.F.K. Typesetting Ltd., Hitchin, Hertfordshire
Reproduced, printed and bound in Great Britain by
Athenæum Press Ltd, Gateshead, Tyne & Wear

Reprinted 1990
Reprinted 1997

British Library Cataloguing in Publication Data
Griffith, J.A.G. (John Aneurin Grey)
   Parliament.
   1. Great Britain. Parliament
   I. Title   II. Ryle, Michael
   328.41

   ISBN 0-421-35280-9
   ISBN 0-421-43970-X Pbk

PARLIAMENT

"The Government has had its summer recess – a delicious time for any Government. Now we have got to settle down to the dreary, nagging strain of Parliament."

From the entry for Sunday October 17, 1965, in Richard Crossman, *The Diaries of a Cabinet Minister*, Vol. 1, at p. 352.

"Constitutional theory always has and always will emerge from the hard facts of politics rather than from the text-books of professors."

From the leading article in *The Times* newspaper of December 24, 1985.

PREFACE

Sir Ivor Jennings first completed his comprehensive study of the working of Parliament in 1939[1]. A second edition was published in 1957 and reprinted in 1961, but although there have been many changes since 1957, no detailed examination of the functioning of the two Houses has subsequently been written. This work attempts to fill that gap. Our use of the same simple title as that chosen by Jennings may be seen as a tribute to our distinguished predecessor.

The authoritative description of the law of Parliament and of the procedures of the two Houses is to be found in Erskine May's *Parliamentary Practice*[2], but that work does not describe in detail how those procedures are used today. Numerous other works – many of them are included in our Bibliography – comment on the ways the Houses work, procedurally, without describing the rules themselves. This book attempts both to set out clearly all the main rules, procedures and practices and to examine how they operate.

We have also adopted a new pattern of analysis. Instead of describing the various processes – legislation, debates, Questions, financial procedures, etc., – as separate and self-contained, we have emphasised how all procedures are essentially means of achieving ends, often involving overlap and inter-relationship. We base our description on an analysis of the functions of Parliament and we seek to show how procedures operate to fulfil those functions. In particular we identify three principal participants in the parliamentary arena – the Government, the Opposition and back-bench Members on both sides – and we concentrate on describing how each of them (and to some extent pressure groups and others from outside) use procedures as tools for political purposes.

We must emphasise that we do not consider those political purposes as such. This is not a comprehensive study of the influence of Parliament on British politics in the twentieth century (although such a book needs to be written). Neither is this book an historical assessment of the working of Parliament. We are essentially concerned with describing activities within the two Houses in recent years. Most of our statistics and examples are drawn from the 1983 to 1987 Parliament, with a number of references to events or decisions in more recent months. However, when seeking to compare practices under different Governments, or by different Oppositions, we have analysed the use of procedural opportunities in earlier years. Elsewhere we have drawn attention to recent significant changes in procedures or practices.

The book falls into four Parts. In Part I we analyse the functions, powers, and membership of the modern British Parliament. In Chapter 1 we identify as central the role of Parliament as a forum where the various participating elements secure, in the words of Leo Amery, "full discussion and ventilation of all matters,"[3] and we analyse the time available for each of these participants. This role of Parliament essentially relates to the accountability of Government, and we examine this concept in some detail, as well as the processes, involving Parliament, whereby Governments are made and

---

[1] *Parliament*, Cambridge University Press, 1939
[2] Butterworths, 20th Edition 1983
[3] L S Amery, *Thoughts on the Constitution* (1947), p 12

unmade. Chapter 2 considers the nature of membership of the House of Commons and discusses the centrally important relationship of Members with those whom they represent: the communications between Parliament and the people. In Chapter 3 we describe the basic powers and privileges of Parliament on which the effective functioning of both Houses ultimately depends. And in Chapter 4 we examine how MPs organise and work through political parties. We consider in particular the growing willingness of back-benchers to dissent from the party line.

In Part II we turn to the framework for parliamentary business. Chapter 5 describes the physical setting, the Officers and the organisation of the House of Commons. Chapter 6 discusses the nature of parliamentary procedure, describes the way the business of the Commons is arranged, and sets out in detail the procedures by which its business is conducted.

Having described membership and procedures of the Commons, we turn, in Part III, to how those procedures are used in that House by the various participants. Chapter 7 looks particularly at the powers available for the Government to control business, and the use of time, on the floor of the House of Commons. Chapter 8 describes the use made by the Government of various procedures for securing the passage of legislation and for bringing other matters before the House. Chapter 9 examines the use made by the Opposition of the opportunities available to it and to other smaller parties. Chapter 10 similarly describes how back-bench Members use opportunities to initiate business. Chapter 11 describes and discusses the important development of select committees as instruments for enhancing Commons scrutiny of Government.

Part IV deals with the House of Lords. Ideally, in a book which examines the working of Parliament in a number of different ways, it would be desirable to examine the part played by the Lords in each of those areas at the same time as describing the processes in the Commons. In practice this would be extremely cumbersome and confusing. Except where matters apply equally to both Houses – in parts of Chapters 1 and 3 for example – we have devoted most of the book to describing the workings of the House of Commons. However Chapter 12, which has been contributed by M.A.J. Wheeler-Booth, seeks to describe the practice and procedures of the House of Lords as they work at present. The House has changed extensively over recent years, and this Chapter adheres to the traditional treatment of composition, powers and functions, concentrating in particular on those areas where there are differences from the Commons.

Chapter 13 draws together some of the main themes of the book and sets out some conclusions on how effectively Parliament works in various ways today.

The book does not deal in detail with one procedural area which is important in both Houses, namely private business. Except where otherwise stated all description and analyses relate to the conduct of public business. We have largely ignored private legislation for three reasons – shortage of space, its limited relevance to the central functions of Parliament, and the fact that these procedures were, at the time of writing, under review by a Joint Committee on Private Bill Procedure the adoption of whose recommendations might well render out of date any description of private legislation procedure we attempted.[4]

---

[4] See Report of the Committee, HL 97, HC 625 of 1987–88

We complete this work with a Bibliography. These books may be of help to those who wish to study alternative descriptions to those we have given or who wish to follow up particular aspects in more detail. We emphasise however that, apart from a few matters, acknowledged in each case, we have not generally relied on these published sources in our own studies or in reaching our conclusions. An important exception is Erskine May's *Parliamentary Practice* (1983 edition) from which we have drawn most of our older precedents or examples, particularly regarding parliamentary privilege in Chapter 3. We are grateful for the help derived from this authority.

Essentially this work is based on our own personal experience and our own detailed research. In undertaking such research, especially regarding statistics of procedural events and analyses of the use of time on the floor of the House for different purposes, we have drawn extensively on procedural records – many unpublished – kept by the Journal Offices of the two Houses. Other sources frequently used have been the Journals and Official Reports of both Houses, various Sessional Returns (some unpublished) and reports and minutes of proceedings of committees. Where appropriate these have been cited, but in many cases information has been derived by us, personally, from a variety of sources.

When conducting our researches over a period of nearly three years and when preparing this book for publication, we have been greatly helped by a number of people, too numerous to mention individually, whom we have interviewed or with whom we have discussed various details or who have advised on earlier drafts of certain sections. These have all been people with direct experience of the workings of the two Houses. They include past and present Members and officers of both Houses, civil servants, officials of the political parties, and commentators. We also acknowledge the help given by the staff of the Libraries of both Houses and of the British Library of Political and Economic Science. We are grateful to them all for their advice and assistance; the final product is, however, totally our responsibility.

Specific detailed research, involving much laborious counting, was undertaken for us by Richard Lambert and Roger Phillips of the Clerks Department, House of Commons, and by William Sleath of the Clerks Department, House of Lords, assisted by Christine Bolton.

A number of secretaries typed, corrected and further corrected successive drafts. We mention in particular Colleen Etheridge, Sarah Meade, Jenny Mitchley and Sandra Southgate. We thank them for all their willing help.

Finally, as the work was extended over the years, we have tested the patience of two groups of people. Our publishers awaited the final text with experienced understanding; we appreciate the professional guidance and encouragement we were given by members of staff at Sweet and Maxwell. Our wives accepted the rival demands of "work on the book" with toleration. We hope its publication may be some consolation.

J.A.G.G.
M.T.R.

June 1989

NOTE ON REFERENCES

Footnote abbreviations have been used as follows:

H.C.Deb., Vol. 100, col. 999 (April 1, 1979) – The volume number and column references of the House of Commons Official Report (Hansard) for the date shown. Similar references to the House of Lords Hansards use the abbreviation H.L.Deb. When column references are italicised, they refer to columns of written answers to Questions.

Earlier Hansard references give the column numbers of the bound volumes, but many more recent references have been taken from daily Hansards and in some of these cases the column references may be slightly altered when the relevant bound volumes of Hansard are published.

H.C. 100 of 1981–82 – A House of Commons paper, such as a select committee report, published with the serial number given in the session indicated. References to the House of Lords papers use the abbreviation H.L.

Cd., Cmd., Cmnd., Cm.100 – The number of a Command paper in the successive series of such papers.

C.J. (1962–63) p.100 – The page of the Commons Journals for the session indicated.

May p.100 – Erskine May's *Parliamentary Practice*; unless otherwise stated the page reference is to the Twentieth Edition (Butterworths, 1983).

CONTENTS (GENERAL)

CONTENTS (DETAILED)

Chapter 1

Chapter 2

Chapter 3

Chapter 4

Chapter 5

Chapter 6

Chapter 7

Chapter 8

Chapter 9

Chapter 10

Chapter 11

Chapter 12

Chapter 13

IS PARLIAMENT EFFECTIVE?

TABLE OF STATUTES

TABLE OF STANDING ORDERS

HOUSE OF COMMONS

HOUSE OF LORDS

PART I

FUNCTIONS, POWERS AND MEMBERSHIP

CHAPTER 1

PARLIAMENTARY GOVERNMENT

THE MEANING OF PARLIAMENT

When Parliament is spoken of today, it is commonly understood to refer to the House of Commons and the House of Lords, and the institution of Parliament is sharply distinguished from the institution called the Executive or the Government. The latter is understood to mean the Queen's Ministers, the Cabinet and the central Departments and, in shorthand, is called White-hall. The shorthand for the Houses of Parliament is Westminster. The two institutions are rightly seen as separate both geographically and functionally and this separation is not weakened by the constitutional requirement that Ministers should also be members of one or other of the Houses. There is some duality of membership but the institutions are distinct.

All this is clear so far as it goes, but it is inadequate to explain the nature of the relationship between the Queen's Ministers and the two Houses. It suggests what is not true: that Parliament is merely a single word to describe what we call the two Houses of Parliament. From earliest times and after the Norman conquest the sovereign took counsel with the most powerful of his subjects and during the thirteenth century, especially under Edward I, the Knights of the shires and representatives from the towns were also from time to time invited to attend what was called the King's Council in his Parliament. The King wanted more than advice. He wanted money and he needed to gather around him those who could supply it through taxes. Soon the Knights and the burgesses from the towns began to meet separately in what became the House of Commons, and the powerful barons and Church leaders became the House of Lords. By the reign of Edward III (1327–1377) it was established that taxation was illegal without the consent of the two Houses and that the concurrence of the Houses was necessary for all statutory legislation.

Parliament meant, in common medieval speech, any meeting for speech or conference.[1] But in political terms, the parley, the speech, the conferring, was one which essentially and necessarily involved the sovereign. Of course, as the House of Commons began to make more demands of the sovereign and particularly to petition for the making of particular laws, the separateness of the Houses from the sovereign became more apparent. But still, the sovereign was an integral part of the Parliament and it was the sovereign who summoned the Houses to meet or who decided not to summon them. Under the Tudors, the Houses were weak in relation to the sovereign's powers which extended once again, for example, to the making of new laws by proclamation rather than by parliamentary process. The dramatic events of the seventeenth century—the opposition by the Commons and the lawyers to James I, the civil war, the execution of Charles I, the Cromwellian Commonwealth, the restoration of Charles II, the further struggle with James II and his flight in 1688—all led to the revolutionary settlement of 1688–1689. From the early eighteenth century emerges the practice of Ministers of the Crown sitting in one or other of the Houses of Parliament.

---

[1] See C. H. McIlwain, *The High Court of Parliament and its Supremacy* (1910), p. 27.

So it is said by constitutional lawyers today that legislative sovereignty—
the power to make laws—rests in the Queen in Parliament. The Queen (in
person if she is in the country) opens Parliament each session in the House of
Lords, her physical presence demonstrating this central principle of the
constitution. The enacting words of an Act of Parliament spell this out:

> "Be it enacted by the Queen's most Excellent Majesty, by and with the
> advice and consent of the Lords Spiritual and Temporal, and Commons,
> in this present Parliament assembled, and by the authority of the same."

Moreover the Queen's Ministers may act only within the legislative
powers they enjoy or within the remaining powers of the royal prerogative
(most importantly in the conduct of foreign affairs). But those Ministers are
also accountable to the Houses of Parliament where they may be criticised
and challenged. All this must be seen against the background of the principal
political consideration: that those Ministers, as the Government, are Ministers because their party commands a majority in the House of Commons, at
least in the sense that no combination of other parties is able and willing to
defeat them in the division lobbies of the House. The Ministers represent the
Executive power which is vested in the sovereign; and "Parliament" means
both the parley between the Executive and the elected representatives and
peers, and the institution where that discussion takes place.

All this is not to seek to present Parliament as an institution that has
remained essentially the same throughout the centuries. In particular the
nature and significance of party has altogether altered over the last 150
years. Whether we lay more emphasis on the Reform Act of 1832 or on the
great enlargement of the franchise in 1867 and 1884 (and again in 1918 and
1928), the significant fact is that during the period after 1870 political parties
became national bodies and acquired new and different relationships with
the electorate. Inevitably, concepts like the political responsibility of
governments both to the Houses of Parliament and to that electorate also
changed their nature.

Governments spend a large proportion of their time administering
services along lines laid down by previous governments. The policies, the
administrative structures, and the operation of the services concerned with
education, social security, health, housing, land use, law and order, energy,
trade and industry, employment, fisheries and food, transport, foreign
affairs, defence and the rest are all, in large part, continued from one
government to the next, irrespective of election manifestos and party
politics. Governments inherit a large collection of regulatory and promo-
tional powers under statutes which had their origins, in forms recognisable
today, between 75 and 140 years ago. The foundation years of the regulatory
state, including public health and housing, were the middle decades of the
nineteenth century, modern school education began in 1870, the welfare
state dates from 1911. Governments have been involved in overseas trade,
defence and foreign affairs since the middle ages.

The more obvious and the more publicised activities of governments are
inevitably those which are a departure from the practices of previous
governments. In many fields, but not all (see pages 8, 9), new policies
require new powers for their implementation. And new powers are obtained
by legislation. All Governments in all countries must control the legislature.
In some, such as the United Kingdom, Governments are Governments
because they exercise that control. In others, such as the United States of

America, the Government has more indirect means of control. But a Government that had not the means to make laws could not exercise its proper authority.

In the United Kingdom, Governments make laws by promoting bills in Parliament and, by using their majority in the House of Commons and the willing or reluctant acquiescence of the House of Lords, obtaining the assents of those Houses which will turn those bills into Acts of Parliament. The constraints imposed by parliamentary procedure mean that only a limited number of bills which are controversial between political parties can be passed through Parliament during a single session. The preparation of the Government's legislative programme is the scene for inter-departmental struggles as Ministers seek to obtain places for their own bills. And time must be found for the various financial bills authorising taxation and the appropriation of moneys to the spending departments. If bills are not passed, new policies cannot be implemented. And, as bills require parliamentary approval, there is no way Governments can avoid the parliamentary struggle.

One constant has remained since the early eighteenth century: the key to understanding how the constitution works still lies in the relationship between the Government and the House of Commons as the representative body. This relationship is directly and greatly conditioned by the dominant presence in the representative assembly of the Ministers of the Crown. It follows that no account of Parliament and its working can be attempted without considering this relationship and that involves first considering the functions of Parliament.

THE FUNCTIONS OF PARLIAMENT

Parliament as a debating forum

Neither House of Parliament in the United Kingdom was created by a Constituent Assembly or the "Founding Fathers of the Constitution." Nowhere are the functions of Parliament laid down in a single constitutional document. Both Houses emerged in response to certain constitutional and political requirements; they acquired certain purposes of their own; and they survive today fulfilling or participating in a wide range of functions.

It is a central feature of Parliament, however, that it performs a responsive rather than an initiating function within the constitution. The Government—at different levels—initiates policy, formulates its policy on legislation and other proposals, exercises powers under the prerogative or granted by statute and, in all these aspects, performs the governing role in the state. Both Houses of Parliament spend most of their time responding, in a variety of ways, to these initiatives, proposals or executive actions.

The Government, however, is not the only source of input of business for Parliament. Much business is originated by the Opposition front-bench, and by back-benchers on either side of the two Houses. The inspiration for their input is largely found in general public opinion, outside pressures or interest groups, newspapers, radio and television, and in the minds and attitudes of millions of citizens represented in the Commons by Members.

Parliament, therefore, finds itself the recipient of a wide range of external pressures and proposals, broadly divided in origin between the Government of the day on the one hand and the outside world—the public—on the other. Only in a limited context does either House have a policy of its own or initiate "parliamentary" proposals. For example the House of Lords has a long-standing concern with its own composition and powers. The Commons (and, to a lesser extent, the Lords) have jealously established, preserved and exercised "all their ancient and undoubted rights and privileges" (to quote the claim made to the sovereign on their behalf by the Speaker at the beginning of each Parliament). And both Houses adopt a "parliamentary" stance and concern themselves with their own interests when initiating or influencing policy on such matters as their own procedures and the pay, accommodation, facilities and conditions of service of Members or Peers. But for most matters the initiative comes from outside Parliament.

Two observations illustrate this: first, unlike many Parliaments imbedded in written constitutions, neither House has a "bureau" or steering committee charged with the organisation of the business. In the Lords the Lord Chancellor, as their Speaker, does not control in any way the business of the House (although, under one of his other hats as a Cabinet Minister, he may exercise considerable influence on the Leader of the House in deciding the agenda). In the Commons the Speaker has only limited powers to regulate the business (see page 148). In practice, particularly in the Commons, the occasions, duration and content of business are largely controlled by the Government of the day exercising its majority, and by the Opposition parties and back-benchers using the opportunities available to them.

Second, although both Houses frequently come to resolutions expressing opinions in some such words as "This House believes . . . " or "condemns . . . " or "welcomes . . . " which purport to express the views of the House, these conclusions normally in no way summarise the opinions of the House as a whole. In the Commons they are rather the opinion of the Government side secured by the exercise of their majority in the division lobbies. Therefore, except in respect of certain "House of Commons matters," when the Speaker can be said to speak for the House as a whole, no single spokesman can claim to represent the views of the House. Each party expresses its own views and each one of the 650 Members is his own public relations officer. And all this is true, also, of the Lords.

The two Houses, therefore, cannot properly be described as governing bodies, nor correctly analysed as being institutions with initiating or law making functions within the constitution. They are better presented as forums within which the contending powers—the parties and those whom they represent, and the individual Members or Peers—publicly debate the issues of the day and matters of their choosing, and through which the Government may secure the authority it needs for the implementation of its policies and the exercise of its powers. If these forums can be said to have a principal function, it is that of exercising constant scrutiny over those who have the powers of government and debating all matters brought before them from whatever source, and, through the operation of the Government's majority in the Commons, of enabling the members of the Government to fulfil their constitutional role.

It is therefore as a debating forum, not as a governing body, that Parliament should be assessed. As Leo Amery wrote in *Thoughts on the Constitution*, referring particularly to the House of Commons, "the main task of Parliament is still what it was when first summoned, not to legislate or govern, but to secure full discussion and ventilation of all matters."[2] It is in

---

[2] L. S. Amery, *Thoughts on the Constitution* (1947), p. 12.

this sense, by ensuring that Ministers are always liable to be required to explain and publicly justify their policies and their actions, that Parliament may be said to be the custodian of the liberties of the people.

The business of Parliament

The parliamentary processes operate within two separate theatres: the two Houses of Parliament. Although the emphasis differs between the two Houses, and although the balance of influence of the participating elements also differs significantly, the nature of the debating role in each chamber is essentially the same. We here describe it primarily in terms of the processes of the Commons; the role of the Lords is described more fully in Chapter 12.

The occasions and opportunities for debate, and indeed to some extent the procedures employed, depend largely on the nature and the origin of the business brought before the House. The business, for this purpose, falls broadly into two categories.

First there is business which involves, sometimes only formally, sometimes more substantially, some process of authorisation or approval by the House, where a decision must be reached by the House. The main forms of such business are proposals for legislation, including in particular proposals for taxation and proposals for certain expenditures. The main originator of this type of business is the Government, although private Members play some part in proposing primary legislation (see pages 385–400) and outside bodies can promote private bills.[3] Other forms of business requiring formal authorisation include changes in parliamentary procedures by new or amended standing orders or sessional resolutions, daily regulation by "business of the House" motions, and regulation of the organs of the House, such as the appointment of, and references of matters to, committees. Again the initiative for these matters lies mainly with Ministers.

What types of governmental decisions and policy involve legislation, and hence Government initiative and parliamentary authorisation, is partly a function of the legal system and partly a function of historical custom and convention. Clearly, decisions to impose duties on citizens or to extend or restrict their rights—ranging from the duty to observe speed limits to the right to claim tax reliefs for certain types of expenses—must involve precise legislation, justiciable and enforceable in the courts. The same applies to benefits, such as the disability allowance, which some citizens, but not others, may claim. The powers of Ministers to make orders or give grants or issue licences, for example, must also be statutorily specified if the dangers of arbitrary government are to be minimised.

More broadly, over the whole field of administration, Ministers and other public authorities need general powers so that they may exercise their many and diverse regulatory powers (as land-use planning, food and drugs control, health regulations), their provision of services (as education and housing), and their management of nationalised industries. They need general powers to acquire land, to employ and pay officials, to enter premises, to build hospitals and motorways. They need to provide police and fire services and to equip and man the armed forces. All this requires legislative authority obtainable only through bills assented to by Parliament.

There is one other important function of government which is statutorily

---

[3] In this book we do not deal in detail with private business, but the role played by back-bench Members in its consideration is discussed on pp. 411–412.

regulated, namely public expenditure of money voted by Parliament. By the application of Votes broadly drawn, Ministers are statutorily limited in the amounts of cash they may spend in each financial year for specific purposes. This is a strange kind of law, ephemeral in its effect and barely justiciable, but nevertheless requiring parliamentary authority. But, as history has shown, much of the power and influence of the House of Commons has derived from this requirement that the expenditure of the Crown be authorised by Parliament each year. And, as we shall show, many of the debating opportunities of the House are based on this formal constitutional requirement.

Whatever is thought to require legislation involves in most cases Government initiative in Parliament; and this also guarantees opportunity for debating in both Houses the proposals set out in the bills. However the question of what needs to be included in legislation is to some extent arbitrary. It is noteworthy that in some other countries much discretion is left to Ministers to interpret and fulfil the broadly stated purposes of legislation, subject to the rulings of the courts. The present British practice—where Acts usually spell out in considerable detail their requirements—is largely an historical inheritance reinforced by continuing suspicion, on the part of politicians of all parties, of both Ministers (and their advisers) and of the judges.

The second category of business is that which does not require formal parliamentary authorisation and for such business debating opportunities are not automatically guaranteed. This non-legislative business falls under a number of different heads. First, there are major areas of government policy and administration where Ministers act under prerogative powers—by right of appointment by and as advisers to the Crown—and where little or no legislation is required.

In foreign affairs, few matters require formal approval by the House. Treaties do not require approval by either House of Parliament, and in the great majority of cases go undebated, although under what is known as the "Ponsonby rule" when a treaty requires ratification the Government does not usually proceed with ratification until after 21 days from the date when the text of the treaty was laid before Parliament. In respect of matters not requiring even a treaty (and many aspects of foreign policy fall into this category) there is no question of formal parliamentary sanction being sought or given for the policies concerned.

The position is similar in respect of economic policy. Admittedly one of the main regulators of the national economy is taxation policy, and this is subject to detailed scrutiny by the House of Commons and formal and specific parliamentary sanction. Another regulator is the level of public spending and, in respect of both central government and local government, spending is subject to some degree of formal parliamentary authorisation. These two determinants condition the public sector borrowing requirement (the third economic regulator) although it is not specifically and separately sanctioned by Parliament. But other important regulators are not subject to formal approval by either House. No specific approval (or even formal notification) is required for changes in the minimum lending rate, for government borrowing by various means, or for decisions that influence exchange rates.[4]

---

[4] For more details of this analysis, see D. Coombes and S. A. Walkland (ed.), *Parliament and Economic Affairs* (1980), Part II.

Little legislation is required in defence matters, except in respect of naval, military and air force law, and here again Ministers largely operate without formal parliamentary sanction. This is particularly true in respect of the deployment of forces, and the use made of resources and equipment already in being. Certainly the research, development and procurement of new weapons or equipment and the recruitment, pay, accommodation etc. of servicemen involves authorisation of expenditure, but such authorisation is treated with a broad brush (a lump sum for all weapons research, development and procurement, for instance) which gives the House no opportunity for formal authorisation of major policy decisions. Two examples illustrate this point. For several years, no mention was made in either House of the original decision to develop a British atomic bomb; the relevant expenditure was buried under the broad headings of weapons research and development. More recently the Government's decision to acquire the Trident missile to replace Polaris did not require the formal ratification of the House, although it was publicly debated[5] and the costs of the programme were examined by the Defence Committee.[6] Most remarkably, no formal parliamentary authority is required for a declaration of war.

In addition to these sectors of policy where Ministers act under prerogative powers, there are many other areas where Ministers, acting under statutory powers, have wide discretion to take policy decisions without specific parliamentary sanction. This is particularly true of major capital projects. No specific parliamentary sanction is required for the building of a new hospital, the creation of a new motorway or the construction of new government offices; nor for investment for which other bodies are responsible but over which Ministers have some control or veto, such as major capital projects in the nationalised industries or local authority capital expenditure involving loan sanctions.

Lastly, there are the wide areas where Ministers may, subject to broad statutory powers, take policy decisions without seeking the authority of the House, other than broad financial approval. For example the Secretary of State for Health can, under his broad statutory duty to "secure improvement in the physical and mental health of the people,"[7] switch the emphasis, through the allocation of resources, from acute medicine to care of the elderly or from physical to mental health. The Secretary of State for Transport may decide to give more assistance to rail services than to roads, or vice versa. The Secretary of State for the Environment may list historic buildings or designate areas of special interest. More generally a number of Ministers—or indeed the Prime Minister—may decide to intervene and play a positive role (or alternatively not to do so) in trade disputes.

Even when the Government does not need formal parliamentary sanction, it may choose to bring a matter before the House for debate. But the main initiative for discussion of non-legislative matters rests with other groups—the official Opposition, leaders of other Opposition parties, and back-benchers on either side of the House.

How Members who are not Ministers choose what matters to bring forward cannot be simply stated. Many topics will be chosen simply because

[5] H.C.Deb., Vol. 997, col. 151–162 (January 20, 1981); H.C.Deb., Vol. 5, col. 160–244 (May 19, 1981) and col. 292–380 (May 20, 1981).

[6] H.C. 36 of 1980–81; and later reports.

[7] National Health Service Act 1977, s.1(1)(a).

the Opposition believe the Government is not doing well in that field and that the publicity created by a debate in the House of Commons will damage the Government's image. For example the Conservative Opposition between 1974 and 1979 initiated a number of debates on the problems of inflation, for which they blamed the Government; the Labour Opposition after 1979 similarly chose to draw attention to the problems of unemployment and the health and social services. Other topics will be chosen by the Opposition because it wants to give publicity to its own alternative policies, and to urge new policies on the Government of the day. Other matters are raised because it is felt that the relevant Ministers should explain and justify what they have done. A great range of policies and administrative decisions are debated, questioned or otherwise scrutinised because they concern one or more back-benchers, either reflecting constituency pressures, or expressing the interests of various groups outside Parliament, or simply because the Members involved have a personal interest in the matters they choose to raise.

In these multifarious ways almost anything that involves ministerial power can be discussed or publicly aired in Parliament. One advantage of the large numbers of Members in the House of Commons is that almost every minority interest or anxiety can find a sympathetic ear somewhere in the House and thus secure public consideration. No issue is too big or too small for parliamentary consideration. All matters ranging from the future of mankind in the nuclear age to Mrs. Smith's disability pension may be raised in Parliament.

From the parliamentary view, the significance of those practices and procedures (especially legislation) which involve formal parliamentary authorisation is that they guarantee the opportunity for debate in some form or other. But this also secures opportunities for the Opposition and others to look critically at those Government policies, decisions and actions that do not require formal parliamentary sanction. For unless the Government is willing to allow some time and procedural opportunity for the Opposition parties, and for back-benchers generally, to initiate business, either to criticise the Government or to advance their own ideas, the Government will find the passage of its own business obstructed and made more difficult.

Thus, despite the control the Government can exercise over the House of Commons by the use of its majority, Ministers can obtain the parliamentary legitimation they require for their own business only if they also allow opportunities and procedures for debate or other forms of scrutiny on both the business they must initiate and on matters brought forward by others. This is the meaning of the phrase "parliamentary government": not government by Parliament, but government through Parliament. The Government may govern, but Parliament is the forum for the public debate and criticism of those acts of government. Parliament is essentially a debating body.

The opportunities for debate in the Commons

Effective debate, in its broad sense, requires two things. First, there must be adequate opportunities for debate to be initiated by the various participants. Second, there must be appropriate procedures and techniques for looking critically at different kinds of business; in particular there must be methods for obtaining the information necessary for effective and influential debate or scrutiny.

There are three principal participants: the Government itself, as represented by Ministers, headed by the Prime Minister; the Opposition comprising the official Opposition front bench, and the leaders of the smaller parties; and the back-benchers from all parties. As will be shown, all these participants also have close links with and are sometimes heavily dependent on outside groups, which have special interests or represent major elements of the public.

The opportunities for the Government are simply summarised in Standing Order No. 13(1):

"Save as provided in this order, government business shall have precedence at every sitting."

Time is provided by this standing order for the Opposition and for back-benchers, but on approximately 75 per cent. of the sitting days Government business has priority (although, on some of these days some of the business actually debated is initiated by other participants). Government business is mainly, but not wholly, legislative, and is taken in standing committees as well as on the floor of the House.

The official Opposition front-bench have, under Standing Order No. 13 (2), 17 days each session on which matters selected by the Leader of the Opposition have precedence over Government business. Since 1985, three days a session have also been at the disposal of the Leader of the second largest Opposition party (defined by reference to the number of Members elected as members of that party). On approximately 12 per cent. of sitting days, Opposition business has priority under the standing order. The Opposition also have other opportunities for initiating business (see Chapter 9).

Before leaving Opposition opportunities, an important historical development must be noted. In the last century there were no Opposition days as such. The official Opposition had to compete or share with back-benchers in taking its opportunities on Government Supply days (when the estimates were debated) to raise matters which concerned them. After the introduction in 1896 of a system of guillotining debate on the estimates which gave the Government a firm guarantee of getting its estimates approved by a specified time, Ministers suggested that the choice of estimates for debate should be left to the Opposition (although it was some years before this new concept became generally accepted). In 1967 the need to relate Supply debates to particular estimates was removed. Finally, in 1982 the reality was recognised in standing orders: Supply days were abolished and Opposition days, as provided for in Standing Order No. 13, were established in their place.[8]

The opportunities for back-benchers are much more varied. Under Standing Order No. 13 private Members' bills and motions have precedence on a number of days (mostly Fridays) in each session. These days comprise 13 per cent. of sitting days. Back-benchers' opportunities for initiating business are not limited to these days, however. The full range of their opportunities and how they exercise their initiative are discussed in Chapters 10 and 11.

The first Table below shows, for the most recent normal length and typical session, the number of days on which Government, Opposition and private Members' business had precedence, as defined by Standing Order No. 13 (as amended by sessional orders). This illustrates the official division of days

---

[8] For full details of this story up to 1978, see S. A. Walkland (ed), *The House of Commons in the Twentieth Century* (1979), Chapter VII by Michael Ryle.

between the three participants; it does not show who initiated business within those periods.

Division of Days under Standing Order No. 13, as sessionally amended, in 1985–86

	No.	%
Opposition Days	20	11.6
Private Members days		
Bills (Fridays)	12	
Motions (Fridays)	9	
Motions (Mondays)	2	
	23	13.4
Government Days	129	75.0
Total:	172	100.0

The next Table gives a totally different analysis. It shows in simplified form, for this typical session of 1985–86, the time spent on the floor of the House on business initiated by, or subjects chosen by, the three participants, irrespective of how the days may have been allocated under Standing Order No. 13.

Analysis of time of House by initiating participants, 1985–86[9]

	hours	minutes	%
A. Business initiated by the Government			
1. Primary legislation and related proceedings	460	40	
2. Motions, including adjournment motions	257	02	
3. Debates on Address to the Queen	25	22	
4. Other proceedings	89	53	
Total	832	57	55
B. Business initiated by the Opposition			
1. Motions	127	20	
2. Amendments to the Address	11	20	
3. Other proceedings	7	54	
Total	146	34	10
C. Business initiated by back-bench Members			
1. Primary legislation	68	30	
2. Private business	42	16	
3. Motions	101	17	
4. Estimates days	17	33	
5. Debates on adjournment motions etc.	148	45	
6. Questions and other proceedings	157	57	
Total	536	18	35
Grand Total	1515	49	100

[9] Journal Office, House of Commons, as published in Sessional Information Digests.

The fact that a piece of business, say the report stage of a bill, is put down by the Government, in "Government time," does not mean that the debate is wholly inspired, directed or developed according to the Government's wishes. Much of the debate will be on amendments moved by the Opposition and, to a lesser extent, by back-benchers. Even on the second reading of a Government bill, or on a Government motion, most of the time will be taken up by the Opposition (setting out, to some extent, their alternative policies) and by back-benchers. The reverse is true on Opposition motions. Therefore one cannot properly say that so much time of the House is "Government time" or "Opposition time" or "back-benchers' time." Indeed, and paradoxically, it could be argued that the time spent on debate on Government bills and other business should be classified as Opposition and back-benchers' time since they are the participants that want the debate and spend time on it. Left to themselves, Ministers would usually be happy to see their bills passed with little or no debate.

As Erskine May says, "in a sense, all Government time is equally Opposition time."[10] However, control of how time is spent is not the only relevant factor. Control of business to be initiated is of equal (or perhaps greater) importance. Here the analysis in the above Table remains relevant. The majority of business is initiated by the Government, but a significant part is initiated by the Opposition and even more by back-benchers.

Two confrontations

There are essentially two confrontations underlying all parliamentary business. The first, as reflected in the very shape of the Chamber, is the confrontation between the Government and the Opposition. This is at the heart of the British political system: the Government of the day is faced by, and challenged by, the alternative governing party, the party that formed the Government not so long ago and hopes to form a Government again before too long. The Government is required to defend everything it does or proposes to do, while the Opposition is given the opportunity to expound its alternative policies and, if critical of the Ministers in power, to answer the challenge of what it would do if it were in office. It is a confrontation which is symbolised most dramatically when the Prime Minister and the Leader of the Opposition face each other across the dispatch boxes for Prime Minister's Questions, or on other big occasions. But it is a confrontation which is also revealed and articulated in almost every parliamentary action of every Member in the House. In nearly everything they do or say, Ministers are speaking for or defending their administration and attacking the Opposition: equally, shadow Ministers are attacking and criticising the Government and fighting to defend their own policies. Of course, in both cases there are also internal struggles within both parties to determine what those policies should be and who should be the leaders of the party charged with expounding them, and these parallel "in-party" confrontations may also be manifested in the House. But back-bench Members on both sides are primarily conscious of their role as supporters of their parties and of their leaders in Government or Opposition.

The second confrontation is equally important, although less obviously manifested and usually less fiercely demonstrated. It is the inherent confron-

---

[10] p. 304.

tation between the Government with its executive responsibilities, and all other Members who without such responsibilities are free to criticise Ministers or their department on behalf of their constituents, or of interest or pressure groups, or on their own personal account. It is to a large extent the historical, constitutional confrontation between Parliament (answerable to the people) and the Executive appointed by the Crown. It is this confrontation which provides much of the material for Question Time, when constituency issues are often to the fore, and for other occasions, described in Chapter 10 when business is initiated by back-benchers. Many topics then raised result from or express discontent with some aspect of Government policy or administration which often cuts across the party divisions. For example, Members of all parties may come together to oppose a proposal for a new London Airport, or to urge more Government help for a particular industry. Other issues (say Mrs. Smith's disability allowance) may involve a direct conflict between back-bencher and Minister with little relation to the confrontation between the parties.

A notable forum for this latter confrontation is the select committee (see Chapter 11). Here back-bench Members of all parties come together to examine Government policy and administration, usually in a largely non-party way, with little influence from the Whips, and to agree (sometimes on cross-party votes and often unanimously) reports commenting on the Government's handling of issues, criticising or praising, coming to conclusions and making recommendations. This work, although essentially advisory rather than decision-taking, has increased greatly in recent years and has focused, in a systematic way, the confrontation between back-benchers on both sides and Ministers of the Crown.

In such confrontation the official Opposition frequently find themselves in a somewhat uneasy alliance with the Government. As a body of people who may have already exercised the powers of Ministers, and who aspire to do so again, they tend to sympathise with the predicaments and reactions of Government; they tend to be impatient of the claims of the back-benchers; they may find the activities of some of their own supporters embarrassing; they may find time and attention paid to private Members' business or back-bench initiative at best irrelevant and at worst an unwelcome distraction from the confrontation which interests them—that across the floor of the House. Thus on such matters as the powers and rights of select committees (of which they are not members), or the allocation of time to back-benchers, or the moving of amendments to Government bills by Government back-benchers which may upset an agreed timetable for a debate, the Whips on the Opposition front bench often find themselves in sympathy with the Government business managers. In this context, it is perhaps significant that the official Opposition, as such, never initiates its own legislation in the way both Government and back-benchers do; they know the difficulties such confusion of roles could cause.

The two confrontations are also distinguished by the procedures employed. When Government business is at stake, especially Government legislation, there are questions before the House to be decided. The Whips are put on; the decision of the House is taken and the majority wins. The same process largely applies to Opposition motions on which the Opposition wishes to register a vote and which the Government wishes to amend or defeat. For such business the procedure of debate followed by vote is ideally suited to the participants concerned: the Whips can control the business and (on the Government's side) the result. Here, procedures are employed which are eminently amenable to Whip control.

The procedures employed for the confrontation between Minister and back-benchers do not, in the main, have these characteristics. Here the legislature is performing what, in America, is called its oversight function— not legislating but keeping Government policies and administration and the day-to-day decisions and actions of Ministers and their civil servants under review and subject to cricitism. Although to some extent the process of debate followed by vote may still be used (on private Members' bills and motions for example) the main procedures employed are those which do not usually end in a vote. Much back-bench scrutiny of Ministers and their departments is also conducted by correspondence, by deputations, by discussion in their offices, or even in the bars and corridors, or party meetings and committees. For all these confrontations, procedures not amenable to Whip control are largely employed, and Members have considerable latitude in the topics they choose to raise and in the line they take on these matters in the House, in committee or on more private occasions (although awareness of the Whips is always present).

Procedures and the search for information

We said earlier that effective debate, in the broad sense, also requires appropriate procedures and techniques, especially for obtaining information.

For examination of policy the formal process of debate is generally employed. Policy issues may, however, also be canvassed at Question Time and in Ministerial statements and the exchanges and Questions that follow such statements. Select committees are also increasingly engaged in policy issues.

Public legislation is almost entirely examined, in the House and in committee, by the process of debate. Information relevant to the discussion on a bill may be sought by Questions for a written answer. Delegated legislation is similarly examined by the process of debate.

For the more detailed examination of how policy is being administered by Ministers, by civil servants or by agencies of one sort or another, the whole range of procedures are available: debate of various sorts, Questions, and committee scrutiny. Taxation is examined in detail in debates on the Finance Bill. But for expenditure the situation is completely different. The details of expenditure, as such, are nowadays hardly debated in the House at all but following the Gladstone maxim that "expenditure flows from policy," the House has concentrated more and more on debating the policies that determine public expenditure. The detailed examination of expenditure plans, current spending or past spending has been increasingly left to select committees. The only other technique that is commonly employed in scrutinising expenditure involves seeking information by means of Questions.

Securing information is at the heart of the debating or scrutiny process. Ill-informed debate cannot be effective. The Government knows most of the facts on any matter that comes up for debate. The Opposition and back-benchers on both sides must therefore also possess the necessary information or have means of seeking it, if debate is to be effective. The right to ask is inherent in the parliamentary process.

Moreover, government today has become so complex and many of the issues so technical that if Parliament is to match the decision-taking processes of government (which includes detailed study of the relevant information) with anything like effective scrutiny, then the House must be able to inform itself. It would clearly be wrong for Members to be limited, in the supply of information, to that which Ministers choose to make public without request, plus whatever they may learn from the press and other outside sources. Parliamentary procedures must therefore be available to enable the House as a whole, committees, or individual Members to obtain further information.

Much information is volunteered by Ministers. They publish White and Green Papers, make statements in the House, issue press releases and publish numerous reports and accounts. Ministers give such additional information as they choose in the course of debates on bills or motions. Ministers are also willing to give much information if specifically requested by Members in the course of debate or by means of parliamentary Questions.

There is a further range of information which cannot, or will not, be readily given in general debate or even in answer to Questions. Sometimes this is because it is complex and voluminous. But some information Ministers may not be anxious to give, but may be obliged to give if asked persistently and pressed to do so. For extraction of such information the select committee technique is essential. It is easy in debate in the House or even in answer to Questions for a Minister to avoid giving information if he wishes to do so. But a committee which requests detailed papers and whose Members persist in asking searching questions is far harder to deny. Furthermore such committees have, through other witnesses, alternative sources of information which sometimes force a government to come clean (or cleaner), if only to defend their policies or decisions from misinformed criticism.

Two other developments have also given Members more effective access to information. First, the growth of the House of Commons Library's research services has enabled Members to be better briefed on many topics that come up for debate. And second, the increasing employment by Members of personal research assistants has worked to the same end.

At the end of these processes, however, there still remains a great deal of information in the possession of Ministers that will never be disclosed. To what extent further disclosure should be sought remains a matter of argument. Totally open government might mean timid and temporising government. But equally, without some openness by Ministers, and at least the techniques for seeking to secure the production of further information, there would be government behind closed doors, which is a total negation of the British parliamentary system. The price of democracy is eternal scrutiny. The ever increasing extent, power and complexity of Government requires that that scrutiny be well informed.

The influence of Parliament

It may be thought that if Parliament is not a decision-taking body but is simply a forum for debate it must lack power and therefore influence. Although debate itself can influence the way Government policy evolves and the way Ministers conduct their administration, yet, if Parliament operated in a vacuum, these influences would have little effect. Ministers could choose to ignore them and to rely on support by the party majority.

But Parliament does not operate in a vacuum. The House of Commons is created by and is in the end responsible to the electorate. Parliament's influence ultimately depends on its relations with the people.

First, the House of Commons draws its authority from the fact that it is elected by and represents the people. Secondly, the House of Commons secures its influence by reflecting public opinion and by forming and conditioning public opinion. As Lloyd George said, the House is the sounding board of the nation: it both speaks for and speaks to the people.

This process of communication inevitably influences Government. In so far as Members are reflecting public opinion they will be heeded by both the Government and by the Opposition parties. And in as far as parliamentary debate influences public opinion, Ministers and Opposition leaders will take that debate seriously. Taken in isolation, politicians can ignore the criticisms of Members. But they cannot ignore the voters in elections. Governments and parties are ultimately sensitive to public opinion and so are sensitive to that which reflects and conditions that opinion: the proceedings in Parliament.

PARLIAMENT AND GOVERNMENT

The making of Governments

We have said that the principal political consideration determining the way in which Parliament works is the party system. The electoral system results in one party having more seats in the House of Commons than any other and most frequently results in that party having more seats than all the other parties put together. However this "overall majority" is by no means always achieved and, we shall see, minority Governments face special problems and test the flexibility of the constitution.

Election

A Government comes into existence as a consequence of the result of a general election held to secure the return to the House of Commons of Members of Parliament. In each of 650 separate geographical constituencies the candidate having the most votes is elected, this system being commonly called "first-past-the-post". The great majority of candidates are selected by one or other of the principal political parties and stand as party candidates. The party with the largest number of seats in the House of Commons forms the Government,[11] its Leader becoming Prime Minister. The principal British parliamentary parties are now the Conservative Party, the Labour Party, and the Social and Liberal Democratic Party.[12]

The results of general elections since the Second World War are summarised below[13]:

---

[11] The only exception in this century followed the general election in Deceber 1923 when the Conservatives won 258 seats, Labour 191 and Liberals 159. When Parliament met, the Liberals joined with the Labour Members to defeat the Conservatives. Labour then formed the Government.

[12] In 1983 and 1987, the Liberal Party and the Social Democratic Party formed an Alliance for electoral purposes. After the 1987 election, the S.D.P. split, all but three of its Members joining all the Liberal Members in the newly formed Social and Liberal Democratic Party.

[13] D. Butler and G. Butler, *British Political Facts 1900–1985* (1986). From 1974, Members from Northern Ireland parties are included in Other. The Speaker is included in the party to which he belonged before his election as Speaker.

		Seats				Votes %				Con/Lab Overall
Year	Total	Con	Lib	Lab	Other	Con	Lib	Lab	Other	Majority
1945	640	213	12	393	22	39.8	9.0	47.8	3.4	Lab 146
1950	625	298	9	315	3	43.5	9.1	46.1	1.3	Lab 5
1951	625	321	6	295	3	48.0	2.5	48.8	0.7	Con 17
1955	630	344	6	277	3	49.7	2.7	46.4	1.2	Con 58
1959	630	365	6	258	1	49.4	5.9	43.8	0.9	Con 100
1964	630	304	9	317	–	43.4	11.2	44.1	1.3	Lab 4
1966	630	253	12	363	2	41.9	8.5	47.9	1.2	Lab 96
1970	630	330	6	287	7	46.4	7.5	43.0	3.2	Con 30
Feb. 1974	635	297	14	301	23	37.9	19.3	37.1	5.7	Lab –33
Oct. 1974	635	277	13	319	26	35.8	18.3	39.2	6.7	Lab 3
1979	635	339	11	269	16	43.9	13.8	36.9	5.4	Con 43
			Lib/SDP				Lib/SDP			
1983	650	397	17/6	209	21	42.4	25.4	27.6	4.6	Con 144
1987	650	376	17/5	229	23	42.3	22.6	30.8	4.3	Con 102

The disparities resulting from the "first-past-the-post" system are apparent. In 1951 Labour had a higher percentage of votes than the Conservatives but 26 fewer seats. That situation was reversed in February 1974. Throughout, the Liberals were greatly under-represented in seats as a proportion of votes cast in their favour. They obtained nearly one-fifth of votes cast in the two elections of 1974 but were rewarded with only one-fiftieth of the seats to be won. In 1983, the Liberal-SDP Alliance won only 3.5 per cent. of seats on 25.4 per cent. of the total vote, the Conservatives winning over 60 per cent. of seats on 42.4 per cent. of the vote, and Labour 32 per cent. of seats on 27.6 per cent. of the vote.

From 1945 until 1977, either the Conservatives or Labour provided a single party Government, with no commitment to any other party in the House of Commons as the price of support. Despite Labour's very small overall majority of five after the general election of 1950, no attempt was made by the Government to gain Liberal support during the 18 months of that administration and no seats were lost in 16 by-elections. But when the Conservatives won the election of 1951 with an overall majority of 17 seats, the Prime Minister (Mr. Churchill) offered a Cabinet post to the leader of the Liberals (Mr. Clement Davies) who did not accept.[14] This was part of a general approach adopted by some Conservatives during the 1950s to bring the Liberals into an anti-Labour coalition. It did not succeed.

When Labour were again returned with a very small overall majority of four in 1964, the Government made no positive approaches to the Liberals and 18 months later Labour were returned with a good majority of 96. So also Mr. Heath's victory in 1970 with a majority of 30 was solid enough for most purposes.

The result of the election of February 1974 gave no party anything like an overall majority. Labour won 301 seats, the Conservatives 297, the Liberals

---

[14] On all this, see David Butler (ed.) in *Coalitions in British Politics* (1978), Chapter 5.

14, the Ulster Unionists 11 and others 12—out of a total of 635 seats. Mr. Heath remained as Prime Minister for a few days while he tried to persuade the Liberals to join a coalition. He promised to support the setting up of a Speaker's Conference "to consider the desirability and possibility of a change in our electoral arrangements"—the Liberals were pressing for proportional representation—but the Liberals rejected the offer. Mr. Heath resigned and was succeeded by Mr. Wilson as head of a Labour Government.

The Labour victory in October 1974 gave them an overall majority of only three seats but a majority over the Conservatives of 42 seats, with 13 Liberals and 26 "others" (including 12 from Northern Ireland and 11 Scottish Nationalists). Labour made no immediate overtures to other groups. Indeed at the Party Conference the previous year the Leader of the Party had most explicitly rejected the possibility. By-election defeats and the defection of two Members to form the Scottish Labour Party meant that by the beginning of 1977, the Government was in continuing danger of defeat. Then from March 1977 until the summer of 1978, Labour survived with the help of the Liberals in the House of Commons—"the Lib-Lab pact" (see page 41). The Government held on to office during the "winter of discontent" of 1978–79 but was finally defeated in the House on March 28, 1979 by one vote whereupon Parliament was dissolved (see pages 41–42).

The Conservative victory at the general election of 1979 restored one party Government based on an overall majority of 43. This was not much more than the majority of 1970, but the Government was not threatened by internal dissension. It was the Labour Opposition that was greatly weakened in the House and in the country by the emergence of the Social Democratic Party in March 1981 and the Parliamentary defections that followed. After the Party was launched, 26 Labour MPs and one Conservative MP joined its ranks. Two by-election victories brought the total to 29 at the time of the general election in 1983.

The general election of 1983 resulted in a large Conservative majority of 144, a considerable decline in the Labour party vote (from 11.5 million in 1979 to 8.5 million in 1983) with the Liberal-Social Democratic Alliance coming close to Labour in votes (7.8 million). But the Social Democratic Party representation was reduced to six seats, the Liberals winning 17 seats. The general election of 1987 saw some revival in the Labour vote (up 3.2 per cent) and a decline in the Liberal-SDP Alliance vote (down 2.8 per cent) with the Conservatives maintaining their share of the vote and their firm hold on office with an overall majority of 102.

Prime Minister and other Ministers

The Government of the United Kingdom is most commonly thought of as the Prime Minister and the Ministers in the Cabinet, together with other Ministers, the Departments of State and senior civil servants. Excluded from this description but having governmental functions are local authorities, public corporations managing the nationalised industries and welfare services, and administrative tribunals; and the public servants who are employed by those bodies.

With a few exceptions this distinction between the inner circle of central governmental bureaucracy and the outer circle of public authorities of many kinds reflects the distinction between those institutions with which Parliament is directly concerned and those with which it is not.

The Prime Minister is the leader of the political party which can command a majority in the House of Commons. Each party elects its own leader (see below, pages 105–107).

When a Prime Minister resigns in office, he can make his resignation effective from a date after his successor has been elected as leader—as did Mr. Wilson in 1976. If he dies in office, no doubt the Cabinet would nominate a temporary Prime Minister for the Queen's approval until the election of the new leader took place.

After Parliament has been dissolved so that a general election may be held, Ministers remain in office and, if their party is returned with a majority, they continue in office. If a different party is returned with an overall majority, the previous Government resigns and the Queen asks the leader of that other party to accept the seals of office as Prime Minister and to form a Government.

If, after a general election, no party commands an overall majority in the House of Commons, there may be a period of negotiation between the parties before it becomes clear whom the Queen should send for.[15]

The first task of the newly appointed Prime Minister is to form a Cabinet. This involves two closely connected problems. The first problem is whom to appoint. By convention, a Minister must be a Member of the House of Commons or the House of Lords; or, if not so at the time of appointment, must quickly be found a place in one or other House. This can be done either by persuading a back-bencher to give up his or her seat (generally on promise of a peerage) so creating a vacancy which, it is hoped, will be filled, after a by-election, by the Minister[16]; or by making the Minister a Peer. Except where a coalition Government is formed, the Prime Minister will choose Ministers exclusively from Members or Peers of the Prime Minister's party.

A Conservative Prime Minister is not otherwise restricted in choice of Ministers. There will be those who are regarded (and regard themselves) as more senior, more eminent than others. Some will have been Ministers in earlier Governments. Some will have long been supporters of the Prime Minister. Some will have held important positions within the party. Some will be particularly popular with party members in the constituencies.

These more senior party members who are also Members of Parliament, or are Peers, will be expecting Cabinet office, Not all will have their expectations fulfilled. The Prime Minister may decide that some are too old; or that their previous record does not justify high office; or that for some personal reasons their appointment is not acceptable. Their political position within the party (whether they are on the right or the left) presents complications. The Prime Minister will not wish to be surrounded by politically unsympathetic people. But the diversity of opinion within the party must be considered and, within limits determined by the Prime Minister, given some measure of representation within the Cabinet. Geographical and occupational spread, businessmen and trade unionists, women, all are to be considered.

---

[15] This happened after Mr. Heath's defeat in February 1974 before Mr. Wilson took office. See above, p. 19.

[16] In January 1965, P. Gordon Walker failed to win such a by-election and resigned as Foreign Secretary. After the general election of June 1987, Mr. Peter Fraser lost his seat but continued as Solicitor-General for Scotland.

A Labour Prime Minister may not be so free. Standing orders of the Parliamentary Labour Party since 1980 provide that on taking office the Leader shall appoint as members of his Cabinet those who were elected members of the Parliamentary Committee at the dissolution and have retained their seats in the new Parliament. There are 18 such members, all drawn from and elected by Labour Members of the House of Commons.[17] In what follows this restraint on the power of a Labour Prime Minister must be borne in mind. He retains the right to appoint members of his Cabinet to specific jobs but not to form his Cabinet initially of those whom he chooses. But party standing orders say nothing to limit his power to dismiss and to fill vacancies thus created. Moreover it is doubtful whether they can constitutionally limit his right to recommend to the Queen as her Ministers whom he chooses. None of this has been tested in practice.

The second problem that faces the Prime Minister is the allocation of jobs within the Cabinet. This is not so much a question of which jobs to have represented in the Cabinet (that almost answers itself) as of which jobs to give to which Ministers. Some jobs in the Cabinet—Chancellor of the Exchequer, Foreign and Home Secretaries, for example—are more prestigious jobs than others and the most senior or eminent of persons within the party will not be pleased with and might not accept the lesser jobs. The Prime Minister may also appoint a few individuals to jobs which, in terms of departmental responsibility, are sinecures (the Chancellorship of the Duchy of Lancaster for example) and so leave them free to be used for such special jobs as the Prime Minister may allot while having their general advice at hand whenever it is needed.

Some representation in the House of Lords is also necessary. The Lord Chancellor will be the most senior of that group which may contain a few of the most eminent: Lord Carrington as Foreign Secretary from May 1979 to April 1982 was an example. The conferment of a peerage is also a way of bringing into the Cabinet someone from outside the House of Commons (as was Lord Young, for example, in 1985).

At the end, the Cabinet will therefore be composed for the most part of some 22 or so of the most senior and eminent members of the party in the House of Commons (the exclusion of Mr. Heath, the former Prime Minister, from Mrs. Thatcher's Cabinet in 1979 being the most striking post-war exception). The Cabinet will also contain a few of the younger men and women who have proved their abilities in previous office or elsewhere and who are seen as likely to rise to the highest posts; and one or two of the Prime Minister's favourites.

Not in the Cabinet are the four Law Officers (the Attorney-General and the Solicitor-General, the Lord Advocate and the Solicitor-General for Scotland) and 30 or so senior Ministers. Of these most are Ministers of State in different departments. In addition, there are over 30 Parliamentary Under-Secretaries of State and Parliamentary Secretaries; and others including Whips totalling over 20. This gives a full number of over 100 ministerial appointees on the Government's payroll distributed among more than 20 Departments of State.

Subject to what we have said about the possible limitations on the powers of a Labour Prime Minister, all these persons are appointed and dismissible

---

[17] The 18 are made up of the Deputy Leader, the Chief Whip, the Chairman of the P.L.P. and 15 M.P.s.

by the Prime Minister. Moreover, it seems that in practice Prime Ministers today do make the great majority of these decisions. The Prime Minister having made the most important appointments in the Cabinet will take advice from those appointed, including the Chief Whips, about the other dispositions, senior and junior. But the evidence indicates that all appointments at all levels are effectively made by the Prime Minister who may seek to balance political opinion within departments by appointing a Minister of State or Parliamentary Under-Secretary or Parliamentary Secretary whose political views are known to be somewhat to the right or to the left of the Minister who is the head of the department. Certainly the Prime Minister does not normally delegate to the senior Minister in the department the power to appoint his juniors, though he may express his preference, more or less strongly.[18]

This account has emphasised the extent of the power of patronage of the Prime Minister in the making of these appointments. But this does not mean that the Prime Minister can simply adopt an attitude of "take it or leave it," particularly where the more senior posts are in issue. There are many examples of bargains being made between the Prime Minister and those to be appointed.[19] The list of Cabinet Ministers indicates a hierarchy and some Ministers have insisted on keeping their place in that list when moved to other jobs. Some have attempted to obtain assurances for future promotion or have sought to lay claim to specific Ministerial posts, or to specific provisions concerning terms and conditions of office. R. K. Alderman estimated in 1976 that more than 20 persons had refused offers of Cabinet membership since 1918 and that there had been many more refusals of non-Cabinet office, sometimes on financial grounds.[20]

All of this shows that the Prime Minister's job in seeking to fill specific posts requiring particular qualifications is not easy. The patronage power is real and no doubt the great majority of Members and Peers on the Government side will take anything that is offered especially on first appointment or on promotion. And some will accept out of loyalty or because refusal would be damaging to their personal reputation. But in the bargaining process, not all the power is on the Prime Minister's side. Malcontents on the back-benches can be a considerable nuisance to any Government.

As many Ministers at all levels spend an important part of their time answering for the Government in the House of Commons their ability to hold their own in the face of parliamentary criticism is an important attribute. It is on the floor of the House or in committee that a Member has the best opportunity of impressing the Prime Minister and other senior colleagues with his or her abilities. Another attribute much appreciated is that of loyalty, that of being "a good party man." As in other walks of life, a combination of individual ambition and personal deference, or at least the appearance of both, is not always easy to achieve.

The House of Commons is a genuine testing ground of certain political qualities, some of which are valuable, if not indispensable, in Ministers. But a good parliamentary performer does not necessarily make a good Minister.

---

[18] But see J. Prior, *A Balance of Power* (1986), p. 190 where he records that he was given a free hand to choose his Ministers for the Northern Ireland Office.

[19] See R. K. Alderman, "The Prime Minister and the Appointment of Ministers: An Exercise in Political Bargaining" in (1976) 29 *Parliamentary Affairs* 101.

[20] See last note. In 1963, Mr. Enoch Powell and Mr. Iain MacLeod refused to serve in Sir A. Douglas-Home's Cabinet.

Being the head of a large department of State, even holding a ministerial post at a lower level within a department, calls for other important qualities. Ministers are also decision takers. The officials in the department will collate and present the material on which the decisions must be based and will present alternatives or preferred choices. The Minister must be able to assess the merits and demerits of the arguments put to him and even of the arguments not put to him. He must also have a keen political sense, which his officials may lack, of the way in which particular decisions will or may be received by the affected public. Misjudgment may lead to considerable political embarrassment, even when the decision itself, in purely administrative terms, is the correct decision. Some excellent House of Commons men and women, including those who appear popular or well-liked in the general community, have proved to be less than competent Ministers. So also the reverse is true.

Prime Ministers also dismiss Ministers both from the Cabinet and from junior Ministerial appointments, and a vacancy in the Cabinet is often the occasion of a re-shuffle of posts. The most comprehensive exercise in dismissal from Cabinet in recent times was when Mr. Macmillan replaced seven members on July 13, 1962 in an attempt to rejuvenate the Cabinet. The Prime Ministerial years under Mr. Wilson (1964–1970 and 1974–1976), Mr. Heath (1970–1974), and Mr. Callaghan (1976–1979) saw few dismissals of importance, except that by Mr. Callaghan of Mrs. Castle from the Department for Social Services in 1976. Under Mrs. Thatcher (from 1979) there have been a dozen or more dismissals or forced resignations from the Cabinet on grounds of personal or policy differences (see page 27).

Responsibility and accountability

Collective responsibility

The principle of collective responsibility, as applied to Cabinet Ministers, means that each Minister accepts responsibility for the decisions of the whole Cabinet. Inside the Cabinet, a Minister may argue for a different course of action but he is expected not to express public disagreement with the course decided on though dispensation may be given to a Minister on a matter particularly affecting his constituency (see pages 70–71). If he feels very strongly on a matter he may resign in which case he will have an opportunity to make a statement in Parliament. This version of the doctrine applies in the simplest case where Ministers are present at the Cabinet meeting where the decision is taken. But it also applies to Cabinet Ministers who are not present and so could not be said to participate in the making of the decision; and to those decisions of Cabinet committees which are not required to be endorsed by the full Cabinet and the existence of which some Ministers may be unaware. The chairman of each Cabinet committee decides, after consultation with the Prime Minister (where the chairman is not the Prime Minister), whether decisions of the committee may be taken by a dissident Minister to the full Cabinet.

The institution of Cabinet committees with limited membership inevitably results in the fragmentation of Cabinet government.

A major exception to the principle of collective responsibility was made in April 1975. The Labour Cabinet was divided on the question whether the United Kingdom should remain in the Common Market. It was agreed that Ministers should have a limited right, outside Parliament, to express views at variance with the official view of the Government that the United Kingdom should remain in.[21] Seven Cabinet Ministers openly campaigned, in the period leading to the referendum on the question, against the majority view. And the clashes between Ministers sometimes seemed to go beyond the "agreement to differ." Difficulties arose when dissident Ministers answered supplementary questions in the Commons and gave answers which could be interpreted as stating their own rather than the Government's view. In the event, in the division after the debate on April 7–9, 1975, seven Cabinet and 31 other Ministers voted against the official Government view which was approved by 396 votes to 170.[22]

Introducing the "Lib-Lab" agreement on March 23, 1977,[23] the Prime Minister (Mr. Callaghan) said that the Liberal Party had reaffirmed its strong conviction that a proportional system should be used as the method of election to the European Assembly. The Government allowed a free vote on the issue. Mr. Callaghan let it be known that he supported proportional representation for this purpose. In the event, 146 Labour M.Ps voted in favour and 115 (including four Cabinet Ministers) against, but proportional representation was lost by 87 votes. The Leader of the Liberal Party noted: "The Tories' three-line whipped 'free' vote does the trick with a huge anti-PR vote on their side."[24]

Ministers not in the Cabinet are ill-advised to make statements which seem to depart from Government policy. Indeed one reason why an offer of ministerial office is sometimes refused is because acceptance effectively prevents personal expressions of opinion. Any Minister outside the Cabinet who deliberately defies this ban is almost certain to be dismissed.[25]

Collective responsibility is said to be one of the more important conventions of the constitution. But, like so many important conventions, its use and scope are determined by the ordinary practicalities of politics. No Government wishes to demonstrate in public its internal dissensions and so decisions once come to are presented by all Ministers as the policy of the Government. This deprives outside critics of the opportunity to declare that individual members of the Cabinet are dissatisfied with the decision. Speculation may continue but deprived of hard evidence of dissension.

Most Cabinet Ministers most of the time adhere to Cabinet decisions whatever their private misgivings. But some Ministers who either are generally less able to accept decisions of which they disapprove or are particularly incensed by particular decisions, may be unwilling to keep private their disagreement. So, one way or another, they let their doubts be known. At this point, the Prime Minister has to decide what, if anything, to do to restore discipline.[26]

Most recently, disagreement within the Cabinet on the Westland affair led

---

[21] There was a similar agreement in January 1932 on the levy of tariff duties.

[22] H.C.Deb., Vol. 889, col. 1365–1371 (April 9, 1975).

[23] H.C.Deb., Vol. 928, col. 634–758 (March 23, 1977).

[24] David Steel, *A House Divided* (1980), p. 110; H.C.Deb., Vol. 941, cols. 299–422 (December 13, 1977).

[25] This may even apply to Parliamentary Private Secretaries to Ministers: see B. Sedgemore, *The Secret Constitution* (1980), pp. 12, 218–228. Nowadays there are 50 or more P.P.Ses. and they are expected to support the Government, although they are not Ministers and receive no salary except as ordinary Members.

[26] In 1969, Mr. Callaghan, then Home Secretary, disapproved, in part, of the Government White Paper *In Place of Strife* and this became known. He was removed from an inner Cabinet committee: see Harold Wilson, *The Labour Government 1964–70* (1971), pp. 789, 805, 816.

to a major crisis in the life of Mrs. Thatcher's administration.[27] In 1985, Westland, a company building helicopters in the United Kingdom, was in need of additional capital. A largely American-based consortium—popularly known as Sikorski-Fiat—was interested in becoming a minority shareholder for this purpose. The Secretary of State for Defence (Mr. Michael Heseltine) preferred a European consortium and he publicly promoted its cause. In the Prime Minister's view this promotion conflicted with the Government's position of not favouring either bidder and was in breach of the convention of collective responsibility. The Prime Minister required all Ministers to refer statements they intended to make about this matter to the Cabinet Office for approval. Mr. Heseltine refused to accept this constraint and resigned from the Cabinet on 9 January 1986.

Collective responsibility is a useful, often necessary, principle for the conduct of government. The political success of a Government rests to a considerable extent on the confidence it manages to generate among the electorate and that confidence is damaged when Ministers are seen to be divided. How far individual Ministers may be allowed to express personal doubts depends in the last resort on the Prime Minister. As Mr. Callaghan said in 1977: "I certainly think that the doctrine should apply, except in cases where I announce that it does not."[28]

Collective responsibility requires Ministers either to accept Government policy or to resign. Famous examples of resignation on policy grounds are those of Sir Samuel Hoare, then Foreign Secretary in Baldwin's Government, in 1935, when a plan agreed with the French premier (Pierre Laval) was disowned by the Cabinet because of adverse public opinion[29]: and of Sir Anthony Eden, Hoare's successor at the Foreign Office, over Chamberlain's policy towards the Italian leader (Benito Mussolini) in 1938.[30]

The most momentous resignation was that of Neville Chamberlain himself when he was succeeded by Winston Churchill as Prime Minister in May, 1940. This followed a debate in the House of Commons on the Norwegian campaign when, on a motion for the adjournment, 41 Government supporters voted with the Opposition, some 60 abstained and the Government's official majority of over 240 fell to 81.[31] But, as Mr. Chamberlain remained in the Cabinet his resignation cannot be listed as an operation of the doctrine of collective responsibility.

Other examples of Cabinet resignations because of disagreements on policy include those of Aneurin Bevan (Minister of Labour and National Service) and Harold Wilson (President of the Board of Trade) in 1951, the immediate occasion being the Budget proposals, including the making of charges for dental and ophthalmic treatment under the National Health Service.[32]

One well documented and much cited example of resignation is less usually included as one of policy disagreement but seems to have been so. This concerned 725 acres of Crichel Down which had been compulsorily

---

[27] For a detailed account, see the Fourth Report from the Defence Committee (H.C. 519 of 1985–86) and the Minutes of Evidence (H.C. 169 of 1985–86); for the Government Response, see Cmnd. 9916.

[28] H.C.Deb., Vol. 933, col. 552 (June 16, 1977).

[29] H.C.Deb., Vol. 307, cols. 2007–2017 (December 19, 1935).

[30] H.C.Deb., Vol. 332, cols. 45–50 (February 21, 1938).

[31] H.C.Deb., Vol. 360, cols. 1364–1368 (May 8, 1940).

[32] H.C.Deb., Vol. 487, cols. 34–43, 228–231 (April 23, 1951).

acquired and was later transferred to the Ministry of Agriculture and Fisheries who decided to let the land as a single fully equipped holding. In 1953 it was decided to appoint a particular tenant without honouring a promise to go to public tender. Eventually the Minister (Sir Thomas Dugdale) set up an inquiry. Rumours of bribery, corruption and personal dishonesty were found to be without substance but some civil servants were severely criticised.[33]

Sir Thomas made statements to the House of Commons on two occasions. On June 15, 1954 he said that the inquiry, in finding no bribery, corruption or personal dishonesty, had achieved his main purpose in setting it up, and he defended his civil servants.[34] His second statement was in a full debate on the whole affair on July 20, 1954. He accepted full responsibility for the actions of his civil servants and said he had been much criticised since his first statement for attaching too little importance to their faults. He said he had never sought to obscure the fact that mistakes and grave errors of judgment had been made which undoubtedly merited severe censure and reprimand. The Government, however, had changed the decision on the disposal of the land and Sir Thomas announced his resignation at the end of his speech.[35]

It seems however that Sir Thomas's resignation was not because of his responsibility for the faults of his civil servants. Certainly he did not explicitly say so and his resignation surprised the Opposition front bench. It seems that Sir Thomas disagreed with the Government's decision to reverse, so far as it was able, his own decision in this particular case.[36]

In 1957, Lord Salisbury resigned from the Cabinet in disagreement with the Government's policy over Cyprus.[37] In 1958 Mr. Thorneycroft resigned as Chancellor of the Exchequer over economic policy.[38] Other resignations from the Cabinet on policy grounds were those of Mr. Cousins as Minister of Technology on incomes policy in 1966,[39] the Earl of Longford as Lord Privy Seal on education policy in 1968,[40] Mr. Gunter as Minister of Power on general dissatisfaction with the Government in 1968,[41] and Mr. Prentice as Minister for Overseas Development similarly in 1976.[42]

Akin to resignations on grounds of particular policy are those of Mr. George Brown in 1968 and Mr. Heseltine in 1986. During an international financial emergency in March 1968 a meeting of the Privy Council was held late at night when, according to Prime Minister Wilson's account,[43] George Brown, then Foreign Secretary, was not consulted because he could not be found for some hours. Mr. Brown resigned. He complained strongly of "presidential" government. This was also, in very different circumstances,

---

[33] See report of the public inquiry Cmd. 9176.

[34] H.C.Deb., Vol. 528, cols. 1745–1747 (June 15, 1954).

[35] H.C.Deb., Vol. 530, cols. 1178–1298 (July 20, 1984).

[36] See Lord Boyle, "Ministers and the Administrative process" in 58 *Public Administration* 1. (1980). Dugdale was severely criticised by many Conservative back-benchers at meetings of the 1922 Committee: see I. F. Nicolson, *The Mystery of Crichel Down* (1986).

[37] H.L.Deb., Vol. 202, cols. 953–959 (April 2, 1957).

[38] H.C.Deb., Vol. 580, cols. 1294–1297 (January 23, 1958). He was joined by his junior Ministers, Mr. E. Powell and Mr. N. Birch.

[39] H.C.Deb., Vol. 731, cols. 1787–1799 (July 14, 1966).

[40] H.L.Deb., Vol. 288, cols. 1–10 (January 22, 1968).

[41] On July 1, 1968.

[42] H.C.Deb., Vol. 923, cols. 516–525 (December 21, 1976).

[43] *The Labour Government 1964–70* pp. 640–8; and see George Brown, *In My Way* chapter 9; H.C.Deb., Vol. 761, col. 55–57 (March 18, 1968).

part of Mr. Heseltine's reason for his resignation during the Westland affair (see page 25). In constitutional terms, he made clear that he thought the Prime Minister should act as (in the old phrase) *primus inter pares* and that she was instead assuming greater powers.[44] Both these resignations were in part by way of protest against the way government was being conducted.

Frequently the reason for ministerial resignations is personal. Sometimes these are the result of conduct which is deemed not acceptable. In the last 25 years instances include the conduct of Mr. Profumo[45] in 1963, Mr. Maudling[46] in 1972, Lords Lambton and Jellicoe[47] in 1973, and Mr. Parkinson[48] in 1983. Personal blunders are less common: Mr. Hugh Dalton's[49] almost inadvertent leaking of budget secrets, minutes before he was due to make them public in 1947, is an example.[50]

Individual Ministerial responsibility

MINISTERS AND CIVIL SERVANTS: Members of Parliament are concerned with all aspects of the machinery of central Government including the relationship between Ministers and civil servants. So long as the system is retained whereby political Ministers are put in charge of departments of State which are staffed by permanent civil servants, there will be conflict as well as co-operation between those Ministers and those servants. If Ministers seek to push civil servants into actions or procedures which go against what civil servants regard as legitimate, sooner or later (on recent evidence, later) civil servants will rebel. If civil servants seek to impose their views of what is in the public interest too strongly on reluctant Ministers, Ministers will look elsewhere for advice. On the floor of the House and in select committees, Members investigate this relationship and criticise and suggest reforms.[51]

It is often said that traditionally civil servants are anonymous. But, in the ordinary meaning of that word, this is not so. The names of many senior civil servants are well known. *The Civil Service Year Book* shows in what part of what department each civil servant works from the rank of principal upwards. Civil servants sign letters in their own name and take decisions in their own name, and they appear publicly before select committees. This greater visibility of civil servants means that Members are more aware today of whom in the departments to approach for information or assistance.

What is true is that, normally, all actions by civil servants are taken on the nominal instruction of Ministers. Legally and constitutionally, civil servants are not the servants of Ministers but, like Ministers, are servants of the Crown. But the Minister is the departmental head, the statutory powers are

---

[44] *The Times*, January 10, 1986; Mr. Brittan's resignation in January 1986 is discussed below pp. 28–29.

[45] Then Secretary of State for War.

[46] Then Secretary of State for the Home Department.

[47] Then Parliamentary Under Secretary of State, Ministry of Defence; and Lord Privy Seal, respectively.

[48] Then Secretary of State for Trade and Industry.

[49] Then Chancellor of the Exchequer.

[50] H.C.Deb., Vol. 444, cols. 651–652 (November 13, 1947); see also H.C.20 of 1947–48.

[51] See, for example, the Report and Minutes of Evidence of the Treasury and Civil Service Committee on Civil Servants and Ministers: Duties and Responsibilities (H.C. 92–I, II of 1985–86).

vested in him, and he provides the authority under which civil servants operate.

The Parliamentary Commissioner for Administration is empowered to inquire into the activities of individual civil servants when investigating a complaint of maladministration and although it is not his practice to name names his reports may clearly indicate where, within the service, the fault or responsibility lay.

Permanent secretaries are the accounting officers of departments and have the responsibility to ensure that funds voted by Parliament are spent for the purposes appropriated.[52] This can give rise to conflict with Ministers and disagreements may be recorded. If the safeguarding of public funds or the regularity of expenditure is in question the accounting officer may ask for written instructions from his Minister before he will take action; and he may report the matter to the National Audit Office. In 1975 Sir Peter Carey, second permanent secretary and accounting officer at the Department of Industry recorded his objection to the Minister's interpretation of the Minister's powers under section 7 of the Industry Act 1972 to use public funds to establish three workers' co-operatives.

If serious faults are discovered in a department, an official inquiry may be set up, often after parliamentary pressure, and its report made public. In extreme cases, an investigation may be made under the Tribunals of Inquiry (Evidence) Act 1921; it is held in public and evidence may be called from Ministers, civil servants and others. Public inquiries often lead inevitably to the naming of officials found to be at fault.

In 1972, a tribunal of inquiry reported that an under-secretary in the Department of Trade and Industry was negligent in not taking appropriate action which might have prevented the collapse of the Vehicle and General Insurance Company. Two other named civil servants were also criticised.[53] A committee of inquiry in 1977[54] and a tribunal of inquiry in 1982[55] were both severely critical of public servants in their activities as Crown Agents.

In December 1980, three category A prisoners escaped from Brixton prison. The Governor accepted primary responsibility for the human errors found by the official inquiry and was moved to another post.[56] Similarly, the inquiry into the breakout at the Maze prison in Belfast in September 1983 led to criticism of public officials. The report said that "at all levels the quality of managerial control, direction and leadership proved inadequate."[57]

In recent times, parliamentary criticism of civil servants became sharpest during the investigations into the Westland affair (pages 24–25). The Secretary of State for Defence (Mr. Heseltine) in January 1986 made public a letter he had written to advisors to the European consortium. The Prime Minister suggested to the Secretary of State for Trade and Industry (Mr. Brittan) that he should seek the advice of the Solicitor-General about the accuracy of some of the statements in that letter. He did so and the Solicitor-General wrote to Mr. Heseltine saying that, on the basis of the limited

---

[52] Exchequer and Audit Departments Act 1866, s.22; see H.C. 576 of 1977–78 Appendix 3.
[53] See report of the tribunal H.C. 133 of 1971–72; H.C.Deb., Vol. 831, cols. 419–428 (February 16, 1972) and H.C.Deb., Vol. 836, cols. 33–161 (May 1, 1972).
[54] H.C. 48 of 1977–78; and see H.C. 49 of 1977–78.
[55] H.C. 364 of 1981–82. The Crown Agents were brought under statutory control by the Crown Agents Act 1979.
[56] See H.C.Deb., Vol. 998, cols. 20–26 (February 2, 1981).
[57] H.C. 203 of 1983–84 para. 8.29 and below, pp. 35–36.

information in documents he had seen, there seemed to him to be "material inaccuracies." Mr. Brittan, on receiving a copy of the Solicitor-General's letter, authorised his officials, without the Solicitor-General's knowledge but subject to the agreement of the Prime Minister's office, to disclose certain excerpts from this letter to the press by telephoning the Press Association. The Defence Committee found "quite extraordinary" the acceptance by five senior officials "apparently without demur" that giving extracts from the Solicitor-General's letter to the Press Association was the only way to do it in the time available. This, said the select committee, was "a wrong decision"[58] and it found "extraordinary" the fact that no disciplinary action was to be taken against any of these officials.[59] Of Sir Robert Armstrong, the select committee said:

> "It is to the Head of the Home Civil Service that all civil servants have to look for example and a clear lead in such things. In this case that lead has not been given."[60]

And the committee concluded:

> "Ministers may express regret at the naming of individual officials in proceedings of the House. Yet when the conduct of individual officials is a matter of general comment and controversy, Ministers discharge their obligations to officials by satisfying the House that those officials have behaved properly. Officials who do their duty have a right to expect that support from their Ministers. If Ministers cannot demonstrate that officials have behaved properly, the question of disciplinary proceedings arises."[61]

In its report on efficiency and effectiveness in the civil service, the Treasury and Civil Service Committee in March 1982 drew attention to the Management Information System for Ministers which the Secretary of State for the Environment (Mr. Heseltine) had introduced. Each directorate[62] of the department prepared an annual statement for the Secretary of State which provided him with regular information about all the activities of the department so that he could review in detail the work done, systematically, comprehensively and on a continuing basis. The select committee recommended that the system should be adopted in all departments and the statement published.[63]

In its observations on the select committee report just referred to, the Government announced the setting up of the Financial Management Initiative (FMI) designed to promote in each department an organisation and system under which managers at all levels would have a clear view of their objectives, a well-defined responsibility for making the best use of their resources, and the information needed to exercise their responsibilities

---

[58] H.C. 519 of 1985–86 paras. 159–160.

[59] *Ibid.* para. 213. The Government considered that disciplinary proceedings were not called for: Cmnd. 9916, para. 3.

[60] *Ibid.* para. 214. The Government did not agree with this suggestion: Cmnd. 9916, para. 34.

[61] *Ibid.* para. 237.

[62] Usually a section of the Department headed by an Under-Secretary.

[63] H.C. 236–I of 1981–82 paras. 23–26. Mr. Heseltine later introduced the system into the Ministry of Defence; H.C.Deb., Vol. 52, cols. 155–156 (January 17, 1984). See also Cmnd. 9841 paras. 5, 6, 13, where the Government in July 1986 endorsed these developments.

effectively. Essentially this is a value-for-money exercise. It has consequences for the structure of Supply estimates and so for parliamentary
scrutiny.[64]

Both of these innovations may have the result of indicating more specifically than hitherto the duties of individual civil servants who may then be
called to account by Members of Parliament in select committees and
elsewhere.[65]

Recent developments indicate that this personal responsibility may soon
be carried further. In February 1988 the Prime Minister announced that the
Government had accepted the main recommendations of its Efficiency
Unit.[65a] These were contained in a report entitled Improving Management in
Government: The Next Steps. The central recommendation was that "agencies" should be established to carry out the executive functions of government within a policy and resources framework set by a Government
department. Chief Executives of agencies would be personally responsible
for operational matters while Ministers would remain responsible for policy.

The Treasury and Civil Service Committee emphasised that, with this
greater delegation to agencies, there must be "rigorous accountability to
Parliament, and to the public", and urged the Government to modify the
existing arrangements to ensure that the Chief Executive gave evidence to
select committees on his own behalf about what he had done as head of the
agency.[65b] The Government agreed that where a committee's interest was
confined to day-to-day operations, Ministers would "normally regard the
Chief Executive as being the person best placed to answer on their
behalf".[65c]

From time to time, civil servants have disclosed confidential information
to Members believing they had a duty to do so in the general public interest.
In the 1930s, Sir Robert Vansittart, permanent Under-Secretary at the
Foreign Office, passed information to Winston Churchill who also received
more detailed and more regular information from Desmond Morton who
was head of the Government's Industrial Intelligence Centre and from many
other civil servants, serving officers in the armed forces, and other public
officials.[66]

The most recent case had wider consequences. In July 1984 Mr. Clive
Ponting, an Assistant Secretary in the Ministry of Defence sent two documents to Mr. Tam Dalyell M.P. who passed them to Sir Anthony Kershaw
M.P. the chairman of the Foreign Affairs Committee. Sir Anthony handed
the documents to the Secretary of State for Defence (Mr. Heseltine) who
called in the Ministry's police to investigate. Two days after the investigation
began Ponting signed a statement admitting that he had sent the papers to
Dalyell. Ponting then resigned from the Civil Service but was later charged

---

[64] Cmnd. 8616, 9058, 9297. And see H.C. 92–II of 1985–86 pp. 3, 125; Q. 34, 215, 229. These
"executive responsibility budgets" are said to cover £3 billion of annual public expenditure:
H.C. Deb., Vol. 103, col. 355 (October 29, 1986).
[65] The Council of Civil Service Unions has recorded widespread scepticism and mistrust of
FMI among middle and lower management grades: see report from Public Accounts Committee (H.C. 61 of 1986–87 para. 42 and pp. 18–22).
[65a] H.C.Deb. Vol. 147 col. 1149 (February 18, 1988).
[65b] H.C. 494–I of 1987–88 para. 46.
[65c] Government reply to Treasury and Civil Service Committee: Cm 524.
[66] M. Gilbert, Winston S. Churchill vol. 5, (1976) esp. pp. xx–xxii, 554–555, 625. Vansittart
and others also passed information "sometimes illicitly" to Hugh Dalton M.P., then Opposition
spokesman: B. Pimlott, Hugh Dalton (1985), pp. 254–256.

under section 2 of the Official Secrets Act 1911 for communicating official information without being authorised to do so. In February 1985 Ponting was acquitted, the jury returning a unanimous verdict.

The two documents contained information about the sinking of the cruiser Belgrano in May 1982 during the Falklands conflict. Ponting claimed that his justification for disclosing the documents was that he believed Members of Parliament were being deliberately misled by ministerial statements about the sinking of the cruiser and that it was his duty to reveal this.[67]

In these cases, therefore, the civil servants claimed that they acted as they did principally because they believed that they owed a duty of disclosure to Parliament or the general public which transcended their duty to their Ministers or to the Government.

On February 16, 1985, the head of the Home Civil Service issued a note of guidance stating the duties and responsibilities of civil servants in relation to Ministers. The note was issued after consultation with permanent secretaries in charge of departments, with their agreement and with the consent of the Prime Minister.[68] A revised version was published on December 2, 1987.[69] The note stated the general principles governing the conduct of civil servants and emphasised that the duty of the individual civil servant was first and foremost to the Minister in charge of the department. The note also stated:

"A civil servant should not decline to take, or abstain from taking, an action because to do so would conflict with his or her personal opinions on matters of political choice or judgment between alternative or competing objectives and benefits; he or she should consider the possibility of declining only if taking or abstaining from the action in question is felt to be directly contrary to deeply held personal conviction on a fundamental issue of conscience.

A civil servant who feels that to act or to abstain from acting in a particular way, or to acquiesce in a particular decision or course of action, would raise for him or her a fundamental issue of conscience, or is so profoundly opposed to a policy as to feel unable conscientiously to administer it in accordance with the standards described in this note, should consult a senior officer. If necessary, and if the matter cannot be resolved by any other means, the civil servant may take the matter up with the Permanent Head of the Department and also has a right, in the last resort, to have the matter referred to the Head of the Home Civil Service through the Permanent Head of the Department . . . If the matter still cannot be resolved on a basis which the civil servant concerned is able to accept, he or she must either carry out his or her instructions or resign from the public service—though even after resignation he or she will still be bound to keep the confidence to which he or she has become privy as a civil servant."

This Note does not cover precisely the situation in which Mr. Brittan's civil servants found themselves during the Westland affair when ordered to disclose to the press the contents of the letter from the Solicitor-General to

---

[67] For his own account, see Clive Ponting, *The Right to Know* (1985). And see H.C.Deb., Vol. 73, cols. 733–826 (February 18, 1985).

[68] See H.C.Deb., Vol. 74, cols. 130–132, as amended in H.C.Deb., Vol. 84, col. 195 (October 24, 1985).

[69] See H.C.Deb., Vol. 123, cols. 572–575.

the Secretary of State for Defence (Mr. Heseltine). The Note does not make clear whether those civil servants were entitled to refuse to make the disclosure in this way if they thought it would be improper (though not illegal) to do so, when they did not have the opportunity to consult superior officers.[69a]

Lord Hooson asked some of these questions in a debate in the House of Lords on February 26, 1986:

"What are the duties, if any, of civil servants to Parliament? Do they owe any duty to Parliament if Ministers lie and a civil servant knows that it is a lie? Do they owe any duty to Parliament if the Minister refuses to be answerable to Parliament? In other words, what are the limits of a civil servant's duty to Government?"[70]

The Armstrong Memorandum as it came to be known led to much discussion and the Treasury and Civil Service Committee in 1985 appointed a sub-committee to inquire into the duties and responsibilities of civil servants and Ministers.[71] The committee was critical of the Memorandum and found remarkable that it should be considered an appropriate answer to today's problems. Observing that loyalty should not be a one way street, the committee recommended that the Prime Minister should, after consultation with the leaders of the other political parties represented in the House of Commons formulate and publish guidelines for Ministers which would set out their duties to Parliament and responsibilities for the civil service.[72] The committee also recommended that the Head of the Home Civil Service should enter into discussions with the Civil Service trade unions with a view to producing an agreed text of a new note of guidance for civil servants.[73] It emphasised that Ministers should be able to play an active role in selecting the key officials who were going to work with them in planning and implementing their policies and generally encouraged the "infusions, temporary and permanent" of highly motivated people of proven ability into the higher Civil Service.[74] Specifically on the issue that gave rise to the Memorandum, the select committee said that it could not regard as justified any leak by a civil servant which was designed to frustrate the policies or actions of a Minister and that civil servants who leaked information "should face the sack or internal discipline."

The Defence Committee ended its report on the Westland affair in July 1986 by inviting anyone who felt traduced by the findings of the committee to give oral or written evidence, in public or in private, to the committee.[75] Responding to the select committee the Government proposed to make clear to civil servants giving evidence to select committees that they should not answer questions which were or appeared to be directed to the conduct of themselves or of other named individual civil servants.[76] In a

---

[69a] Members of the security and intelligence services may seek guidance from a specially appointed staff counsellor (H.C.Deb. Vol. 121 col. 508; November 2, 1987).

[70] H.L.Deb., Vol. 471, col. 1093.

[71] See H.C. 92-I, II of 1985-86.

[72] The Government did not accept this proposal but did state certain principles which it repeated in the revised version of the Armstrong Memorandum (see above note 69): Cmnd. 9841 paras. 10–12.

[73] The Government said Sir Robert Armstrong would discuss this with the civil service unions: *ibid.* paras. 16–18.

[74] The Government did not accept this: *ibid.* paras. 21–25, 26–28.

[75] H.C. 519 of 1985–86 paras. 237, 239–240.

[76] Cmmd. 9916 para. 44.

subsequent debate, the Leader of the House (Mr. Biffen) indicated that there could be further discussion before new guidelines to civil servants were finally and formally issued.[77]

The Treasury and Civil Service Committee responded with a report on Ministers and Civil Servants. It distinguished "actions" of civil servants from their "conduct," defining "actions" as those activities which were carried out on the instructions of, or were consistent with the policies of, the Minister concerned. It noted that select committees regularly took evidence from officials concerning their actions and had no doubt that it would be quite wrong and entirely unacceptable for any restriction to be placed on the giving of such evidence. The select committee defined "conduct" as activities falling outside its definition of "actions"; such conduct might amount to misconduct. It agreed that it would only on rare occasions be necessary for select committees to investigate "conduct."[78]

The Liaison Committee also reported a few days later on the accountability of Ministers and civil servants. It drew attention to the special position of the Public Accounts Committee, and of the select committee on the Parliamentary Commissioner for Administration; and to the obligations falling directly on managerial civil servants under the Financial Management Initiative (see page 29). The Liaison Committee accepted the distinction between "actions" and "conduct" at least to the extent of agreeing that a select committee finding something amiss in conduct would pursue the matter with the Minister before reporting to the House. It recommended that the guidelines proposed by the Leader of the House should not be issued. Drawing on the experience of the Westland affair, the Liaison Committee asked for an undertaking that in future the Government would always ensure that a Minister was accountable to the appropriate select committee.[79]

The Government replied to both these reports. It accepted that if civil servants giving evidence to a select committee were unable to answer a question to the committee's satisfaction because they were inhibited by their duty to or the instructions of Ministers, the relevant departmental Minister should be prepared himself to attend the committee. The Government also accepted that there was no intention to place restrictions on the giving of the evidence about "actions" subject to national security, confidentiality and the preservation of collective responsibility.

To its reply the Government appended draft supplementary guidelines for officials giving evidence to departmental select committees. These stated that civil servants were accountable to Ministers and Ministers accountable to Parliament. So civil servants were subject to the instructions of Ministers and remained bound to observe their duty of confidentiality to Ministers. When questions appeared to be directed to the "conduct" of individual civil servants, carrying the implication of allocating individual criticism or blame, it was for the Minister to make inquiry and to inform the select committee what had happened and what had been done to put the matter right and to prevent a recurrence.[80]

---

[77] H.C.Deb., Vol. 103, cols. 415–416 (October 29, 1986).

[78] H.C. 62 of 1986–87, paras. 15, 26. In March 1988, the committee pursued some of these matters further with the newly appointed Secretary of the Cabinet and Head of the Home Civil Service (Sir Robin Butler): see H.C. 370–i of 1987–88.

[79] H.C. 100 of 1986–87, paras. 8, 9, 13, 15, 18.

[80] Cm. 78, para. 4, 6, Appendix.

Subject to one small alteration, requested by the Liaison Committee to avoid a possible impression that the select committee had approved or were in some way a party to the guidelines, the guidelines were sent to civil servants and appended to a new edition of "The Memorandum of Guidance for Officials appearing before select committees" which was issued in March 1988.[81]

PERSONAL RESPONSIBILITY AND ACCOUNTABILITY: The Minister in charge of a department of State is responsible for the decisions and actions he takes and for those taken in his name by his subordinates. Within the limitations imposed on him by decisions taken by the Government as a whole or by the need to ensure in special circumstances that he has the approval of the Prime Minister or the Treasury, the Minister is responsible for the policy of the department and for the application of that policy in particular cases. In Parliament, he represents the department, answers for it, introduces departmental bills, appears before committees on its behalf, and is expected, either personally or by sending a junior Minister, to be present to respond to criticisms of the department. He fights for the department's needs with other Ministers, in and out of Cabinet, and he is interviewed by the press, on television and on radio as his department's representative. If, as is most common, the Minister is a Member of the House of Commons, there will be a spokesman for his department in the House of Lords. If he is a Peer, he will have a Ministerial spokesman in the Commons.

Although Ministers may frequently seek to evade criticism and although their critics will frequently be dissatisfied with the answers they receive, Ministers only rarely refuse to answer. When they do, it is on the ground that disclosure would be contrary to the national interest, or that the matter is one for which they are not responsible.

The opportunity to hold Ministers accountable arises whenever Parliament is sitting for it is the essence of debate that Members and especially Opposition spokesmen will be enabled to respond to ministerial proposals or to initiate criticism of ministerial actions to which Ministers must reply. These opportunities are discussed at length in later chapters. Debate also provides opportunities for back-bench supporters of Ministers to reply to criticism. Some debates will end in a vote but the impact of criticism on Ministers, and so on the Government as a whole, is not nullified by the Government's almost inevitable victory in the divisions. Sometimes it will be apparent that although the Government has won the vote, it has lost the argument or at least that some part of the criticism has not been adequately answered. If so, the matter will be pursued on other occasions. And outside comment in the press and elsewhere may continue to reflect concern. In a real sense, the process of debate is continuous and a successful Opposition will be able to keep up the pressure. It is not unusual for Ministers to be forced from one position where they deny all blame to other positions where they admit some fault and possibly to a position where they are obliged to retract their earlier protestations of rectitude.

Much discussion has centred on the question of the extent to which Ministers are accountable for decisions and actions taken in their names

---

[81] Unpublished but placed in the House of Commons Library for the use of Members.

by civil servants in their department. It is accepted that Ministers can be personally involved only in policy decisions or in administrative matters of a particularly controversial kind. The day-to-day decisions of civil servants are taken supposedly within the limits of policy but inevitably involve varying degrees of discretion. Often these decisions are of great importance to the individual persons or corporations affected. For all such decisions Ministers are responsible and so accountable to Parliament if questioned there. Parliament is a forum where Ministers frequently learn for the first time what decisions have been taken in their name.

In 1954, during the debate on the Crichel Down affair (see pages 25–26) Sir David Maxwell Fyfe (then Home Secretary) suggested four different sets of circumstances in which the question of ministerial responsibility might arise. First, a Minister might explicitly order a civil servant to take certain action or, secondly, a civil servant might act properly in accordance with the policy laid down by the Minister. In both cases, the Minister must protect and defend the civil servant. Thirdly, "where an official makes a mistake or causes some delay, but not on an important issue of policy and not where a claim to individual rights is seriously involved, the Minister acknowledges the mistake and accepts the responsibility, although he is not personally involved." In this case the "corrective action" is taken in the department and the official is not exposed to public criticism. But fourthly "where action has been taken by a civil servant of which the Minister disapproves and has no prior knowledge, and the conduct of the official is reprehensible, then there is no obligation on the part of the Minister to endorse what he believes to be wrong, or to defend what are clearly shown to be errors of his officers" although he remains constitutionally responsible to Parliament.[82]

There is, however, a further responsibility which the Minister carries. In evidence to the Select Committee on Expenditure in 1977, Sir John Hunt, then Secretary to the Cabinet, said that a Minister had a responsibility, which he could not devolve to his permanent secretary, for "the efficiency and drive" of his department.[83] On the other hand, it is not easy for a Minister to achieve efficiency and drive if his permanent secretary lacks those qualities. Nevertheless, the Minister remains responsible.

If a Minister is culpable and the fault is serious he may be called on to resign. But it is extremely rare for a Minister to do so. Resignation of a Cabinet Minister in such circumstances is a serious event for a Government which is bound to suffer in reputation for a period. A Prime Minister must assess how much damage will result from the resignation and from the failure to resign. And so the political climate at the time and all the circumstances must be considered. The extent of culpability is obviously important.

In September 1983 there was a mass break-out of republican prisoners from the Maze prison in Belfast. The Secretary of State was Mr. Prior and the Under-Secretary, responsible for the prison service, was Mr. Nicholas Scott. The report of the official inquiry found a major failure in security at the prison "for which the Governor [of the prison] must be held accountable"; and a divisional head in the Prison Department of the

---

[82] H.C.Deb., Vol. 530, col. 1290 (July 20, 1954).
[83] H.C. 535–I of 1976–7, para. 95 citing Q. 1855.

Northern Ireland Office "must be held responsible for some of the short-comings".[84] The Governor resigned but no Minister did so.

The Secretary of State accepted in the debate on the report that he would have been obliged to resign if the report had shown that what had happened had been the result of some act of policy that was his responsibility, or that he had failed to implement something that he had been asked to implement, or should have implemented. He continued:

"I do not accept—and I do not think it right for the House to accept—that there is any constitutional or other principle that requires ministerial resignation in the face of failure, either by others to carry out orders or procedures or by their supervisors to ensure that staff carried out those orders. Let the House be clear: the . . . report finds that the escape would not have succeeded if orders and procedures had been properly carried out that Sunday afternoon . . . The question I have to ask myself is whether . . . I was to blame for those prisoners escaping."[85]

Mr. Enoch Powell disagreed. He said:

"The Secretary of State . . . drew a distinction, which I believe to be invalid, between responsibility for policy and responsibility for administration. I believe that this is a wholly fallacious view of the nature of ministerial responsibility . . . Even if all considerations of policy could be eliminated, the responsibility for the administration of a department remains irrevocably with the Minister in charge."[86]

This example demonstrates that the question of ministerial resignation always carries wider political implications. Given the choice, Prime Ministers must consider whether the resignation of a Cabinet Minister will damage the Government more or less than non-resignation. In this case, Mr. Prior's resignation, whether or not it would have accorded with constitutional convention, could have boosted the morale of the Irish Republican Army. The Opposition did not call for the Minister's resignation. Its spokesman said:

"We must consider whether Northern Ireland would benefit if a particular Minister resigned . . . I cannot envisage [Mr. Prior] being replaced from among members of the present Administration by anyone more compassionate or more politically sensitive."[87]

Ministers seldom resign, or offer their resignation, because of faults in their departments. Indeed, if as we have suggested Sir Thomas Dugdale's departure was on policy grounds (see pages 25–26) it is difficult to find a single clear case in recent times.

In the Westland affair (see pages 28–29), Mr. Brittan resigned and accepted full responsibility for the disclosure of the Solicitor-General's letter and for the form in which it was made. He expressed profound regret for the manner of the disclosure. It does not appear, however, that Mr.

[84] Report of an inquiry by H.M. Chief of Inspectors of Prisons into the security arrangements at H.M. Prison, Maze: H.C. 203 of 1983–84.

[85] H.C.Deb., Vol. 53, col. 1042 (February 9, 1984).

[86] *Ibid.* cols. 1060, 1061.

[87] Mr. P. Archer H.C.Deb., Vol. 53, col. 1056 (February 9, 1984), though he did suggest that a former Minister of State in the Northern Ireland Office should cease to be a member of the Government.

Brittan resigned because of any mistakes made by his officials. Indeed he explicitly told the House of Commons that at all times they acted in accordance with his wishes and instructions, that what they did was with his full authority and that they were not to be blamed.[88] He resigned because he had authorised the disclosure in a way subsequently disapproved of by the Prime Minister though she said she would have approved of the fact of disclosure; and because he lost the support of his ministerial colleagues and of Conservative back-benchers.

The nearest example of ministerial resignation for faults within the department was that of Lord Carrington, then Secretary of State for Foreign Affairs, soon after Argentine troops had invaded the Falkland Islands in 1982. In his letter of resignation, Lord Carrington wrote[89]:

"The Argentine invasion of the Falkland Islands has led to strong criticism in Parliament and in the press on the Government's policy. In my view, much of the criticism is unfounded. But I have been responsible for the conduct of that policy and I think it right that I should resign . . . [T]he invasion of the Falkland Islands has been a humiliating affront to this country."

Lord Carrington added that he had concluded that the undivided support of Parliament and of the country for the Government's policy would more easily be maintained if the Foreign Office were entrusted to someone else. The Committee of Privy Councillors who later reported on the events, criticised a number of decisions and actions (and failures to act) of both Ministers and the Foreign and Commonwealth Office.[90] That department had suffered a blow to its credibility and these faults, both of Ministers and officials, led to Lord Carrington's resignation.

Ministerial responsibility remains a strong convention because where Ministers are seen to be evasive, their reputation and that of the Government suffer both in Parliament and outside. Unless some measure of personal culpability can be attached to the Minister, or a scapegoat is needed, he can however usually expect to be retained, or moved to another equivalent post, so long as he has the Prime Minister on his side. The reaction of Parliament, especially the House of Commons, is often crucial. In a departmental crisis, back-bench opinion may determine whether or not a Minister resigns. If the Minister seems to have lost the confidence of the House, he becomes a liability to the Government and not even a strong Prime Minister may be able to save him. Press opinion also plays a part. These external influences seem to have been decisive in the resignations of both Mr. Brittan and Lord Carrington.

The Defence Committee, reporting on its inquiry into the Westland affair stated:

"A Minister does not discharge his accountability to Parliament merely by acknowledging a general responsibility and, if the circumstances war-

---

[88] H.C.Deb., Vol. 90, col. 671 (January 27, 1986). This was an emergency adjournment debate, and the Opposition may have hoped to persuade some Government back-benchers to abstain or even vote against the Government. None did.

[89] Letter to the Prime Minister of April 5, 1982; the Lord Privy Seal (Mr. Humphrey Atkins) and a Minister of State (Mr. R. Luce) also resigned; and see H.L.Deb., Vol. 429, cols. 1–4 (April 5, 1982).

[90] Cmnd. 8787, paras. 291–2, 296, 30, 302, 315.

rant it, by resigning. Accountability involves *accounting* in detail for actions as a Minister.[91]

But Ministers or former Ministers may decide not to account for their actions. As the select committee reported:

> "We asked Mr. Brittan whether he authorised that the whole document should be published. He refused to tell us. We asked Mr. Brittan who selected the passages to be quoted. He refused to tell us. We asked Mr. Brittan whether he knew the facts that would enable him to answer the previous questions. Again, he refused to tell us. We put the following question to Mr. Brittan: 'Why was the Solicitor-General not told that his letter was going to be leaked?' Mr. Brittan would not tell us."[92]

After the report of the select committee had been published, the Prime Minister was questioned in the House of Commons. Mrs. Thatcher expressed her total confidence in the officials referred to (and criticised) in the report, including the head of the home Civil Service (Sir Robert Armstrong). She repeated this statement three times and refused to answer further questions.[93]

MINISTERS AND QUANGOS: The nationalisation measures of the Labour Government of 1945 to 1951 used the public corporation as the principal institutional device. And it has continued to be used for many purposes by successive Governments. At present (1989) the coal, electricity and railway industries are governed by managerial boards appointed by the appropriate Minister. So are other undertakings like civil airways, the Post Office and the Bank of England. Ministers exercise special statutory powers over investment, borrowing and other activities of the boards. But the day-to-day administration is in the hands of the boards so that they may be free of close departmental control and able to operate more easily in the commercial world. Ministers therefore have refused to answer parliamentary questions about those matters for which they have no direct responsibility. At the same time Ministers keep in close touch with the chairman of the boards and exert influence over a wider field than the statutes provide for. Most of the statutes expressly empower Ministers to give general directions to the boards on matters affecting the national interest and although this power is very seldom used its existence helps to shape the relationship between Ministers and the boards.

The former pattern of largely autonomous industries, run by public corporations and subject to forms of ministerial control, is being increasingly replaced by subordinate bodies and, in many cases, by privatisation itself which of course removes parliamentary control.[94] Powers exercised by select

---

[91] H.C. 519 of 1985–86, para. 235.
[92] *Ibid.* paras. 167, 178; and see H.C. 169 of 1985–86 Qq. 946–960.
[93] H.C.Deb., Vol. 102, cols. 587–590 (July 24, 1986).
[94] On January 28, 1988 the Prime Minister stated that on April 1, 1987 there were 524 fewer non-departmental public bodies than in 1979 and that further reductions were planned (H.C.Deb., Vol. 126, cols. 313–314).

committees remain however in an attenuated version and are considered elsewhere.[95]

The relationship of these boards to Parliament is therefore not easily described. Ministers are accountable so far as they have powers and for any exercise they have made of extra-statutory influence, but tend, when it suits them, to seek to avoid accounting for the exercise of their important indirect influence. Questions used to be put down asking Ministers to give general directions to a board and these were usually answered. The affairs of a board may be debated if a public bill concerns the board (often to increase its borrowing powers) or if the board promotes a private bill, or where statutory instruments are made, or on substantive motions or on the adjournment (see page 264). On these occasions debate may range beyond the narrower bounds of Ministerial responsibility. But, although Ministers are empowered to obtain information from the boards, they have refused to answer questions seeking information on day-to-day administration, unless they have intervened directly.

There are other statutory and non-statutory governmental bodies which stand outside the central governmental machinery. One group is of bodies, composed mostly of persons not in Government, which are advisory to Ministers. As they have no other powers the question of their accountability raises few problems. The appropriate Minister is accountable for the appointments he makes and for terms of reference, payment and other such matters. The advice given is usually confidential and the Minister is of course accountable for any action he takes or does not take. It is sometimes useful for Ministers to disclose the advice given so as to support policy decisions they have come to.

A second group consists of administrative tribunals, whose members are appointed by Ministers. They adjudicate on claims arising out of the administration of many functions performed by departments, particularly in social security. Although governed by statutes and statutory instruments, they act independently of departments in coming to their decisions. For these decisions they are, like the courts, accountable to no-one, although there often are rights of appeal to superior tribunals. Again, the appropriate Minister is accountable for the appointments he makes. Both the advisory bodies and administrative tribunals are usually staffed by civil servants whose responsibility to Ministers remains.

The third group consists of executive bodies carrying out a wide range of operational or regulatory functions, various scientific and cultural activities, and some commercial or semi-commercial activities.[96] These are the bodies most commonly referred to as quangos (quasi-autonomous non-governmental organisations) though that word is also sometimes used to include advisory bodies and tribunals. The executive bodies are usually created by statute and include New Town Development Corporations, regional water authorities, the research councils, the Atomic Energy Authority, the Manpower Services Commission and industrial training boards, the British Council, the Commonwealth Development Corporation, and the Housing Corporation. Also to be included in this group, though not covered by the

---

[95] See below, Chapter 11. In 1951 the Select Committee of the House of Commons on Nationalised Industries was set up and after a false start was given new terms of reference in 1956. It became an influential body but ceased to exist as a result of the reform of select committees in 1979.

[96] Cmnd. 7797, para. 1.

Government survey, are public corporations as diverse as regional health authorities, the British Broadcasting Corporation and the Independent Broadcasting Authority. Finally, there are a number of major companies in which the Government has a shareholding.

About so various a collection of executive bodies it is difficult to generalise. Some are as independent as nationalised industries but many are financed in whole or in part by the Government. Some, on the other hand, like the water authorities and, more indirectly, the new towns, charge for their services as does the BBC (for its domestic services) through its licence fees. Where finance is provided at the expense of the taxpayer by way of outright grant, the money is voted by Parliament and the appropriate department approves the body's expenditure and has oversight of the numbers, grading and pay and conditions of staff. The Accounting Officer of the department is responsible for the relevant vote and the Accounting Officer of the body is responsible for the efficient and proper application of the money. The accounts are audited by the Comptroller and Auditor General and through him come before the Public Accounts Committee.[97]

In the event, ministerial accountability to Parliament for these "executive" bodies varies considerably. For appointments, salaries and conditions of work of the members, the Minister generally is fully accountable where these matters are in his hands. For some of them, particularly (amongst those listed) the health authorities, he is answerable to Parliament as fully as he is for his own department. For others, like the BBC, his powers are restricted and so is his accountability.

Quite separate from the bodies discussed above are local authorities. Here ministerial powers are many. Members of local authorities are elected directly and their powers are directly conferred by statute. But Ministers are also given many statutory controls over the raising of revenues and over expenditure, over borrowing, over standards. They have powers of inspection; powers over land acquisition; powers of appeal in connection with land-use; powers to act in default; sometimes powers to give policy directions, to offer advice through circulars, to issue regulations through statutory instruments. Each local authority function must be examined in detail to determine what is the extent of ministerial powers, and in recent years these controls, especially over finance, have greatly increased. In the special case of local police authorites, the powers of the Home Office are great and in the metropolitan police district the Home Secretary is the police authority.

The unmaking of Governments

Government defeats

Government defeats in the division lobbies of the House of Commons between 1945 and March 1972 took place on only 34 occasions. But Norton records that from April 1972 to April 1979 there were 65 defeats—a number which, for a seven year period, had not been equalled since the 1860s.[98] The

---

[97] Cmnd. 7797, para. 71. Some of these bodies are now subject to the jurisdiction of the Parliamentary Commissioner for Administration: see the Parliamentary and Health Service Commissioners Act 1987.

[98] P. Norton, *The Constitution in Flux* (1982), p. 112; and see his *Dissension in the House of Commons 1945–74* (1975); *Conservative Dissidents* (1978); *Dissension in the House of Commons 1974–79* (1980).

change began, as the dates indicate, during Mr. Heath's administration (1970–74) when his policies provoked some dissent among his Conservative back-benchers and he suffered six defeats of which the most important was on the Immigration Rules on November 22, 1982.[99]

Not surprisingly the minority Labour administration of February to October 1974 was defeated on 17 occasions but on none of these did the Government seek a vote of confidence. The re-elected Labour Government was defeated 42 times between October 1974 and March 1979. A serious defeat was on March 10, 1976 by 284 votes to 256. The division was after a debate on the Government's White Paper on expenditure when 37 Labour back-benchers abstained, all except four being members of the left-wing Tribune group though more than half the group voted with the Government. The matter before the House was of central importance to the Government's economic policy. However, the Government on an adjournment motion the next day, which the Prime Minister declared to be a vote of confidence, carried the day by 297 votes to 280.[1]

Early in 1977, the Government suffered a defeat when the second reading of the Reduction of Redundancy Rebates Bill was refused by 130 votes to 129.[2] There were no defections and such misfortunes are almost inevitable when a Government has no overall majority. The bill was replaced in a slightly different form by the Redundancy Rebates Bill which was given a second reading by 220 votes to 183.[3]

Part of the Labour Government's policy at this time was devolution to Scottish and Welsh assemblies and this encouraged the 14 members who were Scottish Nationalists or members of Plaid Cymru not to oppose the Government while there was some chance of these measures being successful. Losses at by-elections and other defections weakened the Labour Government which lost its overall majority in April 1976. On March 17, 1977 the Opposition tabled a motion of censure for debate on March 23. The Government sought the help of the Ulster Unionists and the Liberals. The Prime Minister (Mr. Callaghan) promised the Unionists an examination of their case for an increase in the number of Commons' seats in Ulster and this persuaded three Unionist M.P.s to abstain on the vote. On March 22, the Liberals came to an agreement with the Government under which a Consultative Committee was to be set up with Government and Liberal Members who would regularly examine government policy and Liberal proposals and some specific issues. Thus the Lib-Lab pact was born and the Government survived the vote of censure by 322 votes to 298.[4]

The pact lasted until the summer of 1978, the Government surviving a vote of no confidence on June 14, 1978[5] by the abstention of the Liberals. In December 1978 the Government was five votes short of an overall majority in the House of Commons. On December 13, the Opposition successfully,

---

[99] H.C.Deb., Vol. 846, cols. 1343–1459 (November 22, 1972).

[1] H.C.Deb., Vol. 907, cols. 634–758 (March 11, 1976).

[2] H.C.Deb., Vol. 925, cols. 1126–1186 (February 7, 1977).

[3] H.C.Deb., Vol. 928, cols. 915–960 (March 21, 1977).

[4] H.C.Deb., Vol. 928, cols. 1285–1418 (March 23, 1977). For opposition to the pact within the Cabinet and the Parliamentary Labour Party, see B. Sedgemore, *The Secret Constitution* pp. 96–98; and see A. Michie and S. Hoggart, *The Pact* (1978); and David Steel, *A House Divided* (1980).

[5] The wording of the motion was to reduce by half the salary of the Chancellor of the Exchequer; it was lost by 282 votes to 287 (H.C.Deb., Vol. 951, cols. 1013–1142).

by 285 votes to 279, moved an amendment condemning the Government's policy of using economic sanctions against firms that breached the Government's limit of 5 per cent. on pay rises. Four Labour Members abstained and two were absent. The Scottish Nationalists voted against the Government; so did the Ulster Unionists except two who abstained. One Plaid Cymru Member voted with the Government and two abstained. On the main question which followed the Government was defeated by 285 votes to 283.[6] The Prime Minister immediately announced that there would be a vote of confidence the next day. The Government abandoned its economic sanctions and won the vote by 300 to 290 votes.[7] There were no Labour abstentions and the comparatively large majority was the result of abstentions by Members of smaller parties, especially the Ulster Unionists who had been promised that the bill to increase Parliamentary representation in northern Ireland would be expedited."[8]

Eventually, on March 28, 1979, the Opposition parties combined successfully in a vote of no confidence defeating the Government by 311 votes to 310.[9] The Government immediately advised the Queen to dissolve Parliament.

The first administration under Mrs. Thatcher from May 1979 to June 1983 had an overall majority of 43. There were no defeats for the Government in the division lobbies of the House of Commons during these years. The story in the House of Lords was a little different (see Chapter 12).

Mrs. Thatcher's second administration of 1983–87 was elected with the large majority of 144 and lost only four seats as a result of by-elections. The possibility of a defeat in the House of Commons in a division when the whips were on and the matter at issue was part of the Government's programme seemed wholly remote. Yet on April 14, 1986, the Shops Bill was refused a second reading in the Commons, despite a three line whip, by 296 votes to 282.[10] The bill was intended to repeal the central provisions of earlier legislation and to enable the legal opening of shops on Sundays. The vote was in no sense an ambush in which the Government was taken by surprise. At least 70 Government back-benchers had stated their intention to oppose although no doubt the Government believed the number would be much smaller when the division was called. Before the debate the Secretary of State for the Home Department, as the Minister in charge of the bill, took a firm line indicating that he would prefer to abandon the bill rather than weaken its provisions. Members who criticised the bill did so for different reasons but in the event it appeared that those reasons were strong enough for 68 government supporters and 14 Ulster Unionists to vote against the bill. There were those who considered that the defeat might in the longer run have benefited the Government as it relieved the Government of the burden of trying to pilot a highly controversial measure through the committee and other stages of the bill.

Dissolution

Under the provisions of the Parliament Act 1911 the maximum duration

---

[6] H.C.Deb., Vol. 960, cols. 673–810 (December 13, 1978).

[7] H.C.Deb., Vol. 960, cols. 920–1050 (December 14, 1978).

[8] This was provided for in the House of Commons (Redistribution of Seats) Act 1979.

[9] H.C.Deb., Vol. 965, cols. 461–590. See D. Butler and D. Kavanagh, *The British General Election of 1979* (1980).

[10] H.C.Deb., Vol. 95, cols. 584–702; see below pages 27–28.

of a Parliament is five years. A Parliament usually ends, before that period has elapsed, by being dissolved by a royal proclamation which also orders the issue of writs for the election of a new Parliament. The occasion for a dissolution is the request by the Prime Minister to which the Sovereign accedes. Usually the time chosen is one which the Prime Minister considers most likely to result in a victory at the election.[11] But the Prime Minister may advise dissolution because the Government is defeated when seeking a vote of confidence. Alternatively the Opposition may carry a motion of no confidence in the Government or of censure. Also the Government may say in advance that it regards a particular vote as one of confidence, as did the Prime Minister (Mr. Heath) during the debate on the second reading of the European Communities Bill in 1972.[12] In October 1924, the minority Labour Government, which had taken office in January of that year, went to the country when the Liberal Members voted with the Conservatives.[13] And, as we have seen, dissolution followed when the Labour Government was defeated on March 28, 1979 on a vote of confidence.

The Government does not resign on the dissolution of Parliament but waits until the result of the election is clear. Even when all the returns from the constituencies are in, the effect may not be conclusive. As we have seen, the result of the general election of February 1974 gave no party an overall majority and had Mr. Heath come to an agreement with the Liberals, it is possible that he might have been able to stay in office. But no agreement could be reached, so he resigned and the Queen asked the Labour leader (Mr. Wilson) to form a Government.

---

[11] It is sometimes asserted that the decision is particularly one for the Prime Minister alone but the matter has in recent times frequently been discussed in Cabinet.

[12] H.C.Deb., Vol. 831, col. 752 (February 17, 1972). A Prime Minister might decide, after an adverse vote, to treat it as one of no confidence and to ask for a dissolution.

[13] H.C.Deb., Vol. 177, cols. 693–704 (October 8, 1924). The occasion was the withdrawal by the Government of criminal proceedings against J. R. Campbell, the editor of *Workers Weekly*.

Chapter 2

THE COMMONS AND THE PEOPLE

PARLIAMENTARY ELECTIONS

The electorate

A person entitled to vote at a parliamentary election in any constituency is one who is resident there on the qualifying date (three months' continuous residence is required in Northern Ireland), is not subject to any legal incapacity to vote, is either a Commonwealth citizen or a citizen of the Republic of Ireland, is aged 18 years or over, and is registered in the electoral register.[1] A person may not vote more than once in the same constituency or in more than one constituency. The qualifying date is October 10, for Great Britain (September 15 for Northern Ireland), for elections to be held within 12 months beginning on February 16, in the next following year. Members of the forces and certain persons employed by the Crown or the British Council who live outside the United Kingdom, and their spouses, may acquire a service qualification and so be entitled to vote. Others may qualify as overseas voters or as absent voters (including those on holiday).[2] Such persons are entitled to vote by proxy or by post but these methods require foresight and initiative. Other voters must vote in person at polling booths within the constituency where they reside.

Peers, other than Irish Peers, persons of unsound mind, and convicted persons in prison are incapable of voting; persons found guilty of corrupt or illegal practices at elections are disqualified for five years from voting.

Electoral registration officers have the duty to compile the registers based on compulsory returns made by heads of households which are made public and are open to correction.

It follows that the register is always more or less out of date. Those who move and so are residing in a constituency where they are not registered may use a postal vote or journey to the constituency where they are registered. But only a minority do so. Again, it is scarcely feasible to enforce the requirement placed on the head of the household to make the return on which the register is based; or to ensure its accuracy. Some heads of household may not understand what is required of them. Others may be reluctant, for good or bad reasons, to record their presence or that of others in the house. It is equally difficult to detect false returns, made knowingly or not, so names appear on the register which should not be there.[3]

Many of these defects could be remedied (by more frequent registers and by employing inspectors) but only at an expense which recent governments have been unwilling to meet.

---

[1] The law is contained in the Representation of the People Acts esp. that of 1983 and statutory instruments made thereunder.

[2] Representation of the People Acts 1983 and 1985.

[3] A survey in 1981 suggested that in England and Wales, 6.7 per cent. of those eligible were left off the register and up to 7 per cent. of those included were not qualified by residence: see H.C. 32 of 1982–83, Cmnd. 9140 and H.C.Deb., Vol. 62, cols. 1017–1092 (June 27, 1984).

Constituencies

The United Kingdom is divided into 650 constituencies, each of which returns one Member to the House of Commons.

Under the House of Commons (Redistribution of Seats) Acts, there are four permanent Boundary Commissions, one each for England, Scotland, Wales and Northern Ireland. Each is required to report with proposals for changes in the number and boundaries of constituencies once every ten to 15 years. A Boundary Commission may also make recommendations at any time about any particular constituency. The Speaker is nominally the chairman of each Commission. But each Commission has a superior judge as its deputy chairman and he is the effective principal. Each Commission has two other members, not Members but usually barristers. The Surveyor General and the Registrar General act as assessors. The Commissions publicise their provisional proposals for changes in groups of constituencies and invite representations. Local inquiries may be held presided over by barristers as Assistant Commissioners. Not surprisingly, political parties are the most usual objectors. The Assistant Commissioners then make their reports with recommendations which are usually accepted by the Commissioners. If the Commissioners propose to alter the provisional proposals, there is an opportunity for further representations.

At the election of 1987, there were 523 constituencies in England, 72 in Scotland, 38 in Wales and 17 in Northern Ireland. So far as is practicable having regard to those figures, county and London borough boundaries are not to be crossed. This rule predominates over the next which is that the electorate shall be as near the electoral quota as is practicable.[4] A wide general discretion is given the Commissioners if special geographical considerations make departure from these rules seem desirable but in practice this applies mainly to Scotland and Wales.

The Redistribution Acts provide that where a Boundary Commission makes a report recommending changes, the appropriate Secretary of State shall lay before Parliament a draft of an Order in Council giving effect to the recommendations with or without modification, any modifications being accompanied by a statement of the reasons therefor. If the draft is negatived or withdrawn, the Secretary of State may lay an amended draft. An order in Council has no effect until after the dissolution of the Parliament which approved the draft. Once Parliament has approved the draft the Home Secretary must submit it to the Queen who makes the Order in Council which cannot be called in question in any legal proceedings whatsoever.

After the passing of the 1949 Act, the first reviews by the Boundary Commissions were completed in 1954.[5]

The second periodical set of reports was presented to Parliament in 1969.[6] These resulted in great controversy because the Labour Government refused to implement the Reports, claiming that a radical reform of local government was planned, which would necessitate another revision of the constituencies in the near future. It was alleged that Labour stood to lose 10

---

[4] Electoral quota means a number obtained by dividing the electorate for that part of the United Kingdom by the number of constituencies in it.

[5] Cmd. 9311–9314. In *Hammersmith Borough Council* v. *Boundary Commission* (1954) (*The Times*, December 15, 1954) and in *Harper* v. *Home Secretary* [1955] 1 Ch. 238, the reviews were unsuccessfully challenged in the courts.

[6] Cmnd. 4084–4087.

to 20 seats in the forthcoming general election if the Reports were implemented. The Government proposed that the constituencies should remain
as they were except in the case of Greater London (where the reform of local
government had already taken place) and a small number of very large
constituencies. A bill was brought in to provide for this but it was drastically
amended in the House of Lords and the Government had to drop it. Instead
the Home Secretary introduced draft Orders into the Commons to give
effect to the recommendations and then the whips were put on to defeat
them.[7] The letter of the law was thus complied with. The 1970 general
election was therefore held on the basis of the 1954 distribution of constituencies, which meant that the variation in the size of the constituencies was
in some cases quite considerable. When a Conservative Government was
returned after the general election the Reports were implemented in full.[8]

The third periodical reports were made in 1983.[9] The report for England
was challenged in the courts, the Leader of the Opposition, the Opposition
Chief Whip, the General Secretary and the National Agent of the Labour
Party seeking an order of prohibition or an injunction restraining the
Boundary Commission for England from submitting its report to the Home
Secretary.[10] The basis of the challenge was the allegation that the Commission had failed to propose constituencies which were as near the electoral
quota as practicable and evidence was given to show wide disparities. But
the Court of Appeal held that the discretion enjoyed by the Boundary
Commission was wide enough to cover their proposals and that the applicants had not shown that the Commission had failed to abide by the rules
that governed it. Leave to appeal to the House of Lords was refused. The
Commission's recommendations were approved by both Houses[11] and the
number of constituencies increased from 635 to 650 for the election of 1983
and for the election of 1987.

The electoral quotas for 1983–84 were derived as follows:

	Total electors	Total seats	Electoral quota
England	35,569,230	523	68,010
Wales	2,138,384	38	56,273
Scotland	3,934,220	72	54,642
Northern Ireland	1,061,185	17	62,423
TOTAL	42,703,019	650	65,697

Discrepancies between constituencies when compared with electoral quotas are still considerable. In 1983, the largest electorate in England was
95,357; and the smallest was 46,507. The largest electorate in Wales was
68,741; and the smallest was 30,798. In Scotland the largest was 66,244; and
the smallest was 23,020. In Northern Ireland the largest was 68,913 and the
smallest was 54,115. In size, the 10 smallest constituencies in England (all in
London) averaged 725.5 hectares; the 10 largest averaged 220,318 hectares.
In Scotland the contrasts were even greater, the smallest constituency being
of 1,270 hectares while the largest (including inland water) covered 954,680
hectares.

---

[7] H.C.Deb., Vol. 791, cols. 428–571 (November 12, 1969).
[8] S.I. 1970 Nos. 1674, 1675, 1678, 1680.
[9] Cmnd. 8797–I.
[10] R. v. Boundary Commission for England ex p. Foot [1983] Q.B. 600.
[11] H.C. Deb., Vol. 38, cols. 249–346 (March 2, 1983); H.C.Deb., Vol. 440, cols. 21–37
(March 7, 1983) (the Order for England).

The work of the Boundary Commissions has been criticised. The process is slow. As long as seven years can elapse between a Commission beginning its investigation and the publication of its final recommendations. And much can happen during such a period. Thus the electorate in England at the start of the reviews in 1976 was 33,928,554 and this formed the basis of its recommendations. As we have seen the figure was 35,569,230 by 1983. The procedure itself, with its independent geographical inquiries, may lead to inconsistency, for example in how to reform an urban area whose population has become too large or too small to justify its previous number of constituencies.

The time taken to produce reports is in part the result of the procedure which tries to give every opportunity for objections to be heard. Moreover, the Boundary Commissions cannot control other events and between 1976 and 1983 reports were delayed by the need for the boundaries of wards within local authorities to be reviewed following the major reorganisation of local authorities coming into effect in April 1974.

Disqualifications

The following are disqualified for membership of the House of Commons:

Aliens: Not included in this category are naturalised subjects, Commonwealth citizens and citizens of the Republic of Ireland.

Persons under 21 years of age: When the Family Law Reform Act 1969 reduced the age of majority to 18 years, membership of the House was excluded from the change.

Lunacy: Lunacy or idiocy is a disqualification under common law. Under the Mental Health Act 1959 a Member who is authorised to be detained on grounds of mental illness loses his seat if the detention continues for six months.

Peers: Peers of England, Scotland, Great Britain and the United Kingdom are disqualified. Irish Peers may sit. Under the Peerage Act 1963, a person who succeeds to a peerage may disclaim his peerage within 12 months or, if he is under age when he succeeds, he may disclaim within 12 months of reaching the age of 21 years. If he is a Member of the House of Commons when he succeeds, he may disclaim within one month of succeeding. In certain special cases, these periods may be extended.

Bankruptcy: Generally, a bankrupt may not be elected or, if a Member, sit or vote. Under the Insolvency Act 1986 disqualification ceases if a person is discharged from bankruptcy or if an adjudication is annulled. If a Member continues to be disqualified for six months after being adjudged bankrupt his seat is vacated. The same law applies if a Scottish court awards sequestration of an individual's estate.

Treason: Persons convicted of treason are disqualified for election or sitting or voting in either House.

Other convicted persons: Under the Representation of the People Act 1981 a person sentenced or ordered to be imprisoned or detained indefinitely or for more than one year is disqualified for membership of the House of Commons while detained anywhere in the British Islands or the Republic of Ireland or while unlawfully at large. If a person so disqualified is elected or nominated, his election or nomination is void. If a Member becomes disqualified under this provision, his seat is vacated.

Corrupt or illegal practices at elections: Persons so convicted may be incapacitated for five years from election in any constituency or for 10 years from election in the constituency where the corrupt practice was committed.

Clergy: Clergymen of the Church of England and of the Church of Ireland[12] and Ministers of the Church of Scotland may not be elected Members of the House. Nor may Roman Catholic priests. But holders of ecclesiastical office in the Church of Wales and Ministers of Non-conformist churches are not disqualified.

Office-holders: The House of Commons Disqualification Act 1975 lists offices the holders of which are disqualified for Membership of the House of Commons. The Act also provides that the list may be amended by Order in Council approved by resolution of the House.[13] Subsequent Acts frequently provide that offices thereby created shall be added to the list. The Act of 1975 disqualifies, amongst others, whole-time or part-time civil servants, active members of the regular armed forces, the police, Members of the Seanad and Dail of the Republic of Ireland, holders of many judicial offices including the most important (but excluding Justices of the Peace), ambassadors and high commissioners, election and boundary commissioners and electoral registration officers. In addition there are many public bodies, including boards of nationalised industries, tribunals and various statutory bodies, the members of which are disqualified; and certain offices, such as Lords Lieutenant, disqualify for particular constituencies.

Especially preserved as disqualifying offices are those of steward or bailiff of Her Majesty's three Chiltern Hundreds of Stoke, Desborough and Burnham, and of the manor of Northstead. Members of Parliament who wish to resign from membership of the House apply to the Chancellor of the Exchequer and are appointed to one or other of these offices. The office ceases to be held when another Member applies for it or until the holder asks to be released from it—as would be necessary if he wished to stand for election to the House again.

The Act of 1975 provides that anyone who claims that a person purporting to be a Member is disqualified under the Act may apply to Her Majesty in Council for a declaration. The application is referred to the Judicial Committee of the Privy Council for determination. The House itself may resolve that a matter be referred to the Judicial Committee.

Under the Act of 1975, not more than 95 holders of ministerial offices are entitled to sit and vote in the House of Commons at any one time. These offices are listed in the Act and the list may be amended but not so as to increase the number of offices. The offices of Secretary of State and Minister of State may be held by more than one person. In the Ministerial and other Salaries Act 1975, the offices are put into four classes. Part I includes the Prime Minister and other Cabinet members. Part II includes Ministers not in the Cabinet. Part III covers the Law Officers. Part IV includes parliamentary secretaries and assistant Whips. Not more than 21 salaries may be paid for those in Part I, nor more than 50 for those in Parts I and II, nor more than 83 when Parliamentary Secretaries are added.

---

[12] In 1950 the Judicial Committee of the Privy Council reported that a priest of the Church of Ireland, disestablished since 1869, was disabled from sitting and voting in the House (Cmd. 8067).

[13] For example, see H.C.Deb., Vol. 40, cols. 752–778 (April 12, 1983) and S.I. 1983 No. 608.

Elections

The proceeding for a general election is begun by a royal proclamation which dissolves the old Parliament and orders the issue of writs for the election of the new Parliament. Returning officers appointed under the Representation of People Act 1983 are responsible for holding of elections, all on the same day which is the tenth day after the last day for delivery of nomination papers; that last day is the sixth day after the date of the proclamation. Under the Act of 1983 the maximum expense which may be incurred by a candidate or his agent is £3,240 plus 3.7p for every entry in the electoral register in a county constituency and £3,240 plus 2.8p for every entry in a borough constituency.

The same amounts apply to candidates in a by-election. Any Member, but usually the Chief Whip of the party whose Member held the seat, may move a motion for an order of the House to the Speaker to make out his warrant for the issue of a writ for a by-election following the vacation of a seat by death or for any other reason. The Speaker's Conference in 1973 recommended that the motion should be moved within three months of the vacancy arising.[14]

The Act of 1983 provides for the trial by judges of allegations that an election is invalid on any ground; and requires the House to make orders necessary for carrying the decisions of the judges into execution.

Candidates

The great majority of candidates are selected by the representatives of the major political parties in the constituencies. At the general election in June 1987, the Conservative and Labour parties and the Liberal/SDP Alliance each put up 633 candidates, none of them contesting any of the 17 seats in Northern Ireland. Six parties put up candidates in Northern Ireland: the Ulster Unionists put up 12, the Democratic Unionists 4, the Social Democratic and Labour Party 13, Sinn Fein 14, Alliance 16, Workers Party 14, and there were four other candidates. Plaid Cymru put up 38 candidates in Wales, Scottish Nationalists put up 71 in Scotland, the Green Party 133 and others (excluding Northern Ireland) 106. By-elections attract eccentric candidates because of the publicity given to the campaigns. At the Fulham by-election in April 1986, eight such candidates stood as, respectively, England Demands Repatriation, Democratic Rights for Northern Ireland, the Connoisseur Wine Party, Captain Rainbow's Universal Abolish Parliamentary Party, Fellowship Party, All-Party Common Market Group, Humanist Party, and Official Monster Raving Loony Party.

In all the major parties the wishes and decisions of the local constituency parties when selecting candidates usually predominate but the offices of the national party may seek to influence the decision. Such intervention may cause local resentment and be counter-productive. However the national executive of the Conservative and Labour parties (differently designated)

---

[14] Cmnd. 5500. The recommendation has been breached on four occasions. For occasions when writs have been moved by Members other than the Whips, see pp. 193, 403.

may in extreme cases veto the local selection, as happened most recently when the Labour leadership was seeking to expel members of the Militant Tendency. A Member who has the party whip withdrawn will certainly have his renomination vetoed by headquarters of the party (unless he has recanted); even more so if he has been expelled from the party.[15]

Because selection is locally in the hands of small numbers of party representatives, demands from time to time have been made that the process should be widened to involve all party members in the constituency, along the lines of a "primary" selection in the United States. Occasionally local members have been balloted to resolve particularly contentious disputes.[16]

It was the usual practice for any elected Member of Parliament to be renominated as candidate at subsequent elections so long as he held the seat and wished to continue. But D. and G. Butler recorded 76 cases from 1923 to 1985 when the local party failed to renominate "a sitting and willing M.P. who was still in receipt of the party whip." Of these 32 were Conservatives, 41 Labour and 3 Ulster Unionists.[17] Since 1980 re-selection has been mandatory within the Labour party,[18] but in 1987 only six Members who wished to stand failed to secure re-selection.

Under the Representation of the People Acts before 1985, each nominated candidate was required to deposit £150 with the returning officer and this was forfeited if the candidate failed to receive at least one-eighth of the valid votes cast. From 1945 to 1979 at 11 general elections, Conservative candidates lost a total of 81 deposits, Labour lost 82, Liberals 1348 and others 3944. At the 1983 election, the Conservatives lost five deposits, Labour lost a wholly unprecedented 119, the Liberal/SDP Alliance 10 and others 605. By the Act of 1985, the amount was increased to £500 and the qualifying proportion for forfeiture lowered to one-twentieth. At the 1987 election, no Conservative or Labour candidate (out of 633) lost a deposit, the Liberal/SDP Alliance (out of 633) and Scottish Nationalists candidates (out of 71) lost one each, the Green party's 133 candidates all lost their deposits, Plaid Cymru candidates (out of 38) lost 25, Northern Ireland parties' candidates (out of 77) lost 23 deposits. So did 105 (out of 106) other candidates.

BACKGROUND OF MEMBERS

The educational background of Members reveals possible changes in the class structure of the Conservative and Labour parties.[19]

In public school recruitment the percentage shows some decline and recovery between 1945 and 1966, followed by a decline to 1979 and, in 1983, a considerable and sudden drop. This trend was continued at the election of 1987 when public school recruitment was 62.7 per cent. Old Etonians declined by 1979 to almost half of their 1945 numbers and to below half in

---

[15] As happened to five Labour M.P.s during the Parliament of 1945–50.

[16] See G. Alderman, *British Elections: Myth and Reality* (1978).

[17] D. Butler and G. Butler, *British Political Facts 1900–1985* (1986), pp. 239–240. Of the 76, 25 (seven Conservative, 18 Labour) occurred in 1983, some as a result of the re-drawing of constituencies.

[18] Alison Young, *The Reselection of M.P.s* (1983).

[19] See Martin Burch and Michael Moran, "The Changing British Political Elite 1945–1983" in (1985) 38 *Parliamentary Affairs* 1, from which are drawn the tables which follow. For 1987 figures, see M. Rush in M. T. Ryle and P. Richards (ed.) *The Commons under Scrutiny* (1988). See also D. Butler and D. Kavanagh, *The British General Election of 1987* (1988), Chapter nine, by Bryon Criddle.

Background of All Conservative Members 1945–83 (%)

	1945	1950	1951	1955	1959	1964	1966	1970	Feb. 1974	Oct. 1974	1979	1983
All Public Schools	83.2	83.1	70.2	79.7	75.8	77.9	78.9	74.2	75.0	74.6	73.0	64.1
Eton	27.1	26.7	23.7	23.1	19.4	22.2	21.8	19.0	18.2	17.0	15.0	12.4
Oxbridge	53.3	54.0	54.3	53.7	50.6	54.3	57.1	51.3	55.7	55.1	49.2	45.7
Public/ Oxbridge	50.3	51.9	51.0	51.3	46.5	49.3	51.6	44.7	48.3	47.5	37.4	37.1
Elem/Sec only	3.7	5.3	6.4	7.2	7.9	8.2	5.1	7.5	7.7	7.2	8.2	8.8
State Sec/ Univ	7.0	6.0	6.8	6.6	8.2	7.8	9.0	10.0	11.4	11.9	16.2	17.9
All Universities	64.7	64.7	64.6	65.9	60.7	63.8	67.0	63.5	66.9	67.4	68.0	71.7
Local Government	14.1	16.8	16.6	20.7	25.5	27.2	28.9	30.4	32.0	31.0	35.0	38.1
Numbers	213	298	321	344	365	304	253	330	297	277	339	396

1983. The Oxbridge figures held up well to October 1974 and declined thereafter until 1987 when they rose slightly to 46.1 per cent. Those Conservative Members who attended only state schools increased from 3.7 per cent. to 8.8 per cent. over the whole post-war period and those who graduated after state schools rose from 9 per cent. in 1966 to 17.9 per cent. in 1983. In 1987 the percentage of all graduates rose further to 73.1. The considerable increase in Conservative Members with local government background perhaps indicates that more Conservative Members have been embarking on politics as a career.

The background of new Conservative Members emphasises some of the overall figures.

Background of New Conservative Members 1945–83 (%)

	1945	1950	1951	1955	1959	1964	1966	1970	Feb. 1974	Oct. 1974	1979	1983
All Public Schools	81.2	76.5	68.7	70.5	73.1	82.9	84.5	67.0	85.6	87.5	53.2	47.0
Eton	26.1	21.4	25.0	20.5	16.3	21.9	15.4	12.1	14.5	—	13.2	6.0
Oxbridge	42.1	46.9	53.1	50.0	45.2	56.3	46.1	40.7	59.7	62.5	36.0	35.0
Public/ Oxbridge	43.5	44.9	43.8	47.4	39.4	50.0	46.1	34.1	53.2	62.5	30.4	25.0
Elem/Sec only	6.9	9.8	11.7	10.3	5.7	3.1	7.6	11.1	1.6	12.5	16.0	12.0
State Sec/ Univ	2.7	8.8	11.7	7.7	9.6	9.3	—	13.3	11.2	—	22.6	30.0
All Universities	50.8	61.3	56.3	66.3	53.8	70.4	62.0	57.2	72.6	75.0	73.2	72.0
Local Government	10.8	22.5	22.1	35.9	36.5	34.4	38.7	32.5	27.4	25.0	41.2	52.0
Numbers	72	102	34	77	104	64	13	90	62	8	75	100

The large number of new Members in 1983 makes that a significant year. Public school recruitment is much lower in 1979 and 1983 as is that of Oxbridge graduates. Those with local government experience jumps to over 50 per cent. in 1983. Old Etonians looked like becoming an endangered species in 1983. Burch and Moran conclude that there has been a marked shift in the social character of the Conservative party in Parliament and that this is not merely a product of the majority of 1983 but reflects deeper and more enduring developments.

The parliamentary Labour Party is also undergoing important changes.

Background of All Labour Members 1945–83 (%)

	1945	1950	1951	1955	1959	1964	1966	1970	Feb. 1974	Oct. 1974	1979	1983
All Public Schools	19.4	22.2	23.4	23.5	24.6	24.0	22.8	19.4	15.7	16.4	17.0	13.4
Oxbridge Public	14.5	15.4	16.8	16.4	17.2	17.7	19.3	20.4	19.3	20.8	20.4	14.4
Oxbridge State Sec/	10.4	14.5	13.7	13.1	12.9	12.9	12.7	12.8	9.7	10.4	11.2	9.1
Univ. Elem/Sec	18.7	18.6	18.8	18.6	20.3	24.6	29.8	35.0	39.0	40.3	37.1	38.2
only All	52.4	49.2	36.9	59.9	47.2	39.4	35.5	31.0	26.5	24.4	28.9	21.5
Universities Manual	34.2	37.7	38.7	38.2	39.5	43.9	48.5	51.2	53.0	55.7	57.0	54.1
Workers Teachers/	27.6	27.6	26.2	25.3	21.1	18.4	16.6	13.2	12.3	12.0	19.8	15.3
Lecturers Local	12.1	13.9	14.8	14.3	14.9	16.5	20.1	20.9	25.8	28.1	24.2	25.8
Government	43.5	41.4	40.8	40.8	39.3	42.9	43.7	41.3	46.6	46.4	37.6	47.8
Numbers	393	315	295	277	258	317	363	287	301	319	269	209

Many of these numbers moved up and down over the whole post-war period. This is true of the Oxbridge recruitment (15.7 per cent. in 1987), though that of public school Members has declined overall since 1959 and reached 12.7 per cent. in 1987. Those who attended State schools and universities other than Oxbridge more than doubled between 1945 and 1983 but this may reflect more an increase in the number of graduates in the population than any change in the social structure of the Labour party. Graduates from all universities rose to 57.6 per cent. in 1987. Manual workers declined sharply to October 1974 and then showed some increase. Teachers and lecturers doubled over the whole period.

The picture changes somewhat when we look at the figures for new Labour Members.

Background of New Labour Members 1945–83 (%)

	1945	1950	1951	1955	1959	1964	1966	1970	Feb. 1974	Oct. 1974	1979	1983
All Public Schools	21.5	27.4	13.3	15.4	11.9	19.8	15.3	12.5	6.5	18.2	18.0	22.5
Oxbridge	17.7	19.4	13.3	7.7	4.8	17.9	23.6	18.8	15.2	22.7	5.0	11.8

Public/ Oxbridge	12.2	16.1	6.7	7.7	2.4	11.3	8.3	9.4	6.5	9.1	2.5	11.8
State Sec/ Univ.	19.4	19.4	26.7	26.9	26.2	29.2	48.6	43.7	41.3	50.0	52.5	38.2
Elem/Sec	51.9	38.7	46.6	50.0	59.5	32.3	22.2	23.4	26.0	13.6	40.0	20.6
All Universities	37.6	43.6	40.0	34.6	31.0	45.3	63.9	56.2	47.8	72.7	52.5	55.9
Manual Workers	19.7	17.6	20.0	19.2	23.8	18.9	12.5	6.2	19.6	4.6	20.0	20.6
Teachers/ Lecturers	13.3	17.7	20.0	23.1	9.5	18.9	34.7	29.7	19.9	50.0	15.0	17.6
Local Government	42.2	45.2	40.0	53.0	54.7	51.9	43.1	39.1	56.5	45.4	62.5	64.7
Numbers	227	62	15	24	42	105	72	64	46	22	40	34

The figures for manual workers show an end to the decline of that group while teachers and lecturers are lower in 1979 and 1983 than at any time (except for 1959) since 1945. But the total number of new Labour Members is small (40 and 34 in 1979 and 1983) so that percentage changes may exaggerate apparent trends.

If we consider only those elected as Conservative and Labour Members in 1983 we find that two-thirds were between the ages of 40 and 59 years and that the difference between the parties was negligible. However nearly one quarter of Conservative Members were under 40 years of age, but only 15 per cent. of Labour Members. Conservatives over 60 accounted for 11 per cent. of their Members and Labour's over 60s for 18 per cent. of theirs.

Occupational background disclose important differences between the two principal parties. Three major groups are the professions (legal, medical and academic being the most numerous); business (including company directors and executive, and those otherwise in commerce and insurance); and manual, skilled, semi-skilled and unskilled workers.[20]

Conservative %

	1951	1955	1959	1964	1966	1970	Feb 1974	Oct 1974	1979	1983
Professional	41	46	46	48	46	45	44	46	45	45
Business	37	30	30	26	29	30	32	33	34	36
Misc.	22	24	23	25	23	24	23	20	20	19
Workers	—	—	1	1	1	1	1	1	1	1
	100	100	100	100	100	100	100	100	100	100

Labour %

	1951	1955	1959	1964	1966	1970	Feb 1974	Oct 1974	1979	1983
Professional	35	36	38	41	43	48	46	49	43	42
Business	9	12	10	11	9	10	9	8	7	9
Misc.	19	17	17	16	18	16	15	15	14	16
Workers	37	35	35	32	30	26	30	28	36	33
	100	100	100	100	100	100	100	100	100	100

[20] See D. Butler and G. Butler, *British Political Facts 1900–1985* (1986), p. 178.

In more detail, the composition of the two main parliamentary parties after the 1987 general election was[21]:

Occupation	Conservative	Labour
Professions		
Barrister	43	9
Solicitor	21	9
Doctor/dentist	3	2
Architect/surveyor	7	—
Civil/chartered engineer	6	—
Chartered sec./accountant	17	2
Civil Servant/local govt.	13	8
Armed services	15	—
Teachers:		
University	6	11
Adult	2	15
School	17	29
Other consultants	3	2
Scientific research	3	6
Total	156	93
	(42%)	(40%)
Business		
Company director	39	2
Company executive	75	12
Commerce/insurance	18	9
Management/clerical	4	16
General business	3	2
Total	139	41
	(37%)	(10%)
Miscellaneous		
Miscellaneous white collar	8	18
Politician/pol. organiser	21	12
Publisher/journalist	26	14
Farmer	16	2
Housewife	7	—
Local administration	—	4
Total	78	50
	(20%)	(21%)
Manual workers		
Miners	1	16
Skilled worker	2	44
Semi/unskilled worker	—	6
Total	3	66
	(1%)	(29%)
Grand Total	376	229

Over the 11 elections between 1951 and 1987, the percentages in the

---

[21] Butler and Kavanagh *op. cit.* (1988), pp. 204–205.

different categories are remarkably constant. But from year to year, there are also marked changes. Business recruitment among Conservatives varies from 26 per cent. in 1964 to 37 per cent. in 1987 in which latest year professional recruitment fell to its lowest since 1951 and the difference between these two groups to 5 per cent., with professional still in the lead. Lawyers, chartered secretaries and accountants make up 52 per cent. of professional Conservative Members.

For Labour, the decline in workers recruitment from 37 per cent. in 1951 to 26 per cent. in 1970 suggested a gentrification of the party. This was sharply reversed in later 1970s followed by a further decline in workers recruitment to 29 per cent. in 1987. Among Labour professionals, 59 per cent. are teachers.[22]

We may tentatively conclude that the social composition of both the two major parties is changing. The Conservative Members are becoming less upper class, being recruited less from public schools, less from Oxford and Cambridge; more of them are career politicians, serving apprenticeship in local government. For Labour the picture is less clear. The proportion from public schools of new Members has increased in recent years but for all Labour Members dropped in 1987 to its lowest (12.7 per cent.) since the war. The increase in the number of those with local government background may suggest that, like the Conservative Members, politics is being seen more and more as a career. The relative absence of pattern may be a reflection of the conflict within the Labour party which showed itself so dramatically by the defections of Labour Members to the S.D.P. in the early 1980s and in the expulsions of Militant leaders in 1986.

Women were first given the right to vote at 30 years of age, and to stand for election, in February 1918 and then admitted to full adult suffrage in 1928. In 1929 Margaret Bondfield was appointed Minister of Labour as the first woman Cabinet Minister. In 1979 Mrs. Thatcher became the first woman Prime Minister. The Labour Party and the Social and Liberal Democratic Party are committed to including at least one woman in each shortlist of candidates. Women were candidates in 280 seats in 1983—70 more than in 1979 and almost twice as many as in 1974. From a peak of 28 women Members elected in 1964, only 23 succeeded in 1983. By-elections brought this total to 28 when Parliament was dissolved in May 1987. The general election of 1987 resulted in a marked increase, 41 women being elected, 21 of whom were Labour, 17 Conservative, two SDP/Liberal Alliance, and one Scottish Nationalist.

In 1987, the main parties selected 28 black or Asian candidates (10 more than in 1983) of whom 14 were Labour, six Conservative and eight Alliance. Three blacks and one Asian were elected (all Labour), a mere 0.6 per cent. of the Members of the House.

MEMBERS' INTERESTS

"Surely this place is about pressures" said Mr. Speaker on November 12, 1984.[23] And susceptibility to pressures is closely associated with Members' personal interests.

The diversity of background from which Members are drawn, their pre-

---

[22] See last table.
[23] H.C.Deb., Vol. 67, col. 407.

vious education and occupations, and their future aspirations mean that they have a very wide range of interests. On top of these are the concerns arising from the particular constituencies they represent. Any attempt to itemise their political and social interests results in scores of Members being listed under the headings of economic and financial affairs, defence, education, energy, environment, foreign affairs, health, trade and industry.[24]

To become something of an authority on special subjects may advance a Member's career. Parliamentary experience, such as membership of the standing committee on a particular bill or of a select committee, may be the result of special interest and may itself create or foster that interest.

Nor are these interests confined to parliamentary duties. According to the Register of Members' Interests in December 1987, 159 Members were remunerated directors of companies, and 52 were members of Lloyds.[25] Many Members have outside activities, not remunerated and not registered, for example as members of local authorities, hospital authorities, governors of schools and membership of a large number of other charitable and non-charitable organisations. The mean time spent on outside work is estimated to be 10 hours a week and this covers a wide range of hours. Some Members strongly argue that parliamentary duties should absorb all the working time of those elected. But this is a minority view and shows no sign of becoming widespread. On the other side it is equally strongly argued that for Members to have outside occupations is positively beneficial to the conduct of parliamentary business.

Members of Parliament, being perceived as persons able to exert influence on decision-makers in Government, have long been subjected to pressure by groups concerned to promote their own interests. The emergence of political parties was rooted in interest whether of the landowning aristocracy, of industrialists, or of workers. And the history of the country, certainly since 1832, has been one of the competing claims of such groups. Today the relationships between the major political parties, business interests and trade unions, still dominate politics.

Nor is the Government to be seen as primarily an impartial arbiter between rival economic interests. No doubt on occasion it performs some such function. But the Government is deeply involved with the direction of the economic affairs of the nation and will seek to promote these interests which it sees as most in keeping with its own political philosophy. For governments, and more indirectly for Members generally, the most powerful agencies are those of industry, commerce and finance. The two major parent organisations are the Confederation of British Industry and the Trades Union Congress but no less powerful within their own areas are individual large companies and trade unions. Many of these bodies have their own sections whose main function is to keep in touch with those Members and Peers whom they believe to be sympathetic to their purposes.

From the early nineteenth century, professional groups began to be formed: civil engineers in 1818, mechanical engineers in 1847, the British Medical Association in 1832, the Law Society in 1825, architects in 1834. The philanthropic societies also had their origins in the same period: the Anti-Slavery Society in 1823, the Royal Society for the Prevention of Cruelty to Animals in 1824, the National Society for the Prevention of

---

[24] See *Dod's Parliamentary Companion*.
[25] H.C. 200 of 1987–88.

Cruelty to Children rather later in 1884.[26] In recent years the growth of specialised groups having particular interests to promote has been remarkable. Many of these are concerned with the poor such as the Child Poverty Action Group, Age Concern, War on Want, Oxfam and the Low Pay Unit; others with health (such as MIND and MENCAP) and housing (like Shelter and SHAC); others are more directly political such as the Anti-Apartheid movement, the Anti-Nazi League, the Campaign for Nuclear Disarmament and Greenpeace; others are less directly political like Amnesty International, Justice, the National Trust, Friends of the Earth.

In the early 1980s, a survey was conducted[27] in which environmental groups in the community were asked how far Members and Peers were prepared to assist on a continuing basis. Sixty-two out of 74 groups could count on the assistance of at least one Member or Peer, the median number being nine per group, and most of the other 12 groups were such that parliamentary business was not their concern. Nineteen groups claimed over 30 Members or Peers in regular working relationship. These included such well known and influential groups as the Royal Society for Nature Conservation and the Royal Society for the Protection of Birds. Such groups employed parliamentary agents and had close connection with all-party parliamentary groups such as the Conservation Committee and the Arts and Heritage Group.

Fifty-nine of the groups were asked what were the most significant kinds of assistance given to Members and Peers. Most placed first helping to safeguard or promote the group's aims in legislation. Other kinds of assistance were acting as spokesmen for the group inside and outside Parliament, providing information and parliamentary intelligence, providing links to Ministers and departments. Less significant were service within the group on committees and providing links between the group and political parties.

Conflicts of interests and the Register

On July 17, 1811 Mr. Speaker Abbot ruled: "no Member who has a direct pecuniary interest in a question shall be allowed to vote upon it" and this was understood then to be an ancient practice. But he distinguished an interest "in common with the rest of His Majesty's subjects or on a matter of state policy"; the vote of a Member would not be disallowed solely because of such interests[28] and this is the governing doctrine today. In practice Members may vote on all business before the House except private legislation where they have a direct pecuniary interest. So in 1983, the Speaker ruled that Members who were solicitors might vote on the Home Buyers Bill (intended to remove their exclusive rights on conveyancing) as the bill was on a matter of public policy.[29] But on a private bill to regulate Lloyds, members of that corporation were advised not to vote.

Although Members may vote freely on all matters of public business, they are required to disclose any relevant pecuniary interest they have in matters in debate. Following a report of the Select Committee on Members' Inter-

---

[26] See generally G. Alderman, *Pressure Groups and Government in Great Britain* (1984).
[27] P. Lowe and T. Goyder: *Environmental Groups in Politics* (1983), pp. 68–74.
[28] H.C.Deb., Vol. 20, cols. 1001–1007 (1811).
[29] H.C.Deb., Vol. 50, col. 679 (December 12, 1983).

ests (Declaration)[30] the House agreed two resolutions in 1974. The first related to oral declarations:

> "That, in any debate or proceeding of the House or its committees or transactions or communications which a Member may have with other Members or with Ministers or with servants of the Crown, he shall disclose any relevant pecuniary interest or benefit of whatever nature, whether direct or indirect, that he may have had, may have, or may be expecting to have."

The second resolution was for the establishment of a public Register of Interests:

> "That every Member of the House of Commons shall furnish to a Registrar of Members' Interests such particulars of his registrable interests as shall be required, and shall notify to the Registrar any alterations which may occur therein, and the Registrar shall cause these particulars to be entered in a Register of Members' Interests which shall be available for inspection by the public."

The House also agreed to the appointment of a Select Committee on Members' Interests which in the terms of Standing Order No. 128 now provides that the committee shall examine the arrangements made for the compilation, maintenance and accessibility of the Register; consider any proposals made by Members or others as to the form and contents of the Register; consider any specific complaints made in relation to the registering or declaring of interests; consider what classes of persons (if any) other than Members ought to be required to register; and make recommendations upon those and other matters which are relevant. The committee consists of 13 Members and has the usual power to send for persons, papers and records (see pages 448–452).

The requirement that interests shall be declared does not apply to the asking of oral supplementary Questions nor to the tabling of a Question, a motion or an amendment or to the adding of a Members' name to a motion or amendment already on the Order paper.

On June 12, 1975, the House further resolved that any interest disclosed in the Register should be regarded as sufficient disclosure for the purpose of taking part in any division in the House or in any of its committees. The report of the select committee endorsed by the House defined the purpose of the Register as: "to provide information of any pecuniary interest or other material benefit which a Member of Parliament may receive which might be thought to affect his conduct as a Member of Parliament or influence his actions, to speeches or vote in Parliament."

Nine classes of pecuniary interest or other benefit are required to be registered:

1. Remunerated directorships of companies, public or private.
2. Remunerated employments or offices (excluding Ministerial offices).
3. Remunerated trade, professions or vocations.

---

[30] H.C. 57 of 1969–70.

4. Names of clients when the interests referred to above include personal services by the Member which arise out of or are related in any manner to his membership of the House.
5. Financial sponsorships (a) as a parliamentary candidate where to the knowledge of the Member the sponsorship in any case exceeds 25 per cent. of the candidate's election expenses or (b) as a Member of Parliament, by any person or organisation, stating whether any such sponsorship includes any payment to the Member or any material benefit or advantage direct or indirect, such as the services of a research assistant.
6. Overseas visits, relating to or arising out of membership of the House where the cost of any such visit has not been borne wholly by the Member or by public funds (with some exceptions, *e.g.* on behalf of the Council of Europe or EEC institutions).
7. Any payments or any material benefits or advantages received from or on behalf of foreign Governments, organisations or persons.
8. Land or property of substantial value (excluding a Member's home) or from which a substantial income is derived.
9. Names of companies or other bodies in which a Member has to his knowledge either himself or with or on behalf of his spouse or infant children, a beneficial interest in share-holdings of a nominal value greater than one-hundredth of the issued share capital.

The amount of the remuneration or benefit is not required to be registered. The Register is compiled from returns made by Members and failure to make a return, or the making of a false or misleading return, might be considered by the House as a contempt. The Registrar is also the clerk of the select committee. Disputes about entries are dealt with by the select committee and ultimately by the House. A member of the public or a Member may complain that an entry is incorrect or incomplete and this also is dealt with by the Registrar, by the committee, and ultimately, if need be, by the House.[31]

The nine classes have their ambiguities and imprecisions and the entries, as a result, are not wholly consistent with one another.

Mr. Enoch Powell from the beginning refused to file an entry considering that the resolution was not binding "in as much as it purports to impose obligations which can only lawfully and constitutionally be imposed by legislation."[32] The select committee from time to time sought to persuade the House to take action to enforce the requirement to register but no action was taken against Mr. Powell.[33]

The Register is usually published in January or February of each year.

Under rules made by the Prime Minister, not the House, Ministers are required on appointment to resign from directorships in all companies

---

[31] See, for example, an unsuccessful challenge in relation to the Prime Minister (Mrs. Thatcher) H.C.Deb., Vol. 52, cols. 1072–1074 (January 26, 1984), H.C.Deb., Vol. 53, cols. 24–29 (January 30, 1984), H.C. 330 and 370 of 1983–84.

[32] H.C.Deb., Vol. 893, col. 745 (June 12, 1975) and H.C. 479 of 1975–76. In December 1986 Mr. Powell explained his position in detail to the select committee: H.C. 110 of 1986–87. He lost his seat at the general election of June 1987.

[33] H.C. 479 of 1975–76, 84 of 1976–77, 337 of 1979–80, 110 of 1986–87.

except those concerned with family estates. Although not expected to dispose of all investments, Ministers should divest themselves of any controlling interests if there is any danger of a conflict of interest. They should scrupulously avoid speculative investments in securities about which they have or may be thought to have early or confidential information likely to affect the price of those securities.[34]

Lobbying

In 1982–83, the Select Committee on Members' Interests decided to enquire into the position of those who sought for reward to influence the decisions of the House of Commons by direct communication with Members and were popularly called "parliamentary lobbyists." The select committee made its First Report in May 1985[35] and in December 1985 the House by resolution confirmed that the scope of the requirement for Members to register remunerated trades, professions or vocations included any remunerated activity in the fields of public relations and political and parliamentary advice and consultancy; and agreed in regard to the registration and declaring of clients that the services which required such registration and declaration included, as well as any action connected with any proceedings in the House or its committees, the sponsoring of functions in the Palace, making representations to Ministers, civil servants and other Members, accompanying delegations to Ministers and the like.[36] The select committee considered but did not recommend the registration of lobbyists.

The nature and extent of pressure brought to bear on Members by outside bodies—commercial, industrial, financial or those concerned with special issues—vary considerably. Many, like the environmental bodies, seek merely to interest sympathetic Members from time to time in particular matters, urging them to take action which may include joining demonstrations, approaching Ministers, writing letters to the press, chairing meetings, and receiving deputations. Occasionally, the initiative may come from the Member suggesting to the outside group some action that might be taken. And Members may be willing to have their names publicly displayed as official sponsors or even office-holders of the body. In no sense are Members employed by such bodies and no fees are expected or given.

More direct and more continuous involvement by Members arises when they act as consultants to specific outside bodies. Sometimes the consultancy arises out of the Members' previous occupation. He may have been an active member of a professional firm and, on becoming a Member, be elevated to the level of a consultant which generally means that he ceases to act on a day-to-day basis for the firm. But much more frequently a Member acts as a parliamentary consultant or parliamentary adviser. He is appointed as such by a company or other outside body and is paid a retainer or a fee, which may amount to £5000 or more each year, in return for which he is expected to keep the company or body informed on matters which arise or may arise in Parliament and, as occasion arises, to lobby actively on its behalf. Such appointments are required to be recorded in the Register of Members' Interests. So, from 1955 for several years, Mr. James Callaghan M.P., the

---

[34] H.C.Deb., Vol. 496, cols. 701–703 (February 25, 1952); H.C. 57 of 1969–70, App. II.
[35] H.C. 408 of 1984–85.
[36] H.C.Deb., Vol. 89, cols. 216–254 (December 17, 1985).

future Prime Minister, was the parliamentary adviser to the Police Federation and his immediate successor was Mr. Eldon Griffiths M.P. In 1972, Mr. Brian Walden (then an M.P.) was parliamentary consultant on a five year contract to the National Association of Bookmakers and has been credited with "stopping the Tote from setting up shops on high streets because it would have taken about a million pounds away from the bookies."[37] These associations are open and are accepted and permitted by the House so long as parliamentary privilege is not infringed.[38] In January 1987, 165 Members were consultants or advisers to 289 concerns[39]; in December 1987, 113 Members supplied this service to 272 concerns.[40]

In 1985, 1986 and 1987, heavy lobbying took place on behalf of the contenders for the fixed cross-Channel link. Individual Members helped some of the competing groups. Wimpey were part of one group. Interviewed on Newsnight, the BBC programme, the Member who was their parliamentary consultant was recorded as saying:

"I have arranged meetings with Ministers, I have made sure that everything connected with the Channel Tunnel has been brought to Wimpey's attention, and if they have some particular say at a moment, then I would make sure that their voice has been heard . . . Also Parliamentary Private Secretaries, they are Members of Parliament who help Ministers in the background, and making sure they have adequate knowledge of the scheme, holding perhaps a lunch here, an afternoon tea there to make sure Members and interested parties do know of our scheme . . . I believe in one particular scheme, and I have made sure as a member of the Transport Select Committee, as Wimpey's Parliamentary consultant, that they basically have come up with what I think is the right scheme . . . My fee is eight thousand five hundred per annum."

The Member declared his interest, and the BBC commentator remarked that by a majority of one the select committee expressed its preference for the scheme he supported.[41]

In 1981, a private Member's bill which sought tighter control of cigarette advertising was blocked by the setting down of 164 amendments to another bill dealing with zoos which preceded it. It would seem that many Members having financial links either directly with the tobacco industry or with advertising and public relations firms handling tobacco company accounts were responsible for ensuring that the bill on cigarette advertising was blocked in this way.[42]

In the Westland affair,[43] one Member was paid parliamentary adviser to British Aerospace (part of the European Consortium) and a member of the Select Committee on Defence. Another prominent back-bencher was parliamentary adviser for Bristow Helicopters. In addition, Westland employed their own public relations firm as did several of the other parties to the controversy.

---

[37] H.C. 408 of 1984–85 Q. 14 (Mr. J. Ashton M.P.). The parliamentary consultant is now Mr. J. R. Holt M.P.
[38] See Chapter 3.
[39] H.C. 155 of 1986–87.
[40] Register of Members' Interests; H.C. 200 of 1987–88.
[41] Transcript of "Newsnight," December 9, 1985.
[42] See G. Alderman *op. cit.*, pp. 61–62.
[43] See above pp. 24–25; and M. Linklater and David Leigh, *Not with Honour* (1986).

This brings us to a more intimate relationship between outside bodies and the House. Some of these bodies, perhaps because they lack adequate direct links with Members or because they prefer their activities to be handled by more expert agencies, employ professional public relations companies to promote their interests. Some of these companies range widely over the whole field of public relations and advertising. Others specialise in parliamentary work.

Sir Trevor Lloyd-Hughes was formerly a political correspondent, press secretary to the Prime Minister 1964–69, and chief information adviser to the Government 1969–70. When he left the civil service he formed Lloyd-Hughes Associates and in 1982 gave evidence to the Select Committee on Members' Interests. In a document submitted to the committee he claimed that his company had "masterminded the parliamentary campaign which rescued the United Kingdom ship repairing industry from Government proposals to nationalise ship repairing as well as shipbuilding"; also "obtained important tax concessions from the British Government over their legislation on North Sea oil revenues"; also "changed Government laws on the press and trade unions"; also "secured British Government planning permission for an oil platform building site." Sir Trevor explained that this was a "commercial document" wherein he was trying to sell his services.[44]

Public relations consultancies may pay fees or retainers to Members. An employee of a consultancy may also obtain a pass, which entitles him to enter the Palace of Westminster, as research assistant to a Member. "Are you happy" asked a member of the Select Committee on Members' Interests in 1984 "about performing that research function?" "No," replied a member of the Institute of Public Relations, "I think it is an essentially bogus relationship but one I would gladly shed if I could gain access to information which my clients, I believe, have a right to have." Such information includes documents published or available to Members which are not readily available outside through commercial channels. So also a member of a consultancy may provide a Member with a part-time or full-time research assistant as a form of payment for that Member's advice and guidance.[45]

There remains an even closer relationship between parliamentary consultants and Members. This arises when a Member acts as director of a public relations company. For example, in the Registers of Members' Interests published in January and December 1987,[46] different Members were listed as directors of, or shareholders in, Kingsway Public Relations Ltd., Westminster (Communications) Ltd., Westminster and City Programmes Ltd., Westminster and Whitehall Consultants Ltd., Political Research and Communication International Ltd., and Charles Barker Group Ltd. Such specialist firms provide an information service covering governmental and parliamentary activities and also operate as a link between clients and Members.[47] Entries in the Register in early 1988 indicated that about 50 Members had connections with parliamentary consultancies or research services or public relations.[47a] Lobbyists, on behalf of outside interests,

[44] H.C. 408 of 1984–85, Q. 2, 27, 34.
[45] H.C. 408 of 1984–85, Q. 92, 121, 124, 136, 140.
[46] H.C. 155 of 1986–87; H.C. 200 of 1987–88.
[47] See M. Davies, *Politics of Pressure: The Art of Lobbying* (1985).
[47a] Second Report of Select Committee on House of Commons (Services): H.C. 580 of 1987–88 para. 49.

research and prepare information which they present to Members in the form of parliamentary Questions or amendments to bills or which provides background material for speeches or for evidence to select committees. In this way lobbyists use procedural opportunities as means of persuasion.

All-party and parliamentary subject groups

Members having common interests frequently form unofficial groups open to those of all political parties. Some 90 of these groups exist today. Their primary function is to keep Members, the Government, and to a lesser extent the Opposition, informed of parliamentary and outside opinion, at least so far as it is not seen as controversial between the parties by the members of the group.

In recent years the number of these groups has grown considerably and the criticism was made that some of them were using the House's status, as well as its heat, light and space, for non-parliamentary purposes. This criticism was particularly directed at those groups who admitted to membership persons who were neither Members nor Peers. Pressure on the limited accommodation for meetings was thought by the Select Committee on House of Commons (Services) in 1983–84 to demand some ordering of priorities.[48] It therefore recommended that a distinction should be drawn between "all-party groups" where the membership was limited to Members and Peers, and "parliamentary groups" which admitted outside members. Parliamentary groups would need to be registered in order to benefit from advantages in the booking of rooms. To qualify for registration, parliamentary groups had to be open to all Members with at least five Members from the Government side of the House and five from the Opposition. Officers were required to be Members or Peers; any subscription was not to be more than £5 p.a.

These recommendations were approved by the House in October 1984.[49] Of the subject groups listed on May 30, 1986, 76 were classified as all-party and 21 as parliamentary groups. Several are related to industry, others campaign for wide membership (such as the group against fluoridisation, the United Nations group, the World Government group, the Parliamentary and Scientific Committee).

The range of subject groups includes animal welfare, the environment, the handicapped, health, child care, civil liberties, energy, the motor industry, pensioners, science and technology. During the week beginning January 18, 1988, notice of meetings of all-party groups was given for those on tourism, war crimes, information technology, mental health, population and development, refugees, wool textile, the Channel tunnel and Royal Air Force. Under the auspices of the Commonwealth Parliamentary Association or the Inter-parliamentary Union, there are also over 100 all-party groups associated with particular foreign countries. As groups may be formed overnight and disappear overnight, their precise number is always in doubt. They represent a considerable amount of activity, though attendance may be small.

---

[48] H.C. 256 of 1983–84.

[49] H.C.Deb., Vol. 65, cols. 1362–1374 (October 31, 1984). The rules were further tightened on November 9, 1988, when the house agreed to a resolution of the Select Committee on House of Commons (Services) as set out in its Minutes of October 25, 1988 (H.C. 183–V of 1987–88) which made the requirement for at least five Members from each side apply also to "all-party groups" and provided for the registration of both types of group (H.C.Deb. Vol. 140, col. 456).

Many of these groups are serviced by outside organisations who may pay for the secretarial and other assistance given. Geoffrey Alderman records that one of the best known firms of parliamentary consultants (Charles Barker, Watney and Powell) provides the secretariat for the Parliamentary and Scientific Committee which is paid for out of subscriptions collected from individual and corporate members.[50] Its membership in 1985 included over 200 Members and Peers and representatives of over 150 scientific and technical bodies, 67 companies and organisations, 60 universities and polytechnics. Its object is to provide a permanent liaison between scientific bodies, science-based industry and Parliament. Associate-member companies included the Beecham Group, the Distillers Company, Imperial Chemical Industries and many other large undertakings.

The list of subject groups based on information given by the groups themselves shows that the Royal Society for the Protection of Cruelty to Animals services the Animal Welfare Group, the Chemical Industries Association Ltd. services the Chemical Industry Group, the National Children's Bureau services the parliamentary Group for Children, the Professional Associations parliamentary Support Group services the Personal Social Services parliamentary panel, the Runnymede Trust services the Race Relations Parliamentary Group, the British Youth Council services the Youth Affairs Parliamentary Group. Many other groups are similarly sponsored or assisted. In early 1988 the staff of some 50 Members were also employed by charities or other non-profit making organisations.[50a]

Age Concern England submitted a memorandum to the Select Committee on Members' Interests and gave oral evidence in June 1984.[51] This is a registered charity formed in 1940 and its governing body includes representatives of 70 national organisations and six Government departments. It provides services to elderly people through volunteers, and campaigns on behalf of the elderly. It employs a member of staff to co-ordinate links with Members and Peers and to service the all-party Parliamentary Group for Pensioners. Since 1978, Age Concern has employed a parliamentary officer who spends on average three days a week in the House of Commons working as assistant to the Group. She provides research and administrative support to the Group and brings to the attention of the Group developments affecting elderly people, whether from the media, public bodies, government, pensioner organisations or elsewhere. She also acts as press officer to the Group. There is a part-time secretary, 60 per cent. of whose time is similarly spent on work for the all-party Group.

The support with which the Group is provided by Age Concern extends beyond the presence of a parliamentary assistant as she is able to draw on the expertise of full time specialist members of Age Concern staff, most particularly in the press office and the information and international departments. The parliamentary assistant has stated[52] that she does not act as an agent provocateur for Age Concern England; that the Group remains autonomous, and is entirely independent of Age Concern in every aspect of its work; that the reverse also applies, and the all-party Group is far from the

---

[50] See generally for much of what follows: G. Alderman, *Pressure Groups and Government in Great Britain* (1984), esp. chapter 3.
[50a] H.C. 580 of 1987–88 para. 49 (see above note 47a).
[51] H.C. 408 of 1984–85 pp. 49–58.
[52] In a letter to the authors.

sole channel for the parliamentary activity of Age Concern, although clearly there is a degree of liaison between the two.

The group on Mental Health was serviced by the National Association for Mental Health but the secretaryship has passed to the Royal College of Psychiatrists. The Penal Affairs group is serviced by the National Association for the Care and Resettlement of Offenders. The ASH (Action on Smoking and Health) group and the British Limbless Ex-Servicemen's Association are serviced by the outside organisation also so named. Other examples are numerous.

From all this emerge certain patterns. Those outside bodies some of whose activities touch on the interests of existing groups will make contact with the group as occasion arises. Outside bodies whose interests largely coincide with those of groups may seek a much closer relationship in which the outside body provides secretarial and research services to the group. At this point it may not be clear whose interests (those of the outside body or the group) are being primarily pursued. There is a possibility that the servicing body may take over the group to a greater or lesser extent. Occasionally there have been examples of outside bodies actually sponsoring the creation of a group.[53]

Sir Geoffrey Johnson Smith, chairman of the Select Committee on Members' Interests, put to a witness in 1982 this view:

"Some people think that all-party groups would not exist if it were not for the fact that they are really an extension of the lobbying and that they only exist because their salaried work is financed and they are only alive by the fact that visits to various countries are financed basically by external groups."[54]

As Mr. F. Willey M.P. put it: "The big industries in this country now partly work through all-party committees."[55] Not surprisingly, public relations firms operate in this area also. In June 1986, for example, the public relations company of Charles Barker Watney and Powell appeared to provide the secretariat for at least six groups: those concerned with the Channel Tunnel; Information Technology; Roads; the Motor Industry; Minerals; and, as we have seen, the firm also serviced the Parliamentary and Scientific Committee.

In December 1985, the House of Commons agreed to a recommendation from the Select Committee on Members' Interests that the Members who were officers of all-party and registered groups be required to register and to record the source and extent of any benefits financial or in kind from outside sources which they may enjoy together with any other relevant gainful occupation of any staff which they might have. And where a public relations agency provided the assistance the ultimate client was required to be named.[56] In December 1986, the select committee reported that the Register of parliamentary groups listed 172 Groups.[57] But access to the register is restricted to Members.

---

[53] G. Alderman says that the Council for Nature played a central role in the formation of an all-party group (*op. cit.*, p. 68).

[54] H.C. 408 of 1984–85 Q. 37.

[55] *Ibid.* Q. 53.

[56] H.C. 408 of 1984–85; H.C.Deb., Vol. 89, cols. 216–254 (December 17, 1985); H.C. 261 and 467 of 1985–86.

[57] H.C. 110 of 1986–87.

Sponsorship

The Labour party is historically and structurally closely connected with the trade union movement. Twelve out of the 25 members of the national executive committee of the Labour party are nominated by and elected by trade unions. Trade unions are affiliated members of the party. Trade union branches are part of the structure of the local parties in parliamentary constituencies and so take part in the nomination and selection of candidates. Trade unions may sponsor candidates and undertake to pay part of the expenses of the election campaign and to make donations to the local party. In 1987, 140 sponsored Labour candidates were elected. Of these, the Transport and General Workers Union sponsored 31, the Amalgamated Union of Engineering Workers 12, the National Union of Mineworkers 13, the General Municipal, etc., Union 13. Seventeen other unions sponsored a total of 61 successful candidates. The Co-operative Party sponsored 10 successful candidates.

The constitution of the Labour Party provides that no parliamentary candidates shall be endorsed until the National Executive Committee has received an undertaking by one of its affiliated organisations (which includes constituency Labour parties) that the election expenses of the candidate are guaranteed.

To regulate sponsorship, the Labour Party conference in 1933 instituted the Hastings Agreement under which a sponsoring union may contribute to the election expenses of a candidate not more than 80 per cent. of the maximum expenses allowed by law. Between elections, the maximum annual grant by a sponsoring union to the local party is £600 for borough constituencies and £750 for counties but the union may also pay up to 65 or 70 per cent. of the salary, superannuation and statutory payments of a fulltime agent. None of the sponsored money goes to the candidate.

Members may be subjected to pressure from their unions. Although such pressure if applied too specifically (to a particular vote, for example) might constitute a contempt of the House, sponsored Members may be exhorted to support measures which the union favours and they do attend meetings which may be called by the union to this end. There is also the possibility that sponsorship may be withdrawn and this could have an adverse effect when the Member is up for re-selection. Inevitably a sponsored Member normally supports the policy of the union when matters arise in Parliament.

Three cases have been considered by the Committee of Privileges since 1945 though the first was not strictly a matter of sponsorship. In 1947 W. J. Brown was general secretary of the Civil Service Clerical Association which job he had held since 1923. He was elected as an Independent Member of Parliament in 1943 and re-elected in 1945. He continued as Parliamentary general secretary of the Association with the right to engage in his political activities with complete freedom. As a Member, Brown was critical of the Labour Party and the Trades Union Congress and complained that he was put under pressure by the executive committee of the Association either to moderate the expression of his views or to have his contract terminated or his position made intolerable. The executive committee brought the question of the termination of his contract to the annual conference of the Association. The Committee of Privileges found that the executive committee was entitled to do this, that Brown was not affected in the discharge of his Parliamentary duties, and that no breach of privilege had occurred.[58]

The House in agreeing with the report of the Privileges Committee declared that it was inconsistent with the dignity of the House, with the duty of a Member to his constituents, and with the maintenance of the privilege of freedom of speech, for any Member to enter into any contractual agreement with an outside body controlling or limiting the Member's complete independence and freedom of action in Parliament or stipulating that he should act in any way as the representative of such outside body in regard to matters to be transacted in Parliament, the duty of a Member being to his constituents and to the country as a whole rather than to any particular section thereof.[59]

Secondly, in 1975 the Yorkshire Area Council of the National Union of Mineworkers resolved that they could no longer tolerate the position where a sponsored Member could oppose the Union's policy on major issues and agreed the following guidelines:

(1) No miners' Member should vote or speak against Union policy on any issue which affected the coal mining industry

(2) No Miners' Member should actively campaign or work against Union policy on any other major issue

(3) If any Miners' Member refused to agree to these guidelines or violated them, the Area Council would withdraw sponsorship from that Member.

The Committee of Privileges reported that it was in no doubt that this resolution constituted a serious contempt which represented a continuing threat to Members' freedom of speech and action and which could not be allowed to remain in existence.[60] As a result, the National Executive of the Union nullified the resolution.

Thirdly, in 1977 the national Conference of the National Union of Public Employees passed a resolution calling on the Executive Council of the Union to take swift and positive action in respect of the Union's sponsored Members who were supporting the Government's public expenditure cuts by voting with the Government to implement the cuts; and required the Executive Council to seek an assurance from the six Members sponsored by the Union that they would refrain from supporting the Government's policy on cuts in public expenditure. If such an assurance was not forthcoming the Executive Council was instructed to withdraw the Union's sponsorship. The Privileges Committee was in no doubt that the action called for would have amounted to seeking to use contractual agreements with Members as a means of controlling their conduct or punishing them for what they had done as Members. This would constitute a serious contempt. Referring to Brown's case in 1947, the committee said that the House then decided that there was nothing of itself improper in a Member receiving financial assistance from an outside body so long as the arrangements did not involve the

---

[58] H.C. 118 of 1946–47.

[59] H.C.Deb., Vol. 440, cols. 284–365 (July 15, 1947). In 1986, it was reported that the National Communications Union had "ordered" its recently appointed general secretary Mr. John Golding M.P. to resign his seat in order to devote all his energies to his new job. Shortly afterwards he resigned his seat and at the ensuing by-election in Newcastle-under-Lyme his wife was elected in his stead. No complaint was referred to the Committee of Privileges.

[60] H.C. 634 of 1974–75.

assertion or exercise of any kind of control over the freedom of the Member concerned in Parliament. An outside body might terminate such a relationship where it considered doing so was necessary for the protection of its own interests. But an outside body was not entitled to use the agreement or payment as an instrument of control over the conduct of a Member or to punish him for what he had done as a Member.[61] The result was that the Executive Council decided to take no action on the resolution and to make no change in the existing relationship between the Union and its sponsored Members.

Interests in general

The general line taken by the House is that there is nothing improper in a Member or a group of Members enjoying financial backing from an outside body so long as freedom of speech and action in Parliament is in no way fettered, so long as the money is not an inducement to speak or vote in a particular way on a particular matter, and so long as the financial interest is declared.[62] Nor is there anything improper in a Member holding paid office as a parliamentary consultant to an outside body or even managing a general parliamentary consultancy.

Members do not always find it easy to distinguish legitimate pressure from interference with their duties to constituents and to the nation at large. The most important case in recent years was that concerning the involvement of certain Members in the affairs of J. G. L. Poulson and T. Dan Smith who were convicted for corruption in 1974. The Select Committee on Conduct of Members reported in 1977 on the conduct of a number of Members who had been named in the inquiries and criminal proceedings relating to Poulson and Smith. The committee was unanimous. It found that some statements about six Members or former Members were false and on other matters that their conduct should not be criticised. It concluded however that the conduct of three Members (Mr. John Cordle, Mr. Reginald Maudling and Mr. Albert Roberts) was "inconsistent with the standards which the House is entitled to expect from its Members." In each case the Member had failed to declare his interest when speaking or acting on a matter related to the Poulson businesses in which he had a pecuniary interest; Cordle had also specifically raised a matter in Parliament for reward, and this amounted to a contempt of the House.[63]

When the matter was debated, the House agreed, without division, to a motion moved by the Leader of the House that expressed agreement with the committee's findings related to Cordle (who by that time had resigned his seat); similar motions relating to Maudling and Roberts were however amended on divisions so that the House simply took note of the committee's report in respect of those Members, and other amendments for their expulsion from the House, and for suspension for six months, were defeated by substantial majorities.[64]

---

[61] H.C. 512 of 1976–77.

[62] See also Report from the Select Committee on Members' Interests (Declaration): H.C. 57 of 1969–70.

[63] H.C. 490 of 1976–77, paras. 22–23, 31–33, 38.

[64] H.C.Deb., Vol. 936, cols. 332–460 (July 26, 1977).

MEMBERS AND CONSTITUENCIES

The relationship

The functions of Members are of two kinds and flow from the working of representative government. When a voter at a general election, in that hiatus between Parliaments, puts his cross against the name of a candidate, he is (most often) consciously performing two functions: seeking to return a particular person to the House of Commons as Member for that constituency; and seeking to return to power as the Government of the country a group of individuals of the same party as that particular person. The voter votes for a representative and for a Government. He may know that the candidate he votes for has little chance of being elected. He may then consider that his vote will be counted as one of protest against the successful candidate and his party. He may also know that the party he votes for is most unlikely to form a Government. But even if he votes for a party (such as the regional parties in Scotland, Wales and Northern Ireland) which puts forward only a small number of candidates, he cannot exclude the possibility that the party might participate in the formation of a Government, or might even become part of a coalition.

When a candidate is elected as a Member of the House of Commons, he reflects those two functions of the voter. Whatever other part he may play, he will be a constituency M.P. As such, his job will be to help his constituents as individuals in their dealings with the departments of State. He must listen to their grievances and often seek to persuade those in authority to provide remedies. He must have no regard to the political leanings of his constituents for he represents those who voted against him or who did not vote at all as much as those who voted for him. Even if he strongly disagrees with their complaint, he may still seek to represent it, though the degree of enthusiasm with which he does so is likely to be less great. But secondly, he is also a party man and elected as such. If his party is in office as the Government of the day, his primary duty is to support it and to vote for its measures. If his party is in Opposition, his primary duty is to support its leaders in their criticism of Government policy. He will also be expected to maintain contact with his local party in his constituency.

So put, the life of a Member seems straightforward. But there are at least two complications. The first is that he may feel that the policy of his party, whether it is in office or in Opposition, on a particular matter is not one of which he approves. He may think this because of his personal opinions, or because of its special consequences for his constituents or outside interests or because it reflects a general position within the party with which he cannot agree. On many occasions, he may support the party despite his disapproval. But occasionally the strength of his feeling will be such that he is obliged to express his opposition either by speaking or by abstaining on a vote or even by voting with the other side. Such opposition will not pass unnoticed and, unless the matter is clearly one of conscience, he will not be popular with the party Whips.[65]

The second complication is caused by a special aspect of parliamentary conduct which not infrequently transcends party lines. Members, who are neither Ministers nor front-bench Opposition spokesmen, do regard as an important part of their function the general scrutiny of Governmental

---

[65] On dissent generally see pp. 118–130.

activity. This is particularly the role of select committees which have, as we shall see, gained new prominence since 1979. No doubt it is superficially paradoxical to see Members on the Government side of the House joining in detailed criticism of the administration and yet voting to maintain that Government in office. But as one prominent critic of government has said, there is nothing inherently contradictory in a Member sustaining the Executive in its power or helping it to overcome opposition at the same time as scrutinising the work of the Executive in order both to improve it and to see that power is being exercised in a proper and legitimate fashion.[66]

Although on the great majority of occasions the Member will find himself in agreement with the leaders of his party, there will therefore be the exceptional occasions when he finds himself obliged to consider more closely how he should act. He may be under pressure from some group of his constituents to act in their interest. Edmund Burke is the best known authority on this possible conflict:

> "It ought to be the happiness and glory of a representative to live in the strictest union, the closest correspondence, and the most unreserved communication with his constituents. Their wishes ought to have great weight with him; their opinion, high respect; their business, unremitted attention. It is his duty to sacrifice his repose, his pleasures, his satisfactions to theirs,—and above all, ever, and in all cases, to prefer their interest to his own. But his unbiased opinion, his mature judgment, his enlightened conscience, he ought not to sacrifice to you, to any man, or to any set of men living ... Your representative owes you, not his industry only, but his judgment; and he betrays, instead of serving you, if he sacrifices it to your opinion."[67]

And Burke went on to reject any notions that the Member was bound to obey instructions or mandates from his electorate.

While in the last resort, a Member must exercise his own judgment, having properly considered what are the interests, often conflicting, of his constituents, and come to his own conclusions, the Member does so today, much more than in the eighteenth and the first half of the nineteenth century, within the discipline of his party allegiance. The Member has subscribed to the policy of his party, which he accepted before he was elected, and as a Member taking the party whip he has an obligation to continue to accept decisions made by the party leadership. When he is considering what he shall say or how he shall vote, the policy adopted by the party will be the largest single outside influence on his judgment and he will need to be persuaded by strong moral or political arguments to oppose that policy.

Although the Whips will be displeased by any Member who speaks or votes against party policy, dispensation is possible (for Government backbenchers) where a departmental decision causes special resentment in a constituency. And it is possible, even for Ministers, in exceptional circumstances, to be allowed to express dissent. On February 25, 1986 the Secretary of State for the Environment announced four sites chosen as possible dumping grounds for the disposal of radioactive waste. One was in the

---

[66] B. Sedgemore, *The Secret Constitution* (1980), 181.
[67] Speech to the Electors of Bristol, 1774. There is more than one version of the precise words.

constituency of the Government Chief Whip who immediately issued a statement criticising the decision and saying that the site was "totally unsuitable." And a Conservative backbencher in whose constituency was one of the other sites was reported as saying that he and his constituents would fight a "guerrilla war."

There is a convention that Members do not normally take up individual cases from another Member's constituency unless he is unable or unwilling to act on his constituent's behalf. In 1985–86, an unusual dispute arose regarding the handling of immigration cases. The Home Office issued "guidelines" on the handling of representations by Members. These provided that a Member could ask the Home Office to arrange for the removal of a person seeking entry to be deferred. The Member was then allowed 12 working days within which he could submit written representations. If the Minister upheld the decision to remove the person, the Member had four days to produce new and compelling evidence. Similar provisions applied to representations made where appeal against a decision to remove was exercisable in the United Kingdom. The guidelines then provided:

> "It is not for the Home Office to police the convention that Members of Parliament do not take up cases involving other Members' constituents, but the Home Office will not normally accept a request to defer removal from anyone other than the person who appears to be the constituency Member, or a Member dealing with constituency business on his behalf if he is absent or ill."

This proved to be unacceptable to a number of Members who were anxious to help on immigration cases where other Members refused to act.[68]

The means of contact

The most usual ways in which a Member keeps in touch with his constituents, and in which constituents make contact with their Member, are by correspondence or by the regular opportunities a Member provides by holding "surgeries" in the constituency. A Member will commonly make known that he will be available at one or more offices in the constituency at stated times. Constituents may then bring their difficulties personally to the Member. Or constituents may, though much less commonly, meet the Member in the Palace of Westminster.

Correspondence by letter is a much used way whereby constituents may make contact. When Barker and Rush carried out their sample survey[69] of about 100 Members in the mid 1960s they found about 40 per cent. estimated that they received between 25 and 49 letters a week and about 25 per cent. between 50 and 74 letters a week. Most of the letters raised personal cases and problems, most of those concerning social security and housing.

When Members were asked their views on this part of their work:

> "Nearly 40 per cent. of our 109 respondents felt that the time they spent on their post was the most valuable part of their work as M.P.s, or that it gave them great personal satisfaction, while the role of the M.P. as a welfare officer was welcomed or accepted by 60 per cent. But 20 per cent.

---

[68] See H.C.Deb., Vol. 84, cols. 825–839 (October 29, 1985); H.C.Deb., Vol. 94, cols. 399–401 (March 20, 1986) and cols. 952–1041 (March 26, 1986).

[69] A. Barker and M. Rush, *The Member of Parliament and his Information* (1970), Chapter IV.

say that many matters are not really for them (usually local government responsibilities) and nearly 12 per cent. feel that the welfare role has been taken too far."[70]

An analysis of the correspondence of Mr. Tony Benn, then Member for Bristol Southeast, over 12 months in 1972–1973, showed that he received an average of 24 letters a week from constituents (a total of 1266 in the year) and wrote 37 letters a week to constituents (1958 in the year). The view advanced by some analyses that letter-writers were predominantly middle-class was not supported by this survey. The Member wrote 286 letters to central government departments. Of these by far the most (118) were written to the Department of Health and Social Security, the others being Employment (29), the Treasury (28), the Home Office (24) and the Environment (24). Ten other Departments were written to in 16 or fewer letters. The Member wrote 424 letters to local authorities of which 176 concerned housing, no other subject involving 70 letters or more.[71]

Certainly it seems to be increasingly true that constituents expect their Members to respond directly and usefully to their personal problems. The growth in this "welfare" function has undoubtedly much increased both during this century, since 1945, and again during the last 20 years. It has done so, predictably, with the growth of the welfare state itself but also with the emergence of a general population itself much more aware politically.

As more constituents are approaching Members by post and in local surgeries so also the number of approaches made by Members to departments has progressively increased. It has been suggested that Members take up 100,000 cases each year with the departments centrally and perhaps as many more with the local offices of departments.[72]

Perhaps one important reason why so many Members are involved by constituents who have grievances against departments is that constituents believe their cases are more likely to be treated sympathetically if put forward or supported by Members. Letters from Members are dealt with by Ministers' private offices in the first instance and are likely to be dealt with by civil servants at a higher level than letters addressed by the member of the public directly to the department.

In 1986, the Letter Writing Bureau (sponsored by pen and stationery manufacturers, allied retailers and the Post Office) published the results of a survey carried out in May 1986 to which 196 Members[73] responded by completing a questionnaire. From this it appeared that 47 per cent. of these Members received between 20 and 35 letters (excluding circulars) a day with a further 28 per cent. receiving between 36 and 50 letters a day. This indicated a substantial increase since the 1960s. Letters from constituents made up the greatest part of Members' postbags, 73 per cent. indicating that more than half the letters came from that source.

Asked what constituency matters people had written to Members about most frequently in the past year, 59 per cent. of Members mentioned housing; 31 per cent. health and social security benefits; 20 per cent. education and the teachers' dispute then current; 14 per cent. rates; 10 per cent.

---

[70] *Ibid.* p. 194.

[71] Frances Morrell, *From the Electors of Bristol* (1977).

[72] A. C. Page, "M.P.s and the Redress of Grievances" in [1985] *Public Law* 1; P. Norton, "Dear Minister" in (1982) 35 *Parliamentary Affairs* 59.

[73] Of whom 111 were Conservative and 67 Labour. All 650 Members were circulated.

immigration; eight per cent. unemployment; seven per cent. N.H.S. and hospital closures; three per cent. roads, three per cent. tax; three per cent. Sunday trading. Members for Scotland, the North East, and Yorkshire were most likely to mention housing (those for East Anglia and East Midlands the least likely).

Asked what topical or national issues people had written to Members about most frequently, 76 per cent. of Members mentioned Sunday trading (the bill being debated about this time), 24 per cent. education and the teachers' dispute; 22 per cent. animal welfare and experiments; 19 per cent. embryo experiments and abortion (a private Member's Bill was before the House); 17 per cent. student grants (also then very much in the news); 10 per cent. African famine and Third World aid.

The mixture of the perennial (housing and social security) and the topical (Sunday trading and teachers' dispute) was to be expected. But the growth in "surgery" hours has not led to a lessening in letter writing which again suggests that overall constituents are seeking to use their Members' services more and more.

Whenever major controversies especially on domestic issues arise, campaigners will urge those affected to write to their Member of Parliament advocating a course of action. And it is generally believed that Members receiving a large number of letters from their constituents on one topic do consider this to be a good indication of public opinion, though the effect is reduced when the letters are in common form and obviously not a reflection of spontaneous feeling.

So although some back-bench Members consider that the amount of "welfare" work they are nowadays expected to do, whether in correspondence, or in weekend surgeries in their constituencies, unduly interferes with their major responsibilities (as they see them) in Westminster, others, as we have seen, welcome this personal activity. This may be particularly so for those back-benchers (especially on the Opposition side) who feel frustrated by their inability to influence events.

Constituents expect Members to put local interests and local opinion above all their other considerations. Based on a survey, Ivor Crewe concluded:

> "Thus the ideal M.P. appears to be a local resident who devotes his full time to the job of dealing with constituency problems and conscientiously attending local meetings; who occasionally sallies forth from the constituency to express his views in the 'national debate' at Westminster; and who in cases of conflict gives precedence to constituents' views over those of party, to the local over the national party, and to the party's over his own. Above all, the electorate expect proximity in the sense of the Member's physical accessibility and the priority of his concerns."[74]

This view of what the individual constituent expects of his Member thus coincides with what are often the primary pre-occupations of the back-bench Member. Indeed all Members, including Ministers, must be careful not to neglect their constituents. The difference is that Ministers (and to a less extent Opposition front-benchers) must also concern themselves with their national responsibilities. And no Member can afford to forget his loyalty to his party.

---

[74] "M.P.s and their Constituents in Britain: How Strong are the Links" in V. Bogdanor (ed.), *Representatives of the People?* (1985).

HOURS AND CONDITIONS OF WORK

Members who are not Ministers are likely to be in or about the Palace of Westminster three or four days a week. Some will be attending standing or select committees for five or more hours a week. Party meetings and party committees, all-party groups and non-party organisations, meeting constituents, greeting visitors, all take time. Many will be spending some hours most days pursuing their own professional, commercial or industrial interests outside the House; others will be abroad on international delegations or out of London on committee visits. Only a few will wish or be able to act as gentlemen or ladies of leisure, dropping in to the House only occasionally or only for important divisions.

In May 1983 the Review Body on Top Salaries reported on Parliamentary Pay and Allowances. Questionnaires were sent to 632 Members and 52 per cent. responded. The Review Body found that over one year Members (excluding Ministers and other paid office holders) spent, on average, just over 62 hours each week on all forms of parliamentary work (including constituency and preparatory work) averaging 69 hours when the House was sitting and 42 hours during recess.[75]

All this applies in general terms to back-benchers. For Ministers, life is very different. Their working life is in their departments and, for the most senior, in Cabinet and Cabinet committees. Accounts of ministerial life (for example, in the Crossman diaries) indicate that Parliament, although ever present as part of the background, is seen as a place where they must appear at length for a few hours each week when the business of their department is being debated and must attend for the time it takes to vote in divisions on matters which frequently do not particularly concern them. But Whitehall, and not Westminster, is the centre of their activity. Something similar is true of shadow Ministers. They do not have departments to absorb their time, but their primary interest and what fills their days are governmental activities and the effect of those activities on the public. Their job is to lead the criticism of the Government and, if they are conscientious (which, being hopeful of office when the Opposition becomes the Government, they usually are), there is no limit to their possible endeavours.

More than in the past, and especially with re-selection becoming more common in the Conservative party as well as being mandatory for the Labour party, Members are made very conscious of their relationship with their local constituency organisations. The link between the Member and the local chairman has almost always been close. But all local party officials and members of local party committees expect to be kept in close touch with the Member. So also it is clearly in the interest of the Member that he is continuously informed about the issues that are concerning those in the constituency.

Another analysis, on January 10, 1989, gave the following figures of staff directly employed by Members and paid out of office costs allowance: 25 Members employed no staff; 196 employed one each; 265 employed two; 121 employed three; 29 employed four; and 12 employed more than four.[76a]

---

[75] Cmnd. 8881–II. And see pp. 140–141.

Secretaries and research assistants

In November 1987 the number of staff employed by Members was said to be[76]:

	Number of Members	Number of staff
Conservative	307	641
Labour	173	417
Liberal	17	63
Social Democrat	5	20
Plaid Cymru	2	4
Scottish Nationalist	1	1
Ulster Unionist	3	3
Democratic Unionist	2	2
	510	1151

There are five main categories of Members' staff: permanent research assistants, limited in number to 200 with passes; permanent private secretaries; temporary research assistants employed for more than four months; temporary private secretaries employed for less than one year; research assistants from overseas for short periods, limited in number to 50 with passes at any one time. All who work in the precincts must obtain passes, counter-signed by a Member and validated by the Serjeant at Arms. The passes give access to different parts of the Palace of Westminster, according to category, only permanent research assistants having limited access to the Main Library, others (except temporary secretaries) having access to the Branch Library.

In recent years, the numbers of all categories having increased, concern has been expressed that some passholders were using the facilities for outside interests, including pressure groups and public relations firms,[77] and, following inquiry by the House of Commons (Services) Committee, the House resolved in January 1986 that access should be more tightly controlled.[78]

In December 1985 the House resolved that holders of passes as Members' secretaries or research assistants should register any relevant gainful occupation which they pursued other than that for which the pass was issued.[79] In December 1986 it was reported by the Select Committee on Members' Interests that 1401 had completed registration forms and 295 of these had registered relevant paid occupations.[80]

In November 1987 the House, after divisions, endorsed the recommendation in paragraph 23 of the Second Report of the Services Committee in

---

[76] H.C.Deb., Vol. 122, col. *389* (November 16, 1987). Numbers fluctuate and those published are never up-to-date. The total of 1151 is almost certainly too low. Also research assistants often undertake secretarial work (see report of Select Committee on House of Commons (Services) H.C. 195 of 1984–85).

[76a] H.C.Deb. Vol. 144 col. 475; and see evidence of Deputy Serjeant at Arms to the Society Committee on House of Commons (Services) in 1988 (H.C. 580 of 1987–88 pp. 18–20).

[77] See First Report of Select Committee on Members' Interests, H.C. 408 of 1984–85 Q. 294 (evidence of Mr. G. R. Russell, Deliverer of the Vote).

[78] H.C. 195 of 1984–85, para. 24; H.C.Deb., Vol. 90, cols. 1047–68 (January 29, 1986).

[79] See H.C. 408 of 1984–85 (see note 77) and H.C.Deb., Vol. 89, cols. 216–257 (December 17, 1985); "relevant" meant remunerated activity advantaged by privileged access given by the pass.

[80] H.C. 110 of 1986–87.

1984–85 that a Member who applied for a pass for a secretary or research assistant, whether permanent, temporary or substitute,[81] should be required (i) to provide reasonable details on the background of the appointee (ii) to allow a short period to elapse between the making of the application and the issue of a photo-identify pass and (iii) not to pursue the application in the face of an adverse (and confidential) report on the security status of the applicant. A Member dissatisfied with the explanation of a refusal to issue a pass was at liberty to make representations to the Accommodation and Administration Sub-Committee whose decision on the issue of a pass would normally be regarded as final. In the case of temporary research assistants whose stay was likely to be less than four months and who were sponsored by third parties, the sponsoring body was required to provide such details as the Serjeant at Arms might require on the background of the applicants before a pass was issued. The House also invited the Select Committee on House of Commons (Services) to consider the wider implications for control over access to the precincts of the House and in particular to consider whether the numbers of Members' personal staff should be reduced, bearing in mind the pressure on the capacity of the facilities of the House.[82]

Consequentially, access was further restricted in January 1989 when the House agreed to the Second Report of the Services Committee of 1987–88. This decision limited (save in exceptional circumstances) the number of staff passes per Member to three (non-transferable); it also prohibited overseas "interns" from using temporary secretarial passes. The House agreed however to an amendment, granting limited access to Members of the European Parliament.[82a]

Salaries and allowances

Members were first paid what was then called an "allowance" in 1911. Since then the pay for Members has been a sensitive and controversial matter. A number of attempts have been made to devise a basis that would be seen to be fair but not too generous.[83] In 1970, Members' pay and allowances were referred to the Top Salaries Review Body which made recommendations from time to time, found acceptable by the Government of the day only in part.

On July 21, 1987, the House of Commons resolved that in 1988 and subsequently the salaries of Members (except those receiving a salary under the Ministerial and other Salaries Act 1975)[84] should be at a yearly rate equal to 89 per cent. of the maximum point of the scale for Grade 6 officers (senior principal) in the Home Civil Service.[85] In January 1989 the scale of annual pay and allowances was:

(1)	Basic salary (other than those under the Act of 1975)	£24,107
(2)	Ministers and others under the Act of 1975	£18,148
(3)	London supplement for those with constituencies in inner London; and for Ministers	£ 1,222
(4)	Additional expenses necessarily incurred by a Member staying overnight away from home	£ 9,298 (max.)

---

[81] For illness or holidays, a substitute may stand in for a permanent secretary.

[82] H.C.Deb., Vol. 122, cols. 169–229 (November 10, 1987).

[82a] H.C. 580 of 1987–88; H.C.Deb. Vol. 146, cols. 109–139 (January 30, 1989).

[83] For an authoritative account of the history see R. S. Lankester, "Determination of Pay of Members of the United Kingdom House of Commons" in (1983) 51 *The Table* 36.

[84] For payments to Leaders of the Opposition and Opposition Whips, see p. 77.

[85] H.C.Deb., Vol. 120, cols. 295–344.

Members may also claim reimbursement of expenses incurred in performance of parliamentary duties on secretarial and research assistance and general office expenses (now called Office Costs Allowance). In 1986 the top limit for these expenses was increased by over 50 per cent. when the Government on a snap vote was unable to muster enough support, more than 30 of its back-benchers voting with the Opposition.[86] The amount has now been linked to the salaries of senior personal secretaries in the civil service[87] and in January 1989 was payable at £22,588.

Members are entitled to free travel between Westminster and their constituency, between Westminster and their home, between their constituency and their home, within their constituency, and between their constituency and Government and local authority offices. Members' spouses and children under 18 years may make 15 return journeys per annum between London and the Members' constituencies or between London and home. Members may also claim travel and other expenses when on parliamentary business. Free postage and telephone facilities (with some limitations) are also available.

A resettlement grant is payable to a Member under the age of 65 on the day of dissolution who does not stand for re-election or fails to be re-elected. The grant is assessed as a percentage of salary determined by age and length of service. All Members must contribute 9 per cent. of their salary to a pension fund.[88] The basic scheme provides a pension of one-sixtieth of relevant terminal salary for each year of reckonable service up to July 19, 1983 and one-fiftieth for each year thereafter. Contingent family benefits are also provided.

Ministers and other paid office-holders receive parliamentary salaries at a rate equal to 67 per cent. of Grade 6 officers in the Home Civil Service. They are entitled to draw Ministerial salaries which range from about £15,000 p.a. to about £35,000 p.a. in addition to their reduced salaries as Members of £18,148 p.a. The Leader of the Opposition has a salary of £49,707 (including his parliamentary salary). Salaries are also paid to the Opposition Chief Whip and to two Assistant Opposition Whips (see page 118).

THE REPORTING AND BROADCASTING OF THE HOUSE OF COMMONS

The reporting of the Commons

Ministers, shadow Ministers, Members and Peers, the press, the broadcasting authorities, and the public all have interests in making public what happens in Parliament. But these interests do not always coincide and the principal political parties seek to obtain the terms and conditions most favourable to themselves. Official and parliamentary reports and papers are considered on pages 167–171).

To the press, what happens in Parliament, especially in the House of tion in paragraph 23 of the Second Report of the Services Committee in

---

[86] H.C.Deb., Vol. 101, cols. 1130–43 (July 16, 1986).
[87] H.C.Deb., Vol. 120, cols. 296–344 (July 21, 1987).
[88] See Parliamentary Pensions Acts 1972–1987 and orders made thereunder; and H.C.Deb., Vol. 134, cols. 103–4 (May 24, 1988).

Commons, is a source of information and of stories.[89] The House can be full of drama and the Palace of Westminster is a fruitful area to pick up gossip and more authoritative pronouncements. So also the press informs Members of events taking place in the country and in the world outside and provides much of the material for debates and Questions within the Chamber and in committees. Local and personal difficulties and complaints of constituents often reflect national policy or administration. They may first be voiced in the local press and then raised in Parliament by a Member. Or they may first be put to the Member, raised in Parliament and find their way into the local press. So also national or local journalists may report events which then become parliamentary issues, whence they flow back into the press. Comment on the shortages of staff in National Health Service hospitals, with its personal, local and national consequences, has shown how an issue may move from the personal experience of constituents into the local press, through the national media, into and out of Parliament and, so long as the interest lasts, each stage feeds the next. What is said in Parliament by Ministers or Opposition spokesmen or back-benchers becomes news which creates more comment which becomes a further part of the parliamentary debate.

Members like to see their speeches in Parliament reported in the press, in local if not national newspapers. And this is particularly important for the Opposition front-bench whose criticisms of Government activity or inactivity have little impact unless they are reported.

The development of the system of select committees since 1979 has greatly helped the press and the Opposition. Reports abound and often provide excellent copy for the quality press and sometimes good stories for the tabloids. For a week before publication in July 1986, the Fourth Report of the Defence Committee on the Government's decision-making process on the Westland helicopter company[90] was eagerly awaited with much speculation about its likely revelations. The report itself was given considerable coverage in the press. Only in recent years have the reports of select committes received such attention. They have proved to be a source of valuable information.

All journalists working in the House of Commons must be accredited by the Serjeant at Arms. They are nominated by the newspaper or other agency (such as the BBC or ITN) which employs them. The Serjeant at Arms controls the entry onto two lists: that of the Parliamentary Press Gallery and, within it, that of the Lobby. Over the years, the numbers on both lists have increased as various kinds of newspapers have won accreditation: provincial evening papers were admitted in 1947 and were followed by Sunday papers and by political weeklies. Today those on the whole Gallery list total nearly 500 names, of which around 200 are Lobby journalists.[91] Of the 200, some 150 are active members in the sense that they attend at least one Lobby meeting a week. The 300 who are not members of the Lobby include over 80 from the British Broadcasting Corporation employed in the sound broadcasting of the House and responsible for the recording of

---

[89] See C. Seymour-Ure, "Parliament and Mass Communications" in S. A. Walkland (ed.) *The House of Commons in the Twentieth Century* (1979).

[90] H.C. 519 of 1985–86.

[91] These totals are based on lists of names made available to us. But the lists are continuously changing and it is likely that the totals overstate the true situation at any time.

proceedings for public distribution, another 80 or so official Hansard reporters responsible for the verbatim account of proceedings, and a large number of reporters employed by the press and other agencies to report proceedings, and within the Chamber for use by their employers.

The 150 or so active Lobby journalists are drawn from the national daily and evening newspapers, the BBC, independent television and radio, the Sunday newspapers, the political weeklies and representatives of the provincial evening press. A newspaper or other agency which falls within one or other of the recognised groups is entitled to Lobby membership, the number of members (usually one or two) being determined by the Serjeant at Arms after consultation with the secretary of the Lobby committee. Of the 150 active Lobby members, some 60 are alternates so that a newspaper may be allotted two Lobby places but, officially, only one of these is to be present in the Members' lobby at one time. Both the Serjeant at Arms and the Lobby members have an interest in not allowing the facilities to be overcrowded.

In addition, a number of correspondents from the Commonwealth, American and other foreign press are admitted to the premises but may not attend Lobby meetings.

The primary role of those members of the Gallery who are not members of the Lobby is to report what takes place on the floor of the House of Commons and in its committees. These reporters provide the material from which their press, radio and television employers compile their accounts of events. Lobby journalists on the other hand are concerned to relate what happens at the Palace of Westminster to events outside. Their role is interpretive. They include "sketch writers" giving a traditionally ironical view of the House in action, as well as serious political journalists. They may frequent the Members' lobby and Annie's Bar (from both of which the public is excluded) and talk to Members there and on the Terrace. They receive embargoed copies of many Parliamentary papers including ministerial statements and select committee reports. And they may attend Lobby meetings at which they will be addressed by departmental press secretaries, or Ministers, who appear as guests of the Lobby.

The press secretary of the Prime Minister's office holds briefings for Lobby journalists every morning from Monday to Thursday at No. 10 Downing Street (mostly for the evening papers attended by 15 to 20 journalists); and every afternoon from Monday to Wednesday in the Lobby room at the House of Commons (for the dailies attended by 30 to 40 journalists). On Thursday afternoons the Leader of the House briefs the journalists primarily on the parliamentary programme for the following week. He is usually followed by a briefing given by the Leader of the Opposition. Leaders of other political parties in the House also give regular press conferences. On Fridays, the Prime Minister's press secretary gives a briefing for the Lobby journalists of the Sunday papers. Also on Fridays, the Leader of the House of Lords speaks about the following week's work in the Lords. At all Lobby meetings, statements by Ministers or official spokesmen or others may be followed by questions but the Lobby's Practice Notes insist that Lobby correspondents should bear in mind that the purpose of a meeting is to elicit information and not to score political or debating points.

The proceedings traditionally are very strictly on the basis of confidentiality or of non-attributability. From 1984, however, those who address the Lobby may choose to speak on the record or on any other terms. The Government sources normally still prefer to remain anonymous.

The Lobby is a controversial system and has been criticised as creating too great passivity on the part of Lobby journalists and too great willingness to accept the Government's version of events and so allowing themselves to be used as part of the Government's management of politics.[92] Over the years the relationship between Ministers, particularly Prime Ministers, and journalists, particularly the Lobby, has varied from the wary to the distrustful. Harold Wilson began by seeking to establish more openness but later made known his animosity towards particular journalists.[93] The authorisation of selective disclosures to the Press Association by Mr. Brittan of part of the Solicitor-General's confidential letter to Mr. Heseltine during the Westland affair was a notable example of using the Press for political ends.[94] Mrs. Thatcher's press secretary was reported as having referred to one of her Cabinet as "a semi-detached member of the Government," and to others in similar terms at times when these Ministers had made public statements from which the Prime Minister wished to distance herself.[95]

In 1986, the newly launched *Independent* newspaper announced that it would not attend the mass Lobby meetings at which the Prime Minister's press secretary spoke on a non-attributable basis. *The Guardian* newspaper stated that its Lobby journalists would continue to attend but would treat the statements as attributable and on the record. The leaders of the three principal Opposition parties responded by saying that if they were elected to office, they would discontinue unattributable briefings.[96] Earlier in 1986 Mr. Callaghan, former Prime Minister, had told the sub-committee of the Treasury and Civil Service Committee that the Lobby was now too big, that the basis of confidentiality and trust had gone, that he would abolish it, and that the Prime Minister's press officer should give an open press conference on the record.[97] In March 1987, the Lobby journalists voted to preserve non-attributability (*i.e.* "Government sources" or "Whitehall sources" rather than "Downing Street spokesmen" or a named source) by 35 to 26, with nearly 100 abstaining either out of apathy or because they believed the vote (whichever way it went) would not change the practice.

Both the Lobby journalists[98] and the Parliamentary Press Gallery[99] have their own Code of Practice which, amongst other things, states that Press Gallery and Lobby facilities are made available on the strict understanding that they shall be used solely for the dissemination of news to the general public through newspapers, news agencies, television, radio, news magazines and the specialist press. It is an abuse of Gallery membership for members to pass information gained through Gallery facilities, and not available elsewhere, to interests outside journalism. In no circumstances, says the Code, should advance copies of documents or information in them

---

[92] See M. Cockerell, P. Hennessy, D. Walker, *Sources Close to the Prime Minister* (1984).

[93] J. Margach, *The Abuse of Power* (1978); Richard Crossman records that Wilson told the Cabinet in June 1966 that a particular political journalist "must be denied interviews by any of us": *The Diaries of a Cabinet Minister* (1975), Vol. 1, p. 552.

[94] See pp. 28–29.

[95] See *The Guardian*, September 25, 1986.

[96] *The Guardian* October 2, 1986.

[97] H.C. 92–II of 1985–86 Q. 776–777.

[98] Second Report from Committee of Privileges H.C. 555 of 1984–85, Appendix 18.

[99] First Report from Select Committee on Members' Interests: H.C. 408 of 1984–85, pp. 60–61.

to be provided to such outside interests. The Lobby Code of Practice provides similarly and adds that any breach may be followed by a recommendation to the Serjeant at Arms that Lobby facilities be withdrawn from the member concerned.

In evidence to the Select Committee on Members' Interests in 1984, a member of the Institute of Public Relations stated that paid relationships existed between outside interests and some Lobby correspondents[1]; similar evidence was given by the Deliverer of the Vote.[2] The witnesses for the Lobby journalists and the Press Gallery admitted there had been allegations but said they had found no positive evidence identifying offenders.[3]

In December 1985, following the report from the select committee, the House of Commons resolved that those holding permanent passes as Lobby journalists, or journalists accredited to the Parliamentary Press Gallery or for parliamentary broadcasting, should be required to register not only the employment for which they had received their pass, but also any other paid occupation or employment where their privileged access was relevant. As with the Registers for secretaries and research assistants and for officers of all-party and parliamentary groups, access to the Register for journalists is restricted to Members and there is no requirement to state the amount of any remuneration received.[4] In December 1986, the select committee reported that 459 completed registration forms had been received from journalists, of whom 100 had registered other relevant occupation or employment.[5]

The broadcasting of the Commons

After unsuccessful attempts by the British Broadcasting Corporation in the 1920s to be allowed to broadcast special occasions, little happened until August 1966 when the Select Committee on Publications and Debates Reports recommended[6] that continuous live broadcasting in sound and vision was impracticable and undesirable; that the "feed" could be supplied to broadcasting organisations, for recording and editing, by a Commons Broadcasting Unit; and that a closed-circuit experiment should be made on the basis of which the House could decide. But the proposal was defeated by 131 votes to 130.[7] However the next year an experiment in sound broadcasting, not publicly transmitted, was agreed. It took place in May 1968[8] and was reported on in October[9] but because of the cost nothing was done,[10] although back-benchers kept the matter alive. In February 1975, the experiment in sound broadcasting was approved by the House by 354 votes to 182.[11] The Services Committee reported favourably on the sound experi-

---

[1] *Ibid.* Q. 103.

[2] *Ibid.* Q. 294, 308 (Mr. G. R. Russell).

[3] *Ibid.* pp. 59–72.

[4] H.C.Deb., Vol. 89, cols. 216–254 (December 17, 1985); H.C. 261 of 1985–86.

[5] H.C. 110 of 1986–87.

[6] H.C. 146 of 1966–67. See R. Rogers, "The Broadcasting of the United Kingdom Parliament" in *The Table* (1981), 10.

[7] H.C.Deb., Vol. 736, cols. 1606–1732 (November 24, 1966).

[8] H.C.Deb., Vol. 756, cols. 94–137 (December 11, 1967).

[9] H.C. 448 of 1967–68.

[10] H.C. 48 of 1968–69.

[11] H.C.Deb., Vol. 887, cols. 48–178 (February 24, 1975).

ment[12] and the House approved the principle in March 1976 by 299 votes to 124.[13]

A Joint Committee of both Houses was set up and reported in March 1977[14] and the House of Commons resolved in July 1977[15]:

That pursuant to the Resolution of the House of March 16, 1976 and certain Recommendations made in the Second Report of the Joint Committee on Sound Broadcasting—

(1) The British Broadcasting Corporation and the Independent Broadcasting Authority ('the broadcasting authorities') be authorised to provide and operate singly or jointly sound signal origination equipment for the purpose of recording or broadcasting the proceedings of the House and its committees subject to the directions of the House or a committee empowered to give such directions ('the committee');

(2) the broadcasting authorities may supply signals, whether direct or recorded, made pursuant to this Resolution to other broadcasting organisations, and shall supply them to any other organisation whose request for such a facility shall have been granted by the committee, on such conditions as the committee may determine;

(3) no signal, whether direct or recorded, made pursuant to this Resolution shall be used by the broadcasting authorities, or by any organisation supplied with such signal, in light entertainment programmes or programmes designed as political satire; nor shall any record, cassette or other device making use of such signal be published unless the committee shall have satisfied themselves that it is not designed for such entertainment or satire;

(4) archive tapes of all signals supplied by the broadcasting authorities shall be made, together with a selection for permanent preservation, under the direction of the committee.

A select committee was appointed to give the directions referred to in the resolution,[16] and sound broadcasting began on April 3, 1978. The most contentious matter in these many debates was how control was to be exercised and what part was to be played in this by the House. Under the resolution, editorial control and responsibility rest entirely with the broadcasting authorities, subject to the power of the House or any of its committees to exclude strangers and to the power to give directions. Such directions have dealt with many detailed matters and have required that recordings provided to Members may be used only on private occasions and may not be used in party political broadcasts.[17] Proceedings in select and standing committees may also be broadcast.[18]

---

[12] H.C. 142 of 1975–76.

[13] H.C.Deb., Vol. 907, cols. 123–64, 1132–96 (March 8 and 16, 1976).

[14] H.C. 284 of 1976–77.

[15] H.C.Deb., Vol. 936, cols. 539–72 (July 26, 1977).

[16] H.C.Deb., Vol. 942, cols. 1748–81; 943 cols. 1097–1154 (January 26 and February 6, 1978); see Standing Order No. 129 and p. 447.

[17] H.C. 376 of 1981–82, paras. 18, 25.

[18] The BBC programme "In Committee" covers the work of these committees. "Today in Parliament" and "Yesterday in Parliament" are daily summaries. "The Week in Westminster" is a discussion programme. For lists of BBC broadcasts on Radio 4, other destinations, and select committee coverage see proceedings of Sound Broadcasting Committee (H.C. 377 of 1986–87). B.B.C. Television also broadcasts a weekly programme on proceedings in the House of Lords.

The recorded proceedings of the House are used to provide and supplement news items and other programmes and as backing to television (with the speaker often shown in an accompanying still photograph). Independent Radio News which is the contractor for this purpose under the Independent Broadcasting Authority supplies independent local radio stations and independent television companies (including Independent Television News).[19] A number of overseas broadcasting organisations have been authorised to receive a feed of live proceedings as have the Press Association, the British Forces Broadcasting System and the Central Office of Information. Recordings may be used by bodies other than the BBC or the IBA only with the permission of the committee which requires to be told how they will be used.

Many problems arose out of the decision to allow sound broadcasting. They concerned the difficulties of recording select and standing committee proceedings, archives, copyright, legal and parliamentary privilege including contempt and defamation, advertising and the relations with the Official Report. The Select Committee on Sound Broadcasting dealt with these problems in the first instance.[20]

In 1981–82 the select committee conducted a general review of the progress of sound broadcasting.[21] The select committee sent a questionnaire to all Members inviting their reactions. Some 300 Members responded, of whom 76 per cent. were satisfied with the way broadcasting was handled (though with some reservations), 21 per cent. were dissatisfied, and three per cent. gave no opinion. However only 51 per cent. thought (without qualification) that broadcasting gave a fair impression of the House, and 33 per cent. thought the contrary. Three principal criticisms were that too much emphasis was placed on Question Time (17 per cent.), that there was too much extraneous noise (23 per cent.), and that the coverage of select and standing committees was insufficient (25 per cent.). Many Members felt there was an inevitable tendency on the part of broadcasters to use the material which produced the liveliest and most entertaining programme, to the detriment of more serious appraisal of the work of the House; and that not enough time was given to speeches by back-benchers. Members felt little disquiet that the introduction of broadcasting had affected the way the House behaved though there had been a formal complaint when interruptions from the Strangers' Gallery, during the debate on the Abortion Bill on February 8, 1980, were subsequently broadcast. The select committee instructed the broadcasting authorities not to broadcast such interruptions as not being a "proceeding" of the House within the Resolution. After protest from broadcasters this was somewhat modified to allow broadcasts of a Member's speech made over an interruption.

Direct live broadcasting from the House of Commons has been used on an average of 10 to 12 occasions each session including Prime Minister's Question time, major Ministerial statements and debates on the Falkland war and the Westland affair.[22]

From time to time since 1975, attempts were made to persuade the House

---

[19] Channel 4 (TV) broadcasts "The Parliament Programme" four days a week.

[20] For the earlier period see especially H.C. 284 of 1976–77 (a report of the Joint Committee of Commons and Lords); and see H.C. 270 of 1982–83, H.C. 282 of 1986–87.

[21] H.C. 376 of 1981–82.

[22] H.C. 281 of 1986–87, First Report from Select Committee on Sound Broadcasting which recommended a direct broadcast by telephone.

of Commons to introduce television. In November 1983, Mr. Austin Mitchell was given leave under the ten minute rule to bring in a bill.[23] Two years later there was a substantial debate on a motion to approve in principle the holding of an experiment into televising the proceedings of the House. But it was defeated by 275 votes to 263.[24] However on February 9, 1988 the House by 318 votes to 264 approved in principle the holding of an experiment in the public broadcasting of its proceedings by television, and the appointment of a select committee to consider the implementation of the experiment.[25] On March 29, 1988, a select committee of 20 Members was appointed (including the Leader of the House and the shadow Leader), after a division occasioned by protests from some of the smaller Opposition parties (especially the Ulster Unionists) at their lack of representation on the committee.[26] On November 4, 1988 the committee was continued for the following session and reported on May 8, 1989.[27]

---

[23] H.C.Deb., Vol. 47, cols. 876–878 (November 2, 1983).
[24] H.C.Deb., Vol. 87, cols. 277–366 (November 20, 1985).
[25] H.C.Deb., Vol. 127, cols. 194–288.
[26] H.C.Deb., Vol. 130, cols. 1037–1054.
[27] H.C. 141 of 1988–89.

Chapter 3

PARLIAMENTARY PRIVILEGE

THE NATURE OF PARLIAMENTARY PRIVILEGE

All actions of Members of Parliament, in the course of parliamentary proceedings, are protected by parliamentary privilege. Parliamentary privilege, even though seldom overtly cited or relied on in debates, Questions or other proceedings of the House, thus underpins the status and authority of all Members of Parliament. Without this protection, as we shall show, individual Members would be severely handicapped in performing their parliamentary functions, and the authority of the House itself, in confronting the executive and as a forum for expressing the anxieties of the citizen, would be correspondingly diminished.

On the other hand the fact that the House, and its individual Members, claim certain privileges not available to the ordinary citizen, and may seek to punish those who infringe them, tends to set the House apart from the people it represents and makes it liable to criticism—and even ridicule—if it appears to be asserting privileges which are not obviously essential for its functions.

The reconciliation of these two claims—the need to maintain parliamentary privileges and the desirability of not abusing them—has been the hall-mark of the House of Commons treatment of privilege issues in recent years. As our study concentrates on how the procedures and practices of Parliament operate today, we will not attempt to describe in detail the somewhat complex (and in certain respects still uncertain) law of parliamentary privilege, or the story of its evolution.[1] We confine ourselves to describing how privilege issues have been dealt with in recent years and assessing the significance of parliamentary privilege for Members in the conduct of their normal work in the House. But first we clarify the nature of privilege.

The very definition of parliamentary privilege indicates both its continuing relevance for Parliament and its potentially provocative nature. Erskine May defines it thus: "Parliamentary privilege is the sum of peculiar rights enjoyed by each House collectively ... and by Members of each House individually, without which they could not discharge their functions, and which exceed those possessed by other bodies and individuals,"[2] or as

---

[1] For a systematic description see Chapters 5–11 of Erskine May's *Parliamentary Practice* (20th ed.). For an examination of its development in this century and its application up till then, see Geoffrey Marshall, The House of Commons and its Privileges, in *The House of Commons in the Twentieth Century*, ed. S. A. Walkland (1979). For a comprehensive discussion of many of the issues raised by parliamentary claims to privilege, see the Report of the Select Committee on Parliamentary Privileges, (H.C. 34 of 1967–68) and particularly the evidence given to that committee by L. A. Abraham (pp. 89–129, 133–142) and an account of privilege jurisdiction in Commonwealth legislatures (Appendix IV). For a comparative study of the privileges and immunities of members of other Western European parliaments and of the European Parliament, see Eighth Report of the House of Lords Select Committee on the European Communities (H.L. 105 of 1985–86), especially Appendix 4; Appendix 6 of that Report summarises the history of U.K. parliamentary privilege, and evidence given by Michael Ryle (pp. 42–67) deals with the application of privilege in the House of Commons today.

[2] May, p. 70.

Hatsell, the great eighteenth century authority, said, the privileges of Parliament are rights which are "absolutely necessary for the due execution of its powers."[3] It should be emphasised that these privileges are essentially those of the House as a whole; individual Members can only claim privilege in so far as any denial of their rights, or threat made to them, would impede the functioning of the House. Unlike members of many continental parliaments, individual Members cannot claim various privileges, immunities or benefits (*e.g.* tax benefits or protection from criminal charges) that are unrelated to their functions in the House.

What Parliament has considered "absolutely necessary" has varied over the centuries but certain principles have become established. Neither House, individually, can extend its privileges; either House can, by resolution, decide not to claim or apply privileges it has hitherto claimed; either House can apply its privileges to new circumstances, so, in some cases, creating new instances of contempt (see pages 92–94); each House can individually adjudicate and punish in case of breach of its privileges; and new privileges can only be created or old privileges extended, by Act of Parliament.[4] It may also be held that as the privileges of Parliament are part of the common law of Parliament, established privileges could not be abolished (as opposed to not claimed) except by statute. The extent of privilege has, indeed, been defined from time to time by Act of Parliament—most famously by Article 9 of the Bill of Rights (see below) and most recently by section 214(7) of the Insolvency Act 1985 (denying the protection of privilege to Members against whom proceedings for bankruptcy have been commenced).

THE PRINCIPAL PRIVILEGES

The principal privileges, as claimed by the Speaker from the Sovereign at the beginning of each Parliament, are freedom of speech in debate, freedom from arrest, and freedom of access to the Queen "whenever occasion shall require."

The latter two privileges can be dealt with briefly. Freedom from arrest[5] has for many years applied only to arrest in civil causes, but this presents little problem today as imprisonment in civil process has practically been abolished by statute. Some uncertainty continues regarding imprisonment for contempt of court in cases not involving a criminal charge, but it has been held that a Member may not be imprisoned as part of a civil process for the recovery of a debt.[6]

Members cannot claim freedom from arrest or imprisonment on criminal charges. A Member of the House of Commons is in exactly the same position as any other citizen if he is suspected of, charged with, or found guilty of a crime (provided it is unrelated to proceedings in Parliament, see pages 88–89). He may even be arrested in the House itself,[7] and writs may be served on Members in the precincts of the Palace, provided, in both cases,

---

[3] *Hatsells Precedents*, 1818, Vol. 1, p. 1.

[4] May, p. 75.

[5] For this privilege generally, see May, Chapter 7.

[6] May, p. 115.

[7] In 1815 a Member, who had escaped from prison, was arrested while sitting on the Government front-bench in the Chamber (but before the sitting); the Committee of Privileges concluded that no breach of privilege had been committed (Lord Cochrane's case, May, p. 110).

that the House gives leave if it is a sitting day. The Houses of Parliament cannot be used to give a Member sanctuary from the application of the law.[8] The only special procedure relating to the arrest or imprisonment of a Member of Parliament is that if detained for any significant time (for example, if remanded in custody) the police or court concerned must notify the Speaker. Similarly, if a Member is sent to prison after a conviction, the House is informed.

The original justification from the privilege of freedom from arrest lay in the need for the House to secure attendance and service of as many Members as possible. This principle survives in the excusal of Members and Officers of the House from jury service (now confirmed by section 9 of the Juries Act 1974) and in the exemption of a Member from obligation to give evidence in a court. A Member may give evidence voluntarily, but if a *subpoena* is issued he is not obliged to comply. In cases where a Member receives a *subpoena* and does not wish to give evidence on the day in question because of his service to Parliament, the Speaker has frequently drawn the courts attention to the privilege and asked that the Member be excused; another date for the evidence may be agreed. On other occasions the House has given leave to Members to give evidence in court.[9] The same principle requires the leave of the House to be given before a Member or Officer gives evidence before a committee of the House of Lords. Standing Order No. 120 now gives general leave for this purpose for Members.

The third claimed privilege, that of freedom of access to the Sovereign, is now merely a matter of occasional ceremony. For especially important historical or other occasions both Houses may attend on the Queen, as Houses. The most recent was on July 20, 1988 when Addresses were presented to the Queen to mark the Tercentenary of the Revolutions of 1688–89, and of the Bill of Rights and the Claim of Right (the Scottish equivalent to the English Bill).[10]

The Bill of Rights (finally enacted in December 1689) gives statutory expression to the first, and much the most important, of the parliamentary privileges claimed by the House, that of freedom of speech. Article 9 sets it out fully: "That the freedom of speech, and debates or proceedings in Parliament, ought not to be impeached or questioned in any court or place out of Parliament." There are a number of characteristics of this freedom.

First, freedom of speech in Parliament is laid down by statute, but it may also be considered to be constitutionally established. It would be difficult, for instance, by an ordinary Act of Parliament, to abolish or amend such an historic freedom,[11] and indeed the freedom was claimed and accepted by the Sovereign (sometimes with qualifications) long before 1689.

Second, in earlier times, Kings had sought to restrict the freedom of the House to responding to and voting on the demands made by the Crown, and to deny the House the right to initiate business of their own,[12] but the freedom that was claimed by the Commons and finally enshrined in the Bill

---

[8] See also First Report of the Committee of Privileges (H.C. 365 of 1986–87), para. 17.

[9] May, pp. 107–108.

[10] H.C.Deb., Vol. 136, col. 1233–1263 (July 7, 1988); H.C.Deb., Vol. 137, col. 1081 (July 20, 1988); see also H.C.Deb., Vol. 714, cols. 1433–1438 (June 22, 1965) and H.C.Deb., Vol. 931, cols. 421–425 (May 4, 1977).

[11] See opinion (requested by the House) of the Judicial Committee of the Privy Council in 1958 (Cmnd. 431).

[12] See May, pp. 79–80.

of Rights admitted no such limitations. As Chapters 6, 9 and 10 show, initiatives other than those of the Crown are an essential feature of Parliament today.

Third, although the original challenge to freedom of speech in the House came from the Crown, the terms of Article 9 not only protect Members from action by the Crown but also prohibit action of any kind, and by any person outside the House, against Members for what they may say or do in Parliament. Although the possibility of action by Ministers of the Crown against Members for their conduct in the House may not be entirely a matter of past history,[13] the main benefit of Article 9 of the Bill of Rights, as far as individual Members are concerned, is to enable them to speak freely in the House or in committee without fear of actions for defamation.

Fourth, although Article 9 prevents attempts by outside bodies or the courts to limit freedom of speech in Parliament, it does not mean that Members can say whatever they like at all times, because the House itself, and the Speaker on behalf of the House, can restrict the content of speech in debate and other proceedings, such as motions and Questions (see pages 203–205, 208–212 and 255–258).[14]

Finally, Article 9 contained three very significant words—"proceedings in Parliament." Here Parliament was confirming the ancient right of the House to regulate its own proceedings.[15] This means that it is not only the content of speeches which cannot be called in question in the courts, but the very decisions of the House itself, either in the process of passing legislation[16] or on other matters, such as the control of business or the punishment of Members for breach of its privileges or rules. The House is solely responsible for deciding its own procedure (with minor exceptions where procedures are embodied in statute (see pages 179–180)) and is solely responsible for adjudicating on them in case of dispute and for their enforcement. This position has been accepted by the courts.[17] On no matter is there any appeal to the courts regarding anything that constitutes a proceeding in Parliament. The House is sovereign over its own business.

The term "proceedings in Parliament," has not however, proved easy to interpret, and much of the recent application of parliamentary privilege has turned on its meaning. The Select Committee on the Official Secrets Acts said (following the Sandys case) that the term "covers both the asking of a Question and the giving written notice of such Question, and includes everything said or done by a Member in the exercise of his functions as a Member in a committee of either House, as well as everything said or done in either House in the transaction of parliamentary business."[18] Certain things—speeches in debate in the House—are obviously covered, but this still leaves grey areas. What are a Member's "functions as a Member"; what

---

[13] See, for example, the Sandys case of 1938, where a Member was threatened with action under the Official Secrets Acts in respect of things he had done in the House (H.C. 101 of 1938–39).

[14] See First Report of the Committee of Privileges, H.C. 365 of 1986–87, para. 38 (the Banks case).

[15] See May, pp. 88–91.

[16] See *British Railways Board* v. *Pickin* ([1974], 2 W.L.R. 208) when the House of Lords found unanimously that the courts could not "go behind" an Act to question whether a particular section should have been agreed to by the House.

[17] See May, p. 90.

[18] H.C. 101 of 1938–39, p. v.

is "parliamentary business?" The committee in 1939 concluded that there were some things, such as "communications between one Member and another or between a Member and a Minister, so closely related to some matter pending in, or expected to be brought before the House, that, although they do not take place in the Chamber or a committee room, they form part of the business of the House," and they instanced (it was the matter at issue in the Sandys case), a Member consulting a Minister or other Member on a draft Question.[19] Here the committee seemed to think that private communications between Members related to the business of the House were protected by privilege. The House agreed with the committee's conclusions.[20]

A contrary view has been taken. In 1957 Mr. George Strauss forwarded to a Minister, for his advice, a copy of a letter from a constituent critical of an electricity board; the Minister passed it to the board for their comments; and the board sued Strauss for libel. Strauss believed that in corresponding with a Minister in this way, on a matter which he might wish to raise in the House, and where the Minister had an ultimate responsibility, he was performing a proper parliamentary function. He therefore believed that his actions were protected by privilege and complained that the issue of a writ by the electricity board was a breach of that privilege. The matter was referred to the Committee of Privileges who found that the letter written to the Minister by Strauss was a proceeding in Parliament and that therefore the board had committed a breach.[21] However, when the matter was debated, the House agreed to an amendment rejecting the finding of the committee.[22] The Strauss letter was therefore not a proceeding in Parliament.

Two other relevant decisions in recent years should be mentioned. In 1974 Mr. Tony Benn complained that a body had threatened to sue him for a speech he had made in the country which repeated points he had made in the House. The Committee of Privileges found no contempt as the action did not relate to a proceeding in Parliament.[23] In 1987 in the Zircon case (see pages 103–104) the Committee of Privileges decided that the showing of a film in a committee room could not, of itself, be held to be a proceeding in Parliament.[24]

There is thus considerable uncertainty as to the precise meaning and limits of the term "proceedings in Parliament." Various committees have recommended that it should be statutorily defined, and indeed have suggested definitions,[25] but no action has been taken. Perhaps this is not surprising. The House is judge of its own proceedings and has never entrusted interpretation of its rules or adjudication of disputes to the courts.[26] [27] It has always preferred to retain some flexibility in interpreting and applying its privileges according to circumstances—usually politically judged. To accept a binding

---

[19] *Ibid.*

[20] H.C.Deb., Vol. 353, cols. 1071–1084, (November 21, 1939).

[21] H.C. 227 of 1957–58.

[22] H.C.Deb., Vol. 591, cols. 208–346 (July 8, 1958).

[23] "The Aims of Industry" case (H.C. 246 of 1974).

[24] First Report of the Committee of Privileges H.C. 365 of 1986–87, para. 16.

[25] See *ibid.* Appendix 12.

[26] The House has sought the opinion of the Judicial Committee of the Privy Council regarding interpretation of Article 9 of the Bill of Rights in the light of the Parliamentary Privilege Act 1770 and other similar Acts (Cmnd. 431), and regarding the entitlement of a priest of the Church of Ireland to sit in the House (Cmd. 8067, and see Chapter 2, p. 48).

[27] See Select Committee on Parliamentary Privilege, H.C. 34 of 1967–68, paras. 138–146.

statutory definition of its own proceedings would be to move nearer to adjudication by the courts and would considerably restrict the House's own freedom in enforcing its privileges.[28]

The "grey areas" remain. Members may be confident of protection regarding their speeches in the House and other formal proceedings, but can never be certain how far their freedom of speech and parliamentary action extends. However one major area of Members' activities is generally understood to be unprotected by privilege, namely their conduct of constituency business (unless, perhaps, it be very closely related to a proceeding in the House itself). There have been no clear test cases, but neither the House, nor the Committee of Privileges on its behalf, has ever held that protection of privilege extends to Members' activities in their constituencies or to constituency business such as housing complaints or immigration cases. Members are regularly advised by the Speaker or by the Clerks that such matters are not proceedings in Parliament.

There is one other qualification. The parliamentary privilege of freedom of speech applies only to speech in the House and other proceedings of the House itself, but not to reports of proceedings or debates by newspaper or others outside Parliament (although such publication may attract "qualified privilege" in a court action). Thus parliamentary privilege does not protect a Member publishing his own speech apart from the rest of a debate.[29] However, in addition to qualified privilege, certain publications are absolutely protected by statute. Under the Parliamentary Papers Act 1840 (passed in consequence of the *Stockdale* v. *Hansard* case when the courts found that a person who publishes papers printed by order of the House was not protected by parliamentary privilege[30]) neither criminal nor civil proceedings can be taken against a person for publishing papers printed by order of the House or under its authority (thus Hansard itself is covered). This was extended to cover publication by broadcasting by section 9 of the Defamation Act 1952. And, by section 7 of that Act, a fair and accurate report of the proceedings of public meetings, including those of select committees, published without malice and for the public benefit, is privileged.

THE HOUSE'S PENAL POWERS

Laws are meaningless unless there is power to enforce them by imposing penalties on those who break them. The House does not rely on the courts but has its own penal jurisdiction.

The severest and historically most important power is that of commitment. As some thousand cases recorded in the Commons Journals show, the House for many years committed to prison those, including Members, who challenged its authority, infringed its privileges or otherwise offended against it. This power was also used to secure compliance with its orders, such as for the attendance of witnesses. The power of commitment (which Parliament shares with the courts) has been described as "the keystone of

---

[28] This argument was also advanced by the Select Committee on the Official Secrets Acts, H.C. 101 of 1938–39 para. 22, who quoted with approval Sir William Blackstone: "The dignity and independence of the two Houses are in great measure preserved by keeping their privileges indefinite" (*Commentaries*, 164).

[29] Abingdon's case, 1795; Creevey's case, H.C.Deb., Vol. 26, col. 898 (1812–13); for details see May, pp. 85–86).

[30] *Stockdale* v. *Hansard* (1837) 9 A. & E. 1.

parliamentary privilege"[31] and for many years has been accepted by the courts.

In modern times, as the powers and privileges of Parliament have become better defined, more generally accepted and less challenged by the Crown, by the courts, or by other persons—the battle has been fought and won—and as, on the other hand, the House has become more restrained in asserting its authority, the power to commit offenders to prison, or into the custody of the Serjeant at Arms, has fallen into disuse. The last person to be committed by order of the House was Bradlaugh in 1880.[32] It is unlikely that the power would be used today,[33] but it could be in extreme cases of disobedience if the general political sense so allowed.[34]

The House can also, in cases which both breach privilege and are criminal offences, allow the offender to be prosecuted. If a stranger causes a serious disturbance, such as the man who threw a CS gas cannister into the Chamber on July 23, 1970, instead of the House dealing with this as a contempt, he can be handed over to the police for criminal proceedings.

The other penalties which the House can impose on any offender are limited. It is generally accepted that the Commons has now no power to impose fines.[35] The only other penalties are reprimand or admonishment by the Speaker. Since 1945, two Members (Mr. Walkden in 1947[36] and Mr. Tam Dalyell in 1968[37]) and one journalist (Mr. Heighway in 1947[38]) have been formally reprimanded. Mr. John Junor (editor of the "Sunday Express") was summoned to the bar to explain his actions regarding an article in his newspaper, but after he made an apology to the House, the House decided to take no further action.[39] Again these are penalties which may be thought less effective or appropriate today.[40]

Two other punishments can be ordered for Members who offend the House—namely expulsion, or suspension from the service of the House for a specified period or until the end of the session. The latter penalty is nowadays mainly imposed in a limited form as a disciplinary penalty under Standing Order Nos. 42 and 43 (see pages 213–215). Mr. Ron Brown, however, was suspended for 20 sitting days on April 20, 1988 for damaging the mace and for his later conduct towards the Chair when claiming to make a personal statement. (He was also held responsible for the damage sustained by the mace.)[41] As a punishment for breach of privilege, suspension has not been used since 1911.[42]

---

[31] May, p. 123.

[32] H.C.Deb., Vol. 25, cols. 629–664 (June 23, 1880).

[33] Although it survives in a minor form in the power to order a person who misbehaves in the gallery to be detained until the end of the sitting (see Standing Order No. 141).

[34] The Australian House of Representatives committed two journalists to prison in 1955.

[35] May, p. 136. Although, if the Commons did order a fine, it being a lesser penalty than commitment which is not challenged, it is difficult to see how anyone outside could challenge this, as the proceedings of the House cannot be questioned by the courts. Select Committees in 1967 (H.C. 34 of 1966–67, para. 197) and 1977 (H.C. 417 of 1976–77, para. 15), have recommended that legislation should be introduced to give the Commons this power. Nothing has been done.

[36] H.C.Deb., Vol. 443, cols. 1198–1228 (October 30, 1947).

[37] H.C.Deb., Vol. 769, cols. 587–666 (July 24, 1968).

[38] H.C.Deb., Vol. 443, cols. 1197–1198 (October 30, 1947).

[39] H.C.Deb., Vol. 563, cols. 403–405 (January 24, 1957).

[40] See also Second Report from the Committee of Privileges, Premature Disclosure of Proceedings of Select Committees, H.C. 55 of 1984–85, para. 48.

[41] H.C.Deb., Vol. 131, cols. 675–677 (April 19, 1988) and ibid. cols. 929–954 (April 20).

[42] H.C.Deb., Vol. 21, cols. 1553–86 (February 20, 1911).

Expulsion is the ultimate sanction against a Member. It is an outstanding demonstration of the House's power to regulate its own proceedings, even its composition. The expulsion of a Member cannot be challenged. It may best be understood as a means available to the House to rid itself of those it finds unfit for membership, rather than as a punishment. Indeed one of the Members expelled since 1945 (Baker, see below) had committed no offence against the House. Members have been expelled for perjury, fraud, corruption or "conduct unbecoming the character of an officer and a gentleman"[43]; only a few had offended against the House itself or committed a breach of privilege or contempt.

There have been two expulsions since 1945. In 1948 Mr. Garry Allighan was found to have lied to a committee (he had wrongly accused fellow M.P.s of accepting money for disclosing to the press proceedings of private party meetings, when that was precisely what he had done himself) and generally to have behaved dishonourably in a way that amounted to aggravated contempt.[44] The Leader of the House moved that he be reprimanded and suspended for six months (without pay), but the House, on a division on an amendment moved by Mr. Quintin Hogg (now Lord Hailsham), ordered his expulsion.[45] It is significant that Mr. Allighan was a Member of the Labour Party which held office with a large majority at that time; on such matters the House does not always act on party lines. In 1954, Mr. Peter Baker was convicted of forgery after pleading guilty, and was sent to prison for seven years; the House expelled him.[46]

CONTEMPTS

As the House has power to punish those who offend it (a power which the courts do not challenge) so the House is competent to define and decide on those actions which it may punish. Thus, out of much case law, has grown the concept of "contempt." The law of contempt is also grounded on the basic privilege of freedom of speech, for a contempt consists of "any act or omission which obstructs or impedes either House of Parliament in the performance of its functions, or which obstructs or impedes any Member or officer of such House in the discharge of his duty, or which has a tendency, directly or indirectly, to produce such results."[47] Such obstruction or impedence is essentially restricting freedom of speech in the House (for example by intimidation of those who might speak) or freedom of its proceedings.

The nature of a wide range of contempts, based on hundreds of decisions of the House or of the Committee of Privileges, are described in Chapter 10 of May's *Parliamentary Practice*. Decisions of the House have greater authority, but in the absence of a House decision, later committees and Speakers, when considering complaints of contempt or breach of privilege, naturally have regard to findings of earlier committees; in recent years only a minority of cases have been finally decided by the House (see pages 98–101 below). Here we list, adopting the classifications used by May, the main

---

[43] For a full list of cases, see May, pp. 139–140.

[44] H.C. 138 of 1947–48.

[45] H.C.Deb., Vol. 443, cols. 1094–1198, (October 30, 1947).

[46] H.C.Deb., Vol. 535, col. 1986 (December 16, 1954). This was a somewhat strange decision as, under the Forfeiture Act 1970 (then in force), the Member was automatically disqualified from sitting, having been convicted of a felony and sentenced to imprisonment for more than 12 months (see May, pp. 43–44).

[47] May, p. 143.

types of contempt, and give a few examples of actions (by Members and others) which have been found to be contempts:

(i) Misconduct in the presence of the House or its committees.
— interrupting the proceedings of a committee.[48]
— a witness persistently misleading a committee.[49]

(ii) Disobedience to rules or orders of the House or committees.
— refusal to attend as a witness.[50]
— refusing an order to withdraw from the House.[51]

(iii) Presenting a forged or falsified documents to House or committee.
— forging signatures to petitions.[52]

(iv) Misconduct by Members or officers as such.
— deliberately misleading the House.[53]
— corruption by acceptance of bribes.[54]

(v) Constructive contempts.
— speeches or writing reflecting on the House (this needs some explanation; offensive comments about the House or its Members have frequently been punished on "the principle that such acts tend to obstruct the Houses in the performance of their functions by diminishing the respect due to them" (but see page 98 below)).[55]
— wilful misrepresentation of debates.[56]
— premature disclosure of committee proceedings or evidence.[57]
— other indignities offered to the House, such as fighting in the lobbies[58]; using the badge and the name of the House in connection with an unofficial publication[59]; and serving a writ on a Member in the precincts, while the House was sitting, without leave of the House.[60]

(vi) Obstructing Members in the discharge of their duty.
— molesting or insulting Members attending, coming to, or going from the House.[61]
— attempted intimidation of Members, including publishing threatening posters regarding Members voting in a forthcoming debate[62]; and threatening to stop public investment in a Member's constituency if that Member persisted in making speeches of the kind he had made in a recent debate.[63]
— molesting Members on account of their conduct in Parliament, for example by inciting newspaper readers to telephone a Member to

---

[48] Ashworth, H.C.Deb., Vol. 61, col. 1003 (1842).
[49] Allighan, C.J. (1947–48) 22.
[50] Grissell, C.J. (1878–79) 366.
[51] Bradlaugh, H.C.Deb., Vol. 253, col. 620 (1880).
[52] Bidmead, C.J. (1887) 306.
[53] Profumo, C.J. (1962–63) 246.
[54] Sir John Trevor (Speaker), C.J. (1693–97) 274.
[55] Duffy, H.C. 129 of 1964–65; Ashton H.C. 228 of 1974.
[56] "The Daily News," C.J. (1893) 324.
[57] The Times, H.C. 376 of 1985–86 (and see page 102 below).
[58] Piratin (a Member) and Lucy (a journalist), H.C. 36 of 1946–47.
[59] Statement by the Speaker, H.C.Deb., Vol. 3, col. 789, (April 29, 1981).
[60] Carter, H.C. 144 of 1972–73.
[61] Lucy, C.J. (1946–47) 54, 91.
[62] Mrs. Tennant, H.C. 181 of 1945–46.
[63] Campbell-Savours and MacGregor, H.C. 214 of 1980–81.

complain of a Question he had tabled.[64]

— speeches or writings reflecting on Members conduct in the House, for example accusing the Speaker of partiality in the Chair.[65]

(vii) Obstructing officers of the House while in the execution of their duty.

— resisting the Serjeant at Arms when enforcing an order of the House.[66]

(viii) Obstructing witnesses. (Witnesses have full protection of privilege when "coming, staying or returning" in response to a summons to give evidence before a committee.[67] Parliamentary privilege does not however protect persons giving information voluntarily to Members in their personal capacity.[68]

— calling a person to account or censuring him for evidence given by him to a committee of the House.[69]

APPLICATION OF PRIVILEGE TODAY

Parliamentary privilege has been developed over a very long period. Some matters are firmly established, especially the freedom of speech in debate and other proceedings; the central point has not been challenged since 1887 when, in *Dillon* v. *Balfour*, the court declared that it had no jurisdiction in a matter involving words spoken in the House.[70] This freedom is essential for the effective working of the House. Under it, every day, Members are able to make statements or allegations about outside bodies or persons—and sometimes in offensive language—which they would hesitate to make without the protection of privilege. This is often criticised and undoubtedly the privilege may occasionally be abused. However, the freedom to make allegations which the Member genuinely believes at the time to be true or at least worthy of investigation is fundamental. Such allegations, for example, might relate to possible corruption by a policeman, or abuse of power by some powerful person or public body, or sale of dangerous toys, or fraud by financial businesses, or breaches of health and safety regulations in a factory, although the Member might not be able to present detailed evidence in support of his statements which would stand up in a court of law. Without this freedom parliamentary scrutiny of the executive would be muzzled and individual Members' defence of the interests of their constituents and others would be severely constrained. As in the courts themselves, the House of Commons could not work effectively unless its Members were able to speak and criticise without having to account to any outside body. Freedom includes the freedom to make mistakes. There would be no freedom of speech if everything had to be proved to be true before it was uttered.

Other ancient privileges have been less firmly maintained. We have seen

---

[64] "*Sunday Graphic,*" C.J. (1956–57) 31, 50; H.C. 27 of 1956–57.

[65] "*The Daily Worker,*" C.J. (1937–38) 213.

[66] Maxton and others, C.J. (1930–31) 335, 338.

[67] Resolution of the House of March 8, 1688 (C.J. (1688–93) 45).

[68] May, pp. 167–168.

[69] Cumbrian Railway Directors, H.C. 125 of 1892; H.C.Deb., Vol. 3, cols. 595, 698, 883 (1892). Following this case the Witnesses (Public Inquiries) Protection Act 1892 made it an offence to "punish, damnify or injure" witnesses before committees of either House, on account of their evidence, unless such evidence was given in bad faith.

[70] (1887) 20 Ir. L.R. 600.

already how the House has become decreasingly ready to enforce its privileges with effective punitive action (and see pages 101–102), and correspondingly it has become less concerned to claim privilege, especially in respect of contempts.

The whole scope and application of privilege was reviewed by the Select Committee on Parliamentary Privilege in 1967–68.[71] Prior to the committee's appointment some concern had been expressed about the number of occasions when complaints had been raised in the House of breaches of privilege or contempt regarding relatively trivial matters. The committee concurred: "Members are too sensitive to criticism and invoke too readily the penal jurisdiction of the House; they do so not merely in respect of matters which are too trivial to be worthy of that jurisdiction, but also on occasions when other remedies (*e.g.* in the courts or by way of complaint to the Press Council) are available to them as citizens."[72]

The committee came down against any major changes in the law of privilege, especially the suggestion that jurisdiction in privilege cases should be transferred to the courts, but it recommended a number of significant reforms in the way privilege complaints should be considered.

One reform was apparently radical. On July 16, 1971, the House resolved that "notwithstanding the Resolution of the House on March 3, 1762 and other such Resolutions, this House will not entertain any complaint of contempt of the House or breach of privilege in respect of the publication of the debates or proceedings of the House or of its Committees, except when any such debates or proceedings shall have been conducted with closed doors or in private, or when such publication shall have been expressly prohibited by the House."[73] At the same time the House also permitted the publication of information about how Members had voted, about Questions and motions that had been tabled or about Members intentions in such matters.[74] In practice the House was simply bringing its formal rules into line with the practice of nearly 200 years. It will be noted, however, that the House still retains ultimate control over the right to have its proceedings reported or not, or indeed to meet in private or public.

The House also clarified the criteria to be applied when considering privilege complaints and modified the procedure for their examination.

First it adopted the self-denying principle that the House, while not relinquishing its privileges, would not always seek to enforce them. It was agreed on February 6, 1978 "that the House should exercise its penal jurisdiction (a) in any event as sparingly as possible and (b) only when it is satisfied that to do so is essential in order to provide reasonable protection for the House, its Members or its Officers from such improper obstruction or attempt at or threat of obstruction as is causing, or is likely to cause, substantial interference with the performance of their respective functions."[75] The House agreed at the same time to recommendations that the Speaker was entitled, when considering whether to give a complaint prece-

---

[71] H.C. 34 of 1967–68.

[72] *Ibid.*, para. 10.

[73] H.C.Deb., Vol. 821, cols. 993–94.

[74] *Ibid.*, col. 993.

[75] H.C. 34 of 1967–68, para. 48(i); H.C. 417 of 1976–77, para. 4; H.C.Deb., Vol. 943, cols. 1155–1198.

dence (see below), to take into account the probability that the complainant could seek a remedy in a court of law[76] and, to the mode and extent of the publication of a contempt.[77]

The crucial words in these decisions were "substantial interference." The House no longer entertains complaints about actions which do not cause actual or threatened damage to the working of the House in a substantial way. This has almost eliminated the pursuit of trivial complaints.

The second major change was procedural. Traditionally privilege complaints had been raised and ruled on in the House. In 1978 the House decided that all privilege complaints (except of something happening in the House itself which required immediate attention, such as molestation of Members in the lobbies) should first be submitted to the Speaker privately, and in writing, as soon as possible after the alleged breach of privilege or contempt.[78]

When the Speaker receives a written complaint from a Member,[79] with any supporting documents or evidence, he must first consider whether the matter has been raised as soon as possible and whether it is in the field of privilege at all. Many matters involve some obstruction of a Member, but not in his function as such or do not relate to proceedings of the House (see above). If the Speaker is satisfied that the matter does appear to involve privilege or a contempt, then he must also consider whether there has been "substantial interference" as described above, or whether the matter is too trivial. Only if he is satisfied on this test will the Speaker allow the complaint to proceed.

If the Speaker decides for any of these reasons not to allow the complaint to go further, he writes to the Member who raised the complaint to explain his decision. He normally gives no public ruling (exceptionally, if he considers that a novel point of privilege ought to be explained to the House he may make a statement[80]) and he has ruled that Members should not publish his private ruling in any way,[81] nor may it be read out in the House.[82] If the Speaker turns down a complaint in this way, that is the end of the matter except that the Member is still entitled to publicise his complaint (without referring to the Speaker's decision) in other ways, for example by tabling an early day motion.

If, on the other hand, the Speaker decides that there may have been a serious breach of privilege or contempt he writes to the complainant to tell him that he will allow him to move a motion relating to the complaint, and he so rules publicly in the House. The motion is normally put down for debate the day after the Speaker's ruling and, as a privilege matter, has precedence over all other business.

A privilege motion may simply consist in declaring a certain matter to be a breach of privilege or a contempt (sometimes a "gross contempt") of the

---

[76] H.C. 417 of 1976–77, para. 5.

[77] *Ibid.*, para. 6.

[78] *Ibid.*, paras. 9–12; H.C.Deb., Vol. 943, col. 1198 (February 6, 1978).

[79] Nearly all complaints are raised by Members. If a stranger wishes to complain he must do so by petition. This procedure is seldom used; the last recorded case was in 1864 (see May, pp. 178–80), apart from the occasion when Mr. Tony Benn, who had lost his seat by succession to a peerage, petitioned the House for the matter to be considered by the Committee of Privileges, which the House so ordered (H.C.Deb., Vol. 631, col. 171 (November 29, 1960)).

[80] *e.g.* H.C.Deb., Vol. 3, col. 789 (April 29, 1981).

[81] See, H.C.Deb., Vol. 72, col. 747 (February 5, 1985) and H.C.Deb., Vol. 106, col. 1094 (December 4, 1986).

[82] H.C.Deb., Vol. 114, cols. 303–304 (April 8, 1987).

House.[83] It is normal however, for a privilege motion to refer the matter to the Committee of Privileges for its examination. The motion is usually debated and often divided on (nearly all privilege matters have a political flavour). Since 1945, however, such motions have, with two exceptions,[84] always been agreed to, if moved and not withdrawn. Sometimes, especially if an apology has been received, such a motion may be withdrawn[85] or not moved[86].

The Committee of Privileges is appointed for a Parliament under Standing Order No. 121, but, exceptionally, it has no specified orders of reference. It has however an ancient pedigree and by tradition its functions are fairly clearly defined. It has no power to examine issues other than the specific matters referred to it by the House or a matter closely related to one so referred.[87]

The size of the Committee of Privileges has varied, but in the 1983 to 1987 Parliament there were 17 members. The Chairman was the Leader of the House; other members included the Attorney-General, the shadow Leader of the House, a senior Member of the Liberal Party (for some time the Leader) and senior back-benchers from both sides, mostly Privy Councillors. Under the standing order, the committee has most of the usual powers of select committees, in particular the power to send for persons, papers and records (see pages 281 and 448–449).

After a complaint has been referred to the committee it normally takes evidence from the complainant and from those whose words or actions are complained of. It receives evidence on the relevant aspects of privilege law and the precedents from the Clerk of the House. It does not seek to act like a court of law. The precise rules of evidence as applied in a court are not applied here; counsel are not normally heard; and those whose actions are being investigated are not usually legally represented. The committee approaches its work, however, in an objective and quasi-judicial manner. Its task is simply to see how, if at all, the law of privilege applies to the case before it, to decide whether a breach or contempt has been committed, and to recommend what action, if any, should be taken. It rarely finds itself inquiring in depth into the facts of a matter, which are seldom in dispute.[88]

If the Committee of Privileges finds that there has been no breach or contempt, or if it recommends that no action be taken—perhaps after an apology has been received—it has not been the practice in more recent years for the House to debate the report,[89] and the matter rests there.

If however the committee finds that there has been a serious breach or contempt and recommends further action of some kind, especially the

---

[83] e.g. H.C.Deb., Vol. 481, cols. 653–662 (November 24, 1950).

[84] H.C.Deb., Vol. 485, cols. 2491–2544 (March 21, 1951); H.C.Deb., Vol. 709, cols. 576–642 (March 24, 1965). A motion to "re-affirm that an attempt to influence Members in their conduct by threats is a serious contempt of the House" was negatived without a division on April 21, 1983 (H.C.Deb., Vol. 41, cols. 448–453).

[85] e.g. H.C.Deb., Vol. 765, cols. 1093–1117 (May 24, 1968); H.C.Deb., Vol. 499, cols. 891–898 (April 25, 1952); H.C.Deb., Vol. 129, cols. 193–206 (March 8, 1988).

[86] e.g. H.C.Deb., Vol. 679, cols. 1145–1146 (June 25, 1963); H.C.Deb., Vol. 877, cols. 673–674 (July 18, 1974).

[87] H.C.Deb., Vol. 443, cols. 1242–1245 (October 30, 1947).

[88] For a case where the facts were disputed see the MacGregor case, when the evidence of the Chairman of the British Steel Corporation conflicted with that of a Member. The Committee made no finding on the truth of the matter, but confined itself to concluding that if the Member's version of the story were correct, there would have been a serious breach of the privilege of freedom of speech (H.C. 214 of 1980–81; and see pp. 93 and 101 above).

[89] For earlier practice see May, p. 171.

punishment of an offender, then the Government provides an opportunity to debate the Committee's report, usually on a motion in the name of the Leader of the House to agree with the committee's findings. Only the House can actually order one of the penalties described above. On occasions the House has not agreed to the committee's recommendations.[90]

The overall effect of the new guiding principles and of the procedures adopted in 1978 has been significant. First, the use of the word "privilege," to gain the Speaker's ear and to secure the chance to raise a political issue unrelated to real privilege (which was fairly common before 1978 and is still frequently experienced in some other parliaments) is now almost unknown; indeed if a Member even mentions the word, the Speaker will almost certainly stop him going further.

Second, there are now far fewer trivial privilege cases referred to the Committee of Privileges. In particular no cases of "constructive contempt" involving rude or derogatory reflections on Members have been referred to the committee since 1978[91]; between 1971 and 1977, inclusive, there were five such cases.

Third, the total number of privilege matters of all kinds referred to the committee has been reduced. In the seven years 1971 to 1977, inclusive, there were 17 cases (including one matter reported on by a Committee on Conduct of Members); in the 10 years 1978 to 1987, inclusive, there were 12 (see Table below) and not all of these arose from complaints. Lest it be thought, however, that Members have almost stopped complaining about breaches of privilege, it should be remembered that complaints are still made to the Speaker privately. The figures in recent years are of interest—

Privilege Complaints Submitted to Speaker[92]

Session	Number submitted	Number granted precedence for a debate in House
1982–83	11	3
1983–84	7	1
1984–85	20	1
1985–86	24	1
1986–87	12	—

Privilege is still a living parliamentary animal; but it less frequently comes into the open.

RECENT CASES

The nature of privilege issues today is best shown by the following Table listing those cases referred to committees since 1977.[93]

---

[90] See Strauss case, (page 89 above), *The Economist* case in 1975 (page 101 below) and *The Times* case in 1987 (page 102 below).

[91] A Member complained in March 1988 of offensive and inaccurate words in a *Guardian* "sketch," which alleged that the poor attendance of Opposition Members in the House for a certain debate was because they were "drunk, lazy or incompetent"; the Speaker allowed the complaint precedence, but after a short debate the motion to refer the matter to the Committee of Privileges was withdrawn (H.C.Deb., Vol. 129, col. 27 (March 7, 1988) and cols. 193–206 (March 8, 1988)).

[92] Source: Clerk of the Committee of Privileges, and see evidence given by Michael Ryle (then Clerk of the Committee) to the Lords select committee on European Communities, (H.L. 105 of 1985–86), Q. 279–280.

[93] This is a slightly modified and up-dated version of part of the Table published on pages 45 to 51 of H.L. 105 of 1985–86 as an Appendix to Ryle's evidence. The references to "tacit acceptance" in the fourth column are to recommendations not debated by the House.

Privilege Cases in The House of Commons since 1977

Date and relevant Report	Subject of Complaint or matter otherwise referred	Report and Recommendations of the Committee of Privileges	Action by the House
January 1977 H.C. 176 of 1976–77	Allegation that Members' conduct was influenced by payments received from bookmakers ("*Sunday People*" case).	Serious contempt, but editor's apology acceptable. The source of the allegation (identified by the editor) denied that he had made such an accusation, for which there was no evidence. A similar libel in the *New Statesman* did not merit further attention.	Tacit acceptance.
May 1977 H.C. 512 of 1976–77	Threat by a Union to withdraw sponsorship of Members if they acted in a certain way (NUPE case).	The Union had attempted to impose unacceptable conditions on Members. In the light of their undertaking to let the matter lapse, no further action required.	Tacit acceptance.
March 1978 H.C. 376 of 1977–78	Newspaper reports of contents of a Draft Report before a select committee (*Guardian* and "*Daily Mail*" case).	A contempt. The prime offender was the Member who provided the information, but he could not be identified. No action recommended.	Tacit acceptance.
November 1978 H.C. 102 of 1978–79	Reference in a Court to the Official Report without prior leave (Court proceedings case).	No contempt on the facts. The practice of petitioning for leave to refer to the Official Report should be ended.	The practice formally ended on *October* 31, 1980 (Including published committee proceedings).
May 1978 H.C. 667 of 1977–78; H.C. 222 of 1978–79	Privilege affecting reporting debates where sub-judice matters are involved, and the application of the sub-judice rule to a particular case. (The Colonel 'B' case).	Members had broken the sub-judice rule. There should be a statutory privilege for fair and accurate reports of Parliamentary proceedings.	No action.
April 1981 H.C. 214 of 1980–81	Remarks by the Chairman of British Steel Corporation to the Member for Workington alleged to amount to a threat to cease investment there (MacGregor's case).	Conflict of evidence: Committee not satisfied that there was a contempt.	No action.

March 1982 H.C. 233 of 1981–82	Threat to use a Member's speech in the House (if not withdrawn) as intensification of a damages claim against a third party (Makin's case).	Apology received. The 'threat' was of little substance. No further action recommended.	Tacit acceptance.
December 1982 H.C. 336 of 1982–83	Allegation that witnesses did not tell the truth to a select committee (Abortion (Amendment) Bill case).	A subsequent court case appeared to indicate that they had not told the truth, but they denied this and the Committee did not wish, in effect, to re-try the issue.	Tacit acceptance.
January 1983	Alleged threat that London Members not supporting the Greater London Council (Money) Bill would have fewer new services provided in their constituencies (Livingstone's case).	Enquiry terminated by Dissolution.	
April 1983	Account in *The Times* newspaper of the contents of the draft report of the Chairman of the Foreign Affairs Committee (*The Times* case).	Enquiry terminated by Dissolution.	
June 1984 H.C. 564 of 1983–84	Threat by a Member in debate that he would vote in the Greater London Council for less expenditure in the constituencies of Members voting for an Instruction (Bank's case).	A breach of privilege for a Member, in exercising his freedom of speech, to seek to limit the freedom of action of his colleagues. But as the threat was ignored, the House should take no further action.	Tacit acceptance.
March 1985 H.C. 308 of 1984–85	Leak to the press of a draft report of the Home Affairs Committee (*The Times* case).	A contempt, but no purpose would be served by trying to identify the culprit in the light of previous cases. The Committee would consider further the issues raised in relation to select committee confidentiality.	Tacit acceptance.
July 1985 H.C. 555 of 1984–85	See previous case.	Substantive report on Disclosure of Proceedings of Select Committees.	The House (on division) agreed to the committee's report (*March* 18, 1986).

May 1986 H.C. 376 of 1985–86	Leak to the press of a draft report of the Environment Committee (*The Times* case).	Lobby correspondent in contempt; should be suspended from Lobby for six months. Editor also responsible, and number of passes issued to *The Times* should be reduced by one.	The House (on division) disagreed with the Committee's recommendations; it would be proper to punish a Member who leaked, but "it would be wrong to punish a journalist merely for doing his job" (*May* 20, 1986)
May 1987 H.C. 365 of 1986–87	Speaker's order of *January* 22, 1987 on a matter of national security (The Zircon case).	Speaker's order did not breach privilege and was within his powers. No changes required in the privileges, practices or procedures of the House regarding court injunctions or matters of national security.	Tacit acceptance.

In recent years there have been no cases of equal constitutional significance to some of the leading cases of the last century although important reports were made in 1986 and 1987 regarding confidentiality of committee proceedings, and the privileges, practices and procedures of the House in relation to matters of national security (see below). Scargill's case of 1975 and the N.U.P.E. case of 1977 were of some importance in confirming that trade unions have to be careful in seeking to control the actions of their sponsored Members (see also pages 66–68). The case of the Members investigated by the Committee on the Conduct of Members in 1976 was serious and the findings were significant (see page 68). The findings in the MacGregor case in 1981 and the Banks case in 1984, that threats against a Members' constituency or constituents could be treated as a threat against a Member, may prove to be important in future. In general, however, it is difficult to trace a general pattern in these cases.

The most common complaint has been of premature disclosure of proceedings ("leaks") from select committees—six cases since 1971—all concerned with leaking of draft reports. This continuing problem has caused the House some difficulty. In none of these cases was the original source of the leak discovered[94]; journalists always refused to name them. Although the journalists who were actually responsible for any damage to the work of the committee by the act of publication were readily identified, the House has shown itself unwilling to punish the publisher if it could not identify and punish the original leaker.[95]

---

[94] In 1967–68 a Member freely admitted that he had leaked some evidence given in private to a committee (see Report of Committee of Privileges, H.C. 357 of 1967–68); the Member was reprimanded, but no action was taken against the journalists.

[95] See, for example, *The Economist* case of 1975, where the Committee on a Wealth Tax was unable to agree any report after an extensive leak of one of the drafts; the Committee of Privileges recommended that the editor and the journalist be excluded from the premises for six months; the House, on a division, disagreed H.C.Deb., Vol. 902, cols. 1303–1356 (December 16, 1975).

The issue came to a head in 1985 and 1986. After *The Times* case of 1985, when a draft report of the Home Affairs Committee had been leaked, the Committee of Privileges examined the whole problem in some depth.[96] Starting from a resolution of 1837, which categorically prohibited the publication of unreported evidence and documents presented to committees,[97] the committee made a fresh examination of the problems involved, in the light of the growth and evolution of select committee work. It concluded that privilege need not be enforced in every case (paragraph 50); the rules should be retained for dealing with really serious cases where a leak has caused, or was likely to cause substantial interference with the functions of the House or a committee (paragraph 51); a Member responsible for such a leak or journalist publishing the same should be punished; in the latter case suspension from working in the precincts might be appropriate (paragraphs 56 and 70). Recommendations were also made as to how committees should handle confidential papers and how more serious leaks should be investigated.

On March 18, 1986, on a free vote, the House agreed to the committee's report by 104 votes to 22; a number of Ministers voted in support of the committee.[98]

The House's willingness to follow its own conclusions in practice was soon tested. In December 1985 *The Times* published a leaked version of a draft report of the Environment Committee on radioactive waste. Following the procedures agreed by the House, the Environment Committees examined the matter, failed to identify the source of the leak, and made a special report stating that the publication of the leak had caused serious interference with its work.[99] Under a new procedure agreed to by the House on March 18, 1986, this special report was automatically considered by the Committee of Privileges. Having taken evidence from the Chairman of the Environment Committee and from the Editor of *The Times* and the Lobby correspondent concerned, the committee concluded (by a majority of 11 to 1) that the publication had caused a substantial interference with the work of the Environment Committee and that a serious contempt had been committed by the anonymous leaker and by the journalists who published the story. By the same majority it recommended that the Lobby correspondent be suspended from the Lobby for six months and that *The Times* should forfeit one of its Lobby passes for the same period.[1]

The House debated, on May 20, 1986, a motion, moved by the Leader of the House, to agree to the recommendations of the Committee of Privileges. An amendment was carried, by 158 votes to 124 stating "that it would be proper to punish an honourable Member who disclosed the draft report of a select committee before it had been reported to the House; but that it would be wrong to punish a journalist merely for doing his job."[2] A number of Ministers who voted in support of the Committee of Privilege's recommendations on March 18, 1985, voted on this occasion against them.

---

[96] Second Report from the Committee of Privileges 1984–85, Premature Disclosure of Proceedings of Select Committees (H.C. 555).

[97] *Ibid.*, para. 5; see May, pp. 153–154.

[98] H.C.Deb., Vol. 94, cols. 260–265.

[99] H.C. 211 of 1985–86.

[1] First Report from the Committee of Privileges, H.C. 376 of 1985–86.

[2] H.C.Deb., Vol. 98, cols. 293–332.

Thus it would appear that select committees can no longer rely on parliamentary privilege to protect them against the damage done by premature publication of their proceedings. Except possibly under circumstances as yet untested (obtaining information by theft, blackmail or for payment, for example) the House seems unwilling to punish journalists who act in contempt of the rules of the House.[3]

One other recent report of the Committee of Privileges should be mentioned.[4] On January 21, 1987 it became known that certain Members proposed to show a film (about a secret security project code-named Zircon), the publication of which had been banned by an interim court injunction earlier that day. Ministers sought to have the proposed showing stopped by the Speaker or by the House that evening, but this did not prove possible. The next day the Attorney-General sought another injunction against the Members concerned to prevent them showing the film in the House of Commons until the House could decide whether or not to allow it. The judge in chambers refused this request, apparently because he considered that the matter could and should be under the control of the House of Commons authorities.[5] Later that morning, having received advice "on Privy Councillor terms" the Speaker agreed to issue an order banning the showing of the film in any room under the control of the House. This, he later explained, was intended to be a holding operation, pending a decision by the House.[6]

On January 27, 1987 the Leader of the House moved a motion to confirm the order of the Speaker, but after a full debate the House agreed an amendment, without a division, to refer the matter to the Committee of Privileges.[7] This was a major parliamentary occasion, when the will of the House prevailed over that of the executive.

The committee reported on three main matters. First it found that the showing of a film was not a proceeding in Parliament and therefore was not protected by privilege; the Speaker's order of January 22, had therefore not restricted the protection afforded by privilege; the Speaker had acted within the powers vested in him; in the light of the information then available to him, and in order to enable the House to decide for itself, the Speaker had acted wholly correctly.[8]

Second, in regard to court injunctions, the committee concluded that no changes need be made in the privileges, practices or procedures of the House; the courts could consider injunctions relating to matters which were not "proceedings," but would normally use their discretion to refuse injunctions on matters which fell within the powers of the House to regulate; and the issue or refusal of an injunction neither required nor prevented corresponding action by the House.[9]

Third, the committee considered whether any changes were required in the privileges, practices or procedures of the House in relation to matters of national security. It started from the essential point, as concluded by the

---

[3] A fuller account of this matter may be found in Two Recent Privilege Issues at Westminster, by Michael Ryle, *The Table*, (1986) (Vol. LIV).

[4] First Report, H.C. 365 of 1986–87, sets out the full story.

[5] *Ibid.*, para. 3; for the reasoning of the Attorney General in seeking the injunction see Appendix 5.

[6] *Ibid.*, paras. 4–6.

[7] H.C.Deb., Vol. 109, cols. 207–275.

[8] H.C. 365 of 1986–87 paras. 15–27.

[9] *Ibid.*, paras. 29–34.

Select Committee on Official Secrets Act 1938–1939,[10] and agreed to by the House,[11] that, under Article 9 of the Bill of Rights, "disclosure by Members in the course of debate or proceedings in Parliament cannot be made the subject of proceedings under the Official Secrets Acts." The House itself imposes almost no restrictions on reference in debate or other proceedings to matters relating to national security. Members are therefore free to say what they liked on these subjects and this might be damaging from the Government's point of view. There was a potential clash of requirements: preservation of freedom of speech and protection of national security.[12]

In striking the balance the committee carefully considered a spectrum of restrictions on freedom of speech and parliamentary conduct which had been suggested, ranging from removing by legislation (which would have to qualify Article 9 of the Bill of Rights) the immunity of Members from prosecution under the Official Secrets Acts for things said or done in Parliament, to banning damaging disclosures at meetings on the precincts which were not subject to protection of privilege. All these proposals were rejected by the committee, both because of the practical problems of enforcement and because of the undesirability of giving the executive power to "muzzle its critics," which "would strike at the very heart of the ancient privilege of freedom of speech."[13] The committee therefore made no recommendations for changing the privileges, practices or procedures of the House relating to matters of national security.[14]

Given the circumstances, and the political pressures under which the Committee of Privileges was working, its firm conclusion set out above was of the greatest importance.

CONCLUSIONS

Our description of the privileges of Parliament has concentrated on their practical application in recent years in the House of Commons and their relevance for Members in their daily work. Privilege issues may rarely be publicly raised, and the protection of privilege is often taken for granted. It remains, however, essential for the proper working of the House. Although it has proved desirable not to claim or enforce privilege in every case where a contempt may have been committed, the basic privileges, especially freedom of speech, have not been abandoned.

---

[10] H.C. 101 of 1938–39, para. 10.
[11] H.C.Deb., Vol. 353, cols. 1071–1084 (November 21, 1939).
[12] H.C. 365 of 1986–87, paras. 35–44.
[13] *Ibid.* para. 52.
[14] *Ibid.* para. 59.

CHAPTER 4

PARLIAMENTARY PARTIES

PARTY ORGANISATION IN THE HOUSE OF COMMONS

Political parties in the United Kingdom are organised in three different ways.

First, the Conservative, Labour, and Social and Liberal Democratic Parties have organisations which cover Great Britain. The Scottish National Party, Plaid Cymru and the Northern Ireland parties are organised over their limited geographical areas. Other minor parties may similarly limit their activities to less than the whole country. Second, parties are organised within parliamentary constituencies. Third, Members of parties represented in the House of Commons are organised within Parliament. It is with these parliamentary parties that this chapter is concerned.

The nature of party politics and of the relationship between Parliament and Government imposes on both the principal parties in the House of Commons a similar parliamentary organisation which nevertheless contains important differences. Each parliamentary party is organised on four levels: the Leadership, the general body of party Members, an executive body, and party committees.

The Leadership

The Leader of the Conservative Party in Parliament is elected by all those Members of the House of Commons who take the Conservative whip. No Conservative Member has ever been nominated to stand against a Leader who was in office as Prime Minister.

The rules for elections, drawn up in 1965 and amended in 1975, require that, if the position of Leader falls vacant, an election will be held as early as possible. Otherwise there will be an election within 28 days of the opening of each new parliamentary session. But if the new session is the first of a new Parliament, the election is to be held not earlier than three months nor later than six months from the date of the assembly of that Parliament. The actual date of the election is determined by the Leader in consultation with the chairman of the 1922 Committee (who is responsible for the conduct of the election).[1] Candidates are proposed and seconded but the identity of these nominators is not made known. During the five days between the close of nominations and the ballot, it is the responsibility of the constituency associations representing Conservative Members to inform those Members of their views concerning the candidates. The views of other constituency associations are obtained by area chairmen. Those of Conservative peers are also obtained. All these views are presented to the executive committee of the 1922 Committee on the day before the ballot and through them, by a somewhat imprecise process, to those Members who inquire.[2]

For the first ballot, each voter indicates one choice. For outright success a candidate must receive, of those entitled to vote, both an overall majority

---

[1] See P. Goodhart, *The 1922* (1973), esp. Chapter 9.
[2] N. Fisher, *The Tory Leaders* (1977), Chapters 7, 8, Appendix 1,2.

and 15 per cent. more than any other candidate. If no one achieves this, a second ballot is held based on new nominations. An overall majority alone is then sufficient. If no candidate achieves this, the top three candidates at the second ballot go to a third ballot where each voter indicates first and second preferences. The candidate with the lowest number of first preference votes is eliminated and the votes of those giving him as their first preference are distributed among the other two candidates in accordance with their second preference. The candidate thus elected is presented for confirmation as Party Leader to a Party meeting of Conservative members of Commons and Lords, adopted Conservative candidates and members of the executive committee of the National Union of Conservative and Unionist Associations.

In 1975, Mr. Heath on the first ballot received 119 votes, Mrs. Thatcher received 130, Mr. Hugh Fraser received 16 and there were 11 abstentions or absentees. For an overall majority 139 votes were required. Heath and Fraser withdrew and on the second ballot, Mrs. Thatcher was elected, receiving 146 votes over Mr. Whitelaw (79), Mr. Prior (19), Mr. Howe (19) and Mr. Peyton (11).

No office of Deputy Leader formally exists but the Leader may choose to designate a person as such, as was Lord Whitelaw until his resignation in 1988.

Apart from the general requirement to hold an election as early as possible, the Conservative Party has no rules to deal with the death in office or other sudden withdrawal from office of the Leader. If there were a Deputy Leader, presumably he would take over temporarily. If there were no Deputy, presumably the Cabinet or shadow Cabinet would nominate a caretaker until the election of a new Leader.

In the Parliamentary Labour Party (P.L.P.) the Leader and Deputy Leader are elected from amongst the Commons Members of the P.L.P. at the Party conference, in accordance with the standing orders of the Party.[3] Those standing orders provide that voting in the election of Leader and Deputy Leader shall take place in three sections: the Commons Members of the P.L.P., the constituency delegates, and delegates from affiliated organisations (overwhelmingly, trade unions). The votes for each nominee in a section are calculated as a percentage of the total votes cast in that section and then apportioned respectively as P.L.P. Members 30 per cent, constituency delegates 30 per cent, affiliates 40 per cent. The votes so apportioned are totalled and the candidate receiving more than half the votes is elected. If no candidate reaches this total on the first ballot, further ballots are held on an elimination basis. When the party is in opposition, the election of the Leader and Deputy Leader takes place at each annual party conference. When the party is in government and the party Leader is Prime Minister, the election takes place only if requested by a majority of the conference on a card vote.

When Mr. Kinnock was elected Labour Leader in 1983, the result of the voting was:

---

[3] *Constitution of the Labour Party* clause VI and *Standing Order*. See generally *Standing Orders of the Parliamentary Labour Party.*

	Mr. Kinnock	Mr. Hattersley	Mr. Heffer	Mr. Shore	%
Constituencies	27.45	0.58	1.97	0.00	30
Trade Unions	29.04	10.88	0.45	0.03	40
Labour MPs	14.78	7.83	4.29	3.10	30
Total	71.27	19.29	6.30	3.14	100

For the Deputy Leadership, the result of the voting was:

	Mr. Hattersley	Mr. Meacher	Mr. Denzil Davies	Mrs. Dunwoody	%
Constituencies	15.31	14.35	0.24	0.10	30
Trade Unions	35.24	4.73	0.00	0.03	40
Labour MPs	16.72	8.81	3.28	1.19	30
Total	67.27	27.89	3.52	1.32	100

If the Leader of the P.L.P. dies or for whatever reason becomes permanently unavailable, the deputy party Leader becomes party Leader until a new party Leader is elected at party conference. The Cabinet or the Parliamentary Committee, in consultation with the National Executive Committee of the party, appoints one of their number to serve as deputy party Leader until the next party conference.

The membership in the House of Commons of the other parties being so small, their organisation is not comparable with that of the two large parties.[4] The Liberal Party had an electoral college for the election of its Leader, representing constituency associations. In 1976, Mr. Steel received 12,451 votes and Mr. Pardoe 7032. The Social Democratic and the Social and Liberal Democratic parties elect their Leaders by a ballot of all members of the party in the country.

When in office, the Conservative or Labour Leader as Prime Minister, as we have seen, appoints the members of the Cabinet and other Ministers, subject to various restrictions.

When in opposition, the Conservative Leader nominates a consultative committee, usually known as a shadow Cabinet, drawn from amongst the more senior and experienced Members but also reflecting the Leader's preferences. Areas of responsibility are allocated. Some members of the shadow Cabinet will be Peers. Between 1975 and 1979, a total of 29 Members and Peers served in the Shadow Cabinet, 19 of them for the whole period.

The Labour Leader in opposition does not have so free a hand. The formal similarities in organisation between the parties here conceal considerable differences. The Labour shadow Cabinet or Parliamentary Committee consists of the four officers of the P.L.P.—the Leader and Deputy Leader, the Chief Whip in the Commons and the Chairman of the P.L.P.— together with 15 Labour Members of the House of Commons, the Leader and Chief Whip of the Labour Peers and one other Labour Peer. We have noted how the Leader and Deputy Leader come to hold their posts. The Chief Whip, the Chairman and the 15 Members are all elected by the P.L.P.

---

[4] Effectively, in the 1983–87 Parliament, all Members of the Liberal party and of the Social Democrats in the House of Commons participated in the parliamentary responsibilities which in the two principal parties are performed by the Leadership groups.

The three Peers are elected by Labour Peers. In addition, the Leader appoints another 50 or so Members as junior spokesmen. He allocates areas of responsibility amongst these 70 or so persons. The Leader's list of these additional front-bench spokesmen is formally submitted to the P.L.P. for its approval. The total number of front-benchers is meant to be of the order of one-fifth of the P.L.P. Non-elected front-benchers are placed under some limitations on speaking in the Commons on matters outside their responsibilities.

The sessional election of the 15 Members to the Parliamentary Committee is keenly fought, and to a considerable extent is determined by the relative strengths of groups within the P.L.P.

The general bodies

The general body of Conservative Members in the House of Commons is the Conservative Private Members (1922) Committee. When the party is in office it consists of all back-bench Members but excludes Ministers. When the party is in opposition, it consists of all Members except the Leader. Each session the members of the 1922 Committee elect a chairman, two vice-chairmen, a treasurer and two secretaries.

The 1922 Committee meets weekly while the House is sitting. It discusses the business before the House in the coming week and receives the Whip's recommendations (if in opposition) or instructions (if in office). Matters of controversy within the party may be discussed especially when these arouse the fears and misgivings of Members. If these are strongly expressed and appear to have wide support—for example, the effect of the Conservative Government's distribution of the rate support grant between cities and shire counties—they will at least give the Government pause. Direct and open conflict between the 1922 Committee and the Leadership is rare but indirect pressure can be effective. No Leadership can afford to ignore its back-benchers.

When the Leadership, especially if it is the Government, is doing well, the 1922 Committee is quiescent but it can quickly become an active place for debate if things begin to go wrong. Sometimes it appears as the conscience of the party—by which is generally meant a voice insistent that the Leadership shall not forget Conservative principles (as seen by those protesting).

Reports may come from party groups, especially the specialist committees, but not on a regular basis. Visiting speakers are rarely invited but Ministers may be asked to speak, or may themselves seek to speak, when some reassurance is called for. In opposition, shadow Ministers are expected to attend especially if matters affecting their areas of responsibility are under discussion. Attendance fluctuates.

The Chairman of the 1922 Committee holds a key position in the Parliamentary party. He is looked on by more junior back-benchers as their spokesman and adviser on intraparty matters. He has direct access to the Leader and is the obverse of the Chief Whip. Each has a role to play in the relations between back-benchers and the Leadership but from distinct standpoints.

The Parliamentary Labour Party meets twice a week during the session. The main meeting considers reports from the Parliamentary Committee, from any meeting of the Trades Union Congress and Labour Party Liaison Committee, from any joint meeting of the National Executive Committee and the Parliamentary Committee, from any Departmental Committee;

also any motions of which notice has been given. The other weekly meeting considers the next week's business in the House of Commons, the Chief Whip indicating what the whipping will be.

Special meetings of the P.L.P. may be held at any time as decided by the Parliamentary Committee. When a general election is imminent, the Parliamentary Committee meets with the National Executive Committee under Clause V of the Party Constitution to decide which items from the party programme shall be included in the manifesto. Before this, one or more meetings of the P.L.P. are held to discuss the preparation of the manifesto and the items to be included in it. Immediately after the party has attained office at a general election, a meeting of the P.L.P. is held to consider priorities for the Queen's speech. This meeting is then required to be held annually in May each year during that Parliament.

The Chairman of the P.L.P. presides over its meetings. In his absence the Chief Whip (when the party is in opposition) or the Deputy Chairman (when the party is in office) presides.

When the party is in opposition, members of the Parliamentary Committee and other front-bench spokesmen attend meetings of the P.L.P., especially when any matters under discussion affect their areas of responsibility. When the party is in office, Ministers attend less frequently but are expected to attend when some aspect of the work of their departments is under scrutiny.

The relationship between the Leadership and the general body in the two parties seems to be broadly similar. Labour Ministers attend meetings only when under pressure to do so. Conservative Ministers attend only on invitation. But as Norton observes, the right of Labour Ministers to attend meetings of the P.L.P. means that back-benchers have to contend with their presence.[5] Shadow ministers in both parties are in no position to stay away if their presence is requested. Back-benchers will not usually seek to rock the party boat by attacking the Leadership, and the Leadership has nothing to gain by coming into conflict with appreciable back-bench pressure. Each group needs the other, so disputes are not common, but when they do occur, they can be fierce.

The executive bodies

The Executive Committee of the 1922 Committee consists of the six officers already referred to and 12 other elected back-bench Members. It meets immediately before the meeting of the 1922 Committee where it introduces topics for discussion. One of its roles is to act as a link between the back-benchers and the Leadership, and membership of the shadow Cabinet precludes election to the Executive. Although in no sense does it set itself in opposition to the Leadership, it is the representative body of the back-benchers, and is more concerned to present their view to the Leadership than vice versa. Membership of the Executive Committee is much sought after and Goodhart[6] describes its members as "steady men whose faces have become familiar."[7] At the beginning of 1988–89, two officers failed to be

---

[5] P. Norton in S. A. Walkland (ed.), *The House of Commons in the Twentieth Century* (1979), p. 30.

[6] *Op. cit.*, p. 210.

[7] Of the 18 members elected in the Autumn of 1987, six had not been members of the Executive Committee during the previous year. The six included the Treasurer and both secretaries.

re-elected following their votes, contrary to the party whip in the House. In 1987–88, nine of the Executive Committee were also chairmen or vice-chairmen of party specialist committees and five of these nine were also chairmen of select committees of the House. They form a crucial body in the Conservative Parliamentary Party. Their influence can be of the greatest importance at critical times when disputes arise over the policy the party should pursue when in office or in opposition as their views are frequently formative to the attitudes adopted by the 1922 Committee itself. Such views are transmitted not only through the 1922 Committee but also independently of it. They played a vital role in the pressure put on Mr. Heath when he was persuaded to submit himself under new rules for re-selection in 1975 when he was, in the event, replaced by Mrs. Thatcher as Leader.

Reference has already been made to the Parliamentary Committee of the Parliamentary Labour Party in its role as part of the Leadership when the party is in opposition.

When the Labour Party is in office, the Parliamentary Committee consists of the four officers of the P.L.P.[8]; six back-bench Members of the party in the House of Commons elected by those back-bench Members; one elected back-bench Labour Peer; four Ministers (one from the Lords and three from the Commons, one being the Leader of the Commons) appointed by the Prime Minister or elected by a method decided by him. When the party is in office, the Parliamentary Committee is chaired by the Chairman of the P.L.P. The Member with the highest number of votes of the six elected back-benchers becomes the Deputy Chairman of the P.L.P. The Chief Whip in the House of Lords has the right to attend meetings of the Parliamentary Committee.

The functions of the Parliamentary Committee include deciding when P.L.P. meetings are to be called and the subjects to be discussed; ensuring the effective functioning of the regional groups and party committees; easing difficulties arising between individual Members and the Whips; ensuring proper liaison between the P.L.P. and the National Executive Committee of the Party, including appropriate representation of the P.L.P. on the Party's policy-drafting working-parties and study groups; dealing with the business of the House; and in office maintaining an effective two-way channel of communication between the Government and back-benchers in both Houses.

The Parliamentary Committee meets once a week while Parliament is in session and at such other times as may be determined. The Committee is required to make weekly reports to the P.L.P.

Party committees

The Conservative Party in the Commons in 1988 had 24 specialist committees: agriculture, fisheries and food (with four sub-committees); arts and heritage; aviation; constitutional affairs; defence; education; employment; energy; environment (with one sub-committee); European affairs; finance; foreign and Commonwealth affairs; health and social services; home affairs, legal; media; Northern Ireland; smaller businesses; sports; tourism; trade and industry (with two sub-committees); transport; urban and new town affairs. In addition are seven regional groups for East Midlands, Greater

---

[8] The Leader and Deputy Leader, the Chief Whip in the Commons, the Chairman of the P.L.P.

London, North-West, Scottish, Welsh, West Country, and Yorkshire. There is also a committee on party organisation; and another on unpaired members. These 33 chairmen are supported by over 50 vice-chairmen and over 50 secretaries (who are all Members).

The specialist committees meet regularly (often weekly). Every Conservative Member is automatically a member of every committee. Although policy issues are the principal matters on the agenda, votes are not taken. Attendance fluctuates (averaging between five and 25 members) but each committee has a hard core of regulars. When the party is in office, the chairmen are elected by the committees and these appointments are keenly sought after. To some extent they reflect the political tendencies (towards the right or the left within the party) prevalent at the time on the particular subject. In 1987 and 1988, such intraparty conflicts were reported for the chairmanship of the European affairs, trade and industry, social services, defence and agriculture committees. As all Conservative Members belong to all the specialist committees, the elections for each committees attract a high proportion of those Members. As we have seen, some of those elected to the Executive Committee of the 1922 Committee are also elected chairmen of specialist committees. In contrast, when the party is in opposition, these chairmen are appointed by the Leader from amongst, and according to their responsibilities in, the shadow Cabinet. The vice-chairmen are elected. None of the appointed chairmen is eligible for membership of the 1922 Executive.

When the Conservative Party were in opposition, the chairmen and vice-chairmen and other officers of the specialist committees came together in a Business Committee, chaired by the Leader, and including the Opposition Chief Whip. The Committee met weekly to discuss the next week's business, with shadow ministers in attendance if their subject was to figure prominently on the floor of the House. Virtually all members of the Executive of the 1922 Committee would also be members of the Business Committee which was intended to keep Members in touch with what was going on to provide a formal channel for putting forward any complaints.

The Conservative specialist committees provide a forum for discussion of policy issues, both long term and short term. When the party is in office, they may become the focus of disquiet between the back-benchers and Ministers. In such circumstances, Ministers are expected to address the committees, to explain policy in more detail and to justify action or proposed action. Members who become concerned about some aspect of Government policy are normally expected to raise the matter first in the appropriate committee. In these circumstances, the committees act as early warning systems for the Government and as places where Members may obtain re-assurance. In opposition, the committees, chaired by shadow ministers, may have a more direct contribution to make to the emergence of party policy in its different aspects. But, because the party is in opposition, they can have little or no effect on the course of political events except by way of developing lines of criticism of Government. Visiting speakers are frequently invited to address specialist committees.

Some commentators suggest that the development of select committees of the House since 1979 has diminished the importance of party specialist committees by moving the centre of party discussion on specific issues from specialist party committees to those select committees. But their roles are very different and the party committees can be of great significance especially when critical questions arise quickly, and opinion in the parliamentary

party demands expression. In this sense they may supplement and complement the debates in the 1922 Committee.

The Parliamentary Labour Party has established 14 committees to match
and monitor the departments of Government and the work of their respective select committees except those on Scottish and Welsh Affairs. They are
agriculture; defence; education, science and the arts (with one sub-committee); employment; energy; environment (with one sub-committee); foreign
affairs; health and social security; home affairs; Northern Ireland; parliamentary affairs; trade and industry (with three sub-committees); transport;
Treasury and civil service. They meet at various intervals, often fortnightly
when Parliament is sitting. Notice of a meeting is normally given on the
whip. Sub-committees may be set up only with the agreement of the Parliamentary Committee. Members may become registered members of not
more than three committees. Non-registered Members may attend any
meeting but may not vote. Front-benchers when in opposition and select
committee Members are expected to attend regularly at their appropriate
committee meetings. Ministers are expected to attend when asked. Each
committee appoints its own chairman.

Considerable administrative duties are formally imposed on these committees. In collaboration with front-benchers, they are required to ensure,
in relation to their subjects, an adequate attendance and number of speakers
in any debate; full and effective Question Time; the organisation of opportunities in the House for discussion; the co-ordination of the work of
members of standing committees; the recommending of members to be
appointed to select committees; liaison with those members; the briefing of
all colleagues in the P.L.P. How far they fulfil all these duties may be
doubted. When the party is in office, the chairmen of the committees are
entitled to regular consultation with appropriate Ministers.

Despite the considerable administrative responsibilities placed on these
committees, their influence in the P.L.P. is not great. Except from time to
time when particular issues arise, attendance may be small, down to half a
dozen or so. But election to the chairmanship and other official positions in
the committees is important as, when in opposition, those elected become
part of the policymaking machinery of the party on the joint committee of
P.L.P. and the National Executive Committee of the party. When the party
is in office, the committees form pressure groups urging on Ministers particular lines of policy.

These committees in the P.L.P. are generally regarded as having less
significance than specialist committees in the Conservative party. This may
be because of the difference in organisation between the parties when in
opposition. The Parliamentary Committee of the P.L.P., being an elected
body, perhaps carries more weight within the party than the appointed
shadow Cabinet of the Conservatives. And so the committees are relatively
diminished in influence. From time to time, a committee may be the scene
for an important debate on a controversial issue. But generally, these
committees appear to have less impact than the regional committees of the
party.

Every Member of the P.L.P. belongs to one regional group of which in
1988 there were eight: East Midlands, Greater London, Northern, North-
west, Scotland, Wales, West Midlands, Yorkshire. Frequency of meetings is
usually fortnightly. They pick up local issues and are in touch with local
institutions and this in turn exerts pressure and influence on Members.

Issues which centre around the situation in the great cities unify Members from those areas. Attendance is usually high. Whether the party is in office or in opposition, events in London, Birmingham, Manchester, Newcastle or Liverpool may set much of the agenda in the House of Commons. Members from those cities and their environs with intimate knowledge of the circumstances and alerted by local political and other organisations can bring an immediacy to debates in the House which more general discussions on policy often lack. Regional groups provide the forum within which attitudes are first determined.

The 22 chairmen of committees and regional groups are supported by over 50 other officers.

The Whips

The Government Chief Whip is the Parliamentary (or patronage) secretary to the Treasury. In addition there are three officers of the Household (one of whom is Deputy Chief Whip), five Lords Commissioners of the Treasury and five assistant Whips; all these are in the Commons. In the Lords, the Government Chief Whip holds the office of Captain, Gentlemen-at-Arms, and the Deputy Chief Whip is Captain, Queen's Bodyguard of the Yeoman of the Guard; five assistant Whips are Lords-in-Waiting. All Government Whips are paid as Ministers, and are appointed by the Prime Minister, after consultation with the Chief Whip.

The Opposition Chief Whip in the Commons and not more than two assistant Whips are salaried. So is the Opposition Chief Whip in the Lords. There are 8–10 additional assistant Whips. Other opposition parties also appoint Whips. As already noted, the Labour Chief Whip and the Deputy Chief Whip when the party is in opposition are elected by the Commons Members of the P.L.P. In opposition, the Conservative Chief Whip and all other Whips are appointed by the Leader after consultation with the Chief Whip.

Whether a party is in office or in opposition, the Whips operate as links or contacts between the party leadership and the ordinary Members of the parliamentary party in the House of Commons (with comparable functions exercised by Whips in the House of Lords). Each week they inform those Members about the forthcoming business of the House, indicating when their attendance is required on vital business (a three-line whip), when it is expected because there will be a division (a two-line whip), or when it is simply requested (a one-line whip). These instructions will also tell Members when other party meetings are to be held. They are the channel through which pairing may, subject to the approval of the Whips, be arranged whereby the absence of a Member on one side of the House may be balanced by the absence of a Member on the other side.

The Whips also act as communicators between the leadership and the ordinary Members, in both directions, seeking to ensure that conflicts are avoided, that the leadership does not by inadvertence take a course of action which will cause offence or even rebellion amongst its supporters, and that those supporters do not themselves by inadvertence take action which conflicts with the wishes of the leaders. Such conflicts will of course arise from time to time and it is a function of the Whips to seek to bring the two sides together in the hope that at least each knows where the other stands. In this sense, Whips will seek to persuade back-bench Members not to oppose the leadership. For these purposes, Whips are assigned both to regional groups of Members and to functions of Government. Their attendance at meetings of specialist and regional committees of party Members is an important part of their responsibilities.

The Whips of each party put forward to the Committee of Selection the names of Members to serve on certain of the select and all standing committees of the House (see pages 271, 280). In the P.L.P. the Whips, before doing so, must consult the front-bench spokesman or Minister and the chairman of the appropriate party departmental committee or regional group.[9] Whips also nominate members of select committees directly appointed by the House. Members except front-benchers will usually be asked to indicate their areas of interest and these will appear also through their attendance at or membership of the party's subject committees. Sometimes, Whips are obliged to nominate Members against their wishes to serve on certain committees, especially standing committees on bills which have little political interest. If a Member refuses to serve on such a committee, he must not expect his future wishes to be readily met.

The Chief Whip on each side of the House is influential with the party Leader in suggesting the names of back-benchers who might be appointed as assistant Whips. Such appointments are not universally sought but they do enable a Member to put his foot on the lowest rung of the ladder of promotion and to be involved, to some extent, in the inner councils of his party.

The Government Chief Whip is also influential in the process of appointment of junior Ministers generally and may well be consulted on more senior promotions. We have already seen (page 22) that the Prime Minister in making ministerial appointments is concerned to maintain certain ideological as well as geographical balances within the party and within departments. The Chief Whip is far better placed than the Prime Minister to assess the impact amongst back-benchers of the appointment to the office of assistant Whip, or other junior ministerial post, of one back-bencher rather than another. This is only one factor in the appointment. But it may be significant, and pressure will be brought to bear on the Chief Whip by back-benchers, who have otherwise relatively few opportunities to influence appointments. In both parties, the Chief Whip has other powers of patronage. He can recommend which Members may be sent on delegations abroad, who may be appointed to outside bodies, who may represent the parliamentary party on radio or television appearances.

In 1968, the Parliamentary Labour Party adopted a Code of Conduct which became part of the Standing Orders of the P.L.P. This provided that it was the duty of Members to conduct themselves at all times in a manner consistent with membership of the P.L.P. and in particular to act in harmony with the policies of the P.L.P., to attend the House regularly and maintain a good division record and to refrain from personal attacks on colleagues. No organised group was permissible unless approved in writing by the Chief Whip. Before tabling any motion or amendment, Members were required to consult the Chief Whip. The "conscience" clause provided:

"While the Party recognises the right of Members to abstain from voting in the House on matters of deeply held personal conviction, this does not

---

[9] Where nominations are made by order of the House and not to the Committee of Selection, a similar procedure is followed. All nominations are formally submitted to the P.L.P. but motions to add or remove particular names are not in order.

entitle Members to vote contrary to a decision of a Party Meeting, or to abstain from voting on a Vote of Confidence in a Labour Government."

This Code is still in operation. The Chief Whip may take or recommend disciplinary actions in respect of any breach of these various provisions. A reprimand may be given by the Chief Whip in writing and reported to the Parliamentary Committee. On the recommendation of the Chief Whip, that Committee may seek approval of a meeting of the P.L.P. for the suspension of a Member for a specified period. A suspended Member is still expected to comply with the party whip. The period of suspension may be extended, or the Chief Whip, after consultation with the Parliamentary Committee, may reduce it. Withdrawal of the whip (which is expulsion from the P.L.P.) may be decided by a meeting of the P.L.P. at which prior notice of motion has been given by the Parliamentary Committee. If suspension or withdrawal is proposed, the Member concerned has a right to be heard at the P.L.P. meeting. There were several suspensions or withdrawals of the whip in the 1940s and 1950s, but no such disciplinary action has been taken in recent years.

The Conservative Party has no such code, and although it would, at any time, be possible for the party to decide to withdraw the whip from any Member, no procedure to effect this is provided and there are no precedents.

Despite these differences in rules between the parties, the practice is similar. Neither Chief Whip has true disciplinary powers. Both have levers of persuasion. Loyalty to party is strong and Members are reluctant to take action which might damage the party in the eyes of the public. Members with ambitions to rise in the party, in the hope of becoming Ministers in some future administration, or to be appointed to high office within Parliament, will not wish to acquire the reputation of being unreliable. But for those with no such ambitions or with unwavering principles or with a preference for minority views, such considerations will not persuade them to conform to the party line. They may by their actions lose the support of party officials in their constituencies; but it is frequently the case that their dissent is stimulated by particular circumstances in those constituencies, or by the political views of local party activists.

Pressure by the Whips will no doubt often persuade a few doubters not to express their doubts in the division lobbies. Such pressure may be decisive in terms of votes as when the Government in 1985 managed after much difficulty to obtain a majority of 17 votes on the motion to give large increases to top salaries in the public sector (see page 129). The failure of Government Whips to produce a majority for the second reading of the Shops Bill in 1986 is an outstanding example of pressure not always being effective (see page 42). If Governmental proposals are shown to be unpopular in the country amongst those electors likely to be habitual supporters of the party, the Whips may be powerless, as for example over the proposal in 1986 to strengthen the means test for university grants (see page 129) or to apply particular formulae to the distribution in the same year of the rate support grant to the disadvantage of the shire counties (see page 130).

The disciplinary actions of the Whips are directed primarily towards securing the support of their Members in the division lobbies. The one rule on which Whips in both parties insist is that they should be informed in advance by a Member who intends to vote against his party or to abstain.

Political groups within parliamentary parties

It is commonly said that every political party is a coalition of differing views. However defined or described, every party has its right wing and its left wing, its wets and its dries. Sometimes the strain for one sub-group of remaining within the party is too great and individuals join other parties or give up politics or even set up new parties.

In the House of Commons, the sub-groups in the Conservative and Labour parties are organised and important. Whenever elections take place within the parliamentary parties, the battle lines are drawn. In the P.L.P. and the Conservative Party, the most important election is that of Leader; in the P.L.P., to this must be added the post of Deputy Leader. At the next level is the election by the P.L.P. of the Parliamentary Committee and by the Conservative members of the Executive Committee of the 1922 Committee. Below these come the elections of chairmen and officers of the subject committees. All these are seen as important contests in the continuing struggle involved in trying to push the party more in one direction than another on matters such as defence, the social services, the environment, employment, taxation. The appointment of new assistant Whips or junior Ministers when, as we have seen, the Chief Whip has much influence, is also seen as an opportunity to seek to have appointed someone from one sub-group or another. In the P.L.P., the election in opposition of the parliamentary Party chairman, the Chief Whip and the Deputy Chief Whip provide other occasions.

At the beginning of the 1988–89 session there were two principal groups in the P.L.P. The left-wing Campaign group had some 35 to 40 members. The more centrist Tribune group had about 110 members. In the voting for P.L.P. chairman, Chief Whip and the Parliamentary Committee, members of these groups do not vote rigidly for candidates put forward by their groups. The result of the elections does not therefore give more than a general indication of the relative strengths of the groups within the P.L.P.

Members of the Conservative Party in the House of Commons also form groups, but with less formality than the P.L.P. In 1989 the "No Turning Back" group contained a dozen or so Members. All or most of its members also belonged to the right wing "92 Group" which had some 90 members. They were opposed by the centre-left "Lollards" with a membership of some 120. Both groups campaigned strongly for the election of its members as chairmen and officers of back-bench party groups, and of the Executive of the 1922 Committee.

When their party is in power, groups measure their relative success or failure, above all, by the number of their members who are given ministerial office or who are appointed as parliamentary private secretaries to Ministers.

Similarities and differences

The overall structure and functioning of the House of Commons inevitably imposes on the two large parties a similar organisation. The leadership group with Whips as its agents, and the general membership of party working also through specialist and regional committees are the two principal levels of operation, and are common to both parties. So also is the separateness of the leadership group when the party is in office. The relationship between leaders and the general membership when those leaders are Ministers is quite different from the relationship when the party is in opposition. Ministers see themselves as having obligations of government which transcend their obligations to the party machine. This does not mean that they cut themselves off from contact with their back-benchers. If they do so, they will quickly be reminded who it is that sustain them in office. But the lives of Ministers are mostly spent in their departments, they have access to information others cannot enjoy, and they are served by a professional and highly experienced corps of public servants to whose advice and warnings they must pay attention.

Some of the differences between the parties are significant. Policymaking is formally more centralised in the leadership in the Conservative Party in Parliament but this is in part offset by the greater influence of the Conservative specialist committees compared with the Labour counterparts. If we compare, when the parties are in opposition, the Parliamentary Committee of the P.L.P. and the Conservative Leader's consultative committee, the most obvious difference is that the former is elected and the latter appointed. When to this we add the appointment by the Conservative Leader (in opposition), out of that consultative committee and others, of the chairmen of the specialist committees and contrast it with the election of those chairmen in the P.L.P., the line of command from the Conservative Leadership seems to be much stronger. But the Labour Party in the House of Commons, when in office, has no body comparable to the Executive Committee of the 1922 Committee. Conservative Ministers are excluded from the 1922 Committee whose Executive Committee may then become a centre of elected back-bench pressure which the Labour Parliamentary Committee (containing at least seven senior Ministers) cannot be.

To push these comparisons and contrasts too far is dangerous. So much depends on personalities. Leaders, in or out of office, can seek to lead forcefully from in front or more subtly from behind. The chairmen of the P.L.P. and of the 1922 Committee can be strongly influential, or not so, depending both on their character and on their relationship with the Leader. Members of Parliament themselves range from the most active and ambitious to those who regard their membership of the House as sufficient achievement. And there are other Members who find their greatest satisfaction in serving on, perhaps becoming chairmen of, committees of the House of Commons.

These patterns change from party to party and from time to time. The balance of power within the parties also changes, as different ideologies come to prominence. Some party organisation is essential and it is held together less by the Whips than by loyalty, belief and self-interest.

Financial assistance to Opposition parties

On March 12, 1974, the Queen's speech introducing the first session of the newly elected Labour Government included an intention to consider the provision of financial assistance to enable Opposition parties more effectively to fulfil their parliamentary functions.[10] Discussions were entered into between the parties and on March 20, 1975 the House of Commons resolved that provision should be made. As amended the resolution provides that each Opposition party shall be entitled for each calendar year to £2550 for each seat won by the party plus £5.10 for every 200 votes cast at the

---

[10] H.C.Deb., Vol. 870, col. 47 (March 12, 1924).

preceding general election. For entitlement, a party must have at least two Members or, if only one Member, have received at least 150,000 votes at the election. The payments are made monthly and an independently certified statement must be made annually that the amounts claimed have been expended on purposes in accordance with the resolution of the House and incurred exclusively in relation to the party's parliamentary business.[11]

The effect is that from June 1987 the Labour party annually received £839,700, the Social and Liberal Democrats £187,200, the Social Democrats £56,100, the Official Ulster Unionists £30,000, the Scottish National Party £18,300, the Democratic Unionists £9,800, Plaid Cymru £10,800 and the S.D.L.P. £11,600.[12]

The Labour Opposition distributed their allocation in three broadly equal parts between the Leader's Office, the maintenance of the office of the Parliamentary Labour Party, and the elected members of the Parliamentary Committee and some of the non-elected spokesmen.

On January 1, 1989 the salaries of the Leaders of the Opposition in the Commons and in the Lords, the Opposition Chief Whips in both Houses and two assistant Whips in the Commons were:

	£
Leader of the Opposition (Commons)	49,707
Leader of the Opposition (Lords)	30,647
Chief Opposition Whip (Commons)	42,357
Assistant Opposition Whips (Commons)	33,497
Chief Opposition Whip (Lords)	27,377

The salaries for office holders in the Commons include a reduced parliamentary salary of £18,148 per annum. The Opposition Whips Office in the Commons in 1988 had four staff at a cost of £55,000, and a photocopier and postal services costed at £16,500. In the Lords, the Whips Office had postal services and other supplies costed at £13,500. The Leader of the Opposition in the Commons had a car service costed at about £36,000.[13]

From time to time, proposals are made for further financial aid to be made to political parties to assist their extra-parliamentary activities. But they have not been implemented.[14]

INTRA-PARTY DISSENT

Of all the factors that go to make up the general characteristics of the House of Commons, party is the strongest. It is because of party that Members are in the House. Party determines whether they sit on the Government side or on the Opposition side. Party indicates where their support lies in the country. Party will decide whether they are re-selected. The Leader of the Party in the House may exercise the greatest influence on their future political careers and party Whips on their day to day activities.

---

[11] H.C.Deb., Vol. 134, cols. *104–105* (May 24, 1988).

[12] Exceptionally the Social and Liberal Democrats were given an allocation although the party did not exist at the time of the general election in 1987. This reduced the allocation to the Social Democrats.

[13] H.C.Deb., Vol. 127, col. *659* (February 17, 1988).

[14] See Report of the Committee on Financial Aid to Political Parties (Chairman, Lord Houghton) in August 1976 (Cmnd. 6601).

But it is mistaken to suppose that Members, especially new Members, always find so-called party discipline irksome and oppressive. On the contrary the structures of party can be helpful. Loyalty to party is the norm, being based on shared beliefs. A divided party is looked on with suspicion by the electorate. It is natural for Members to accept the opinion of their Leaders and spokesmen on the wide variety of matters on which those Members have no specialist knowledge. Generally Members will accept majority decisions in the party even when they disagree. It is understandable therefore that a Member who rejects the party whip even on a single occasion will attract attention and more criticism than sympathy. To abstain from voting when required by party to vote is to suggest a degree of unreliability. To vote against party is disloyalty. To join with others in abstention or voting with the other side smacks of conspiracy.

Philip Norton has made extensive and detailed studies of the history of intra-party dissent in recent years.[15] The following Table summarises dissenting votes from 1945 to 1979 in divisions on the floor of the House of Commons.[16]

Divisions Witnessing Dissenting Votes

Parliament (Number of sessions in parenthesis)	Number of divisions witnessing dissenting votes			Number of divisions witnessing dissenting votes expressed as a percentage of all divisions
	Total:	Lab:[a]	Con:[b]	
1945–50 (4)	87	79	27	7.0
1950–51 (2)	6	5	2	2.5
1951–55 (4)	25	17	11	3.0
1955–59 (4)	19	10	12	2.0
1959–64 (5)	137	26	120	13.5
1964–66 (2)	2	1	1	0.5
1966–70 (4)	124	109	41	9.5
1970–74 (4)	221	34[b]	204	20.0
1974 (1)	25	8	21	23.0
1974–79 (5)	423	309	240	28.0

[a] As one division may witness dissenting votes by Labour *and* Conservative Members, the Labour and Conservative figures do not necessarily add up to the totals on the left. A dissenting vote is where one or more Members, Conservative or Labour, enters a lobby to vote against their party whip or the apparently clear wishes (sometimes implicit) of their front bench.
[b] Excluding the untypical Labour back-bench "ginger group" votes of February–March 1971.

The dissent within the party of Government shown by these figures

---

[15] See his *Dissension in the House of Commons 1945–74* (1975), *Dissension in the House of Commons 1974–79* (1980), *Conservative Dissidents 1970–74* (1978), also his chapter 2 in P. Norton (ed.), *Parliament in the 1980s* (1985), We have drawn heavily on this material in what follows.
[16] Reproduced from P. Norton, *Dissension in the House of Commons 1974–1979* (1980), p. 428.

increased sharply towards the end of the long Conservative rule from 1951 to 1964. The very small Labour majority in 1964–1966 helped to keep that dissent under control but it re-emerged after the 1966 election and the influx of more than 70 new Labour Members. As the Table shows, the noteworthy dissents were those of Government back-benchers in 1966–1970 and in 1970–1974, and of back-benchers on both sides of the House in 1974–1979. As a phenomenon of party, occasional dissents by small numbers of Members are much less significant than dissents on special issues by groups of Members. Dissents by Government back-benchers are, in their possible effects, much more significant than dissents by Opposition back-benchers.

1966–1970

During this Parliament the most effective revolt against the Government was one where back-benchers on both sides of the House combined and forced the Government to withdraw the Parliament (No. 2) Bill which sought to reform the House of Lords. In November 1968, the Labour Government white paper[17] on that reform was debated and the Opposition spokesman gave it general support. With a three-line whip on the Government side and a free vote on the Opposition side (the front-bench Conservatives "advising" support), an amendment to reject the white paper was defeated by 270 votes to 159.[18] In the minority were 47 Labour Members and 103 Conservatives. Many others abstained, including between 40 and 50 Labour Members.[19] On February 3, 1969, the Parliament (No. 2) Bill, based on the white paper, was given a second reading by 285 votes to 135. There was a two-line whip on the Government side, the Opposition taking the same view as on the white paper. In the minority were 27 Labour and 105 Conservative Members.[20] The committee stage of the bill was taken on the floor of the house, as befitted a measure of constitutional importance. Between February 12, and April 14, 1969, there were 55 divisions. A number of Labour back-benchers voted consistently against the bill but the figures are misleading as the strategy, with many Conservative back-benchers of the same mind, was to keep the House sitting late and to disrupt the Government's legislative programme. Opposing Members on both sides took turns in keeping a presence. As the Prime Minister later wrote: "the ingenious hostile coalition found little difficulty in moving and debating amendments on a scale which brought progress almost to a standstill."[21] On April 17. 1969, the Prime Minister announced that the bill would be withdrawn to make way for industrial relations legislation.[22]

That legislation was to be based on another contentious White Paper *In Place of Strife,*[23] which had been debated on March 3, 1969. The motion for its approval was passed by 224 votes to 62, the Opposition abstaining. In the minority were 55 Labour Members and some 40 more abstained.[24] This

---

[17] Cmnd. 3299.

[18] H.C.Deb., Vol. 773, cols. 1429–1434 (November 20, 1968).

[19] See J. P. Mackintosh in D. Leonard and V. Herman (ed.), *The Backbencher and Parliament* (1972).

[20] H.C.Deb., Vol. 777, cols. 167–172. Subsequently, the Opposition generally allowed a free vote without advice.

[21] H. Wilson, *The Labour Government 1967–70* (1971), p. 767.

[22] H.C.Deb., Vol. 781, cols. 1838–1841.

[23] Cmnd. 3888.

[24] H.C.Deb., Vol. 779, cols. 163–166.

expression of dissent reflected considerable disquiet in the Labour Party, inside and outside Parliament, and contributed to the eventual decision not to proceed with legislation but instead to seek the voluntary co-operation of the trade union movement, announced by the Prime Minister on June 19, 1969.[25]

Both these major conflicts between the Labour Government and some of its back-benchers took place in the last 18 months of the Parliament. But there had been appreciable dissent earlier. Much of the early controversy in 1966 and 1967 within the Parliamentary Labour Party, and more widely, centred on prices and incomes policy but the Government's back-benchers largely restricted themselves to abstentions, with the result, for example, that on August 3, 1966 an opposition motion to debate the committee stage of the Prices and Incomes Bill on the floor of the House was defeated by only 52 votes.[26] In October 1966, the motion to approve the activation of Part IV of the Act was agreed by 307 votes to 239, with some 30 Labour back-benchers abstaining.[27] The next Prices and Incomes Bill was given a second reading on June 13, 1967 with some 40 Labour abstentions, a situation repeated on the second reading of the third such Bill on May 21, 1968.[28] On June 25, 1968, 23 Labour back-benchers voted against the continuation of prices and incomes measures and some 20 abstained.[29]

In April 1967, a motion calling for the cessation of bombing of North Vietnam ended in an unsuccessful closure motion in which 59 Labour back-benchers voted against Government policy.[30] In February 1968, 22 Labour back-benchers defied the whips on a proposal to increase national insurance contributions[31] followed by 37 (with up to 50 abstentions) on the same day on school milk.[32] The next day, the Home Secretary successfully moved the second reading of the Commonwealth Immigrants Bill (to control the entry of Kenyan Asians) by 372 votes to 62. In the minority were 35 Labour Members with perhaps 40 abstentions.[33] The remaining stages of the bill were pushed through at one sitting and dissenting votes by Labour Members of 46, 41, 34, 26, 8, and 16 were recorded.[34]

Increase in national health service charges brought about 49 dissenting votes from the Labour back-benchers on one occasion and 55 (plus a large number of abstentions) on another.[35]

A vote in May 1967 on the principle of joining the European Communities was opposed by 36 Labour back-benchers with 50 abstentions.[36] Three divisions on the Nigerian situation in 1969 produced adverse Labour votes of

---

[25] H.C.Deb., Vol. 785, cols. 700–714.

[26] H.C.Deb., Vol. 733, cols. 605–610. The Government majority at this time was 96.

[27] H.C.Deb., Vol. 734, cols. 842–970 (October 25, 1966).

[28] H.C.Deb., Vol. 765, cols. 419–424.

[29] H.C.Dcb., Vol. 767, col. 397–402.

[30] H.C.Deb., Vol. 745, cols. 1049–1050 (April 21, 1967).

[31] H.C.Deb., Vol. 759, cols. 1041–1044 (February 26, 1968).

[32] H.C.Deb., Vol. 759, cols. 1103–1106 (February 26, 1968).

[33] H.C.Deb., Vol. 759, cols. 1363–1368 (February 27, 1968).

[34] H.C.Deb., Vol. 759, cols. 1595–1600, cols. 1601–1604, cols. 1627–1630, cols. 1669–1672, cols. 1687–1690, cols. 1711–1714 (February 28, 1968).

[35] H.C.Deb., Vol. 765, cols. 2305–2308 (May 30, 1968); H.C.Deb., Vol. 787, cols. 1399–1402 (July 21, 1969).

[36] H.C.Deb., Vol. 746, cols. 1645–1656 (May 8–10, 1967); 26 Conservatives also voted against.

35, 20 (with up to 70 abstentions), and 24.[37] The Government was also opposed by 51 of its back-benchers on the "Fearless" proposals for settlement of the Rhodesia revolt in October 1968.[38] The next day, considerable back-bench dissent was inspired by a proposal in the Justices of the Peace Bill to agree with a Lords Amendment retaining the Lord Mayor and Aldermen of the City of London as *ex officio* justices of the peace. Into the Government lobby went 116 Conservatives, 80 Labour Members and one Independent Conservative. Opposing were 75 Labour Members, eight Liberals and one Plaid Cymru Member.[39]

Finally, almost the last division of this Parliament was on an emergency motion by a Government back-bencher to protest against American military activities in Indo-China. The motion was negatived, the Opposition voting with the Government, and 61 Labour Members were in the minority, many more abstaining.[40]

1970–1974

The figures in the Table on page 119 support Dr. Norton's thesis that there was a significant increase in the incidence of intra-party dissent within the parliamentary Conservative party in the Parliament of 1970–74, although it is also to be noted that Conservative Members voted against their party to an appreciable extent during the Macmillan and Home administrations of 1959–64. Dr. Norton attributes the increase in Conservative dissent during 1970–74 to the leadership of the Prime Minister, Mr. Heath: to the measures he introduced, the manner in which they were introduced and in which they were pushed through the House of Commons; to Mr. Heath's failure to communicate with his back-benchers, either at the personal level of friendship or at the intellectual level of explaining and justifying his actions; and to his failure to use judiciously his powers of appointment and patronage. In 1971–72, when dissent increased on the Conservative back-benchers, by far the most important single cause was the introduction of the European Communities Bill, during the debates on which Conservatives dissented in 85 divisions. In 1972–73, Northern Ireland was the subject of most Conservative dissents, followed by the Government's economic policy. These two matters also aroused dissent in the short session of 1973–74.

The Conservative Party during the 1970–74 Parliament had an overall majority of 30 so the dissent of one or two of its Members was of no great significance. But 64 of the 204 divisions recorded in the Table involved 10 or more dissenters. We have seen that on six occasions the Government was defeated during that Parliament (see page 41) and it carried the Second Reading of the European Communities Bill on a vote of confidence with a majority of only eight, 15 of its back-benchers voting against and a further five abstaining.[41]

Too much emphasis can easily be placed on dissents where the number of M.P.s is small. In 1971–72, 38 Conservatives cast only one dissenting vote

---

[37] H.C.Deb., Vol. 779, cols. 1693–1696 (March 13, 1969); H.C.Deb., Vol. 786, cols. 1709–1712 (July 10, 1969); H.C.Deb., Vol. 793, cols. 367–372 (December 9, 1969).
[38] H.C.Deb., Vol. 770, cols. 1227–1230 (October 22, 1968).
[39] H.C.Deb., Vol. 770, cols. 1329–1332 (October 23, 1968).
[40] H.C.Deb., Vol. 801, cols. 267–270 (May 5, 1970).
[41] H.C.Deb., Vol. 831, cols. 729–758 (February 17, 1972).

and 36 cast between two and nine dissenting votes. In 1972–73, 47 Conservatives cast only one dissenting vote and 52 cast between two and nine dissenting votes.

Nevertheless these figures show a considerable increase on those between 1945 and 1970. Looking back from 1988 they do not seem surprising and so the question arises how far Mr Heath's style of management—inevitably criticised by some at the time as "presidential"—was primarily the cause; or whether there has been more of a general willingness since the late 1960s on the part of back-benchers, especially those belonging to the party in power, to assert themselves. This might have less to do with the style of individual Prime Ministers and more to do with a changing perception of the role of back-benchers.

Of the 34 occasions during the Parliament of 1970–74 when Labour Members in opposition voted against the whip (or against front-bench advice), more than 30 Members combined to do so on nine occasions. At the end of the six-day debate to approve the Conservative Government's decision of principle to join the European Communities, 69 Labour Members voted to support the Government in defiance of a three-line whip[42] and some 20 abstained. Divisions on Northern Ireland produced 68[43] and 32[44] Labour dissenters when the official Labour Opposition abstained. Increase of pay for judges, on which the Opposition abstained, saw dissents of 39 and 40.[45] Against other official abstentions, dissenters numbered 43 on defence policy,[46] 31 on the second reading of the Civil Aviation Bill[47] and 30 on the continuation of emergency powers regulations.[48] The other occasion was a large dissent of 54 Labour Members on the election of Mr. Selwyn Lloyd as Speaker in January 1971,[49] though some part of this vote (which was additionally supported by three Conservative Members) was a protest against the procedure for the selection of Speaker from which back-benchers were largely excluded (see page 143).

To attribute the resurgence of dissent among Conservative back-bencher M.P.s primarily to Mr. Heath's handling of the parliamentary party may therefore be too simple. There were, and are, ideological differences amongst Members of all parties. An alternative theory is that the elections of 1964, 1966 and 1970 introduced a new breed of younger, better educated Conservative Members with a more professional attitude to their careers as parliamentarians. This could be said also of Labour back-benchers of the period. One analysis suggests that neither of these theories is clearly supported by voting behaviour and that if Members of both the major parties have recently shown greater disloyalty to their leaders than was usual hitherto, the reasons are several and complex.[50]

---

[42] H.C.Deb., Vol. 823, cols. 2211–2218 (October 28, 1971).

[43] H.C.Deb., Vol. 823, cols. 327–330 (September 23, 1971).

[44] H.C.Deb., Vol. 848, cols. 101–104 (December 11, 1972).

[45] H.C.Deb., Vol. 808, cols. 1515–1518 (December 16, 1970).

[46] H.C.Deb., Vol. 831, cols. 1653–1656 (February 24, 1972).

[47] H.C.Deb., Vol. 814, cols. 1279–1282 (March 29, 1971).

[48] H.C.Deb., Vol. 804, cols. 193–196 (July 20, 1970).

[49] H.C.Deb., Vol. 809, cols. 21–26 (January 12, 1971). It seems also that there was a large number of abstentions, the total of those voting being 353 (including tellers).

[50] M. Franklin, A. Baxter, M. Jordan "Who Were the Rebels? Dissent in the House of Commons 1970–74" in *XI Legislative studies Quarterly* (1986) 143.

1974

During the short Parliament of March to October 1974 (when the Government did not have an overall majority), the tactics of the official Conservative Opposition for the first three months were to avoid defeating the Labour Government and precipitating a general election. In the 21 divisions when back-bench Conservatives acted against this policy and voted, the Opposition abstained in 18 and supported the Government on three occasions. In the eight divisions when Government back-benchers dissented, the Opposition supported the Government on six occasions and abstained once. The eighth occasion was a Conservative amendment to the Finance Bill to restrict the rate of pool betting duty. This was carried by 291 votes to 274, a Government defeat. But only one Labour back-bencher voted with the Opposition.[51]

1974–1979

The Parliament which lasted from October 1974 until March 1979 was remarkable. The conventional wisdom was that no Government could operate effectively for more than a few months unless it had an overall working majority of at least 20 to 25 seats. It was true that a Labour Government had lasted from October 1964 to March 1966 with an overall majority of only four but this was regarded as most unusual. Yet Labour held office for four and a half years after winning an overall majority of only three in October 1974 and being in an overall minority from April 1976.

The Table on page 119 shows that Labour back-benchers dissented in 309 divisions, a much higher percentage than in any previous Parliament since 1945, and a total that exceeded the total of all other divisions involving Labour dissents since that year.

As for previous Parliaments, the weight of dissent is more significant than the total number of dissenters. Norton has analysed this as follows[52]:

Number of Labour dissenting voters	Number of divisions 1974–1979
1 only	53
2–9	87
10–19	49
20–29	31
30–39	20
40–49	25
50 or more	44
	309

Of the 69 divisions in which 40 or more Labour MPs voted against the whip, members of the leftwing Tribune Group[53] constituted a clear majority in all but five of those divisions. The proportion of Tribuneites in the 69 divisions ranged from 39 per cent to 87 per cent.

The two issues which caused the most serious dissents were United Kingdom membership of the European Communities (E.C.) and devolution to assemblies in Scotland and Wales. Neither of these followed a simple

---

[51] H.C.Deb., Vol. 877, cols. 355–360 (July 16, 1974).
[52] *Dissension in the House of Commons 1974–79* (1980), p. 439.
[53] Some 86 Labour M.P.s were members of the Group for all or part of the Parliament.

left-right division, some of the most important dissents being inspired by the rightwing of the Parliamentary Labour Party. Abstentions by two right-wingers (Mr. John Mackintosh and Mr. Brian Walden) on November 10, 1976 deprived the Government of a majority in divisions on the Dock Work Regulation Bill[54]; votes against the Government by Mr. Richard Crawshaw and Mr. George Strauss on August 4, 1975 on a clause of the Housing Finance (Special Provisions) Bill, with others abstaining, also resulted in a Government defeat.[55] Mr. Douglas Jay and Mr. Nigel Spearing were prominent opponents of Government policy on E.C. membership as were Mr. Tam Dalyell and Mr. George Cunningham on devolution.

The Scotland and Wales Bill proposing assemblies with devolved powers for those countries was given a second reading on December 16, 1976 by 292 votes to 247, 10 Labour Members voting against the whip and 31 abstaining.[56] On February 22, 1977, the Leader of the House (Mr. Michael Foot) moved a guillotine motion which was defeated by 312 votes to 283, 22 Labour Members voting with the majority and 21 abstaining.[57] The Government abandoned the Bill, which was replaced by two bills, one for Scotland and one for Wales.

The Scotland Bill received its second reading on November 14, 1977, 11 Labour Members voting against it and four abstaining.[58] The next day, six Labour Members voted against the second reading of the Wales Bill and at least two abstained.[59] On January 25, 1978, Mr. George Cunningham moved an amendment to the Scotland Bill to provide that if it appeared to the Secretary of State that less than 40 per cent of the persons entitled to vote in the referendum (which was to be put to Scottish voters before the Act could come into effect) had voted in favour of the Act, he should lay before Parliament the draft of an Order in Council for the repeal of the Act. This amendment was carried against the Government by 168 votes to 142, the majority including 37 Labour Members.[60] A similar amendment was made to the Wales Bill. The bills, so amended, were passed and on March 1, 1979 the referendums were held. In the event, 52 per cent voted in favour in the Scottish referendum but they constituted only 33 per cent of the electorate and so the Act was repealed. So was the Wales Act which was supported by only 20 per cent of voters (12 per cent of the electorate).

The effect of the Labour dissents and abstentions particularly on the guillotine motion on the Scotland and Wales Bill and then on the Cunningham amendment to the Scotland Bill was to defeat the Government's devolution policy. The collapse of the proposals meant that the Scottish and Welsh nationalists had no particular reason to vote for the continuance of the Labour Government. And, the Lib-Lab pact having ended, the early defeat of the Government became inevitable.

The Table on page 119 shows that Conservative M.P.s were also often willing to vote against their Whips during the Parliament of 1974–1979. Compared with Labour, proportionately fewer Conservative Members dissented frequently. This is perhaps explained in part by the greater organ-

---

[54] H.C.Deb., Vol. 919, cols. 581–614.
[55] H.C.Deb., Vol. 897, cols. 199–204.
[56] H.C.Deb., Vol. 922, cols. 1871–76.
[57] H.C.Deb., Vol. 926, cols. 1361–1366.
[58] H.C.Deb., Vol. 939, cols. 207–214.
[59] H.C.Deb., Vol. 939, cols. 507–512.
[60] H.C.Deb., Vol. 942, cols. 1545–1548.

isation (by the Tribune Group) of dissidents on the Labour side of the House. Devolution, the E.C. and the economy were principal issues dividing the Conservatives.

The number of occasions when the Conservative back-benchers defied the Whips in any appreciable numbers (compared with the numbers of Labour Members who did so from time to time) is very small. Early in the session, on January 30, 1975, on the second reading of the Prices Bill, the official party policy being to abstain, 41 Conservative Members nevertheless voted against.[61] The Opposition decided to vote against the second reading of the Scotland and Wales Bill on December 16, 1976 and this resulted in the resignations of Mr. Buchanan-Smith and Mr. Rifkind from the shadow Cabinet. They were joined by only three colleagues in voting for the second reading but 29 other Conservative back-benchers abstained.[62]

The most substantial revolt on the Conservative side came on November 8, 1978 when 116 Conservative Members voted against the Government motion to continue sanctions against Rhodesia despite the party's decision to abstain.[63]

These three occasions scarcely add up to evidence of significant intra-party dissent amongst Conservative Members.

To compare dissent within the Parliamentary Labour Party with that amongst the Conservative Members during the Parliament of 1974–1979 is not to compare like with like. Dissent amongst Government back-benchers when the Government has a very small majority, or none at all, makes the business of governing very difficult. It was remarkable that the Labour administrations were able to last for so long. It seems even more remarkable that they were able to do so despite the level of dissent within the parliamentary party. This points to a danger in looking at the operations of party through the spectacles of dissent. More important are the unifying elements. Although there were those who were willing to cause the Government embarrassment, they supported the Government when support was needed. The Parliament of 1974–1979 can be held up as an example of unprecedented dissent by back-benchers, but the Government held office, by one device or another, for five full years (if we include the Parliament of March to October 1974) during which period its overall majority never exceeded three. Moreover the Government showed, if further showing were needed, that a large number of defeats could be borne. The Government of the 1974–1979 Parliament was defeated on the floor of the House on 42 occasions, 23 of which were caused by Labour Members voting in the Opposition lobby.[64]

1979–1983

The overall Conservative majority of 43 seats at the general election of 1979 was large enough to withstand minor dissents without much inconvenience. Nor was it greatly tested in the lobbies though the Government suffered one defeat.

Norton lists 18 main occasions when Conservative Members either voted against their Government or abstained.[65] On 11 of these occasions, the

[61] H.C.Deb., Vol. 885, cols. 755–758.
[62] H.C.Deb., Vol. 922, cols. 1871–1876.
[63] H.C.Deb., Vol. 957, cols. 1141–1146.
[64] See P. Norton in P. Norton (ed.), *Parliament in the 1980s* (1985), pp. 26–27.
[65] *Ibid.* Chapter 2.

number of dissenters was 20 or fewer, on three between 21 and 30, and on four occasions over 40. Of those four occasions, two concerned immigration,[66] one concerned the closed shop[67] and the other was a number of divisions on the 5 per cent. abatement in the real value of unemployment benefit. The Government defeat was on the second of the debates on immigration rules.[68] Norton points to the occasions when the threat of large scale back-bench dissension forced the Government to change its course as described below. Other proposals withdrawn under threat of defeat included charges for eye tests, reductions in the BBC's external services, a three-stage pay rise for Members, and "hotel" charges for patients in N.H.S. hospitals.

The first serious rebellion was over the Iran (Temporary Provisions) Bill. This was the result of the holding as hostages in the United States Embassy at Tehran a number of nationals of the United States Diplomatic corps and, legal efforts to have them freed having failed, the EC governments agreed on April 22, 1980 to extend their support to include economic measures. The bill to impose sanctions on trade with Iran was read a second time on May 12, 1980, and received the Royal Assent two days later.[69] On May 19, the Government announced that orders made under the Act would affect contracts entered into after November 4, 1979. This retrospective element was strongly opposed by Conservative back-benchers and others.[70] Leave was immediately given to raise the matter under Standing Order No. 20,[71] and the Government quickly changed their mind and announced that there would be no retroactivity.[72]

On April 22–23, 1980, more than 40 Conservative back-benchers voted against the Government on the Employment Bill supporting amendments which would have had the effect of requiring ballots to be taken before strike action[73] and otherwise lessening trade union immunities.[74] A proposal in the Education (No. 2) Bill debated on February 13, 1980 to allow local authorities to charge for transport to schools was opposed and 13 Conservative back-benchers voted with the Opposition, the amendment being defeated by 302 votes to 279.[75]

On November 6, 1981 a Local Government Finance Bill was presented by the Secretary of State for the Environment (Mr. Heseltine) and read a first time. It proposed further restrictions on the freedom of local authorities to determine the level of the rates they levied. In the Conservative back-bench committees on finance and on the environment and in the 1922 Committee, strong opposition was expressed to certain provisions of the Bill. A Labour motion on November 12, upholding the autonomy of local government and opposing the principle of the bill produced some 20 abstentions[76] by Conservative back-benchers. The bill was withdrawn.

---

[66] H.C.Deb., Vol. 31, cols. 755–759 (November 11, 1982) and H.C.Deb., Vol. 34, cols. 435–439 (December 15, 1982).

[67] H.C.Deb., Vol. 983, cols. 639 644 (April 23, 1980).

[68] See note 66 above.

[69] H.C.Deb., Vol. 984, cols. 913–1012, 1833.

[70] H.C.Deb., Vol. 985, cols. 30–44.

[71] H.C.Deb., Vol. 985, cols. 44–48 (Mr. T. Dalyell).

[72] H.C.Deb., Vol. 985, cols. 254–263 (May 20, 1980).

[73] H.C.Deb., Vol. 983, cols. 227–320.

[74] H.C.Deb., Vol. 983, cols. 581–644.

[75] H.C.Deb., Vol. 928, cols. 1595–1660. Subsequently the Government was defeated in the House of Lords and did not seek in the Commons to re-instate the relevant clause.

[76] H.C.Deb. Vol. 12, cols. 672–754. The motion was defeated by 299 votes to 249.

Though much more detailed analysis would be required before it could be clearly shown that pressure, other than that shown by dissenting votes or abstentions, from the back-benchers on the Government side, was stronger in the Parliament of 1979–1983 than in earlier Parliaments, the divisions within the Conservative Parliamentary Party, between "wets" and "dries," between those who supported the Government's reductions in public spending and those who wished the Government to be less restrictive, were apparent. Because Conservative Governments since 1979 have been less willing than most Governments to compromise, to seek a middle way, the divisions within the party in the House have been more obvious and the attempts by some back-benchers to persuade Ministers to change their minds have been more publicised than is usual.

Mrs. Thatcher's first administration could not be said to have had a hard time from its supporters in Parliament. But they continued the tradition begun by Conservative back-benchers under Macmillan's premiership, carried on by the Labour left under Wilson between 1966 and 1970, by Conservative back-benchers under Mr. Heath's premiership, and by the Labour left again between 1974 and 1979, of a willingness to embarrass their Government front-benches.[77]

The strongest statement of dissent is for a Member, elected as a member of one party, to transfer allegiance to another party. In recent times, until 1981, such changes were rare. In July 1974, Mr. Christopher Mayhew left the Labour party for the Liberals and in October 1977 Mr. Prentice transferred from Labour to Conservative. Less significant are the occasions when Members have refused to continue to take their party whip (or have had the whip withdrawn or suspended) and have continued to sit as independent Members. In July 1976 two Labour Members broke away to form the Scottish Labour party until defeated in 1979.

The outstanding defections occurred between February and December 1981 when 25 Labour Members and one Conservative Member joined the Social Democratic Party. Two other Labour Members defected in March and June 1982. One of those who had defected sat later as independent Labour. Only four of the defectors retained their seats in the 1983 election and one of those lost his seat in 1987. One defector (Mr. Douglas-Mann) resigned, stood at the ensuing by-election, and lost his seat.[78]

1983–1987

After the general election of 1983, the Conservative Party was returned with an overall majority of 144 seats in the Commons. It was difficult to imagine that the Government would ever be defeated on a major measure. Norton[79] has recorded that during the first session there were 62 divisions in which 137 Conservative back-benchers cast a total of 416 votes against the Government. Of these, the highest number of dissenting votes was on April 2, 1984 when 43 voted for an amendment to the Trade Union Bill to require contracting in for paying the political levy[80]; on various other amendments to the same bill there were 37 dissenting votes.[81] On the second reading of the

---

[77] See the discussion in D. Judge (ed.), *The Politics of Parliamentary Reform* (1983).
[78] For these and other details see D. & G. Butler, *British Political Facts 1900–1985* (1985), 223–228.
[79] See P. Norton in P. Norton (ed.), *Parliament in the 1980s* (1985), Chapter 2.
[80] H.C.Deb., Vol. 57, cols. 721–744.
[81] H.C.Deb., Vol. 64, cols. 853–960 (July 24, 1984).

Rates Bill, 13 Conservatives voted against the Government (including Mr. Heath and five former Ministers) and at least 25 abstained. The Bill was primarily designed to curb what the Government regarded as overspending by some local authorities. Mr. Heath considered that it was a centralising measure and so conflicted with a major Conservative principle.[82] Between nine and 20 Conservative Members opposed the bill on different occasions.[83]

Various amendments to the Local Government (Interim Provisions) Bill, which was to pave the way for the abolition of the Greater London Council and other metropolitan councils, attracted 22 Conservative dissenters.[84] When the abolition bill had its second reading, a dozen or so Conservative abstained[85] and in committee a Conservative back-bench amendment for a directly-elected replacement for the G.L.C. was rejected by only 23 votes.[86] On November 22, 1984, eight Conservatives voted against the possibility of a cut in overseas aid and some 40 abstained.[87] In November and December, Conservative back-benchers rebelled against a proposal to increase parental contributions for the maintenance of students from wealthier families.[88] By December 2, 180 Conservative Members had signed critical early day motions and much back-bench activity had taken place. On December 5, the Government substantially reduced the increase.[89]

On July 18, 1985, the recommendations of the Top Salaries Review Board were laid before Parliament.[90] They aroused considerable opposition which was voiced in the debate on July 23. The Government carried the day by the narrow margin of 249 votes to 232, some 48 Conservative back-benchers voting with the Opposition. Had the Opposition polled its full strength, the Government would have been soundly defeated.[91]

On March 7, 1986, the Government consented to the sale of Vickers Shipbuilding and Engineering Ltd. to the V.S.E.L. Employee Consortium as a result of strong pressure from Conservative back-benchers.[92] More serious was the battle over General Motors' desire to purchase British Leyland interests. This was opposed by many Conservative Members, including apparently some Cabinet Ministers, but initially was strongly supported by other Ministers, including, it was understood, the Prime Minister. The back-bench pressure was successful and General Motors withdrew.[93] April 1986 was a cruel month for the Government. Some 41 Conservative back-benchers defied the Government on the Airports Bill fearing that one of its consequences would be to promote Stansted airport at Manchester's expense.[94] On April 14, came the massive defeat on the second reading of the Shops Bill when the interests of the Church, the trade unions and amenity groups combined and persuaded 68 Conservative back-benchers to vote against the bill, as did 14 Ulster Unionists.[95] On April 17, 12

---

[82] H.C.Deb., Vol. 52, cols. 165–260 (January 17, 1984).
[83] H.C.Deb., Vol. 57, cols. 148–260, cols. 309–384 (March 27, 28, 1984).
[84] H.C.Deb., Vol. 59, cols. 891–1057, cols. 1090–1170 (May 9, 10, 1984).
[85] H.C.Deb., Vol. 69, cols. 27–131, cols. 173–274 (December 4, 1984).
[86] H.C.Deb., Vol. 69, cols. 1181–1184 (December 12, 1984).
[87] H.C.Deb., Vol. 68, cols. 417–500 (November 22, 1984).
[88] H.C.Deb., Vol. 67, cols. 239–240 (November 14, 1984).
[89] H.C.Deb., Vol. 69, cols. 360–381 (December 5, 1984).
[90] H.C.Deb., Vol. 83, cols. 220–226 (July 18, 1984).
[91] H.C.Deb., Vol. 83, cols. 990–1012 (July 23, 1985).
[92] H.C.Deb., Vol. 93, cols. 594–598 (March 7, 1986).
[93] H.C.Deb., Vol. 94, cols. 787–798 (March 25, 1986).
[94] H.C.Deb., Vol. 95. cols. 168–400 (April 9, 1986).
[95] H.C.Deb., Vol. 95, cols. 584–702 (April 14, 1986) (see pp. 42, 115, 314, 327–328).

Conservatives rebelled on a vote on milk quotas during the report stage of the Agriculture Bill.[96] On April 23, 11 Conservatives opposed the second reading of the European Communities (Amendment) Bill which was to give legal force to the Single European Act agreed to by EC Ministers in Luxembourg in December 1985. These and other dissents directly involved 114 Conservative back-benchers, not counting abstentions absences.

We have already noted (page 77) the ambush set by Conservative and other back-benchers in July 1986 which resulted in a large increase in Members' allowances for secretaries and researchers. Over 30 Conservatives led the way and ended the debate 50 minutes earlier than expected, the amendment being carried by 172 votes to 128.[97] Towards the end of 1986, the Secretary of State for the Environment (Mr. Ridley) came in for harsh criticism at meetings of the 1922 Committee and the Conservative back-bench environment committee on his proposals for the allocation of the rate support grant on the ground that it was unfair to the shire counties. As a result the Minister modified his allocation.[98] Disquiet was also caused among some Conservative back-benchers in December 1986 over the Government's proposal to reduce mortgage protection for the unemployed,[99] and over the bid by B.T.R. for Pilkington Bros.,[1] while 15 Conservative back-benchers opposed in the lobbies plans to impose new charges for health and hygiene inspections at dairies.[2]

Conclusion

The growth of dissent during the last 30 years (which was sustained during the beginning of the new Parliament in 1987) is, as we have noted, not attributable to any single cause. But some emphasis must be placed on the decline in numbers of old-style rural Conservative and trade union Labour Members who were largely content to give loyal backing to their party. In both parties it may be that more of those recently elected look upon their Membership of Parliament as being their principal career, and the House of Commons now provides the procedure and structures within which such back-bench activity can be more vigorously pursued. So also, demands from constituents have increased. In these senses Members have gained in status (though not necessarily in popularity) and this may have led them to be more willing to criticise their leaders.

---

[96] H.C.Deb., Vol. 95, cols. 1036–1106 (April 17, 1986).
[97] H.C.Deb., Vol. 101, cols. 1130–1143 (July 16, 1986).
[98] H.C.Deb., Vol. 106, cols. 685, 931–934 (December 3, 1986); H.C.Deb., Vol. 108, cols. 147–160 (January 13, 1987).
[99] H.C.Deb., Vol. 107, cols. 1123–1154 (December 16, 1986).
[1] H.C.Deb., Vol. 107, cols. 871–892 (December 15, 1986).
[2] H.C.Deb., Vol. 111, cols. 680–703 (March 2, 1987).

PART II

THE FRAMEWORK OF PARLIAMENT

CHAPTER 5

ORGANISATION AND INSTITUTIONS OF THE COMMONS

Sir Winston Churchill once said "first we shape our buildings and afterwards our buildings shape us."[1] Many writers have described, with either relish or resentment, the overwhelming psychological experience of coming to and working in that strange latter-day Gothic masterpiece which is the Palace of Westminster, the home of the two Houses of Parliament.[2] Their experience has shown how dominant are the influences of tradition and well-tried practices and how elusive seems the possibility of reform or the introduction of new ideas.[3] The very design of the building conditions the way people work, in both Houses, and their attitudes, style and ultimate achievement. Around and within the building have grown organisations and patterns of work that together form a framework within which the Member of Parliament is required to operate. In this chapter we describe that framework.

THE PALACE OF WESTMINSTER

The two Houses of Parliament are tenants in a Royal palace which dates back to 1099 (when Westminster Hall was completed) and which was originally the residence of the Kings of England. To this palace the Kings summoned their Parliaments—first the Lords spiritual and temporal, and later the representatives of the "communes" who formed the House of Commons. Indeed it was not until the King vacated the Palace in 1547 that the Commons came to meet there as well, and so the building became the Houses of Parliament.

The Palace remains, however, in the ownership of the Crown and is managed for the Crown by the Government (currently by the Property Services Agency (P.S.A.) on behalf of the Department of the Environment). This means that, although both Houses now exercise full control over the use made of their respective areas of the Palace, they have strictly limited powers in respect of the fabric. This is looked after by the P.S.A., who also provide heating, lighting, ventilation, furniture and maintenance and decorating services. If the Lords or the Commons want some alteration to their accommodation (extra rooms for Members, for example, or alterations to one of the cafeterias) they need to make a case to the P.S.A., on whose budget the cost is borne. A considerable sum (over £24 million for example in 1989–90)[4] is set aside for these purposes, but the need to obtain Government approval for physical changes intended to be of benefit to Members or staff of the two Houses restricts the independence of the legislature. This has somewhat limited the development of services needed by the Commons for scrutiny of the executive. There has not been enough space, within the present Palace and adjoining buildings used by Parliament, for all the offices for Members and their staff, and for the staff of the House itself, which many Members believe desirable.

---

[1] H.C.Deb., Vol. 393, col. 403 (October 28, 1943).
[2] For a description of its inspiration and creation see "*Mid Victorian Masterpiece*" by Sir Barnett Cocks (Hutchinson, 1977).
[3] See, for example, Aneurin Bevan, "*In Place of Fear*," (Heinemann, 1952) pp. 5–11.
[4] This is the estimate (Class XX, Vote 18, Section G), for P.S.A. works services for both Houses.

The nature of the building is also influential. The present Palace was mostly built in the last century, after the fire of 1834. Sir Charles Barry and Augustus Welby Pugin were masters of an elaborate Gothic, ecclesiastical style, and although this has been moderated in the House of Commons itself, which was redesigned and rebuilt in 1950 after the Chamber was destroyed by bombing in 1941, the style, redolent with historical references, still exercises some influence. The mood of pervading tradition, of historical authority, of elaborate ceremony and of ancient forms of order is difficult to escape.

Of greater significance are the shapes and size of the two Chambers and of other rooms where Members work. As shown on the plan below, the Commons' Chamber is rectangular, with benches facing each other as they were in the former chapel in which the House met from 1547 to 1834. At one end, raised up, is the Speaker's Chair and in front of it the Table of the House, where sit the Clerk of the House (on the Speaker's right), the Clerk Assistant and other Clerks at the Table. To the right of the Speaker sit Ministers on the front–bench, and behind and around them the back–benchers of the Government party. To the Speaker's left are the Opposition front–bench spokesmen and their supporters. Below the gangway (a short flight of steps half-way down the Chamber) on the Opposition side there are also benches for Members of smaller parties such as the Social and Liberal Democrats, and the Scottish, Welsh and Ulster parties; the Democratic Unionist Party support the Government and sit on its side of the House. Thus the very shape of the Chamber expresses and re–inforces the confrontational characteristics we described in Chapter 1. This is highlighted by the confrontation of the Prime Minister and the Leader of the Opposition when they face each other across the Table and speak from the despatch boxes.

The remaining occupants of seats on or adjacent to the floor of the House are the Serjeant at Arms (or one of his deputies) at the far end of the Chamber facing the Speaker, the civil servants in the Officials Box to the right and behind the Speaker, who are there to assist their Ministers, and others particularly concerned with the business in hand who have the use of a small gallery at the far end of the Chamber on the Opposition side. In addition Officers of the House may stand behind the Speaker's Chair or at the Bar of the House. And doorkeepers, commonly called "badge messengers", go in and out (though not right onto the floor of the House) with messages for Members.

Above the Speaker there is a large Press Gallery for Hansard reporters (in the front row), lobby correspondents and reporters for newspapers, television etc., including many from overseas. At the other end is the Strangers' Gallery for those who wish to listen to proceedings, including special areas reserved for Members of the House of Lords, diplomats, guests of the Speaker, Commonwealth visitors and other distinguished strangers. Down the two sides of the Chamber are other galleries reserved for Members themselves. These are technically part of the House and on occasions Members have spoken from them. However Speaker Thomas, after some Members had used the gallery to demonstrate their disapproval of the Government's Irish policy, stated that in future Members seeking to speak from the galleries would be unlikely to "catch the Speaker's eye."[5]

The size of the Chamber is also significant. Members sit on benches not at

---

[5] H.C.Deb., Vol. 13, col. 165 (November 17, 1981).

PLAN OF THE COMMONS CHAMBER
(slightly simplified)

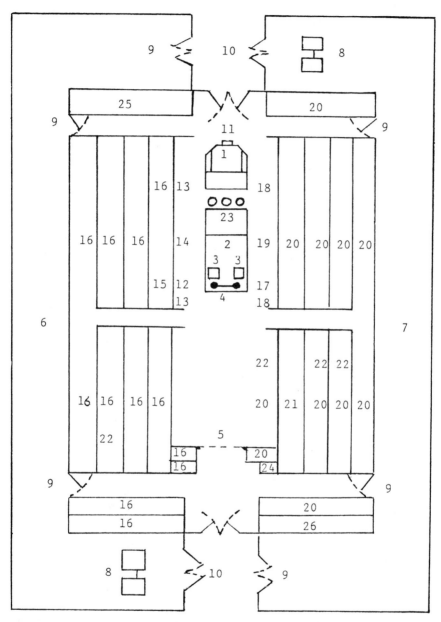

1 Speaker's Chair	10 Exits from Lobbies	18 Opposition Whips
2 Table of the House	11 Petition Bag	19 Shadow Ministers
3 Dispatch boxes	12 Prime Minister	20 Opposition Back-benches
4 The Mace	13 Government Whips	21 Democrats
5 The Bar of the House	14 Other Ministers	22 Other smaller Parties
6 Aye Division Lobby	15 Parliamentary Private	23 Clerks at the Table
7 No Division Lobby	Secretaries	24 Serjeant at Arms
8 Division Clerks' Desks	16 Government Back-benches	25 Civil Servants
9 Entrances to Lobbies	17 Leader of Opposition	26 Strangers

desks, and there are no permanently reserved places. Even the places occupied by the Prime Minister, other Ministers, the Leader of the Opposition, and former Prime Ministers are only theirs by courtesy and convention.[6] Therefore there is no fixed number of Members who may sit in the House. But the number of slots where Members who were present at prayers place their name-cards, in accordance with Standing Orders Nos. 7 and 8, to reserve a seat for the day indicates that 364 places are available, without uncomfortable over-crowding, on the floor of the House. On big occasions a further 50 Members can sit on the steps of the gangways, crowd in behind the Speaker's Chair or stand at the Bar. Those who cannot find a place on the floor must use one of the side galleries. But not every one of the 650 Members can sit in comfort.

Paradoxically this has certain beneficial consequences. On many occasions attendance in the House is not high. Members are increasingly specialist, and business becomes more voluminous and complex. No Member attends every debate, and the majority of Members attend only those debates in which they have a special interest. Thus it is not unusual for only some 20 or 30 Members to be in the Chamber for the major part of many debates with somewhat higher attendances for the opening and closing speeches from the front-benches. A Chamber seating 650 would often be intolerably empty. The small Chamber also makes it possible to maintain the intimacy of debate. Other than front-benchers (who use the dispatch boxes), Members speak from their places and there is much argument and counter-argument across the Chamber, with interruptions and reactions from supporters and opponents. A larger Chamber would need a special rostrum for speakers, who would tend to practice oratory and deliver set, pre-prepared speeches, rather than enter into proper debate. Finally, it may be thought that when the House is crowded, for Prime's Minister's Questions, for example, or for the Budget or some other big debate, this adds to the drama of the occasion.

Much of the work of the House is conducted in committees, and the architecture of the committee rooms is again significant. The House is fortunate that when the Palace was rebuilt after the fire of 1834, Parliament was going through one of its phases when committees were heavily employed for private bills and for investigating various social problems; this would not have been so 50 years earlier or 50 years later. As a result Barry incorporated into the new Houses of Parliament a magnificent committee corridor, stretching almost the whole length of the building, with 16 committee rooms, of varying sizes, overlooking the river; other committee rooms were provided elsewhere in the building. For many years these rooms were little used, but today, nearly every one of these rooms is in use most days, for official committees of either House, for party meetings, or for other meetings sponsored by Members. Extra committee rooms—and many extra conference and interview rooms for unofficial meetings—have been added in recent years.

Today there are 18 committee rooms in the Commons and seven in the Lords available for standing committees, select committees and committees

---

[6] On one occasion, Dame Irene Ward, a Government supporter, sat in the place of the Prime Minister, Harold Macmillan; she was breaking no rule and was not required to move. On other occasions Liberal Members have occupied seats on the Opposition front-bench.

on private bills. Some of their characteristics are manifested in the layout of the rooms they occupy.

Standing committees of the Commons debate in much the same way as does the House itself. Thus these rooms are arranged like the House. The Chairman sits on an elevated dais, or at a separate table. The benches are arranged facing each other—Government and Opposition. The public sit in a railed off area at the far end of the room. It is a confrontational forum, reflecting most of the work they do.

Select committees have a totally different function. They investigate and deliberate, but do not debate. They usually seek consensus. The select committee rooms reflect this. The Chairman sits at a horse-shoe shaped table, with the Clerk of the committee beside him, and other Members down the two sides of the horse-shoe. They sometimes align themselves by party, but often they sit in random order. There is no obvious confrontation between them. Witnesses give evidence at a table facing the open-end of the horse-shoe. Other staff of the committee, and the press, sit at tables on either side of the room. A shorthand writer sits in the middle of the horse-shoe recording the evidence verbatim (or tape recordings may be used). The public are normally admitted to evidence sessions and sit at the back of the room. Private bill committees meet in similar rooms to those of select committees.

We have primarily described the Chamber of the Commons and its committee rooms. The House of Lords is essentially similar, except that the Lords Chamber is dominated by the raised Throne at one end, where sits the Queen at the opening of Parliament, with the Bar at the other, where the Commons come on the same occasion. In front of the Throne is the Woolsack, used by the Lord Chancellor or other presiding officers of the House of Lords. Unlike the arrangement in the Commons, the Clerk of the Parliaments and other Clerks sit at the Table facing the Lord Chancellor, and some way away from him. On the right of the Throne, and of the Woolsack, are the Government benches and also the Bishops' bench; on the left are the benches of the Opposition parties; and at the far end, facing the Throne, in front of the Bar, are some cross-benches (unknown in the Commons), where sit the Law Lords and other Peers who do not wish to take the whip of any of the parties. The Lords do not usually use debating committees (such as the Commons standing committees), but their rooms for select committees and for private bill committees are similar to those in the Commons.

The Palace of Westminster houses many people other than Members and there are numerous rooms other than the two Chambers and committee rooms. Leaving aside the Lords' accommodation, there are the Speaker's offices and his private apartments[7]; offices for Ministers and leaders of Opposition parties; offices or desk space for other Members; the Library and storage space for its vast collection of books, records and other documents; interview rooms where Members can meet their visitors; offices of the staff of all the House departments (see pages 152–159 below); rooms for other supporting services such as the police and custodians, telephone operators, the Post Office, maintenance engineers, etc.; accommodation for

---

[7] The Speaker is the only Member of the Commons provided with living accommodation in the Palace. The Serjeant at Arms, the Deputy Serjeant, the Speaker's Secretary and two Office Keepers also live within the precincts but are shortly to be re-housed nearby. The Clerk of the House also has an apartment in a nearby building.

associated bodies such as the Commonwealth Parliamentary Association and the Inter-Parliamentary Union, and for the press, including radio and television studios; rooms for Members' research assistants and secretaries; cloakrooms and toilets; a barber's shop; space for recreation or relaxation (including a gymnasium, a miniature rifle range and a chess room); and accommodation for providing and consuming food and drink. In the Commons alone there are 10 separate rooms where meals can be eaten and a further seven bars; much political and parliamentary business is there conducted.

Apart from Members, some 2,500 people work daily in the House of Commons alone, and a further 700 staff are employed by various bodies performing functions on behalf of the two Houses.[8] They all require some accommodation. In February 1987, within that part of the Palace of Westminster (i.e. excluding outside buildings) allocated to the House of Commons, there were 273 offices for Members, 55 desk spaces for Members' secretaries, 91 offices for parliamentary staff, and 31 offices for other organisations.[9] Altogether the Palace covers eight acres; it has 11 courtyards, 100 staircases, 35 lifts, two miles of passages and some 1,100 rooms.[10] The total floor area of the Palace is approximately 790,000 sq. ft.; 530,000 sq ft. for the Commons and 260,000 sq. ft. for the Lords.[11]

The pressure on limited space, even in the large Palace of Westminster, is very great. It has grown significantly in recent years as a result of the growth of parliamentary work and the increasing employment of Members' secretaries and research assistants; in May 1987 desks were provided for 410 secretaries.[12] The conclusion forced on Parliament in the 1960s and 1970s was that this demand could not all be contained in the old Palace. Today Members or staff of the House (or associated bodies) occupy three large buildings on the Embankment downstream from Westminster Bridge (including the former New Scotland Yard), one building across the road in Old Palace Yard, and other offices near Westminster Abbey.

Some of the main offices and working areas of the House departments are located near the Chamber, including in particular offices of the Clerk's Department, the main Library, the Serjeant's offices, the Official Report and most of the refreshment facilities. These have to be convenient for Members, whose main areas of work lie in the Palace itself.

Other departments and offices, especially the Administration Department, the greater part of the Committee Office, and a major branch of the Library, including the Public Information Office, are located off the main building. So are the offices of many Members and the great majority of their secretaries and research assistants; many of the latter work in one of the Norman Shaw buildings on the Embankment, where they can use the Branch Library. Plans for the future, as worked out by the House of Commons (Services) Committee are to provide as many Members as possible with offices or desks in the Palace itself, and to move some House of Commons staff out of the main building. The main accommodation and

---

[8] H.C.Deb., Vol. 105, col. 176, (November 20, 1985).

[9] H.C.Deb., Vol. 110, col. 16, (February 9, 1987).

[10] *The Houses of Parliament—An Illustrated Guide to the Palace of Westminster*, 13th Edition, pp. 24–26.

[11] H.C.Deb., Vol. 93, col. 359 (March 10, 1986).

[12] Second Report from Select Committee on House of Commons (Services), H.C. 378 of 1986–87, para. 46.

work areas for Members' staff would remain in the out-buildings. The policy will be advanced significantly by the proposed creation of the first stage of a new parliamentary building in Parliament Street (at the foot of Whitehall) in about 1991.[13]

Other facilities for Members should be mentioned. In their offices Members are provided by the House authorities with essential furniture—a desk, a couple of chairs, a filing cabinet, a telephone, etc.—but other office equipment, such as word-processors and computers, they have to buy themselves, using their allowances. Outside their offices a number of major facilities are at their disposal free of charge. For example photo-copying machines (for creating more material for others to read) and shredding machines (for reducing surplus reading matter) are provided.[14] Computer terminals with access to various data banks may be used in the Library (or access can be achieved from Members offices). The Grand Committee Room off Westminster Hall is equipped for use as a cinema, and films on matters of current political interest are often shown by Members who are anxious to interest or influence their fellow politicians. A major facility of practical importance is the five-storey underground car park beneath New Palace Yard, with space for 495 cars. And finally there is a terrace beside the Thames for fair-weather relaxation, entertaining guests, casual chatter or serious political plotting.

Members' guests and many other visitors to the House play a central role in Parliament, for they (although termed "strangers") are the ultimate reason for its existence; these are the people the Members represent. Their rights and facilities are therefore important.

Any citizen has the right to come to Parliament to contact Members. Although all visitors are subject to a physical security check (the House is sadly aware of past attacks on its Members, with one Member killed in recent years within the precincts[15]) they can pass freely to the Central Lobby without need for an appointment, and can then seek the Members they desire to see by completing a "green card." This is taken round the building and, provided the Member is in the Palace and is free (he may well be busy in a committee or other meeting), he will normally come to the Lobby to see his visitor, especially if it be a constituent. Other visitors come having first made an appointment. Many people write to Members and others telephone; if a Member is not available his secretary may take the call or a message can be left with a telephone answering service.

As well as individuals wishing to "lobby" a Member, once or twice a week there are "mass lobbies," when people from a particular area or industry or profession (sometimes in large numbers from all over the country) wish to raise a single issue with their Members. On these occasions up to 100 people at a time may be admitted to the Central Lobby; other groups may be taken by Members to interview rooms where they can discuss the problem.

Many people come to listen to proceedings from the public gallery of the House; the average annual number in the years 1985–1987 was 160,201.[16] Question time is particularly popular and the gallery is usually full till about

---

[13] See Second Report of the House of Commons (Services) Committee, H.C. 378 of 1986–87, para. 3.

[14] In June 1986, there were 74 photocopying machines in use in the House of Commons and parliamentary outbuildings: H.C.Deb., Vol. 99, col. 90 (June 9, 1986).

[15] Mr. Airey Neave, killed by a bomb in the car park in 1979.

[16] H.C.Deb., Vol. 128, col. 646 (February 29, 1988).

4.00 p.m.; for admission at this time it is necessary to obtain a ticket in advance, which can best be done by writing to a Member. At other times the public can be admitted without prior issue of a ticket, but there is often a queue on the pavement outside St Stephen's Porch (the public entrance), and the more interesting the debate, the longer the queue.

People wishing to attend public meetings of standing and select committees do not need tickets. But many committee meetings attract a number of representatives of interest or pressure groups and other specialist observers, and school parties or students are often taken to committee meetings as part of an educational visit; the limited public seating is often full.

Large numbers of people seek to tour the Palace of Westminster each day simply to see the Queen's Robing Room, the Royal Gallery, the Chambers of the two Houses and the historic Westminster Hall, without attending any debates. Total numbers have to be limited, and all such visitors have to be escorted in parties of not more than 16. Members frequently arrange such visits for constituency groups or for schools.

Lastly, Members, Officers and staff have many friends and other visitors whom they meet personally, and whom they may entertain in the Strangers Dining Room, the cafeteria or in various other dining rooms or bars.

All these contacts between Members and the public are an essential part of the working of Parliament. The throng of people in the Central Lobby each day is a testament to parliamentary democracy.

THE WAY MEMBERS WORK

Accommodation and facilities greatly influence the way Members work. Today, all Members who so wish (a few require nothing) have either a room of their own, a shared room, or at least a desk of their own in a larger room shared with as many as a dozen other Members.[17] It was not always so.[18] Thirty years ago most Members (other than Ministers, the leaders of Opposition parties, and one or two chairmen of committees) had no private space except a small locker from which they would have to remove their papers each day to work in the Library or to dictate to their secretaries in the corridors. But even today accommodation is far from generous for many Members. In effect there is an awkward choice for most of them. Either a Member can have a reasonably-sized, and often very comfortable room in one of the out-buildings (in some cases up to five-minutes walk from the Chamber but near enough for the Member to be able to get to the House for divisions), with a secretary and assistant fairly near by, or he can have a small, overcrowded room or desk space in the main building, near the Chamber, but with the secretary at least five minutes walk away. Furthermore, Members' parliamentary work and social life take them away from their offices for long periods—to the Chamber, to committee rooms, to the Library, to the Central Lobby to meet constituents, and thence to interview

---

[17] In May 1987, 111 rooms were provided in the Palace itself for 124 Ministers, front-bench Opposition Members and other office-holders (excluding the Speaker); 158 rooms, of which 61 were single rooms, were provided for other Members; and 171 rooms, of which 96 were single rooms, were provided for Members in other buildings. Overall there were 261 single rooms; most of the remaining 388 Members have to share; often with three other Members. (H.C. 378 of 1986–87, paras. 39–40).

[18] For the expansion of accommodation since 1971, see H.C.Deb., Vol. 121, col. 17 (October 26, 1987).

rooms or bars or the Terrace, or again to committee rooms for party, all-party and other meetings, or to the dining rooms or cafeterias.

Therefore, although many Members use their offices for part of the day (dealing with mail with a secretary in the morning for example, and signing letters in the evening) and although some Members do much work in their offices, the use of a suite of offices (Member, research staff and secretary) where a Member can see constituents, hold meetings and concentrate his political and parliamentary work (which is the normal pattern, for example, in the U.S.A. and Canada) is almost impossible in Westminster. Members therefore spend relatively little time working alone or with their personal team; they spend much time with other Members within one working or relaxation area or another. Because they are gregarious they are communicating with each other, influencing each other and developing their reactions to a multiplicity of political issues.

Most of these gatherings, other than the formal meetings of the House or of select and standing committees, are one-party rather than multi-party. There a number of all-party groups and a little cross-socialising, especially through such bodies as the Inter-Parliamentary Union and the Commonwealth Parliamentary Association. When Members drink in the bars, they are sometimes politically mixed. But when eating, be it in the Members Dining Room, the Tea Room or the Cafeteria, they nearly always sit with Members of their own party. Leaving aside the work of the House itself and its committees, serious political work is mostly done within strict party bounds at meetings of the parliamentary parties and their committees, at gatherings of like-minded Members within the party, or when seeing Ministers or party-leaders in their rooms; at many of these meetings party-supporters from outside the House may also be present.

Thus the accommodation and the social habits of M.P.s reinforce the role of the House of Commons as a communications medium, rather than a workshop. Members may spend some time as solitary craftsmen assembling and fashioning their own instruments of influence, but they spend as much or more time in the company of their fellow Members (particularly those of their own party), combining together to exercise that influence. This is a peculiar and central feature of the House of Commons.[18a]

THE OFFICERS AND DEPARTMENTS OF THE HOUSE OF COMMONS

Every organisation requires office holders who can exercise authority, speak on its behalf, administer its business and serve its members. In the House of Commons these functions are divided among elected officers, who are Members of Parliament, and the permanent officers and their staff who are employed by or for the House.

The elected officers

The Speaker

The Speaker is the senior officer of the House.[19] His is one of the great

---

[18a] For a detailed description of the working life of a back-bench M.P. see L. Radice, E. Vallance and V. Willis, *Member of Parliament*, esp. Chapters 3, 4, 5 and 8.)

[19] For a full description of the history and nature of this office see Philip Laundy, *The Office of the Speaker*, and *The Speaker and his Office*, by the same author, in *The Commons in the Twentieth Century*, ed., S. A. Walkland.

offices of State (ranking sixth in the official order of precedence after the Royal Family). He receives a salary (including a small parliamentary salary) slightly greater than that of a Cabinet Minister.[20] Under the House of Commons (Speaker) Act 1832, his Speaker's salary is charged directly to the Consolidated Fund and is not voted annually by Parliament; this symbolises and reinforces his independent position. His parliamentary salary is voted by the House, as for all Members. He has the use of magnificent official apartments and a private residence in the Palace of Westminster. On retirement from the Speakership he is always immediately made a Member of the House of Lords.

The Speaker is always a Member of the House. When a vacancy arises consideration has to be given to which Member could best hold the office. On many occasions in the past a back-bencher, with no ministerial experience, has been chosen. He might possess the advantage of being well-known among other back-benchers on both sides of the House, over whom he would have to exercise authority, and he would know them. He would have the disadvantage, perhaps, of carrying less authority with the senior Ministers and ex-Ministers on the front-benches. On other occasions a senior former Minister has been called to the Chair. He might have advantages and disadvantages which are the reverse of those of a back-bencher; he might also be thought to be—or to have been—a more partisan figure, and therefore possibly less acceptable in the neutral role of the Chair.

Practice since 1945 has tended towards selection of a man with Ministerial experience. Col. Clifton Brown, Speaker until 1951, had come from the back-benches. Mr W. S. ("Shakes") Morrison, elected in 1951 had been a Cabinet Minister and front-bench spokesman in Opposition. His successor, Sir Harry Hylton-Foster, elected in 1959, had for the previous five years been the Solicitor-General. On his death in 1965, he was succeeded by Dr. Horace King, who had been Chairman of Ways and Means and Deputy Speaker since 1964 but had previously served the whole of his parliamentary career on the back-benches. His successor was exceptional. When Mr Selwyn Lloyd was chosen in 1971 he had held nearly all the highest Cabinet posts except that of Prime Minister (Minister of Supply, Minister of Defence, Secretary of State for Foreign Affairs, Chancellor of the Exchequer and Lord Privy Seal and Leader of the House of Commons). He was followed in 1976 by yet another ex-Minister, but one who had also served as Deputy Speaker since 1974, Mr George Thomas. Finally, when he retired at the general election of 1983, another Deputy succeeded to the top post, the present Speaker Weatherill. Prior to his appointment as Chairman of Ways and Means in 1979 he had been Deputy Chief Whip of the Conservative Party while they were in opposition from 1974 and indeed had spent nearly all his parliamentary career since 1964 as a Whip in government or opposition. This was an unusual but far from unhelpful background for one who was called to be Speaker of the House.

Traditionally, most Speakers have been lawyers, but since 1945 there have only been three lawyers (Morrison, Hylton-Foster and Selwyn Lloyd) against four non-lawyers (Clifton Brown, King, Thomas and Weatherill). Several Speakers had previously held the post of Chairman of Ways and Means (Deputy Speaker). This was true since 1945 of Speakers Clifton

---

[20] H.C.Deb., Vol. 119, col. *582–584* (July 16, 1987).

Brown, King, Thomas and Weatherill, but as the Select Committee on Procedure made plain in 1972, there should be no automatic presumption that experience in that post constitutes a qualification for the office of Speaker.[21]

When a vacancy occurs, following the resignation or death of a Speaker, the new Speaker is always chosen from among the Government supporters. It used to be left to the Government to make a choice and propose a name to the House. More recently, particularly after some criticisms had been expressed at the time of Selwyn Lloyd's call to the Chair,[22] wider-ranging consultations have been conducted, including discussion with back-benchers and the Opposition, with a view to agreeing on a broadly acceptable person. The consequence has been that the most recent Speakers—and this appears to have been particularly true in the case of Speaker Weatherill— have been men who have been chosen, on first being called to the Chair, by the Members generally, and who have not necessarily been the first choice of the Prime Minister of the day.

The principle that the Speaker should be chosen by the House as a whole is reflected in the procedure for his election. At the beginning of a Parliament, the House first meets for the election of a Speaker. Under a new procedure adopted in 1972 and embodied in Standing Order No.1, the Chair is taken by that Member, not being a Minister of the Crown, who has had the longest continuous service as a Member of the House (commonly known as "the Father of the House").[23]

The House is then summoned to the Lords to hear a Commission read "for the opening and holding of Parliament," at which time the Lords Commissioners also direct the House to proceed to the election of a Speaker, and to present him the next day, in the House of Peers, for the Royal Approbation.

When the Commons return to their Chamber, the presiding Member calls a senior back-bench Member on the Government side to propose the election of a Member of the House "to be their Speaker." Another Member then seconds the motion; in almost every case this is nowadays done by a senior back-bench Member of the principal Opposition party so emphasising the cross-party nature of the choice being made. The only exceptions since 1945 were in 1951, when the election of the Speaker was contested by a candidate from the Labour Party (Major Milner, former Chairman of Ways and Means), and 1959, when the Labour Party, although they did not support a rival candidate to Hylton-Foster, were unhappy about the choice of yet another Conservative to be Speaker.

The choice of a new Speaker is therefore normally unopposed. The only exception since 1945 in addition to those mentioned above was in January 1971 when several back-benchers on either side wished to criticise the choice of Selwyn Lloyd as a prominent former Minister, and to protest against the lack of consultation among back-benchers before this choice was announced. They proposed Sir Geoffrey de Freitas, without his agreement, as a rival candidate, simply to force a division to record their protest. However when a Member who has already been Speaker wishes to continue

---

[21] First Report for the Select Committee on Procedure, H.C. 111 of 1971–72, para. 26.

[22] *Ibid.*, para. 10. For a fuller discussion of the process of choosing Speakers since 1945 see Philip Laundy, *The Office of Speaker in Parliaments of the Commonwealth*, 1984, pp. 74–78.

[23] S.O. No. 1(1). Until this Standing Order was passed in August 1972, the Clerk of the House presided until a Speaker was elected.

in that office, he is nowadays always re-elected, at the beginning of Parliament, without opposition.

Under the new procedure laid down in Standing Order No.1 the Chair is now taken by the retiring Speaker when he is retiring in mid-Session, so that his successor may thereupon be chosen.[24] If the Speaker has died or otherwise ceased to be a Member of the House, the Chair is taken by the Father of the House as already described.

A person or persons having been proposed and seconded the House may debate the choice before it, although if there is only one candidate there is usually no further debate except that the person chosen submits himself[25] to the House. The relevant questions are then put and, if necessary, there may be a division (or divisions). Eventually a name is agreed upon. After a short speech, thanking the House for the honour conferred upon him, the successful man is conducted to the Chair by his proposer and seconder, demonstrating as he goes a traditional resistance to acceptance of this high office in memory of those of his predecessors who found its occupation far from enjoyable and in some cases prematurely terminated (eight Speakers have been executed). On arriving at the Chair he makes, from the steps, one more formal expressing of thanks and then takes the Chair as Speaker elect. The Mace is then placed on the Table, and the Prime Minister, and Leader of the Opposition and other party Leaders congratulate the Speaker on his election. The House is then adjourned.

The choice of a Speaker is not, however, a matter for the Commons alone. The Speaker has a constitutional function as "spokesman" for the House, and on behalf of the House has right of access to the Queen. It is therefore necessary for the Speaker elect to receive the Royal Approbation. This is given on the day after his election, in the House of Lords.[26] At the same time the Speaker claims, on behalf of the Commons "all their ancient and undoubted rights and privileges." After the Lord Chancellor has, on behalf of the Queen, confirmed these, the Speaker and the Commons return to their Chamber and the Speaker's election is complete.

The non-political status of the Speaker, the nature of his working life and the related question of duration of his tenure of office is different from that in most other parliamentary systems. First, although the Speaker is elected originally to Parliament as a party politician, on being chosen Speaker he drops all party connections and activities. He relinquishes for life all offices in his party; he does not attend party meetings at Westminster or party conferences in the country; and he plays no party role in his constituency. He may continue to deal, privately, with constituency correspondence and the problems of his constituents in much the same way as any other Member, although he cannot table Questions or raise their problems in debate (in compensation his correspondence with Ministers about constituency cases is given most careful consideration).[27]

At Westminster he leads a somewhat cut-off life; for example he does not use the dining rooms or the Members' Smoking Room, or other bars or the

---

[24] See proceedings on February 3, 1976.

[25] It might, of course, be "herself," but this has not yet happened. Here, as throughout the book, the male pronoun is used for simplicity.

[26] Approbation has only once been refused: to Sir Edward Seymour in 1678.

[27] For a description of how the Speaker's constituency work may be handled, see Report from the Select Committee on Parliamentary Elections (Mr. Speaker's Seat) H.C. 98 of 1938–39.

Library. However he has his own accommodation where he does most of his work away from the Chamber. Here he is able to meet any Members individually to discuss problems they wish to raise with him. He has regular meetings with party leaders, the Leader of the House or the Whips from either side to discuss the business of the House. He has daily meetings with the Clerk of the House, the Serjeant at Arms and other Clerks, and with the Deputy Speakers when he is briefed on the business for the day and other procedural matters. And he receives many visitors and entertains Members of the House and their wives (on a strictly non-party basis) as well as Speakers and Members of other parliaments from all over the world.

In all this he is assisted by a Secretary and some six other staff who are personally appointed by him or under his authority to serve in the Speaker's Office. There is also a Speaker's Chaplain, who says prayers in the House each day, and two Speaker's Counsels, who are usually former civil service lawyers. The first advises the Speaker and the Officers of the House on legal matters (for example in relation to the terms of employment of staff) and has other major responsibilities regarding private legislation and statutory instruments (see page 445). The Second Speaker's Counsel is the legal adviser to the Select Committee on European Legislation (see page 436).

In the Chamber itself the Speaker is the principal presiding officer. Unless he is unavoidably absent or has obtained the leave of the House to be absent,[28] (in which cases his absence is notified to the House by the Clerk, and a Deputy Speaker takes the Chair) he always goes to the House in formal procession, preceded by the Serjeant at Arms carrying the Mace, for prayers at the beginning of each sitting. On Mondays to Thursdays he then remains in the chair during Question time and for ministerial statements and other business before the main business for the day. If the main business is a major debate, the Speaker may remain until both front-bench spokesmen have spoken; and he usually returns for an hour or so in the earlier part of the evening and again for the wind-up speeches at the end of a debate and for the division. He often presides at other difficult or important moments, when feelings may be running high and his authority and experience will be called upon. But he also takes his share of some of the more routine debates, including the occasional adjournment debate at the end of the day.

As presiding officer the Speaker has a number of functions. He is charged with numerous responsibilities and powers, many of them involving personal discretion for the control and conduct of proceedings of the House. There are some 40 matters on which the Speaker has discretion, ranging from adjourning the House in case of grave disorder to appointing chairmen of standing committees (both under standing orders) and from calling Members to speak in debate or ask supplementary Questions[29] to giving his casting vote when numbers are equal in a division. Details of most of these powers and discretions are described in Chapter 6.

The Speaker is both master and servant of the House. As master he has power to control debate and the conduct of Members in the Chamber. Here he is essentially playing the role of the referee. He is neutral in the argument, but is concerned to see fair-play between the parties. He must seek at all

---

[28] See, e.g. H.C.Deb., Vol. 39, col. 1024 (March 24, 1983).
[29] Some of the difficulties experienced by the Speaker in carrying out these duties, and the sort of factors he bears in mind, are described in H.C.Deb., Vol. 127, cols. 1259–1260, (February 19, 1988).

times to protect minorities and to ensure that all points of view may be expressed, but he must also do his best to see that the wishes of the majority are not unduly frustrated by minorities abusing the rules of the House. He has a particular responsibility to look after the interests of back-benchers (on both sides) to ensure that their rights are not eroded and their opportunities are not denied them by the actions and pressures of the Government and Opposition front-bench.[30] He must rule on the interpretation and application of the rules of procedure[31] while leaving it to others to advise on how Members may use those rules for their own advantage.[32] He frequently has to deal with points of order—some genuine, some less so (see page 196)— inviting him to intervene to prohibit one thing or to allow another. And he has to impose discipline and occasionally punish Members for breaches of the rules or defiance of his rulings or orders. His authority is extensive; when he rises to give a ruling or to exercise his formal powers, all other Members must remain seated and he should be heard in silence.

In all these matters he acts in accordance with powers given him by the House or inherited by well-established practice. In this way he is the House's servant. He fulfils its commands and acts to ensure the enforcement of its decisions, but he is not the manager of the House's business. In particular he has no power (except in certain limited circumstances) to decide on what days the House shall meet, the hours of meeting, the business to be taken at any sitting (except when selecting amendments to motions or bills), the duration of that business, the duration of debate or the duration of speeches in a debate. These matters can only be decided by the House itself, either ad hoc or by standing order, and that means essentially by the Government of the day who, through its majority, has secured control over the arrangement of business (see Chapter 7). Members frequently appeal to the Speaker for time to be provided to debate such and such a matter, or for more time to be allowed for another debate, or for a statement to be made about something else. This may give them publicity, but otherwise their appeals are pointless. The Speaker, as he always replies, has no power to intervene on such matters.

On many matters where he has power the Speaker takes decisions privately. Some of these decisions are later announced in the House, for example on the selection of amendments to motions or to bills at report stage or on private notice Questions (PNQs) which he has allowed. Many other decisions never come up in the House, for example on applications for priority to be given to privilege complaints which he has not allowed, or on out of order Questions, or on disallowed PNQs.

The Speaker's decision on any of these matters, whether it be a public ruling or a decision taken privately, cannot be formally challenged except on a substantive motion of which notice has been given (although Members

---

[30] For example, he keeps careful notes of Members whom he has not been able to call on one occasion, so as to give them an opportunity on some other occasion (see, e.g. H.C.Deb., Vol. 81, col. 29 (June 17, 1985); H.C.Deb., Vol. 118, col. 510 (July 1, 1987)). For a general assessment of the role of the Speaker in protecting back-benchers, see Robin Oakley, "Umpire with a backbench bias," The Times December 24, 1987.

[31] For a case where the Speaker ruled that a Minister had acted contrary to the rules of the House, following which the Minister apologised, see H.C.Deb., Vol. 103, col. 1103 (November 6, 1986).

[32] See, e.g. H.C.Deb., Vol. 106, col. 23 (November 24, 1986); H.C.Deb., Vol. 90, col. 207 (January 21, 1986); H.C.Deb., Vol. 134, col. 723 (June 7, 1988).

frequently seek clarification or urge reconsideration of a ruling by points of order). Such motions are rare. Only three motions critical of the Speaker were debated from 1945 up until the end of Session 1987–1988 (there were also nine debates on motions critical of other occupants of the Chair); 11 other such motions were tabled regarding the Speaker but not debated (and five regarding other occupants of the Chair). If such a motion is tabled by senior Members the Government provides time for it to be debated reasonably promptly. Motions of this sort in recent years have all been negatived or withdrawn. As the statistics show, however, individual back-benchers have also criticised the Chair's decision on a specific matter: for example the acceptance or refusal of the closure, or the failure to call someone in a debate, in motions which have not been debated. Sometimes these are formally withdrawn (perhaps tempers have cooled); on other occasions they lie dormant among the early day motions and are quietly forgotten. In one way or another the authority of the Chair is upheld.

Behind the scenes the Speaker can exercise considerable informal influence, especially in persuading the Government and Opposition to get together "through the usual channels" to reach agreement on certain matters; he can seek to cool the passions; he can encourage down-hearted Members; he can discourage the over-confident; he can offer hope—and suggest outlets—to the frustrated. And he can advise Members from all sides on the action they propose to take in the House.

Away from the Chamber the Speaker has responsibilities for the administration of the House. Some of these have been statutorily defined by the House of Commons (Administration) Act 1978 and other legislation (see pages 160–162), but others are inherited from his predecessors or are inherent in his office. He is responsible, for example, for decisions regarding security in the House and other matters regarding the use of accommodation and facilities; on these matters he is advised by the House of Commons (Services) Committee and the Serjeant at Arms. He appoints the heads and deputy heads of several House departments (see pages 152–159) and is advised by them and consulted by them in cases of difficulty. He is consulted on other senior appointments in the House departments. He greets official visitors to the House, and occasionally represents the House at international conferences, such as the Conferences of European Speakers and Commonwealth Speakers. And from time to time he presides over Speaker's Conferences which consider and recommend changes in electoral law.

In all his actions, both public and private, the Speaker is guided by two considerations. First he must always enforce—and be seen to enforce—the rules of the House and to apply consistently the established practices of the House; so long as he follows the rules and practices he is on firm ground.[33] Second he has to handle the House and its personalities with tact and with a sense of humour but above all both firmly and fairly. To be firm but not fair is the character of the tyrant: to be fair but not firm is the mark of a weak man. Neither will be respected by the House. The Speaker's task is not easy; but it is for such qualities that he has been chosen, by his fellow Members, to be their Speaker.

A major question regarding the Speakership relates to the tenure of his

---

[33] As Speaker King put it, "The bedrock of this House is allegiance not so much to the individual in the Chair as to the sound wisdom, the procedure, customs and courtesies of which he is the guardian and the exponent" (H.C.Deb., Vol. 808, col. 671, (December 10, 1970)).

office. Here again practice is very different from that in many parliaments. The Speaker ceases, like other Members, to be a Member of Parliament once the House is dissolved. (Although, under section 3(2) of the Ministerial and other Salaries Act 1972 and Schedules 1 and 2 to the House of Commons (Administration) Act 1978 the Speaker continues to be deemed to be Speaker for certain statutory purposes (for example in regard to the employment of staff) until a Speaker has been chosen in the new Parliament). If he wishes to continue, the Speaker contests the election simply as "The Speaker" without a party label. In recent years the major parties have often not contested such elections, (although there were such contests in 1945, 1964, both elections in 1974 and in 1987) but other candidates have sometimes stood; Speaker Thomas, for example, was opposed by Plaid Cymru and the National Front in Cardiff West in 1979. The Speaker has usually experienced little difficulty in being returned to the House.

Once re-elected as a Member, the principle of the continuity of the Speakership (first established in 1841) is now so well accepted that no Speaker in modern times has been challenged when nominated for re-election to the Chair, although the formal processes are all repeated. Thus the Speaker, once elected, continues as Speaker so long as he wishes to do so, whatever his political origins and whatever the party in power. Clifton-Brown (originally Conservative) was continued as Speaker by the Labour majorities in 1945 and 1951, as was Hylton-Foster in 1964, and Selwyn Lloyd in 1974; King (originally Labour) was re-elected when the Conservatives won the election in 1970, as was Thomas in 1979. This continuity of office, making a Speaker, in effect, no longer dependent on party backing for his continuance in office, both reflects and underlines the unique impartiality and independence of the modern Speaker in the British House of Commons.

Finally, there is the process and timing of the Speaker's retirement. For many years Speakers retired at the end of a Parliament simply by not standing in the general election. This was the way Clifton Brown and Morrison retired in 1951 and 1959. However Hylton-Foster died in office, during the 1965 Summer recess. His successor, King, was thus elected in mid-Parliament, and he also retired in mid-Parliament as did his successor, Selwyn Lloyd, in 1976.

This pattern, of continuing in office after an election but then retiring, has several advantages. First, it may, depending on election results, facilitate the choice of Speakers from different parties. For example, given that Speakers are chosen from the majority party at the time of their first election, such alternation of party would not have been possible if King had stayed on till 1974 or Selwyn Lloyd until 1979. Second, the choice of a new Speaker in mid-Parliament is made much easier. There is more time for consultation than during the flurry of activity (especially in the filling of ministerial offices) after a general election when a hurried choice may have to be made before the House meets. Third, those who elect a Speaker in mid Parliament all know the probable candidates. Not all Members have such experience when a choice has to be made immediately after an election.

It was no doubt for these reasons that the Procedure Committee in 1972 expressed the hope "that whenever possible the Speaker should retire in the middle of a session."[34] It is interesting to note that Speaker Thomas did not follow the recent practice or this advice.

---

[34] H.C. 111 of 1971–72, para. 22.

The office of the Speaker is of great importance in any examination of how the House works. But the advice and support given to the Speaker by other officers and departments, and the work they do under his authority or on his behalf are also important. To these other officers we now turn.

The Chairman of Ways and Means and the Deputy Chairmen

The Chairman of Ways and Means, and the First and Second Deputy Chairmen of Ways and Means (the title derives from the time when they chaired the now defunct Committee of Ways and Means) are also the three Deputy Speakers. They are always senior Members of the House, often with experience of chairing standing committees, but sometimes being ex-Ministers; they often have had experience in both these fields.

The Chairman and his Deputies have for many years been appointed from either side of the House. They never vote in the House or committees—except to give a casting vote—and therefore, to ensure that the balance of strength between the Government and Opposition is not affected by the appointments to the Chair, it is now the practice to ensure that the four occupants of the Chair, namely the Speaker and the three Deputy Speakers, are drawn equally from the two sides. In 1989 the Speaker originated from the Conservative side, the Chairman of Ways and Means was Labour, the First Deputy Chairman was Conservative, and the Second was Labour.

The Deputy Speakers are appointed by motion in the House at the beginning of each Parliament, usually on the day of the Queen's speech. There is normally consultation between, as well as within, the parties, as it is important that all the occupants of the Chair should be acceptable to Members on both sides. However once such informal agreement has been reached, the formal appointment by the House is usually made without debate, and without any of the ceremony attending the election of the Speaker. Appointments have not usually been challenged in recent years.[35] The functions of the Deputy Speakers, when presiding in the House, are largely the same as those of the Speaker. Under Standing Order No.3(1) the Chairman of Ways and Means or a Deputy Chairman may take the Chair, as Deputy Speaker, when asked to do so by the Speaker, without any formal communication to the House. Such informal sharing of duties of the Chair is the regular practice, and one or other of the Deputy Speakers (working an agreed roster of duties) occupies the Chair for much of the sitting time.

By long established practice, the powers of the Chairman of Ways and Means, when acting as Deputy Speaker, are, with one exception, the same as those of the Speaker, including his disciplinary powers and the power to accept the closure. However, other than in respect of consideration of the estimates, he has, by specific provision of Standing Order No.31(5), no power in the House to select amendments to motions or bills (see page 217); this can only be done by the Speaker. Under Standing Order No. 2, the two Deputy Chairmen have the same powers as the Chairman.

If the Speaker is ill or is away from some important occasion his absence may be formally notified to the House by the Clerk or he may be given leave of absence. In such circumstances, under Standing Order No.3(2) and the Deputy Speaker Act 1855, the Chairman of Ways and Means assumes all the

---

[35] For a division when the appointment of a Deputy Chairman of Ways and Means was opposed, see H.C.Deb., Vol. 652, cols. 708–718 (January 29, 1962).

powers of the Speaker in the House until the next sitting or until the Speaker returns (or, if the House adjourns for more than 24 hours, for a period of 24 hours after that adjournment); these powers include the selection of amendments and also various powers outside the House, such as those relating to the issue of writs and the powers conferred on the Speaker by the House of Commons (Administration) Act 1978.[36] Under Standing Order No. 12(3) the Chairman (or one of the Deputies) may act for the Speaker regarding emergency recalls of the House during a recess, if the Speaker, for any reason, is unable to act himself.

When the Chairman is similarly unable to be present in the House, and this has been announced, the First Deputy Chairman would (under Standing Order No.3(3)) assume the duties and exercise the authority of the Speaker; and if he was also away, the Second Deputy Chairman would be given those responsibilities. But neither of these situations has ever occurred. All these formal temporary replacements must be renewed daily.[37]

As Chairmen, the Chairman of Ways and Means and his Deputies have particular responsibilities for committees of the whole House, where the Speaker never presides. Here they have full powers regarding the conduct of the committee's proceedings, including the selection of amendments (although in practice the primary responsibility for such selection rests with the Chairman himself and not with the Deputies). On such matters, there can be no appeal from their decisions to the Speaker, who always refuses to be drawn into arguments about committee proceedings. But as Chairmen they do not have powers relating solely to the House, such as the suspension or adjournment of the sitting in cases of disorder, or putting the question for the suspension of a named Member (see pages 213–216).

The Chairman of Ways and Means also usually presides over the House for the annual presentation of the Budget by the Chancellor of the Exchequer because it used to be presented in the Committee of Ways and Means.

Outside the House and its committees, the Chairman has certain particular responsibilities, especially in connection with private legislation; he is charged with the organisation of private business in the House, with seeing that all private bills are given a fair opportunity to make progress, and with moving their various stages, such as second and third readings. The Chairman himself takes the chair of the Court of Referees and the Standing Orders Committee, and the two Deputies share the work of chairing committees on unopposed private bills.

Under Standing Order No.4, the three Chairmen are *ex-officio* members of the Chairmen's Panel. The remainder of the Panel, not less than 10 in number, are nominated by the Speaker at the beginning of each session. He may add further Members or make substitutions in the course of the session. In 1988 there were 21 nominated Members, and this has been standard in recent years. Members of the Panel may take the chair in committees of the whole House, when asked to do so by the Chairman of Ways and Means, and typically two Members act in this way for a few hours whenever there is a prolonged committee stage of a bill. When presiding in committee of the whole House, temporary chairmen have all the powers of the Chairman of Ways and Means except that of selection of amendments (see Standing

---

[36] Schedule 2(2) to that Act.
[37] See for example April 17, to April 25, 1985, inclusive, during a period of illness of the Speaker.

Order No. 31(2)) and acceptance of the closure (see Standing Order No. 35 (4)). They do not normally occupy the chair when feelings are running high and the firm discipline of the Chair is required; they would not normally name a Member, for example.

As members of the Chairmen's Panel the Chairman and Deputy Chairmen of Ways and Means are entitled to take the chair of standing committees, and occasionally do so, when other members of the Panel are unavailable. For example, in session 1984–1985, the Second Deputy Chairman of Ways and Means chaired a Standing Committee on four occasions. The duties of the chairman of a standing committee are described elsewhere (see pages 272–273), but collectively the Panel considers from time to time procedural matters relating to such committees, and agrees sessional resolutions relating to the order in which bills allocated to a committee shall be considered and the procedure for resuming adjourned proceedings.[38]

The Chairman of Ways and Means and the two Deputy Chairmen, so long as they hold these posts, cease to play an active political role in the House; they do not attend party meetings or committees; they do not speak or vote in the House save in their official capacity; and they seek to avoid public comment on controversial political issues, both inside and outside the Chamber.[39] However they do not distance themselves as far from party politics as the Speaker. They remain members of their parties and when the next general election comes they resume a full political role and fight under their party banner. In their constituences they retain membership of the local party, and play a political role, though perhaps in a lower-key. In the House they are not withdrawn, socially, like the Speaker, but make full use of the dining rooms, cafeterias and bars. They sometimes listen to debates in the House, although they do not normally sit on the Government or Opposition benches when doing so. Finally, while the Speaker is always dressed in his official uniform in public rooms within the precincts, the three Chairmen are less formally attired: they wear morning dress (for men) when in the Chair, but otherwise wear ordinary day attire.

Another important difference from the Speaker is their tenure and duration of office. They normally serve, once elected, for a full Parliament, and they may be continued in office by the House for another Parliament—but not necessarily so. If a Chairman ceases to hold that office, he may, unlike the Speaker, remain in the House of Commons; Mr Harry Gourlay, Deputy Chairman of Ways and Means from 1968–1970, continued to sit until 1987. If a Chairman wishes to relinquish his office in mid-Parliament, he does so by announcement to the House or by letter to the Speaker.

The Chairman of Ways and Means is made a Privy Councillor. When he eventually leaves the Commons he is sometimes given a peerage. The Chairman's salary is linked to that of a Minister of State, and the salaries of his Deputies are linked to those of junior Ministers. All of these are borne on the House of Commons Vote.

Staffing the House

Elected members need professional and administrative support. In the

---

[38] *e.g.* C.J. (1985–86) 140.

[39] For an example of criticism of a Chairman for expressing political views in the country, and of his explanation, see Mr. Harold Walker's personal statement in H.C.Deb., Vol. 56, col. 408 (March 14, 1988).

House of Commons a great variety of services are provided by the staff of six "House departments" whose ultimate purpose is to enable Members to perform their functions as effectively and conveniently as possible. Other services are provided by other bodies and by the staff employed by Members themselves.

The main responsibilities of those who serve the House as a whole are to advise on parliamentary procedure and practice, to provide administrative and professional services, and to provide objective, factual research and information for Members. Such functions require people with training, acquired specialist skills, experience and objectivity. Much of the help and advice given by staff is for the benefit of the Opposition and of back-benchers on either side. For these reasons, the House of Commons has for many years had a non-political, permanent, and professional staff system. Senior and middle-seniority staff are mostly appointed in their early twenties and normally serve a full career until retirement at about 65. This maximises experience and continuity. More junior clerical, secretarial and industrial staff are less likely to serve the House for a whole career, although some do so.

Individual appointments and promotions (with the exception of a few of the most senior posts) and postings are made by senior management and not by Members. Recruitment for the more senior grades is by public advertisement and interviews and, in some cases, after public competitive examinations. The more senior staff may not belong to or be active in any political party or express their opinions publicly on any politically sensitive issue.

Staff are organised into separate and operationally autonomous departments within the House of Commons service, where they acquire and develop specialised skills, knowledge, and experience. They may be employed in a variety of duties within these departments, so broadening their experience and giving some variety to their work, but the more senior staff do not normally move from one department to another.

The staff in the House of Commons service are not members of the civil service although their pay and conditions of service are linked to those of equivalent ranks in the civil service. They are servants of the House. Their overriding loyalty is to the House of Commons itself.

The House departments

The House departments which together form the House of Commons service are the Clerk's Department, the Serjeant at Arms Department, the Department of the Library, the Administration Department, the Department of the Official Report, and the Refreshment Department.

The Clerk's Department

The Clerk's Department is responsible for the procedural services of the House and is the oldest of the House departments. The Clerk of the House is the senior permanent officer of the House and the principal adviser to the House and to the Speaker on the privileges, procedures and practices of Parliament.[40] Under him various offices are concerned with the daily pro-

---

[40] For a short history of the evolution of the Clerk, and of his department, with a summary of his present responsibilities, see W. R. McKay, "*The Office of Clerk of the House,*" *The House Magazine* February 27, 1987; and see also W. R. McKay, *Clerks in the House of Commons 1363–1989: a biographical list* (House of Lords Record Office, 1989).

ceedings of the House and the administration of the business of the House itself and of its committees. The Clerk is also the Accounting Officer for the House, and so has overall responsibility for the expenditure of all the departments. And he presides over the Board of Management, which comprises the heads of all the departments. He is ranked for salary as equal to a Permanent Secretary in the civil service.

The first Clerk of the House (then called the Under Clerk of Parliaments) was appointed in 1363 and in 1640 the first Clerk Assistant was appointed. In this century the Clerk Assistant in post at the time has usually succeeded to the top post on the retirement of a Clerk, which makes the appointment of the Clerk Assistant particularly important. The Clerk is appointed by the Queen on the advice of the Prime Minister, who first consults the Speaker, who in his turn may consult the House of Commons Commission (see pages 160–162). The Clerk Assistant is appointed by the Queen on the advice of the Speaker (after a similar consultation process) from among the more senior officers of the Clerk's Department. The Clerk himself appoints the remaining staff in his department (using the procedures described on page 155), though he may discuss the more senior appointments with the Speaker. The Clerk and the Clerk Assistant are both appointed by the Crown for life. Although in practice today they retire at about the age of 65, this security of office ensures an important degree of independence for the Clerk and his department in relation to the executive. As servants of Parliament they can be fearless and objective in the advice they give, regardless of whether it is welcome or not to Ministers of the Crown.

The Clerk of the House, the Clerk Assistant, the Principal Clerk of the Table Office, with four other Principal Clerks comprise the Clerks at the Table, one of whom is always present when the House is sitting, and often two or three. They advise the Speaker, the Whips on either side, and Members generally on procedural aspects of the immediate business of the House, and record all the decisions of the House. When the House goes into a committee of the whole House, the Clerk leaves the Table and the Clerk Assistant is the principal adviser to the Chairman of Ways and Means and other chairmen. The Clerk Assistant is linked to the civil service grade of Deputy Secretary.

The Clerk's Department is organised into offices charged with specific functions. The first regular committee clerks were appointed as "clerks without doors" (i.e. outside the Chamber of the House itself) in 1696, and now comprise the Committee Office. Here, under the supervision of the Clerk of Committees (also linked to the Deputy Secretary grade), with two Clerks of Select Committees (who oversee groups of committee staff) and the Clerk of Financial Committees, are found the staff of numerous select committees (see Chapter 11). Such has been the growth of committee work that the Committee Office has increased from some half-dozen people in 1950 to over 80 full-time staff in 1988. It is bigger than all the other offices of the Department put together. Staff in the Committee Office are largely responsible for the administration of their committee's work, for organising programmes for inquiries, and for conducting the committee's correspondence. But they also become closely involved in the substance of their committee's investigations, for example by advising on the choice of witnesses or lines of questioning, and by drafting reports and other papers. Committee clerks also advise on the procedures and practices of Parliament as they affect their committees. We further describe the staffing of select committees in Chapter 11.

The Public Bill Office has responsibilities for public legislation at all stages—from advising on procedural points during drafting, through various prints of the bill (each of which is thoroughly checked) almost up to the preparation of the Act copy (this last stage being the responsibility of the Public Bill Office in the House of Lords). The Clerk of Public Bills has particular responsibility for the examination of Government bills before they are presented, and therefore he deals closely with the Government's Parliamentary Counsel on such matters as what may or may not require a money or Ways and Means resolution, or Queen's Consent or on whether particular provisions would make a bill hybrid, (see page 227). Five other clerks in this office—with assistance from other offices—serve standing committees and are responsible for preparing amendment papers and advising chairmen and other Members on the admissibility and selection of amendments. Much time is also given by this office to helping Members with private Members' bills.

The Private Bill Office fulfils equivalent functions regarding private bills. The Clerk of Private Bills is, together with his opposite number in the House of Lords, one of the Examiners of Petitions for Private Bills, whose job it is to satisfy themselves that the numerous private business standing orders have been complied with at various stages, and to report to the House.

The Table Office under its Principal Clerk provides immediate support for the Clerks at the Table and has particular responsibility for the preparation of the Order Paper and of notices of Questions and motions for future days. Much of the work of the clerks in the Table Office consists in vetting Questions and early day motions and advising Members on how to get them in order. The Editorial Supervisor of the Vote and his assistants, who come under the Principal Clerk, also supervise much of the printing for the House (done by H.M.S.O. at their special Parliamentary Press) of the working papers in the Vote bundle (see pages 167–168). Finally, the Table Office, being situated close to the Chamber behind the Speaker's Chair, is handy for Members seeking immediate procedural advice, although more complex inquiries will be referred to other offices.

The Clerk of the Journals and his team in the Journal Office are responsible for preparing and publishing the daily Votes and Proceedings and the sessional Journal of the House. Statistics of time spent on different items of business and other procedural records are also maintained. Because it is the office of procedural record, it has naturally become the office of procedural research and hence a source of procedural advice. The Journal Office is responsible for the initial drafting of business of the House motions and standing orders. It accumulates material for the periodic revisions of Erskine May's *Parliamentary Practice*. The clerk of any Procedure Committee is often provided from that office. Finally the Clerk of the Journals himself is clerk of the Committee of Privileges, and advises Members and helps prepare advice for the Speaker on privilege matters.

The Overseas Office was created in 1953, primarily to advise colonial legislatures on procedural matters and to draft their standing orders as they moved towards independence. Today it is mostly concerned with the House's relations with other parliaments all over the world (especially in the Commonwealth) and with international assemblies of which M.P.s are members, such as the Council of Europe, Western European Union and the North Atlantic Assembly; it also maintains some contact with the European Parliament, and the staff of the European Legislation Committee are in the

Overseas Office. Much of the work of the Principal Clerk of the Overseas Office, who also serves at the Table, is concerned with visits by members and staff of other parliaments seeking procedural advice or training, and arranging for visits to other parliaments to study their proceedings or to give advice. He maintains close relations with the Commonwealth Parliamentary Association and the Inter-Parliamentary Union.

The total establishment of the Clerk's Department in April 1988 was 150, comprising 61 professional clerks and 89 support and secretarial staff. The professional clerks circulate in the course of their careers through most of the offices of the department, which enables them to develop a broad understanding of the problems of Parliament and a mastery of all aspects of their craft of parliamentary procedure. Higher posts are filled by promotion within the department, and therefore new clerks should have the potential for promotion right to the top. Candidates must possess a good honours degree and must pass the same competitive examination, run by the Civil Service Commission, as is used for recruiting the higher grades of the civil service. Once appointed clerks learn the work from their seniors and by experience. Very few clerks leave the service early; most serve some 40 years or more before retiring at 65, usually as head of one of the offices, and occasionally as Clerk of the House.

The middle ranks in the Clerk's Department are filled by senior and higher executive officers (S.E.O.s and H.E.O.s) who are promoted from officer clerks, who provide administrative and support services in all the offices and to all committees.

The Department of the Serjeant at Arms

The Serjeant's Department is the next most senior department. The first Serjeant at Arms was appointed in 1415, and his original function was to enforce the orders of the House in the exercise of its penal jurisdiction. He soon became an established senior officer of the House, though appointed for life by the Sovereign. Under the House of Commons (Offices) Act of 1812, he was entitled House Keeper of the House of Commons, and in this capacity, under the directions of the Speaker, he has charge of all the House's committee rooms and other buildings. The Serjeant at Arms remains a Crown appointment and is linked to an Under Secretary in the civil service. Posts of Deputy, Assistant and two Deputy Assistant Serjeants at Arms were later created. Today the Deputy Serjeant at Arms is appointed by the Speaker; the other officers are appointed by the Serjeant. The Serjeant at Arms Department is a large one with a total establishment of 186 in April 1988, and with a wide range of responsibilities, falling broadly, into two categories.

First, the department is concerned with order and security, ceremonial, and communications. This involves enforcement of order in the Chamber and its galleries, and in the precincts of the House, and control of admission or access to them, particularly the admission of visitors to listen to debates. Numerous ceremonial duties survive, for example carrying the Mace in the daily Speaker's procession at the opening of the sitting. The Serjeant's responsibilities for communications involve liaison with the Post Office and other agencies over the functioning of telephone and telegraph services, division bells, and sound amplification systems.

The duties of the Serjeant's Department under the second category of house-keeping include the allocation and booking of accommodation;

cleaning; the supply of stationery, laundry, and other stores; and liaison with the Property Services Agency on building maintenance, repairs and redecorations, and the provision of furniture, heating, lighting and ventilation for the House of Commons building and seven outbuildings. Recent extensions of these functions include the supervision of a large underground car park, the provision of a first-aid service and supply and control of photocopying machines.

The Serjeant himself advises the Speaker directly on security matters and he and his deputies advise the Services Committee which, in its turn, advises the Speaker on accommodation policy (see pages 162–164).

The five Serjeants thus require a wide range of talents. For many years it has been the policy to appoint persons with administrative and managerial experience from outside the House of Commons rather than by promotion from within the service of the House. In modern times the Serjeants have been retired officers of the Navy, Royal Marines or Army (but not, as yet, the Royal Air Force—unlike the House of Lords where distinguished Royal Air Force officers have held the post of Gentleman Usher of the Black Rod).

The Department of the Library

The Library was not created as a separate department until 1967, but the first Librarian (linked to Under Secretary) was appointed in 1818, and an Assistant, now Deputy Librarian, was added shortly afterwards. For many years the Library's functions were primarily concerned with the creation and custody of a good parliamentary library, but in the last 30 years there has been a major growth in the demand by Members for information relevant to their parliamentary work, and the Library has responded by establishing and developing a research and information service designed to provide Members with quick factual answers to their enquiries. The total establishment of the Library in April 1988 was 155½.

The Library itself is now organised into two main divisions. The Parliamentary Division stocks some 130,000 books and pamphlets, including almost all types of books except modern fiction. It provides parliamentary and legislative references, documentation and information; it staffs the reference room, where are kept newspapers, periodicals, press releases and official circulars. It provides a special European and international documentation service. There is also a comprehensive, computer-based index to parliamentary Questions, debates in both Houses, and other current parliamentary information.

The Research Division staff undertake politically neutral research for individual Members and offer advice, derived from their specialist knowledge, published material, and information gained from Government departments and other authoritative sources. The division operates through five sections dealing respectively with economic affairs; education and social services; home and parliamentary affairs; science, environment and defence; and Members' statistical enquiries. In addition to replying to oral enquiries from Members and officers, the division supplied 7683 written answers to individual Members in 1987, and 87 to other bodies (in addition the International Affairs section in the Parliamentary Division answered 1278 enquiries). The Research Division also prepares background papers, reference sheets, and briefer research notes relating to current legislation and other matters of contemporary political interest for the use of Members generally; 78 such papers were issued in 1987 (and eight by the International Affairs section).

Other special services provided by the Library included access to various macro-economic models, a collection of videotapes of politically interesting T.V. programmes, a Public Information Office (which answers factual outside enquiries about the work and operations of the House and publishes a Weekly Information Bulletin and a Sessional Information Digest), on-line access to certain external data bases, and an educational service on the working of Parliament for schools and teachers.

The Vote Office, which is responsible for the provision and distribution of papers required by Members and staff of the House, is also part of the Department of the Library. The Deliverer of the Vote, as the head of the office is called—reflecting his ancient duties of delivering the Votes and Proceedings to Members' homes—holds an historical post, dating from 1731. He is appointed by the Speaker. Today the Vote Office is divided into three main sections. A parliamentary section provides free copies to Members and officers of all parliamentary papers and certain non-parliamentary publications relevant to the work of Members in the House. Members living within three miles of the House still receive the daily Vote bundle and copies of bills by hand delivery, free of charge. The European Communities Section provides, on request, documents published by the European Commission, the European Parliament and the Council of Ministers. The Sale Office sells documents to Members, and parliamentary and non-parliamentary papers to certain outside customers.[41]

The Librarian is assisted by a Deputy Librarian and both are appointed by the Speaker. There are also two Assistant Librarians. The number of staff in some of the more senior grades rose from eight in 1950 to 35 in 1988 (including those in the Vote Office). These are mostly graduates. Those working in the more specialist posts in the Research Division (the majority of the younger graduate staff) require subject knowledge and skills of a high order. Library clerks are therefore appointed after open, competitive interviews following advertisement. Because of subject specialisation, jobs are not changed frequently, but promotion brings opportunities to broaden experience and responsibility.

Support staff in the Library and Vote Office include library executives, of various ranks, many of whom possess professional library qualifications and degrees, a number of clerical staff and attendants and personal secretaries and typing staff.

The Department of the Official Report

The Official Report, or Hansard, was created as a separate department in 1978. William Cobbett had started the regular reporting of the House in 1807, but it was soon taken over by Luke Hansard. Reporting did not become an official service of the House, with staff paid out of the House of Commons Vote, till 1909. Today the department is responsible for reporting all speeches made in the House and in standing committees. Hansards, for both House (up until about 10.30 p.m.) and committees are normally published the following day.

Hansard staff possess rare skills. Few shorthand writers outside those working for Parliament can boast their speeds, and most of the reporting of

---

[41] For a list of regular customers, see H.C.Deb., Vol. 112, cols. 467–468 (March 2, 1987).

the House itself is undertaken in shorthand. Many of the debates in standing committees are, however, recorded on tape and the transcribers of these tapes work long hours at a difficult task. Such people must be properly trained when recruited (although further training is given by the department), and some previous working experience is often invaluable. Some of the more senior staff were previously journalists. For the skilled reporters promotion opportunities are open to the top. The Editor of the Official Report is head of the department, and he is assisted by a Deputy Editor and eight Assistant Editors of varying ranks. The Editor and Deputy Editor are appointed by the Speaker. In April 1988 the total Hansard establishment was 84.

The Administration Department

The Administration Department was created as a separate department in 1968. It comprises two offices. The Fees Office, under the Accountant, is responsible for the initial preparation of the House of Commons estimates; the payment of salaries, allowances, expenses and pensions of Members and staff; payment of the expenses of select committees; and preparation of the annual accounts.

The Establishments Office is of growing importance. The head of the office is the secretary to the Board of Management. It has had special responsibilities in relation to grading reviews. The office provides advice and assistance to other departments, as requested, on staff matters. It assists in appointment and promotion processes. It has various functions in respect of negotiations and consultations with trade unions representing most grades of staff.

The work of the department is supervised by the Head of the Administration Department (linked to Under Secretary). He, the Accountant and the Head of the Establishments Office, are appointed by the Speaker. As a member of the Board of Management, the Head of the Department has an overall responsibility for administrative services and, in particular, for the development of staff policy and, reporting to the Clerk of the House as Accounting Officer, for financial control throughout the House of Commons. The Computer Officer, who advises both Houses on the application of computers and word processors to the work of both Members and the departments, and his assistants also come under the Administration Department, as does an internal auditor, a staff inspector and a staff welfare officer (who also works for both Houses).

Because of the technical skills they possess, such as accountancy or personnel management, many of the more senior staff in the Administration Department originally worked in the civil service, in industry, or in commerce, and have only come to the House in mid-career. However, having come, few of them leave before normal retirement, and promotion opportunities exist up to the top posts of the department. The total establishment of the department in April 1988 was 92.

The Refreshment Department

The Refreshment Department is the most recent of the House departments, having only been created in 1980. Although no doubt the services it provides have been required since the Commons were first summoned to meet at Westminster in 1265, "in-house" refreshment services were only started in 1773 by John Bellamy, the Deputy House Keeper of the day. The General Manager is appointed by the Speaker. Under the scrutiny of Members—a sub-committee of the Services Committee—the department provides a wide range of catering services for Members, staff, the press and guests.

The skills of this department are not peculiar to Parliament, and the more senior staff are recruited from outside the House of Commons Service. In April 1988 the department's establishment was 238.

The total establishment of staff of all grades in the six House departments as at April 1, 1988 was 905½.

OTHER STAFF EMPLOYED AT WESTMINSTER

The House departments described above do not by any means comprise all those who serve the House of Commons and its Members. Although these other groups will not be described in detail, their existence and functions should be noted.

First, there is the Speaker's Office. The officers and staff of this office were listed on page 145. Like those in the House departments, they are all part of the House of Commons service, paid for on the Vote of the House, but unlike the former, the Speaker's staff are appointed by the Speaker personally and are not employed by the House of Commons Commission.

Other important services are the responsibility of various Government departments or other bodies. Such essential services as heating and lighting, the alteration, repair and maintenance of the fabric of the building, provision of furniture, and decoration are the responsibility of the Property Services Agency. The Post Office and British Telecom serve all those working at Westminster. The Official Shorthand-writer (a private firm which reports the proceedings of select or private bill committees in both Houses) and Thomas Cook, the travel agents, have offices there. The police who work in the Commons, though under the control of the Serjeant for security and operational purposes, are employed by the Metropolitan Police as are other custodians and firemen who keep an eye on the building day and night. A major service is provided by H.M.S.O., which does all the parliamentary printing (although not on the precincts) and provides many other supplies and equipment including photo-copiers and stationery. Lastly the Central Computer and Telecommunications Agency has provided, on repayment by the House, certain computer services and some office equipment such as word-processors for use in the House departments (but not for Members, who must buy their own). The total number working for these various bodies in the Palace of Westminster or its precincts (many of these staff serve both Houses) in 1988 was some 900.

In contrast to the situation in some other parliaments, the House of Commons does not provide secretarial services for individual members, and the only official research services available are those in the Library. The arrangements regarding Members' personal research and secretarial staff were described in Chapter 2, and party offices in Chapter 4.

Other bodies housed in the Palace and working closely with or for Members of both Houses include the press and broadcasters working in the Press Gallery or the Lobby (see pages 78–79), the U.K. Branch of the Commonwealth Parliamentary Association, and the British Group of the Inter-Parliamentary Union. They receive many parliamentarians from overseas, and send many parliamentary delegations to other countries.

THE ADMINISTRATION OF THE HOUSE OF COMMONS

For many years the administration of the House of Commons was largely in the hands of the senior officers of the House, principally the Clerk, the Serjeant and the Librarian, although their freedom of action was severely limited by the fact that all expenditure was subject to Treasury control. The departments of the House were largely autonomous, with little co-ordination and only limited co-operation between them. In 1978 some fundamental changes were made. In 1975 a committee appointed by the Speaker and chaired by Mr Arthur Bottomley (now Lord Bottomley) had reviewed the administration of the House. It emphasised the need for more closely co-ordinated services, and, rejecting proposals for a single department, recommended a federal structure, under the ultimate control and authority of a body of senior Members.[42] This was implemented by the House of Commons (Administration) Act 1978.

The House of Commons Commission

The 1978 Act created the House of Commons Commission, consisting of the Speaker (in the chair) the Leader of the House, a Member nominated by the Leader of the Opposition, and three back-benchers appointed by order of the House (in practice one comes from the Government side, one from the official Opposition and one from one of the smaller parties). The Commission makes an annual report to the House.

The Commission is the employer of all staff in the House departments (except that it has no power to appoint the Clerk of the House or the Clerk Assistant or the Serjeant at Arms, who are appointed by the Crown). It has a statutory duty to ensure that the complementing, grading and pay of staff in the House departments, and, so far as is consistent with the requirements of the House, their other conditions of service, are kept broadly in line with those in the Home Civil Service; pension arrangements are similarly linked. Thus the Act created, for the first time, a unified House of Commons Service, with a single employer.

Section 3 of the Act contains a constitutional innovation of some importance. Before 1978 all the estimates for the public service had been presented to the House by Ministers after scrutiny and approval by the Treasury. These included the House of Commons estimates covering pay, allowances etc of both Members and staff and other expenses of running the House. Under the 1978 Act, the Commission is required to prepare and lay before the House estimates incurred from the service of the House.[43] Although the Leader of the House clearly has a major say, on behalf of the Government, when the Commission is considering the House's estimates, especially for major new services (and on such matters the Commission would not approve additional spending without a resolution of the House), the Treasury have no formal control over this aspect of the House's expenditure. Nor is this expenditure subject to cash limits. This is a far cry from the days when Treasury approval had to be secured for the appointment of an extra part-time cleaner. This control by the House of its own administrative expenditure has proved important in respect of the staffing and operational expenses of select committees, including overseas travel, and the develop-

---

[42] Report of Committee on House of Commons (Administration) H.C. 624 of 1974–1975.
[43] Similar provision is now made for the Public Accounts Commission to prepare and present the estimates of the National Audit Office (section 4(2) and (3) of the National Audit Act 1983).

ment of research services in the Library. In these matters the elected House of the legislature can boast a precious degree of independence.

The House's administration expenditure is borne on Class XX, A, Vote 1, of the Estimates. Under section 3(1) of the House of Commons (Administration) Act the Commission has appointed the Clerk of the House to be the Accounting Officer for the House's expenditure. He oversees the preparation of the estimates for all the House departments for submission to the Commission, and is accountable to it, and ultimately to the House, for ensuring that all expenditure is contained within these estimates as approved in the House of Commons Vote.

The powers given to the Commission to present estimates do not extend to Member's pay, allowances, or pensions, or to expenditures in support of Opposition parties (see pages 117–118). These estimates are still subject to Treasury control, although the rates of Member's pay and allowances are determined by the House itself (see pages 76–77).

Section 4 of the House of Commons (Administration) Act defines the House departments and gives the Commission power to allocate functions between them and to create, divide, amalgamate or abolish any House department. One of the first acts of the Commission was to re-organise the House departments that existed in 1978 and to create the six House departments described above.

The 1978 Act gave the House of Commons Commission wide powers. In practice, it has delegated many of its functions in respect of staff. In particular it has delegated to each of the Heads of Departments the power to remit, appoint and promote staff in each of their departments and to allocate their duties. Consequently, the Commission (or indeed any other Member) has no say in the appointment or career management of individual members of the staff, apart from the most senior appointments. This protects the political neutrality and independence of the staff of the House.

The Commission has also delegated to the Heads of Departments jointly certain responsibilities for management within the House of Commons by the creation of a Board of Management, consisting of all the Heads of Departments under the chairmanship of the Clerk of the House. Through the Clerk, who attends meetings of the Commission for this purpose, the Board advises the Commission or the Speaker on all matters affecting more than one department and is responsible for implementing the decisions of the House, the Commission, or the Speaker in such matters.

In particular, the Board has responsibility for developing, subject to policy decisions by the Commission, more unified staffing arrangements. It has been concerned, for example, in such matters as grading reviews for the whole House of Commons Service, and relations with trade unions. An Administration Committee, consisting of Deputy Heads of Departments, under the chairmanship of the Head of the Administration Department, advises the Board on such matters, particularly on detailed establishment questions. The Commission also has the advice of the staff inspector, who works in the Administration Department.

The Commission has delegated detailed financial control in other areas. A major item on the House Vote is for overseas travel by select committees. The estimate for this purpose in financial year 1988–89 was £360,000. In practice allocation of this money could not easily be undertaken by the Commission, nor could control of such expenditure by committees be properly delegated to an officer of the House, such as the Accounting Officer;

only Members themselves can judge what is and is not justified in this field. It has been agreed therefore that, within the overall total approved by the Commission, the detailed allocation of money for overseas travel by committees should be delegated to the Liaison Committee, comprising the chairmen of nearly all select committees (see pages 434–435).[44] Similar delegations have been made for expenditure by members of select committees, and by members of international assemblies, such as the Council of Europe, attending international conferences.

Other matters have directly concerned the Commission. It has overseen and finally approved a grading review of all the staff of the House, as recommended by the Board of Management. It has approved a new telephone exchange and associated equipment for the Palace of Westminster (a share of the costs being borne on the House of Commons Vote). It has sought to reach agreements with the various trade unions representing staff in the House departments on recognition of unions and on procedures for settlement of disputes. It has approved new proposals for the internal mail delivery system and for the delivery of Hansard to Members. It has approved the use of surpluses on the Refreshment Department's trading fund for certain capital works in that department. And it has considered the arrangements with H.M.S.O. for payment for their services; the Commission was not prepared to accept a repayment system, so printing and stationery continue to be borne, as an "allied service," on the Vote of H.M.S.O. and not that of the House of Commons.[45]

The duty of the Commission to control the expenditure of the House has involved it in many detailed matters and it now meets up to eight times a year. The arrangements for these meetings are made by the Secretary to the Commission, who is a senior officer of the Clerk's Department. Others attending the Commission's meetings are the Clerk of the House, as Chairman of the Board of Management, any individual head of department directly involved in an item on the agenda, and the Speaker's Secretary.

The Services Committee

While the Board of Management co-ordinates and provides advice on matters affecting the House departments and their staff, the advice of Members on the services and facilities provided for themselves comes from the House of Commons (Services) Committee. (See also page 446.)

The Services Committee, as it is commonly called, is appointed under Standing Order No. 125, and consists of 20 Members under the chairmanship of the Leader of the House; as with all committees, the party-membership is proportionate to that of the House. The quorum is five. The Deputy Chief Whips of the Government and Opposition are usually members of the committee. Its terms of reference are "to advise the Speaker on the control of the accommodation and services in that part of the Palace of Westminster and its precincts occupied by or on behalf of the House of Commons, and to report thereon to the House." Most of the work of the committee is done by its Accommodation and Administration, Catering, Computer, Library and New Building Sub-Committees.

The committee is advisory and mainly concerned with representing back-

---

[44] For details of how this money has been allocated see the periodic Minutes of Proceedings of the Liaison Committee, (e.g. H.C. 396 of 1987–88).
[45] See Annual Reports of the House of Commons Commission.

bench opinion or looking at ways of improving the working conditions of back-benchers. It takes up problems of accommodation or facilities referred to it by Members, or sometimes by officers of the House (especially the Serjeant at Arms and the Librarian) on behalf of Members, or by the Leader of the House or the Whips from either side. The various sub-committees examine these matters, working closely with the relevant officers of the House. Architectural advisers have also been appointed. The sub-committees also take formal evidence, written or oral. They then make recommendations to the full committee in the form of either a report or a resolution, which the committee usually agrees to.

Controversial proposals, or matters of wider interest or greater complexity, or matters on which formal evidence has been taken, are usually dealt with in a report to the House. More straight forward proposals will be embodied in resolutions. All resolutions of the committee are reported to the Speaker and to the House in the published minutes of proceedings. Reports are made direct to the House and are published. In session 1985–86, the committee made three reports[46] (on additional accommodation for the House, on cancer screening and on proposals for a Hansard Year Book) and agreed to 32 substantive resolutions or orders. They ranged from approval of a parliamentary book shop in the new building to the choice of the House of Commons Christmas card.

Some reports are for information only, involve no decision, and are unlikely to be debated. Others include recommendations which the authorities concerned can comply with (in many cases the Property Services Agency (P.S.A.) on accommodation and re-building matters) and again no debate is needed. But other reports, especially those involving significant policy decisions or expenditure on the House of Commons or P.S.A. Votes will be debated so that the House itself can decide the matter. For example, on November 22, 1983, the House debated and agreed with the report of the committee on Phase 1 of the new parliamentary building.[47]

Recommendations and resolutions involving expenditure on the House of Commons Administration Vote must be commented on by the Accounting Officer before they are considered by the Services Committee. They must also be submitted by the Speaker to the House of Commons Commission for its approval. Thus the Commission receives advice from three main sources before reaching decisions: from the Services Committee on new or improved services requested by Members, from the House departments on the problems and practical aspects of providing them and from the Accounting Officer on their cost. Co-ordination of this advice and decision-taking is achieved at three levels: the Speaker chairs the Commission and is advised by the Services Committee; the Leader of the House, representing the Government's point of view, chairs the Services Committee and is a member of the Commission; and the offices of Secretary to the Commission and Clerk of the Services Committee are held by the same person, namely a Deputy Principal Clerk in the Clerk's Department who keeps the Clerk of the House, as Accounting Officer and Chairman of the Board of Management, regularly informed of all proposals and decisions.

Many matters are referred directly to the Speaker himself, who has an historical, but non-statutory, responsibility for accommodation, services

---

[46] H.C. 144, 266 and 570 of 1985–86.
[47] Third Report of the Committee, H.C. 269 of 1982–83; H.C.Deb., Vol. 49, cols. 261–292.

and facilities, protocol and security questions. He approves the great majority of these (perhaps after consultation with the Leader of the House, the
Whips or officers of the House) on his own authority. Only rarely does he
not agree to a resolution from the Services Committee.[48]

Finally, on the most routine or uncontroversial matters, the sub-committees do, in effect, take decisions which are simply reported to the Speaker
and the main committee. These include choice of materials for curtains or
wallpaper, purchase of periodicals in the Library or changes in the menu in
the dining room. The Catering Sub-Committee still performs many of the
quasi-executive functions that its predecessor, the Select Committee on
Kitchen and Refreshment Rooms, used to exercise.

OVERALL STAFFING AND EXPENDITURE

The growing importance of the procedural, administrative, research and
other services of the House is shown by the growth of staff and the volume of
expenditure required for the work of the House. The following Table shows
the establishment (full-time equivalent) of the Speaker's Office and each
House Department at April 1 in 1979 and 1988, with the percentage increase
over that period.

Departmental Establishments

	1979	1988	Percentage Increase
Speaker's Office	10	11½	15
Department of the Clerk of the House	119	150	26
Department of the Serjeant at Arms	181	186	3
Department of the Library	118	155½	32
Administration Department	60	92	53
Department of the Official Report	70	84	20
Refreshment Department	*234	238	1
Totals	782	917	17

* This figure is as at April 1, 1980, since the Refreshment Department was
not previously a Department of the House.

The increase in the Clerk's Department is almost entirely attributable to
the growth of select committee work. The growth of the Library reflects the
enlargement of research services for Members' to match increasing requests
for information from Members' research assistants and from the public. The
additional staff in the Administration Department has largely been required
for processing and advising on Members allowances (which have grown in
number and complexity) and those of their staff (also rapidly expanding).
Membership of the House is becoming more active, more full-time and more
sophisticated. But it all costs money.

[48] In December 1981, Speaker Thomas did not approve the placing of a memorial plaque in
the Chamber for Rev. Robert Bradford M.P., who was murdered in Northern Ireland. A
similar plaque had earlier been approved in memory of Mr. Airey Neave, M.P., who was
murdered in the precincts of the House.

Class XX, A, Vote 1 (House of Commons: Administration) showed the estimated expenditure in the 1988–89 financial year on running the House—

Expenditure on House of Commons Administration

	1988–89 £'000
Office of the Speaker	423
Department of the Clerk of the House	4,613
Department of the Serjeant at Arms	2,514
Department of the Library	2,842
Administration Department	1,661
Department of the Official Report	1,972
Refreshment Department	2,592
Retired Allowances, etc.	1,766
Police	3,842
Common Services (Postage, telecommunications, etc.)	2,780
Computer Services	1,706
Gross Total	26,711
Deduct: Appropriations in aid	248
Net Total	26,463

Other allied services in support of this vote were—

	£,000
Stationery and Printing	12,200
Rates on Government Property	900
Total	13,100

Other expenses are borne on Class XX, Vote 21 (Parliament and Privy Council: House of Commons) of the Estimates. These include Members' pay, expenses and allowances, pension contributions, and financial assistance to Opposition parties. The estimate for 1988–89 was as follows—

		£'000
Salaries, etc., of 650 Members of Parliament		15,800
Members' expenses:		
(a) Travelling expenses	5,467	
(b) Payment for office expenses	14,601	
(c) Payments for the additional cost of staying overnight away from main residence	5,174	
(d) Pension provision for Members' secretaries and research assistants	876	
(e) Secretarial redundancy payments	30	
(f) Miscellaneous	18	
		26,166
Contributions to the Members' Pension Fund		3,065
Financial assistance to Opposition parties		685
Contribution to the Members' Fund which makes grants and payments to ex-Members and dependants		115
Total		45,831

It is noticeable that Members expenses now considerably exceed Members' salaries.

The net total cost of the House of Commons in 1988–89 was therefore estimated to be—

House of Commons: Administration	£26,463,000
Allied service costs	£13,100,000
Parliament and Privy Council: House of Commons	£45,831,000
Total	£85,394,000

To arrive at the total cost of Parliament we must add the estimated net cost of the House of Lords in the same year—

Parliament and Privy Council: House of Lords	£13,234,000
Allied service costs	£4,320,000
Total	£17,554,000

and the estimated cost of Property Services Agency works services for both Houses (Class XX, Vote 19), which was £19,567,000.

Thus the grand total of the annual cost of Parliament in 1988–89 was estimated to be £122,515,000. This is roughly the same as the estimated expenditure on driver and vehicle licensing; administration of housing benefits; or the Manpower Services Commission in Wales. It is only slightly more than expenditure on the Secret Services (£113 million). It is only one-tenth of expenditure on overseas aid. The country gets its Parliament fairly cheaply.

WORKING PAPERS OF THE HOUSE OF COMMONS

The reliable provision of printed papers is essential for the efficient functioning of Parliament. Very few items of business are sprung on the House without warning which means that notice previously given has to be printed, published and available for Members and other users. All decisions, acts and debates of the House must be precisely and speedily recorded, and maintained in a readily accessible form. Documents relevant to any matter to be debated in the House must always be readily available for those wishing to participate in the debates. These characteristic requirements are fulfilled by the working papers of the House.

Future business of the House is announced each Thursday after Questions by the Leader of the House, either as a business statement or in response to a private notice Question by the Leader of the Opposition or the shadow Leader of the House. The statement covers the whole of the following week and the Monday of the week after that. It deals only with the business of the House and of committees of the whole House, and with the main business of the Government and Opposition and other important debates, but not Question time, or minor or unopposed business, or technical procedural motions, or less time-consuming private Members business (*e.g.* motions for leave to bring in bills or the daily half-hour adjournment debates). And it obviously excludes unforeseen business such as private notice Questions and in particular, all Government statements. The statement is circulated to all concerned in typescript and is, of course, published in Hansard.

The daily working papers comprise the "Vote" which is prepared by the relevant offices in the Clerk's Department, published by H.M.S.O., and delivered by hand to all Members living within a three-mile radius of the House and otherwise made available in the Vote Office. The Vote (or Vote bundle as it is sometimes called) includes papers relating to the proceedings of the previous day, and the business for the day (printed on white paper), and notices of motions, Questions, etc., for future days (printed on blue paper). The contents of the Vote are as follows.

The Votes and Proceedings are the daily record of the formal decisions, transactions, and other business of the House; they also include some things deemed to be done in the House, which nowadays are done by a formal "book entry" without any actual proceedings in the Chamber itself, such as reports from committees, the laying of papers by Ministers and presentation of some public petitions. They do not however, record certain things which do happen in the House, but which do not involve any decision or formal action, such as Questions or statements by Ministers. The Votes and Proceedings are compiled in the Journal Office, mainly from the minutes kept by the Clerks at the Table. They are published under the authority of the Speaker, and unlike the minutes of many bodies, they are not subject to the approval of the House at its next sitting.[49]

The Division Lists show the names of those voting in every division and the matter on which they were voting. The Proceedings of Standing Committees is a simplified record of the business done in each standing committee on a bill in the form of an annotated amendment paper indicating what

---

[49] For a motion to expunge an entry, see H.C.Deb., Vol. 634, cols 938–1020 (February 13, 1961); it was negatived. For a complaint regarding a division following which the Speaker ordered the figures to be corrected, see H.C.Deb., Vol. 80, col. 845 (June 11, 1985); *ibid.* col. 892 (June 12, 1985).

decision, if any, was taken on each amendment. A full minute of all such committees is published after the bill or other matter has been reported.

Turning to the current day, the Order Paper sets out all the business to be taken in the House that day; it is the House's daily agenda. The normal order of business is described in pages 192–203, and the Order Paper follows this so far as notice has been given. The main items include Questions for oral answer; business at the commencement of public business; the orders of the day or notices of motions which are the main business of the House that day; a list of committees meeting that day, showing time and place; and Questions for written answer in Hansard. At the end, and clearly distinct, there are numerous "Remaining Orders," which are items of business (nearly all governmental) which are technically down for that day but which will not be actually taken. They are deferred daily until the Government are ready to transfer them to the effective orders for the House to consider. The remaining orders offer a handy indication of pending Government business. Any private business to be taken and notices, etc., relating to private bills are separately listed on the Private Business sheets.

The business for each standing committee sitting that day—mainly lists of amendments to bills marshalled in the correct order—are published in the Supplement to the Vote. This also includes marshalled lists of amendments to bills before committees of the whole House or to be considered on report.

Turning to future business, a major section of the Vote bundle is the Notice Paper which lists notices of Questions and motions given the previous day for various future days, and notices of motions for which no day is fixed, called early day motions (EDMs). The Notice Paper published each Saturday contains all outstanding orders, motions and Questions for future days, and a list of all EDMs tabled that session. A white Order Book is also published each day giving all business set down for future days.

Finally, published also as a Supplement to the Vote, there are numerous Notices of Amendments given on the previous day to bills in committee or awaiting their report stage; marshalled lists of all amendments of which notice has been given are also often published before a committee stage begins.

A very different publication is the sessional Journal of the House of Commons. This is prepared from the Votes and Proceedings and is published, with a procedural and subject index, as the permanent official record of the House's proceedings and of all things formally done or deemed to be done in the House in that session. The Journals of the House have been maintained since 1547. Under section 3 of the Evidence Act 1945, a printed copy of the Journal is accepted as evidence in a court of law. A General Index to the Journals is published every 10 years. The Journals and their indexes are invaluable records for those conducting procedural research.

The Official Report of Debates (or Hansard as it is commonly called) is the full report of speeches, Questions and answers, statements and all things said in the House itself; separate papers report debates in standing committees. It also includes written answers to Questions (including those tabled for oral answer but not reached) and certain other matters going beyond what was actually said in the House, such as occasional detailed supplementary information relating to answers to Questions. But Members are not allowed to insert undelivered speeches into Hansard. Other information published in Hansard includes the lists of all Members voting in divisions, essential procedural information on the business transacted, and (at the beginning of each volume) a list of Government ministers and of the principal officers and staff of the House.

Hansard provides a full report of debates, being defined as one "which, though not strictly verbatim, is substantially the verbatim report, with repetitions and redundancies omitted and with obvious mistakes corrected, but which on the other hand leaves out nothing that adds to the meaning of the speech or illustrates the argument."[50] Members cannot change the substance of what they have said but may correct the record of their speeches before publication. If the Editor's interpretation of the rules is challenged, the matter is decided by the Speaker. The House of Commons Hansard is published daily by H.M.S.O. There are also weekly volumes, bound volumes with indexes, and a sessional index.

An essential working document is a bill. Bills are published after presentation and again from time to time as amended. Any amendments to Commons bills made by the Lords are similarly printed for consideration by the Commons. Each print and reprint of the bill is given a number in a sessional series. We describe the structure of bills on page 228.

When a bill receives the Royal Assent, it is published as an Act. Acts are numbered as chapters of the annual statute book.

Other parliamentary papers are reports from select committees with associated minutes of evidence and memoranda. When evidence is taken in public, each day's evidence is usually printed separately as a "daily part" but is reprinted in a bound volume with the final report to which it relates. Reports and evidence are printed by order of the House and are numbered in the House of Commons papers series (*e.g.* H.C. 222) for each session.

Other documents published by or for the use of the House include the Public and Private Business Standing Orders, a Manual of Procedure, an Alphabetical List of Members, the Weekly Information Bulletin, the Sessional Information Digest, such essential working papers as wall-sheets showing membership of committees or allocation of bills and other business to standing committees, and the menus in the dining rooms.

Other papers, which are also relevant to the business of the House, may be presented to Parliament by outside bodies. These fall into three categories.

First there are papers presented, nominally, by command of the Queen, and known as Command papers. These are mainly documents which Ministers wish to publish or to present to Parliament but which are not required by statute. They cover major policy statements (for example the annual Defence White Paper, or the Financial Statement that accompanies the Budget, or new policy proposals), treaties, annual reports of various departments and bodies, reports of Royal Commissions or departmental committees, and accounts of certain bodies. They are given a continuing serial number; the Cmnd. series finished with Cmnd. 9846, and a new series, Cm., started in 1986. There are, on average, 330 printed Command papers presented each year (a number of them on detailed matters, such as statements of Treasury guarantees of nationalised industries' borrowing, are not printed).

Papers are often laid before the House pursuant to statutory requirements. Many of these are statutory instruments which is the main form by

---

[50] Definition used by the Select Committee on Parliamentary Debates (H.C. 239 of 1907).

which delegated legislation is now exercised under the Statutory Instruments Act 1946. Every Order in Council is a statutory instrument and so is every other instrument (order, regulation, etc.) made by a Minister if the parent Act so provides. Over the five years 1981–1985, an average of 1,924 statutory instruments were laid before Parliament each year, filling 5,987 pages, in six to seven volumes. Other papers laid in this way are called "Act papers" and include a wide range of documents which Ministers and other statutory bodies are required by Act to lay before Parliament, such as annual reports and accounts, numerous statistics on various areas of Government and the economy, audit reports by the Comptroller and Auditor General, Church of England measures, and statements of salaries of members of boards of nationalised industries. Most Act papers are printed and published, but a few are not printed though available for Members to see in the Library of the House.

The third category of papers laid before the House, usually by Ministers, occasionally by officers of the House, and sometimes by other bodies, are returns. These are specifically ordered by the House and frequently relate to statistics, including details of the business of the House in the previous session. Occasionally a report of an inquiry which contains possibly defamatory material may be ordered as a return so that it may, being printed by order of the House, benefit from the protection of the Parliamentary Papers Act 1840 (see page 90).[51] Command papers do not have this protection. Most returns (but, until the consolidated returns for 1987–88, not all House sessional returns) are published as House of Commons papers.

The power to order a return is ancient and of historical importance. Although less used by the House itself today than it was up until the middle of the last century, it is regularly activated in the powers given to select committees to send for persons, papers and records (see pages 448–449).

Command Papers may be presented to the House (under Standing Order No.137) and statutory instruments (but not drafts) may be laid (under Standing Order No. 138) by being delivered to the Votes and Proceedings Office (part of the Journal Office) on any day during the existence of a Parliament, though by practice this is not done on Saturdays, Sundays, and Bank Holidays. Draft statutory instruments and other Act papers, returns, etc., can only be laid on sitting days, until the rising of the House. Copies are also placed in the Library. Papers presented or laid may also be withdrawn. Nowadays nothing actually happens in the House when a paper is presented, laid or withdrawn, but the fact is recorded in the Votes and Proceedings and the Journal.

All papers presented or laid before the House or printed for the use of the House are made available for Members, lobby correspondents and other regular parliamentary users in the Vote Office and are sold to the public by H.M.S.O. Parliamentary papers must be made available to Members before being sent to Government departments or sold to the public outside, although advanced copies of Command papers may be given to the press provided the information is not published before it is available to Members.

---

[51] See, e.g. the Hennessy Report on the escape of prisoners from the Maze Prison (H.C. 203 of 1983–84); Report of the Investigation into the cause of the 1978 Birmingham smallpox occurrence (H.C. 668 of 1979–80); two reports of inquiries relating to the Crown Agents and a Government statement thereon (H.C. 48, 49 and 50 of 1977–78); and the report of an inquiry into security and HM Prison, Leicester (H.C. 202 of 1976–77).

There are no formal rules to this effect, and it has not been held to be a breach of privilege to release information to the public before it is announced in the House. Such prior release has, however, frequently been strongly deprecated by Speakers.[52] The Speaker has suggested that summaries of some Command papers, as issued by Ministers to the press could also be put in the Vote Office for the use of Members.[52a]

One other record of the House's business should also be mentioned. Tape recordings of debates and other proceedings of both Houses, and of some committees, which have been made for sound broadcasting have been retained in the Sound Archives Unit of the House of Lords Record Office, which also holds film material relating to either House and tapes of radio programmes containing parliamentary material. Members of both Houses have unrestricted access to the archives, and the unit can supply tape cassettes of recorded proceedings to the public for a fee. There are, however, restrictions on the use that may be made of recordings (see page 82).[53] The Sound Broadcasting Committee has also prohibited their use for party political broadcasts or at election meetings. Their primary value is educational and documentary. In future, the great occasions and speeches in Parliament will be available for all to hear.

Finally, we must not neglect one essential working paper, namely Erskine May's Parliamentary Practice,[54] or "Treatise on the Law, Privilege, Proceedings and Usage of Parliament" to give it its full title. This is not, as is sometimes suggested, a work which attempts to say what must be done in Parliament. It is rather a compilation, edited for some 140 years by the Clerks of the House of Commons, of what parliamentary procedure has become, based on ancient practice and on what the Houses themselves have decided should be done in the conduct of parliamentary business. It gives numerous references to Speaker's rulings in the Commons and to precedents in both Houses for the interpretation and application of these practices and rules. It is descriptive of procedure; not prescriptive. It is not essential for the daily use of the ordinary politician; it is essential for those who must advise him on his opportunities and methods of proceeding—especially the clerks and other officers of the two Houses. It is studied with gratitude by those (including the present authors) who seek, in other publications, to describe the House as a working institution. It is to the procedures of the House that we now turn.

---

[52] See, *e.g.* H.C.Deb., Vol. 203, col. 1240, (March 9, 1927); H.C.Deb., Vol. 91, col. 791 (February 11, 1986); H.C.Deb., Vol. 145, col. 173 (January 17, 1989); and H.C.Deb., Vol. 385, cols. 1574–1578 (December 9, 1942).
[52a] H.C.Deb., Vol. 140, col. 45 (November 7, 1988).
[53] Resolution of the House, see H.C.Deb., Vol. 936, col. 539 (July 26, 1977).
[54] Published by Butterworths; 20th ed. 1983. The next edition is expected to be published in 1989.

CHAPTER 6

THE PROCESSES OF THE HOUSE OF COMMONS

PROCEDURES FOR THE CONDUCT OF BUSINESS

The Nature of Parliamentary Procedure

All institutions need clearly recognised processes for the transaction of their business. For a political assembly, embodying conflicting elements, combatting parties and competing individuals as does the House of Commons, agreed procedures (to use the parliamentary term) are essential for the orderly conduct of proceedings. In the case of the British Parliament, being the sovereign legislature of a country that has no comprehensive written constitution by which to protect and safeguard the right and interests of the citizen, the acceptance and application of clear procedures is all the more important for, if business is not conducted in the correct way, there is no appeal to any outside court against the decisions of that parliament. As it has been put in respect of legislation, you cannot look behind the Royal Assent (and see page 88).

Thus good procedures and their consistent and correct application are essential for the protection of citizens against improper adoption of laws that affect them. As has been said, in the absence of a written constitution the rights of the subject are to be found in the interstices of parliamentary procedure. Or, to quote an older authority, Hatsell:

> "as it is always in the power of the majority, by their numbers, to stop any improper measures proposed by their opponents, the only weapons by which the minority can defend themselves against similar attempts by those in power are the forms and rules of proceedings, which . . . become the standing orders of the House; by a strict adherence to which the weaker party can also be protected from those irregularities and abuses which these forms were intended to check, and which the wantonness of power is but too often apt to suggest to large and successful majorities."[1]

Procedures of some sort are therefore essential, but they are not sacrosanct. Procedures are servants, not masters. Procedures, once adopted, must be followed, but if they do not work well, or produce results unacceptable to those whose operations are conditioned by them, they can and should be changed. Speaker Denison in the nineteenth century recalled that "old Mr. Ley" (Clerk of the House of Commons from 1820 to 1850) used to say "what does it signify about precedents? The House can do what it likes. Who can stop it."[2] The House remains the master of its own procedures.

It is however the House which is the master and the House which can do what it likes, not individual Members, not majority or minority groups and not the Speaker or its other officers. Unless and until the House, collectively and formally, changes its procedures, those procedures currently in force are binding on all its Members and officers.

---

[1] Hatsell, *Precedents of Proceedings in the House of Commons*, 1818 Edition Vol. II, p. 237.
[2] Quoted by Sir Barnett Cocks, Clerk of the House, in his Preface to the 18th Edition of Erskine May's *Parliamentary Practice*.

It is this binding quality which provides the first essential characteristic of good parliamentary procedures. They should have mandatory effect on those persons or parties to which they apply, and they should be applied consistently on all occasions to which they relate. They should therefore be certain and not arbitrary. Those affected by them should know the procedural consequences of pursuing any given course of parliamentary action. For these reasons—and despite Mr. Ley—where procedures are based on precedent rather than a written rule, those precedents should be followed consistently by those entrusted with the enforcement of those procedures (unless, of course, following Mr. Ley, the House deliberately decides otherwise). For these reasons Speakers and other occupants of the chair do not lightly "pick and choose" among the precedents, following one on one occasion and another at some other time (though, occasionally, bad precedents— normally decisions which did not accord with earlier decisions—are quietly forgotten or laid aside.[3]) They seek to maintain a consistent pattern of decisions that follow previous practices.

The advantages and desirability of this certainty and consistency are generally recognised. As Mr. Enoch Powell put it when arguing against a certain procedural change, "Any unnecessary alteration of our procedure and rules must tend to weaken the forces of habitual convention and behaviour upon which the success of our proceedings depends."[4] However it is increasingly true that governments have used their majorities to set aside for particular occasions the standard rules and practices of the House when this seems to them to be necessary. There are numerous examples, such as restricting the time for debate on particular motions, providing that certain matters be decided without debate, or guillotining the debate on bills. A particularly dramatic exercise of such power was the decision to dispense with the standing orders applying to the proceedings on the Aircraft and Shipbuilding Industries Bill in 1976 which appeared to be hybrid; if the orders had been applied, this would have delayed the Bill's passage.[5]

On the whole, despite their varied nature and the varied authority on which they are based (see pages 175–180 below) the practices and procedures of the House of Commons do have binding effect, are respected as such, and are applied consistently, so that their import is usually clear.

This leads to the second characteristic of good procedures, that business conducted according to the rules should be predictable and that no business should be sprung on the House without adequate notice. As will be seen, this is strongly entrenched in the procedures of the House of Commons. Historically these features were rooted in a desire to avoid decisions being taken hastily, without opportunity for proper consideration and reconsideration and with the participation of all interested Members. In earlier times, this was achieved by the multiplication of questions[6] to be decided by the House. As late as 1848 for example, 18 separate questions (excluding amendments) had to be proposed before a Bill was passed,[7] and until relatively recently financial business was first discussed in committees of the whole House after

---

[3] The House has occasionally ordered that certain proceedings "should not be drawn into a precedent."

[4] H.C.Deb., Vol. 525, col. 2185 (March 31, 1954).

[5] H.C.Deb., Vol. 912, cols. 632–766 (May 27, 1976).

[6] For the meaning of this procedural term see pp. 177 and 203.

[7] Kenneth Mackenzie, *The English Parliament*, (1968) p. 134.

which there could be another debate in the House itself on motions to agree with the resolutions passed in committee.

Today the procedures have been greatly simplified and the multiplicity of questions reduced, although there are still three readings, plus a committee and report stage, for the passage of bills. The development of speedy printing has meant that advance notice can be given to all Members of the business to be considered each day.[8]

Predictability of business is ensured in a number of ways. First, the days on which the House sits, and the time when sittings begin are enshrined in standing orders, and cannot be altered without the decision of the House on a motion of which notice must be given. To a lesser extent, the time of rising is also predictable; although business is often exempted from the rules and may sometimes continue to any hour.

Second, all important business is announced in advance. The form of the weekly business statement, which mainly deals with Government and Opposition business, was described in Chapter 5, page 167. In the case of private Members' bills and motions, these are usually put down for days well ahead of the time when notice is given, so again there is ample advance warning. The topics for the daily adjournment debates for the following week are published each Friday.

Third, nearly all business of any substance is discussed on a motion or a bill, of which printed notice has been given; advance notice is also given of Questions for oral answer. Thus nearly all business to be dealt with appears on the Order Paper.[9] The Speaker declines to propose the question on bills unless they are printed.[10] Although there is no rule to this effect, notice is usually given of amendments to motions and of amendments to bills, but if business has been hurried or some other unforeseen occurrence makes it unavoidable, manuscript amendments may be selected for debate.

The third characteristic of good procedures, namely that they should be clear and readily comprehensible by all those whom they effect, including those charged with their interpretation and enforcement, is less easily achieved.

On nearly all major matters, and on all matters of regular occurrence, the practices and procedures of the House are clearly established; and for the great majority of Members, who are happy to be guided by their Whips or their senior colleagues, this is all that is required. But for other matters—less common, but perhaps of great procedural significance—the procedures are

---

[8] This process of modernising procedure was begun some time ago, as the following extract from evidence given by Erskine May to a Select Committee in 1854 shows:

"When the greater part [of these ancient forms] were adopted the proceedings of the House were very different, in many respects, from what they are at present. Motions were made without notice—there were no printed votes—the bills were not printed—petitions relating to measures of public policy were almost unknown—parliamentary reports and papers were not circulated—strangers were excluded—and debates unpublished. In all these respects the practice has changed so materially that I think a smaller number of forms is now necessary than probably was found consistent with due notice to every one concerned in former times." (Select Committee on Business of the House, H.C. 212 of 1854, Q. 197).

Since then the practice has changed still further and the number of "forms" employed has been greatly reduced.

[9] For some exceptions, see pp. 193–197.

[10] Occasionally a private Member's bill which has not yet been printed appears on the Order Paper for second reading, and this rule is then applied.

not always so clear and decisive, precedents may be lacking. Here, very careful thought must be given by the clerks to the advice to be tendered to the Chair or to the partisans on either side. On such matters, the decisions and rulings of the Chair are inevitably unpopular with one side or other, however technically correct they may be, and are often challenged by points of order. Here the authority of the Chair becomes of great importance.

The firm and fair enforcement of the rules, however, is not enough to secure their acceptance and the orderly conduct of business. Precedents themselves may be neutral, but it does not necessarily feel that way to the man whose motion or amendment or Question or speech is ruled out of order. It is therefore important that procedures be applied in a constructive way, so that if one course of action is not permitted, some alternative way of raising a matter on the floor or in committee may be suggested instead. It also helps to warn Members in advance of an adverse ruling. "Rolling the pitch" in this way may avoid tiresome and time-consuming points of order at a later stage; and sometimes, there is some room for compromise. Speakers, chairmen and clerks spend much time in giving such helpful advice and advance warnings, and in this way, while not managing the business, assist its orderly conduct.

Over the last 100 years, the House of Commons has largely succeeded in developing parliamentary procedures which have binding effect, which secure predictable business and which are mainly, though not totally, clear in their interpretation and application. This, together with the large extent of agreement between the Government and Opposition on the arrangement of business (see pages 297–298) has secured general acceptance of the processes for the transaction of business. Political issues may be hard fought in the House but, on the whole, not procedural matters—or not for long. The debate is on the issues, not about how it should be conducted. This is a most significant feature of the House of Commons today.[11]

The Sources and Development of Procedure

The procedures of the House of Commons have never been totally codified. They are not contained in any one document, though they are conveniently analysed and summarised, with many cited precedents, in some 1000 pages of Erskine May's *Parliamentary Practice*. There are no special procedures for their adoption or modification—a simple majority of the House is all that is necessary to agree or amend a standing order—and hence they have frequently been changed in response to new circumstances, requirements or moods of the House.

The ease with which procedures may be changed encourages a constant concern with procedural reform (though that term is sometimes disputed— one man's reform is another man's phobia). In modern times, especially since 1945, Procedure Committees have frequently been appointed by the House to review and report on various aspects of the "procedures in the public business of the House," or to consider specific matters referred to them. Procedure Committees with broad terms of reference were appointed in the sessions covering 1945–46, 1957–59, 1964–67 (with some specific instructions), 1968–73, 1975–79 and 1984–87; another such committee was

---

[11] It is different elsewhere; in Canada, for example, much of the party battle has often centred on procedural matters, such as the prolonged ringing of the division bells (for two weeks) in 1982 (see The Table, Vol. LI (1983) pp. 46–53).

appointed on May 27, 1988.[12] Committees to consider specific subjects sat in 1955–57, 1967–68, 1974–75, 1980–81 and 1981–83. A slightly different type of committee was appointed in 1961–64 and again in 1975–78 to consider more minor matters referred to it by the House from time to time.[13]

Not all these committees came up with substantial proposals for procedural reform, and by no means all their recommendations have been accepted by the House and implemented. Some recommendations, such as enabling standing committees to hear evidence on some bills or for the development of specialist select committees were made by several procedure committees before their final acceptance. But increasing concern with how business is conducted by the House and particularly with the opportunities for Members to play a useful role—contrast the fact that only four procedure committees were appointed between 1918 and 1939—has served to keep the procedural reform pot on the boil and has substantially changed the way the House works. Every new edition of Erskine May—now roughly every six or seven years—includes a large number of up-dating alterations and even as this book was being written, procedures were changed and sections had to be revised.

All this means that the procedures of the House of Commons have remained lively and purposeful—and worthy of study in their own right— not fossilised nor, in the main, related to obsolete purposes. Much of the dead wood—what Mr. Emrys Hughes, a former M.P., called the "mumbo-jumbo" of Parliament[14]—has been removed. What is left—though not ideal and partly derived from older forms and customs—is mainly of practical use. This is illustrated by a description of the sources of parliamentary procedures and of the nature of its evolution.

The four principal sources of procedure are, (i) practice, (ii) the standing orders and occasionally other orders or resolutions of the House, (iii) rulings from the Chair, including enforcement of many customs of the House, and (iv) a few statutory provisions. It should be noted that, with the rare exception of the last category, these can all be modified by the House itself, and the House is the sole determiner and arbiter of its own procedures.[15] This distinguishes parliamentary procedure from the law of Parliament which applies to both Houses (including parliamentary privilege) and defines the composition and powers of each House. Such law can only be changed by statute passed by both Houses.

Practice of the House

The authority for many of the most important components of parliamentary procedure can only be found in the practice of the House. The earliest origins of some of these practices—what is sometimes called "ancient usage"—are lost in history, but early records of such practices survive in the Journals of the House. Such ancient usage includes the various stages in the passage of bills. The first, second and third readings, with intervening committee and report stages, as employed today, are nowhere

---

[12] H.C.Deb., Vol. 134, col. 682.

[13] For a full list of Procedure Committees in the years 1958 to 1987, with the matters on which they reported and the dates of debates on those reports, see H.C.Deb., Vol. 130, cols. *521–6* (March 30, 1988).

[14] *"Parliament and Mumbo-Jumbo,"* 1966.

[15] See also page 88 on the privilege of Parliament.

prescribed by standing orders or other formal decisions of the House. The use of select committees is equally founded in ancient usage. Another example may be found in the procedures for financial business. Other practices are more recent; for example the procedure of Ministers making statements which may be followed by Questions, and indeed, the procedures for questioning Ministers, are not laid down in any formal rule but have evolved in practice, although themselves exceptions to what may be called "basic procedure" of Parliament.

This basic procedure is perhaps the most fundamental of all practice that has evolved from ancient usage, for it regulates the very process of debate and decision-taking by the House; it is nowhere laid down in standing orders. Stated simply, the House decides everything on a question put to it. This is the process of debate, described more fully on pages 203–208 below.

This process of debate—motion made; question proposed; debate arising; question put and agreed to (or negatived); resolved or ordered—is common to most of the main business of the House and to much of its committee work. It has one essential feature, which is distinctive of British parliamentary procedure, namely that at any one time, after a question is proposed, there is only one question before the House, and each question and each amendment is decided separately (though to avoid unnecessary duplication, several motions or amendments may, by modern practice, be debated together). This facilitates the essential clarity of parliamentary proceedings.

These elements of the basic procedure of Parliament are still employed. Other features of this ancient procedure have been largely modified, restricted or even abolished in the Commons (although still surviving in many cases in the Lords) but it is useful to understand them, as so much of modern procedure is partly founded on these aspects of basic procedure. By basic procedure any Member could, at any time when no motion was already before the House, move a motion (or when a motion was already being debated it could be superseded by another motion, for example a motion to adjourn the debate). Any Member could speak, though only once, to every motion; there were no restrictions on length of speeches; and debate on motions could thus continue until all those who wished to speak had done so. The only restriction was that speeches had to be relevant to the question before the House. Thus there were no time limits on debate. Nor were there limits on the hours of sitting of the House; the House would rise when there was no more business to be done, or at any other time when it decided to do so on a motion to adjourn, and any Member had the right to move the adjournment of the House.

Another feature of these old procedures was that all business was regulated by ad hoc motions. For example, a debatable motion would be moved to provide for the next stage of a bill to be taken on some future day, or for the House to resolve itself into a committee, or for resolutions reported from a committee to be considered forthwith, or on a future day.

Finally, all Members were equal, and had equal rights to bring forward business. There was no priority for government business, and indeed in the earliest periods there was no identifiable government.

It is doubtful whether this procedurally idyllic Garden of Eden ever fully existed. From the earliest times practices were established that restricted, in various ways, the unimpeded operation of basic procedure. What is certain is that, although the principles of basic procedure—the process of debate and the right of every Member to initiate debate and to speak—continue to apply in modern procedure, these processes and rights have always been subject to the right of the House itself to order otherwise. In practice the House has "otherwise ordered" to a marked extent.

Standing Orders

Modern procedures, while founded on the older practices of the House, are essentially the product of modifications and restrictions of those practices expressed mainly in standing orders. This is the second primary source of parliamentary procedure.

Standing orders are orders passed by the House for regulating its own proceedings—mainly the conduct of its business, but also, to some extent, the conduct of its Members and of others involved in the business of the House. In particular standing orders have given specific powers to the Speaker and other occupants of the Chair for the control of debate and other proceedings.

There is no special procedure for the making of a standing order. They are carefully drafted, in accordance with the instructions of the Government so far as their substance is concerned, by the Clerk of the House and his staff and moved, after notice, by the Leader of the House. The only thing that distinguishes them from sessional orders or resolutions or other business of the House motions, is that they are normally in general terms (while the former frequently relate to a specified item or items of business) and that the House also orders "that this order be a standing order of the House." Once passed, standing orders remain effective indefinitely, until repealed or modified by further standing orders, or unless suspended for particular business by order of the House (as quite often happens with some standing orders, especially those regarding the time for ending consideration of the business for the day).

There are at present (May 1989) 147 public business standing orders. They are published in a slim paper-back which is reprinted from time to time when new orders are made or old ones amended. The public business standing orders are also published in full as an Appendix to Erskine May's *Parliamentary Practice*.

The principal characteristics of the present public business standing orders (which were re-arranged in a more logical order in 1986) are that they modify and restrict basic procedure so as to limit the occasions for and, in some cases, the duration of debate, and they give priority to the Government in organising the business of the House and in securing the passage of its own legislation. However they also specify the rights of the Opposition and of private Members. We return frequently to this theme in later chapters.

There are also 274 private business standing orders, which almost completely codify the proceedings on the various forms of private legislation.

Occasionally "temporary standing orders" are made. This somewhat paradoxical term describes orders which apply for more than one session yet do not have indefinite effect. The main orders of this type are orders for the nomination of members of select committees, and sometimes for the appointment of select committees, which are effective for the remainder of the Parliament, and orders making provision for the carry-over of private and hybrid bills from one session to the next, so that they are not lost at the end of a session if proceedings on them have not been completed.

Sometimes orders are made which regulate procedure for one session only and so are not standing orders, for example the order made at the beginning of each session allotting specific days for private Members' bills and motions. Occasionally there are experimental orders, which are tried out for a session or two as sessional orders before being made (if the experiment is thought successful) standing orders; Standing Order No. 45A), permitting the Speaker to impose time limits on certain speeches in certain debates, was operated intermittently on a sessional basis before the standing order was passed in 1988 (see page 209).

Other orders, although not specifically stated to be standing orders, have a continuing effect. Some of these are very old, declaring, in effect, practices that are now recognised as such without incorporation in standing orders, such as the rule, affirmed in 1604[16] against "speaking tediously, impertinently and beside the question"; and others relate to the privileges of the House (see Chapter 3). Even today the House sometimes takes decisions regarding its procedures in this way, by agreeing to recommendations of procedure committees. For example, the procedure for considering privilege complaints, which was adopted in 1978 (see page 96), resulted from such a resolution and is not incorporated in standing orders.

Rulings from the Chair

Much modern practice is based on rulings by the Speaker or other occupants of the Chair, and such rulings are also particularly important in achieving consistent interpretation and application of the standing orders. Such case-law is the third source of the House's procedures. In some areas almost all the procedures are based on decisions of the Chair, and very little is laid down by standing order. For example, almost none of the rules regulating the admissibility of amendments to bills or of the rules regarding the form and content of Questions to Ministers are set out in standing orders, but depend on the consistent application of Speaker's rulings (some of them given in private) which in their turn create binding precedents.

Other procedures largely laid down in this way include the rules for the content of speeches and for the behaviour of Members in the House. Many of the customary conventions of the House, if not based on, are at least sustained and continued by Speakers' rulings. To take an apparently trivial example, the rule against smoking in committees (except when deliberating in private) is supported by more recent rulings by Speakers and chairman, although the House itself resolved in 1693, "That no Member of the House do presume to take tobacco in the gallery of the House" or "at the Table, sitting at Committees."[17] This inter-relationship between formal decisions of the House and their application by the Speaker to later, different circumstances, is typical of the way many procedures have evolved and become established.

Statutory Procedures

Finally there are a few areas where the procedures of the House are laid down by statutes. This applies to procedures which bear directly on people outside Parliament. For example, under the Provisional Collection of Taxes

---

[16] C.J. (1547–1625), 172, 946.
[17] C.J. (1693–97), p. 137.

Acts 1913 and 1968, provided certain procedures are followed in the House of Commons, immediate effect can be given to Budget resolutions before they are agreed to by the House. Legislative authority is also required for procedures involving both Houses, as illustrated by the Parliament Acts 1911 and 1949, and the Royal Assent Act 1967.

Sometimes, however, detailed Commons procedures which concern that House only and could have been laid down in standing orders, have been prescribed by statute—notably for Scottish provisional order bills, under the Private Legislation Procedures (Scotland) Act 1936, and for special procedure orders, under the Statutory Orders (Special Procedures) Acts 1945 and 1965.

In addition, although these are not part of the internal procedures of the House, it should be remembered that some of the powers and privileges of the House, which clearly affect its operations, are laid down by statute—for example Article 9 of the Bill of Rights protects freedom of speech in Parliament. And the composition of the House, the processes for electing its Members and the duration of their competence are all defined by Acts of Parliament.

PROCEDURAL FRAMEWORK

Parliaments, Sessions and Sittings

The House works within a time framework which comprises Parliaments, sessions and sittings. The first two dimensions are imposed on both Houses and are not under their direct control; the daily sittings of each House are controlled by that House.

Parliaments

A Parliament is summoned by the Sovereign to meet after each general election and the duration of a Parliament is from that first meeting until Parliament is dissolved by the Sovereign, prior to the next general election. Each Parliament is given a series number. The Parliament summoned on June 17, 1987 is the 50th Parliament of the United Kingdom since its creation in 1801.

Parliaments are summoned and dissolved by proclamation issued by the Queen with the advice of the Privy Council. The continuity of Parliament is today secured by including in the same proclamation the dissolution of one Parliament, the order for the issuing of writs for the election of a new Parliament and the summoning of that Parliament to meet on a specified date at Westminster. Under section 21(3) of the Representation of the People Act 1918, the interval between the date of the proclamation and the meeting of Parliament must be not less than 20 clear days, although this period can be further extended by proclamation. During this interval the general election is held.

The timing of each general election, and hence the duration of Parliament, is essentially decided by the Prime Minister of the day (see pages 42–43), subject to the operation of section 7 of the Parliament Act 1911 which provides that a Parliament, if not previously dissolved, ceases to exist five years from the day on which by writ of summons, it was first appointed to meet. During the first and second world wars, the life of Parliament was extended by annual Acts. Apart from that, Parliaments have lasted, in this century, for an average of three years one-and-a-half months. The most popular times for holding general elections have been the Spring and the Autumn, but the timing and the duration of Parliaments are almost entirely determined by political considerations. The duration of more recent Parliaments is shown in the following Table:

Duration of Parliaments

No. of UK Parliament	Date first met	Date dissolved	Duration Years	Months
38	August 1, 1945	February 3, 1950	4	6
39	March 1, 1950	October 5, 1951	1	7
40	October 31, 1951	May 6, 1955	3	6
41	June 7, 1955	September 18, 1959	4	3
42	October 30, 1959	September 25, 1964	4	11
43	October 27, 1964	March 10, 1966	1	4
44	April 18, 1966	May 29, 1970	4	1
45	June 29, 1970	February 8, 1974	3	7
46	March 6, 1974	July 31, 1974	—	5
47	October 22, 1974	April 7, 1979	4	5
48	May 9, 1979	May 13, 1983	4	—
49	June 15, 1983	May 18, 1987	3	11
50	June 17, 1987	—	—	—

Each Parliament begins, in the Commons, with a meeting for the election of the Speaker (see pages 143–144). The Clerk of the Crown in Chancery also delivers to the Clerk of the House of Commons a Return Book, showing the names of Members elected for each constituency. There are then sittings of both Houses to enable Members to take the oath or make an affirmation of loyalty to the Crown. The ordinary form of oath prescribed by section 1 of the Oaths Act 1978, which is administered in the Commons by the Clerk of the House, is "I swear by Almighty God that I will be faithful and bear true allegiance to Her Majesty Queen Elizabeth, her heirs and successors, according to law, so help me God." Members who so prefer may make a similar solemn affirmation, under section 5 of the Oaths Act 1978 and Standing Order No. 5. Members returned after by-elections also take the oath or affirm. Following the death of a Sovereign, Parliament must immediately meet, pursuant to the Succession to the Crown Act 1707, and all Members of both Houses again take the oath, or affirm.

A Member of the House of Commons who votes or sits in the House during debate after the election of the Speaker, without taking the oath or making an affirmation, is liable, under the Parliamentary Oaths Act 1866, to a fine of £500 for each such offence and his seat is vacated. A Member cannot draw his parliamentary salary until he has taken the oath or affirmed, but there are some functions of an M.P., not involving his participation in the House, which he can fulfil (including resigning his seat by accepting the Chiltern Hundreds or some other disqualifying office).

Sessions

After the election of the Speaker and the swearing in of Members (which takes about four sitting days), the first session of Parliament is opened, normally by the Queen in person but sometimes by Lord Commissioners on her behalf. This is done with magnificent ceremony. The Queen, having come in formal procession accompanied by the officers of her Court, takes her seat on the Throne in the House of Lords. The Gentleman Usher of the Black Rod (appointed by the Queen to attend the Lords) is then sent to summon the Commons. In accordance with the spirit of several resolutions agreed by the House in 1642 after Charles I sought to arrest the five Members, the Queen's messenger is not automatically admitted, but knocks on the doors of the House, which have been shut in his face, in effect to ask permission to enter. He then enters and firmly, but courteously, informs the House that the Queen commands it "to attend Her Majesty immediately in the House of Peers." Led by the Speaker, attended by the Clerk of the House and the Serjeant at Arms, with the Prime Minister and the Leader of the Opposition closely behind, the Commons then go to the Bar of the House of Lords. The Queen, having been handed the Speech by the Lord Chancellor, reads the Speech from the Throne which is addressed to both Houses and sets out her Government's policies and legislative programme for the session. One short section is however addressed to Members of the House of Commons only ("Estimates for the public service will be laid before you") thus indicating the Commons sole responsibility for initiating the authorisation of expenditure in response to requests from the Crown.

The Speech having been read, the Queen and her courtiers depart; the Commons return to their Chamber and the Lords remain in theirs. Both Houses are now free to proceed with the work of the session, because no business can be transacted until Parliament has been opened by the Crown.

The pageantry of the State Opening of Parliament is undoubtedly grand and colourful, but within this ceremony is encapsulated the central feature of the British Constitution, namely the sovereign supremacy of the Queen in Parliament.[18] In the absence of a written constitution to provide for this, it is appropriate for the constitution to be physically demonstrated once a year in this way.

The session thus opened will normally be the first of several sessions of a Parliament. Sessions usually last for about a year, although there is no requirement, other than a well-established convention and certain practical convenience, for this to be so; business could be conducted in sessions extending over several years and in some countries, for example Canada, this is frequently done.[19] In practice, apart from those sessions beginning after a spring or summer election, Parliament is normally opened early in November and prorogued about a year later; the normal length session has been about 170 sitting days in the Commons, as the following Table shows:

---

[18] Except in so far as U.K. laws may be found to be in breach of Treaties of the European Communities.

[19] There used to be a convention that no business should be transacted after Supply for the year had been appropriated—the main purpose of the Crown in summoning Parliament having thus been accomplished—but this is no longer followed, and legislation is frequently passed after the Appropriation Act.

Duration of Sessions

Session	No. of Sitting Days
1970–71	206 (1st year of new Parliament)
1971–72	180
1972–73	164
1973–74	60 (Dissolution)
1974	87 (Short Parliament)
1974–75	198 (1st year of new Parliament)
1975–76	191
1976–77	149
1977–78	169
1978–79	86 (Dissolution)
1979–80	244 (1st year of new Parliament)
1980–81	163
1981–82	174
1982–83	115 (Dissolution)
1983–84	213 (1st year of new Parliament)
1984–85	172
1985–86	172
1986–87	109 (Dissolution)

Note

The practice of starting the first session after a general election in months which would normally have been included in the last session of the previous Parliament has lengthened some sessions; similarly other sessions are prematurely terminated by a general election.

A session is opened by the Queen (or a Commission) as described; it is closed by the Queen on the advice of her Ministers, normally by the process of prorogation (followed, at the end of a Parliament, by dissolution) or by immediate dissolution. The House is normally prorogued, while sitting, by a Commission in the House of Lords when the Royal Assent is signified to any outstanding Acts and a Speech from the Throne is read summarising the work of Parliament during the session. If either House is adjourned, however, Parliament may be prorogued by proclamation. The instrument of prorogation will also specify the day when Parliament is to meet again. Even when Parliament is prorogued prior to a general election, a nominal day is named for its resumption, but this is then superseded by a proclamation dissolving Parliament. In recent years, however, the practice has been to dissolve Parliament by proclamation while the Houses are adjourned, without it first being prorogued; this was done for the second election in 1974, and in 1979, 1983 and 1987.

The prorogation of Parliament is a prerogative act of the Crown and relates to both Houses. Its effect is to suspend nearly all proceedings of both Houses until Parliament is summoned again; nor may committees sit while Parliament is prorogued.[20] It is therefore not desirable for Parliament to be prorogued for an extended period (although by proclamation, Parliament while prorogued could be summoned for an earlier day than originally provided for, pursuant to the Meeting of Parliament Acts 1797 and 1870 and section 34 of the Parliament (Elections and Meetings) Act 1943), and in practice Parliament is usually only prorogued for a few days—typically from a Thursday till the Opening of Parliament on the following Tuesday or Wednesday.

---

[20] Judicial business may continue to be transacted in the House of Lords and the Speaker may exercise certain powers, including the issue of writs for by-elections.

Another effect of prorogation is to bring to an end all the business of a session. Thus all public bills which have not been passed by the end of a session fall, and if it is desired to proceed with them again in the next session, they must start again from the beginning.[21] Similarly, adjourned debates and all notices of Questions and motions for future days lapse. However, standing orders may be made in one session regulating business for the remainder of a Parliament and in this way, for example, select committees can continue their work from session to session within a Parliament, almost without interruption (see page 280).

Sittings

Within each session each House controls its own sittings, and the consequences of this freedom in the Commons are the cause of frequent critical comment, for the House "sits more often and longer and later than any other Western democratic legislature."[22]

The normal sitting days and times of the Commons are laid down in standing orders. Under Standing Order No. 9 the House meets on Mondays to Thursdays at 2.30 p.m., and Standing Order No. 11 provides for Friday sittings at 9.30 a.m. Unless the House otherwise ordered, it would therefore sit five days a week throughout the year. In practice, however, the House does not sit on Bank Holidays and other public holidays, and nowadays usually adjourns for about three weeks at Christmas, for a week at Easter, for the same time over the Spring Bank Holiday and for the Summer during the whole or most of August, the whole of September and part of October. The longer adjournments are called recesses.

The date of rising for the Summer recess is often a topic of anxious speculation, especially by Members and staff with children of school age (most anxious of all are those with children at Scottish schools which break-up earlier). The Leader of the House never commits himself long in advance on the date of rising and the threat of "sitting late into August" is sometimes used to encourage awkward back-benchers to come to heel.[23] Between 1970 and 1987 (inclusive) the House adjourned on one occasion before July 23, on five occasions between July 23 and 26, on five occasions between July 27 and 31, and on seven occasions in August. The latest rising was on August 9, 1972. The two Houses take their recesses largely at the same time; unlike the total period of sessions, each House regulates its own adjournments.

As the days and time of sitting are prescribed by standing order, the House does not appoint at the end of each sitting the day and time of the next sitting. A motion is simply made, "That this House do now adjourn", and the House automatically meets again according to the standing order.

However, if the House is to adjourn till a later day after a recess, a date for meeting again must be specified. It is now the practice for a motion to be made several days in advance to the effect that the House, at its rising on Friday May 23 (say), will adjourn till Tuesday June 2, then, on the Friday,

---

[21] Provision may be made for hybrid, private and personal bills to be "carried over" from session to session.

[22] First Report from the Select Committee on Procedure, H.C. 588–I of 1977–78, para. 9.1.

[23] See, for example, Mr John Biffen, speaking on the need to restrict debate on the European Communities (Amendment) Bill, July 1, 1986: "it is not an ignoble consideration to take into account the desire of the House to adjourn for the summer recess no later than early next month." (H.C.Deb., Vol. 100, col. 932).

the ordinary adjournment motion is all that is needed. Under Standing Order No. 22, debate on such motions for the adjournment of the House for a specified period is limited to three hours, at the end of which time the Chair puts the question on any amendment that may have been moved (the Opposition sometimes moves amendments to reduce the length of the recess in protest against some aspect of the Government's policy or conduct) and on the main question. These short debates before each recess are mainly used by back-benchers to raise a wide range of matters that concern them (see page 406).

Similar motions are sometimes made for the House to sit at an earlier time on a future day than provided for in Standing Order No. 9. For example, the House usually sits on Maundy Thursday, before the Easter Recess, at 9.30 a.m. and sometimes has a Question hour before a debate on the adjournment, and a motion moved several days before is needed to amend the standing orders accordingly. Standing Order No. 22 does not apply to such motions, but they are not usually debated.

In cases of emergency, as for example on the outbreak of war in 1939 and following the Argentine invasion of the Falkland Islands in 1982, the House has sat on Saturdays and even Sundays. If the House is sitting when the need for such a special sitting becomes apparent, a motion is moved to permit this, but if the House is adjourned for a recess, it may be recalled early for this purpose. The House has also sat at the weekend on the demise of the Crown, and following the abdication of King Edward VIII for the swearing of Members. In this century there have been 22 Saturday sittings (mostly before the first World War) and one on a Sunday (on September 3, 1939).

If it is decided to recall the House earlier during a recess this can be done under Standing Order No. 12, but only at the request of the Government.[24] If the Speaker is satisfied that the public interest so requires (and there are no cases of his failing to agree), he appoints a day for the House to meet. The first business on this day is appointed by the Government. Emergency recalls have been fairly frequent since the last war, especially during the Summer recess. For example, the Commons were recalled to debate devaluation in 1949, the Korean War in 1950, the Suez crisis in 1956, the Berlin crisis in 1961, Czechoslovakia and Nigeria in 1968 and Northern Ireland in 1971 and 1974. On April 3 (a Saturday) and 14, 1982 the House was recalled to debate the Falkland Islands situation. Other recalls have been to permit a prorogation before a dissolution. In all there were 15 occasions when Standing Order No. 12 was applied from 1945 up to the end of Session 1986–87.

It is usual, once the business for which the House has been recalled has been debated, for the House to adjourn again to the day originally planned and not to proceed with other routine business.

The length of sittings is not as precisely determined or as specific as their beginning. Standing Order No. 9 provides that the business of the House shall be interrupted at 10.00 p.m., on Mondays to Thursdays (under Standing Order No. 11, at 2.30 p.m. on Fridays); and, unless otherwise provided, no opposed business (other than divisions on questions necessary to dispose of the interrupted business) can be taken after the moment of interruption. But this does not mean that the House usually stops work soon after 10.00 p.m., for on most days something else is "otherwise provided."

---

[24] The date of meeting of both Houses, when adjourned, can also be altered by proclamation, pursuant to the Meeting of Parliament Acts 1797 and 1870, but this is no longer the practice.

First, under standing orders, certain types of business are "exempted" from the ten o'clock rule (or the 2.30 p.m. rule on Fridays) (see pages 201–202). In addition to such exempted business, Standing Order No. 14 also enables the ten o'clock rule to be suspended for other business. In this way the Government can provide (with the approval of the House) for extra debating time on business of their choosing—usually their own business, but occasionally an Opposition motion or "prayer."

The power to take extra time is used on a wide range of occasions. For example, the Government, in response to demands from Members on both sides, or sometimes from the Opposition only, may decide to give an extra two hours for the second reading debate on some bill that has attracted a lot of interest. It is unlikely to allow a longer extension because divisions on major matters—involving larger attendance on a three-line whip—are not popular after midnight. Similarly extra time may be given for a debate on a Government motion or for the first day of a two-day debate on a wide matter, say a general foreign affairs debate. One of the main occasions for late sittings, however, is the unlimited suspension of the rule for the report stage of a Government bill. Unless such indefinite extension were given, the Government would have no certainty of getting the bill through because opponents could engage in prolonged debate on early amendments and exhaust the allotted time and further consideration of the bill would have to be adjourned. If there is no fixed stopping time the Opposition usually accepts that the bill will go through eventually and do not artificially prolong debate. Nevertheless consideration of controversial bills, with many amendments, frequently continues all through the night and often for two, three or even four days. Proceedings in committee of the whole House and consideration of Lords Amendments are similarly extended.

Other business is often not started until after 10.00 p.m. and the rule has to be suspended for such business—sometimes for a limited period, sometimes "till any hour"—(unless the business itself is exempted under Standing Order No. 14 or Standing Order No. 15). Examples include the various stages of minor bills, and motions on House of Commons matters such as Members' pay and allowances, privilege matters, reports of the Procedure Committee and amendments to standing orders.

The following Table shows how many hours were spent after 10.00 p.m. (or after 2.30 p.m. on a Friday, which is unusual) in Session 1985–86 (the last full session in the last Parliament) on the main types of business involved.

Main Causes of House sitting late, 1985–86

Business	Hours spent after moment of interruption [a]	
	hours	minutes
Government Bills:		
Second readings	23	44
Committee of the whole House	10	56
Committal motion[b]	10	33
Consideration stages	42	32
Third readings	8	42
Lords Amendments	12	18
Government motions:		
European Community documents	21	14
Other substantive motions	11	22

Private business	8	05
Adjournment debates		
After proceedings on Consolidated Fund Bills under S.O. No. 54	30	0
Daily motions at end of business	75	40
Delegated legislation		
Affirmative motions on S.I.s etc.	37	12
N Ireland affirmative motions	6	46
Prayers against S.I's, etc.	13	17

Notes

(a) Including time spent on divisions
(b) This was an untypical motion to commit the controversial Channel Tunnel Bill to a select committee (H.C. Deb., Vol. 98, cols. 1195–1327 (June 5, 1986)).

The overall effect is that the duration of a sitting is frequently considerably more than the period of eight hours (5½ hours on Friday) envisaged by the standing orders. In 1985–86, for example, the House sat after midnight on 73 days and after 3.30 p.m. on a Friday on two days. And as the following Table shows, there are many sittings extending even later into the night.

Occasions when the House sat after 1.30 am

Session	Number	Session	Number
1979–80 (a)	41	1983–84 (a)	34
1980–81	28	1984–85	35
1981–82	22	1985–86	18
1982–83 (b)	13	1986–87 (b)	6

(a) Unusually long session
(b) Unusually short session

Some sittings, lasting till after 8.00 a.m., are called "all-nighters." The following Table shows the average duration of sittings in recent sessions.

Session	Average duration of sittings	
	Mon–Thursdays	Fridays
1981–82	9h 36 mins	5h 20 mins
1982–83	9h 24 mins	5h 26 mins
1983–84	9h 26 mins	5h 15 mins
1984–85	10h 05 mins	5h 25 mins
1985–86	9h 42 mins	5h 20 mins
1986–87	9h 22 mins	5h 31 mins

Over this period, the average time of rising on Mondays to Thursdays was six minutes past midnight. This means that a Member's working day at the House is potentially very long, especially when committee meetings, party meetings, appointments with constituents and others, correspondence and necessary reading (much of which occupies the morning as well as the sitting hours) are taken into account. However, not all Members attend to the end every night. Business is increasingly specialised and Members have become increasingly specialist. For detailed and not particularly controversial business put down for consideration after 10.00 p.m.—for example, an affirmative resolution on a technical statutory instrument—a high attendance would be neither expected nor particularly praiseworthy. Such business is for the specialists and the rest can have an evening off.

The figures for divisions illustrate this. The number voting is largely conditioned by the subject-matter, its degree of controversy and the extent of the Whips' anxiety to ensure a good turn-out for their side (or in the case of Governments with a small majority, simply to ensure they are not defeated). But average figures give some indication of the pressure on the 650 Members to be present, (although such pressure does not apply at all on many days and falls off markedly after 10.00 p.m.). The following Table gives the figures for a selection of sessions in recent Parliaments.[25]

Total Numbers Voting in Divisions (Mondays to Thursdays)

Session	% of days with divisions before or at 10 pm	Average number in divisions before or at 10 pm[(a)]	% of days with later divisions	Average number in later divisions
1974–75	59	406	34	343
1980–81	62	384	39	300
1985–86	65	375	38	272

(a) including divisions immediately following divisions at 10 pm

It is noticeable how, although the frequency of divisions appears to have risen slightly (see also page 206 below), the number of Members voting has fallen. This may be the consequence of more relaxed whipping when Governments have larger majorities.

Put simply, the above Table shows that, on average, not much more than half the membership of the House is required to be present even on days when there are divisions, and considerably less than half stay on for later business. Even the relatively low figures in later divisions are not as low as they would be if the Government did not consider it necessary to keep at least 100 Members in the House in order to be able to obtain a closure if that proved necessary to secure their business (see page 222). And of course there is often business taken late at night on which no votes are expected; indeed that kind of business, of interest only to a handful of Members, often runs late because there is no pressure from numerous other Members, anxious to get home to bed, to bring it to an end.

Thus, for many Members, (other than the Speaker, the Deputy Speakers and the Whips themselves who are required, by their job, to attend or be available as long as the House is sitting) late sittings as such are not the real menace to their lives that is sometimes suggested. By pairing, by tolerance of the Whips, and sometimes by straight absenteeism, they can get many evenings off (especially after 10.00 p.m.). The real problem for Members—and even more for their wives, families and friends—is the unpredictability of late sittings and required attendance. Three-line and running whips (when Members are tied to the House) may be announced at only a few days notice (say on Thursday for the following Tuesday) and this can cause havoc

---

[25] For figures for earlier sessions, see First Report from the Select Committee on Procedure, H.C. 588–I of 1977–78, Table X, p. cx.

for a Member's social and family life, or even for political and constituency engagements.

For the staff of the House the situation is different. Not all of them work in the evenings or at night, but each department maintains essential staff to ensure that Members get all the services they need up to the rising of the House, and some staff have to work later still to complete their work. But night work is shared (and financially rewarded) and typically a man or woman may work on a regular basis till slightly after the House rises one or two nights a week.

A Typical Session

Before describing the procedures in more detail it may be helpful to outline the sequence of business in a session as a whole. The session begins with the Queen's Speech from the Throne which she delivers in the morning in the House of Lords. When the Commons resumes its sitting in the afternoon it first passes a number of largely formal sessional resolutions and orders relating to elections; the conduct and treatment of witnesses; the need for the Metropolitan Police to maintain free passage for Members to and from the House and to ensure that "no disorder be allowed in Westminster Hall or in the passages leading to this House ... and that there be no annoyance therein or thereabouts," and the preparation and printing of the Votes and Proceedings and the Journal. These traditional proceedings are now of mainly historic importance and remind us of times when the authority of the House was frequently challenged and the Commons had to assert its rights. The Outlawries Bill "for the more effectual preventing Clandestine Out-lawries" is also read a first time, symbolising the right of the House to consider business of its own choosing before proceeding to consider the Queen's Speech and business laid before it by Her Majesty's Ministers. None of this formal business is normally debated today, although on November 6, 1984 the Liberals forced a short debate on their rights as a party in the House and forced a division on the motion for the printing of the Votes and Proceedings.

Next the Speaker reminds the House of the Queen's Speech by referring to the copies available in the Vote Office, though he no longer reads it to the House. Then begins the first major debate of the session, the Debate on the Address thanking Her Majesty for her Speech. This usually lasts for five days and gives an opportunity for a broad review of the Government's programme and policy. Two Government back-benchers move and second the Address (now almost the only occasion when a motion is formally seconded). They are customarily a contrasted pair (rural and urban, old and new, Scottish and English, etc.,) and traditionally pay respects to their constituency, essay a certain amount of humour and attempt to be polite and not too controversial. Next comes the Leader of the Opposition, who gives a quick, off the cuff reaction to the Government's programme as announced in the Queen's Speech (for he has had little time to study it) (see pages 339–340). He is followed by the Prime Minister who makes a major speech outlining and defending the Government's attitudes, beliefs, policies and programme. The general debate is then open, with Members from both sides commenting on the Government's programme and responding to it from party political, constituency and personal points of view.

The debate on the first day, which in recent years has usually been a Wednesday, but is sometimes a Tuesday and sometimes a Thursday (here we assume a Wednesday) is totally general; any topic is in order. On the Thursday and Friday there will be specific topics agreed through the usual channels, for example social services or foreign affairs or the state of the economy, on which most Members will concentrate, although not obliged to (for the motion before the House is still the motion for the Address which itself refers to the whole of the Queen's Speech).

On the following Monday and Tuesday the debate is more formally restricted by the moving of amendments by the Opposition relating to specific areas of policy (for typical examples see pages 339–340). Debate is then confined to the matter of the amendments. The form of amendment is always to add to the Address some qualifying regret, critical of the Government itself, and not to leave out any of the traditional and somewhat flowery language in which the House expresses its thanks to the Queen.

Each amendment is separately debated for a day and is voted on and defeated at 10.00 p.m. on the Monday and Tuesday. Traditionally, the Leader of the House winds up the debate on the Address on the last night with a general reply to points made throughout the five-day debate, and he often gives a good-humoured (in some hands—for example those of Capt. Harry Crookshank in the early 1950s, and Mr John Biffen more recently— witty) defence of the Government's position.

Another unusual feature on the last night is that two amendments are selected by the Speaker for divisions. The first is tabled by the official Opposition; the second by another party. Normally such a second amendment is not possible at the end of a day's debate because after the first is voted on at 10.00 p.m. the second amendment cannot be called, as no new opposed business such as the amendment can be taken after the moment of interruption, pursuant to Standing Order No. 9(6). This used to mean that the smaller parties or other minority groups were never able to put proposals or criticisms of their own to the House for a vote at the end of the debate on the Address. However, Standing Order No. 32, first made in 1979, now permits the Speaker to put one further amendment to a vote (but not further debate) on these occasions. Normally an amendment moved by the second largest opposition party (in recent years the Liberal (or Democrat) party) has been selected.

Another early piece of procedural business is the annual order appointing the days when private Members' motions and bills shall have precedence over government business, pursuant to Standing Order No. 13 (for further description and discussion of the allocation, see pages 11–12, 385 and 400). This motion is usually moved and agreed to without debate in the first few days of the session.

During or soon after the debate on the Address, the Government presents some of its bills—those wanted most urgently and one or two of the biggest or more important on which an early start is desirable. Soon after the debate on the Address, the House therefore turns to the second readings of those bills and this is its main work until Christmas. Statistical examples may be given from the most recent normal length session, 1985–86. In this session 10 Government bills[25a] starting in the Commons and one Lords bill were read a second time before Christmas. Some urgently required bills, (e.g. three in

---

[25a] In these and equivalent statistics below, Consolidated Fund Bills and provisional order bills have been excluded.

1985–86) will complete their committee stage at this time, and even later stages.

Other items of business before Christmas are the Vote on Account for the next financial year and the Winter Supplementary Estimates for the current financial year. Nowadays these are usually passed without debate but there is usually a debate on the Chancellor of the Exchequer's Autumn Statement (see page 320).

Fridays during this period up to Christmas are mainly used for Government business, but normally the last three Fridays before the House rises are appointed for private Members' motions.

Between Christmas and Easter second readings of Government bills continue to bulk large (19 Commons bills and three Lords bills in 1985–86), but much of the work of Members in this period will be in standing committees. It is not unusual for some eight or nine such committees, each considering a different bill, to be sitting at the same time each Tuesday and Thursday morning at this time of the year, and for four or five of those to be sitting in the afternoon or evening as well. As a result, some bills are reported from committee and the House itself begins to spend time on their consideration stages; others are considered and reported from committee of the whole House (altogether seven Government bills were considered on report in this period in 1985–86).

Before Easter the House votes Supply covering the remaining supplementary estimates for the current financial year. There is usually one Estimates Day for debating one or two of these estimates, as chosen by the Liaison Committee (see page 250). Approval is also given to the excess votes for the preceding financial year (see page 249). An opportunity for a general discussion of the Government's expenditure plans has been provided in recent years by a debate on the Public Expenditure White Paper (but see page 320). Questions relating to the armed services may also be debated at this time in three debates, on the adjournment, on the Navy, Army and Royal Air Force.

A major item of financial business in this period which does provide lengthy debate is the Budget. This is normally presented towards the end of March or early in April, before the House rises for the Easter recess. Debate lasts for four days, typically with the Budget being presented on a Tuesday, debated on Wednesday and Thursday and concluding with debate and divisions on the more controversial Ways and Means resolutions on the following Monday.

Another important piece of financial business at this time is the debate on, and approval of the annual Local Government Rate Support Grant Report (England) for which a whole day is usually devoted. Further time will be allowed for debating similar reports for Wales and similar orders for Scotland.

The first six Fridays in the weeks after Christmas are normally appointed for the second readings of private Members' bills, so some of these Fridays (if there is a controversial Bill), become important days in a Member's diary[25b]; others may give him a day away from Westminster. The other Fridays before Easter are mainly devoted to private Members' motions, when attendance may be less important.

[25b] 509 Members voted on the second reading of the Protection of Official Information Bill on Friday January 15, 1988; others were present but abstained.

Between Easter and the rising for the Summer recess the Government's main legislative business is the second readings of bills sent down from the Lords (six in 1985–86, including the Shops Bill, which was negatived), a few further second readings of new Commons bills (seven in 1985–86), and the remaining stages of both Commons and Lords bills (23 Government bills were reported out of committee in the period April to July 1986). Towards the end of July there are usually a number of Lords Amendments to Commons bills (and a few Lords Amendments to Commons Amendments to Lords bills) to be considered (relating to nine bills in 1985–86). As a result, the majority of Government bills obtain their Royal Assent in this period (in 1985–86, 24 such bills were given Royal Assent between Easter and the Summer recess compared with two before Christmas and nine between Christmas and Easter).

An important, though not time-consuming, item of financial business in this period is the passage of the Consolidated Fund (Appropriation) Bill at the end of July. Before its passage, however, two further days will have been devoted to consideration of estimates selected by the Liaison Committee.

Much more time, however, is required in this period for consideration of the Government's fiscal proposals as set out in the Finance Bill (see pages 252–254 and 319–322).

Another major policy area on which the House concentrates some attention in the Summer is defence. Two days are usually devoted to a debate on the annual Defence White Paper and the Defence estimates.

Private Members' business continues to occupy some time. The first five Fridays after Easter are mainly devoted to the report and remaining stages of private Members' bills which have emerged from committees, and one Friday towards the end of July is reserved for completion of such bills, in particular the consideration of Lords Amendments. Private bills may also require a significant amount of floor time in this period.

At the end of July a rather exhausted House rises thankfully for the Summer recess. After the recess the House usually has a "spill-over" period of one or two weeks in October before the end of the session. This is primarily required because the phasing of Government legislation between the two Houses leaves the Lords with a considerable amount of work to do on Commons bills that only reach them in June or July, and consequently they often have a shorter summer recess than the Commons. The results of their labours, in the form of Lords Amendments, fall to be considered by the Commons in this "spill over" period (six Government bills in 1985–86). There may also be a few late bills—for example consolidation bills—originating in the Lords (three in 1985–86). Finally the Royal Assent is given to all outstanding bills which have been agreed by the two Houses (13 Government bills in 1985–86) and the House is prorogued. So ends one session of the House of Commons.

The Daily Arrangement of Business

We will not, at this stage, describe in detail most of the procedural events in the House of Commons day, as many of the formal procedures will be described later in this chapter, and how these procedures are used is the theme of Chapters 7 to 11. There are some events, however, which do not fit naturally into those sections and are briefly described here. It should be emphasised that not all the following events happen each day.

Prayers

The House sits at 2.30 p.m. from Monday to Thursday (the differences on Fridays are described on pages 202–203). When the Speaker arrives in the House bells are rung throughout the precincts (and beyond) and the sitting of the House begins with the prayers for Parliament, as set out in the Church of England Prayer Book, read by the Speaker's Chaplain. The Speaker and the Chaplain kneel at the Table in front of the Speaker's Chair.[26] Members stand in their places and face the benches instead of kneeling. (A non-religious purpose in their attendance is that they thereby reserve for themselves a fixed place on their chosen bench for the rest of the day). Apart from the Chaplain and the Serjeant at Arms (who comes in with the Mace) only Members attend prayers. Prayers last for about four or five minutes and when completed the Speaker takes the Chair; the bells are rung again; the Chaplain leaves; the Clerk of the House, the Clerk Assistant and the Principal Clerk of the Table Office (listed from right to left as they face the House) take their places at the Table; strangers, Hansard reporters and the press are admitted to the galleries; and the work of the House begins.

Business Immediately After Prayers

Some unopposed formal business can be taken without debate at this stage. This includes the Queen's Answer to Addresses presented to her by the House which are conveyed by one of the Government Whips in his capacity as an officer of the Court (usually the Vice-Chamberlain of the Household); formal communications by the Speaker, most commonly reporting the death of a Member; motions for new writs for by-elections which are normally moved by the Chief Whip of the party that formerly held the seat, although any Member may so move, and occasionally does so if it be thought that a by-election is being unduly delayed (if opposed they stand over till after Questions); proceedings on private bills if unopposed, but if objection is signified the business is deferred till another day; and motions for unopposed returns, that is unopposed by the department who will make the return (see page 170).

Questions

Questions for oral answer, as set down on the Order Paper, are next taken; these are followed by private notice Questions (PNQs). In accordance with Standing Order No. 17, Questions begin no later than 2.45 p.m. (but in practice always begin within a minute or two of the Speaker taking the Chair as all the preceding business is undebated), and apart from PNQs no new Question is called after 3.30 p.m.

Business After Questions

After Questions, the House may be faced with a variety of matters, mostly of a strictly informal nature in that they do not involve any decision of the House by order or resolution. None of these matters requires notice, and so (except for ballots) no reference to them appears on the Order Paper.

---

[26] If the Speaker is ill or otherwise unavoidably absent, or has been given leave of absence by the House, this is announced by the Clerk of the House before prayers are read, and the Speaker's place is taken by a Deputy Speaker.

Although not officially provided for, the first thing that sometimes happened in the past at this stage was that the Speaker heard and ruled on "points of order" raised by Members arising directly out of Questions that day. Unless something unusual has happened that requires the immediate attention of the Chair,[27] the Speaker declines to hear points of order during Question time because they take time and deprive other Members of the opportunity to ask Questions. In 1987, however, the Speaker, concerned about the increasing use of points of order as a means of extending Question time, decided that he would no longer take points of order arising out of Questions or other matters until after statements and other such business. Consequently they are now normally heard immediately before the business of the day printed on the Order Paper.[28] This change was not at first popular with all Members (even the Opposition front-bench expressed some reservations) but since points of order have been deferred in this way (it is not possible every day, as sometimes there is nothing else before the main business) fewer points of order appear to have been raised (and see pages 196–197 and 377 below).

After Questions and any points of order taken at that stage, the Speaker calls Ministers who have given notice (usually by 12 noon) of their intention to make a statement on some matter of policy or some recent event (see pages 262–263).

The Speaker himself may also make statements, giving rulings on matters raised with him, announcing arrangements for debates under his control, (e.g. adjournment debates before recesses) or dealing with certain privilege applications.

Next may come the introduction of new Members elected at by-elections (usually on the Tuesday after their election). They are introduced by two sponsors from their own party—usually a Whip and another Member known to them; they get a good cheer from their own side; they take the oath or make the affirmation; they sign the Test Roll; they are introduced to the Speaker; and they are led away to find their feet as best then can in the strange new world for which they have been chosen.

The next item is almost a daily occurrence (except on Fridays), namely applications, lasting not more than three minutes, to move an emergency adjournment of the House under Standing Order No. 20 (see pages 264–265).

Ceremonial speeches are also taken at this time, for example on the death of distinguished statesmen who were former Members of the House or on the occasion of royal jubilees or marriages. Such speeches are made by party leaders and back-benchers with some personal link with the persons referred to; the "father of the House" often speaks for all back-benchers on such occasions. Occasionally, by leave of the House (that is if no one objects) motions have been moved without notice, for example on the death of the Duke of Windsor in 1972 (when the reactions of the House were reflected in an amendment, that was agreed to unanimously, to add condolences to the Duchess of Windsor).[29]

Next come ballots for the right to move private Members' motions. In a

[27] See, e.g. H.C.Deb., Vol. 132, cols. 1021, 1024, 1031–1034 (May 5, 1988).
[28] H.C.Deb., Vol. 109, col. 1142 (February 5, 1987) H.C.Deb., Vol. 110, cols. 459–460, 471–474 (February 12, 1987), and H.C.Deb., Vol. 128, cols. 161–162 (February 23, 1988).
[29] H.C.Deb., Vol. 838, cols. 37–49 (June 5, 1972).

normal length session, these are held on 13 days specified in the order made at the beginning of each session (see page 400). Members sign the ballot book during Question time and when the time comes to hold the ballot the Clerk Assistant draws three numbers and the Speaker reads out the names of the fortunate Members whose motions will have priority on the day concerned. But they need not give notice of their motions at this stage.

Occasionally personal explanations are, with the Speaker's permission, made at this point. These may relate to a range of matters. Examples in the last forty years include: a Member drawing attention to erroneous statements about himself with consequent apologies[30]; an explanation by the Chairman of Ways and Means on why he acted in a professional capacity (as a solicitor) for one Member against another[31]; a statement made by a Minister challenging allegations made in the House by certain Members about his personal conduct which reflected on his suitability to hold his office (the allegations were later shown to be true, and the Minister, by making a personal statement which deliberately misled the House, was found to have committed a grave contempt)[32]; vice versa, a statement withdrawing a charge that Philby was the "third man" in the Burgess and Maclean case (the House later formally resolved that this withdrawal was based on wrong assumptions and that the original allegation had been justified)[33]; and even a statement on the reasons for a Member resigning his seat (because he had promised to do so if he ever left the party for which he stood at the election).[34] In all these cases, the agreement of the Speaker has to be given to the terms of the statement, which should not be controversial or provocative.[35] Personal statements are normally heard without interruption.[36] Debate or questions are not allowed following a personal statement, though another Member who is involved in the matter may then also make a statement, for example to apologise.[37]

There is one other kind of personal statement which is not subject to prior vetting by the Speaker, namely those sometimes made by Cabinet Ministers when resigning from the Government; again no debate is permitted. Post war examples include Mr. Aneurin Bevan and Mr. Harold Wilson,[38] Mr. George Brown,[39] and Mrs. Judith Hart.[40] Sir Thomas Dugdale made a similar statement during a debate.[41]

Somewhere around this stage, points of order may be raised. A point of order as properly understood relates to the practices or procedures of the House and essentially to a matter on which the Chair has power to take action—for example whether a Member is in order in using certain language

---

[30] H.C.Deb., Vol. 535, cols. 2609–2610 (December 21, 1954).

[31] H.C.Deb., Vol. 448, cols. 2584–2586 (March 22, 1948).

[32] H.C.Deb., Vol. 674, cols. 809–810; (March 22, 1963), H.C.Deb., Vol. 679, cols. 655–665 (June 20, 1963).

[33] H.C.Deb., Vol. 545, cols. 29, 2014 (October 25 and November 10, 1955); H.C.Deb., Vol. 681, col. 682 (July 17, 1963).

[34] H.C.Deb., Vol. 23, cols. 38–39 (May 4, 1982).

[35] For a case where the Member did not adhere to the terms of the statement approved by the Speaker, see H.C.Deb., Vol. 131, cols. 675–677 (April 19, 1988).

[36] H.C.Deb., Vol. 23, col. 38 (May 4, 1982).

[37] H.C.Deb., Vol. 535, col. 2609 (December 21, 1954).

[38] H.C.Deb., Vol. 487, cols. 34–43, 228–231 (April 23 and 24, 1951).

[39] H.C.Deb., Vol. 761, cols. 55–57 (March 18, 1968).

[40] H.C.Deb., Vol. 893, cols. 418–420 (June 11, 1975).

[41] H.C.Deb., Vol. 530, col. 1194 (July 20, 1954).

which might be "un-parliamentary" or whether a motion or an amendment or a Question is within the rules of the House. In practice so-called "points of order" are more usually related to matters over which the Chair has no powers, such as the arrangement of government business, or the choice of Minister to reply to a debate, or indeed the content of a Minister's answer or statement. On such matters the Speaker frequently has to reply, with whatever degree of patience or impatience he thinks appropriate, "that is not a point of order" or "that is not a matter for the Chair."

What the Chair has called "fraudulent points of order"[42] are however frequently employed by Members to enable them to make a political point against a Minister or against their opponents. This is possible because genuine points of order, relating to the enforcement of the rules of the House, must be raised without delay, and therefore the very use of that phrase gives a Member the right to be heard, even in the middle of another Member's speech. The difficulty for the Chair is that until the point of order has been explained, he has no knowledge of whether it is genuine or not, so he must hear it. And even if it is not a proper point of order, one such "point of order" leads to another, and another and another—and the Chair must hear them all, unless, as sometimes happens, he decides that he must bring the exchanges to an end and refuse to hear any more points of order on that matter.[43]

Where a genuine point of order is raised, the Chair will rule on it and, if necessary, immediately enforce the rule, for example by requiring a Member to withdraw an un-parliamentary expression. If the matter is complicated, for example, whether a particular bill is hybrid or a particular amendment outside the scope of a bill, or if the facts require investigation, the Chair will undertake to consider the point of order and to rule on it later or on another day. If a Member is seeking guidance on how to raise a matter in the House, the Speaker declines to give him a lesson in parliamentary procedure there and then. If the matter raised relates to the organisation of business, the Leader of the House, if present, will note the point (sometimes the Speaker will, in effect, nod in his direction) and, particularly if the Opposition front-bench are involved, may himself rise "on a point of order" and defuse the situation by indicating his willingness to look into the problem—probably by "discussion through the usual channels" (see Chapter 7). The Speaker has, however, deprecated Ministers making prepared statements in response to alleged points of order, as they cannot then be properly questioned on them.[44]

As shown by the following Table, the practice of raising points of order after Questions or before the main business appears to have increased somewhat in recent years, or at least it is taking more time (including time on Speaker's rulings in reply to points of order)—

[42] e.g. H.C.Deb., Vol. 503, col. 277 (July 1, 1952).
[43] See, e.g. H.C.Deb., Vol. 971, cols. 100–105 (July 23, 1979), H.C.Deb., Vol. 109, col. 812 (February 3, 1987), and H.C.Deb., Vol. 112, cols. 935–936 (March 18, 1987). But even then Members may try to raise "a different point of order," and so prolong the matter.
[44] H.C.Deb., Vol. 91, cols. 560–565 (February 7, 1986); col. 794 (February 11, 1986), cols. 960–962 (February 12, 1986).

Time taken on points of order and Speaker's rulings (a)

Session	Time	
	hours	minutes
1976–77	6	23
1977–78	8	56
1978–79(b)	4	55
1979–80(c)	14	38
1980–81	2	34
1981–82	5	20
1982–83(b)	5	33
1983–84(c)	14	39
1984–85	14	12
1985–86	14	21
1986–87(b)	9	30

(a) After Questions at 3.30, not in the course of debate.
(b) Unusually short session.
(c) Unusually long session.

Lastly, at this stage, urgent matters relating to privilege may be taken (excluding complaints of breach of privilege which do not require immediate attention, as these are now raised privately by letter to the Speaker, see page 96) including debate on motions for new writs for by-elections, if they have been opposed when first moved before Questions.

The above business may take anything between no time at all to some two hours if there are several PNQs or Ministerial statements. So the House sometimes does not reach the next block of business until after 5 o'clock.

Business Taken "at the Commencement of Public Business"

This block comprises a number of events of an essentially brief and often formal nature, of which notice has been given on a previous day and which appear on the Order Paper under the heading "At the Commencement of Public Business." Unlike most business in the preceeding group, this business also involves some formal decision by the House which will therefore be recorded in the Votes and Proceedings and Journal. Some business in this category is taken on most Mondays to Thursdays.

The business falls under three heads. First is the presentation of public bills under Standing Order No. 39, by either Ministers or back-benchers (see pages 228–229 and 384). As this does not involve any debate, the time spent is minimal. In 1985–86, 26 Government bills and 51 private Members' bills were presented in this way (20 of the latter being presented on the same day following the ballot).

Next come business motions moved by Ministers, usually in the name of the Leader of the House. These fall into two classes. First those made pursuant to a Standing Order and decided without amendment or debate. The most common of these are motions under Standing Order No. 101(3) to refer statutory instruments to a standing committee for consideration (see page 246); if more than one such motion is on the paper, the Speaker frequently, with the leave of the House, puts one question on all of the motions together. Other motions are made under Standing Order No. 102 (3) to refer European Community documents to standing committees; under Standing Order No. 100(3) to refer matters relating to regional affairs to the Standing Committee on Regional Affairs and similar motions under Standing Order No. 99(2) to refer matters to the Northern Ireland Committee (these are now rare, see pages 274–275 and 277); motions under Standing

Order Nos. 96 and 97(1) to refer Scottish estimates, and matters relating exclusively to Scotland to the Scottish Grand Committee; similar motions under Standing Order No. 98(2) and (5) to refer Welsh bills or matters to the Welsh Grand Committee; and motions under Standing Order No. 90(1) to refer public bills to a second reading committee. None of these motions may be debated; they are rarely opposed; and they consume little time.

Of more interest are motions, for which standing orders do not provide, to modify the procedure of the House for specified business. Frequently these business motions suspend, or vary the provisions of standing orders. These are fully debatable motions, and may, within limits, be amended. Sometimes they are controversial, but more often they have been agreed through the usual channels (see Chapter 7). Examples of such motions include: motions to vary the normal sitting days or the hours of a particular sitting; motions to limit the time for which a specified motion may be debated, and sometimes to provide that questions necessary to dispose of proceedings on that motion and on selected amendments shall be put automatically at the end of that debate; motions to enable the House to consider several motions together (for example a mixture of Government affirmative motions and Opposition prayers) with separate questions being put, as required, at the end of a specified time (under such procedures several motions have been debated together for three hours whereas under Standing Order No. 3(1) (b), they would only be debatable for 1½ hours each); motions to vary the days available for private Member's business; and, finally, motions to permit certain bills to be taken through more than one stage on the same day or to enable an urgent bill to be hurried through all stages at one sitting. Guillotine motions for limiting time for consideration of specified bills (see pages 225–227) are not considered at this stage.

It will be noted that many of these business motions involve a somewhat artificial "packaging" of the House's debates—so many hours for this motion; the question to be put automatically (whether or not anyone is still wishing to speak) on that motion; several motions to be debated together, etc. And increasingly such business motions are being put down not in relation to that day's business but to regulate business on some future day; the figures for recent sessions being as follows:

Business of the House motions

(excluding ten o'clock suspension motions)

Session	Relating to the same day	Relating to a future day
1980–81	17	2
1981–82	20	1
1982–83(a)	6	2
1983–84(b)	9	16
1984 85	3	10
1985–86	3	21
1986–87(a)	3	6

(a) Unusually short session
(b) Unusually long session

In this, as in other ways, the Government, using their majority, and largely with the acquiescence of the Opposition (who rarely oppose and often benefit from such motions) have increased their detailed control over the business of the House and, especially, over the time spent on each item of business. It is a far cry from the "basic procedure" of Parliament under which each motion was debatable almost without limit (see page 177); but it appears to be the way the majority of Members wish things to be. The convenience of the majority—the Government gets its business through; the Opposition knows precisely when to marshal their forces for divisions; and the mass of back-benchers do not suffer from lengthy debate and late sittings—has increasingly predominated over the rights of minorities and individuals who might wish to debate matters long after others have lost interest.

The third item of business that is taken "at the commencement of public business" on most Tuesdays and Wednesdays,[45] are motions by back-benchers for leave to bring in bills under what is known as the "ten-minute rule" (see pages 228–229 and 390–391). These motions, if unopposed, take only about 10 minutes, but if opposed, and if followed by a division, the proceedings can take over half-an-hour. The time spent on 58 ten-minute rule motions in Session 1985–86 was a little over 11 hours.

Privilege Motions of which Notice has been given

If the Speaker has granted precedence to a privilege complaint (see page 96), the relevant motion will be taken at this stage, because privilege business takes precedence over all other business. Only about one such motion is normally allowed each session (see page 98).

Orders of the Day and Notices of Motions

At any time between 3.30 p.m. and around 5.30 p.m., depending on what other business has been taken after Questions, the House comes at last to the main business of the day. This has, of course, been announced in the weekly business statement and details appear on the Order Paper.

All the items to be considered consist of either notices of motions or orders of the day. The differences are largely technical and for most Members have little practical significance although there are some procedural nuances. Notices of motions are put down by named Members to be moved by one of them when called; they can be removed from the Order Paper by the same Members; and the Member who moves has a right of reply at the end of the debate. Motions are used to express opinions or to regulate some proceedings. Orders of the day are items of business appearing on the paper by order of the House. When an order of the day is read by the Clerk at the Table, any Member may move any related motion (for example, "That the bill be read a second time"), but he does not have a right of reply. Orders of the day can be discharged (that is, withdrawn or deferred to a later day) only by order of the House, although such orders are often made by "book-entry" (formally, on the private instruction of the Member in charge of the business, without anything being said in the House); such entries are recorded in the Votes and Proceedings and Journal (but not in Hansard). Orders down

---

[45] Not on Budget day, when the Government Whips do all they can to avoid such a motion delaying the Chancellor's speech by seeking to secure a place for one of their supporters, who then withdraws when it is too late for anyone else to fill the gap.

for future days may similarly be discharged (but may not be advanced to an earlier day). Most orders of the day are the various stages of bills, but an adjourned debate on a motion is also of this class. Put another way, a notice of motion is new business; an order of the day is a later stage of business previously initiated.

Notices of motions and orders of the day are disposed of—agreed (with or without amendment), negatived or withdrawn—in the order in which they appear on the Order Paper, pursuant to Standing Order No. 24, although various events, such as motions for the withdrawal of strangers, the "naming" of Members, urgent statements between orders, or the suspension or adjournment of the House in cases of grave disorder, can occasionally interrupt the orderly dispatch of business. Only Ministers can move the adjournment of the House between orders of the day; this has sometimes been done to permit a statement and short debate on a matter of urgency (for example, on the signing of the Brussels Treaty on March 17, 1948), although a simple statement would now usually be permitted by the Speaker for such purposes.

Also under Standing Order No. 24 Government business is arranged on the Order Paper in whatever order the Chief Whip decides. For private Members' business, where each item, be it a motion or a stage of a bill, belongs to different Members (often with rivalling interests) the business is taken strictly in the order (subject to certain priority for the later stages of bills) in which it was first set down for that day (see pages 388–389 and 396).

Orders of the day not disposed of, and adjourned debates, are set down for such future days as the Member in charge may appoint; and orders (but not motions) not reached that day automatically stand over till the next sitting, unless the Member in charge otherwise instructs the Clerk at the Table (Standing Order No. 9(5)). The latter is a daily occurrence for Government business, as nearly all Government business is formally put down for each day; only some items are actually taken, however, and the rest (set out as "remaining orders," see page 168) are deferred. For private Members' bills however, all the orders are read over on each occasion when such business has priority (see page 393). If no instructions are given about an order which has been read, it becomes a dropped order (it disappears from the Order Book), but it may be revived by a "book-entry" on the instruction of the Member in charge; this happens frequently with private Members' bills.

Moment of Interruption and Ten o'clock Business Motions

At 10.00 p.m. on Tuesdays to Thursdays the business under consideration is interrupted (unless it be business which is automatically exempted from such procedure—see pages 201–202). This is termed "the moment of interruption." If a decision is expected at this point (for example, on the second reading of a bill or on a motion on an Opposition day), the Minister replying to the debate sits down just before 10.00 p.m. and, provided no one else tries to speak, the question is then put and there may, if desired, be a division. But if the Member speaking does not sit down, or if someone else seeks to "catch the Speaker's eye," the closure may be moved (see page 222). Thus divisions at 10.00 p.m. are not automatic as is often thought, but the closure does guarantee their possibility providing the majority are so agreed. The closure may be claimed before or at the moment of interruption.

In practice the closure is quite often claimed at 10.00 p.m. on Opposition days by the Opposition, which wishes to ensure that it gets a chance to divide on its motion, and is then regularly granted by the Chair and agreed to by the House without division; it is similarly claimed by the Opposition when it wishes a division at the end of a debate on the adjournment. It is rarely claimed by the Government at 10.00 p.m. on the second readings of its bills or after debate on a Government motion as the House is usually ready to vote without a closure. It is the possibility of the closure—not its actual use—which effectively ensures that debates end, and divisions are held, at 10.00 p.m., however many further Members would have wished to speak.

After the moment of interruption and the disposal of business in the way described, the Government Whips may move a business motion under Standing Order No. 14(2) to (4) of which notice appears on the Order Paper, to permit specified further business to be proceeded with though opposed for a specified, or for unlimited, time. This is sometimes to enable business being considered before 10.00 p.m. to be continued, and sometimes to enable new opposed business that would otherwise not be permitted at that hour of the night to be debated and disposed of. Such motions are moved on a large number of days each session. In accordance with the standing order, they must be moved by a Minister and are not amendable or debatable. Nowadays they are nearly always agreed without division.

Exempted Business

The House can now consider business which is exempt from the ten o'clock rule, either because the rule has just been suspended for this purpose, or because a standing order so exempts it. Certain business is exempted completely; under Standing Order No. 14(1)(a) proceedings upon a bill brought in upon Ways and Means resolutions (principally the Finance Bill) may continue until any hour (although in practice Finance Bill debates do not go as late as they used to). Other business is only exempted for limited time. Most of the latter category comprises proceedings on delegated legislation under Standing Order Nos. 14 and 15 (see pages 246–247). But proceedings on money resolutions are also exempted under Standing Order No. 14(1)(d) until 10.45 p.m. or for three-quarters of an hour after they have started, whichever is the later. Debate on European Community documents (defined by Standing Order No. 14(1) as comprising draft proposals by the Commission of the European Committees for legislation and other documents published for submission to the Council of Ministers or the European Council, whether or not such documents originate from the Commission) may, under Standing Order No. 14(1)(b) be debated until 11.30 p.m. or for an hour and a half after commencement of proceedings on them, whichever is the later; this is the same limit as for affirmative resolutions on statutory instruments. Lastly, under Standing Order No. 54, the House may debate matters chosen by back-benchers till 9.00 a.m. (8.00 a.m. on a Thursday night debate) on the adjournment motion moved after the passage of each Consolidated Fund Bill (see pages 249 and 265–266). Certain other business that may be opposed, can be taken without amendment or debate, (i.e. the question is put forthwith): motions under Standing Order No. 80(b) to approve recommendations made by a business committee for guillotining a bill (see page 226); motions under Standing Order No. 131(2) for approval of recommendations of the Liaison Committee for the consideration of estimates by the House (see page 250); and affirmative resolutions made under Standing Order No. 101(5) to approve statutory instruments that have already been debated in a standing committee (see page 246). Similar motions may be made pursuant to Standing Order No. 102(5) (and here amendments are permitted) and questions put forthwith relating to European Community documents which have been considered in a standing committee (see page 276). Such motions are rarely opposed.

Presentation of Public Petitions

When all the intended business of the day has been dealt with, and before the motion is moved for the adjournment of the House, back-bench Members on either side may present public petitions. However there can be no debate on such petitions so their presentation takes little time (see pages 267–268).

Adjournment of the House

A motion is now moved formally by a Government Whip for the adjournment of the House which permits a short debate (see page 266).

Thus the House concludes its business for the day. The Speaker (or his Deputy) leaves the Chamber behind the Serjeant (or his Deputy) carrying the Mace. He informs the Serjeant that the House will sit at "the usual time tomorrow." The nearly empty House and lobbies echo the call of the doorkeeper, "who goes home?" Only a few clerks are left to write up the Votes and Proceedings and to send the proofs of the next day's Order Paper to the printer; the staff in the Library begin to turn out the lights; the late duty Hansard reporters dispose of the last of their copy; the bars, tea-room and Post Office are closed; and the Palace is handed over to the police and custodians for the night. The House has risen.

Arrangements on a Friday

The arrangements for a Friday sitting are similar, with the following exceptions provided for in Standing Order No. 11. First, the House sits at 9.30 a.m. and business is interrupted at 2.30 p.m. It is unusual for the rule to be suspended or for exempted business to be taken after 2.30 p.m., although this very occasionally happens when Government business is taken.[46] Time limits of such exempted business are consequently adjusted: for instance affirmative resolutions started before or at 2.30 p.m. end not later than 4.00 p.m. In the 1983–87 Parliament, the House debated opposed business after 2.30 p.m. on only two occasions. The latest time of rising on a Friday since 1979 was 6.30 p.m. on July 31, 1981.

Secondly, there are some variations in the business arrangements. Unopposed private business may be taken, but rarely is: opposed private business may not be set down for a Friday (Standing Order No. 16). Petitions are presented at the beginning of the sitting instead of the end.[47] There is no Question hour. Business may be interrupted, however, at 11.00 a.m. for

---

[46] The Leader of the House gave an assurance in 1980, that the Government would only move to suspend the 2.30 p.m. rule "in special circumstances of urgency and importance" (H.C.Deb., Vol. 976, col. 2048 (January 12, 1980).

[47] In the spring of 1988 the Government tabled a revised standing order to limit the number of petitions taken at this time, but this was not proceeded with and had not been tabled again in the 1988–89 session at the time we went to press.

ministerial statement (including business statements), private notice Questions or personal statements, although the Speaker has deprecated statements on Fridays which eat into private Members' time.[48] Members may not seek to move emergency adjournment motions under Standing Order No. 20 on Fridays, and such motions, if allowed, cannot be set down for such days. Nor can Members move for leave to bring in bills under Standing Order No. 15 (the "ten-minute rule").

On 21 Fridays each session, in recent years, private Members' business has had priority over Government business (see pages 11–12). Opposition days are not, in practice, taken on Fridays.

FORMS OF PROCEDURE

It is convenient at this stage to describe the principal forms of procedure used by the House. How they are used—by the Government, by the Opposition and by back-benchers,—is the theme of Chapters 7 to 11.

Debate

The process of debate, as established by basic procedures (see pages 177), is the main process used for most of the House's business—but not all; it is not used in Questions or Ministerial statements, or in select committee proceedings, for example. The process is essentially simple: a motion is made ("That this House approves . . . "); a question is proposed by the Chair in the same form; debate arises; the question is put; it is agreed to or negatived; if agreed a resolution (expressing an opinion) or an order (requiring action by the House, or a committee or individual Members or officers) results. There are all sorts of variations or modern qualifications of this basic process: amendments may be moved on which a question is again proposed and each amendment must be disposed of separately, before the main question (as amended if it has been) is put; there may be amendments to amendments; some motions may not, by standing order, be amended or others may not be debated; debate on motions or amendments may be adjourned; debate may be closured; and motions or amendments may be withdrawn. But the essentials are plain; only one motion is considered at a time and in the end all motions (and amendments) must either be agreed to, negatived, or withdrawn.

The logic of this procedure is binary. Decisions are taken in sequence, singly, and each decision on each motion and each amendment is a simple "yes" or "no." With a few exceptions (for example, in the House, 100 Members must vote in the majority for a closure to be effective, and 20 or more Members can block a motion to refer a statutory instrument to a standing committee) there are no qualified majorities; there is no requirement on any question for an absolute majority; and, as we will see, there are not even any procedures for registering abstentions in a division. This binary process is mirrored in—or is a reflection of—the two-sided, confrontational nature of the House's proceedings (see pages 13–15). The systematic logic of these procedures protects the clarity of decision taking.

Motions

Any Member may give notice, and have printed on the Order Paper or as

---

[48] See, *e.g.* H.C.Deb., Vol. 102, col. 363 (July 23, 1986).

a Notice of Motion, almost any motion on any subject, provided it is in proper parliamentary language, and is not in some other way "not a proper subject for debate." Such matters are ultimately decided by the Speaker. Speakers have disallowed notices of motions which have reflected on a Member's mental condition, which are clearly ironic or "tendered in a spirit of mockery," which have included obscenities, or are merely designed to give annoyance. Motions which are unduly long have also been disallowed; Members are not permitted, in effect, to write their speeches into the record.[49]

A more significant reason for not allowing a notice of motion is if the matter is *sub-judice*; the same rule also applies to debate and Questions. The *sub-judice* rule does not however apply to legislative business. In accordance with long-standing practice which was confirmed by resolutions of the House of July 23, 1963 and June 28, 1972, and always subject to the discretion of the Chair, matters awaiting or under adjudication in a criminal court in the United Kingdom must not be referred to; this is normally taken as applying from the moment charges are preferred. The same applies to civil actions once the case has been set down for trial or has been appealed. Under this rule, which comes into operation in relation to some half-dozen cases a session, motions (or Questions) may be kept off the paper until the case is settled, or until the case otherwise ceases to be *sub-judice* under the rules of the House, for instance after a decision by a lower count but before formal notices of appeal has been lodged with a higher count. If a motion has been tabled before the matter became *sub-judice*, it is taken off the paper until the case ceases to be *sub-judice*. Occasionally this has led to complaints in the House, but usually the Speaker, by using his discretion and the power given to him by the 1972 resolution to allow references to "issues of national importance such as the national economy, public order on the essentials of life," has avoided unduly restricting the wishes of Members to table motions or refer in debate to current political issues such as strikes. This has been true even where injunctions have been sought in the courts. References to current criminal trials are, however, more rigidly excluded.

Subject to these rules, Members may give notice of motions on any subject because the House, being subordinate to no other authority save Parliament as a whole, is able to express its opinion on any matters. It is not quite true to say that there is no such thing as an "out of order motion," because motions which repeat motions which have already been agreed to or negatived in the current session, or which anticipate a matter already due to be considered by the House which is likely to be debated in the reasonably near future (see Standing Order No. 26), or which would have the effect of imposing a charge (expenditure) or a tax without the Queen's recommendation, may all be ruled out of order and not called for debate even though they have been allowed on the paper. But these circumstances are exceptional. By and large, Members can table motions on almost anything: whether they have a chance to move them and have a debate is quite another matter.

Amendments

Amendments are more subject to procedural restrictions. They may not be moved and so will not be selected for debate if they are not relevant to the motion they seek to amend; they must not have the effect of rendering the

---

[49] For more details of irregular notices, see May, pp. 381–383.

motion, if amended, unintelligible or self-contradictory; they must be consistent with other amendments already agreed; and they must not, in effect, directly negative the motion itself without explanation (an amendment to a motion "That this House approves ... " which was simply to leave out "approves" and insert "does not approve" would be out of order, but an amendment which sought to add reasons for the disapproval would be in order). Amendments which prove to be out of order may however be tabled and will be printed on the Notice and Order Papers unless they are out of order for the following reasons.

It is an important rule, which has quite frequently to be applied, that the personal conduct or character of a limited group of people cannot be criticised except on a substantive motion, and therefore amendments may not even be tabled, let alone debated, which include such criticism. These protected persons are the Queen and other members of the Royal Family, the Lord Chancellor, the Speaker and other Members of either House, and judges of the superior courts of the United Kingdom. These restrictions have frequently caused difficulty for some Members: references to judges in amendments or debate which go beyond criticism of their judgments and decisions in court and imply, for example, political bias, have been ruled out of order. Members may however incorporate such criticism in a substantive motion—and they frequently do so.

Notice given

Apart from certain procedural motions, which by custom or standing order can be moved without notice, formal notice, given at least one day previously, is required for all substantive motions before they appear on the Order Paper. One day's notice is sufficient for many less controversial motions and for business of the House motions, but on more controversial matters such as motions on Opposition days, longer notice is sometimes (but not always) given, which helps the tabling of amendments. Longer notice is occasionally required by standing order (see pages 281, 390 and 400). In cases of emergency or for some ceremonial occasions, the House has by agreement (one Member's objection, if sustained, would be sufficient veto) waived the need for notice of a motion. Notice is usually, but not necessarily, given of amendments.

Members give notice by handing in the text of the motion, including its title, to the Table or Table Office. Nothing is nowadays said in the House. The motion may be in the names of as many Members as wish to sign it. Many have only one name; traditionally principal Government and Opposition motions are signed by six names; many "early day motions" are signed by large numbers of Members (see pages 268 and 381).

Motions Made and Questions Proposed

Apart from Ministers (who can act for each other) only a Member who gave notice (ie. any signatory) can make a substantive motion; any Member who has not already spoken in a debate can move an amendment which has been selected by the Chair (see page 217). When called by the Chair a Member moves the motion, either formally or with a speech. A seconder is not required. Suppose the motion "That this House fully supports the economic policies of Her Majesty's Government" has been moved by a Minister for a debate in Government time, the question is then proposed from the Chair in the same terms. The debate is now open and the first person called will be an Opposition front bench spokesman on economic affairs. In the course of his speech he may propose an amendment (which will be on the Order Paper) in terms such as these: leave out from "House" to end and add "totally condemns the failure of the Government to tackle the growing problem of unemployment." When he sits down, the Chair proposes the question on the amendment thus: The question is "That the Amendment be made,"[50] and on this question the remainder of the debate takes place. At the end of the debate the two front-benches wind up and the mover of the original motion has, if he wishes, a right of reply. The Minister usually speaks second. When all who wish to take part have spoken (or after a closure) the Chair puts the question, first on the amendment and then on the main question in the same form as it was originally proposed, or as amended if it has been.[51]

Divisions

Many motions are agreed to without divisions; on others the Opposition may wish to register an oral protest when the question is first put, but do not press the matter to a division (particularly after midnight or on some less important business when their supporters may be thin on the ground). But divisions are frequently called—an average of 320 a session in the 1979–87 Parliaments on all forms of business. The process is as follows. First the Speaker (or Chairman) orders "Division. Clear the Lobbies." The news of a division is shouted round the corridors by the policemen and the division bells are sounded throughout the House and in various restaurants and homes (for those who "live on the bell") in the neighbourhood. Members come crowding in and enter one of the two lobbies on either side of the Chamber (Ayes to the right and Noes to the left of the Speaker), where their names are recorded by clerks from the Clerk's Department. At the exit from each lobby they are counted by the tellers who have been appointed by the Chair on the nomination of the Whips or other Members concerned. For each lobby, the tellers are a supporter and an opponent of the question at issue (usually Government and Opposition Whips). On a whipped vote, the Government teller counts and the Opposition teller checks the figures. When everyone has voted the four tellers go to the Table, give the figures to a Clerk at the Table, and one of the tellers on the winning side reads out the numbers; these are then repeated by the Chair who declares the result.

All this takes some considerable time. Two minutes elapse before the naming of the tellers and a further eight minutes are allowed for a Member to come to the division before the entrance doors to the lobbies are locked. The whole process lasts for between some 12 and 20 minutes (depending on the numbers to be counted), which means that in an average session some 80 hours are spent in this way. Procedure Committees have several times

---

[50] This is the standard form of question on an amendment. Exceptionally, under S.O. No. 30, on Government amendments to leave out the effective words and add others on motions on Opposition days, the question is proposed in the form "That the original words stand part of the question", followed (if that is negatived) by "That the proposed words be there added." This enables a vote to be held first on the wording proposed by the Opposition and then on the wording proposed by the Government.

[51] Exceptionally under S.O. No. 30, on Opposition days a further question is not put on the main question; after the divisions on the original words and the Government amendment, the Chair simply declares the motion (as amended) to be agreed to. In effect a further question would be redundant as the decision of the House was taken on the amendment.

examined different systems of recording and counting votes, including electronic methods, but have confirmed each time that the present system
should continue.[52] All studies have shown that little saving of time would
result from any other method so long as Members have to come to the
Chamber from offices and other places which are several minutes away. The
practice is unlikely to change and indeed is favoured by most Members; it
provides a good opportunity to contact Ministers and other fellow-Members
as they walk through the lobbies.

There are various ways in which a division can be nullified: it is called off,
for example, if either side cannot produce two tellers; and it may have to be
called again if something goes wrong in the course of the division (for
example a failure to ring the bells). If fewer than 40 Members take part in the
division (35 voting, plus four tellers, plus the occupant of the Chair) the
division is not effective and the business stands over till the next sitting
(Standing Order No. 40). This happens quite often on private Members'
business.

Under Standing Order No. 39, if the Chair believes that a division has
been unnecessarily claimed—if, for example, a small minority, having been
defeated in one or two divisions on a series of amendments to a bill, seek to
press further amendments in that series to a division—it can, after two
minutes, require Members to vote by rising in their places (and so avoid time
being taken up by walking through the lobbies) and can declare the result on
that evidence. The procedure is rarely used,[53] but its availability is a protection against the use of divisions by a few people for purely obstructive
purposes. It is not suitable for use when a major party wishes to divide the
House.[54]

The numbers of those voting in divisions are recorded in the Votes and
Proceedings and Journal; the numbers and names on each side are shown in
Hansard; and official division lists, corrected as required (sometimes Members are missed out or the wrong name is marked off by mistake) are
published from time to time and bound up each session.

It should be emphasised that only actual votes are recorded; there is no
official way of showing dissent by abstaining, but Members sometimes let
the press (and their Whips) know of their intention to defy their party Whip
and often indicate their position by remaining firmly in their seats while the
House divides. Abstainers on significant occasions (unless paired) are thus
noted and may be listed in the newspapers. Abstentions for personal convenience, which have no political significance, occur all the time by what is
called "pairing." Pairing arrangements, which are registered with the Whips
on either side, involve two Members from opposed parties agreeing not to
vote in a particular division, or between particular hours or on specified

[52] See, for example, Second Report of the Committee, H.C. 58 of 1945–46, p. V; Report of
the Committee, H.C. 92 of 1958–59, paras. 36–37; Third Report of the Committee, H.C. 283 of
1966–67.

[53] There have been five occasions since 1945 when the procedure has been used (some
involving several claimed divisions). The most recent case was on May 25, 1988, on the report
stage of the Firearms (Amendment) Bill, when a small number of Members protested against
the imposition of a guillotine by voting on every Government amendment; Standing Order
No. 39 was used 51 times (H.C.Deb., Vol. 134, cols. 458–485).

[54] For example, on March 23, 1971, the Labour Opposition divided the House 57 times after
midnight on Government amendments put under a guillotine, without debate, to the Industrial
Relations Bill; Standing Order No. 39 was not used, H.C.Deb., Vol. 814, cols. 413–441.

days; thus their potential votes are cancelled out and the Members are free for other official,[55] or personal engagements. This obviously suits the Members concerned and the Whips and parties are happy as long as the margin of votes is unaffected. The Whips on both sides are usually anxious to keep up the spirits of their troops by allowing Members some free evenings; thus pairs are even allowed, to a limited degree, on many three-line whips.[56]

An occasional cause of controversy concerns Members who may have a personal, pecuniary, interest in the subject-matter of a debate. These have to be declared (see pages 57–58) but as far as votes are concerned, the possibility of disallowances is only effective in restricting Members' rights to vote on certain private bills. (See May, pp. 411–416 and page 57 above).

Casting Vote of the Chair

A matter of keen concern at times when the Government enjoys only a slim majority is the casting vote of the Chair. In the Commons, if the numbers in a division are equal, the Speaker or his deputy or a Chairman of a committee (who does not normally vote) has to give a casting vote.[57] It is now well established that the Chair votes according to well-defined principles and not according to its own views of the merits of the issue. Thus, following the ruling of Speaker Addington in 1796, its first guiding principle is to vote to provide opportunity for further discussion (the Chair will, for example, vote Aye on the second reading of a bill). Another principle, laid down by Speaker Denison in 1867, is that the Chair should not allow a final decision of the House to be taken on its casting vote (it will, for example, vote No on any substantive resolution or on the third reading of a bill). A further guidance, which was also expressed by Speaker Denison in 1860, is that the Chair should vote to keep a bill in the form so far approved by the House; it therefore normally votes against amendments, including Lords Amendments to a bill.

A notable occasion on which the Speaker might have had to give a casting vote was on the motion, moved on March 28, 1979, "That this House has no confidence in Her Majesty's Government." In the event this was carried by 311 to 310, one Ulster Independent Member having abstained, and the Government fell. It may be assumed that if the Ulster Member had voted against the motion, and the numbers had been equal, that the Speaker would have given his casting vote with the Noes (following Speaker Denison's decision of 1867) and the life of the Callaghan Government would have been spared (on that day at least).

Rules Governing Speeches

There are rules for debate. Speeches must be addressed to the Chair; they must be in English (although Latin tags were formerly liberally used by those who wished to exhibit their classical education, and occasional quotations in other languages—Welsh for example—have been tolerated); and, with the exception of Ministers' speeches from the dispatch box, they should not

---

[55] For example, Members away on select committee business may agree to pair.

[56] Sometimes no pairs (even for sickness) are allowed. For example on March 28, 1979, for the vote which resulted in the fall of the Labour Government, no pairs were permitted and all but one Member (who was very ill) were present; three by-elections were outstanding.

[57] Exceptionally, in an opposed private bill committee, the Chairman has an original and a casting vote. (Private Business Standing Order 135).

normally be read (although Members have sometimes got away with refer- ring to "copious notes"). The order in which Members are called is entirely a matter for the Chair, but some precedence is usually given to Privy Council- lors and to those wishing to make their maiden speeches; the latter are traditionally heard without interruption.

A Member, once called, has the floor, and, subject to time limits described below, he may speak as long as he likes provided he is relevant to the question before the House and is not guilty of "tedious repetition" (see page 213). In sessions 1984–85 and 1985–86 the House experimented with a rule under which the Speaker could impose a 10-minute limit on speeches in debates on second readings of public bills, Opposition motions on Oppo- sition days and Government motions,[58] during a two-hour period in the early evening; in effect this applied to back-benchers but not to front-bench spokesmen.[59] A permanent rule to this effect, extending also to the debate on the Queen's Speech, and covering either 6 to 8 p.m. or 7 to 9 p.m. on Monday's to Thursdays (and 11.30 a.m. to 1.00 p.m. on Fridays) was made on July 13, 1988.[60] However, the most effective practical restraint on length of speeches is the number of Members wishing to speak and the consequen- tial pressure from colleagues. If many Members are anxious to be called, those speaking will be expected—and urged by the Chair—to be as brief as possible, and will talk for only about 10 to 15 minutes. On other occasions few Members wish to take part in a debate and longer speeches, say 30 or 40 minutes, may be tolerated. Indeed on some occasions the Whips, anxious lest a debate collapse before the agreed time for a division, may encourage their Members to speak at length. On yet other occasions, Members attempting to delay business or to talk out a private Member's bill may make very long speeches indeed. The record in modern times is held by Mr John Golding who, in a standing committee, once spoke for 11¼ hours.[61]

As can be seen, it is not possible to produce a meaningful average for the duration of speeches, but for an ordinary, whole-day debate, with average demand for participation, speeches by back-benchers usually range from 10 to 20 minutes in length. On such occasions the opening front bench spokes- men usually speak for 30 to 40 minutes each, and the winders-up would typically require 20 to 30 minutes. When the detailed stages of bills are being debated, or less important business, speeches are often much shorter.

In the House itself no Member, with certain exceptions, may speak more than once on any question. The mover of an amendment speaks on the main question and cannot speak again, but a Member who speaks to an amend- ment may also speak to the main question or on other amendments. Nowa- days, however, amendments to motions (as opposed to bills) are seldom debated separately from the motion itself. The exceptions to this rule are that the mover of a substantive motion (though not of an order of the day, such as the second reading of a bill) has a right to speak again, usually at the

---

[58] An earlier experiment, in session 1979–80, had applied only to debates on second readings of public bills (see First Report of the Select Committee on Procedure, H.C. 570 of 1983–84.
[59] Reports of the Procedure Committee H.C. 570 of 1983–84, H.C. 623 of 1984–85 and H.C. 592 of 1985–86.
[60] H.C.Deb., Vol. 137, cols. 503–524. The standing order is now S.O. No. 45A.
[61] On the Telecommunications Bill, 1982–83 (Standing Committee Debates (Stg Co H), cols. 795–913 (February 8, 1983)). As a result of this experience Standing Order No. 28 was passed to prevent its repetition (see pp. 224–225).

end of a debate; and, under Standing Order No. 74, when a Bill is considered after being reported from a standing committee, the Member in charge of the bill and the mover of any amendment or new clause, may speak more than once in respect of that amendment or new clause. Otherwise Members may only speak again by leave of the House (which means unanimous consent of those present); this is frequently granted to Ministers to enable them to reply to debates on bills or an adjournment debate, but is occasionally refused when a Minister has annoyed the House—or one section of it—in some way.[61a] There is no restriction on the number of times a Member may speak in any committee.

On the whole a Member can speak freely (protected as he is by privilege from possible actions for defamation (see page 88), subject to compliance with certain conventions and rules of the House. It is, for example, out of order to quote from speeches made in the House of Lords in the current session, other than speeches by Ministers. References to the Queen should be in respectful terms (in earlier centuries Members were sent to the Tower for offending against this rule, but it has not created such problems in recent years).

The rule requiring criticism of the conduct of various people to be debated on a substantive motion (see page 205) obviously restricts what can properly be said in debate on other occasions. This rule has to be enforced from time to time; for example several Members have been named or ordered to withdraw from the House (see pages 213–215) in recent years for refusing to withdraw charges against the personal conduct or honour of various people: accusing Ministers of lying[62]; suggesting that the Prime Minister would be prepared to bribe judges to get her own way[63]; referring to "tame Tory judges"[64]; alleging that "the Chancellor of the Exchequer is perverting the course of justice"[65]; and suggesting that the company of a certain Lord had stolen £9 million from the Post Office and imputing that certain Lords were "a load of thieves and rogues."[66] On many more occasions Members have obeyed the request of the Chair and withdrawn such remarks or other un-parliamentary expressions.

Various words have been ruled "un-parliamentary," including a wide range of abusive terms some of which now have a distinctly old-fashioned flavour, such as "cad," "corrupt," "dog," "guttersnipe," "humbug," "hypocrite," "behaving like a jackass," "cheeky young pup," "stool-pigeons," "swine," "vicious and vulgar," and even the simple "wicked." (It is interesting how often the animal kingdom is called in aid when venting abuse on opponents.[67]) When considering whether an expression is unparliamentary, the Chair (and Members generally) have to consider the context: some people may be accused of dishonesty, others not; heated language in some circumstances may be readily understood or overlooked, in other cases it may be deliberately damaging to the debate; one man's despicable jackass

---

[61a] For a recent example see H.C.Deb., Vol. 139, col. 705 (November 11, 1988).

[62] H.C.Deb., Vol. 2, col. 950 (April 8, 1981); H.C.Deb., Vol. 59, cols. 345–349 (May 2, 1984).

[63] H.C.Deb., Vol. 64, cols. 181–185 (July 17, 1984).

[64] H.C.Deb., Vol. 65, cols. 218–221 (July 31, 1984).

[65] H.C.Deb., Vol. 86, cols. 256, 313–316 (November 8 and 11, 1985).

[66] H.C.Deb., Vol. 954, cols. 416–419 (July 18, 1978).

[67] For a fuller list, see Erskine May, 19th Edition, p. 445, but this list was discontinued in later editons.

may be another's amiable old donkey. Any abusive words which are likely to create disorder may be ruled out, but the main guiding principle is that charges should not be made against Members (or other persons in the protected category listed on page 205 above) which question their honesty or integrity, for example by imputations of false motives, charges of lying, deliberately misleading the House and other falsehoods. A Member cannot be both honourable and dishonest.[68] Erskine May says, "good temper and moderation are the characteristics of parliamentary language" (although "ought to be" might be more realistic).[69] However, as the Speaker has said "we have controversy politics in this Chamber and I hope we shall always have a robust Parliament and not be mealy-mouthed."[70]

It is also a convention, though a matter of courtesy rather than a rule which the Chair can enforce, that Members give notice to each other if they intend to raise matters concerning another Member's constituency[71] or to criticise his conduct in some way.[72]

There are other, more specialised, rules of debate. Reference must not be made to matters which are *sub-judice* (see page 204). Care must be used when criticising the other House. It is not in order to quote directly from speeches made in the Lords, other than the speeches of Ministers. Ministers must not quote (as opposed to summarise[73]) from unpublished dispatches or other state papers unless they are prepared to lay them before the House; this rule does not apply to quotations from private letters and memoranda, and Ministers can still excuse themselves from the rule by claiming that compliance would injure the public interest. On the other hand Ministers do sometimes lay documents, from which they have quoted, in the Library.[74]

Members cannot flourish weapons in the Chamber but have been allowed to exhibit other articles to illustrate an argument: one Member produced an English apple to demonstrate his support for the fruit-growers of his constituency. References to the strangers in the gallery are frowned upon and the presence of even the most distinguished foreign statesman goes unremarked. Finally, Members are required, by resolution of the House, to declare in debate (though not during oral questions) any personal pecuniary interest they may have in the matter under discussion; Members frequently

---

[68] Allegations of collective lack of integrity—"the hypocrisy of the party opposite"—have however been allowed; and the Speaker has ruled that while it may be permitted to describe a party as "racist" it would be out of order to apply that term to an individual Member (H.C.Deb., Vol. 103, col. 127 (October 27, 1986).

[69] May, p. 432.

[70] H.C.Deb., Vol. 128, col. 666 (February 24, 1988).

[71] See, *e.g.* H.C.Deb., Vol. 92, col. 37 (February 17, 1986).

[72] See, *e.g.* H.C.Deb., Vol. 96, col. 312 (April 23, 1986); H.C. Deb., Vol. 143, cols. 1107–1110 (December 15, 1988).

[73] A case where the Speaker insisted that his decision as to whether a Minister had quoted or not, must be based on what was said in the House, whatever other evidence was produced, arose from the Westland Affair in 1986. A Minister, having made full reference to the official minutes of a meeting he had had with certain industrialists, was not required to lay the minutes on the Table as his account of the minute was in reported speech and did not purport to be a quotation (H.C.Deb., Vol. 90, col. 205 (January 21, 1986)). Although support for the contention that the Minister had quoted directly was provided in the form of a leaked copy of the minutes of the meeting, the Speaker pointed out that he had no authority to send for Cabinet documents; he had to decide, and rule, on the basis of what was said in the House, and he could not tell whether Ministers were quoting or not except from what the Minister himself said (H.C.Deb., Vol. 90, col. 461, (Janaury 23, 1986)).

[74] See, *e.g.* H.C.Deb., Vol. 91, cols. 629, 641 (February 10, 1986).

begin their speech with such words as "As a farmer (or director of a company, etc.) I must declare an interest." They are not required to declare the value of their interests (see also pages 58–59).

Rules Applying to Members not Speaking

Other rules and conventions apply to Members who are not speaking. Members bow to the Chair when entering or leaving the Chamber.[75] Members should not read books or newspapers unrelated to the business, or deal with their correspondence (although it is not unknown for a Member to sign his letters as he waits for the next division). Smoking is not permitted. Although informality and variety of dress and fashion are now more general (especially in warmer weather) a certain sense of propriety in dress is maintained: Speaker Thomas said that it was "the custom in every Parliament" for Members to wear jackets and ties[76] (but customs change so this may not remain true for ever).

Members are expected to remain reasonably silent while someone else is speaking and not disturb the person addressing the House by unruly interruptions. Clearly this last rule cannot always be enforced, and indeed the House would be a duller place if all speeches were heard in total silence; reasonable reactions are a natural part of a critical assembly representing a wide range of opinions. But some restraint is required if the minimum essential requirement—that all Members may be heard, however unpopular their remarks—is to be observed. Although the House today seldom hears the crowing of cocks and other animal noises which have been condemned in the past, the multiplication of reactions ("nonsense," "come off it," "what about your friends," "go back to . . . ") and other derisory comments which singly might be harmless, often result in a level of noise which makes it almost impossible to hear the person speaking. This happens quite frequently, especially during Prime Minister's Questions and the wind-up speeches at the end of a controversial debate when the House is crowded awaiting a division. It is then necessary for the Chair to intervene and to call the House to order. This is not a new problem, although the sound broadcasting of the House has made a wider public more aware of it, and it has been experienced throughout Parliament's history. No doubt noisy debate will continue so long as Members feel strongly about the issues of the day and ordinary human beings are elected to the House of Commons.[77]

Powers of the Chair to Control Debate

As will be seen from the description of the conduct of debate, much depends on the powers of the Chair to control debate and enforce order. The Speaker, his deputies and the chairmen of committees are therefore given certain disciplinary powers, which they can exercise on their own initiative.

---

[75] It is sometimes argued that the bow is directed to the altar that used to be behind the Speaker's Chair when the House sat in the St. Stephen's Chapel after 1547; the fact that the Speaker himself bows when entering the Chamber supports this theory.

[76] H.C.Deb., Vol. 27, col. 468 (July 8, 1982).

[77] Ministers of all parties are liable to suffer in this way. One of the authors remembers seeing Sir Winston Churchill, when Prime Minister from 1951 to 1955, shouted down on more than one occasion. His response was simple but effective: instead of trying to raise his voice over the hubbub he would lower it almost to a whisper and the noise would subside; you cannot readily heckle a speaker if you cannot hear what he is saying.

The first power of the Chair, which is exercised many times a day, lies in the simple authority of the Speaker's office. When he rises, all other Members should sit down; when he speaks others should be silent; when he calls for order (conventionally simply by saying "order, order") his wishes and orders must be obeyed (for example, a Member may be required to withdraw an un-parliamentary expression). It is only when the wishes of the Chair are not respected or his directions disobeyed that the Chair needs to resort to formal disciplinary powers, given him by standing order, to restore order or enforce his authority[77a]. Although these powers only occasionally need to be formally activated, their very existence supports the Speaker and other occupants of the Chair in the daily exercise of their authority.

Standing Order No. 41 gives the Chair power to deal with irrelevance in debate or undue prolongation of a speech (a form of filibustering in which the Irish nationalist Members specialised in the last century and which led to the adoption of this standing order in 1882). If a Member is roaming wide of the question before the House or committee and introducing a lot of irrelevant material or if he repeats facts or arguments at length which have already been advanced, the Chair will first require him to speak to the question or to shorten his remarks. If he persists in going wide or in repetition, the Chair warns him that he must come to order. And if he fails to respond, the Chair can order him to discontinue and resume his seat on the grounds that, to quote the standing order, he has persisted in "irrelevance or tedious repetition either of his own arguments or of the arguments used by other Members in debate." This standing order is seldom actually used; there were only 17 occasions in the Chamber from 1945 till the end of Session 1987–88 (four of them in committee).[78] It has normally been applied to deal with irrelevance rather than repetition; and there are no cases in recent years where a Member has been disciplined, or even restrained, for repeating the arguments already used by other Members.

If a Member is "grossly disorderly" or persists in disorderly conduct, particularly if he disregards the authority of the Chair and usually after several warnings, the Chair can use its powers under Standing Order No. 42 and require the Member to leave the House for the remainder of that day's sitting. This power was used on 30 occasions from 1945 up till the end of Session 1987–88 (18 times after 1979). On two of these occasions the power was exercised by the chairman in a Committee of the whole House. On only five of these occasions was the suspended Member a member of the ruling party. In 11 of these cases the order of the Chair was not obeyed and the Member had to be named (see below). The offences for which Members have been ordered to withdraw from the House include refusal to withdraw un-parliamentary language, refusal to discontinue a speech when ordered to do so under Standing Order No. 41, challenging the discretion of the Chair in selecting amendments or calling Members to speak in a time-limited debate, and imputing partiality to the Chair in exercising its powers.

For the most serious cases of disorder by individual Members in the Chamber itself and the most flagrant flouting of the Chair's authority,

---

[77a] The powers of the Chair to deal with disorderly conduct by Members were under review at the time we went to press, following a report by the Procedures Committee (First Report, H.C. 290 of 1988–89).

[78] For recent examples see H.C.Deb., Vol. 125, col. 928 (January 19, 1988); H.C. Deb., Vol. 148, cols. 720–722 (March 7, 1989).

including cases where Members have refused to withdraw from the Chamber when ordered to do so, the Chair may find its own authority is insufficient and may need the support of the House itself. In such circumstances the Speaker or his deputy names the Member or Members[79] concerned. He simply says "I name Mr ... " and the procedures laid down by Standing Order No. 43 then come into operation. If a Member is named in the House a motion is immediately made by the Leader of the House (or by another Minister on his behalf) "That Mr ... be suspended from the service of the House." If the offence is committed in a committee of the whole House, the Chairman or Deputy Chairman[80] names the Member and then suspends the proceedings until the Speaker resumes the Chair, when the Chairman reports that a Member has been named for whatever reason, and the motion for his suspension is then moved as if the offence had been committed in the House itself. The motion is not amendable or debatable and the question is therefore put forthwith; there may be a division, even at the time of unopposed business. When such a motion is agreed, the Speaker orders the Member to withdraw.

Suspension under this procedure lasts for five sitting days (including the day of the offence) on the first occasion in a session; if the same Member is again named and suspended in the same session, his suspension then lasts for 20 sitting days[81]; if he were to incur this penalty a third time he would be suspended for the remainder of the session, unless the House reprieved him. A Member ordered to withdraw under Standing Order No. 42 or suspended under Standing Order No. 43 is required by Standing Order No. 44 to leave the precincts of the House entirely, except for service on private bill committees. While suspended he can perform no other parliamentary function, such as the tabling of Questions or motions.

If the orders of the Chair, under either Standing Orders Nos. 42 or 43, for a Member to withdraw from the House are not immediately complied with, the Speaker may order the Serjeant at Arms to ensure compliance with the order, and if necessary to use force to remove the offending Member; if this power is necessary, the Member is automatically suspended for the remainder of the session. (Standing Order No. 43(4)).[82]

---

[79] Two or more Members may be named at the same time only if they have jointly disregarded the authority of the Chair. See, for example, the naming of three Ulster Members on November 16, 1981, following an organised protest from the galleries reserved for Members. H.C.Deb., Vol. 13, cols. 24–25.

[80] This power would not normally be exercised by a temporary Chairman.

[81] There have been two cases since 1945. On April 8, 1981, a Member was suspended for refusing to withdraw a charge that a Minister had lied, (H.C.Deb., Vol. 2, cols. 950–951); he was again suspended on July 15, 1981, for "grossly disorderly conduct" (seeking to lay documents on the Table during Questions) (H.C.Deb., Vol. 8, col. 1159). His latter suspension extended until after the Summer recess. In Session 1987–88, another Member was suspended twice, on both occasions following accusations that the Prime Minister had lied to the House (H.C.Deb., Vol. 122, cols. 567–570 (November 12, 1987) and H.C.Deb., Vol. 138, cols. 17–20 (July 25, 1988).

[82] There are no cases of the Serjeant at Arms having to remove Members forcibly since 1945, although on one or two occasions he has been required to intervene, whereupon the Member has withdrawn voluntarily. Mr Denis Skinner on one occasion, when the Speaker ordered the Serjeant to ensure his exit, said contemptuously "What, him? Get back in your chair," and stalked out. (H.C.Deb., Vol. 987, col. 218 (June 24, 1980)). On another occasion Dame Irene Ward, having made a protest from in front of the Table, was named and suspended and refused to withdraw until the Serjeant was directed to escort her out, whereupon, having said "Do you want my right or my left arm" they walked out together as if going in to a formal dinner party. (H.C.Deb., Vol. 765, cols. 893–895 (May 23, 1968)).

Members were named and suspended on 23 occasions from 1945 up till the end of Session 1987–88, (there were 8 suspensions under the standing order in that session alone), on all but one for offences in the House itself. Only one of the offending Members was of the Government party. The occasions for naming Members have been similar to those when the Chair has ordered Members to withdraw,[83] the decision on what disciplinary power to use depending greatly on the Chair's judgment of the severity of the offence, the mood of the House, the character of the offender and sometimes perhaps on the undesirability of using the naming procedure (which could lead to a division) on certain occasions or at certain times during a sitting. And no doubt the mood of the Speaker of the day (or his Deputy in the Chair) has varied. It is difficult to establish any clear guiding criteria, in the post-1945 cases, in distinguishing between these procedures. What is certain is that if the Chair cannot secure compliance with his orders on his own authority then he can secure the support of the House by naming a Member.

It is, of course, theoretically possible for the House to refuse to suspend a named Member,[84] and on 15 of the 23 occasions between 1945 and the end of Session 1987–88 political colleagues of the named Member forced a division against his suspension, so, in effect, lending some support to his behaviour and challenging the decision of the Chair. However, it has nearly always been a minority of the Opposition party who have adopted this position, and with few exceptions[85] the Leader, Whip and front-bench Members of the official Opposition have abstained or voted with the majority when one of their colleagues has been named, so supporting the authority of the Chair.

The Chair's disciplinary powers under Standing Orders Nos. 41, 42 and 43 serve to deal with disorderly conduct by individual Members or one or two acting in isolation; they are not suitable for dealing with mass demonstrations or wider-spread defiance of the Chair, or for total rowdiness or disorder involving large numbers from both sides of the House. In such cases of grave disorder the Chair is empowered, by Standing Order No. 45, either to suspend the House till a stated time (a cooling-off period) or to adjourn the House on its own authority. If grave disorder of this kind occurs when the House is in committee, the Chairman leaves the Chair to report the circumstances to the House, the Speaker (or a Deputy), resumes the Chair and the House itself can then be suspended or adjourned.[86]

Such events are fortunately not frequent. From 1945 till the end of Session 1987–88 the House was suspended under the standing order on 14 occasions;

[83] An exceptional occasion was on January 11, 1988, when a Member was named, and suspended, for seeking to protest during prayers against cuts in the N.H.S., before the Speaker took the Chair. The terms of his protest went unrecorded as Hansard and the press are not present during prayers. (H.C.Deb., Vol. 125, cols. 1–3).

[84] This has never happened in the U.K., but on February 28, 1975, the House of Representatives in Australia refused to suspend a Minister who had been named by the Speaker. The Speaker felt obliged to resign.

[85] One exception was on March 13, 1972, when a motion to suspend a Labour Member, who had been named by the Deputy Speaker for making offensive remarks to the Chair, was carried by 299 to 220, with the official Opposition putting tellers in for the Noes. (H.C. Deb., Vol. 833, cols. 168–178). In 13 divisions since then, up till the end of Session 1987–88, the highest vote against suspension has been 102, on the naming of a Member for stating that the Prime Minister had lied to the House (H.C. Deb., Vol. 122, cols. 567–570 (November 12, 1987)).

[86] There is only one committee precedent: grave disorder in the form of protracted points of order challenging the rulings of the Chairman of Ways and Means, in committee on the Commonwealth Immigrants Bill, 1961 (H.C. Deb., Vol. 650, cols. 1455–1476, (December 6, 1961)).

on two of these the cooling-off period was not able to produce a return to normality, the disorder continued, and the Speaker had to adjourn the House; on one occasion the Deputy Speaker adjourned the House without first suspending it. The details of these cases are as follows:

List of adjournments or suspension of the House under Standing Order No. 45 in cases of grave disorder, 1945–1988

1 November 1956	Suspended	Suez: No more questions on statement
8 February 1961	Adjourned	NHS contributions: closure
6 December 1961	Suspended (half-hour)	Commonwealth Immigrants Bill: selection of amendments in committee of the whole House
23 July 1970	Suspended (2 hours)	Stranger having thrown C.S. gas cannister
25 January 1971	Suspended (15 mins)	Industrial Relations Bill: guillotine (Member standing before the Mace)
20 January 1972	Suspended (11 mins)	PMs Questions: 1 million unemployed – "Heath out!"
4 March 1975	Suspended (20 mins)	Norton Villiers Triumph assistance: Finance Bill guillotine
27 May 1976	Suspended (20 mins) and Adjourned	Aircraft and Shipbuilding Industries Bill: Mace-swinging
6 July 1978	Suspended (20 mins)	Stranger having thrown horse dung
13 November 1980	Suspended (10 mins)	Council house rents: obstruction of Black Rod
16 November 1981	Suspended (twice, 10 mins each)	Northern Ireland (Security): naming of three Members
21 November 1984	Suspended (10 mins) and Adjourned	Social Security contributions by persons on strike: several Members standing before the Mace
17 January 1985	Suspended (20 mins)	Continuing demands for debate on miners strike
15 March 1988	Suspended (10 mins)	Persistent protest during Chancellor's Budget statement

The value of a suspension is that it often gives time for an agreement to be reached between the Government and Opposition, sometimes involving the Speaker, on the future conduct of business, or simply for tempers to cool. Sometimes the same can be achieved by an informal suspension, even where there is no grave disorder, and in recent years Speakers have occasionally sought to calm things down in this way.

Informal suspensions are occasionally used for practical convenience, for instance if certain business finishes early before the appointed time for taking the next business, such as private business at 7.00 p.m., or private Members bills to be read over at 2.30 p.m. on a motions Friday (see page 393), or for other reasons of mutual convenience or propriety (on the sudden collapse of a Member for example). On the first day of each session the House is suspended after the Opening of Parliament in the morning until the normal time of sitting in the afternoon. Before the House adjourns for a recess the Speaker is often authorised to suspend the sitting, when business is finished, until Royal Assent has been notified to outstanding bills; in practice this rarely proves necessary. Standing Order No. 10, which was made in 1968, also provides for the House to be suspended at night, on a motion, till 10.00 a.m. the next morning, to permit a morning sitting; this standing order has not been used since 1969.

An important power conferred on the Speaker (and on the Chairman of Ways and Means and Deputy Chairman in a committee of the whole House) by Standing Order No. 31 is that of selection of amendments; and the power to select some amendments implies the power not to select other amendments. This is particularly important in relation to amendments to bills in committee and on report, and how this power is then used is discussed more fully in pages 233 and 236–237 below. The selection of amendments to motions poses few problems. Normally the termination of debate at 10.00 p.m. permits only one amendment to be moved[87] and, if the motion is a Government motion, the official Opposition's amendment will usually be selected and other amendments not selected; it will be vice versa if the motion is moved by the Opposition. Either way, back-bench amendments to major Government or Opposition motions are rarely called and indeed, apart from amendments tabled by the leaders of smaller parties to ensure that their distinct point of view is on the record, they are rarely tabled.

The practice is different for certain motions. Motions regarding the procedures of the House or the pay and allowances of Members are often complicated and may be amended in detail in the same way as bills. Under these circumstances several amendments may be tabled by back-benchers and selected by the Chair for debate and votes (a special business motion to make this possible in a time-limited debate may be needed (see page 198)). Other motions attract the interest of back rather than front-benches. Three recent occasions when the House worked in this way and back-bench amendments of significance were selected, debated and (in some cases) agreed to were a debate on a report of the Committee of Privileges regarding a leak of the proceedings of a select committee (see page 101),[88] a debate on various procedural changes, especially proposals for timetabling public bills (see pages 306–307),[89] and a debate on Members' office, secretarial and research allowances (see page 77).[90]

The Speaker's (and Chairmen's) exercise of the power of selection is frequently criticised, but it is a purely discretionary power; the Chair always refuses to give reasons in public why a particular amendment has not been selected; and any considered criticism must be by substantive motion. Since 1945, five motions critical of the Chairman of Ways and Means regarding the selection of amendments have been tabled and called for debate; one was not moved[91]; the others were negatived or withdrawn.[92] It should be noted that some of these Motions did not criticise the Chair's discretion or judgment as such, but simply said that the decision should not be treated as a

---

[87] Exceptionally an additional amendment may, pursuant to Standing Order No. 32, be moved at the end of the debate on the Address (see page 190).

[88] H.C. Deb., Vol. 96, cols. 293–332 (May 20, 1986).

[89] H.C. Deb., Vol. 92, cols. 1083–1136 (February 27, 1986).

[90] H.C. Deb., Vol. 101, cols. 1130–1143 (July 16, 1986).

[91] H.C. Deb., Vol. 929, cols. 538–539 (March 30, 1977).

[92] H.C. Deb., Vol. 489, cols. 721–746 (June 21, 1951); H.C. Deb., Vol. 656, cols. 1026–1080 (March 27, 1962); H.C. Deb., Vol. 731, cols. 441–492 (July 6, 1966); H.C. Deb., Vol. 832, cols. 432–454 (March 1, 1972).

precedent. Two critical motions (those of 1951 and 1966) were moved from the Opposition front-bench. In 1964 one other motion, criticising the Speaker's selection on one occasion, was tabled by back-bench Members but was not debated.

Another power of the Chair sometimes proves controversial. In committee on a bill the question has to be put on each clause or schedule "That the clause (or schedule) (as amended) stand part of the bill" (see pages 234–235). This enables the committee to consider the clause as a whole. But it often happens that the debate on the various amendments to the clause has covered everything in the clause and there is nothing new that would be said on the clause as a whole. Sometimes no one wishes to speak further and the question on the clause can be disposed of without trouble, but if it looks as if progress may be unreasonably delayed by continued debate on the clause, largely repeating points already debated and decided on the amendments, the chairman can use powers given him by Standing Order No. 67 to state his opinion that the principle of the clause and all matters arising thereon have been adequately discussed, and put the question on the clause without any debate.

This power has to be used with care. Clearly if a chairman has already told the committee that certain matters are out of order on an amendment, but would be in order on clause stand part, he cannot easily apply the standing order at the end of debate on the amendments. Similarly opponents of the bill have regard to the possibility of the Chair applying the standing order when planning their tactics and moving their amendments; too many amendments or too lengthy speeches may reduce the opportunities for later debate. The power was used in committee of the whole House on six occasions in the 1979 to 1987 Parliaments. On one occasion, on February 26, 1969, a motion was tabled by 20 Opposition Members against a chairman for exercising this power; it was not debated.

Other standing order powers conferred on the Chair to help it control debate relate to the acceptance of the closure and of motions to adjourn a debate; these procedures, which, unlike those described above, are not initiated by the Chair, are described on pages 219–225 below.

Under the natural authority of the office, without any specific standing orders, the Speaker and his Deputies, and the chairmen of committees, have significant powers in the choice of speakers, and of those wishing to ask Questions or raise points of order. In debate, after the mover of a motion or amendment has spoken, the Speaker normally calls Members from the Government and Opposition benches alternately, although he may interrupt this pattern to fit in a representative of one of the smaller parties. If many Members wish to speak, and not all will be able to, the choice of Members (who "catches the Speaker's eye") is one of the most onerous responsibilities of the Chair. Similarly, during Question time and after Ministerial statements, the choice of questioners is often not easy.

Speakers seek to keep a fair balance between parties and between different blocks of opinion within parties, but their choice is not always universally applauded, especially by those whom they have failed to call, and sometimes there is protest and somewhat muffled criticism of the Chair. The Chair is always firm on these occasions: the choice of speakers is entirely a matter for the discretion of the Chair, and no point of order can arise.[92a] If

---

[92a] For a recent case, involving the rights of an Opposition Whip to be called in debate, see H.C. Deb., Vol. 146, col. 440 (February 2, 1989).

Members wish to criticise how the Chair has exercised its discretion in this matter, they must table a substantive motion. Five such motions have been tabled since 1964; they appeared on the notice paper as Early Day Motions, but were not debated (one was withdrawn). Similar sensitivity is required by the Chair in hearing Members on points of order, although here the discretion of the Chair not to call someone cannot be readily exercised as Members have the right to raise such points (if genuine), even while another Member has the floor (see page 196). The skill of the Chair, when faced with persistent points of order, lies in knowing how much rope to give and at what stage he can refuse to hear any more points of order on that matter.

The powers and authority to control debate are, with one qualified exception, exercisable by the Deputy Speakers as well as the Speaker in the House itself (the power to select amendments is vested in the Speaker alone, except for debates on estimates (Standing Order No. 31(5)). In committees of the whole House, all these powers can be used by the Deputy Chairmen as well as the Chairman of Ways and Means; other Members who occupy the Chair at the invitation of the Chairman, as temporary Chairmen, do not have the power to select amendments and would not name Members or deal themselves with grave disorder. The powers of chairmen of standing and select committees are described in pages 272–273 and 282–283.

Other Procedures for Controlling or Curtailing Debate

There are certain other procedures for controlling or curtailing debate where the initiative does not lie with the Chair, although in some cases it exercises some discretion in applying these procedures.

The mildest form of control relates to motions for the adjournment of debate or of proceedings on a bill. Once a question has been proposed, any Member who has not already spoken in that debate can move "that the debate be now adjourned"[93]; on consideration of a bill a motion may be made, when no question is before the House (between amendments), "that further consideration of the bill be now adjourned"; and in committee of the whole House a similar motion may be made "that the Chairman do report progress and ask leave to sit again." The effect of all these motions, if agreed to, is that the business under consideration is ended for the day and may be resumed on a later day.

Such motions, which delay progress on the motion or bill (and are therefore termed "dilatory motions"), are frequently moved by Ministers or Whips when the Government's business plans allow more than one day for a major debate or for consideration of a bill. They are occasionally moved by the Government when it becomes apparent to the Whips that debate on a bill is going to be unduly protracted and that they will not complete the planned business that evening (or not without a lot of fuss); so they accept reality and agree to call it a day.

Dilatory motions are also occasionally moved by the Opposition or by back-benchers when they believe that the business should be postponed (for instance if relevant documents are not available in the Vote Office) or that the House is being asked to sit too late on a bill. For example, on a long committee or report stage, if the Government do not move to report progress or adjourn around about midnight, the Opposition may seek to do so, in order to find from the Minister how long he intends to keep them sitting; and similar motions may be moved later in the night.

---

[93] It is also possible to move "That the House do now adjourn," but this is rarely used.

Dilatory motions, under basic procedure, are debatable (although not amendable) and so offer an opportunity for a minority to frustrate the majority by endlessly debating motions to defer taking decisions. It was the use of such tactics by the Irish nationalists in the last century which led to the adoption of restrictions to prevent abuse of dilatory motions. Under Standing Order No. 34, the Chair, if it believes that a dilatory motion "is an abuse of the rules of the House" may either decline to accept the motion at all or may put the question on the dilatory motion for an immediate decision without debate.

Thus, when a dilatory motion is moved, the Chair has three choices. If it believes the proposal reasonable, or at least worth debating—if moved by the Minister or by the Opposition after a lengthy period of consideration of a bill, for example, it proposes the question to the House for debate and decision. Such debates do not usually last long, and the scope of debate should be limited to the desirability of adjourning or continuing the business, not its merits. If the Chair believes it unreasonable or simply an attempt to frustrate progress, it may put the question forthwith so that the Members themselves may decide whether or not to adjourn. If it is thought to be truly an abuse (for example if such a motion had been negatived not long before or if the House had recently decided that the business could be continued after 10.00 p.m., or if the absence of papers complained of does not involve a genuine obstacle to the proper consideration of the business) the Chair can refuse to accept the motion at all, and the business continues. The following Table shows how the Chair in the Chamber[94] dealt with dilatory motions moved by Members other than Ministers in the 1983–87 Parliament.

Proceedings on Dilatory Motions
(other than those moved by Ministers)

Session	Allowed by Chair	Not allowed by Chair	Question put forthwith
1983–84	–	1	–
1984–85	1	2	–
1985–86	1	1	1
1986–87	1	–	–

A procedure akin to that of a dilatory motion, but which is now very rarely used, is the "previous question". This is moved in the form, "That the question be not now put" and if agreed to has the effect of aborting the debate on the original question (though it could be moved again on another day).[94a] A similar, and equally rare, procedure is the motion "That this House do now pass to the orders of the day.[94b] Neither of these procedures can be used in any committee (see May, page 388).

Dilatory motions seek to control debate by extending it, or at least by deferring a decision. Many other procedures are designed to curtail debate. First, there are a whole series of standing orders requiring the question to be put forthwith on various procedural motions, without amendment or debate. Some examples—motions to refer matters to various committees (pages 197–198), motions relating to matters considered by and reported

---

[94] Dilatory motions are quite often moved in standing committees, and chairmen can exercise the same powers, but relevant statistics are not readily available.

[94a] For a recent case see H.C. Deb., Vol. 145, cols. 649–660 (January 20, 1989).

[94b] For a recent case see H.C. Deb., Vol. 80, cols. 578–586 (June 7, 1985).

from various committees (pages 201–202), motions on clauses already fully debated (page 218) and some dilatory motions (page 220)—have already been cited. Other instances of such rules include: motions to commit Bills to committees of the whole House, or to a select committee or to a special standing committee, if moved immediately after second reading (Standing Order No. 61(2)); motions for the withdrawal of strangers (Standing Order No. 143); motions for suspension of named Members (Standing Order No. 43(1)); motions on Budget Day applying the Provisional Collection of Taxes Act (Standing Order No. 50(2)); motions on the last day of the Budget debate on all the outstanding resolutions (Standing Order No. 50 (3)); questions on the second and third readings of Consolidated Fund Bills (Standing Order No. 54); and business motions moved at 10.00 p.m. to enable the ten o'clock rule to be suspended for certain business (Standing Order No. 14(2) to (4)). Three standing orders permit "brief explanatory statements" for and against the proposal (but not amendment or debate) before the question is put: Standing Order No. 19(1) on a motion to bring in a bill under the "ten minute rule"; Standing Order No. 61(3) on a motion to commit a bill in part to a standing committee and in part to a committee of the whole House; and Standing Order No. 72 on a motion to re-commit the whole of a bill to a committee.

Other standing orders provide for time limited debates but without an automatic decision at the end. Three hours is allowed for emergency adjournment debates under Standing Order No. 20, but at the end of this period, unless the question is previously decided, or the motion withdrawn, or a closure is moved, the motion for the adjournment lapses. Similarly, adjournment motions moved under Standing Order No. 54 after the passage of each Consolidated Fund Bill lapse the next morning at 9.00 a.m. (8.00 a.m. on a Friday) if not previously concluded.

On the other hand, a number of other standing orders enable or require the Chair to put the question automatically after a specified period or at a specified hour (if not previously decided): on money resolutions at 10.45 p.m. or after three-quarters of an hour, whichever is the later (Standing Order No. 14(1)(d)); on affirmative proceedings pursuant to Acts and on European Community documents at 11.30 p.m. or after an hour and a half, whichever is the later (Standing Order No. 14(1)(b)), or on prayers against statutory instruments at 11.30 p.m. (Standing Order No. 15(2)). In the cases of affirmative resolutions, European Community documents and prayers, the Chair can adjourn the debate instead of putting the question if it thinks that the time for debate, bearing in mind the importance of the subject-matter, has been inadequate. But this discretion is very rarely used; there was only one case in the 1979 to 1987 Parliaments.[95] Proceedings on motions to provide for recesses are limited to three hours, with all questions necessary to dispose of those proceedings being put automatically (Standing Order No. 22); and similarly with motions for imposing a guillotine on a bill (Standing Order No. 81).

---

[95] On the Parliamentary Constituencies (Wales) Order 1983; points of order delayed the start of the debate and after the hour and a half the Deputy Speaker adjourned the debate because the importance of the subject-matter meant that there had been inadequate time for debate (H.C. Deb., Vol. 37, cols. 392–423 (February 16, 1983). On July 17, 1985, a decision by a Deputy Speaker not to use his power under the standing order to adjourn a debate on an instrument relating to Edinburgh rates was criticised by some Members. A critical motion was tabled by 8 back-benchers, but was not debated.

All these procedures for putting questions without debate, or after limited debate, although departing far from the basic procedure of Parliament, are now generally accepted and their application is rarely criticised. It may be because of this willingness to accept packaged debates that the Government has increasingly used ad hoc business motions (often moved several days in advance—frequently on the preceding Friday) providing for the question on specified business to be put at specified times or after a specified length of debate (see pages 198–199). In effect this has introduced a procedure for imposing a closure in advance and therefore regardless of the actual course of the debate. But Members do not appear to object, for such motions are rarely opposed.

The closure itself, the next most vigorous restriction of debate, is not open to this potential criticism, and is subject to various conditions to prevent its abuse. Standing Order No. 35 provides that after a question has been proposed any Member may (even in the middle of another Member's speech) claim to move "That the question be now put" (so that the debate must stop), and "unless it shall appear to the Chair that such a motion is an abuse of the rules of the House, or an infringement of the rights of the minority" the closure motion is put forthwith. No debate or even points of order are allowed on the Chair's acceptance (or refusal) of the closure. The decision then rests with the House. For the closure to be applied, there must obviously be a majority in favour but also, under Standing Order No. 36, if there is a division not fewer than 100 Members (not counting tellers) must be included in that majority. If the closure is agreed to, the question on the motion or amendment that is being closured must be put forthwith, and again points of order are not allowed to delay this happening. The discretion of the Chair cannot be challenged at that time.

The conditions attaching to the granting of the closure are important. Nothing is formally laid down, but the Chair, in whose sole, personal, discretion it lies (the advice of the clerks is not usually sought on whether or not to accept the closure, although advice on relevant facts—precedents, length of debate, etc., may be given), does seek to act within certain broad guidelines, based on previous practice and experience. First, it will take account of the Members who have spoken and how many still wish to speak; in particular regard will be had to whether the Government and Opposition spokesmen have been heard and whether minority opinion has been expressed. Secondly, it will consider the length of debate and how much longer it could last. Here, practice and practical considerations are important. For example, a closure will normally be granted just before the moment of interruption at the end of a full day's debate on a substantive motion or second reading of a bill, (including at 2.30 p.m. on a Friday); indeed it may be claimed and granted when the business is interrupted by the Chair. It would not normally be granted on such business significantly earlier than the moment of interruption. These cases are easy. More judgment is required for some business which is not time limited, for example the report stage of a bill. A rough rule of thumb, depending on the importance of the amendment, the numbers wishing to speak, and the extent to which there may appear to be a deliberate attempt to delay progress, is that some two or three hours' debate would usually be allowed before a closure was granted on an important amendment, but on some procedural motions, such as a dilatory motion, the closure might be accepted after half an hour. A lot depends on the occasion, the mood of the House, and no doubt, the patience of the Chair.

Claimed closures are sometimes turned down by the Chair, but not often because most closures are claimed by the Whips on either side, and the Whips (not wishing to be publicly repudiated) may seek the private guidance of the Chair on whether a closure will be accepted, before they claim it. The relative absence of refusals of Government claims (there have been some) does not, therefore, mean that closures are always granted when the Government Whips desire; they are often told, privately, to wait a while.

Occasionally the acceptance by the Chair of the closure has proved controversial (although the usual Opposition protest is against the Government for moving the closure rather than the Chair for accepting it). Since 1945 there have been three motions debated which were critical of the Chair on these grounds (two in 1952[96] and one in 1961[97]), and since 1964 two such motions (one in 1980 and one in 1985) have been tabled but not debated.

The statistics show how the closure has however become a routine part of the House's procedures: (see page 224).

The limited and decreasing use by the Government of the closure in respect of their bills is examined in pages 301–302. But for private Members' bills the continued availability of the closure remains highly significant. Here the need for 100 in the majority on a closure becomes particularly relevant. Whereas this requirement has little effect on the Government, except that it means that they have to keep at least 100 supporters in the House on any controversial business for which a closure may be needed (it is not needed for business where the question is put automatically), it is a very different matter for a back-bencher trying to get a second reading for a controversial bill on a Friday. Although the Chair will always grant the closure at 2.30 p.m. on the second reading of a bill which has been debated all that sitting (and occasionally on bills which have had several hours' debate but which were not the first bills to be considered that day) this is of no use if the Member cannot find 100 supporters to vote for the closure and his opponents are numerous enough or skilled enough—even if only a small minority—to talk the bill out at 2.30 p.m. (see pages 392–393). It takes a fairly popular cause for 100 Members to turn up on a Friday when there is no party Whip requiring their presence. Furthermore, the Member in charge of a controversial bill which was approved by a majority on second reading may still have similar difficulties if faced with numerous amendments at report stage; the continued loyalty of 100 colleagues will again be required. The statistics only give a partial indication of the extent of this problem as they do not show the numerous occasions when a bill was "talked out" because the Member in charge did not bother to claim the closure, knowing he lacked the necessary numbers.

Closure is a procedure for bringing a debate to an end, especially when Members are making unduly long speeches, but there is one circumstance under which it cannot be used, namely when a Member makes an excessively long speech when first moving a motion or amendment; the question "That the question be now put" cannot then be moved because no question has yet

---

[96] H.C. Deb., Vol. 500, cols. 397–417 (May 7, 1952); H.C. Deb., Vol. 509, cols. 43–105 (December 8, 1952). These motions were both withdrawn after debate.

[97] H.C. Deb., Vol. 634, cols. 1025–1074 (February 13, 1961). The official Opposition pressed this motion to a division.

Closure

In House or Committee of the whole House

Session	Claimed	Assent given by Chair	Assent withheld by Chair	Agreed to on division	Negatived on division	Less than 100 in majority	Agreed to without division	Negatived without division
1976–77	36	29	7	11	0	4	13	0
1977–78	37	24	13	7	1	1	15	0
1978–79	18	12	4	6	0	1	5	1
1979–80	44	36	8	18	1	3	12	1
1980–81	23	21	7	6	3	2	10	0
1981–82	23	20	3	9	1	1	9	0
1982–83	7	6	1	2	0	3	1	0
1983–84	23	24	4	4	2	4	14	0
1984–85	29	24	5	13	0	0	10	1
1985–86	41	34	7	8	0	5	21	0
1986–87	12	8	4	1	0	1	6	0
Totals 1976–87	301	238	63	85	8	25	116	2

been proposed. In 1983 this problem was dramatically posed when a Member spoke for 11¼ hours in a standing committee when moving an amendment to the Telecommunications Bill.[98] Nothing could be done to limit his speech—he successfully avoided irrelevance and "tedious repetition"—so the problem was considered by the Procedure Committee. Following its recommendation,[99] the House agreed on February 27, 1986, to a new standing order (Standing Order No. 28), which provides that when a motion or an amendment is being moved at any stage of proceedings on a bill, a Member may claim to move "That the question be now proposed," and unless the Chair (excluding temporary chairmen in committees) considers that this is an abuse of the rules of the House (for example moved too soon) that question shall be put forthwith. The House, or committee, by a majority can thereupon ensure that the debate is opened, provided, as with the closure, that in the House or a committee of the whole House, 100 Members vote in the majority. This procedure has not yet been used in the House,[99a] but certainly its very existence will deter attempts to filibuster by prolongation of speeches when moving amendments.

The most drastic method of curtailing debate is the allocation of time order or "guillotine." This involves a detailed and sophisticated set of procedures whereby the House, on a motion, imposes a timetable on the further proceedings on a bill.

The basic procedure for guillotining a bill is fairly simple; the details are highly complex (guillotine motions customarily cover some three pages of the Order Paper), but need not be fully described here. The first step is that the Government tables an allocation of time motion in respect of a specified bill or specified bills.[1] The main components of these motions include a requirement that the Bill be reported from a standing committee by a stated date (if the bill has been committed to a standing committee), and a limit to the number of days that may be spent in committee of the whole House (if the bill has not been sent upstairs) and on report and third reading. The motion may include a detailed breakdown of the time to be devoted to various parts of the bill or clauses (or of amendments to these clauses) on the floor of the House, but it is more normal for these details to be worked out by the business committee (see below). The motion also makes detailed provision for bringing proceedings to a conclusion at the end of each period allotted to specified business, namely when the knives of the guillotine fall and terminate further debate on a section of the bill, for example, by requiring the question to be put without further debate on the amendment then under discussion and enabling outstanding Government amendments to be decided (with a division if required) without debate. The motion defines "allotted days" when the guillotined bill is taken and frequently permits the House to sit for an additional hour or two after 10.00 p.m.

---

[98] Standing Committee Debates (Stg Co H), 1982–83, cols. 795–913. (February 8, 1983).

[99] Second Report from the Select Committee on Procedure, H.C. 49 of 1984–85 paras. 15–16.

[99a] It was moved on two occasions in session 1987–88 in standing committees: Standing Committee Debates (Stg. Co. D on Immigraton Bill), col. 439 (December 17, 1987); Standing Committee Debates (Stg. Co. C on Protection of Animals (Amendment) Bill), cols. 14–15 (February 10, 1988).

[1] In 1975–76, one order was applied to both the Health Services Bill and the Dock Work Regulation Bill, and on the same day another order to both the Rent (Agriculture) Bill and the Education Bill (H.C. Deb., Vol. 915, cols. 1606–1684 and 1685–1757 (July 20, 1976)).

on such days. The motion protects the time available for debating the bill should an emergency adjournment debate under Standing Order No. 20 be allowed on an allotted day and likewise if opposed private business were set down for such a day, (which is unlikely). It prohibits dilatory motions, unless moved by Ministers, but requires the latter to be decided forthwith. Finally a guillotine motion customarily allows for supplementary motions, especially for guillotining Lords Amendments, to be debated for not more than one hour.

Under Standing Order No. 81, debate on each guillotine motion is limited to three hours, at the end of which the Speaker automatically puts the question. Amendments may be moved, for example, to provide additional time for various proceedings, but nowadays seldom are.

When the motion is agreed (always after a division—traditional hostility still guarantees that degree of opposition), a business sub-committee of the standing committee (if the bill is at that stage), nominated by the Speaker under Standing Order No. 103, works out a detailed timetable for the remainder of the committee stage (clauses 1–8 by day 20; clauses 9–12 by day 22, etc., for example), and specifies when the proceedings will be conducted at each sitting (so restricting evening and night sittings).

When the bill is reported from the standing committee, unless the guillotine motion has included the detailed timetabling within its own terms (as it has on six occasions since 1945), a business committee appointed under Standing Order No. 80, consisting of not more than eight Members nominated by the Speaker under the chairmanship of the Chairman of Ways and Means, and including the Minister in charge of the bill, a Government Whip, and representatives of the Opposition front-bench, agrees a resolution specifying the detailed allocation of time for debating amendments to various parts of the bill within the days allotted by the guillotine motion itself for the report stage, and also for the time to be allowed for third reading. The business committee may also timetable debate on clauses in committee of the whole House, if the bill is not before a standing committee.

The business committee is required by the original guillotine motion to report its resolution by a specified day, and under Standing Order No. 80(b) a motion for the House to agree to this resolution is put without amendment or debate and, when agreed to, becomes in effect an order of the House. In recent years it has been the practice to allow for further resolutions from the business committee, varying their original decisions, which are likewise agreed by the House; such variations have been made on several occasions.

If the Lords amend a Commons bill which has been guillotined, it may be necessary for the original allocation of time order to be supplemented so as to guillotine debate on the Lords Amendments (for example, that the proceedings on Lords Amendments 1 to 3 shall be concluded by 6.00 p.m. on the allotted day, on Amendments 4 to 18 by 7.45 p.m., etc.). As these amendments are often very numerous, it is nowadays normally provided that separate questions be put on the amendment being debated when the knife falls, on Government amendments to Lords Amendments or to the bill itself, and on any Lords Amendment to which the Government moves to disagree; and single questions are then put for the House to agree first to all the remaining Lords Amendments affecting the Commons financial privileges (see page 239), and then to all other remaining Lords Amendments, *en bloc*. Again, the detailed timings and blocks of Lords Amendments are usually agreed with the Opposition; in practice this means that debates and votes take place on the matters of their choosing and that the majority of Lords Amendments to which the Government agrees (many of them concessions towards the Opposition's position) are agreed without debate. It is thus difficult, under the guillotine, for individual Members to oppose specific Lords Amendments, with or without debate.

A description of how the Government uses the guillotine procedure to achieve its legislation programme will be found in Chapter 7, pages 302–307.

Types of Legislation

The general process of debate, described above, applies to debate on all forms of business, and so to legislation as well as motions. However, there are many special legislative procedures that can conveniently be summarised here. How these procedures are used will be more fully described in Chapters 8 and 10.

Legislative procedures are those used for passing bills and other subordinate forms of legislation into law and for enabling bills to be examined, criticised and sometimes amended in detail before they become law. There are two main classes of legislation: private and public. Private legislation confers powers or benefits on particular persons or bodies in excess of or in conflict with the general law. Most private legislation is contained in private bills which are promoted by outside bodies (such as local authorities, charities, companies) or occasionally individuals, but Scottish private legislation is dealt with by provisional order bills introduced by Ministers under the Private Legislation Procedure (Scotland) Act 1936. Debate in the House on private legislation is further considered in Chapter 10, pages 411–412. Public legislation relates to matters of public policy, generally affecting, or liable to affect the rights, duties, powers or benefits of all citizens or all citizens of specified classes (for example, all men over 65).

Some public bills, usually introduced by Ministers, affect private rights (for example by giving Ministers power to acquire specified land for some major capital development, such as the Channel Tunnel). These are termed hybrid bills, and the procedure for their passage may involve examination by a select committee similar to the examination given to private bills.

Public legislation can be divided into public bills, and statutory instruments and other forms of delegated legislation. The first require the full approval of the Queen in Parliament; the second are made by Ministers, under powers given by Acts, although often subject to some form of parliamentary procedure.

Public Bills

Public bills can be further sub-divided into Government bills, introduced by Ministers, and private Members' bills, introduced by back-benchers. In this Chapter the basic procedures for all public bills are described; the special procedures for private Members' bills are dealt with in Chapter 10.

Most bills may be introduced into either House, although bills of "aids and supplies"—that is the annual Finance Bill and other major taxing measures and the Consolidated Fund and Appropriation Bills for authorising central Government expenditure (see pages 247–248)—must originate in the Commons, and normally any bill whose main objects are financial will also start there. For political reasons senior Ministers (who are mostly in the Commons) also wish major and controversial legislation, with which they are closely associated, to start in the Commons. This concentration of major bills in the Commons sometimes causes problems for the Lords; the nature of the legislation starting in the Lords and the legislative procedures of that House are discussed in Chapter 12.

Bills first introduced into the House of Commons are called Commons bills and those starting in the Lords are known as Lords bills; Lords bills have the word [Lords] after their short title, e.g. the Transport Bill [Lords].

The Form of a Bill

Every bill has a short title, which is normally the same as the title by which the eventual Act will be cited, (e.g. the Transport Bill of Session 1984–85 became the Transport Act 1985).[2] It has a long title, which summarises the main purposes and content of the bill; everything in the bill must be covered by that title. There may be a preamble setting out the reasons for introducing the bill, but this is now unusual. And there is always an enacting formula, preceding the effective clauses, which summarises the legislative authority of Parliament (for full terms see page 4).

The main body of a bill may comprise parts or chapters—being groups of related clauses—clauses and schedules (clauses are called sections when the bill becomes an Act and internal references use the latter term). Clauses are sub-divided into sub-sections, paragraphs and sub-paragraphs; schedules are sub-divided into paragraphs and sub-paragraphs. Schedules are always dependent on a clause and have no effect unless that clause is agreed; they contain detail which would be less appropriately contained in the clause. Bills vary in length from one clause[2a] —containing both the substance of the bill and the citation and commencement provisions—to several hundred; the Companies Act 1985 (a major consolidation measure) has 27 parts (broken up into chapters), 747 sections and 25 schedules.

An explanatory memorandum, which has no legal significance, is frequently attached to the first print of a bill in each House; it summarises the provisions of the bill, and, if the bill involves additional expenditure, it explains the financial and staffing consequences of its proposals.

On the back of a Commons bill is listed the Member in charge who presented it and not more than 11 other Members who are supporters. The date when it was ordered to be printed, and a printing number, is shown on all bills.

Introduction

A bill may be introduced into the Commons in one of three ways. First, it may be presented under Standing Order No. 58, notice of the short and long title having been previously given and so appearing on the Order Paper, without any debate or question put. The Clerk at the Table reads the short title, and the bill is then deemed to have been read the first time, and ordered to be printed; and is set down for second reading on a later day named by the Member presenting it (or a Whip for the Government). Second, it may be brought in pursuant to an order of the House, either on a motion for leave to bring in a bill or following certain preliminary proceed-

---

[2] Exceptionally the Consolidated Fund (Appropriation) Bill becomes the Appropriation Act. Also the second bill of a session with the same short title is called (No. 2), but as an Act it may be the first Act of any calendar year.
[2a] See the Abortion (Amendment) Bills of Sessions 1987–88 and 1988–89, which were drafted like that by the private Member who introduced them so as to minimise the number of possible debates in committee; most very short bills have a separate citation clause.

ings such as agreement to the Ways and Means resolutions on which the Finance Bill is founded (see page 252). And third, a bill may be introduced after being passed by the Lords and sent to the Commons. In this case nothing actually happens in the Chamber; a Member wishing to take up a Lords bill simply notifies the Clerk at the Table and, under Standing Order No. 58(3), the bill is recorded in the Journal as having been read the first time, ordered to be read a second time on the day the Member appoints, and to be printed.

Nearly all Government bills (except Consolidated Fund Bills and Finance and other bills brought in on a Ways and Means resolution) are either presented in the Commons under Standing Order No. 58, or brought from the Lords.[3] Private Members' bills are either presented, brought from the Lords or brought in on a motion for leave under Standing Order No. 19 (the "ten minute rule", see pages 390–391).

Bills are presented in dummy form. The actual text of the bill is submitted by the Member in charge to the Public Bill Office. In the case of Government bills this is done by Parliamentary Counsel, who are the Government's draftsmen. They will usually have prepared a draft text in advance, sometimes many days before, so that normally the final agreed text is submitted and sent for printing at the same time as the notice of presentation, and the bill is published on or soon after its first reading. It is the duty of the Clerk of Public Bills to ensure that the text complies with the rules of the House. In particular he checks that everything in the bill is covered by the long title, and that any provisions involving additional expenditure are printed in italics to indicate that a money resolution will be required to permit those provisions to proceed (see page 231). In the case of private Members' bills, he has to satisfy himself that the main object of the bill is not to create a charge on public funds, for, under Standing Order No. 48, such bills may only be presented by Ministers. The Clerk of Public Bills will also decide whether the bill affects Royal interests or the Royal prerogative (in which case the Queen's consent, or Prince of Wales' Consent, will be required at some stage), whether it appears to be hybrid, and whether it could—though this is no bar to presentation—conflict with or duplicate another bill dealing with the same matters that has already been introduced. He will also advise the Speaker if the bill relates exclusively to Scotland, as special procedures are then employed (see page 230).

Any difficulties on any of these matters are normally resolved by discussion between the Clerk of Public Bills and the Member concerned (or Parliamentary Counsel for Government bills). In the rare case that they cannot agree, the issue would be decided by the Speaker. One way or another, no bill is allowed to proceed unless it complies with the rules of the House, most of which are not in standing orders but derive from well-established procedure. In practice few bills are prevented from going ahead; the only significant obstacle is that which prevents back-benchers from bringing in bills whose main object is to increase government expenditure. The bill is then printed by Her Majesty's Stationery Office and published.[4]

---

[3] Exceptionally, if a bill is required with great urgency and notice of presentation cannot be given, leave may be sought for a motion to bring in the bill to be moved without notice. See, for example, proceedings on the Northern Ireland Bill 1972 (H.C. Deb., Vol. 831, cols. 1285–1286, 1297–1298, 1363–1449 (February 23, 1972).

[4] Quite a large number of private Members' bills (26 in session 1985–86 for example) are not submitted for publication, and may not proceed further.

Second Reading

On the appointed day, when the Clerk reads the order of the day for the second reading of the bill, the Member in charge moves, That the bill be now read a second time.[5] This permits a wide debate on the principle and purposes of the bill, what it does and what it does not do and how it will affect various interests. It also permits consideration of why it does not do other cognate things. The Minister explains and defends the bill; the Opposition gives its views; and back-benchers may draw attention to particular weaknesses, especially in regard to those they represent. It is a broad debate. An amendment may also be moved by the Opposition to the second reading of government bills (this is now unusual in respect of private Members' bills), setting out reasons for opposing the measure; other Members may also table reasoned amendments but they are not normally selected for debate.[6] At the end of the second reading debate the House must come to a decision, (unless, as occasionally happens with private Members' bills, the bill is, by unanimous leave of the House, withdrawn). If the bill is read a second time, the House is deemed to have approved the bill in principle. If the second reading is defeated that is the end of the bill.

Although most bills are debated at second reading on the floor of the House, it is possible, under Standing Order No. 90, for the debate on less controversial bills to be taken in a second reading standing committee provided 20 or more Members do not object. If that committee recommends that the bill ought to be read a second time, the actual second reading is decided by the House without amendment or debate. In the 10 sessions up till 1987, an average of five government Bills a session were read a second time in this way (and see pages 312–314). Because only unopposed bills are normally referred to second reading committees, their proceding usually lack controversy and are often speedy.[6a] Similar procedures enable the Scottish Grand Committee, consisting of all Members sitting for Scottish constituencies, to consider the principle of bills relating exclusively to Scotland, but such proceedings can be blocked by 10 Members, under Standing Order No. 93(2), so in effect this procedure can be used only if the Opposition agrees. The Scottish Grand Committee considered, on average, two bills in principle in each of the same 10 sessions.

Committal and Instructions

Bills, having been read a second time, are committed to a committee for examination in detail. Under Standing Order No. 61, when a bill (other than a Consolidated Fund or Appropriation Bill, or a bill for confirming a provisional order) has been read a second time it stands committed to a standing committee unless the House otherwise orders. However a motion to commit a bill to a committee of the whole House or to a select committee or to a special standing committee, or a motion expressing the expediency of

---

[5] Queen's Consent may be signified by a Privy Councillor at this stage if the Royal interests or prerogatives are fundamental; there were two such cases in both 1984–85 and 1985–86.

[6] Amendments to postpone the second reading for three or six months often used to be tabled, but they are not normally employed today as it is simpler, and even more effective, to vote against second reading.

[6a] Most unusually, in session 1988–89 two Members voted against the motion to recommend "that the Civil Aviation (Air Navigation Charges) Bill [*Lords*] ought to be read a second time" in a second reading committee on February 28, 1989 (Standing Committee Debates, col. 8).

the bill being considered by a joint committee of both Houses, may be moved without notice by any Member immediately after second reading and decided forthwith without debate (Standing Order No. 61(2)). The Member in charge of the bill can likewise move under Standing Order No. 61(3) for the bill to be committed to a committee of the whole House for some of its provisions and for the remainder of the bill to be sent to a standing committee; the Finance Bill is now regularly treated in this way, and occasionally other bills.[7]

After a bill has been committed, the House may give instructions to a committee empowering it to do something it would not otherwise be able to do, such as extending the scope of the bill, or, indeed, requiring it to consider certain amendments; but instructions are now rare, and are subject to selection by the Speaker (Standing Order 31(4)).

Financial Resolutions

Before a bill is considered in committee, money and Ways and Means resolutions may be required. These can only be moved by Ministers. Money resolutions are needed to authorise any provisions of a bill involving significant additional expenditure or other charges on central government funds (see pages 247–248). Ways and Means resolutions are similarly needed at this stage to authorise the levying of taxes and other charges on the people which are subordinate to the main purpose of the bill (if taxation was its main purpose, the whole bill would have been founded on such resolutions, see page 252). In the case of Government bills these resolutions are normally moved immediately after second reading, although sometimes supplementary resolutions are needed later to permit Government amendments involving additional charges. Money resolutions for private Members' bills are also sometimes moved by Ministers at a later stage. Unlike money resolutions which are exempted for a limited time under Standing Order No.14(1)(d), Ways and Means resolutions are not exempted business, and it is customary for the Government to move to suspend the ten o'clock rule to enable them to be taken, even if opposed, after a second reading; they are often not debated.

Committee Stage

The proceedings in committee are, in some ways, the most important part of the House's consideration of bills; they certainly absorb most of the time spent on legislation. Here we describe the basic committee proceedings for bills, which are common to both committees of the whole House and standing committees; the special feature of the latter are described in pages 270–274 below.

Committees go through bills clause by clause, and schedule by schedule, although the committee can agree, on a motion, to re-arrange the order, for example, to group the schedules together with the clauses to which they relate. Each clause and schedule must be separately agreed to, and there can be a separate debate (unless the chairman uses his powers under Standing Order No. 67, see page 218) on each one. Before this, however, amendments may be moved to the clause or schedule—to insert or add words, to leave out words, or to leave out and insert or add words—and these are all

---

[7] *e.g.* the Local Government Bill in Session 1984–85.

debatable. New clauses may also be proposed after the existing clauses have been considered and new schedules after the existing schedules. The process and rules of debate in committee are the same as in the House, with one major exception: a Member may speak as many times as he wishes on the same question.

The critical process of examining a bill in detail is subject to rules relating to amendments. Once a bill has been read a second time any Member (be he on the committee or not) may give notice in the Public Bill Office of amendments and of new clauses and new schedules.[8] The clerks in that office are always available to help Members in drafting amendments. The clerks put the amendments into the correct form and they are all published the next day. Before the bill starts in committee, and regularly thereafter, a marshalled list of amendments is published, arranging the amendments in the order they fall to be considered. The chairman can, advised by the clerks, then examine all the amendments with a view to grouping them for debate.

His primary task will be to eliminate any amendments which are out of order. There are numerous rules on this matter, which are not laid down in standing orders but which are derived from common sense and have been defined and applied by the Chair for many years. They are all supported by precedents and rulings. The main rules are as follows.[9] Amendments are out of order—

(a) which are irrelevant to the subject-matter or beyond the scope of the bill. "Scope" is a difficult concept, and requires careful judgment in relation to the content of the bill; for example in a bill with only one limited purpose (say the licensing of dogs), it could be held to be outside the scope to introduce amendments to extend it to cover other purposes (say the licensing of cats), but if the bill already has a number of purposes (say regulating the ownership and treatment of animals in a number of different ways) an amendment to add one more purpose (say to include cats in the relevant list) would be in order. One particular application of this rule is that it is outside the scope of a consolidation bill (which simply re-states the existing law) to move amendments which would amend the law;

(b) which are similarly irrelevant to or beyond the scope of a clause. But here the amendments can usually be brought into order by being moved as a new clause;

(c) which depend on amendments already negatived;

(d) which conflict with amendments, or with parts of the bill, already agreed to;

(e) where necessary consequential amendments have not been tabled, (this rule is relaxed in many less important cases) or the amendment is otherwise incomplete;

(f) which conflict with the decision of the House to approve the principles of the bill on second reading. These are commonly called "wrecking amendments" and often pose thorny problems for the chairman of a committee on a controversial bill;

(g) which leave out or negative the effective words of a whole clause. The same objectives can be achieved by voting against clause stand part;

(h) which would make the clause unintelligible or which are ineffective in

---

[8] Exceptionally, if a bill is to be hurried through, the House may make an order permitting amendments to be handed in before second reading.

[9] For a full list, see May, pp. 555–558.

other ways. This rule is not applied so rigorously as to exclude all amendments which are less than perfectly drafted; so long as the meaning is plain the amendment may be in order although not in as perfect legal language as the draftsmen might choose;

(i) which are "vague, trifling or tendered in a spirit of mockery"; and

(j) which impose charges (expenditure or taxation) beyond those authorised by a money or Ways and Means resolution of the House. This is a most important rule. It allows Members to move amendments to reduce expenditure or taxation, and to move for increases so long as they are within the terms of the relevant resolution, but not for increases beyond those so authorised. For example, if the bill permits a Minister to make grants not exceeding £50,000 for specified purposes and the money resolution simply said "the Secretary of State may make grants" for those purposes, then an amendment to leave out "£50,000" and insert "£75,000" would be in order, but an amendment to extend the purposes for which grants may be made would be out of order; if, on the other hand, the resolution also included a specific reference to £50,000 as the maximum grant, then an amendment to the bill to increase that sum would also be out of order. It will be seen, therefore, that the scope of amendments to a bill involving expenditure is strictly defined by the terms of the money resolution (which means, in effect, by the Government). A detailed, "tight," money resolution—in nearly the same terms as the bill itself—excludes all amendments to increase the levels or purposes of expenditure, but a "wide" resolution ("the payment out of money provided by Parliament of any expenses of the Secretary of State incurred in consequence of the Act"), as is quite common, allows a wide range of amendments to be moved to increase expenditure. The tactical use of these procedures is examined in Chapter 8, pages 330–331.

Having ruled out all inadmissible amendments, the chairman, again advised by the clerk of the committee, uses his powers of selection (see page 217) to group the remaining amendments for debate, so that all those on the same or closely related topics can conveniently be debated together. He may also refuse to select some amendments which, although not technically out of order, can reasonably be omitted, for example very minor amendments, or those which are clearly based on some misunderstanding, or which appear to have been tabled purely for the purpose of delaying progress on the bill—much depends on the general mood and behaviour of the committee, and on the attitude of the chairman. In practice, in a standing committee, nearly all amendments which are in order are selected or grouped in some way for debate; in a committee of the whole House the Chairman of Ways and Means may be somewhat more rigorous in seeking to confine the debates to the major matters which concern Members, as shown by the amendments they have tabled, and may decide not to select certain amendments. This occasionally leads to complaint and points of order.

Amendments may be moved in committee without notice, and occasionally are when some unexpected event makes this reasonable, but normally amendments are selected only if they appear on the notice paper; indeed, except when a bill is being hurried through, and longer notice is not possible, the chairman does not usually select "starred" amendments, *i.e.* amendments handed in the previous day and appearing for the first time. It is proper that all concerned should have full opportunity to study amendments proposed to bills before they are debated.

In exercising his powers, the chairman (often through the clerk) usually keeps the Government and the Opposition (and sometimes other Members keenly concerned) informed in advance of what is proposed. This liaison enables him to explain to the Opposition spokesman why certain amendments may be out of order and to get their reactions to the proposed groupings; they may, for example, prefer to have a group split up to permit two separate debates on related but different matters, or otherwise to have a different arrangement of debates. On questions of order the chairman's decision is final (there is no appeal to the Speaker), although sometimes it is challenged by points of order in the committee, but selection and grouping are matters of discretion, and frequently chairmen are prepared to modify their original decisions to meet the wishes of the committee, provided this is fair to both sides. The Chair must avoid the danger of permitting unnecessarily prolonged debate, but equally it must ensure that all relevant arguments can be heard. This involves the clear and impartial application of the rules of procedure which protect both the majority and the minority. The political clash may be vigorous and the committee is the proper arena for this purpose, but there is no advantage in prolonged disputes about the rules of that arena.

When the committee meets (or when the House is resolved into a committee on the bill) the Chairman announces his selection of amendments—indeed it has usually been circulated in advance—and calls a Member to move the first amendment in the first group of selected amendments (or puts the question on the first clause, if there are no amendments to it). The other amendments in that group may be debated at the same time, but when the first amendment has been disposed of—agreed to (with or without sub-amendments), negatived or withdrawn—the further amendments in the group will not be moved unless, when they are reached according to their place in the bill, the Chairman allows them to be moved formally for a separate vote, but not for further debate. Separate questions on grouped amendments are frequently allowed when there are alternative proposals in a group of amendments or because later amendments are consequential on an amendment which has been agreed to. Amendments consequential on or similar in purpose to negatived amendments fall and are not called.

The debate itself is a simple process. In a standing committee a Member moves an amendment; the Minister may give the Government response; the Opposition front-bench (if they did not move) may speak; other Members from both sides may speak; the Minister may be pressed on various points; the Minister may speak again; the Opposition spokesman may speak again; and so it goes on until the committee is ready to come to a conclusion or the closure is moved (although this, nowadays, is comparatively rare). Unless there is an attempt to filibuster, speeches are often fairly short, and debate is often on matters of detail as well as policy. When bills are considered in committee of the whole House it is usually somewhat different. The issues are largely political; speeches tend to be longer; and it is not normal for anyone, other than the Member who moved an amendment and the Minister dealing with that amendment, to speak more than once. On the other hand back-bench Privy Councillors, on both sides, often contribute to the debates; such Members are not usually nominated to standing committees on bills. Debate on the floor of the House tends to be more formal than debate in a committee upstairs.

When all amendments to a clause have been disposed of, the committee may, unless the chairman uses his powers under Standing Order No.67, (see page 218), debate the question, "That the clause (as amended) stand part of the bill." Debate on this motion should not repeat the debate on the preceding amendments, but it is proper to consider the policy embodied in the clause or to seek explanations or assurances from Ministers about how they envisage the clause being applied in practice.

When all the clauses in the bill have been disposed of, the committee may consider new clauses introducing new matter within the scope of the bill, or designed to replace clauses which have been disagreed to. Sometimes a bill may be almost re-written in this way, especially private Members' bills (see page 395). More drastically a committee, although it has not formally the power to disagree with a bill which the House has approved on second reading, may in practice achieve the same result by negativing all the effective clauses and not replacing them; a formal report to this effect is then made to the House in lieu of reporting the bill. This is naturally a very rare occurrence, and in recent years has only happened with a private Members bill.[10]

After clauses and new clauses, the schedules and any new schedules are considered. If there is a preamble, this may also be debated. Amendments may also be moved to the long title, but only if they are necessitated by amendments that have already been made to the bill. Finally the question is proposed, and in standing committee is sometimes briefly debated, for the report of the bill to the House.

Reporting of Bills

Bills reported with amendments from a standing committee are always reprinted, as amended, before they are considered by the House. Bills amended in committee of the whole House are normally reprinted unless, as sometimes happens, the remaining stages are to be taken forthwith. Amendments can then be tabled for the report (or consideration) stage. All bills reported from standing committees are, under Standing Order No. 71, considered on report by the House, but bills reported from committees of the whole House are only given a consideration stage if amended in committee; unamended bills from committees of the whole House go straight to third reading. The few bills reported from select or joint committees are recommitted to a committee of the whole House, or to a standing committee which enables their content to be debated politically in addition to the detailed scrutiny of the select or joint committee.

Report Stage

The procedures at report stage differ from those in committee in a number of respects. Unless the House varies the order, new clauses are considered before amendments to the bill and new schedules before amendments to schedules (new clauses and new schedules in the name of the Member in charge of the bill having priority). Amendments are related to the page and line of the bill as a whole and not to the clauses. As it is the bill as a whole which is considered, no question is put on each clause. The rule against

---

[10] See proceedings on the Transport (Amendment) Bill in Standing Committee B in 1950–51. A key clause of the Education Bill 1970 (a Government measure) was negatived in a standing committee, but the House re-committed the Bill with an instruction permitting the committee to restore the clause (H.C. Deb., Vol. 800, cols. 424–504 (April 22, 1970)).

speaking more than once is applied, with certain exceptions for bills reported from standing committees (see pages 209–210).

The rules regarding the admissibility of amendments in committee apply equally on report, but the Speaker's exercise of his powers of selection is quite different from that of the chairman of the committee.

The Speaker's guiding principle is to avoid debate on the floor of the House which is simply a repetition of the debate in committee and where exactly the same decision may be expected on the amendment or amendments concerned. Speaker King set out the criteria which have generally been followed. Speakers usually select:

all Government amendments—equally all amendments by the Member in charge of a private Member's bill;

all amendments involving some undertaking by the Government;

new "compromises" or "halfway" proposals;

important issues fully debated in committee, but still containing vital matters worthy of a "last look";

new matters brought in by members of the committee or non-members; and

amendments relating to new developments since the committee examined the bill.[11]

Some of these criteria need explanation. The reference to "undertakings" is to undertakings of many kinds given by Ministers in committee in response to criticism of the bill, ranging from "the Government accepts that the terms of the bill could be improved and will table amendments accordingly," through "we would like to discuss this further with interested bodies," to "we are confident the present proposals are all right but, if the committee so desires, of course we will look at this again." Following such ministerial undertakings amendments are often withdrawn in committee. If, having given an undertaking, the Government tables an amendment on report it is, of course, selected. If the Opposition (or other Members) table the same amendment as the one in committee on which the undertaking was given, or one which is modified in response to committee criticism but which raises the same point, it is also selected, and if the Government has not tabled a relevant amendment, this gives the House an opportunity to ask the Minister to explain his decision. If both the Government and the Opposition table relevant amendments, they will be grouped together for debate. In this and other ways problems may be discovered or exposed in committee but the solutions are brought forward at the report stage; the two processes must be considered together.

"Compromises" are, by definition, different from the amendments debated in committee, and therefore are selected; but they must be genuinely different, not just rewording.

"Vital matters worthy of a last look" means, in practice, amendments fully debated in standing committee, and probably decided on a straight party vote, to which the Opposition attaches a lot of importance; they are too important to be decided by a small committee, and should be voted on by the House as a whole. The Opposition is often asked to limit its choice of such amendments to one or two points as this criterion weakens the general principle of avoiding repetition of debates.

In addition to these criteria, a few other tests are applied. Amendments

---

[11] Sixth Report from the Select Committee on Procedure, H.C. 539 of 1966–67, p. 87.

are selected on report which were negatived in committee on a casting vote of the chairman or which were negatived in a vote involving cross-party voting, or to revise an amendment which was carried on a cross-party vote in committee; in all these cases the decision of the House could be different from that of the committee. In particular amendments are sometimes tabled to reverse Government defeats in committee, and these are always selected.

In general amendments which were debated at length in committee and brought to a vote are not selected by the Speaker for further debate on report; amendments only briefly debated and which were then withdrawn may well be selected if time permits. The overall effect of the Speaker's selection is that, even after grouping, quite a number of amendments are not selected on report. Much depends on the bill, the extent of attempted obstruction, the number of amendments tabled, and the time available.

The time available for the report stage naturally varies according to the bills concerned. In many cases it may only be a matter of minutes (or no time at all if there are no amendments). For a major and controversial Government bill, two or three full days and all-night sessions may be required; for example the report stage of the Police and Criminal Evidence Bill, 1984, without a guillotine, lasted for 18½ hours. Overall, as the Table on page 311 shows, the report stages of Government bills often take up more time on the floor of the House than any other stage. In sessions 1964–84, some 9 per cent. of the total time of the House was spent on the report stages of Government bills.[12]

Third Reading

The third reading of a bill is normally taken immediately following the report stage, in which case the bill is obviously not then re-printed if amended, but occasionally—as often happens with the Finance Bill—when the third reading is to be on a later day, the bill, as further amended on consideration, is again reprinted. Between report and third reading there may also be a recommittal to enable further amendments to be considered, but this is nowadays very rare. The last occasion was in 1962 on the Finance Bill.

The third reading is, today, a largely formal stage; only verbal amendments (which are very rare[12a]) are allowed, and this stage does not usually take up much time (see Table on page 311). If the bill affects Royal interests or the Royal prerogative, the Queen's or Prince of Wales's Consent is usually signified by a Privy Councillor at this stage; there were 10 such bills in 1984–85 and 16 in 1985–86. Third reading permits a final statement by the Minister and the Opposition of their attitudes towards the bill as it now stands and of what they expect its results to be; other Members may comment on aspects of the bill which concern them, but a third reading debate should not extend to discussion of matters omitted from the bill. Reasoned amendments for rejection of a bill are very occasionally moved (see page 362). Sometimes congratulations and thanks are liberally distributed before the bill is sent on its way; sometimes not. Sometimes there

---

[12] Second Report of the Procedure Committee, H.C. 49–II of 1984–85, p. 29.
[12a] For a recent case see H.C. Deb., Vol. 150, cols. 1160–1209 (April 14, 1989).

is no debate at all.[13] Thus the Bill is finally passed in the Commons and sent (or returned) to the Lords.[14]

Lords Amendments

If the Lords do not amend a Commons bill (or the Commons a Lords bill) it is now ready for Royal Assent. If, however, there are Lords Amendments to Commons bills, as there frequently are for bills of any size or substance, whichever party is in power, those amendments are sent to the Commons for their consideration, and are printed. The House cannot, however, consider anew the whole bill, but only the amendments made by the Lords and the relevant text of the bill; parts of the bill untouched by the Lords cannot be further debated.

Each Lords Amendment must be put to the House separately for decision, although they are often grouped, at the suggestion of the Minister, for convenient debate; the Speaker has no powers of selection over the actual Lords Amendments, but can select or not amendments to the Lords Amendments and other related amendments to the bill. Notice is usually given of all such further amendments. On each Lords Amendment one of the following decisions may be made. The House may—

(a) agree with the Lords Amendment;

(b) disagree with the Lords Amendment (and offer reasons for such disagreement);

(c) amend the Lords Amendment and, as amended, agree to it;

(d) agree to the Lords Amendment and make consequential amendments to other parts of the bill (but they must be genuinely consequential—not new points);

(e) disagree to the Lords Amendment but make other related amendments to the bill in lieu thereof; or

(f) disagree to a Lords Amendment to leave words out, but make amendments to the words so restored to the bill.

The above lists the more common procedures but there are other possible varieties (for example dividing of Lords Amendments).[15] One procedural point of great historical importance but of little practical significance today is that attention must be drawn by the Chair to any Lords Amendment which infringes the Commons financial privileges (where the Lords, by an amendment to a Commons bill, propose any alteration, increase or decrease, in any

---

[13] From 1967 to 1985 a standing order prohibited any debate on third reading unless at least six Members gave notice of their wish for a debate; it had little effect on Government bills as it became standard practice of Opposition parties to give such notice.

[14] It may of course, be negatived on third reading. The last occasion was on July 12, 1977, when the Local Authority Works (Scotland) Bill (a Government measure) was defeated by 99 votes to 105 (H.C. Deb., Vol. 935–1, cols. 351–381).

[15] For a full description of the complex procedures on consideration of Lords Amendments, see May, pp. 579–588.

financial charge on public funds, local or national, or any tax or other charge on the people). It is open to the Commons, as very frequently happens with Government amendments, to agree to the Lords Amendment and thus to waive their privileges; occasionally, however, the Commons disagree to a Lords Amendment which trespasses on their financial privileges and the reason for disagreement is then said to be because it infringed privilege. In practice, however, the Commons financial privileges no longer seem to deter the Lords from dealing with the more detailed financial aspects of legislation, and the Commons do not appear particularly distressed by the frequent infringement of their privileges.

When all the Lords Amendments have been considered (and for a long bill this may be a whole day's work and sometimes a night as well) they are returned to the Lords together with reasons for any straight disagreements. These are agreed by a small committee from both sides, but in practice are drawn up by the Government draftsman in pretty terse terms. If the Commons have agreed to all the Lords Amendments and done nothing else, full agreement on the text of the bill between the two Houses has now been reached and the bill is ready for Royal Assent. If the Commons have disagreed with any Lords Amendments or have amended them or made any amendments to the bill, the Lords must now consider what to do about these changes and must convey their decisions to the Commons, who in their turn must decide how to react to the Lords Amendments to the Commons Amendments to the Lords Amendments, or Lords Amendments to Common Amendments in lieu of a Lords Amendment, etc. To follow the path through the whole maze of possibilities would be too tedious an expedition for our readers.[16] Suffice it to say that eventually there must either be agreement, or final disagreement by one House or other insisting on an amendment to which the other insists on disagreeing, or the process is terminated by prorogation or dissolution and the bill falls. In the great majority of cases in recent years when this shuttle process has been conducted, final agreement has ultimately been reached. The only exceptions, among Government bills, taking bills that had been read the third time in each House, being the Trade Union and Labour Relations (Amendment) Bill of Session 1974–75 and the Aircraft and Shipbuilding Industries Bill, of Session 1975–76. The Parliament Bills of Sessions 1947–48, and 1948, which were designed to amend the Parliament Act 1911, were not passed by the House of Lords and so never came back to the Commons.

The procedure for Commons Amendments to Lords bills is similar. Any amendments made by the Commons to a Lords bill are considered by the Lords and, unless they agree to all the Commons Amendments, their decisions on those amendments are returned to the Commons for their consideration, and the process described above may continue. There have been no cases since 1945 of failure to reach agreement on a Lords bill once this stage has been reached.[17]

---

[16] For a case of great complexity see the proceedings on the Trade Union and Labour Relations (Amendment) Bill, 1974–75. The bill went back and forward between the two Houses six times and it was still not agreed when the session came to an end.

[17] Although the Shops Bill [*Lords*] of session 1985–86 was negatived by the Commons on second reading, (see pp. 42 and 327–328) and there are many cases of private Members' Lords bills failing to pass in the Commons (see p. 392).

Overall an average of 12 Commons bills were amended by the Lords in each of the 10 sessions up till 1987, and an average of 10 Lords bills were amended by the Commons per session in the same period. As the Table on page 311 shows, a significant amount of time is spent in the Commons on consideration of Lords Amendments.

Royal Assent

When total agreement has been reached by both Houses on the text of a bill it is ready for Royal Assent. Bills are prepared and presented to the Queen for Royal Assent by the clerks of the House of Lords. Apart from occasions at the end of a session when the Commons go to the Lords for the prorogation of Parliament, when the Assent to any outstanding bills is first signified by Commissioners, the Commons no longer participate in the process of Royal Assent. Under the Royal Assent Act 1967, the Speaker simply notifies the House, at a convenient moment, that the Queen has signified her Royal Assent to certain Acts; this is recorded in the Journal.

Royal Assent is given by the Sovereign on the advice of her Ministers; it has not been refused since Queen Anne refused her Assent in 1707 to a Bill for settling the militia in Scotland.[18]

Parliament Acts

If agreement between the two Houses cannot be reached the Government may decide to assert the political supremacy of the House of Commons and bring the Parliament Acts 1911 and 1949, into play. The fact that these Acts are rarely formally applied must in no way diminish their significance. The very possibility of the Commons overriding, by application of the Parliament Acts, a veto of an essential piece of legislation on the part of the Lords—or even their failure to co-operate in its passage—adds greatly to the power of the Government to achieve, in the end, the passage into law of any bill on which they are determined to succeed, while not eroding completely the ability of the Lords to seek modifications or compromise by process of amendment and delay. The significance of this for the Lords is considered in Chapter 12. Here we describe the basic procedures.

Whenever a public bill is passed by the House of Commons, the Speaker, having consulted in more difficult or politically sensitive cases two Members of the Chairmen's Panel, must decide whether or not it is a money bill within the terms of the Parliament Act 1911, and if it is, certify it as such. Section 1(2) of that Act defines a money bill as a public bill which, in the opinion of the Speaker, contains *only* provisions dealing with central government taxation, or the imposition, variation or repeal of charges on the Consolidated Fund, National Loans Fund or money provided by Parliament, or the raising, guarantee or repayment of loans by Government, or subordinate matters incidental to any of these purposes. Few bills are wholly concerned with taxation or expenditure in these ways and so qualify for the Speaker's certificate: there were 55 certified bills in the eight sessions of the 1979–87 Parliaments (including 28 Consolidated Fund and Appropriation Bills which are always certified). Not all Finance Bills are money bills under the Parliament Acts as they often contain some non-taxing provisions: only four out of 10 in the period analysed.

---

[18] L.J. (1705–09) 506 (1707).

A bill certified as a money bill under the Act which has been passed by the Commons but which is not passed by the Lords without amendment within one month after they receive it, shall, under section 1(1) of the Act, unless the Commons otherwise direct (as on occasions the Commons have done[19]), be presented to the Queen for Royal Assent and become an Act of Parliament. It is possible for a certified bill to be amended by the Lords,[20] but if the Commons then agree to any such amendments the bill can no longer attract the benefit of the Parliament Act to obtain the Royal Assent.

These provisions of the Parliament Act, to prevent the Lords blocking essential financial legislation, had been proved necessary by the Lords rejection of the Finance Bill, 1909, but in practice no money bill has been given Royal Assent in this way.

Under section 2 of the Act of 1911, as amended by the Parliament Act 1949 (which reduced the period of delay to one year), a bill which has been passed by the House of Commons in two successive sessions (whether of the same Parliament or not) and which, having been sent up to the House of Lords at least one month before the end of the session, is rejected by the House of Lords in each of those sessions (and rejection includes failure to pass in an agreed form) shall, on its rejection for the second time by the House of Lords, unless the Commons direct to the contrary, be presented for Royal Assent (the Speaker having certified that the provisions of section 2 of the Act have been complied with). One year must lapse, for the Act to be applied, between the second reading of the bill in the Commons in the first of these sessions and its passing in the Commons in the second session. And the bill must be in substantially the same form in each session, except that it may incorporate amendments made by the Lords in the first session before its rejection by them.

Bills originating in the House of Lords are not subject to the Parliament Acts, nor do the Acts apply to private bills, or provisional order bills, or statutory instruments. Furthermore a bill seeking to extend the maximum duration of Parliament beyond five years is exempt from the Act, so the Lords could block any legislation to postpone the holding of a general election; however (perhaps somewhat surprisingly) amendment of the Parliament Act itself is not exempt (as was shown in 1948 and 1949), and so even the five-year Parliament provision is not totally entrenched.

The only bills to have been passed under the Parliament Act powers we have so far described are the Government of Ireland Act 1914, the Welsh Church Act 1914 and the Parliament Act 1949. There is, however, one other provision of the Act which has also been used. Under section 2(4) of the 1911 Act the Commons may, in the second session, suggest, before the third reading, amendments that should be made to the bill (if they were actually made, the Parliament Act could not be applied, as the bill would no longer be the same as the bill rejected in the first session); such suggestions are sent to the Lords and, if agreed by the Lords, are treated as amendments made by the Lords and agreed by the Commons. This facilitates the reaching of agreement without prejudicing the possibility of still obtaining Royal Assent under the Parliament Act if the bill is eventually rejected by the Lords. The suggested amendment procedure has been used on three occasions: on the

---

[19] See H.C.Deb., Vol. 291, cols. 2202–2204 (July 5, 1934); H.C.Deb., Vol. 848, col. 1531 (December 20, 1972); H.C.Deb., Vol. 917, col. 258 (October 12, 1976).

[20] See, *e.g.* C.J. (1921), pp. 347, 364.

Temperance (Scotland) Bill, 1913 (when the suggestion was negatived by the Commons),[21] on the Trade Union and Labour Relations (Amendment) Bill, 1975–76 (where one suggestion was agreed to and others negatived; the Lords, in effect, agreed to the suggestion and, other outstanding differences having been settled, the bill obtained Royal Assent without the use of the Parliament Act)[22]; and on the Aircraft and Shipbuilding Industries Bill, 1976–77 (where again the suggestions were negatived in the Commons).[23]

Intervals Between Stages of Bills

We have been considering circumstances under which bills are extensively delayed; we now describe more normal practice. It is however very difficult to generalise as circumstances, the nature of legislation, and the degree of urgency vary greatly. Apart from the so-called "practice of the House" which requires each stage of a "bill of aids and supplies" to be taken on a different day (and that rule is now overridden by Standing Order No. 54(1) in respect of Consolidated Fund and Appropriation Bills and is frequently overridden by order of the House for Finance Bills), nothing is laid down in standing orders or by practice which formally regulates the maximum or minimum time between the various stages of a bill.

Leaving aside private Members' bills, where different practices apply (see pages 385–398), the ordinary arrangements for Government bills is meant to be something like this. There are at least two weekends between publication and the bill's second reading. The committee stage starts some 10 or more days after second reading (excluding bills, such as uncontroversial consolidation bills or bills required in an emergency, which are usually taken in committee of the whole House immediately after second reading). The report stage is taken some 10 or more days after the bill is published as amended in committee. The third reading may be held on the same day as the report stage. However, evidence given to the Procedure Committee in 1985[24] shows that these "norms," which were described by the Procedure Committee in 1978,[25] and confirmed by the 1985 Committee,[26] were not always complied with in respect of Government bills in Session 1983–84. Seven, out of 43, bills were debated on second reading with less than the recommended interval since publication; 14 out of 36 Bills began their committee stage before the recommended interval of 10 days had elapsed; and eight out of 34 Bills were considered on report with less than the recommended 10-day interval since the end of the committee stage.

There is sometimes an acute shortage of time for considering Lords Amendments, particularly in the Summer when the Government is anxious to complete a bill before the long recess. Lords Amendments may be considered on the very day they are received, and are frequently considered on the following day. When this happens the Speaker relaxes the notice that is normally required for tabling amendments to Lords Amendments.[27]

---

[21] H.C.Deb., Vol. 55, cols. 470–508 (July 9, 1913).

[22] H.C.Deb., Vol. 903, cols. 1349–1502 (January 21, 1976); H.C.Deb., Vol. 904, cols. 267–388 (January 27, 1976).

[23] H.C.Deb., Vol. 922, cols. 258–374 (December 7, 1976).

[24] Second Report, H.C. 49–II of 1984–85, pp. 135–137.

[25] First Report, H.C. 588 of 1977–78, para. 2.28.

[26] Second Report, H.C. 49 of 1984–85, para. 29.

[27] See, *e.g.* H.C.Deb., Vol. 102, cols. 202–203 (July 22, 1986).

At the beginning of this chapter we emphasised the importance of ensuring that the House has adequate notice of every item of business. Failure by the Government to allow adequate time (in the opinion of many Members) has often been criticised. The inconvenience that can be caused by too hurried proceedings—including the late tabling of numerous amendments—can be a serious matter, not only for Members who have to prepare their amendments and contributions to debate in committee and on report, but also to outside parties and pressure or interest groups, who wish to brief Members on amendments when the bill is published, before and during committee and before the report stage. Select Committees on Procedure have recommended that minimum intervals between stages should be laid down by standing order,[28] but this has not been accepted by the Government.

Even if such rules could be enforced (and standing orders can be suspended), it would still not remove the problem of late tabling of amendments. For example, the 1986 Finance Bill was reported from committee on June 19; it was re-printed as amended and published on June 26; 29 Government amendments were tabled on June 30, 69 on July 3 and 58 (including five important new clauses) on July 4 (this was a Friday, so these latest amendments were not available for most Members and interested persons till Monday July 7); the bill was due to be considered on July 8 and 9. In the event, following complaints that inadequate time had been allowed for the examination of the latest amendments, the Government agreed to defer the second day from July 9 until July 17, when the major Government new clauses were considered. Thus the flexibility of the Houses' procedures enabled the problems for Members to be somewhat alleviated.

There are undoubtedly problems for the Opposition, back-benchers and outside parties when major Government bills are hurried through. On the other hand the need for the Government to work to a tight timetable if it is to succeed in getting its legislation—supported by the majority in the House—on to the statute book without undue delay cannot be ignored.

Bills Passed with Minimum Delay

We have dealt with bills where debate is protracted and the guillotine may be required. The flexibility of procedures make it possible, however, for other bills to be passed with great speed. The Consolidated Fund and Appropriation Bills are always treated in this way (see page 249), but other bills are often hurried through for various reasons; either public policy so requires, or there has been some emergency, or the bills are so uncontentious that little time need be spent on them. The common feature of these bills is that they must be generally acceptable to the House, for if more than a handful of Members are opposed for any reason they can delay progress not only by prolonging debate on the bill itself but by insisting on debating various procedural motions, such as to permit a committee stage on the same day as second reading.[29] Uncontroversial private Members' bills are often

---

[28] First Report, H.C. 588 of 1977–78, paras. 2.27–2.28; Second Report, H.C. 85 of 1984–85, para. 23.

[29] See, *e.g.* H.C.Deb., Vol. 512, cols. 257–264 (March 3, 1953).

hurried through all stages without debate ("on the nod"), usually when time is running out for such legislation[30] (see page 392).

If there is significant opposition, it is almost impossible to hurry a bill through all its stages on one day. But this can readily be done, if everyone is agreed, as on September 1, 1939, when 18 bills were introduced into the Commons, passed, sent to the Lords and given Royal Assent, all between 6 p.m. and midnight.[31] Similarly the Northern Ireland Bill 1972 was introduced and passed all stages to Royal Assent on February 23, 1972, although one Member opposed its second reading.[32]

Passage of second reading and all remaining stages in one House at one sitting is more common. On average, in the 10 sessions up till 1986–87, 12 bills a session (excluding Consolidated Fund and Appropriation Bills) have been read a second time, committed to a committee of the whole House, reported, considered (if amended), read the third time and passed at one sitting; 12 other bills per session have also received their committee and remaining stages at the same sitting.

Commencement

And so a bill becomes an Act. Unless otherwise provided in the Act it comes into affect immediately, but frequently it is administratively necessary for commencement to be delayed, either for the whole Act or for specified parts, and either until a stated day or till such day as the Minister may, by order, prescribe. Such orders, known as commencement orders, are not normally subject to the parliamentary proceedings described below. Commencement of parts of Acts may thus be delayed for some time, without any parliamentary control, until the necessary administrative arrangements have been made; indeed very occasionally a commencement order is never made, and the Act, or parts of an Act, never come into force.[33]

Delegated Legislation

We have described the basic procedures for bills (primary legislation), but the House also has to deal with delegated (or secondary) legislation. Delegated legislation is part of the law of the land, enforceable in the courts, but it is law made by Ministers, under powers given them by Act, rather than direct legislation by Parliament. Although of equal legal effect, there is one important difference between deligated legislation and Acts of Parliament. The latter are made by a constitutionally sovereign authority and are not subordinate to any constitutional limitations within the United Kingdom.[34]

---

[30] Sometimes there is too much hurry. The Protection of Military Remains Bill went through all stages "on the nod" on Friday January 31, 1986; it was later pointed out that the bill should have had a money resolution; the proceedings in committee and on third reading were therefore ordered to be null and void on the following Monday; a money resolution was then agreed to; and the bill went through its remaining stages on the following Friday (H.C.Deb., Vol. 91, cols. 28, 119, 259, 611 (February 3, 4 and 7, 1986)).

[31] H.C.Deb., Vol. 351, cols. 125–220.

[32] H.C.Deb., Vol. 831, cols. 1285–1297, 1363–1450, 1454.

[33] See for example, the Easter Act 1928.

[34] Under the Treaties of the European Communities, domestic legislation must be compatible with those treaties and with legislation made by the Council of Ministers. If it were thought that an Act of the U.K. Parliament was in conflict with Community law, that Act could be challenged in the European Court, and its provisions could be overridden by legislation agreed by the Council. But these external restraints on U.K. legislation do not directly affect the procedures or legislative processes of either House of Parliament.

An Act cannot be challenged in the courts on the ground that it is *ultra vires*. Nor, under Article 9 of the Bill of Rights, can the proceedings in passing a bill in Parliament be questioned in any court. Delegated legislation, however, can be challenged in the courts[35] on the grounds that the Minister had no power, under the parent Act, to make delegated legislation in the terms concerned. But again, parliamentary proceedings, for example in approving an instrument, cannot be questioned in the courts.

Delegated legislation comprises regulations, Orders in Council, other orders, schemes, rules, codes of practice, Rate Support Grant Reports for England and Wales, etc., and even statutes of certain colleges. These are all different forms of making detailed provision for implementing and administering the principles and requirements of the law as set out in the parent Act. Under the Statutory Instruments Act 1946, the great majority of these forms of delegated legislation are defined as statutory instruments, including Orders in Council when the parent Act was passed after 1948 and other instruments made by Ministers where the parent Act so provides. Other forms of delegated legislation, such as Immigration Rules, the Highway Code and Codes of Practice on Industrial Relations, while not statutory instruments, are often treated as such by Parliament. Statutory instruments are numbered, *e.g.* S.I. 1986, No.100.

The parent Act defines the way and by whom a statutory instrument may be made and the nature of parliamentary control, if any, to which it is subject. Some statutory instruments, and many local instruments, are not laid before Parliament at all; some are not even printed. Other less important instruments are laid before Parliament, but are not subject to any parliamentary proceedings. Many of the more significant instruments may be laid and come into operation immediately, or at some specified date, unless either House passes, within a limited time, a motion to annul the instrument; this is known as the negative (or "prayer") procedure. Sometimes the instrument is laid in draft, and either House may similarly resolve that it be not made. Finally, other more significant instruments are laid in draft or are laid in final form and do not come into effect (or in some cases do not continue in effect beyond a specified period) unless one or both Houses pass a resolution approving the document. This is known as the affirmative procedure; only the Commons are given powers of this kind in relation to instruments dealing with taxation, but the approval of both Houses is required for most instruments under the affirmative procedure.

In recent years some 2000 statutory instruments have been made and printed each year (approximately half being general and half local), filling six volumes some two or three inches thick. The extent of parliamentary concern is illustrated by the fact that in session 1987–88, 246 instruments subject to the affirmative procedure and 1240 instruments subject to the negative procedure were considered by the joint or select committee (see below) out of a total of 1947 instruments that fell to be considered by them.

A joint committee of both Houses, sometimes called "the scrutiny committee," considers instruments laid before Parliament, with a view to determining whether the attention of the House should be drawn to it on one of several specified grounds.[36] A select committees of Commons Members

---

[35] See, *e.g. R. W. Paul* v. *The Wheat Commission* [1937] A.C. 139; *Chester* v. *Bateson* [1920] 1 K.B. 829; *Commissioners of Customs and Excise* v. *Cure and Deeley Ltd.* [1962] 1 Q.B. 340.

[36] For details see Standing Order No. 124 and page 445.

considers instruments land before the House of Commons only. We consider the work of the joint committee and select committee on pages 444–446.

With a very few exceptions, statutory instruments cannot be amended by either House.[37] But if debate in either House, or examination by the scrutiny committee, reveals some error or drafting defect in an instrument, or if the Government are otherwise persuaded that the instrument should be amended in some way, the Government can withdraw the instrument and re-lay it in an approved form, as quite often happens. An instrument may also be re-layed if one House negatives an affirmative instrument or agrees to a prayer for anullment. It should be noted that the Parliament Acts do not apply to delegated legislation, so the Commons cannot override the Lords in this field.

Affirmative Procedure

If an instrument is subject to the affirmative procedure, the responsibility lies with the Minister, having laid an instrument, to move the necessary motion for its approval (for example, "That the New Towns (Limit on Borrowing) Order 1983, dated 12 December, 1983, a copy of which was laid before the House on 20 December, be approved"). This motion may be made in the House, often after 10.00 p.m., in which case (unless the House otherwise orders) debate is limited to one and a half hours, at the end of which the question is usually put (see page 221). Alternatively—for the less controversial instruments or those of interest to only a limited number of Members—the Government may, having given notice of the motion to approve, move under Standing Order No. 101 that the instrument be referred to a standing committee on statutory instruments; this is decided without amendment or debate. The procedure in these committees is described on page 275; they have no power actually to approve an instrument. Soon after the committee reports, a motion is moved in the House for the instrument to be approved, and the question is put forthwith, under Standing Order No. 101(5). Thus many affirmative instruments are debated upstairs, although the final approval is still given by the House. Relevant statistics for the 1983–87 Parliament are given on pages 331–334.

The Negative Procedure

The procedure for prayers against instruments is similar, but here the initiative lies with the Opposition parties and back-benchers to table the appropriate motions (for how they use these opportunities see pages 345–350 and 406–407). Unless special provision is made, debates on prayers cannot, under Standing Order No. 15(1) and (2) continue after 11.30 p.m., and given that Government business usually takes up most of the time until then, it is now often extremely difficult to find time for debating prayers on the floor of the House. We consider this question further on pages 345–347. Therefore if a prayer is tabled (usually as an early day motion), unless the official Opposition can persuade the Government to find time for it to be debated on the floor, it will either remain undebated or it must be debated upstairs, with a Minister moving the reference to the committee as for affirmative instruments. If

---

[37] For a list of 18 statutes, from 1850 to 1962, which gave Parliament powers, in various ways, to amend delegated legislation, see Report from Joint Committee on Delegated Legislation, H.L. 184, H.C. 475 of 1971–72, p. 181.

debated upstairs, however, it is not the practice (though permitted by Standing Order No. 101(5)) for opportunity to be found for the House to vote on the prayer itself. The Government do not need a decision on an instrument that is subject only to the negative procedure and the Opposition have no means of forcing a vote (unless they put down a prayer for debate on an Opposition day). Thus, under the negative procedure, although the initiative lies with the Opposition or back-bencher, the Government can, in practice, control the extent to which instruments are debated. We give statistics for recent sessions on page 346.

Financial Procedures

The original need to summon a House of Commons arose from the financial requirements of the Crown, and the House's authority and influence sprung from, and has been based on, its powers to approve—and to consider before approving—taxation and Government expenditure. In this century, however, the procedures for scrutinising and authorising the Government's expenditure proposals have increasingly been stripped to the bare essentials and specific debates on expenditure as such have been greatly reduced. In particular the opportunities that consideration of Supply gave to the Opposition and back-benchers to raise matters of their choosing have been replaced by other procedures (see pages 11, 250 and 340–342). There is no need therefore, in a work which is primarily concerned with what happens in Parliament today, to describe at length the details of financial procedures that were of considerable importance in earlier years. Here only the essential principles and the surviving financial practice will be discussed.[38]

Constitutional Principles and Practices

The central historical and constitutional principles, common to both expenditure and taxation, are that the Crown (which today means Ministers of the Crown) demands money, the Commons grant it, and the Lords assent to the grant; but the Commons do not authorise expenditure or seek to impose taxes unless this be required by the Crown. These requirements are more specifically stated in two financial rules applying to Parliament as a whole. First, that all charges (proposals for expenditure or taxation) must be demanded or recommended by the Crown before they can be considered. Second, all charges must first be considered by the House of Commons but must also be embodied in legislation for approval by both Houses. Subordinate to these are procedural rules of the House of Commons, such as the requirement for proposals for both expenditure and taxation to be first brought forward in the form of resolutions on which legislation, giving full effect to the proposals, may then be founded.

The practical effects today of these constitutional principles and financial rules fall under three heads. First, the Government must lay before the House of Commons each year its estimates for expenditure for the forthcoming financial year, and seek their approval by the House; it must then obtain legislative approval for this expenditure in the form of Consolidated Fund and Appropriation Bills. Moneys so voted by Parliament must be

---

[38] For a full description of Parliament's financial procedures see May, Chaps. 27–32. For an examination of their use and gradual disuse in this century, see Michael Ryle, "Supply and other Financial Procedure," in S. A. Walkland (ed.) *The House of Commons in the Twentieth Century* (1979).

appropriated to specific purposes in the same session as that in which they were first requested in the Government's estimates. This is known as Supply procedure. Second, for any bills involving charges, the Government must move either money or Ways and Means resolutions and this limits the scope of amendments that may be moved to bills (see pages 233 and 330–331). Third, the Government must introduce, each year, a Budget, expressed in Ways and Means resolutions, which finds its legislative expression in the Finance Bill which is scrutinised in detail by the House.

Before describing these proceedings, we must examine more closely the concept of a charge, which brings the financial procedures into play. The tests of a charge upon public funds (expenditure) are as follows. It must be new and distinct, and not already authorised by law. Under Standing Order No. 46, it must be payable out of the Consolidated Fund or National Loans Fund, or out of money to be provided by Parliament; it must therefore affect central government expenditure, not local, and does not extend to payments out of special funds such as the National Insurance Fund. And it must be effectively imposed and not just an expression of opinion or a recommendation. Examples of charges include imposing additional duties on Ministers or Government departments that would involve expenditure; payments out of the Consolidated Fund such as the salaries of judges; Government loans to nationalised industries; increases in the time during which previously authorised expenditure may be incurred; extension of the purpose of previously authorised expenditure; and increasing the amount of money that may be spent.

The Voting of Supply

Supply is voted annually. The Queen announces in her Speech from the Throne "Members of the House of Commons, Estimates for the Public Service will be laid before you," which signifies the royal recommendation. The session 1985–86 which started in November 1985, included the second half of the financial year 1985–86 (April 1, 1985 to March 31, 1986) and the first half of the financial year 1986–87. The first estimates laid in December 1985 were the Winter Supplementary Estimates for 1985–86, covering expenditures additional to, or for different purposes from, those included in the main estimates for 1985–86 (presented in the Spring of 1985) which had been appropriated in the Appropriation Act 1985, passed in July of that year. At the same time the Vote on Account, being a lump sum (amounting to about 45 per cent. of the current year's total expenditure) to keep the Government going for some four or five months pending the voting of the full estimates, was also presented. Under what is known as the Supply guillotine, on a day before February 6 (usually before Christmas) these estimates having been set down for approval by the House and two days' notice having been given, the Speaker, at 10.00 p.m., put the question under Standing Order No. 53(1) and (2), "That a further supplementary sum, not exceeding £1,622,415,000" (to use the 1985 figure) "be granted to Her Majesty out of the Consolidated Fund to defray charges for Defence and Civil Services for the year ending on March 31, 1986, as set out in House of Commons Paper No. 9." He then put a similar question for the total Vote on Account for 1986–87, which is not at this stage appropriate to separate services. Under Standing Order No. 53, the whole amounts are put as single questions and there can be no amendments or debate at this point. The Consolidated Fund Bill was then ordered in on these resolutions, which gave the Treasury the power to issue from the Consolidated Fund the amounts stated in the Supply resolutions and authority for the Government to spend that money.

A few days later the Consolidated Fund Bill was set down as the first order of the day and, pursuant to Standing Order No. 54(1), the questions were put immediately for both the second and third readings. Under the standing order there is no committee stage or debate. However a lengthy debate on the adjournment followed, which was used for debating back-bench matters (see pages 265–266).

In the Spring, further supplementary estimates for 1985–86 were presented, to cover the remaining additional expenditure expected in that financial year. However, it is not always possible to be totally accurate in estimating, sometimes unforeseen expenditures have to be incurred, and every year some votes are over-spent. This excess expenditure must be given retrospective authorisation and so, in February 1986, Excess Votes for 1984–85 (which had been audited by the Comptroller and Auditor General) were presented. Assuming the Public Accounts Committee reports that it has no objection, excess votes may be put to the House for its approval without debate (Standing Order No. 53(3)(c)). Estimates for the maximum numbers of service personnel to be retained in the Navy, Army and Air Force in the year 1986–87 (the Votes A as they are called) were presented at about the same time; when the resolutions approving these numbers were agreed to, the House had fulfilled its constitutional function of approving annually the maintenance of the armed forces of the Crown. Not later than March 18, 1986, under Standing Order No. 53(1) and (3), all these requests—the Spring Supplementary Estimates, the Excess Votes and the Votes A—were then put to the House as single questions and decided without amendment or debate. The Consolidated Fund (No. 2) Bill was then ordered in on the two financial resolutions, and was passed under the same procedure as the first bill.

The main estimates for 1986–87 were presented at the same time as the Budget (up till 1980 they were usually presented in February). No attempt is made to consider them singly or in detail at this stage, but the general import of the Government's expenditure plans can be considered in the Budget debate. During the Summer of 1986 early supplementary estimates for 1986–87 and revised estimates were presented as changing circumstances and new events made necessary. And, just before the summer recess, on a day not later than August 5, a single resolution, authorising all the outstanding sums required for the financial year 1986–87 (that is the total of all the estimates for that year less the amount voted on account back in December) was agreed to, without amendment or debate, under Standing Order No. 53(4).

The Consolidated Fund (Appropriation) Bill was then ordered in. This not only authorised, like the earlier bills, the issue of the total amounts required, but it appropriated specified maximum sums to be spent in the year 1986–87 on specified purposes, giving the details for each vote as set out in the estimates (but not further broken down into sub-heads, items, etc., as in those documents). For example, Class XI, Vote 1, covered expenditure by the Home Office on court services, compensation for criminal injury, including a grant in aid, probation, police, community services, and superannuation payments for police and fire services: £1,895,308,000 Supply Grants and £9,799,000 Appropriations in Aid (the last being receipts that may be used for those services). The procedure for passing the Consolidated Fund (Appropriation) Bill is the same as for the earlier Consolidated Fund Bills, *ie*, under Standing Order No.54(1), there is no debate on the bill itself.

In addition to the three regular Consolidated Fund and Appropriation Bills, there is occasional need, when some major expenditure requires to be authorised urgently, for additional or supplementary estimates to be presented and an additional Consolidated Fund Bill to be hurried through.[39]

So far it would appear that nothing has survived from the old days when individual votes and subheads of the estimates could be debated and the Government's estimates could be considered in detail before legislative authority was given for its expenditure. Certainly the House has abandoned any attempt to debate annual Supply expenditure as such, in a comprehensive way, preferring to consider longer term expenditure policy in the context of the Budget and other economic debates (see pages 319–321). The House has likewise, and inevitably (given the complexity and volume of the task) abandoned any attempt to examine details of expenditure and administration on the floor of the House, as used to be done in the Committee of Supply when approving individual estimates, but has largely left this task to select committee (see Chapter 11).

However, following (with one significant modification) the recommendations of the Select Committee on Procedure (Supply) of Session 1980–81,[40] the House agreed in July 1982 to retain a limited capability for debating estimates as such, and for considering amendments to Supply motions. While accepting the total abolition of Supply days (now replaced by Opposition days) Standing Order No. 52 provides for three days other than Fridays (the committee recommended eight) to be allotted each session for consideration of estimates; one of those can be split into two half-days, (*i.e.* up till 7.00 p.m. or from 7.00 p.m. to 10.00 p.m.). The estimates to be considered on these days are selected—and time may be allocated—by the Liaison Committee under Standing Order No. 131(2). This committee consists of the chairmen of select committees (see page 416) and thus the choice of the estimates to be debated is, in effect, made by the select committees who naturally choose estimates relating to matters on which they have carried out inquiries and reported to the House.

Amendments may be tabled and, if selected by the Speaker, moved to the estimates down for debate, so retaining a vestige of the old right of the House to reduce the estimates; there is no other opportunity to do this under present procedures. However a procedural oddity provides (in Standing Order No. 52(4)) that all questions on the estimates and amendments to them must be deferred till 10.00 p.m. In this way the Whips have avoided having to keep their troops present throughout the day in case any estimate or amendment is put to a division. (For examination of how Estimates days have been used in practice, see page 408–411).

The formal procedure for authorising expenditure in advance of money being spent by the Government, culminating in the appropriation each year of specified sums for specified purposes, is followed by procedures for accounting for such expenditure and scrutiny of those accounts.

---

[39] See, for example. H.C.Deb., Vol. 71, cols. 886–955, 1096 (January 22 and 23, 1985); this was to authorise additional payments to the Budget of the European Communities.

[40] H.C. 118 of 1980–81.

Each year, at about the end of October or beginning of November, the Appropriation Accounts for the financial year ending on the preceding March 31, are laid before the House, together with the reports of the Comptroller and Auditor-General (C. and A.G.) thereon and on certain related trading and storage accounts. The National Audit Office, under the C. and A.G., has audited all these accounts which show how much money was actually spent, for each vote for which money was appropriated in the Appropriation Act, comparing this with the amount granted. It is for these amounts that the Accounting Officer of each Government department is accountable to Parliament. The amounts spent under various programmes and sub-heads are also audited and shown in the accounts.

The Appropriation Accounts and other accounts laid before Parliament are considered by the Public Accounts Committee under Standing Order No. 122. This committee, advised by the C. and A.G., reports to the House not only on the way money has been spent, but also on whether there has been waste or extravagance, on whether there has been bad estimating which has led to over-spending or under-spending, and on whether expenditure programmes are giving "value for money"; it is not meant to consider the merits of policy decisions. The committee's reports are laid before the House from time to time and there is an annual debate when matters raised by the committee can obtain an airing on the floor of the House. The work of the Public Accounts Committee is further examined in Chapter 11, pages 441–444.

We may sum up this description of Supply procedure in this way. The House has largely abandoned all opportunities for direct control of public expenditure by means of debate and vote on the estimates presented to the House. Except on three Estimates days, there is no opportunity to amend or negative any of the individual estimates, and the Government secures formal approval for its expenditure, without debate, in three or four block votes each year. In place of formal direct control by voting Supply, which for many years has been largely theoretical[41] the House has increasingly relied on informal and indirect control through the exercise of its influence on policy, through scrutiny of policy, administration and expenditure by departmentally-related select committees, and by *ex post facto* scrutiny of actual spending by the Public Accounts Committee.

Money Resolutions

The House still formally exercises some direct control of expenditure through the procedures which we described on page 231 above, namely the specific authorisation by money resolutions of new charges on public funds before their incorporation in legislation. Each money resolution, before being tabled, is formally recommended by the Queen, and this is indicated on the Order Paper, so fulfilling the first financial and constitutional rule (see page 247 above). These resolutions are now of little significance as distinct instruments for financial control over the Government, as the expenditure to which they relate may be debated on the bill itself. Indeed the resolutions are often not debated at all. However, as already explained, they have great practical significance as instruments by which Ministers are able

---

[41] The last time the House actually cut an estimate was in 1919 when provision for an additional bathroom for the Lord Chancellor in the Houses of Parliament was deleted from the Royal Palace's Vote, H.C.Deb., Vol. 118, col. 2323 (July 31, 1919).

to restrict the scope for opposition and back-bench amendments to bills. Thus procedures designed in part to limit the powers of Ministers (setting limits to expenditure) have become procedures restricting the powers of the House.

Ways and Means and the Finance Bill

The House plays a much more positive and directly significant role when authorising taxation. The Chancellor of the Exchequer presents his Budget in the Spring. The significance of this, as a major element of the Government's initiative in Parliament, is considered on pages 319–322. Here we outline the procedures involved.

When presenting his Budget the Chancellor gives formal notice of the Amendment of the Law motion which gives broad authority for "amending the law with respect of the National Debt and public revenue and to make further provision in connection with finance," and of the specific Ways and Means motions which authorise all the taxing charges to be incorporated in the Finance Bill; he also gives notice of other money and procedural motions related to that bill. All the provisions in the Finance Bill have to be covered by the resolutions which the House agrees to. Exceptionally, no notice of any of these motions is published in advance of the Budget debate, so as to avoid premature disclosures.

After his Budget speech the Chancellor formally moves a motion to give immediate provisional statutory effect, under section 5 of the Provisional Collection of Taxes Act 1968, to the proposals contained in certain specified Ways and Means motions which he has tabled; this enables, for example, the duty on tobacco or petrol to be increased that evening before the necessary legislation is passed. Under Standing Order No. 50(2) the question on this must be put forthwith, and nowadays it is almost almost always agreed without division.

The Chancellor then moves formally the Amendment of the Law motion, which is before the House for the whole of the Budget debate lasting usually four days. At the end of the last day this motion is agreed to and, under Standing Order No. 50(3), the question is then put, without amendment or debate, on each of the outstanding Ways and Means and other Budget resolutions which are on the order paper. Several of these contain declarations that the resolution shall have statutory effect under the Provisional Collection of Taxes Act. This is the opportunity for the official Opposition or for other opposition parties to indicate their dislike of certain aspects of the Budget by dividing the House against selected Ways and Means motions. In recent years there have usually been some three or four divisions of this kind.

The Finance Bill is then ordered in on the resolutions which have been agreed to, and is published some three or four weeks later. The need to preserve Budget secrecy precludes earlier publication but permits detailed drafting consultations after the Budget has been presented. The bill itself is often very lengthy, and includes many detailed tax reforms that go beyond the purely revenue requirements of the Budget. The Finance (No. 2) Bill, 1988 was, with 139 clauses and 10 schedules, one of the largest in recent years.

The House's procedures for considering the Finance Bill are much the same as for any other piece of Government legislation, with three significant modifications. First, all proceedings on such a bill are automatically exempt, under Standing Order No. 14(1)(a), from the ten o'clock rule. Second, after second reading, which provides an opportunity for a broad debate on the Government's tax proposals against the background of the national economy, the committee stage of the bill is now divided between a committee of the whole House and a standing committee.[42] The motion to commit certain clauses to a committee of the whole House (and sometimes new clauses on specified matters) is moved by the Government, but the choice of which matters should be considered in this way is, in practice, largely left to the Opposition. The outcome is that the more controversial policy aspects of the bill—rate of income tax or petrol tax, for example, or proposals for a major new tax—are debated on the floor for about three days.[43]

The remainder of the bill is examined in detail—and at considerable length—by a standing committee. It is the common practice for this committee to meet in the late afternoon two or three evenings a week, and for some of its sittings to last long into, or even all through, the night. The committee may well hold some 10 to 12 sittings before reporting the bill.

When the bill is reported from the standing committee it is reprinted as amended (including any amendments to clauses considered in committee of the whole House) and the whole bill is considered on the floor at, usually, two sittings. Third reading may also be taken at the same time, although on three occasions since 1976 a separate day has been allowed for a general economic debate on third reading, which strays somewhat from the normal rule that only the content of the bill itself may be discussed at this stage.

The third modification of usual procedures relates to the selection of amendments. Because there is a Finance Bill every year, which provides regular opportunities to propose amendments to tax law, greater use is made of the chairman's powers of selection in committee so as to rule out matters which have been debated on other occasions and may be debated again. This applies particularly to new clauses. A wide range of new clauses proposing reductions in the size or scope of existing taxes may be tabled—some examples from the standing committee on the 1986 Bill were "Relief for technical education and development," "Abolition of general betting duty on course dog track betting," "Maintenance funds for historic buildings, etc." and "Luncheon vouchers"—and therefore only a sample of these topics can be debated each year. Similar restrictions are imposed at the report stage.

In general the Finance Bill provides an annual opportunity for the Opposition and back-benchers from both sides not only to examine critically the Government's proposals for new taxes or for variations in existing taxes, but also to propose their own changes in taxation including (by moving new clauses) reductions in existing tax burdens which the Government themselves do not propose to modify. Many of the latter proposals are consequent upon representations made by a wide range of pressure groups and interested organisations, many of them hardened old campaigners.

---

[42] Until 1967 the Finance Bill was always committed wholly to a committee of the whole House; in 1968 the whole bill was committed to a standing committee, but this was not acceptable to the Opposition, and a guillotine proved necessary to pass the bill (the only other case of a guillotined Finance Bill was in 1975); since 1969 the division of the bill, as described, has been the standard practice, except when it has been necessary, by agreement, to hurry a Finance Bill through before or after a general election.

[43] This has been standard since 1976, except that five days were allotted in 1981, four in 1982, two in 1985 and two in 1986.

The annual Finance Bill offers an excellent opportunity for groups of Members who are familiar with the problems, working closely with outside groups who are even more well aware of the issues, to confront directly, and in extended debate, Treasury Ministers who themselves are usually well experienced, and who are backed by even more experienced civil servants. The issues range from major policies such as the rates of income tax and tax allowances to highly technical questions of tax law. The debates—especially in the standing committee—are often some of the best argued and most effective of any held in the House. The Members know each other well; they know the problems well; the issues are serious; and the protagonists go straight to the point. We examine more fully the nature of the House's scrutiny of taxation on pages 321–322.

Parliamentary Questions

We have so far described debate and other procedures where the House is formally engaged in a process of taking decisions. We next move to a range of procedures where the House is not involved in any kind of decision. We first deal with the rules regarding parliamentary Questions.[44] These provide a prime opportunity for both the Opposition and back-benchers to question Ministers on the wide range of matters for which they are responsible, either to obtain information they need for the continuing political debate or for constituency purposes, or to raise in some way a political point on the floor of the House.

The use the protagonists make of these procedures is examined in pages 352–359 and 366–376; here the basic rules are described.

Types of Questions

There are various types of Questions. Questions of which notice has been given for oral answer are taken every Monday to Thursday, after prayers and private business, till 3.30 p.m. Ministers take it in turns to answer Questions, the rota of Ministers being decided by the Government, after consultation with the Opposition parties. In practice each of the major departments comes top of the Question rota, which is the essentially relevant position, on one day every three or four weeks, and always on the same day of each week. Some Ministers answering for smaller departments, for instance the Minister for the Arts or the Attorney General, have a short, fixed time after other Ministers on Mondays. Exceptionally—and most important—the Prime Minister may be questioned every Tuesday and Thursday from 3.15 until 3.30 p.m.

Notice of Questions

Under Standing Order No. 17(4), (5) and (6) the minimum notice of a Question for oral answer is 48 hours and the maximum is 10 sitting days (in effect, at most times of the session, this means two weeks) Many more Members wish to ask Questions than there is time for on most days,[45] so

---

[44] The proceduralists' joke is that Question time is when there is no question before the House.

[45] It has been the practice of recent Speakers to call several supplementaries on each Question that is reached, and as a result only between 10 and 20 Questions receive oral answer each day although there may be up to a hundred on the Order Paper (see also pages 369–370).

those which are to come first are decided by lot (called "the shuffle"). To enter the shuffle, a Question must be tabled by 4.00 p.m. on the first day on which they may be tabled for the Minister concerned. The maximum notice is therefore the crucial consideration, and Questions handed in later than 4.00 p.m. on the first day, or tabled on later days, are unlikely to be called for oral answer. Questions which are not reached may be withdrawn or deferred but are usually left on the paper and are given a written answer, published in Hansard.

Members are rationed in the number of Questions they may have down for oral answer: eight during any period of 10 sitting days; not more than two on any one day; of which not more than one may be to any one Minister. These rules, which are not in standing orders, are based on a decision of the House approving the recommendations of the Committee on Parliamentary Questions, 1971–72.[46]

There are far fewer restrictions on Questions for written answer. There is no maximum period of notice; Questions can be tabled—and often are—for the following day; and there is no limit to the number any Member may table. Ministers are not obliged to answer ordinary Questions for written answer on the day they are down for answer but they try to answer within a week. If a Member requires an answer on a specific day (perhaps to meet his local weekly paper's deadlines or in time for a debate in the House) he can table a priority written Question under Standing Order No. 17(7), which must be answered on the day for which it is tabled, provided that at least 48-hours' notice has been given; sometimes a holding reply has to be given and a substantive answer is published in Hansard on a later day.

Notices of Questions handed in to the Table Office up till 10.30 p.m. each night while the House is sitting (rising of the House on Fridays), and which are in order, are published in the Notices of Questions and Motions the next day. They are thereafter re-published in the Order Book each day, and finally on the Order Paper on the day they are due to be asked.

Rules Regarding the Form and Content of Questions

The rules of order for Questions, regulating their content, are not in the standing orders. They have accumulated over many years on the authority of Speakers' rulings in response to new situations or problems, and are consistently enforced by the Speaker, and by the Clerks at the Table on his behalf. They have been reviewed from time to time by various committees,[47] but have remained largely unchanged.

The basic rules are that Questions may be asked of Ministers about any matter for which they are responsible and that Questions must ask for information or press for action. Flowing from these are a large number of more specific rules. For example, relating to ministerial responsibility, Ministers have declined to answer Questions dealing with matters for which local authorities or nationalised industries are primarily responsible, even though Ministers may have certain ultimate powers, and consequently these sorts of Questions have been ruled out of order. So have Questions relating to the personal powers of the monarch (for example, ecclesiastical patronage or the grant of honours or the appointment of Ministers), even though Ministers may advise the Queen on such matters. Questions about the

---

[46] H.C. 393 of 1971–72, p. x; H.C.Deb., Vol. 848, cols. 992–1070 (December 18, 1972).

[47] *e.g.* The Committee on Parliamentary Questions, H.C. 393 of 1971–72.

internal affairs of other countries are usually out of order, although if the British Government has been involved, for example, by making representations, Questions about the actions of Ministers are obviously in order; foreign statistical questions are also usually allowed. Members are required to take responsibility for the facts on which their questions are based and, applying this to Ministerial responsibility, Questions asking for confirmation of rumours or for comment on newspaper articles have been ruled out of order.

The "asking for information or pressing for action" rule prohibits Questions which are essentially argumentative or convey or seek expressions of opinion, and also the use of epithets or value-judgments (you can ask a Minister what plans he has for reducing the shortage of geriatric beds in a certain hospital, but not "the appalling shortage"). Many questions have to be edited on these grounds. Questions which are primarily concerned with giving, rather than asking for, information are also out of order, but the essential facts are sometimes stated briefly as a basis of a question asking a Minister to take action or adopt a new policy.

Questions are disallowed which ask for information which is readily available in published documents, or which have already been answered in the current session. Questions are also out of order if Ministers have refused an answer to such Questions in the past. This is an important rule and is much relied on by the Table Office when assessing whether or not there is ministerial responsibility. For example, Ministers sometimes refuse to give information or take action or they say that such and such a matter is the responsibility of another body or that they have no power to do what is asked; such replies block further Questions of that kind. Ministers sometimes answer that it is not the practice to disclose information of a certain kind, especially relating to defence and security (for example, details of arms sales to particular countries), but also including the tax affairs of individuals and information about commercial contracts. A particularly important class of Questions which at one time raised problems was regarding the day-to-day running of nationalised industries (why the 8.13 a.m. from Orpington ran late on Tuesday), and ministerial refusal to answer such Questions required many such Questions to be ruled out of order. Fewer Questions pose difficulties under this head today; instead there are new problems regarding the residual regulatory powers of Ministers in respect of certain monopoly industries which have been privatised. A further extension of the ministerial refusal rule has the effect of disallowing Questions about matters which are, of their nature, secret, such as the operations of the secret service, consultations between Ministers, including Cabinet business, and advice given to Ministers by civil servants.

Other miscellaneous rules on the content of Questions require the disallowance of Questions which ask about matters of past history (unless relevant to a current problem); about ministerial speeches in the country or at party meetings; seek legal opinions (which are matters for the courts); seek the solution of hypothetical propositions; are multiplied with slight variations on the same points (by the same or different Members, so limiting mass-question "campaigns"); "raise questions of policy which are too large to be dealt with in an answer to a Question"; or (at the other extreme) are "trivial, vague, or meaningless." The inclusion of a name of a person in a Question asking for the prosecution of an individual, when the use of the name was not necessary to make the Question intelligible, has also been disallowed by the Speaker.[48]

Some of the rules for parliamentary debate (see pages 208–212 above) also apply, including restrictions on criticism of certain categories of person, prohibition of un-parliamentary language and the ban on raising matters that are *sub-judice*. The latter rule is strictly enforced, subject to the discretion of the Chair to waive the rule in exceptional circumstances.

Given all these rules,[49] it might be thought that they must almost prevent effective questioning of Ministers by the Opposition and back-benchers. Certainly the clerks in the Table Office who advise Members on their admissibility, have to spend much time applying these rules and telling Members that they cannot ask Questions in the form offered to them. But they also seek, if at all possible, to suggest a way in which the Member can raise the matter he is anxious to ask about. For example, if a Question is out of order because a Minister has not the powers needed to take the action requested, a Question may be suggested asking him (without mentioning any individual or local case) to introduce legislation to give himself those powers. A specific Question about unpunctuality on the railways may be out of order, but a substitute question about the need for additional investment by British Rail in rolling stock or signalling equipment or asking about the relevant statistic kept by the department (for which Ministers are responsible) may enable the Member to make his point. And there are a number of fairly standard Questions for oral answer (for example to ask what matters were discussed when the Minister last met the chairman of a board or corporation) which can be used as a peg on which a Member may hang his point in a supplementary Question.

The Table Office clerks discuss most Questions that may fall foul of the rules with Members in person, either as they seek to table them or after careful study. When taking a view on ministerial responsibility, the clerks are guided by statutes, other publications such as Command papers or evidence to committees, and especially by previous ministerial answers. When in doubt about a Minister's powers, or when certain facts are relevant (is a certain hospital a N.H.S. hospital or private, for example) they may consult the Government department concerned—but only for guidance or advice; a Question is never ruled out of order simply because a department says it should be, and in case of doubt the benefit is given to the Member tabling the Question, not the Minister. The Table Office also has the power to edit Questions to put them into the correct form (while not affecting the substance) or to correct minor infringements of the rules. Some Members are happy to leave it to the clerks to put their Questions in order and allow extensive correction without further reference to them; at the other extreme a few Members will not allow a comma to be altered in their Question without their authority.

In the end—sometimes after prolonged discussion involving the Principal Clerk of the Table Office—agreement is nearly always reached between the Table Office and Members. Either the Question, with some amendment, can be put in order and sent to the printer or it is accepted by the Member that it is out of order and cannot be tabled. But in cases of unresolved

---

[48] See, H.C.Deb., Vol. 94, col. 26 (March 17, 1986); and The Table, Vol. LIV, 1986, pp. 106–107.
[49] There are other detailed restrictive rules, see May, pp. 337–344.

disagreement the ultimate decision lies with the Speaker. Indeed, it is Speakers' rulings from which the rules derive and all the advice given and decisions by the Table Office are taken on behalf of the Speaker and with his authority. On occasions, therefore, a Member asks that a disputed Question be put to the Speaker for his decision, or indeed the Table Office may themselves suggest this if the matter seems in doubt or raises problems of particular novelty or significance. The Speaker's decision is final; there is no appeal against the Speaker's ruling and it cannot be raised in the House except by means of a substantive motion critical of the decision. There are no recent cases of this being done.

As a measure of the extent to which Members and the Table Office are able to reach agreement on the applicability of the rules to their Questions, it must be emphasised that some 30,000–40,000 Questions are tabled each session, but nowadays only some two or three Questions a session have to be referred to the Speaker; the rest are settled in the Table Office.

After notice is given of Questions and before they are asked in the House, or given written answers, a few changes may occur. Questions can be withdrawn or deferred till later days. Questions for oral answer may be converted to written answer Questions. And Questions may be transferred from one Minister to another on grounds of responsibility; this is entirely within the rights of Ministers (they cannot even be questioned on the subject) and something over which the Speaker, the Table Office and the Member concerned have no control.

Question Time

Eventually Questions for oral answer appear on the Order Paper to be asked and answered in the House. Each Member is called in turn; he calls the number (the text does not have to be read as it is printed on the paper); and the Minister gives his prepared answer; he may, at his request, answer several related Questions together. Each Member whose Question was asked is then called to ask a supplementary; this is when the Member makes his political point or asks the question he originally had in mind and for which the Question, as printed, was simply a peg. And the Minister answers that supplementary, making his own political points. The control now lies entirely in the hands of the Speaker. If the original Question was a matter of limited interest, or an individual or local case (which is now fairly unusual), he may only allow one supplementary and then move on. If the matter is of wider interest, and a number of Members on both sides wish to join in— including, perhaps, the Opposition front-bench—then he may allow up to half a dozen supplementaries.[50]

Theoretically, the rules for supplementaries are the same as for original Questions. But in practice it is difficult for the Speaker, on the spur of the moment, to decide whether or not Ministers are responsible for certain matters, and it is impossible for him to exclude argument and expressions of opinion. Unless the breach is pretty blatant—the present Speaker, for example, has tried to stamp on Questions to the Prime Minister about the policies or conduct of the Opposition, or trade unions, for which she is clearly not responsible[51]—he usually lets the supplementaries run fairly

[50] e.g. H.C.Deb., Vol. 92, cols. 295–312, 322 (February 19, 1986).
[51] e.g. H.C.Deb., Vol. 91, cols. 428, 429 (February 6, 1986); the same rule applies to Questions to other Ministers, e.g. H.C.Deb., Vol. 128, col. 134 (February 23, 1988).

freely, intervening only to stop excessive length and to cut short points that are clearly irrelevant to the original Question.

Although there are many rules regarding the content of Questions, there are no rules—other than those relating to debate and parliamentary language[52]—that govern ministerial answers. In particular, a Minister cannot be compelled to answer a Question and, although a complete refusal to answer is rare (but is sometimes used to block further Questions on that subject), a Member who is not satisfied with the answer he has received has no redress except to try to ask more Questions on another occasion or to raise the matter in some other way. The Speaker has no powers to intervene, although complaints about unsatisfactory answers are frequently raised as points of order after Questions (see pages 194–197).

Questions to the Prime Minister

The rules apply equally to Questions to the Prime Minister as for other Ministers. In practice, however, Prime Minister's Questions are distinct in a number of ways. First, their substance is different. Originally Members sought to question the Prime Minister on specific matters of policy or Government administration. However there was always the danger, and it sometimes occurred, that the Prime Minister would transfer such Questions to the Minister primarily responsible and that the Member would thus lose this valuable opportunity to challenge the Prime Minister (or to show his support) at prime time. There was also the problem that such Questions, of which two weeks' notice was required if they were to be reached, were often politically stale on the day. Members therefore increasingly resorted in the 1970s to the device of the "open Question," which was on a subject that was personal to the Prime Minister and therefore not transferable, and which could also be used as a peg on which to hang a supplementary on any issue of the day on which it was asked.

The formula which is nowadays almost uniformly adopted is "To ask the Prime Minister if she will list her official engagements for [the day of answer]." Every Tuesday and Thursday over 100 Questions of this kind appear on the Order Paper,[53] with only one or two on specific topics and a few Questions "To ask the Prime Minister if she will pay an official visit to [somewhere in the Member's constituency]" (which is a geographically narrowed form of open Question). Those who, by the luck of the shuffle, come in the first half-dozen on the list will have an opportunity (after the Prime Minister has given a brief factual answer to the first such Question) to fire a supplementary at the Prime Minister on a subject of their own choosing; for example "will the Rt. Hon. Lady, in the course of her busy day, give consideration to the rising unemployment caused by the shut down of factories in my constituency, and what is she doing about it . . . . . . "

Again the Speaker controls the calling of additional Members to ask supplementaries, but here he has further factors to take into account. First, very many Members want to join in and this causes considerable pressure on the Chair. The Speaker calls Members, in turn, from either side. He keeps

---

[52] For example, the Speaker has criticised the use of a written answer to criticise the personal conduct of a Member; such criticism should be embodied in a substantive motion (see page 205). The Minister concerned apologised to the House (H.C.Deb., Vol. 103, col. 1103 (November 6, 1986)).

[53] By the Spring of session 1988–89, the number had risen to over 200 on some days.

records showing how many times back-benchers have been called, so as to be as fair as possible.[54] (For use by back-benchers of these opportunities, see pages 371–372). He usually tries to call some of those who are lower down on the list, but unlikely to be reached.[55] He has also let it be known "that if representations are made to me beforehand that an hon. Member wishes to be called during Prime Minister's Question time, that hon. Member will not be called. I make that absolutely clear."[56]

Secondly, the Leader of the Opposition (or, if he is absent, his deputy), who by tradition never asks any other oral Questions, is by convention allowed up to three, or occasionally four, supplementaries to the Prime Minister; no-one else has more than one. This is a prime opportunity for the Leader of the Opposition to put on the political agenda the issue of the day (see pages 353–357). It is also a valuable right for the Opposition which is sometimes resented by Government back-benchers.

The consequence of the current system of Prime Minister's Questions is that in effect the House now allows—for the Prime Minister only—the system of Questions without notice that is standard procedure in the parliaments of Australia and Canada.[57] All that is different is the artificiality of the standard form Question and consequently a list of questioners (encouraged by the Whips on both sides) whose luck in the shuffle partially limits the Speaker's choice of who shall be able to put a supplementary question, on almost any topic, to the Prime Minister.

Questions to Members other than Ministers

Questions are occasionally put down to Members who are not Ministers, or to Ministers in a non-Ministerial role, but the rules are essentially the same. Questions may be tabled to the Leader of the House as Chairman of the Select Committee on House of Commons (Services) (those relating to the Refreshment Department will be answered by the Chairman of the Catering Sub-Committee), to a Member representing the House of Commons Commission, to the Chairman of the Public Accounts Commission, to a Member answering on behalf of the Church Commissioners of the Church of England, and very occasionally to other chairmen of select committees.

Private Notice Questions

In addition to Questions of which notice has to be given, Standing Order No. 17(3) also provides for Questions "which are, in the Speaker's opinion of an urgent character, and relate either to matters of public importance or to the arrangement of business." These are called "private notice Questions" (PNQs) because, in asking them, a Member says he has given the Minister "private notice."

The rules for PNQs are the same as for ordinary Questions, but in addition the Speaker needs to be satisfied that the matter is sufficiently urgent to justify waiving the normal requirements for notice. An application for a PNQ has to be made to his office by 12 noon (10.00 a.m. on Fridays) and is

---

[54] H.C.Deb., Vol. 103, col. 450 (October 30, 1986).

[55] *Ibid.*, cols. 451–452.

[56] *Ibid.*, col. 450.

[57] The then Second Clerk Assistant in evidence to the Committee on Parliamentary Questions (H.C. 393 of 1971–72, pp. 56–57) recommended that the House should go the whole hog and adopt such a system, but the committee was not persuaded.

not allowed if the matter has not been raised at the first opportunity (it must relate to that day's news, not something that was known about two days before), or if another opportunity for raising it will soon be provided.[58] In particular applications are disallowed if the matter could be raised on a Question already on the paper, which is likely to be reached, on the same or similar subject, or if the Minister proposes to make a statement.

Applications for PNQs are made almost daily, and sometimes three or four on the same day. The Speaker allows, on average (although the practice of Speakers has varied, see Table below and page 358), about one a week. He never gives reasons publicly for allowing or disallowing PNQs, and the fact that he has disallowed an application, or even any indication that an application has been made, is strongly deprecated.[59]

PNQs are called at the end of Questions. The Minister answers and may then be asked a number of supplementaries. The rules for supplementaries are exactly the same as for ordinary Questions, but the Speaker usually exercises his discretion to allow rather more than is normal during Question time (although not as many as on a ministerial statement, see pages 262–263 and 335). An average of 11 or 12 supplementaries is normal nowadays; but the Speaker takes into consideration the importance of the issue, the number of Members wishing to speak and the pressure of other business on parliamentary time. The numbers of supplementaries permitted on a PNQ have ranged from one[60] to 30.[61] For how the Opposition use PNQs see pages 357–359 and for their use by back-benchers see pages 374–376.

Mention should be made of one regular, but rather different PNQ, namely the business Question put each Thursday to the Leader of the House by the Leader of the Opposition, (or, especially since 1987, the shadow Leader of the House) in reply to which the Leader of the House announces the business for the forthcoming week and the following Monday (sometimes a statement is made instead of a PNQ). The questioner is then allowed a fairly lengthy supplementary, pressing for debating time on a number of topics, to which the Leader of the House replies. Then the Speaker calls a large number of Members from either side, who press for debates or statements on matters that concern them (see also pages 363 and 376–377).

The statistics for all forms of Questions highlight some significant changes in the last 40 years. The following Table analyses the numbers of Questions actually asked[62] in several years since 1945, with fuller detail since 1976:

---

[58] See, e.g. H.C.Deb., Vol. 126, col. 860 (February 2, 1988).

[59] See, e.g. H.C.Deb., Vol. 96, cols. 661–662 (April 28, 1986).

[60] H.C.Deb., Vol. 77, cols. 21–22 (April 29, 1985).

[61] H.C.Deb., Vol. 62, cols. 141–152 (June 19, 1984).

[62] Statistics have sometimes been published of Questions tabled for oral and written answer, but these are less significant as a measure of how procedures are actually used as they do not allow for Questions withdrawn, transferred, unstarred, etc., which create double-counting. Nor do they distinguish those Questions for oral answer which nevertheless received written replies.

Number of Questions Asked

Session	Number on Paper for Oral Answer			Number on Paper for Written Answer	Number of PNQs asked (a)
	Reached for oral answer	Received written answer	Total		
1946–47	6795	6702	13,497	3,433	42
1956–57	5151	6617	11,768	6,020	33
1966–67(b)	8464	8850	17,314	16,951	39
1976–77	2488	3975	6,463	25,076	23
1977–78	2648	5034	7,682	28,739	14
1978–79(c)	1272	1368	2,640	13,152	23
1979–80(b)	3787	8881	12,668	39,912	40
1980–81	2532	8472	11,004	22,688	8
1981–82	2554	6202	8,756	23,439	9
1982–83(c)	1793	4833	6,626	17,095	7
1983–84(b)	3226	10650	13,876	40,119	48
1984–85	2393	12398	14,791	31,523	26
1985–86	2480	14852	17,332	31,718	43
1986–87(c)	1484	11722	13,206	21,331	19

(a) Excluding the weekly business Question
(b) Unusually long session
(c) Unusually short session

The most striking feature of the Table is the overall growth of Questions of all kinds. The increase of Questions for written answer is particularly marked. There is also a general reduction in the number of Questions for oral answer which are reached, indicating the greater willingness of Speakers to allow more supplementaries. We look at this in more detail on pages 369–370.

Ministerial Statements

On any day after Questions (at 11.00 a.m. on Fridays), Ministers may, on their own initiative, make statements on any events or policy decisions of their choosing.[63] Although the Speaker is notified, his permission is not required, and the customary opening, "with your permission and that of the House, I wish to make a statement on ... " is purely a courtesy. The use made by Ministers of these opportunities is examined on pages 334–336.

After the statement, which may be fairly short, but sometimes lasts for some five or 10 minutes, the relevant shadow Minister is called and, by custom,[64] is allowed to comment, at roughly equivalent length, and to ask a few questions. After the Minister's reply, the process becomes one of short questions and answers, just as during Question time, with Members being called from both sides of the House. Depending somewhat on the impor-

---

[63] Occasionally, in cases of urgency, or to announce a change in business, statements have been made at other times: between orders of the day, at the end of business, on the motion for the adjournment, or on a dilatory motion; there were 34 such cases in the period 1968–87.
[64] See H.C.Deb., Vol. 102, col. 951 (October 21, 1986).

tance of the subject, the Speaker nowadays allows a fair number of supplementaries and this may continue for quite a considerable time (see page 335). The shadow Minister is traditionally called again for a brief concluding comment or question at the end. In calling Members, the Speaker gives priority to Privy Councillors, and to those who are known to have specialist knowledge or a constituency concern. Inevitably, if there is wide interest in the matter and he needs to protect the business of the day, he has to leave out some disappointed Members. But, overall, many more Members are able to participate, if only briefly, in response to statements than in formal debates.

Occasionally the contents of a Minister's statement have, in some way, come to the attention of the press and may be published before the Minister rises to tell the House. Although this is not technically a contempt or breach of privilege, such practice has been strongly deprecated by the present Speaker who holds the view that the House should always be told first.[65]

Adjournment Debates

Adjournment debates, of various kinds, are all subject to the normal rules of debate (see pages 208–212), with the additional requirement that speeches must relate to matters for which Ministers have some administrative responsibility (this has been allowed, in contrast with the rules for Questions, to include the conduct of nationalised industries) and should not be primarily concerned with arguing the need for legislation (although, under Standing Order No. 29, incidental reference to such matters is permitted and this relaxation is usually liberally interpretted). All adjournment debates provide opportunities for the House to debate matters without coming to any formal decision or expressing a view as in a resolution. The motion in each case takes the form "That the House do now adjourn". This is not to be confused with dilatory motions to defer taking a decision on a question before the House, which are occasionally moved in the same terms (see page 219).

There are four main species of adjournment debates.

Main Business Debates

The first is the use of an adjournment motion moved as a main item of business, and appearing on the Order Paper, which permits a debate on a matter of the Government's choosing,[66] without requiring the House to come to a decision. It is not permissible to move amendments to adjournment motions, so the choice of this type of debate is sometimes tactically advantageous in depriving the Opposition of the chance to move an amendment which might be politically embarrassing. For example, the debate on the Government's handling of the Westland Affair, on October 29, 1986, (following the publication of two reports from the Defence Committee on the subject), was held, by the Government's choosing, on a motion for the adjournment of the House. On other occasions a debate on foreign affairs may be held over one or two days on such a motion, so permitting a wide-ranging discussion.

It is possible, however, for the Opposition to divide the House on the

---

[65] See, e.g. H.C.Deb., Vol. 135, col. 36 (June 13, 1988).

[66] When Opposition debates were held on Supply days (up till 1982), the Opposition quite often chose to hold a debate on an adjournment motion: this has twice been done since the introduction of Opposition days under Standing Order No. 13 (H.C.Deb., Vol.35, cols. 670–709 (January 24, 1983); H.C.Deb., Vol. 80, vols. 640–686 (June 10, 1985)).

motion for the adjournment to express general dissatisfaction with the Government's policies or attitude (although the reasons for and nature of that dissatisfaction will find no formal expression in the Journal of the House). In such cases the Opposition vote for the adjournment of the House and the Government vote against, so as to protect later business (even though a Government Whip formally moved the motion at the beginning of the debate). Some major House of Commons debates have been held on the adjournment and finished with such divisions, including the critical debate on the conduct of the war, on May 7 and 8, 1940, which led to the fall of the Chamberlain Government.

Emergency Adjournment Debates

A second and most important use of the adjournment debate procedure is to provide opportunity for debating urgent and important matters for which time has not otherwise been provided. On any day other than a Friday, a Member may ask leave under Standing Order No. 20 to move the adjournment of the House for the purpose of discussing a specific and important matter that should have urgent consideration. Advance notice must be given to the Speaker by noon that day (unless the urgent happening became known after that time) and he must decide whether to grant the application. The sort of consideration he takes into account will usually include the extent of ministerial responsibility, whether the matter has been raised at the first opportunity, whether other opportunities exist for bringing the matter before the House in reasonable time, whether the matter is really urgent (will irrevocable action be taken if debate is postponed?) whether the matter is specific and clearly identified (not just a rumour or disputed allegation) and, generally, whether it is of sufficient public importance to justify interrupting the arranged business of the House. However, the actual arguments which he considers in any particular case are never publicly known because the Speaker is, by Standing Order No. 20(5), precluded from giving the reasons for his decisions to the House.

There are many applications but few are allowed; those that are tend to be made by the official Opposition (see pages 350–352). But back-benchers take extensive advantage of the opportunity to draw matters to the attention of the House in this way (see pages 377–379). Total figures in recent years are as follows:

Applications for emergency adjournment debates

Session	Number of Applications (including multiple applications on the same matter)	Number granted
1974–75	33	1
1975–76	58	3
1976–77	44	3
1977–78	38	2
1978–79(a)	66	3
1979–80(b)	89	2
1980–81	48	1
1981–82	61	2
1982–83(a)	50	2
1983–84(b)	84	3
1984–85	61	1
1985–86	87	1
1986–87(a)	48	2
1987–88(b)	88	1

(a) Unusually short session
(b) Unusually long session

If the Speaker grants an application for an emergency adjournment debate and assuming that the support of 40 Members, as required by Standing Order No. 20(1), is shown[67] then the debate itself is normally held as first business on the following day, or on Monday if the application is granted on a Thursday. In cases of great urgency, the Speaker can allow a debate at 7.00 p.m. the same day (Standing Order No. 20(2)).[68]

The Motion for the adjournment of the House then appears on the Order Paper (if approved for debate on a later day) in the name of the Member who made the successful application, and only he can move it (the one occasion when the adjournment is moved by someone other than a Minister or Government Whip). Under Standing Order No. 20(6), the rules of debate on such emergency adjournment Motions are the same as they would be on a Motion to take note of the matter at issue, therefore relevant matters outside the responsibility of Ministers may be mentioned, and there is no ban on referring to legislative remedies, but all speeches must relate to the specific matter on which the debate was granted.

Following Consolidated Fund Bills

The third use of the adjournment debate is under Standing Order No. 54 (2) which enables Members to raise topics of their choosing in the all-night debates (till 9.00 a.m., or 8.00 a.m. on a Friday) that follow the passage of

---

[67] There has been only one occasion since 1945 when an application, granted by the Speaker, has failed solely for lack of the support of 40 Members in the chamber (H.C.Deb., Vol. 659, cols. 1542–1552 (May 17, 1962)); on another occasion the House, on a division, refused leave after 40 Members failed to rise (H.C.Deb., Vol. 913, cols. 32–36 (June 14, 1976)).

[68] There have been only three occasions since the standing order was adopted in its present form in 1967 (H.C.Deb., Vol. 776, cols. 1553–1554, 1605–1662 (January 30, 1969); H.C.Deb., Vol. 961, cols. 56–57, 103–166 (January 22, 1979); H.C.Deb., Vol. 962, cols. 30–31, 98–168 (February 5, 1979)).

Consolidated Fund Bills before Christmas, in March and at the end of July.[69] The choice of topics to be debated depends on the luck of a ballot held in the Speaker's Office on a previous day. Debate on two topics, selected by the Speaker, may last for three hours; debate on all other topics is restricted to an hour and a half. For the use made by back-benchers of these opportunities see pages 405–406.

Daily Adjournment

Lastly, we come to the most common adjournment debate, and in some ways the most important: the daily adjournment. Every sitting day,[70] before the House rises, there is a motion "That the House do now adjourn," and this permits a short debate, initiated by a back-bencher on any matter for which a Minister is responsible. The topics that Members wish to raise are first vetted by the Principal Clerk of the Table Office to ensure that they are within the rules (ministerial responsibility, not legislation, not *subjudice*, etc.). A Member's right to initiate such a debate again depends on a ballot held in the Speaker's Office, under rules laid down by him, every Thursday for the Tuesday, Wednesday and Friday of the following week and the Monday after that; the topic for each Thursday is chosen by the Speaker personally. The list of topics is published weekly on the Notice Paper.

If the adjournment is moved at or after the moment of interruption the debate is limited to half an hour. If it is moved first before 10.00 p.m. (2.30 p.m. on Fridays), it lapses at that hour and is moved again. If the adjournment is not previously agreed to, the Speaker automatically adjourns the House at 10.30 p.m. (3.00 p.m. on Fridays) or after 30 minutes (whichever is the later) under Standing Order No. 9(7). There can be no division on a daily adjournment motion after 10.00 p.m. (2.30 p.m. on Fridays) as, under Standing Order No. 9(6), unless otherwise exempted, no opposed business can then be taken. In the debate, the Member who "has the adjournment" speaks for some 10 or 15 minutes; other Members occasionally make short contributions; and then the Minister replies for some 10 or 15 minutes.

Occasionally, if the main business finishes early, there may be time for more than one adjournment debate, and a second or even a third debate may then be allowed, provided the Member concerned can find, before 8.00 p.m. (12 noon on a Friday) a Minister who is willing to reply to the debate. This sometimes results in some smart political manoeuvering, with Government back-benchers being urged by their Whips to apply for additional adjournments to keep out some Opposition Member who may wish to raise some politically embarrassing topic, which might otherwise be undebated.[71] On other occasions there may be extensive debate on the first topic which leaves inadequate time for a second subject to be raised.

---

[69] Until 1982 these debates were held on the second readings of the bills themselves, in accordance with the historic principle of seeking the redress of grievances before voting Supply, but this sometimes restricted the scope of debate to matters for which finance was to be provided by the bills, and nowadays a more wide-ranging debate is in order (although it results in granting Supply before airing the grievances).

[70] Unless the Speaker has adjourned the House, on his own authority under Standing Order No. 45, in cases of grave disorder.

[71] For example, Mr. Tam Dalyell in 1983–84 several times was thought to be wishing to debate the Belgrano question on the adjournment, but others were more fortunate. Eventually, on February 18, 1985, he succeeded in making his points on a Government motion (H.C.Deb., Vol. 73, cols. 769–774).

Similar adjournment motions are moved on the last day before each recess and comprise their main business. On these occasions about eight Members obtain, by ballot, the right to open a short debate, but time limits—of 30 to 45 minutes—are set by the Speaker, and the time at which each debate is due to start is shown on the Order Paper.

The way back-benchers use these adjournment debates is examined on pages 403–404.

Public Petitions

A procedure of great historical importance[72] but of less practical significance today is the presentation of public petitions. Any citizen or group of citizens may prepare and sign a petition to the House on any matter "in which the House has jurisdiction to interfere" which concludes with a prayer "for such relief as is within the power of the House."[73] Given the power of the House to legislate, this covers almost any matter within the United Kingdom. There are, however, many other detailed and very old rules which must be observed when preparing a petition, and those wishing to petition the House are advised to consult the Clerk of Public Petitions in the Journal Office, House of Commons.

A petition has to be presented to the House by a Member. Any Member can present a petition (provided it is in order), either publicly immediately before the adjournment is moved (or at the beginning of business on a Friday), or privately by putting the petition in the petition bag behind the Speaker's Chair. If he presents it publicly to the House he may, under Standing Order No. 132, state who the petitioners are, the number of signatures, and what it is about, and conclude by reading the prayer, but, under Standing Order No. 133 it may not (except under very unusual circumstances[74]) be debated. Members sometimes briefly state their own attitude when presenting a petition (usually in support), but may not make a speech on the matter.

All public petitions which are in order are listed in the Votes and Proceedings for the day of their presentation, and later published with the Vote. They are referred, under Standing Order No. 135, to the relevant Minister. Ministers are not required to reply to petitions, but they frequently do so and any observations they make are presented to the House and also published.

We examine on pages 383–385, the use made of the public petition procedure, but here the basic statistics in recent years may be of interest.

---

[72] Bills were originally founded on petitions, and private bills still are. In the 19th Century public petitions were very numerous.

[73] May, p. 861.

[74] Very occasionally petitions complaining of some present personal grievance may, under Standing Order No. 134, be considered forthwith and debated. For example, on November 29, 1960, a petition relating to Mr. Benn's loss of his seat, following his succession to a peerage, was referred to the Committee of Privileges.

Public Petitions

Session	No. of Petitions received(a)	No. of Ministerial Observations(b)
1967–68	27	–
1977–78	24	1
1981–82	27	20
1982–83	29	19
1983–84	760	43
1984–85	957	42
1985–86	516	24
1986–87	108	8
1987–88	356	55

(a) Often in identical terms and not necessarily separately published.
(b) Often relating to more than one petition.

Early Day Motions

We have already described the procedures for debate in the House, including the rules for giving notice of motions. One particular form of notice of
motion enables back-benchers and sometimes the Opposition, to bring
matters to the attention of the House and the public without the House itself
taking any decision; these are the so-called "early day motions" (or EDMs).
Their use by back-benchers is examined on pages 379–383; here we describe
the procedure.

The term "early day" in this context is really a euphemism for "never—or
hardly ever." Apart from prayers against statutory instruments which are
first tabled as EDMs, these motions do not come up for debate. Notice is
given in the Table Office of the terms of the motion, with a title, and of the
names of the Members who are tabling it, and these are published the
following day. Further names may be added on later days in support of the
motion and these are published each week, with an up-dated total of the
number of supporters, but only the names of the first six sponsors are
re-printed each time. Amendments may also be tabled and are likewise
published from time to time, with any names added therto. An index of
EDMs is published four times a year.[74a]

The rules regarding the content of EDMs are the same as for other
motions (see pages 203–205), for example the matter must not be *sub-judice*
in the United Kingdom.[75] If there is difficulty in deciding the admissibility of
a motion, the question is decided by the Speaker.[76] But disallowance of
motions is rare—perhaps three or four a session—and in principle Members
can table EDMs on almost any topic or problem anywhere in the world. This
is a valuable outlet for many points of view which otherwise would not come
before the House.

[74a] In order to reduce printing costs, the daily re-publication of motions and amendments
after the addition of names was stopped in April 1989, following the recommendations of a
Procedure Committee (Third Report, H.C. 254 of 1986–87); the weekly publication of an index
was also ended.

[75] In November 1986, a number of motions were allowed which referred to the case concerning the book *Spycatcher* by Peter Wright a former officer of M.I.5., which was at the time *sub
judice* in the Australian courts.

[76] See H.C.Deb., Vol. 132, col. 1032 (May 5, 1988).

Committee Systems

As the work of the House has grown, and issues have, in various ways, become more complex the House has, in the last 40 years, increasingly come to rely on the use of various forms of committee. These fall into four categories: committees of the whole House; private bill committees; standing committees; and select committees (including joint committees of Commons and Lords). Some of these carry out functions that the House itself could—and does—do, but where the use of a number of committees enables more work to be done. Others do work that the House as a whole could not do effectively. We consider each of them in turn.

Committees of the Whole House

A committee of the whole House is really the House, without the Speaker, under another name. The device was originally used for a variety of purposes when the House wished certain matters to be considered in detail before being formally approved by the House itself; in particular it enabled Members to debate matters without "the King's man" being in the chair. Many of these matters were financial and for many years it was a basic rule of financial business that proposals for increased expenditure or taxes had first to be considered in committee. The main financial committees—the Committee of Supply and the Committee of Ways and Means (in which the Budget was debated)—did not survive the simplification of financial procedures in 1966 and 1967. Today all financial business is done in the House itself (see pages 247–251) and the only surviving use of committees of the whole House is for the committee stage of some public bills.

Committees of the whole House are presided over by the Chairman of Ways and Means or one of his Deputies, who have most of the powers of the Speaker in the House, (see pages 149–150). Temporary chairmen, who are members of the Chairmen's Panel (see pages 150–151) may also preside in committees of the whole House and frequently do so during longer committee stages on major bills; they have fewer powers than the Chairman of Ways and Means and, in particular, cannot accept the closure or select amendments.

The House goes into committee when an order of the House to that effect, which is on the Order Paper, is read by the Clerk; no further motion is required (Standing Order No. 64). The Speaker leaves the upper chair; the Mace is removed from the Table by the Serjeant and placed on a lower rack; the chairman sits at the Table in the seat usually occupied by the Clerk of the House (who, like the Speaker, plays no part in the business of committees); the Clerk Assistant (or another Clerk at the Table) reads the short title of the bill; and the committee proceedings begin.

The procedures for considering a bill in committee were described on pages 231–235. When consideration of the bill is complete, the chairman puts the question, "That I do report the bill without amendment (or as amended) to the House," and when this is agreed he leaves the lower chair; the Mace is replaced on the Table; the Speaker or a Deputy resumes the upper chair; and the chairman reports that the committee has gone through the bill and directed him to report it (with or without amendment) to the House (if the chairman himself takes the chair as Deputy Speaker, as often happens, a Government Whip makes the report).

Similar proceedings occur when a committee does not complete its work on a bill at a particular sitting, except that the motion then moved is "That the chairman do report progress and ask leave to sit again"; this is debatable, and often is debated when moved by the Opposition (see page 219); if the motion is carried, the chairman leaves the chair and reports accordingly to the Speaker; the Member in charge of the bill (or a Whip) then names a day for a further sitting of the committee.

Private Bill Committees

Private bill committees are used for the detailed examination of private legislation in a way that could not possibly be done by a large body like the House itself. They are small bodies—only four Members for opposed bill committees and seven for unopposed bills—who act in a quasi-judicial way. Committees on opposed bills, for example, hear counsel on behalf of the promoters of the bill and of the petitioners against the bill, who may each call evidence and cross-examine witnesses in front of the committee; they do not debate; they have no power to call for evidence on their own initiative; they deliberate in private; and they have power, in effect, to reject a bill as well as to amend it.

The membership and chairman of an opposed bill committee are chosen, under Private Business Standing Order 111, by the Committee of Selection (see page 447). An unopposed bill committee is chaired by one of the Deputy Chairmen of Ways and Means and comprises members selected by the Chairman from a panel appointed by the Committee of Selection for this kind of work at the beginning of each session. The part played by back-benchers in private legislation is further considered on pages 411–412.

Standing Committees

Standing committees play an increasingly important part in the work of the House, especially—but not solely—on legislation. It must be admitted that their name is a misnomer, which has persistently misled those familiar with the concept of standing committees (or "*commissions permanantes*") in other parliaments. The term is an anachronistic survival from the time when bills were committed to bodies with a largely permanent membership, who examined every bill referred to them. Today the membership is totally ad hoc (except for the Scottish and Welsh Grand Committees and the Northern Ireland and Regional Affairs Committees, see pages 274–275), and members are nominated anew for each bill or matter committed to a standing commit-tee. A better term might be "debating committees" which emphasises the method of working which distinguishes them from most other committees.

Standing committees use the same debating procedures as committees of the whole House, and indeed are much like the House in miniature. They meet in public[76a] Government and Opposition sit facing each other; they have neutral chairmen; and they examine bills, and other matters, in much the same way as the House does. They are indeed doing work that the House could perfectly well do, but which all elements find it advantageous to carry out in committee. The Government gets more business through, with up to eight committees sitting at the same time; the Opposition can concentrate its teams and effort; and many back-benchers are saved—in contrast with committees of the whole House—from having to stay around in large

---

[76a] Under Standing Order No.89(2), a standing committee may order that strangers be not admitted. The only occasion on which this has been done was by the Welsh Grand Committee at its morning sitting on July 13, 1988; this followed the discovery that, by an error, the Secretary of State of Wales (who was present) had not been nominated to the committee.

numbers waiting for divisions on bills, the details of which have not been their concern. The use made by the Government of this committee system is examined on pages 315–318. Its use for private Members' bills is described on pages 392–395.

Standing committees are mainly used for the scrutiny of bills, but the same debating forum may be used for consideration of statutory instruments, European documents and matters of regional or limited national concern. The current use of standing committees for such purposes is described below.

Bills or other matters are referred to standing committees by the House, which means, in effect, by the Government, except that in respect of certain matters the Opposition can exercise a veto (see pages 274–275). The allocation of bills, statutory instruments and European Community documents to particular standing committees (identified for ease of reference as "Standing Committee, A, or B, etc.," or "First, or Second Standing Committee on Statutory Instruments, etc.,") is formally made by the Speaker, but in practice the choice is made for Government business by the Government and for private Members' bills by the Member in charge (see pages 394–395). In effect Ministers can arrange their bills in short queues for each committee, according to their priority in the legislative programme.

Members of standing committees are nominated, under Standing Order No. 86, by the Committee of Selection without need for further approval by the House (in contrast with the procedure for select committees). Except for the Scottish, Welsh, Northern Ireland and Regional Affairs Committees (see pages 274–275) and a committee appointed under Standing Order No. 92 for the consideration stage of certain Bills (a procedure which is no longer employed[77]), committees consist of between 16 and 50 Members drawn from both sides of the House. The actual number depends on the importance of the bill and the extent of interest in it. In the 1983–87 Parliament, committees ranging from 18 to 25 were normally appointed for most Government bills, comprising, for a committee of 19, 11 Government, 7 Opposition and 1 smaller party Member. The Committee of Selection is required, by Standing Order No. 86(2), to have regard to the composition of the House and in practice the parties are represented in strict proportion to the overall party strengths. For particularly important bills, larger committees may be nominated. For example, in 1988 for the Housing and Education Reform Bills there were 31 Members on their standing committees, and for the highly contentious Local Government Finance Bill (which introduced the community charge or poll tax) a committee of 44 was set up. A larger committee, of about 45 Members is always nominated for the Finance Bill (see pages 253–254). The appropriate size of any committee is usually agreed through the usual channels.

The Committee of Selection are also required, by Standing Order No. 86 (2) to have regard to the qualifications of the Members to be nominated. This covers the inclusion, on the Government side, of one or more Ministers[78], a Whip and back-benchers who are known to specialise in the relevant

---

[77] The only instance of its use since the standing order was made in 1967 was on the Water Resources Bill in 1968.
[78] Under Standing Order No. 87, the Law Officers may attend and speak in any standing committee, but not being nominated to the committee they cannot move motions or amendments, vote or be counted in the quorum. Other Ministers, not being on the committee itself, may similarly participate in debate in the standing committee on a Finance Bill.

field or who have indicated an interest, perhaps by speaking on second reading. The Opposition team is similar. Under Standing Order No. 86(2), the Committee of Selection can change the membership of a committee from time to time, but once a committee has started work on a bill, the membership is not changed except in cases of illness or change of ministerial or Opposition office.

In practice, for Government bills (it is different for private Members' bills where the Whips are not usually appointed), the Committee of Selection accepts the teams nominated by the Whips on either side. Occasionally they may note the protests of an independently-minded Member who wishes to be on a committee but who has not been picked by his own Whips, but the Committee of Selection is not anxious to interfere in such internal party wrangles.

The chairman of a standing committee is appointed by the Speaker, under Standing Order No. 85, from the Chairmen's Panel. For longer-running committees additional chairmen are sometimes appointed so they may share the burden, especially when committees are sitting in the evening or through the night. The Speaker may also change the chairman of a committee, though this will not normally be done once it has started work.

Chairmen of standing committees are drawn from both sides of the House (where work is shared there is usually one chairman from each side), with little regard to the nature of the bill; more experienced chairmen, of whatever party, are given the bigger and more controversial bills. While in the chair, a chairman (and that term is used whether the office holder be male or female) plays a completely neutral role so far as partisan argument and the subject-matter of the bill or matter are concerned. Like the Speaker in the House he is only concerned with interpreting and applying the rules, ensuring fair-play, and exercising discipline. For all this he has the assistance of a clerk who advises on procedure and looks after the practical arrangements of the committee's business. Outside the committee room the chairman resumes a normal political life, except that, by convention, he plays no part in further debate or divisions on the bill for which he was chairman.

The powers of a chairman of a standing committee are similar to those of the chairman of a committee of the whole House. He can select amendments and accept a closure motion. He has a casting vote, which he uses on the same principles as the Speaker in the House (see page 208). He can order a Member to sit down, under Standing Order No. 41, if he is persistently irrelevant or tediously repetitious, but otherwise he does not possess the disciplinary powers over Members that the Speaker and chairmen have in the House (see pages 213-216); he cannot order a Member to leave the committee, for example. If a Member persists in disobeying an order of the chair or is otherwise grossly disorderly, the only action the committee can take (after, perhaps, a suspension to see whether tempers may cool or reason prevail) is to make a special report to the House on the conduct of the Member concerned, and then, if necessary, to adjourn.[79] There is no appeal to the Speaker against a ruling by the chairman of a standing committee, nor can he be asked to rule about any matter arising in committee.[80]

---

[79] See, for example, Proceedings of First Scottish Standing Committee, January 23, 1973, and H.C.Deb., Vol. 849, cols. 666–678 (January 25, 1973). This case related to Members not on the committee; for a case involving nominated Members, one has to go back to 1924–25, which is a tribute to the authority of chairmen.

[80] See, e.g. H.C.Deb., Vol. 125, col. 464 (January 14, 1988).

If a stranger misbehaves, the chairman has power, under Standing Order No. 141(2), to direct the policeman (who comes under the Serjeant at Arms) to take him in custody and remove him from the committee room.

Standing committees sit at Westminster, except that under Standing Order No. 94(3) the Scottish Grand Committee may sit in Edinburgh on specified Mondays by leave of the House.[80a] Committees may sit only on days on which the House sits, may sit while the House is sitting, and can continue after the rising of the House. The day and time of the first sitting of a standing committee is appointed by the Chairman, after consultation with the Member in charge of the bill or other matter—in the case of Government business, via the Whips. Further meetings are determined by the committee itself, usually on a motion by the Minister (or other Member) in charge, except that, under Standing Order No. 88, a committee cannot sit after 1.00 p.m. (except for not more than 15 minutes to finish the bill, or to complete proceedings when a closure is moved or a division is in progress) or before 3.30 p.m.[81]

Most committees on Government bills sit on Tuesdays and Thursdays (see page 317), and most committees on statutory intruments and European legislation hold their meetings on Wednesday mornings. Standing Committee C, considering private Members' bills, also sits on Wednesday mornings.

Afternoon sittings continue till the committee decides to stop on a motion to adjourn the debate (if one be in progress) or further consideration of the bill (between debates).

In a standing committee, as in committees of the whole House, there are no restrictions on the number of speeches or their duration; the normal rules of debate and behaviour apply[82], clauses and amendments to bills are considered in the same way as in the Chamber, and the debates and proceedings are published. The main procedures peculiar to standing committees, other than those noted above, are: a quorum must always be present (under Standing Order No. 89(1), the quorum of a standing committee is 17 or one-third of the membership, whichever is less); the minimum number required to support a closure is the same as for the quorum (Standing Order No. 89(3)(b)); and divisions are held by the clerk calling the roll of the committee when Members respond "Aye" or "No" (or "No vote"). Ordinary standing committees have no power to receive written or oral evidence. They are not committees of inquiry, and their procedure is that of debate.

How they debate varies greatly from committee to committee and from bill to bill; it is impossible to generalise accurately. Some bills are short and uncontentious and there are few amendments; a few brief debates in which the Opposition indicate their broad approval and ask for assurances on one or two points—to which the Minister helpfully responds—dispose of the bill. Others are more contentious and numerous amendments may be moved, but debate may be short and precise with brief exchanges between the front-benchers. Other bills may be harder fought, with lengthy debates on

---

[80a] The Committee sat in Edinburgh 11 times during the 1983–87 Parliament; such sittings have been fewer since the 1987 general election.

[81] Exceptional times have been permitted, by order of the House, for the Scottish Grand Committee meeting in Edinburgh, (e.g. H.C.Deb., Vol. 74, col. 752 (March 4, 1985)), and restrictions are normally imposed on the times of sitting of the Welsh Grand Committee when considering matters referred to it (e.g. H.C.Deb., Vol. 82, col. 305 (July 2, 1985)).

[82] However, a somewhat less formal atmosphere can be detected, and as early as 1921 a chairman ruled that when the weather was warm Members could remove their jackets.

major matters of disagreement. And on some bills there is overt filibustering, with large numbers of amendments being tabled, and lengthy debates on each one; the closure may be applied[83]; and such proceedings usually end with a guillotine being imposed. Some committee debates are highly political and exciting (or excited); others are complex, technical and often boring to those who are less expert. Some proceedings are good-tempered; others require frequent intervention by the Chair to require the withdrawal of un-parliamentary expressions and to keep a semblance of order.

There are procedural variations for certain standing committee. Bills certified by the Speaker as relating exclusively to Scotland, if committed to a standing committee, are considered by a Scottish Standing Committee including not fewer than 16 Members representing Scottish constituencies (Standing Order No. 86(2)) unless the House otherwise orders. [83a] A second Scottish Standing Committee is used for Scottish private Members' bills (Standing Order No. 95). The use of Second Reading Committees was described on page 230. The Scottish Grand Committee considers the principles of some purely Scottish bills under Standing Order No. 93 (in effect their second reading), Scottish estimates referred to it under Standing Order No. 96, and specified Scottish matters referred to it under Standing Order No. 97. It comprises, in accordance with Standing Order No. 94(2), all Members representing Scottish constituencies; the quorum is 10. The Welsh Grand Committee appointed under Standing Order No. 98 similarly considers bills[84] and specified Welsh matters referred to it; it consists of all Members sitting for Welsh seats, plus not more than five other Members nominated by the Committee of Selection.

Motions to refer bills, matters and estimates to these Grand Committees are decided without debate under the relevant standing orders, but such references (except for Scottish estimates and Welsh matters) may be blocked if a relatively small number of Members (10 for Scottish bills and matters; 20 for Welsh bills) indicate their objection in the House. Thus, in effect, the Opposition can veto such references. The Scottish Grand Committee when considering Scottish bills, estimates or matters and the Welsh Grand Committee when considering Welsh matters have no power to express opinions on the business referred to them, but only to report that they have considered such business. The Welsh Grand Committee when considering a bill referred to it must recommend whether or not the bill should be read a second time, like a second reading committee.

A Northern Ireland Committee, appointed under Standing Order No. 99 to consider specified matters relating to Northern Ireland, can also report only that it has considered such matters. The Committee consists of all Members sitting for constituencies in Northern Ireland plus not more than

---

[83] The closure is not nowadays extensively used in standing committees. In session 1985–86, in nearly 400 meetings of committees, the closure was only claimed seven times (in all cases by Government Whips); it was refused once and granted thrice in respect of sittings motions and granted thrice in respect of amendments to bills.

[83a] After the 1987 election, when there were few Government supporters from Scottish constituencies, the minimum number of Scottish Members had to be reduced on one occasion (H.C.Deb., Vol. 132, cols. 831–855 (May 3, 1988); on other occasions an unusually large number of English Conservative Members had to be added to give the Government its majority.

[84] Such bills need not relate exclusively to Wales, but all such references are rare. There have been only two cases since the standing orders provided for this in 1974.

25 other Members nominated by the Committee of Selection. Only 27 such references have been made since the standing order was passed in 1975. The work of this committee in recent years is discussed on page 361.

Equally rare, in recent years, has been the use of the Standing Committee on Regional Affairs. This is appointed under Standing Order No. 77 to consider any matter of a regional interest in England which is referred to it on an undebatable Motion moved by a Minister (again blockable by 20 Members). Its composition is, however, somewhat bizarre as it consists of all Members sitting for English constituencies, plus up to five others. It has only sat on 13 occasions since the order was made in 1975. The use made of these committees—and the difficulties experienced by the Government Whips in controlling them—are described on page 361.

Much more common is the use of Standing Committees on Statutory Instruments for debating delegated legislation—although any decisions are still taken by the House. Under Standing Order No. 101, when a Member tables a "prayer" for the annulment of a statutory instrument under the negative procedure, or when a Minister has given notice of a motion for the approval of an instrument or draft instrument, under the affirmative procedure, a Minister may move, at the commencement of public business, for the instrument concerned to be referred to a standing committee. The question must be decided without debate, but can be blocked by 20 or more Members signifying their objection. Thus, the Opposition can ensure that the more controversial and important instruments that are subject to the affirmative procedure are debated on the floor of the House. It has less control over where prayers are debated because, in effect, if it blocks a motion to refer a prayer to a committee upstairs, the Government is not obliged to find time for the prayer to be debated at all (see pages 246–247). The same procedure may, in effect, be used for debating Church of England measures—but rarely is.[85] We consider the use by Government, Opposition and backbenchers of Standing Committees on Statutory Instruments on pages 334, 348–350 and 406–407, respectively.

When an instrument is referred upstairs a standing committee of usually 18 Members may debate each instrument for one and a half hours (or two and a half hours in the case of instruments relating exclusively to Northern Ireland[86]) on a motion "That the committee has considered the instrument." No amendment can be moved to this motion, so the committee is unable, formally, to express any view for or against the instrument or to have a significant vote on it (though occasionally the Opposition registers its disapproval by voting against the formal motion). Often a group of related instruments may be debated together, but again for only one and a half hours.

An unusual feature of a Standing Committee on Statutory Instruments is that, under Standing Order No. 101(2) any Member who is not a nominated member of the committee may attend and speak, but he may not move motions or amendments, vote or be counted in the quorum. Other than this, the procedures are much the same as for a committee on a bill; the Speaker allocates instruments to specified committees and appoints the chairman; the normal rules of debate apply.

---

[85] Only three cases since the system was devised in 1973.

[86] There were 60 such instruments referred to committees between 1975, when the procedure was introduced, and the end of the 1986–87 session.

A similar procedure was adopted in 1980 for debating less controversial or more technical European Community documents as defined by Standing Order No. 14(1) (see page 201). Under Standing Order No. 102, usually following a recommendation by the European Legislation Committee, (see pages 436–439), a Minister may move that a document be referred to a Standing Committee on European Community Documents. The procedure for such motions is the same as for reference of statutory instruments.

The powers of a committee on European Community documents are, however, significantly greater. Under Standing Order No. 102 each document (or group of documents) may be debated on a motion moved by the Government which expresses a view on the merits of the proposals, to which amendments may be moved. A significant debate, ending with a significant vote,[87] is thereby permissible. Debate on these motions may last for not more than two and a half hours. Again any Member may attend and speak. When the committee reports its resolution, a motion (usually in the same terms) is made in the House—and again amendments may be moved and voted on—but without further debate. We consider the use made of these committees on the initiative of back-benchers on pages 407–408.

An important innovation since 1980 has been the use of special standing committees. After several experiments, Standing Order No. 91 was passed in 1986 to enable the appointment of committees which, in addition to having a debating function for the committee stages of bills could also, within limits, take evidence before getting down to their debates. Such committees thus operate partly like select committees (see below) and partly like standing committees.

Under Standing Order No. 16(2) a bill may be committed to a special standing committee on a motion moved by any Member (to be put forthwith if moved immediately after second reading). The members of a special standing committee are appointed by the Committee of Selection. Under Standing Order No. 91(2), the Speaker may appoint any non-Minister as chairman for the evidence hearing sittings; in practice the chairman of the relevant departmentally-related select committee has usually been appointed for this purpose.

A special standing committee has power to hear oral evidence—usually in public—at not more than three morning sittings during a period of 28 days after the committal of the bill; written evidence may also be called for. One other sitting may be used for private deliberation (selecting witnesses or discussing their evidence, for example). At the conclusion of these proceedings, the committee reverts to working like any other standing committee, going through the bill clause by clause and debating amendments; the evidence that has been received is directly relevant to those debates and frequently quoted. These sittings are chaired by a Member from the Chairmen's Panel. The use made of this new procedure is discussed on page 318.

The growing use of standing committees, of all kinds, in the years since 1945 has been most marked, as the Table below shows. They have enabled much work—most of it Government business—to be transferred from the floor of the House to committee rooms upstairs so that more business can be transacted. On the other hand they have also continued to provide opportunities for the Opposition and back-benchers to criticise and debate

---

[87] It is very rare for amendments to be moved—let alone divided on—as only less controversial documents are referred upstairs.

Government policy and administration on a wide range of matters that might well have been squeezed out or severely curtailed if all these critical processes had had to be conducted in the Chamber itself. Given the growth of Government business, and given that there must be some limit to the number of hours the House is required to sit, it has become inevitable that more and more business has to be debated upstairs. The progressive development of the standing committee system has been one of the most important changes in the working of the House of Commons in this century.

Notes (see following Table)

(a) Unusually long session
(b) Unusually short session
(c) Excluding Second Reading Committees, and Scottish and Welsh Grand Committees, but including special standing committees.
(d) Normally only one sitting is devoted to each bill referred for consideration in relation to its principle. At the other sittings Scottish matters and Scottish estimates are considered. In 1947–48 and 1957–58, Scottish estimates were considered by the Scottish Standing Committee.
(e) Almost entirely for consideration of Welsh matters.
(f) Length of sittings can vary enormously from one of a few minutes to one lasting from 4.00 p.m. till lunch-time the next day. The standard sitting is, however, about two-and-a half hours for most forms of business, except for Statutory Intruments Committees, when sittings may be very brief and rarely exceed one-and-a-half hours.
(g) The burden of committee work varies greatly between Members. For example in 1985–86, out of 567 Members summoned to sit on standing committees, 192 attended less than six sittings; by contrast 12 Members attended 50 or more sittings.
(h) Including one meeting of a standing committee to consider a bill on report.

Work of Standing Committees

Sessions

Type of Committee etc.	1937 -38	1947 -48	1957 -58	1962 -63	1967 -68	1972 -73	1977 -78	1979 -80 (a)	1980 -81	1981 -82	1982 -83 (b)	1983 -84 (a)	1984 -85	1985 -86	1986 -87 (b)
Number of standing committees on bills appointed (c)	4	5	6	8	10	10	5	10	10	9	11	12	9	12	8
Number of sittings of standing committees on bills (and number of bills committed)	102 (28)	125 (21)	174 (34)	204 (38)	331 (53)	273 (50)	107 (36)	464 (41)	313 (36)	300 (40)	260 (33)	424 (40)	224 (45)	375 (43)	176 (36)
Number of sittings of Second Reading Committees (and number of bills considered)	–	–	2 (1)	–	6 (6)	3 (3)	6 (6)	1 (1)	4 (4)	8 (8)	7 (7)	6 (6)	4 (4)	8 (8)	5 (5)
Number of sittings of Scottish Grand Committee (and number of bills considered) (d)	–	6	7	15 (4)	12 (5)	9 (2)	9 (3)	10 (2)	8 (1)	13 (2)	7 (3)	11 (2)	13 (4)	10 (–)	2 (1)
Number of sittings of Welsh Grand Committee (e)	–	–	–	4	2	8	5	12	9	6	7	9	10	6	4
Number of sittings of Northern Ireland Committee	–	–	–	–	–	–	4	6	3	2	3	4	1	–	–

Work of Standing Committees (*cont.*)

Sessions

Type of Committee etc.	1937 –38	1947 –48	1957 –58	1962 –63	1967 –68	1972 –73	1977 –78	1979 –80 (a)	1980 –81	1981 –82	1982 –83 (b)	1983 –84 (a)	1984 –85	1985 –86	1986 –87 (b)
Number of sittings of Regional Affairs Committee	–	–	–	–	–	–	2	–	–	–	–	–	–	–	–
Number of sittings of standing committees on statutory instruments (and number of instruments considered)	–			–	–	8 (17)	96 (141)	88 (130)	46 (62)	56 (80)	49 (73)	77 (96)	71 (100)	71 (98)	51 (72)
Number of sittings of standing committees on European Community documents (and number of documents considered)	–			–	–	–	–	–	5 (7)	10 (12)	–	10 (30)	7 (17)	9 (17)	9 (12)
Total number of sittings of standing committees (f)	102	131	183	223	352(h)	301	229	581	388	395	333	541	330	479	247
Total number of Members (including Chairman) appointed to serve on standing committees (g)	376	433	456	489	514	523	556	567	518	538	524	584	570	567	554

Select Committees

Unlike standing committees, select committees fulfil a function which the House itself could not possibly undertake. The way they work and their achievements are more fully discussed in Chapter 11; here we describe the basic procedures.

Select Committees are appointed by the House and are subordinate to it. The House gives them their duties. For example, "Select committees shall be appointed to examine the expenditure, administration and policy of the principal government departments ... etc.," to quote Standing Order No. 130. These are their "orders of reference." The House gives them the necessary powers to carry out those duties. And it nominates their members. Until fairly recently, select committees were appointed and nominated each session only for the duration of that session, and if a committee's work was not completed, or if it had a continuing remit, that committee had to be re-appointed and re-nominated at the beginning of the next session. Sometimes there was considerable delay in re-appointing committees because of difficulties in completing the membership or, occasionally, because of disagreements regarding orders of reference. Such delays handicapped committees by interrupting and unnecessarily prolonging inquiries and by making it difficult for a committee to plan its work ahead from session to session.

As a result of this experience a new procedure was adopted in 1974 under which well-established committees, such as the Public Accounts Committee, were set up for the whole of that Parliament. By 1983 the procedure had been taken to its logical conclusion and all the regular committees are now appointed by standing order and so continue not only from session to session but also from one Parliament to the next. However the membership has to be nominated for the life of one Parliament only, and this has led to delay in re-constituting committees at the beginning of a Parliament.[88]

In addition to these standing order committees,[89] ad hoc committees are sometimes appointed on a sessional basis for particular inquiries, and when their work is complete they report and terminate. If such a committee cannot complete its work by the end of a session, it makes a special report to that effect, and is re-appointed at the beginning of the next session. Occasionally such a committee may be appointed for the whole of a Parliament if its inquiries are likely to be protracted.[90] Exceptionally a committee's life has been extended at the end of one session for one further session.[91]

---

[88] For example, the House met after the general election in June 1987, but most of the departmentally-related select committees were not nominated until December 2. And see pp. 418–419.

[89] For a full list, see pp. 415–417.

[90] This has been the practice with Select Committees on Procedure in recent years (*e.g.* H.C.Deb., Vol.134, Vol. 682 (May 27, 1988)).

[91] Select Committee on Televising of Proceedings of the House, 1987–88 and 1988–89 (H.C.Deb., Vol. 139, col. 1329 (November 4, 1988)).

When a committee has been appointed, its membership is nominated by the House. The standard procedure for nomination is for the motion to be moved by a Government Whip, the numbers having been agreed through the usual channels and the names being those supplied by the Whips of the parties concerned. Under Standing Order No. 104, however, the members of the 14 departmentally-related committees appointed under Standing Order No. 130 must be nominated on a motion, of which at least two days' notice has been given, moved by the Chairman of the Committee of Selection or by another member of that committee on his behalf. We discuss the significance of this procedure, and how it operates, on pages 417–419. After the initial nominations, membership of committees may be changed from time to time by discharging some Members and adding others, using the same procedures as for the original nomination.

The size of a select committee is defined by the relevant standing orders or appointment order and nominations. Although there is no formal requirement to this effect, the party balance on select committees is nearly always proportionate to party strengths in the House. The quorum of each committee is also laid down by order. Under Standing Order No. 107, select committees cannot work unless a quorum is present; the chairman counts in the quorum. The varying sizes and party balance of committees and their quorums are described on pages 416–417 and 434.

When a committee is appointed, the House also gives it powers. The usual powers for a committee with continuing inquiry functions include: power "to send for persons, papers and records," that is, to call evidence (for discussion of the extent and practical exercise of these powers see pages 448–451); power to sit notwithstanding any adjournment of the House, namely, to meet during recesses; power to adjourn from place to place, that is to sit away from Westminster, either in the United Kingdom or overseas; and power to report from time to time so that it can make separate reports on different aspects of its orders of reference at the committee's discretion.[92] All committees having power to call evidence obviously also have power to report that evidence to the House, usually from time to time.

There are occasional variations of these standard powers. For example, some committees, such as the Liaison Committee and the Committee of Privileges, have no power to travel away from Westminster; the power to travel has also been limited to sittings in the United Kingdom.[92a] Committees have been ordered to report by a certain date.[93] A committee has been given power to hear witnesses voluntarily but not to order evidence formally.[94] Standing Order No. 130(5)(d) and (e) gives the departmentally-related committees power to show each other their evidence (which is quite often done) or to have concurrent meetings (which they have not done).

Select committees all have their own permanent staff (see page 153) and many committees nowadays have power to appoint specialist advisers. The usual powers for this purpose are as set out in Standing Order No. 130(5)(b)

---

[92] Ad hoc committees are sometimes not given this last power, so that having reported they are *functus officio*.

[92a] Select Committee on Cyprus, 1975–76; Computer Sub Committee of the House of Commons (Services) Committee, under Standing Order No. 125(12) (until May 1989).

[93] The Select Committee on Cyprus in its second session, 1975–76.

[94] The Select Committee on the Civil List, 1970–71 and 1971–72.

(see page 423), but some committees may have particular requirements.[95] Very occasionally, committees are given power to appoint persons to carry out investigations on their behalf,[96] or to hear counsel to such extent as they see fit.[97] Most unusually the Procedure Committee of 1975–76 was given power to invite persons to attend its meetings and to take part in its deliberations, in other words to co-opt strangers to its membership, but these powers were never used.

Powers are sometimes given to select committees to appoint sub-committees. This may either be without restriction, as for example, the Services Committee, or subject to a limit on numbers, as for example, with the Foreign Affairs, the Home Affairs and the Treasury and Civil Service Committees, which each have power to appoint one sub-committee (Standing Order No. 130(3)). Without such formal powers, sub-committees may not be appointed, but sometimes committees are able to operate *de facto* sub-committees by different groups of Members of a committee specialising in different aspects of that committee's work, often with different Members in the Chair. Sub-committees are usually given the same powers as the full committee except that they cannot report direct to the House; any report prepared by a sub-committee must be considered and agreed (with or without amendments) by the full committee, and reported to the House as its own report. Evidence taken by sub-committees is, however, reported direct to the House.

Papers are sometimes referred to a select committee, particularly reports of previous committees and evidence taken by previous committees.

A select committee having been thus appointed and nominated is now free to use the powers given it by the House as it thinks fit. For example, it interprets its own order of reference; it chooses its own subjects for inquiry within the scope of that order; it determines the days and times of its own sittings; it summons evidence of its own choosing; and it prepares and agrees its own reports and special reports. Subject to the rules and practices of the House it also, in effect, regulates its own proceedings, and there is no appeal to the Speaker on a decision of a committee or of its chairman.

The first meeting of a select committee is at a time fixed by the senior member of the committee (*i.e.* the person who has been an M.P. for the longest cumulative period, irrespective of continuity of service). The first business at this meeting is the election of the chairman. Although, in practice, the choice has usually been made in advance (see pages 419–420), the formal decision still lies with the select committee itself. No deputy chairman is appointed, but if the appointed chairman is not present at any meeting, any other member may be called to the chair for that meeting.

A chairman of a select committee has the same general powers for putting

---

[95] For example the Services Committee, which is concerned, *inter alia*, with the parliamentary buildings, has power to invite an architect to attend its meetings in an advisory capacity (Standing Order No. 125(5)), and its Library Sub-Committee has power to consult with the Librarian of the House (Standing Order No. 125(10)), so that he need not be summoned as a witness. The Joint Committee on Statutory Instruments has power to have the assistance of Speakers Counsel and of Counsel to the Lord Chairman of Committees (Standing Order No. 124(4)). And the Select Committee on European Legislation may similarly be advised by Speakers Counsel (Standing Order No. 127(3)).

[96] For example, Procedure Committee, 1975–76, and Committee on Conduct of Members, 1975–76.

[97] For example, Committee on Conduct of Members, 1975–76.

questions, ruling on matters of procedures and so on as has a chairman of a committee of the whole House, but he has none of the disciplinary powers that are given to the Speaker or chairmen in the House or standing committees. Nor can he accept a closure or restrict in any formal way the questioning of witnesses provided the questions are within the committee's remit.[97a] His formal powers are therefore strictly limited. But his informal influence—his central role in conducting inquiries—is of great importance.

When a select committee is at work its procedures and proceedings are very different from those of the House or of a standing committee. Many of its meetings are deliberative, for example when choosing its chairman, deciding on a subject for inquiry, agreeing a programme for an inquiry, selecting witnesses, discussing visits it may make to institutions in this country or overseas, considering the appointment of specialist advisers, discussing the best lines of questioning for particular witnesses, reviewing evidence received and agreeing the heads of a report, considering the terms of a draft report, going through that draft report formally, deciding on amendments, and finally agreeing the report to be made to the House.

When a committee is deliberating, Members sit round a horseshoe table, with the chairman in the centre and the committee's clerk beside him; any specialist advisers who are assisting the committee sit facing the Members. Members sometimes sit by party but more normally they arrange themselves in a random way on either side of the chairman. The atmosphere is relaxed and casual; Members may smoke, and in warm weather take off their jackets. They do not make speeches as in the House, but discuss and argue and seek to reach agreement. Except when a committee is going through a report formally and occasionally when a formal motion is proposed relating to the proceedings of the committee or on the election of a chairman, there is no single, specific question before the committee. Typically, the chairman sums up and expresses the committee's decisions in some such words as "well I think we are agreed that . . . ," or "The general view seems to be that we should. . . . " Such informal consensus is often accepted, but any Member has the right to seek a decision by a formal procedure by which the views of dissenting Members can be recorded in a division. In general, when all is amicable and party (or personal) conflicts are low-key, informal processes work best; if there is less general agreement or major principles are at stake, more formal procedures may be needed.

When divisions are called—normally on amendments to draft reports— the names are called and the votes are recorded by the clerk, and are published in the minutes of proceedings. Thus, although committees do not publish minority reports as such, minority opinions as expressed in alternative drafts or in amendments are formally recorded and published with the majority conclusions. Although there is no published record of the discussion, every Member has the right to have his own opinions recorded formally. This ultimate safeguard makes it possible to conduct the majority of business by informal consensus.

Such an approach is greatly aided by the fact that all deliberative meetings

---

[97a] The committee itself can formally decide what questions shall or shall not be asked, although this is not usually done. For a striking example, see Proceedings of the Foreign Affairs Committee (relating to its report on the sinking of the *Belgrano*), H.C. 11 of 1984–85, pp. lvii–lxv. The majority of Members from the Government side called a number of divisions to leave out questions that Opposition Members wished to ask, but it was formally agreed that other questions be put to various Ministers and a former Chief of Defence Staff.

of select committees are in private. Apart from the members of the committee, only the committee's staff and specialist advisers are allowed to remain during deliberations.[98]

The practice is completely different when a select committee is hearing evidence. Although public hearings were not uncommon in the nineteenth and early twentieth centuries, they fell out of favour until the middle 1960s. Then some committees—led by the Select Committee on Nationalised Industries—began admitting the public and in 1971 the position was codified by the adoption of Standing Order No. 108 which permits select committees and their sub-committees (unless the parent committee decides otherwise) to admit strangers during the examination of witnesses. Today most committees admit the press and the public to most of their evidence meetings, the main exceptions being those meetings of the Foreign Affairs, Defence and Public Accounts Committees when confidential or classified evidence may be given by Government witnesses, and of committees such as Trade and Industry and Public Accounts when hearing evidence that may be commercially confidential. Some domestic committees, for example sub-committees of the Services Committee, normally take evidence in private, and the Committee of Privileges has always done so. Sometimes a committee will begin a meeting in public and then go private for certain parts of the evidence, or vice versa.

When a committee admits the public, many people may crowd into the back of the room. If the topic under investigation is in any way politically exciting, lobby correspondents will be present, the relevant pressure groups will all be represented, officials from Government departments will be there, and (if there is room for them) students and school parties will come to watch this important side of the work of Parliament. On other occasions interest may be confined to the specialist press and the relevant pressure groups. In the case of disorder the policeman who attends all public committee meetings on behalf of the Serjeant at Arms may, on the direction of the chairman under Standing Order No. 141(2), remove any stranger who misbehaves. Such cases are very few.

When a committee hears evidence in public it may, if the broadcasters so wish, be recorded for broadcasting by the B.B.C. or one of the sound-broadcasting companies. Committees have no power when admitting the public to prohibit broadcasting, but they are alerted by a signal when they are being recorded.

When witnesses are being examined the proceedings are somewhat more formal than during deliberation, but the seating arrangements are just the same, except that the specialist advisers sit at a side table, and the witnesses sit facing the committee. A shorthand-writer is also present (or someone operating a recording machine) to make a verbatim record of all the evidence.

The chairman or another Member, as agreed before the witnesses are called in, usually leads off the questioning, with other Members joining in on matters which interest them. Sometimes (especially in the Public Accounts Committee) Members take it in turns, round the table, to ask their questions; in other committees Members chip in as they wish, although the

---

[98] Clerks from other parliaments attached to the House for training or study have, with the agreement of the committee, been allowed to attend private meetings of select committees as observers.

chairman always ensures that everyone has his opportunity. Questions are usually brief, though the practice of sitting in public seems to have led to slightly longer questions through the introduction of statements showing the questioner's own point of view. Answers vary considerably in length. However it is difficult to generalise about the questioning process; each committee develops its own habits and practices.

Committees use their powers "to adjourn from place to place" extensively by travelling in the United Kingdom and overseas in furtherance of their inquiries. On these occasions they have many informal meetings which are not recorded or reported. We describe how they do this on pages 421–422.

When a committee has taken the evidence—formal and informal, written and oral—that it needs, the time comes to prepare its report. There may, at this stage, be a deliberative meeting to review the outcome of the inquiry and to discuss the main lines of the report. A draft report is then prepared. The first drafts are normally written by the clerk, sometimes with the help of a specialist assistant, or by a specialist adviser, or by two or three of them working together; their agreed draft is then submitted to the chairman, and usually further amended in accordance with his wishes. It is then circulated to the committee as the chairman's draft report.

Having had time to read it, the committee begins consideration of the draft report.[99] It usually takes it informally first, identifying sections or paragraphs that the Members would like to see re-drafted or suggesting additional points that should be made or matter that could be omitted. A further draft will then be prepared and, for a big or controversial report, this process may take several meetings. Finally, the committee is ready to take formal decisions. Agreement has perhaps been achieved on much of the report, but certain matters of disagreement remain; these can only be resolved formally.[1] So the committee then goes through the report, paragraph by paragraph, and considers formally every amendment moved to each paragraph; and as in a standing committee or committee of the whole House, every amendment must be either agreed to, disagreed to or withdrawn. Finally, the question is put, "That the report (as amended) be the report of the committee to the House" and any Member who does not agree with the report can formally register his objection. The minutes of proceedings are published with the report.

The committee also reports the written and oral evidence on which it has based its report (including if possible some of the evidence originally heard in private), and the House orders this to be printed. Sometimes, however, confidential evidence is left out of the reported evidence at the request of witnesses and with the agreement of the committee (this is known as sidelining) and is therefore not published, although omissions are indicated by asterisks in the published record. Other less important evidence—such as numerous volunteered memoranda—may be laid on the Table and placed in

[99] Occasionally another Member may prepare an alternative draft report (on which again the clerk may have helped), in which case the first task of the committee is to decide, usually on a vote, which draft report to consider (see, for example, Third Report from Foreign Affairs Committee (relating to the sinking of the *Belgrano*), H.C. 11 of 1984–85, pp. lxvi–cxxiv).

[1] Quite often total agreement is reached informally, even on potentially controversial material. The relevant part of the Minutes of Proceedings on the Fourth Report of the Defence Committee, on Westland P.L.C. The Government's Decision Making (H.C. 519 of 1985–86), simply reads "Paragraphs 1 to 240 read and agreed to." The minutes of other committees have covered several pages, recording numerous amendments and divisions.

the Library and so become available to Members (and to the public via the Record Office, House of Lords), but is not printed. For a smaller inquiry, the evidence, even if published separately after each public hearing, is re-published with the report in one volume; for a bigger inquiry, the report and the evidence and memoranda may be published in separate volumes.

Select committes may also make special reports, which deal not with the actual matter referred to them, but with other matters arising from their work, such as observations on their orders of reference or powers (for example, requesting the power to appoint sub-committees), indicating topics of inquiry they propose to deal with in future, reporting on the conduct of a witness (for example, in refusing to answer a question[2]), reporting that it has not had time to finish an inquiry before the end of the session (in the case of sessional committees), or otherwise commenting on matters ancillary to their work. Special reports are most commonly used for reporting to the House the observations by Government departments on previous reports of the committee, sometimes with further comments by the committee on those observations. Such observations are also sometimes made in the form of Command papers, which are presented directly to the House, in which case no report is required from the committee concerned unless it wishes to comment further.

The Government has agreed to try to reply, by observations, to all select committee reports concerning Government departments within two months of the publication of the report. It has not always succeeded.

The select committee process and the proceedings of these committees are becoming increasingly important, and the volume of select committee work has grown in recent years, as is shown by the Table below.

CONCLUSIONS

The Growth of Parliamentary Business

Procedures are not static but are constantly changing to match changes in the volume and nature of parliamentary business. Parliamentary business is a product of three factors. First, the amount of business Parliament is required to do by the Government. Second, the amount of business Members themselves choose to undertake in criticising and scrutinising Government. Third, the nature of that business. A ready index of the growth of parliamentary business is therefore the use of various procedures. The growth in legislation, in use of standing committees, in Questions and statements, in the tabling of motions, and in select committee activity have all been referred to or quantified in detail in earlier sections of this chapter, but the

---

[2] See Third Special Report from the Trade and Industry Committee, H.C. 628 of 1985–86.

The Use of Select Committees

Session	No. of select committees (c)	No. of sub-committees appointed	Total No. of meetings of committees and sub-committees	Total No. of reports and special reports (d)
1937–38	11	–	106	11
1947–48	10	6	221	14
1957–58	15	10	224	17
1967–68	14	19	334	47
1977–78	18	22	566	143
1978–79(a)	17	21	337	242
1979–80(b)	26	7	912	180
1980–81	29	7	792	173
1981–82	28	7	747	138
1982–83(a)	28	7	595	144
1983–84(b)	27	7	787	242
1984–85	27	7	769	214
1985–86	28	7	823	222
1986–87(a)	28	6	501	140

(a) Unusually short session
(b) Unusually long session
(c) Excluding business committees on guillotined bills, committees appointed to draw up reasons for disagreeing to Lords Amendments, committees on hybrid bills, and committees concerned with private legislation (including the Committee of Selection).
(d) Since the 1960s this total has been considerably increased by the large number of reports, made almost weekly, by the Joint Committee on Statutory Instruments and the Select Committee on European Legislation, and by the practice of the Public Accounts Committee of making numerous separate reports on separate accounts, rather than (as was done up till 1975) collecting nearly all their work into one large report.

Tables on this page and on page 289 give a convenient overall picture of a much more active House. In our opinion this growth of work and activity is the most noteworthy change in the functioning of the House of Commons in this century. And the process has accelerated in recent years. However, as the Table on page 289 shows, the greatest part of the additional work has been undertaken by committees, there has been no overall increase in either the number of sittings of the House itself or in their duration.

Volume of Public Legislation passed by Parliament
(including delegated legislation)

Year	Public General Acts and Measures		Statutory Instruments	
	Number	Pages (a)	Number	Pages
1900	63	198	N/A	N/A
1910	38	214	303	922
1920	82	560	2,472	1,753
1930	42	805	1,166	1,966
1940	61	506	2,223	1,685
1950	51	1,001	2,144	4,067
1960	67	1,176	2,496	2,820
1970	61	1,516	2,044	6,835
1980	70	2,876	2,051	7,424
1981	72	2,276	1,892	6,558
1982	59	2,130	1,900	5,572
1983	62	1,541	1,966	6,439
1984	62	2,876	2,065	6,099
1985	76	3,233	2,082	6,518
1986	72	2,847	2,356	N/A
1987	57	1,538 (b)	2,279	N/A

Notes

(a) The growth of the statute book in recent years is partly accounted for by exceptionally large consolidation Acts; for example the Income and Corporation Taxes Act 1988 had 1,041 pages.

(b) Published in A4, and therefore with fewer pages.

The Effect of the Growth of Business on the House's Procedures

The growing volume and complexity of work has had three important effects on the conduct of proceedings of the House of Commons. First, procedures have increasingly been devised to give priority to, and expedite Government business, by limiting debates and simplifying the processes for taking decisions. For example, certain motions may be decided without amendment or debate, and time-limited and pre-packaged debates are increasingly used even when the rules do not require this. Debate on the second reading of the Finance Bill is, by the rules, open-ended, yet on April 23, 1987, it finished precisely at 10.00 p.m., as the Whips on each side had arranged, so the House would divide at a convenient hour; and on April 8, 1987, on the third reading of the Northern Ireland (Emergency Provisions) Bill, for which the rule had been suspended so debate did not need to stop at 10.00 p.m., the Liberal Whip rose at 10.01 and said "I shall not disappoint the Government and Opposition Whips who wish to commence the debate on the next

Other Indicators of House of Commons Activity

Session	No of meetings of standing committees (a)	No of meetings of select committees (b)	No of Questions on Order Paper		No of sitting days	Average length of sittings
			For oral answer	For written answer		
1935–36	87	111	8613	1602	137	8 hrs 33 mins
1945–46	152	253	21135	6178	212	8 hrs 15 mins
1955–56	176	340	14775	3501	219	7 hrs 57 mins
1965–66	69	114	4332	3646	65	8 hrs 25 mins
1975–76	552	619	8097	33223	191	9 hrs 21 mins
1985–86	479	823	17332	31718	172	8 hrs 35 mins

Notes:

(a) Length of meetings varies enormously, and cannot readily be indicated.
(b) Including sub-committees

business as close to 10 o'clock as possible." These are typical occurrences. The practice of the House has thus departed from basic procedure as described on page 177 above. This chapter has shown how extensive this departure has become.

Second, an increasing use has been made of committees. Committees have mushroomed to facilitate the passage of legislation and to give additional opportunities for debating other matters. And select committees have evolved which provide greater opportunities for back-benchers to scrutinise the Government's policies and administration, for which the process of ordinary debate would not be suitable.

Third, back-benchers on either side have increasingly used procedures available to them to raise matters of policy of their choosing or to seek for information. The Opposition have also secured more certain occasions for debating matters of their choosing.

Overall Analysis of Current Procedures

The following Table shows how, in the most recent normal length session, the time on the floor of the House was spent in using various procedures.

Time Spent on Different Types of Business, Session 1985–86
(analysed according to the procedure employed)

	hours	minutes
A. LEGISLATION (PRIMARY AND SECONDARY)		
Motions for leave to bring in bills under S.O. No.19	11	15
Second readings	179	59
Remaining stages	304	44
Allocation of time motions (Guillotines)	10	31
Money resolutions	1	37
Ways and Means resolutions	21	04
Affirmative resolutions on statutory instruments and Church Measures	87	14
Prayers against statutory instruments	18	47
Private legislation	42	16
Total for legislation	677	27
Percentage of total time	45%	

		hours	minutes
B.	*MOTIONS*		
	Substantive motions (other than below)	236	10
	Adjournment motions (other than below)	95	41
	Emergency debates under S.O. No.20	3	12
	Privilege motions	1	17
	Motions relating to European Community documents	42	18
	Address in reply to Queen's Speech (including amendments)	36	42
	"Recess" motions (adjournment motions before and motions for recesses)	30	11
	Debate on adjournment following Consolidated Fund Bills (S.O. No.54)	37	26
	Daily adjournment debates	81	08
	Estimates days	17	33
	Total for all motions	581	38
	Percentage of total time	38%	

		hours	minutes
C.	*STATEMENTS, QUESTIONS, PNQs AND S.O. NO. 20 APPLICATIONS*		
	Statements (other than business)	70	51
	Questions to Ministers	127	16
	Private notice Questions	12	13
	S.O. No. 20 applications	5	19
	Total	215	39
	Percentage of total time	14%	

D.	*MISCELLANEOUS*		
	Business statements	19	02
	Points of order and Speaker's rulings	14	21
	Presentation of petitions	2	21
	Other	4	21
	Total	40	05
	Percentage of total time	3%	

It will be seen that in 1985–86 slightly less than half the time of the House was spent on considering legislation (including delegated legislation), while slightly more than half the time of the House was largely devoted to enabling Members to discuss a wide range of matters without necessarily coming to any formal conclusion. This analysis excludes all the work of committees upstairs.

Another analysis illustrates the point made on pages 14–15 that the procedures mainly used for Government business involve some formal decision by the House (or committee). Such proceedings are eminently suited for control by the Whips, who seek, on both sides, to ensure that the decisions are made in the way they wish. This also applies to business initiated by the Opposition. By contrast, the majority of the time spent on business initiated by back-benchers on either side involves procedures where no simple decision results. These include Questions to Ministers, and debates of various kinds on motions for the adjournment of the House. The work of select committees also falls largely into this category. For these procedures, whipping is hardly applicable and back-benchers on either side are accordingly less subject to Whip control.

These fundamental distinctions are brought out in the following Table, which, using the breakdown between Government, Opposition and private Members' business employed in the Table on page 12, analyses the time spent in Session 1985–86 accordingly to whether the procedures used involved a real decision or not. It will be seen that nearly 80 per cent. of Government initiated business involved decision taking and that nearly all business initiated by the Opposition was of this nature, but that 57 per cent. of business initiated by back-benchers did not involve the taking of substantive decisions.

Time Spent on Different Types of Business, Session 1985–86
(analysed according to whether substantive decisions have to be taken or not)

A.   Business Initiated by the Government

		hours	*minutes*	*% of category A*
1.	*Business involving decisions*			
	(a) Primary legislation and related proceedings	460	40	–
	(b) Motions (other than adjournment motions), including debate on the Address	186	43	–
	Total	647	23	78%
2.	*Business not involving decisions*			
	(a) Adjournment motions (topic chosen by Government)	95	41	–
	(b) Ministerial statements (including business statements)	89	53	–
	Total	185	34	22%

B.   Business initiated by the Opposition

		hours	*minutes*	*% of category B*
1.	*Business involving decisions*			
	(a) Motions (other than adjournment motions) including debates on Opposition days initiated by smaller parties, and amendments to Address			
	Total	138	40	95%

2. *Business not involving decisions*

(a) Adjournment motions	–	–	–
(b) S.O. No.20 applications and private notice Questions	7	54	–
Total	7	54	5%

C. Business Initiated by Back-benchers

	hours	minutes	% of category C
1. *Business involving decisions*			
(a) Primary legislation	68	30	–
(b) Debates on private business	42	16	–
(c) Motions	101	17	–
(d) Estimates days debates	17	33	–
Total	229	36	43%
2. *Business not involving decisions*			
(a) Debates on motions for recesses	12	06	–
(b) Various types of debate on Adjournment motions	136	39	–
(c) Questions to Ministers (including private notice Questions)	132	07	–
(d) Applications for S.O. No.20 debates, points of order, presentation of petitions etc.	21	29	–
(e) Miscellaneous	4	21	–
Total	306	42	57%

We have now completed a description of the processes for the conduct of the business of the House of Commons—of their nature, of the framework within which they are operated, and of the occasions for their use. The way they are used by the Government, by the Opposition parties and by back-benchers on either side, is the theme of the next Part of this work.

PART III

THE USE OF OPPORTUNITIES

CHAPTER 7

GOVERNMENT CONTROL OF BUSINESS

In a famous passage, Walter Bagehot described the Cabinet as "a *hyphen* which joins, a *buckle* which fastens, the legislative part of the state to the executive part of the state."[1] If one rule had to be chosen as the most important in the unwritten constitution it would be that the Government is composed of Ministers who are members of the political party which commands a majority of votes in the House of Commons and who themselves are members of one or other House of Parliament. The Government is constitutionally the body which can control the House of Commons. It is Government business which absorbs the greatest part of the time of the two Houses. As we have already noted in Chapter 1, on 75 per cent. of the sitting days of the Commons, Government business has priority and on these days the Government arranges such business as it thinks fit.[2]

The Government could seek to use its majority to deny the Opposition a reasonable opportunity for criticism of Government policy or in other ways to manipulate the business of the House to the Government's advantage. But the Opposition is not defenceless. Time is a valuable commodity which the Opposition has many opportunities to use as it chooses. Since it is the Government that needs to get its business through, obstruction by the Opposition can be a considerable embarrassment. No doubt, at the end of the day, the Government will get its way and win its vote in the division lobbies. But prolongation of the debate will upset the Government's timetable. So the Government has a real interest in ensuring that its relations with the Opposition are as harmonious as can be expected and that the Opposition is given as little opportunity as possible for obstruction.

Similarly the Opposition often has an interest in maintaining reasonably harmonious relations with the Government on the arrangement of business, being dependent on the Government for some of its opportunities to bring matters forward, including the timing of Opposition days. The more reluctant the Opposition shows itself to agree informal timetables (for example, for bills in committee and on report) and the more it obstructs Government business, the more the Government will protect its position by limiting Opposition opportunities in one way or another, including the use of guillotines (see pages 302–307).

This mutual interest in securing, on the whole, agreement over the arrangement and timing of business (but not its content), with much give and take between the two sides, is partly the product of, and certainly reinforced by, a combination of two factors. The first is the relatively frequent alternation of the party in power. The longest period of unbroken party rule in this century has been only 13 years (1951–1964); the average duration from 1900 to 1987 (leaving out coalitions) has been five and a half years.[3]

The second factor is the length of parliamentary service of Members,

---

[1] Bagehot, *The English Constitution* (1922 ed.), p. 14.
[2] S.O. Nos. 13(1), 24.
[3] The "National Government" of 1931–1940 is here counted as Conservative.

especially the more senior. On average, Members spend about 15 years[4] in the House of Commons (sometimes with broken tenure) and many serve for much longer. In March 1988, the average length of service in the House of Commons of Members of the Cabinet was 19 years.

The combination of these two factors means that most Members have experience of being in both Government and Opposition, sometimes several times. Of the Cabinet in 1988, the Prime Minister and four other Members had had three spells on the Government side and two in Opposition; only one Member (Mr. John Major) had never sat on the Opposition benches. In 1988–89 the governmental experience of the Opposition, after 10 years out of office, has been less than usual.

It is for these reasons, among others, that there has grown up in the House of Commons a remarkable degree of understanding between the front-benches on either side as far as management of business is concerned. Mr. John Biffen (then Leader of the House) said on February 27, 1986: "All Governments are tomorrow's possible Opposition, and I think that my right hon and hon friends . . . should consider, at least theoretically, how these proposals [for timetabling of more Bills] would bear upon the Opposition". His remarks were echoed by Mr. Peter Shore for the Opposition.[5] Sometimes, indeed, the front-benchers appear to share a common attitude at odds with that of back-benchers on either side. This mutual understanding is the foundation for the great degree of agreement that is commonly reached through "the usual channels" on the arrangement and conduct of business. One manifestation of this has been the increasingly agreed packaging of debate which we described in Chapter 6.

The control of the Government over the time of the House of Commons limits the occasions when the Opposition can hold the Government to account. But tradition ensures that Opposition speakers are entitled to broadly as much time as Ministers during the course of debate. Usually, as we have seen, the Speaker calls Members alternately from the two sides of the House. Ministers and official Opposition spokesmen have precedence, as have Privy Councillors, but it is important that this is not abused. Back-benchers who wish to speak may notify the Speaker in advance of the debate but the choice by the Speaker remains real, and Government control over its own supporters is limited.

THE USUAL CHANNELS

By putting up candidates for membership for the House of Commons, with the intention that those who are successful will take their seats and attend the House, a political party implicitly accepts the parliamentary system of government.[6]

Supplementing the necessary measure of agreement between the parties

---

[4] Report of the Committee on Remuneration of Ministers and Members of Parliament, 1964 (Cmnd. 2516) para. 78.

[5] H.C.Deb., Vol. 92 col. 1088, 1092–3.

[6] Perhaps the obstructive tactics of the Irish Members in 1880s (which led to the adoption of the closure and other restrictive procedures) were an attempt to prevent the parliamentary system from working.

on how business shall be conducted, day-to-day contact is needed. The programme for the next week is announced by the Leader of the House each Thursday but is discussed with Opposition spokesmen before its announcement. Amongst other matters on which agreement is normally come to, after discussion between Government and Opposition, are the length of debate on a motion, whether a bill is to be debated in committee on the floor of the House or in standing committee, when Government motions are to be moved to approve statutory instruments. A particularly important area of agreement relates to the timetabling of bills as they progress through the House, especially in standing committee when, more often than not, the two sides agree on the number of sittings that will be needed.[7] Only if agreement cannot be reached, or breaks down, will the Government have to resort to other means (such as additional sittings or the guillotine) to make progress. If late night sittings are in prospect, this will also be a matter for discussion, sometimes affected by the desire to debate certain matters earlier so as to catch the morning newspapers. Agreement will also be come to on how long the respective last speakers (the "winders-up") in an important debate will need; and the Speaker will be informed.

Important and sometimes controversial discussions take place on how many chairs of select committees shall be held by the Opposition and, particularly, which chairs. Some proposals—for example to send a bill to a second reading committee or to the Scottish Grand Committee or for a statutory instrument to be debated in a standing committee—can be blocked by the Opposition and so need their positive agreement.

All this does not mean that what takes place on the floor of the House or in committee is ritualised and wholly predictable. The plans may be interrupted and set aside by some unexpected event in the House or in the world outside. Back-benchers on either side of the House may rebel against the arrangements agreed by their leaders and quite frequently do.[8] Chief Whips on both sides of the House have a common interest in placating backbenchers and may work together to this end.

The principal actors in the discussions that take place between the two sides in the House are the Leader of the House and the shadow Leader, and the Government Chief Whip and the Opposition Chief Whip. These are "the usual channels." The Government Chief Whip, together with the Leader of the House, is responsible for seeing that the Government's timetable runs smoothly at all levels: sessionally, weekly and daily. It requires good judgment and careful execution to ensure that Government bills make their way through the Commons and the Lords to emerge as Acts of Parliament in accordance with the Government's timetable.

The Government Chief Whip sits on many important governmental committees and attends Cabinet meetings though he is not a member. His office is at No. 12 Downing Street and he sees the Prime Minister more regularly than does any other Minister. His most crucial role is to deliver the Government's vote in the division lobbies and if he tells the Prime Minister that he cannot guarantee sufficient back-bench support, no one can contradict him.

---

[7] "Most bills go through the House with an overt or tacit agreement as to their broad time schedules" as Mr. Biffen, Leader of the House, has said: H.C.Deb., Vol. 73, col. 77 (February 11, 1985).

[8] Governments sometimes closure debate on amendments moved by their own backbenchers, e.g. on Water (Fluoridation) Bill 1984–85: H.C.Deb., vol. 74, col. 879–932 (March 5, 1985).

On a day-to-day basis, there has to be a considerable flow of information between the parties through the medium of the Whips' offices. The nature of parliamentary business is such that only seldom is anything to be gained by one side keeping its intentions secret from the other side. It is in the interests of neither side to surprise the other. The vast majority of divisions are at agreed and predictable times not least because back-benchers prefer this to be so. Only on rare occasions is a snap vote taken and this is commonly the work of back-benchers. The Government and Opposition Chief Whips meet when some matter is in dispute which intermediaries have failed to resolve; as do the Leader and the shadow Leader.

There is one principal intermediary: the private secretary to the Government Chief Whip. He is a permanent civil servant who holds this same office as Government Chief Whips of the same or different parties come and go.[9] His accountability is to the Government Chief Whip and to the Leader of the House and he is the Government's chief means of communication with the Opposition on parliamentary business. He liaises closely with the Clerk's Department and advises the Government Chief Whip on the many kinds of tactical and other decisions which the Chief Whip must take. At the same time his role is to seek to ensure that the relationship between the two sides is clear and, so far as possible, harmonious. So while his primary duties, like those of any other civil servant, are to his Ministers, it is also his function to convey to those Ministers the reactions of the shadow ministers and to do what he can to promote agreement. R. H. S. Crossman wrote of the present private secretary's predecessor:

> "Freddie Warren is still in control of the parliamentary timetable. The more I see of him the more astonishing I find the influence he exerts. He really is the bridge between the Opposition and the Government. It's as though there had been one staff sergeant-major running the British and the German staffs in World War I and it's this which really keeps the House of Commons running and enables us to have so few misunderstandings between the two Chief Whips on either side."[10]

If the two sides do not agree, this is likely to surface in the House with danger of disruption to the Government's business. As we have already noticed, arguments between the two sides on the conduct of parliamentary affairs are conducted against this background of the pressure of time. Also, ill-will between the parties may well lead to further difficulties in the near future. Occasionally co-operation between the parliamentary parties breaks down and the "usual channels" are closed for a time. Business is then delayed, pairing ceases, votes are called on trivial matters and everyone's personal convenience suffers. Normal relations are soon resumed. For different reasons, therefore, it suits both sides to come to agreements and there is sufficient strength on both sides for genuine compromises to be reached.

CURTAILMENT OF DEBATE

From time to time agreement cannot be reached on the timing of business, and then various procedures may be employed for the curtailment of debate. The procedures for applying the closure to debate and for laying down a

---

[9] Only three people have held the post since it was created in 1919.
[10] Richard Crossman: *The Diaries of a Cabinet Minister* vol. 2, (1976) p. 625.

timetable (or guillotine), in accordance with which a bill is to be debated, have been described in pages 222–227.

The Closure

The Closure was for many years a controversial weapon in the Government's armoury for controlling business, and its imposition was often opposed. Today it is often claimed formally, to ensure the conclusion of a debate at the times agreed by the parties, and is then agreed without division, but its use to restrict debate without such agreement is fairly rare in respect of Government business (it is more common on private Members' bills see Chapter 9, pages 392–393). The number of closure motions in the House or committee of the whole House on which a division had been called in recent years is shown in the following Table (with some earlier years for comparison).

Divisions on Closure Motions

Session	Government Business		Opposition Business	Private Members' Business	Private Business
	Committee or Report stage of Bills	Other Government Business			
1947–48	11	5	–	–	–
1961–62	11	3	–	–	–
1971–72	7	2	–	1	1
1983–84(a)	–	2	1	3	2
1984–85	6	1	–	2	3
1985–86	–	–	–	3	10
1986–87(b)	–	–	–	–	2
1987–88(a)	3	2	–	4	11

(a) Unusually long session
(b) Unusually short session

These figures indicate that the imposed closure, without agreement, is nowadays rarely used in respect of Government business, even to prevent obstruction or undue delay of bills in committee or at the report stage. Governments tend to prefer to proceed by informal agreement and, if that fails, to use the guillotine to timetable debate on amendments to bills rather than claiming a closure at the end of each debate. The same is true in standing committees.

It would be wrong to conclude, however, that the closure has ceased to be important as an instrument for control of business. In many cases agreements can be reached only because the Opposition knows that in the absence of a voluntary time limit to a debate, the Government could impose a limit by claiming a closure and winning the vote with the required number in the majority. This applies to many debates on amendments in committee or on report, but in particular the almost automatic conclusion of debates on Government motions and on second readings of Government bills at 10 o'clock is secured only by the possibility of the closure, even if it is not actually used. If the closure procedures did not exist, or were not generally acceptable, such automatic termination of debate would be far less common, and many second readings and other debates would have to be adjourned and resumed again another day simply because one or two

Members still wished to speak or because the Opposition did not wish to facilitate that business. The closure thus remains an instrument of great potential importance even if less frequently applied.

Guillotines

The guillotine is normally used when the Government finds that progress on a major piece of its legislation is being frustrated by prolonged debate at the committee stage.[11] This will normally be the result of large numbers of amendments being tabled, several Opposition Members speaking to each amendment, and very lengthy speeches on each amendment or group of amendments. Even the regular application of the closure would not succeed in achieving much progress; and many meetings of the committee, often extending late into the night, might prove necessary before even the first few clauses of the bill were agreed. It is at this point that Governments (of all political complexions) introduce the guillotine.[12]

In the past, guillotine debates (which until 1967 were debated for a whole day) were hotly contested occasions when feelings ran high, on the one hand about the wickedness of curtailing debate in this way and stifling legitimate criticism of the bill and, on the other, about the scandalous waste of time, caused by those who were obstructing the proper progress of legislation and frustrating the will of the House. Nowadays less is made of these occasions. It is difficult for either side to make a great case against or for guillotines when each side in its turn in the past has itself imposed or opposed them. Debate today tends to relate to the damaging nature or importance of the bill (justifying lengthy debate, say the Opposition; justifying its speedy progress, say the Government) with relevant details of the delaying tactics employed in committee which are said to confirm the need for the guillotine.

In practice the details of the guillotine—although not of course the overall time limits—are largely as required by the Opposition. The Government, having ensured that the bill will be out of committee by a certain date, is happy to leave it to the Opposition to concentrate its fire, in the limited time available, on those clauses which it considers require most attention. This often means that the more politically controversial clauses are debated at length before the guillotine is imposed, or may be considered briefly before the knives fall at the specified sittings, but other clauses, often containing matters of administrative importance to many people affected by the bill, may not be debated at all. Careful selection by the Opposition of those clauses, new clauses and amendments which should be debated before the knives fall also sometimes has the effect that matters which back-benchers, especially Government back-benchers, wish to debate may be squeezed out and remain undebated (even if selected by the Chair) under the guillotine; this is especially true at report stage when the timetable may be very tight.[13]

The use of guillotine motions has been fairly consistently restrained since 1945. Governments are not anxious to make extensive use of timetabling

---

[11] This will normally be obstruction by the Opposition, but on occasions delay may be caused by some of the Government's back-benchers, *e.g.* on the Northern Ireland Bill 1981–82 (see evidence given by the Leader of the House to the Procedure Committee: H.C. 49–II of 1984–85, Q. 131). And see debate on Firearms (Amendment) Bill 1987–88: H.C.Deb., Vol. 134, cols. 386–486 (May 25, 1988).

[12] For fuller discussion see Second Report of Select Committee on Procedure H.C. 49–I of 1984–85 and H.C. 49–II esp. pp. 3–9, 12–14, 31–3, 73–6.

[13] See, *e.g.* H.C.Deb., Vol. 129, col. 205 (March 22, 1988).

procedures and have confined their use of this powerful instrument for drastically curtailing debate to those bills whose passage, in one session, appeared impossible without the use of the guillotine. Other bills have had lengthy discussion in standing committees, but their ultimate passage was not threatened and the guillotine was withheld.[14] The following Table shows all guillotined bills from 1974–75 to 1987–88.

Use of Guillotine 1974–75 to 1987–88

Session	Bill	Bills guillotined in standing committee		Bills guillotined in committee of whole House		Time allotted for report & 3rd R	Number of hours allotted for Lords' Amendments (incl. debate on supplementary orders)
		Hours in cttee before guillotine	Hours in cttee after guillotine	Hours in cttee before guillotine	Hours in cttee after guillotine		
1974–75	Finance	–	–	–	–	4 days until midnight	
	Industry	75	31	–	–	2 days until 11 pm	1 day until midnight
	Petroleum & Submarine Pipelines	60	22	–	–	1 day until 11 pm; ½ day until 7 pm	
1975–76	Aircraft & Shipbuilding Industries	–	–	–	–	3 days until 11 pm	6 hours
	Health Services	42	32	–	–	1 day until 11 pm	6 hours
	Dock Work Regulation	–	–	–	–	1 day until 11 pm	6 hours
	Rent (Agriculture)	–	–	–	–	1 day until midnight	6 hours
	Education	–	–	–	–	1 day until midnight	6 hours
[1976–77	Scotland & Wales (*negatived*)	–	–	91]	–	–	
1977–78	Scotland	–	–	–	101	2 days until 11 pm	3 days until midnight
	Wales	–	–	–	65	2 days until 11 pm	2 days until midnight
	European Assembly Elections	–	–	22	16	1 day until midnight	
1979–80	Education (No. 2)	82	21	–	–	2 days until midnight	4 hours
	Social Security	60	32	–	–	2 days until midnight	3 hours
	Housing	110	34	–	–	2 days until midnight & ½ day until 7 pm	1 day until midnight

[14] See, for example, the Police and Criminal Evidence Bill 1983–84, which took 59 sittings in standing committee, but was never guillotined. In the same session the passage of the Telecommunications Bill was considered impossible without a guillotine, imposed after 15 sittings of the committee. The controversial and large Electricity Bill 1988–89 went through the Commons without a guillotine, although a guillotine was required for the equally controversial Water Bill of that session.

Use of Guillotine 1974–75 to 1987–88—*continued*

Session	Bill	Bills guillotined in standing committee		Bills guillotined in committee of whole House		Time allotted for report & 3rd R	Number of hours allotted for Lords' Amendments (incl. debate on supplementary orders)
		Hours in cttee before guillotine	Hours in cttee after guillotine	Hours in cttee before guillotine	Hours in cttee after guillotine		
	Social Security (No. 2)	44	20	–	–	1 day until midnight	
1980–81	Transport	55	41	–	–	1 day until 1 am	1 day until 11 pm
	British Nationality	90	46	–	–	3 days until midnight	1 day until 10 pm
1981–82	Oil & Gas (Enterprise)	– 70	-- 29	–	–	1 day until midnight and ½ day until 7 pm	1 day until 10 pm
	Employment	91	19	–	–	1 day until midnight and ½ day until 7 pm	1 day until 10 pm
	Northern Ireland	–	–	61	10	1 day until midnight	
1982–83	Transport	80	16	–	–	1 day until 1 am	
	Telecommunications	110	39	–	–	1 day until midnight & 1day until 1 am	
	Housing and Building Control	90	18	–	–	1 day until 1 am	
1983–84	Telecommunications	80	26	–	–	1 day until midnight & 1 day until 10 pm	
	Rates	80	29	–	–	1 day until midnight & 1 day until 10 pm	
	Rating & Valuation (Amendment) (Scotland)	82	18	–	–	1 day until midnight	
1984–85	Local Government	86	59	–	–	1 day until midnight & 1 day until 10 pm	1 day until midnight
	Transport	94	53	–	–	1 day until midnight & 1 day until 10 pm	1 day until 10 pm
1985–86	Gas	75	39	–	–	1 day until midnight & ½ until 7 pm	2 hours
	Social Security	100	41	–	–	1 day until midnight and 1 day until 10 pm	4 hours

Use of Guillotine 1974–75 to 1987–88—*continued*

Session	Bill	Bills guillotined in standing committee		Bills guillotined in committee of whole House		Time allotted for report & 3rd R	Number of hours allotted for Lords' Amendments (incl. debate on supplementary orders)
		Hours in cttee before guillotine	*Hours in cttee after guillotine*	*Hours in cttee before guillotine*	*Hours in cttee after guillotine*		
	European Communities (Amendment)	–	–	18	4	1 hour	
1986–87	Abolition of Domestic Rates Etc. (Scotland)	76	18	–	–	1 day until midnight & 1 day until 10 pm	3 hours
	Local Government Finance	–	–	15	6	1 day until midnight	2 hours
1987–88	Education Reform	88	78	–	–	4 days until 10 pm	1 day until midnight; 1 day until 10 pm
	Local Government Finance	72	64	–	–	5 days until 10 pm	1 day until midnight
	Social Security	–	–	–	–	–	6 hours
	Firearms (Amendment)	–	–	–	–	5 hours	
	Housing	–	–	–	–	–	4 hours
	School Boards (Scotland)	–	–	–	–	–	4 hours

The figures indicate that since 1974–75, Governments have been reluctant to move for an allocation of time order until a standing committee has sat for 70 to 80 hours, whereas less than 30 hours was common during the period 1946–47 to 1960–61. The Housing Bill 1979–80, the Telecommunications Bill 1982–83, and the Social Security Bill 1985–86 were all in standing committee for 100 hours or more before guillotines were moved.

The largest number of bills guillotined during a session in this period was six (in 1987–88). In February 1977, the guillotine motion on the Scotland and Wales Bill 1976–77 was defeated and the bill was subsequently withdrawn.[15] Such a defeat is, given the Government's majority, extremely unusual. But the Government must be careful not to take too great advantage of the strength of its position. If it seeks to impose too stringent a timetable, especially on a bill of general constitutional significance, the House may show its resentment. This occurred on the European Communities (Amendment) Bill 1985–86 which was to incorporate into United Kingdom law the Single European Act signed by representatives of all members of the European Community. The Opposition objected to the terms of a timetable motion and the Leader of the House had to accept an amendment allowing more time for debate.[16] On another occasion, following a major change of policy when the Government decided to abolish the Inner London Education Authority (which entailed tabling 25 new clauses to replace nine existing clauses) the Government moved a supplementary guillotine for the

---

[15] H.C.Deb., Vol. 926, col. 1234–367 (February 22, 1977).
[16] H.C.Deb., Vol. 100, col. 705–9, 931–82 (June 30, and July 1, 1986).

Education Reform Bill in 1988 allowing two additional days in standing committee and an extra day for the report stage.[17]

In March 1984 the Select Committee on Procedure was required to pay particular regard to the allocation of time in standing committees. The committee reported a year later.[18] Its main concern was that bills in standing committees should be properly considered and this, it reported, was not likely to be achieved if matters were debated very late at night or all through the night and the following morning. This led it specifically to consider the time-tabling (or guillotine) of bills.

One proposal frequently discussed is that all Government bills, or the more controversial, should be timetabled before consideration in committee began or soon thereafter. This would mean that the Government would know from an early stage the date by which debates in committee would be concluded. The principal objection to this reform is that it would deprive the Opposition of one of its strongest weapons, that of delay. It is argued that, in the absence of a timetable, the Opposition does bring pressure to bear on the Government by delaying progress and so force the Government to make concessions or, at least, to give undertakings to re-consider particular provisions in the bill. No doubt this delaying power has been advantageous to Opposition members of standing committees, not least because where undertakings are given, the Speaker will allow debate at the report stage of the bill if the Opposition is dissatisfied with any concession made. So the particular matter is ensured of additional publicity. On the other hand, the number of occasions when it can be shown that the Opposition has gained a clear and substantial concession by means of delay alone is few. Perhaps it can be said only that where other pressures exist, whether from Government back-benchers or outside interests or public opinion, delay is a useful additional weapon. But the constitutional point remains, as expressed by Sir Edward du Cann: "if the Executive wishes to curtail discussion it should seek deliberate authority for doing so."[19]

The Procedure Committee recommended:
(a) That there should be a Legislative Business Committee (LBC), nominated at the beginning of each Parliament by the Committee of Selection, of 13 senior Members of the House, having a Government majority but acting independently in the interests of back-benchers;
(b) If the LBC considered that a Government bill was likely to require more than 25 hours in standing committee, it would recommend that the bill should be reported after a stated maximum number of hours in committee;
(c) A business sub-committee drawn from the membership of the standing committee would determine the details of the allocation of time.

When the report of the Procedure Committee came before the House, the motions put by the Leader of the House (Mr. Biffen) did not include a motion proposing the adoption of this recommendation. An amendment moved by the Conservative chairman of the Procedure Committee and supported by all but one of the other members of the committee, proposing the adoption of the committee's recommendation, was defeated by 231 votes to 166.[20] The majority—on a one-line Whip—included a very large

---

[17] H.C.Deb., Vol. 127, col. 1083–97 (February 17, 1988).
[18] H.C. 49–I of 1984–85.
[19] H.C. 49–II of 1984–85 App. 6.
[20] H.C.Deb., Vol. 92, col. 1083–1130 (February 27, 1986).

number of Ministers and Parliamentary Private Secretaries and only 20 Government back-benchers. Those supporting the amendment claimed that the interests of back-benchers were their first concern.

The Procedure Committee then re-considered its position and put forward new proposals,[21] believing that the real objection to its original recommendations was that the Whips on both sides of the House feared they would lose control of the time of the House. It repeated an original recommendation that business in standing committee should end at 10 p.m. The new proposals would have empowered a business sub-committee, nominated by the Committee of Selection and drawn from members of the standing committee, to meet from time to time and to make recommendations to the standing committee about progress. But the Government took no action on these proposals.[22]

The Government does, on occasion, appear to respond to the main concern expressed by the Procedure Committee that important parts of guillotined bills should not go through the Commons without proper consideration. Two major bills were guillotined in committee in 1987–88, the Education Reform Bill and the Local Government Finance Bill. In the latter case at least the guillotine was imposed rather earlier than usual, but in both cases, as the Table above shows, considerably more time than usual was allowed, both in standing committee and on report, for the further consideration of these bills. These relatively generous guillotines did ensure that few clauses of these important bills went undebated in the House of Commons.

---

[21] H.C. 324 of 1985–86.
[22] See the evidence of the Leader of the House in the Minutes of Evidence: H.C. 324 of 1985–86, Q. 1.

CHAPTER 8

GOVERNMENT INITIATIVES

Government is essentially an active, decision-making and executive function. The ultimate authority of a Government in the United Kingdom to
govern—its legitimacy—derives from its election. It then exercises the
powers vested in Ministers and departments by statute or the royal prerogative. To acquire new powers the Government must prepare new statutes in
the form of bills which it then presents to Parliament for approval. Without
that approval the Government cannot acquire new powers.

In addition, the Government submits itself to the scrutiny of Parliament
by initiating debate on certain policy matters whether or not it already has
the statutory powers to effect those policies. It is an accepted convention
that the more important policy issues are put to Parliament there to be
debated. Exceptionally, Governments sometimes seek to conceal their
intentions in order to minimise parliamentary and other criticism. The
obvious danger in such a course is that it is likely to be uncovered at some
time. Members of Parliament, on both sides of the House of Commons, are
not easily persuaded that certain matters are properly withheld from their
scrutiny.

At the time of a general election, the broad policy intentions of the parties
are set out, in more detail or less, in their election manifestos. Some parts of
each manifesto will clearly commit the party to action, generally involving
new legislation, in certain areas of public administration. The idea of a
mandate operates at least to this extent, that what is firmly promised in the
manifesto the electorate expects to be carried out. The converse is not true.
For a variety of reasons, including the unpredictability of events, Governments will choose or be forced to do certain things which were not included
in the manifesto. Where promises made in the manifesto are not fulfilled,
the Government must then, successfully or not, seek to justify its apparent
breach of faith.

The principal items in the Government's legislative programme for the
coming session are outlined in the Queen's Speech at the opening of Parliament. Other broader statements of intended policy are also made in the
Speech.

The first part of the Queen's Speech deals with foreign affairs and
defence. On June 25, 1987 the Speech at the opening of the first session of
the new Parliament promised that her Government would stand fully by its
obligations to the NATO Alliance, sustain Britain's contribution to Western
defence by modernising the independent nuclear deterrent through the
introduction of the Trident submarine programme, strive for balanced and
verifiable measures of arms control and strongly support the United States'
proposals for the elimination of intermediate range nuclear missiles, strive
for a worldwide ban on chemical weapons, play a leading role in the
development of the European Community, work for the reform of the
common agricultural policy and press for strict controls on Community
spending, and sustain the fight against international terrorism and traffick-
ing in drugs. The people of the Falkland Islands and Hong Kong had special
mention. So did the United Nations and the Commonwealth, the Middle
East and Southern Africa.

After a single sentence, addressed only to the Commons, stating that estimates for public expenditure would be laid before them, the Speech dealt with economic and domestic policy. In 1987, the Speech said that the Government would maintain firm control of public expenditure, consult the Manpower Services Commission with a view to providing a comprehensive employment service, guarantee places on the youth training scheme, and raise educational standards and extend parental choice. Legislation would be introduced to provide for a national curriculum for schools, delegation of school budgets and greater autonomy for schools, reform the structure of education in inner London and give greater independence to polytechnics and colleges. Measures would be introduced to effect major reform of housing legislation. Other items included a bill to abolish domestic rates, to privatise water and sewage functions, to tackle the problems of crime, to reinforce immigration controls, to make licensing hours more flexible, to improve the rights of trade unionists, to reform the law of copyright and intellectual property, to maintain the health and social services, to support farming, to improve rented housing in Scotland, to seek devolution in Northern Ireland, to assist the merchant shipping industry and to improve the arrangements for legal aid.[1]

Government policy, which may or may not require legislation, emerges from debate within the Government party and in discussions between Ministers, civil servants and outside advisers. The number of people who seek to influence Government policy is very large. All the principal interest groups—business people, trade unionists, members of commercial and professional bodies, welfare organisations, consumer and amenity groups—try to get the Government interested in their particular problems. Within Government circles, both inside and outside Parliament, aspects of policy will have been discussed sometimes for many years. The general lines of policy can be seen only in retrospect, not least because it is pressure of day to day events, requiring Government decisions, that frequently determines policy rather than general considerations thought out in advance. Nevertheless, Governments can be seen to have followed certain patterns of policy making. From 1979 to 1988, for example, statutes concerned with the powers of trade unions, with spending by local authorities, with privatisation of public corporations, with education, have reflected the political philosophy of the Conservative party, despite some internal inconsistencies.

While consultations with interest groups take place continuously when Government policy is being determined, this must not be understood to indicate that government is primarily a matter of reacting to such interests. On the contrary, Government policy is formed primarily within Cabinet, committees of Government, and Government departments. Policy-making is multi-layered. At the highest levels it flows from party political commitments, expressed in manifestos, white and green papers and in public statements of other kinds. At lower levels there are always, within departments, many changes being sought, some of departmental policy, others of improvements in administration, not all of which are controversial between Government and Opposition. These may arise because of particular investigation by departments or inter-departmental committees into aspects of policy or administration. How far they are controversial is reflected in the time spent in committees and these are indicated below. It surprises those

---

[1] H.C.Deb. Vol. 118, cols. 38–40.

who see only the proceedings in Parliament which attract the most publicity how much legislation is passed with little argument.

The amount of legislation that can be passed in a parliamentary session is limited by the time available, within the traditions of debate. There are always more proposals coming from departments than there is time for their promotion. The settling of the legislative programme of Government bills for a session is a matter of argument within a Cabinet committee established for this purpose. Many proposals do not find a place in the programme, some being postponed from session to session. Decisions are taken of the order in which different Government bills are to be introduced into Parliament. The most important and the most controversial will be introduced early in the session into the House of Commons. Others will follow later and many bills are first introduced into the House of Lords. Of the 199 Government bills which became acts of Parliament during the Parliament of 1983–87, 85 were first introduced into the House of Lords.

GOVERNMENT BUSINESS

There are four main types of Government business: proceedings on Government bills; Government motions; motions to approve statutory instruments requiring affirmative resolutions; and ministerial statements. Time spent on the floor of the House on these matters during the last Parliament was as follows:

Time spent on Government Business
Hours and minutes

	1983–84	1984–85	1985–86	1986–87	Total
1. Government bills[2]	547:58	435:42	414:27	231:38	1629:45
2. Government motions					
(a) General	76:53	87:44	74:07	28:52	267:36
(b) Adjournment	144:24	81:46	95:41	60:30	382:21
(c) Money resolutions	1:44	3:52	1:37	0:12	7:25
(d) Ways & Means resolutions	22:35	22:27	21:04	24:36	90:42
3. Affirmative resolutions	164:06	127:54	82:29	51:13	425:42
4. Ministerial statements on policy	76:34	67:29	70:51	35:36	250:31

With the general elections of 1983 and 1987 being held in June, the 1983–84 session was some five months longer and the 1986–87 session some five months shorter than the usual 12 months. Over the whole Parliament, Government bills took 53.5 per cent. of the time spent on the main types of Government business listed in the Table, the percentages in each session varying by no more than 1.5 per cent. of the average. Government motions took 24.4 per cent. of that time overall, affirmative resolutions 13.9 per cent. and ministerial statements 8.2 per cent., the variations from session to session being more marked, as the figures for the "normal" length sessions of 1984–85 and 1985–86 show.

Government Bills

Every Government inherits a large number of legal powers conferred in or under Acts of Parliament. As we shall see, in each session, Ministers bring to the House of Commons some 50 or 60 bills comprising the Government's legislative programme. These bills fall into three broad groups:

---

[2] Excluding allocation of time orders and committal motions.

First, there are about 10 major policy bills. They will be debated on the floor of the House on second reading for six hours or so (or, exceptionally, when two days are allotted for this purpose, for some 12 hours). A few of these bills will be committed to a committee of the whole House including some clauses from the Finance Bill. In the 1983–87 Parliament, they also included three Local Government Bills (1983–84, 1984–85 and 1986–87), and bills on parliamentary representation (in 1984–85), the interception of communications (1984–85) and teachers' pay and conditions of services (1986–87). But most will be sent to standing committees where they will often be considered for 50 hours and more. Most will then be further debated on the floor of the House on report, third reading, and consideration of Lords' Amendments.

The second group consists of some 20 other policy bills some of which may take rather less parliamentary time. They will usually have the full second reading debate of six hours or so, and then be sent to standing committees there to be debated for 30 hours or more. Again they will almost invariably be further debated on report, and third reading (and perhaps some consideration of Lords' amendments).

The third group consists of a further 20 or so bills. About a quarter of these have their second reading off the floor of the House. Most pass quickly through the House, some by way of committee of the whole House, and others after a few hours in standing committee, followed by a short report stage and third reading, or passage "on the nod."

We may now look at this in more detail:

Time spent on Government Bills on the Floor of the House of Commons

Hours and minutes

	Second reading	Committee of whole House	Report	Third reading	Lords' Amendments	Total
1983–84	173:37	90:34	175:49	40:20	67:38	547:58
1984–85	162:14	81:29	138:59	26:36	26:24	435:42
1985–86	148:18	34:12	164:19	26:29	41:09	414:27
1986–87	92:36	62:36	59:30	8:27	8:29	231:38

Any stage of a bill may be passed "on the nod" without debate and, as we shall see, some bills are passed without any debate on the floor of the House at any stage. Frequently debates last for a few minutes only.

Government Bills debated on the Floor of the House of Commons and in Standing Committee

Number of bills

	No. read a first time	2R	CWH	Standing Cttee	Report	3R	Lords' Amdts.	No. passed
1983–84	60	47	16	31	24	30	16	60
1984–85	56	37	15	29	28	28	14	54
1985–86	51	38	6	30	26	30	16	49
1986–87	39	29	12	22	19	24	8	36
Total	206	151	49	112	97	112	54	199

The discrepancy between the number of bills introduced and those debated on second reading on the floor of the House is explained by showing how those not so debated were dealt with:

	2R Cttee	Consoli-dated Fund bills	Consoli-dation bills	Scottish Grand Cttee	Special Procedure Act bills	Suspended from previous session	Total
1983–84	6	3	2	2	–	–	13
1984–85	4	4	7	4	–	–	19
1985–86	8	3	1	–	1	–	13
1986–87	5	3	–	1	–	1	10
Total	23	13	10	7	1	1	55

These last six categories of statutes call for further explanation.

2R Cttee. Some uncontentious small bills are debated in second reading committees off the floor of the House under Standing Order No. 90. The debates average some 30 minutes, a few going through virtually "on the nod." All but four of these 23 bills were first introduced into the House of Lords.

Consolidated Fund Bills are, in accordance with Standing Order No. 54, not debated.

Consolidation bills are usually introduced into the House of Lords and sent forthwith to a joint committee of both Houses. They may be briefly debated on second reading in the Commons. During the 1983–87 Parliament, there were 30 such Bills of which 20 were so debated. The power to amend these Bills is restricted and there rarely is any debate in committee or on report.

Scottish Grand Committee: uncontentious bills relating exclusively to Scotland may be debated in this committee off the floor of the House.

Special Procedure Act: under the Statutory Orders (Special Procedure) Act 1945, bills confirming such orders are not normally read a second time.

Suspended bills are those which, being hybrid bills, had been read a second time in the previous session and held over to the following session.[3]

Bills not amended in committee of the whole House are not considered on report. Bills reported from standing committees, whether amended or not, are debated on report only if there are further amendments. Frequently there is no debate on third reading; and the House of Lords often proposes no amendments.

The great variations in the time spent on the floor of the House in debating Government bills at all stages is shown in the following Table, analysing the two sessions of normal length in the last Parliament.

---

[3] The bill under this head in the last Table was the Channel Tunnel Bill. In 1985–86 it was committed to a select committee; in 1986–87, it was again committed to a select committee and then to a standing committee; it was enacted in 1988.

Time spent on Government Bills on the Floor of the House of Commons
Number of bills

Time	1984–85	1985–86	Total
Nil	15	6	21
1 minute–1 hour	8	12	20
1–5 hours	5	7	12
5–13 hours	20	11	31
13–20 hours	2	9	11
Over 20 hours	6	6	12
Total	56	51	107

Of the 21 bills that were not debated at all, seven were Consolidated Fund Bills, and eight were consolidation bills.[4] The others were, in 1984–85, the Child Abduction and Custody Bill enabling the United Kingdom to ratify a Hague Convention and a European Convention; the Enduring Powers of Attorney Bill, a product of the Law Commission; the Industrial Development Bill to improve the operational efficiency of the English Industrial Estates Commission; and the Insurance (Fees) Bill which provided for the payment of fees by insurance companies; and, in 1985–86, the Outer Space Bill arising from a series of United Nations conventions; and the Public Trustee and Administration of Funds Bill to enable the administration of certain private assets within the Lord Chancellor's jurisdiction to be carried out more efficiently. These six bills had all been debated in second reading committees.

Of the 20 bills that were debated for less than one hour, eight were consolidation bills. The other 12 were, in 1984–85, the Brunei and Maldives Bill making minor amendments to United Kingdom enactments to take account of the recently acquired membership of the Commonwealth of those states; the Friendly Societies Bill to protect the legal position of some contractors; the Further Education Bill to enable institutions in the local authority sector to engage in commercial activities arising out of their educational and research functions; the Mineral Workings Bill to wind up the ironstone restoration fund and to enable action to be taken to avoid subsidence. None of these four bills had been debated in second reading committees.

In 1985–86, the bills were the Australia Bill to remove the remaining constitutional links existing between the United Kingdom and the Australian states; the British Council and Commonwealth Institute Superannuation Bill to enable superannuation to be paid to employees; the Commonwealth Development Corporation Bill to extend the powers of the corporation to borrow and to lend overseas; the Crown Agents (Amendment) Bill to extend the period during which the Foreign Secretary might determine the rate of interest payable by Crown Agents; the Education (No. 2) Bill to empower the Secretary of State to pay grants to the Fellowship of Engineering and the Further Education Unit; the Family Law Bill to give effect to three separate Law Commission reports; the Land Registration Bill to give effect to a Law Commission report; the Patents, Designs and

---

[4] Consolidation bills add greatly to the statute book and substantially to the statistics. For a list of 271 consolidation (including statute law revision) bills between 1955 and 1984 see H.C.Deb., Vol. 75, cols. 287–291 (March 15, 1985).

Marks Bill to facilitate the computerisation of Patent Officers' register. Of these eight bills, six had been debated in second reading committees. Excluding the seven Consolidated Fund Bills and the 16 consolidation bills, we are left with 18 bills during these two sessions not debated or debated for less than one hour. Of these, 12 were first introduced into the House of Lords and debated there.

The examination of Government bills in the House of Commons

Procedural aspects of this examination have been considered on pages 227-240. We have already emphasised how varied in importance are bills presented to Parliament and how this is reflected in the time spent per bill on their examination. We have seen that during the two sessions of usual length in the 1983–87 Parliament, 41 out of 107 Government bills (38.3 per cent.) were either not debated on the floor of the House or were debated for less than one hour. The Tables on pages 310–311 show that the average time spent on the floor of the House during that Parliament on Government bills was 9.1 hours in 1983–84, 7.8 hours in 1984–85, 8.1 hours in 1985–86, and 6.0 hours in 1986–87.

Second reading

As we have noted (page 230) a second reading debate is concerned with the broad principle of the bill. The Opposition may oppose it wholly and divide the House at the end of the debate. Or it may accept it in general while stating their intention to seek to amend it in particular. Or it may welcome it with more or less enthusiasm. As an exercise in parliamentary scrutiny, second reading debates achieve little. The published bill has already told the story and the Minister presenting it need do no more than emphasise its main characteristics. Opposition spokesmen will indicate the broad lines of their response and make public (at least in Hansard) their relative concern. Government back-benchers may also draw attention to particular provisions about which they or their constituents or some interest group may have reservations. The result of the division, if there is one, will be in favour of the bill unless the Government has no overall majority in the House and all its opponents (possibly with some help from Government dissidents) combine against the bill.

Having said all this, it has to be remembered that occasionally a Government may be so misguided as to bring before the House a measure which a large number of its supporters in the House so dislike for, perhaps, a variety of reasons, that they will rebel against party discipline, defy the Whips and their own front bench and refuse to give the bill a second reading. This was what famously occurred on April 14, 1986 when the Shops Bill was negatived (see pages 327–328). So also, rebellions (whether indicated by voting against the Whip or abstaining) which significantly reduce the size of the Government's majority warn Ministers that their proposals are not acceptable to all their supporters and that more serious difficulties may lie ahead. Such back-bench dissent can be expressed in many ways but the registering of adverse votes is one of the strongest, because the most public, manifestation. Divisions on the second reading of Government bills are also, though less significantly, occasions when Opposition back-benchers may also show dissent from the policy of their leaders.

Committee stage

As the Table on page 311 shows, 112 Government bills (54 per cent.) were committed to standing committees and 49 bills were actually debated in committees of the whole House during the 1983–87 Parliament (others went through on the nod).

Bills taken in committee of the whole House typically fall into four categories. The first contains bills of constitutional importance such as Representation of the People Bill 1984–85 and the European Communities (Amendment) Bill 1985–86. The second category includes those of major political importance, on which many Members wish to speak, such as the Local Government (Interim Provisions) Bill 1983–84, the Local Government Bill 1984–85, the Teachers' Pay and Conditions Bill 1986–87, the Local Government Finance Bill 1986–87 and those clauses of the Finance Bill so committed. The third category contains bills requiring little more than formal approval such as consolidation bills; it would be a waste of Members' time to nominate a standing committee for such bills. The fourth category are bills which the Government wishes to pass quickly such as the Northern Ireland (Loans) Bill, the Education (Amendment) Bill, and the British Shipbuilders (Borrowing Powers) Bill, all of 1985–86.

By taking a bill to committee of the whole House rather than (as otherwise, in almost all cases, happens automatically) to standing committee, the Government uses valuable time on the floor of the House but, on the other hand, runs little risk of defeat on any vote in committee; it also speeds up the passage of the bill.

The procedure in committee by way of proposing amendments, moved by either Government or Opposition Members, has been described (see pages 231–235). Amendments moved by the Opposition (or possibly by a Government back-bencher) will have one or more of a variety of purposes. They may be intended to cause political mischief, to embarrass the Government, to discover what are the Government's real intentions and whether they include in particular one or more specific possibilities, to placate interests outside Parliament, to make positive improvements in the bill, to set out alternative proposals, to initiate a debate on some general principle of great or small importance, to obtain assurances on how a particular clause or sub-section will or will not be used, to correct grammatical errors or to improve the drafting of the bill. If moved by the Government, the purpose of an amendment is most likely to be to improve the drafting, to make changes consequential on other amendments which have been made, to implement agreements with outside bodies, to introduce new matter or occasionally to meet a criticism made made by a Member either during the second reading debate or at an earlier part of the committee stage, or informally.

On a controversial bill where the Opposition is unlikely to succeed in making any significant amendments, the main purpose of the Opposition is to pursue its general criticism of the policies of the Government.

The business of conducting a bill through committee as the Member in charge requires a Minister to have a detailed understanding of the provisions of the bill. He must know not only the purpose of each clause and its relation to other clauses and the bill as a whole, but also why the draftsman has used certain words or phrases. Sometimes a Minister's understanding of legislative language is not complete and he is obliged to say that he is advised that the words used and not other words are necessary to achieve the purpose sought. It follows that when amendments are tabled the Minister must be carefully briefed as to their meaning, their purpose, and their effect. He must know what he can accept either with profit or at least without loss, what he can give way on and to what extent, what he must resist to the end.

For the performance of all these functions, the Minister is advised and instructed by his department. His relationship with his back-bench supporters in committee is of less importance. He wishes, of course, to carry them with him and he hopes to be able to rely on them to support him with their vote in divisions. When the bill is taken on the floor of the House, the relationship is no different from that of a Minister making a statement of general policy on behalf of the Government on any non-legislative matter. If the party machinery has worked well, Members who are interested will have argued the general issues in party groups or, if the issue is important and central to the party's policy, more generally, even perhaps at party conferences. Members may have served on select committees which were concerned with the issue. Or they may, for constituency or other reasons, be wholly familiar with it and need no help from their Minister. In the case of standing committees, as we shall see, they may have been nominated for membership of the committee because of the positive help they can give the Minister from the back-benches.

The Opposition has no back-up comparable to that of the Minister's departmental staff. The Opposition will take advice from organisations opposed to the purposes of the bill and from its party machinery. Much more than on the Government side, interested and knowledgeable Opposition Members (including members of the standing committee if the bill has been so committed) will meet regularly outside the committee to decide on their strategy and tactics. At least, this is likely to happen on the more important policy bills. On less important bills, one or two leading Opposition spokesmen may carry a large part of the whole burden.

The composition and procedure of standing committees has been described on pages 270–274. The Government will be represented by the Minister in charge of the bill, supported by his Parliamentary Private Secretary, possibly another Minister and a Whip, with other Members added. The Opposition will be represented by one or more official spokesmen on the subject of the bill, by an Opposition Whip, with others added. Back-bench membership on standing committees will be sought after on important bills but regarded as an imposed chore on bills which have little or no public appeal.

Most bills of importance go to standing committees off the floor of the House. Proceedings there may be lengthy or short as the following Table shows:

Sittings on Government Bills in Standing Committee in the House of Commons

Number of Bills[5]

No. of Sittings	1	2–10	11–20	21–30	31–40	over 40	Total bills
1983–84	9	7	6	6	2	1	31
1984–85	8	16	1	2	2	–	29
1985–86	7	11	6	3	2	1	30
1986–87	3	13	4	1	1	–	22
Total	27	47	17	12	7	2	112

The number of sittings gives only a general indication of the length of debate as only morning sittings (10.30 a.m. to 1 p.m.) are limited in duration. Many other sittings take place from 4.30 p.m. for any period until 1 p.m. the next day. In the above Table for most of those meeting on 10 occasions or fewer, the duration of each sitting was 2½ hours only. Where the number of sittings exceeded 10, the average length of each sitting was between 2½ and three hours. To this Finance Bills form an exception. Standing committees on Finance Bills usually hold about 10 sittings on Tuesday and Thursday afternoons and evenings, each of which frequently lasts for five or six hours.

Afternoon sittings were less used until some 10 years ago, but now, with increasing legislative pressure and more sustained and protracted opposition, they have become common place. The normal pattern of standing committee sittings on Bills (apart from the Finance Bill) is for committees to sit on Tuesday and Thursday mornings; if busy, to sit again on the same days at 4.30 p.m. till about 7 p.m.; if very busy to sit again from about 8 p.m. to 10 p.m.; and if really lengthy debate is being experienced (usually as a result of obstruction tactics) to sit late into, or even all through, the night. In session 1985–86 there were 375 sittings of standing committees; 109 of these were afternoon sittings, and nine continued till after midnight. The heaviest load for standing committees is in February and March. On Tuesday March 1, 1988, nine standing committees on bills met in the morning; seven of those met again at 4.30; and four met again after supper.

The immediate and direct impact of the committee stage on the contents of bills is very small: only rarely is an amendment successfully moved against the wishes of the Government and only rarely does the Government accept an amendment moved by the Opposition. Indirectly the impact is greater, Ministers in committee do agree to re-consider proposals from the Opposition (often in order to make progress) and this sometimes results in Government amendments at a later stage which more or less accept the Opposition's argument. Many undertakings to think again, or even to amend the bill, result from debate on matters raised by outside interests. But none of this is likely significantly to modify the principles of the bill.

If, however, the committee stage is viewed as a part of the process which forces the Government to explain and to account for its proposals and Ministers to subject themselves to questioning and criticism by the Opposition, positive results can be seen to be achieved. Piloting a bill through committee can also be a real test of ministerial ability and reputations can be won or lost in the process.

---

[5] H.C. 107 of 1984–85; H.C. 308 of 1985–86; H.C. 169 of 1986–87; H.C. 57 of 1987–88; for Public Bills, see H.C. 16 of 1984–85; H.C. 45 of 1985–86; H.C. 81 of 1986–87; H.C. 56 of 1987–88.

Over the years proposals have been made to provide opportunity for Members to seek to obtain information by calling witnesses as do select committees. Special standing committees with this power are now provided for under Standing Order No. 91.[6] Since 1980 when the practice was first instituted, only five bills have been sent to special standing committees. In the first session (1980–81) the Criminal Attempts Bill, the Education Bill, and the Deep Sea Mining (Temporary Provisions) Bill were so committed; in 1981–82, the Mental Health Amendment Bill and in 1983–84 the Matrimonial and Family proceedings Bill also went to special standing committees. As the procedure has been used only for a few non-contentious bills, it cannot be said to have been tested as a major reform. The Select Committee on Procedure in 1984–85 reported that virtually all the evidence they had received about the operation of special standing committees had been enthusiastic and expressed their hope that it would be possible for a wider range of bills to be committed to such committees.[7] The Leader of the House (Mr. Biffen) was "agnostic" about their value and said that some Ministers had welcomed the procedure while other Ministers had found it irksome and not particularly productive.[8]

Mr. Biffen's formulation was:

"The overriding purpose of a bill's committee stage is, I believe, to provide an opportunity for the scrutiny and elucidation of its detailed provisions. This purpose needs, however, to be achieved within a wider framework that takes account, for example, of the parliamentary time-table as a whole."[9]

This states the conflict. Members want more scrutiny and more elucidation. For Ministers the question is whether a proposed change in procedure will result in the speedier passage of the bill. More explanation may do so but it also may not. Again the Leader of the House put the alternatives starkly.

"Some critics of existing standing committee procedure argue that its failings arise inevitably from its present 'debate and party orientated' basis and that what is required is a fundamental change in the consideration of bills in the committee to an investigatory and questioning basis on the pattern of a select committee inquiry."[10]

The Leader of the House rejected this criticism and as a business manager this was to be expected. While Ministers remain in control of parliamentary time and conventions remain as they are, any move in favour of extending the scope of special standing committees is unlikely.

Report and later stages

The procedure has been discussed on pages 235–240. All that need be added here is that the debate requires the Government to respond further and announce its decisions on matters left over from the committee stage. The Government can also seek to reverse any amendments made when the bill was in committee which the Government is not willing to accept.

---

[6] See above p. 276.

[7] H.C. 49–I of 1984–85 paras. 12, 13; this hope was repeated in their report two sessions later: see H.C. 350 of 1986–87 para. 10.

[8] H.C. 49–II of 1984–85 Q. 120, 121.

[9] *Ibid.* p. 31.

[10] *Ibid.*

Occasionally, the Government decides that discretion is the better part of valour and does not press its view, so avoiding the possibility of a back-bench revolt and public displeasure. The Government will also put forward its own amendments, having had time to re-consider its earlier position, perhaps after being pressed to do so by outside interests. There will be still more Government drafting and consequential amendments. The Opposition has further opportunity to register its views on the important issues and to attack the Government. In general, problems are discussed in committee. Solutions may or may not be produced on report. The Tables on page 311 show that the average time spent on bills considered on report was between five and six hours. But, as we shall see, on major bills the time spent is often three times the average.

The procedure on third reading and Lords' Amendments has been described above (pages 237–238). The former is of little or no importance and proposals are made from time to time for its abolition. Lords' amendments are often part of the tidying-up process, or implementing earlier Government undertakings. However they sometimes result from Government defeats in the Lords and these can give rise to government embarrassment and, even, constitutional crisis.

Financial initiatives

The financial procedures of Parliament have been described above in Chapter 6 (pages 247–254), where it is emphasised that the Government initiates the proposals both for expenditure and for taxation. As the Public Accounts Committee (PAC) reported in March 1987 "Parliament's consideration of the annual estimates—the key constitutional control—remains largely a formality."[11] The examination of the taxation proposals in the Finance Bill, however, is more thorough. The PAC listed the annual cycle of five major documents which indicate the intentions of the Government and give the information on which the House of Commons can consider these initiatives.

The first document is the Financial Statement and Budget Report in which the Government sets out the Budget, the short-term economic forecast and the Medium Term Financial Strategy which provides the financial framework for economic policy for up to five years ahead. This the Chancellor of the Exchequer lays before the House as he opens his Budget in March. In this the Chancellor, as Erskine May says,

> "develops his views of the resources of the country, communicates his calculations of probable income and expenditure, and declares whether the burdens upon the people are to be increased or diminished."[12]

What those burdens are to be in the forthcoming financial year are mainly set out in the Ways and Means resolutions tabled by the Chancellor of the Exchequer at the end of his speech. These resolutions and in particular the general "amendment of the law" resolution form the basis of the general debate which follows for four days or so at the end of which the Opposition may divide the House on a few of the more controversial. The Finance Bill is then introduced. Three or four weeks later the bill has its second reading

---

[11] Para. 2 of H.C. 98 of 1986–87 on which much of what follows is based.
[12] May, p. 831.

and is committed in part to the whole House and in part to a standing committee. The committee of the whole House debates the clauses before it (chosen by the Opposition) for two or three days. The standing committee meets on a number of occasions during the next few weeks with frequent late night sittings. We have seen that in committee and on report, possible amendments are restricted by the Ways and Means resolutions and by the rule that only Ministers can propose, by such resolutions, charges which increase taxes or reduce reliefs (pages 252–253). Throughout the Government retains the initiative.

The second document in the annual cycle is the Autumn Statement, normally published in November, which sets out the Treasury's latest economic forecast and the planning totals for the next three years and provides the broad departmental allocations of expenditure which have been agreed during the public expenditure survey. This last is an exercise carried out by the Government and finalised by a Cabinet committee at which Ministers seek to obtain approval for the expenditure of their Departments for the forthcoming financial year and at which the Treasury seeks to contain them within pre-determined general limits. The Autumn Statement is reported on by the Treasury and Civil Service Committee and debated in the House of Commons.

From 1969 to 1988, the third document was the Public Expenditure White Paper, published in the winter. It provided more detailed programmes of expenditure. Its material has now been transferred in part to the Autumn Statement, and in part to separate departmental volumes containing each department's plans. These are published in March, on or shortly before Budget day. These changes[13] were in response to proposals made both by the Public Accounts Committee[14] and by the Treasury and Civil Service Committee[15] to improve financial reporting to Parliament.

Based on these papers the fourth set of documents are the Supply Estimates. They represent the Government formal request to Parliament for cash to finance the major part of central Government's expenditure for one year. The main estimates are presented to the House of Commons at the same time as the Budget (together with an explanatory Summary and Guide). Other supplementary estimates are presented during the course of the year, as extra funds are needed. Few of these estimates are nowadays debated in the House, however, as explained on pages 248–251.

The Government's initiative in bringing forward expenditure requirements is therefore less significant, in terms of providing opportunity for debate, than it was in earlier years when estimates could be debated at length. Today the real opportunity for scrutinising, influencing and, to some measure, controlling public expenditure lies in the various occasions when, on the initiative of Government, Opposition or back-benchers, policy issues are before the House or its committees: on legislation, on the Autumn Statement and the departmental reports, on Opposition motions, at Question time, on ministerial statements and before select committees. Expenditure, as Gladstone used to argue, flows from policy; to control expenditure one must control policy decisions. The estimates are largely the

---

[13] Cm. 375 published in May 1988.
[14] H.C. 98 of 1986–87; and the Government's reply: Cm. 177.
[15] H.C. 292 of 1987–88.

financial reflection of policy decisions already taken. It is understandable that little time is spent debating them.

Finally, the Appropriation Accounts complete the reporting cycle. Audited by the Comptroller and Auditor General (C and AG) and published in the autumn following the end of the financial year, they record how voted moneys have been spent and include reports by the C and AG where appropriate. They are reported on by the Public Accounts Committee (see page 442).

Time spent on Finance Bills during the 1983–87 Parliament

Hours and minutes

	Second reading	Committee of whole House	Standing Committee	Report	Third reading	Total
1983–84(a)	7:58	25:10	117:55	18:39	2:24	172:06
1984–85	6:34	12:02	57:58	19:58	0:41	97:13
1985–86	5:31	6:49	43:12	12:21	0:04	67:57
1986–87(b)	5:58	7:47	8:52	1:05	–	23:42

(a) Two bills in a long session
(b) An abbreviated bill prior to general election

We may take the proceedings leading up to and on the Finance Bill 1985 as an example. On March 19, 1985, the Chancellor of the Exchequer presented his Budget to the House of Commons in a speech of one hours and 12 minutes. He announced the removal of certain limitations on relief for capital gains tax; abolished many stamp duties and development land tax; made several changes in the taxation of businesses; increased duty payable on cigarettes, certain alcoholic drinks, petrol and derv, and vehicles; applied VAT to newspaper and magazine advertising; increased tax liability on company car use; gave certain relief to charities; made no change in rates of income tax but raised thresholds and starting points; and made major changes in national insurance contributions.

Immediately, provisional statutory effect was given to the changes in taxes affecting spirits, beer, wine, cider, tobacco, hydrocarbon oil and vehicles excise duty. The Deputy Speaker called on the Chancellor to move the motion entitled "Amendment of the Law" on which the Budget debate was to take place. This debate began and continued on March 20, 21 and 25 for a further period of 18 hours and 58 minutes when a division approving the motion was carried by 355 votes to 202. All the other 42 Budget resolutions were then put forthwith pursuant to Standing Order No. 50 and agreed to after two divisions (on petrol duty and vehicle excise duty). The Finance Bill was then ordered to be brought in and was read the first time.[16]

The second reading of the Finance Bill was moved on April 29, 1985 by the Chief Secretary of the Treasury. The debate lasted for six hours and 34 minutes including one division on an amendment moved by the shadow

---

[16] H.C.Deb., Vol. 75, cols. 783–824, 869–958, 1013–1079; Vol. 76, cols. 32–150.

Chancellor and defeated by 278 votes to 172. Seven clauses and three schedules were committed to a committee of the whole House, the remainder of the bill going to standing committee.[17] The committee of the whole House debated on May 7 and 8 for a total of 12 hours and two minutes. The matters debated were increased tax on petrol and derv, VAT on newspaper advertisements, personal tax reliefs, class 4 national insurance contributions, capital allowances on machinery and plant, modification of indexation allowance, abolition of land tax and tax on development gains. All clauses and schedules were reported without amendment after several divisions.[18]

In standing committee the bill was debated for 57 hours and 58 minutes during nine sittings on May 14, 16, 21, 23 and June 4, 6, 11, 13, 18, at an average of 6½ hours for each sitting, beginning usually at 4.30 p.m. with a break at about 7 p.m. for dinner. The bill was reported with amendments and was considered on report on July 9 and 10. The debate lasted for 19 hours and 58 minutes, sitting until 3 a.m. on the night of July 9/10 and, with the third reading, until 1.27 a.m. on the night of July 10/11.[19] Several new clauses were moved by the Government and accepted without division. Many new clauses were moved by Opposition members and defeated in divisions; a few were moved by Government back-benchers and withdrawn after debate. One new clause, on tax credits, was accepted by the Government without division. The debates on new clauses were followed by debates on amendments which were either defeated after divisions or withdrawn.

Government legislation during the 1983–87 Parliament

We now examine in more detail the examination by the House of Government legislative proposals during the last Parliament.

1983–84

Where Government bills were debated for any period on the floor of the House of Commons the number of bills and the time spent were:

Government bills 1983–84
Time spent on the Floor of the House of Commons

Number of bills

	1–15 mins	16 mins –1 hour	1–2 hours	2–5 hours	5–8 hours	over 8 hours	Total
Second reading	14	2	1	5	25	–	47
Committee of whole House	8	–	3	1	1	3	16
Report	–	2	2	5	7	8	24
Third reading	8	10	4	6	2	–	30
Lords' amendments	4	2	1	3	3	3	16

Seven Government bills were debated for more than 20 hours on the floor of the House of Commons.

---

[17] H.C.Deb., Vol. 78, cols. 25–114.
[18] H.C.Deb., Vol. 78, cols. 661–756, 795–846.
[19] H.C.Deb., Vol. 82, cols. 902–1058, 1095–1233.

Government bills 1983–84
Time spent on the Floor of the House of Commons and in standing committee

Bills	Hours and minutes						No. of sittings[20]
	Second reading	Committee of whole House	Report	Third reading	Lords' Amendments	Total	Standing Committee
Local Government (Interim Provisions)	5:43	42:4	–	5:01	11:39	64:27	–
Finance (No.2)	7:58	25:10	18:39	2:24	–	54:11	13
Police & Criminal Evidence	6:36	–	18:19	2:50	13:59	41:44	59
Trade Union	6:24	–	14:36	2:13	8:05	31:18	37
London Regional Transport	5:47	–	14:51	0:58	4:48	26:24	36
Rates(a)	6:48	–	11:59	1:57	3:54	23:38	30
Telecommunications(a)	6:29	–	9:05	3:11	4:00	22:45	22

(a) Under an allocation of time order

The purpose of the Local Government (Interim Provisions) Bill was to pave the way for the bill to abolish the Greater London Council and the six metropolitan councils to be introduced in the following session. Elections to these councils, due in April 1985, were to be cancelled and interim bodies established to govern the areas for 11 months. The Leader of the House (Mr. Biffen) agreed that the committee stage should be taken on the floor of the House because although not "constitutional" the bill was "extremely important." Proceedings were lengthy and contentious with 33 divisions in committee. In the House of Lords the Government suffered a major defeat with the success of an amendment postponing the coming into force of the Act[21] and was forced to introduce a new proposal which enabled the members of the councils to continue in office for an additional year, pending the decision on the abolition of the councils.[22]

As already noted, Finance Bill sittings in standing committee are longer than those on other bills. In 1983–84 the proceedings were on the scale of a marathon, absorbing 117 hours and 55 minutes, an average of nine hours for each sitting, several lasting all night (with breaks).

The Police and Criminal Evidence Bill embodied major extensions and reforms of police powers and was debated in detail in standing committee (creating a record for the number of sittings) without a guillotine being imposed; many amendments were made. The Trade Union Bill was a further step in the limitation of trade unions' power, on this occasion being directed principally at their internal working and organisation. The London Regional Transport Bill has as its purpose the transference of the functions of the London Transport Executive to a new body out of the control of the Greater London Council. The Rates Bill was an instalment of the Government's programme to control local authority expenditure by limiting rates

---

[20] See explanation after Table on page 317.
[21] H.L. Deb., Vol. 453, cols. 1034–1071 (June 28, 1984).
[22] H.C.Deb., Vol. 65, cols. 43–93 (July 30, 1984).

and precepts leviable by certain authorities. The Telecommunications Bill provided for the appointment and functions of a Director General, abolished British Telecommunications' exclusive privileges and provided for the licensing of telecommunication systems.

Nine other bills were considered for more than 10 sittings in standing committee: Rating and Valuation (Amendment) Scotland (28 sittings); Housing and Building Control (27); Data Protection (25); Ordnance Factories and Military Services (24); Health and Social Security (17); Matrimonial and Family Proceedings (12); Prevention of Terrorism (12); Tenants Rights, etc., (Scotland) Amendment (12); Co-operative Development Agency and Industrial Development (11). These are all bills in the second rank of contention taking between 10 and 20 hours of time on the floor of the House and between 25 and 80 hours in standing committee.

1984–85

Where Government bills were debated for any period on the floor of the House of Commons, the number of bills and the time spent were:

Government bills 1984–85
Time spent on the Floor of the House of Commons

	Number of bills						
	1–15 mins	16 mins –1 hour	1–2 hours	2–5 hours	5–8 hours	over 8 hours	Total
Second reading	5	4	–	9	17	2	37
Committee of whole House	6	–	1	2	1	5	15
Report	1	5	5	9	4	4	28
Third reading	6	13	6	3	–	–	28
Lords' amendments	3	6	1	2	2	–	14

Six Government bills were debated for more than 20 hours on the floor of the House of Commons.

Government bills 1984–85
Time spent on the Floor of the House of Commons and in standing committee

Bills	Hours and minutes						No. of sittings[23]
	Second reading	Committee of whole House	Report	Third reading	Lords' Amend-ments	Total	Standing Com-mittee
Local Government(a)	15:28	13:22	12:11	1:12	7:46	49:59	35
Finance	6:34	12:2	19:58	0:41	–	39:15	9
Water Fluoridation	4:53	–	30:15	3:32	–	38:40	4
Representation of the People	5:59	20:54	2:24	0:28	0:59	30:44	–
Interception of Communications	8:28	10:43	4:45	1:13	0:17	25:26	–
Transport(a)	5:26	–	12:17	1:11	3:40	22:34	34

(a) Under an allocation of time order

---

[23] See explanation after Table on page 317.

The Local Government Bill was passed to abolish the Greater London Council and the six metropolitan councils and to transfer their functions. Clause 1, which provided for the abolitions was taken in committee of the whole House. The length of the debate on this one clause reflected the intensity of the opposition to this measure. The average length of each sitting in standing committee was over four hours. The Water (Fluoridation) Bill aroused some strong feelings among libertarians in the House of Commons, particularly some Government back-benchers, although it was given a second reading in a relatively small House by 159 votes to 71. The bill, consisting of only two substantive clauses, empowered statutory water undertakers to make a limited increase in the fluoride content of the water supply to a particular area when requested to do so by the appropriate health authority. The bill was in standing committee for 8½ hours; but was considered on report for over 30 hours, its last sitting which also included the debate on the third reading lasting from 10.57 p.m. on March 5, 1985 until 8.11 p.m. the next day.[24]

The proceedings on the Finance Bill were discussed above.

The Representation of the People Bill was also, as is usual for constitutional bills, taken in committee of the whole House. It extended the right to vote to non-residents, and to those on holiday; it changed the rules about lost deposits; and made other minor reforms. The Interception of Communications Bill was also taken on the floor of the House in committee (because the Government wanted to speed its passage). It was designed to regularise the legal powers of telephone-tapping in the national interest and to create offences for illegal interceptions. The purpose of the Transport Bill was to de-regulate bus services. It abolished road service licensing, provided for the transference of the operations of the National Bus Company and made other provisions for the regulation of transport services in London and the provinces. Discussion on the bill in standing committee and on report and on consideration of Lords' Amendments was made subject to a guillotine on April 1, and October 29, 1985.[25]

Two Government bills failed to pass. The Civil Aviation Bill was intended to limit air transport movements especially at Heathrow airport. On second reading in November 1984, the House approved the principle of the bill by 232 votes to 154[26] but on two successive occasions in standing committee the Government failed to carry the initial sittings motion. Shortly after the second reading debate and before the standing committee met for the first time the inspector's report had been published on airports policy relating to Stansted airport and terminal 5 at Heathrow. This, it was argued, called for a fundamental reappraisal of the principle of the bill. On December 20, the Secretary of State for Transport accepted that further consideration of the bill should be postponed until the Government had decided what to do about the report.[27] On May 9, 1985 he withdrew the bill.[28]

The second failure was the Education (Corporal Punishment) Bill under which parents were to be allowed to exempt their children from corporal

---

[24] On several amendments, and on third reading, the Government moved the closure against some of its own back-benchers: H.C.Deb., Vol. 73, cols. 996–997 (February 19, 1985); H.C.Deb., Vol. 74, cols. 929–931, 950–951, 1010–1012, 1057–1058, 1136.

[25] H.C.Deb., Vol. 76, cols. 907–957; H.C.Deb., Vol. 84, cols. 854–863.

[26] H.C.Deb., Vol. 68, cols. 299–384 (November 21, 1984).

[27] H.C.Deb., Vol. 70, cols. 561–568.

[28] H.C.Deb., Vol. 78, cols. 467.

punishment. It was carried at second reading by 290 votes to 171 and eventually passed the Commons.[29] The House of Lords having passed an amendment effectively abolishing corporal punishment, so destroying the principle of the bill, the Government did not proceed with it.[30]

Three other bills were considered in standing committee for more than 10 sittings: Insolvency (13 sittings), Food and Environmental Protection (11), Law Reform (Miscellaneous Provisions (Scotland) (26)).

1985–86

Where Government bills were debated for any period on the floor of the House of Commons, the number of bills and the time spent were:

Government bills 1985–86
Time spent on the Floor of the House of Commons

	1–15 mins	16 mins –1 hour	1–2 hours	2–5 hours	5–8 hours	over 8 hours	Total
Second reading	4	2	3	12	16	1	38
Committee of whole House	–	1	1	2	1	1	6
Report	2	2	2	4	8	8	26
Third reading	12	10	4	3	1	–	30
Lords' amendments	1	3	4	6	2	–	16

Five Government bills were debated for more than 20 hours on the floor of the House of Commons.

Government bills 1985–86
Time spent on the Floor of the House of Commons and in standing committee

Bills	Hours and minutes						No. of sittings[31]
	Second reading	Committee of whole House	Report	Third reading	Lords' Amend-ments	Total	Standing Com-mittee
European Communities (Amendment)(a)	5:50	22:07	–	0:47	–	28:44	–
Education	6:41	–	17:52	0:22	–	24:55	15
Finance	5:31	6:49	12:21	0:04	–	24:45	10
Financial Services	6:06	–	8:36	0:25	7:14	22:21	22
Social Security(a)	5:12	–	11:00	2:03	3:33	21:48	42

(a) Under an allocation of time order

The European Communities (Amendments) Bill was to give effect in

---

[29] H.C.Deb., Vol. 72, cols. 38–117 (January 28, 1985); H.C.Deb., Vol. 77, cols. 57–92 (April 15, 1985).
[30] H.L.Deb., Vol. 465, cols. 1314–1333 (July 4, 1985); H.L. Deb., Vol. 466, cols. 1097–1098 (July 23, 1985).
[31] See explanation after the Table on page 317.

United Kingdom law to the changes to the treaties establishing the European Community agreed by heads of government and known as the Single European Act. Some of the anti-Common Market Members on the Government side of the House opposed the bill as did the Opposition. Its committee and remaining stages on the floor of the House were guillotined.[32] The Education Bill (which became the Education (No. 2) Act 1986) changed provisions relating to school governors and parents, to the grouping of schools, the curriculum, discipline, appointment and dismissal of staff and other matters. The 10 sittings on the Finance Bill in standing committee totalled 43 hours and 12 minutes. The Financial Services Bill was designed to establish a framework of regulation to provide effective protection for investors while promoting an efficient and competitive financial services industry. The Social Security Bill introduced changes in the system of social security. After the standing committee had held 30 sittings lasting 115 hours a guillotine motion was imposed on April 15, 1986 to require the Committee to report the bill to the House on or before May 1, with further provisions for report and third reading.[33]

In addition, the following eight bills were considered in standing committee for more than 10 sittings: Public Order (34 sittings); Gas (32); Wages (26); Dockyard Services (25); Airports (19); Housing (Scotland) (18); Housing and Planning (15); Building Societies (14). In degree of controversiality, it is not possible to distinguish the Public Order and Gas Bills from those which took more than 20 hours on the floor of the House. If the hours spent in standing committee are taken into account these two bills were debated for longer periods than any except the Social Security Bill. In terms of social and political impact, the Public Order Bill which revised the offences relating to public order introduced new regulations for processions and assemblies, re-enacted and extended the law relating to incitement to racial hatred and empowered the courts to make orders excluding offenders from football grounds, was one of the most important Government bills of the session.

The Okehampton Bypass (Confirmation of Orders) Bill was passed under the provisions of section 6 of the Statutory Orders (Special Procedure) Act 1945. The preliminary stages having been taken, the Act required only report and third reading stages to be taken in the House.[34]

The Shops Bill, which was first introduced into the House of Lords, caused great controversy. It enabled Sunday trading to be legalised and also affected the working hours in shops at all times. Many Government supporters in the House of Commons failed to support it and it was refused a second reading by 296 votes to 282.[35] This was a remarkable Parliamentary occasion which few people would have thought possible on a whipped vote, with all the usual pressures being applied on Government back-benchers to support the bill, in a House where the Government had a majority of over 140 seats. No doubt there were many different, perhaps contradictory, influences at work which all united against the bill. There was the tradition of the British Sunday (to be contrasted with that of the pagan continent); there was the specifically religious pressure; there was a sense that this was not the right

[32] H.C.Deb., Vol. 100, cols. 931–982 (July 1, 1986).
[33] H.C.Deb., Vol. 95, cols. 746–794.
[34] H.C.Deb., Vol. 87, cols. 140–224 (November 19, 1985).
[35] H.C.Deb., Vol. 95, cols. 584–702 (April 14, 1986).

bill to effect the reform; there was trade union opposition; there was, perhaps, some over-playing by Government Whips of their power. Whatever the reasons, the bill was defeated, possibly the Government was relieved, and practices (both legal and illegal) continued as before.

1986–87

Where Government bills were debated for any period on the floor of the House of Commons, the number of bills and the time spent were:

Government bills 1986–87
Time spent on the Floor of the House of Commons

| | Number of bills | | | | | | |
	1–15 mins	16 mins –1 hour	1–2 hours	2–5 hours	5–8 hours	over 8 hours	Total
Second reading	4	1	3	15	6	–	29
Committee of whole House	3	2	1	3	–	3	12
Report	1	7	5	2	2	2	19
Third reading	16	5	3	–	–	–	24
Lords' amendments	3	1	2	2	–	–	8

Four Government bills were debated for more than 20 hours on the floor of the House of Commons.

Government bills 1986–87
Time spent on the Floor of the House of Commons and in standing committee

Bills	Hours and minutes						No. of sittings[36]
	Second reading	Committee of whole House	Report	Third reading	Lords' Amendments	Total	Standing Committee
Teachers' Pay & Conditions	6:03	22:48	–	0:26	3:02	32:19	–
Local Government Finance(a)	5:58	20:51	–	–	1:25	28:14	–
Criminal Justice	4:47	–	16:29	0:16	0:52	22:24	36
Abolition of Domestic Rates etc. (Scotland)(a)	5:34	–	13:37	–	2:02	21:13	27

(a) Under an allocation of time order

The Teachers' Pay and Conditions Bill abolished the statutory negotiating machinery for school teachers, required the Secretary of State to appoint an Advisory Committee and empowered him by order to determine school teachers' pay. The Local Government Finance Bill was introduced to validate certain things done by the Secretary of State and to set up a new method

---

[36] See explanation after Table on page 317.

of calculating relevant and total expenditure for the purposes of rate support grant, and rate limitation systems for local authorities. On January 26, 1987 discussion on the bill was subjected to a guillotine motion requiring the proceedings in committee to be concluded and the report and third reading stages also to be concluded within one day.[37] Both bills were taken in committee of the whole House to speed their passage. The Abolition of Domestic Rates, etc., (Scotland) Bill provided for the phasing out of domestic rates in Scotland and for the introduction of a system of community charge or poll tax. Discussion in standing committee, report and third reading was subjected to a guillotine motion on February 11, 1987.[38]

The Criminal Justice Bill as introduced consisted of 128 clauses and 10 schedules. It dealt with fraud; evidence; jurisdiction, imprisonment and fines; confiscation of the proceeds of an offence; compensation; juries; children and young persons; extradition; probation; and other matters.

In addition, the following four bills were considered in standing committee for more than 10 sittings: Channel Tunnel Bill (15 sittings), Northern Ireland (Emergency Provisions) Bill (13), Petroleum Bill (12) and Banking Bill (11).

When the general election was announced in May 1987, negotiations took place between the Government and Opposition about the fate of Government bills which had not received the Royal Assent. There were 26 of these, in addition to the 14 already passed. Of the 26, three hybrid bills (Channel Tunnel, Dartford-Thurrock Crossing, and Norfolk and Suffolk Broad Bills) were suspended until the next session; and one bill was lost (the Conveyancing Services Bill which had been introduced into the House of Lords and read a first time). The remaining 22 received the Royal Assent on May 15, 1987. But the Opposition insisted that the Criminal Justice Bill and the Finance Bill should be considerably truncated.

We have seen that the Criminal Justice Bill was considered during 36 sessions of the standing committee in the Commons. It received its second reading in the Lords on April 27, 1987.[39] When the bill was considered in committee in the Lords on May 12, the dissolution of Parliament had been announced and negotiations had taken place between the political parties on the fate of this bill. These resulted in only Part I of the substantive provisions of the bill being agreed and amendments were moved in the Lords to negative all other clauses.[40] The Finance Bill began life with 164 clauses and 22 schedules, receiving its second reading on April 22, 1987.[41] As enacted, it had 72 clauses and 16 schedules. All 38 clauses on personal pension schemes, all 16 clauses on profit-related pay, and all 15 clauses on taxes management provisions disappeared. The slaughter took place during committee and on report on May 12, 1987.[42]

Government motions

Substantive motions

Substantive motions deal with many matters. To some extent these are

---

[37] H.C.Deb., Vol. 109, cols. 36–66.
[38] H.C.Deb., Vol. 110, cols. 320–368.
[39] H.L. Deb., Vol. 486, cols. 1266–1347.
[40] H.L. Deb., Vol. 487, cols. 575–606.
[41] H.C.Deb., Vol. 114, cols. 683–765.
[42] H.C.Deb., Vol. 116, cols. 185–205. In addition, the Local Government Bill lose five clauses dealing with financial assistance for privately let housing accommodation.

routine occasions, where by custom the Government allows time for debates on matters which it is accepted the House should debate each year (reports of the Public Accounts Committee, for example); also there are broad reviews of major policy areas (such as defence). But debates also take place on specific new policies based on green and white papers. During the 1983–87 Parliament, white papers on the defence estimates were debated on four occasions for a total of 46 hours and 13 minutes. The Autumn Statement and public expenditure plans were debated on seven occasions for 41 hours and 12 minutes; the Scottish economy was debated for six hours and 20 minutes. Reports from the Public Accounts Committee were debated on three occasions for 13 hours and 33 minutes. Members' pay and allowances were debated on six occasions for 12 hours and 42 minutes. Debates on parliamentary representation, procedure, privileges and Members' interests totalled 17 hours and four minutes.

The remaining hours were taken with debates lasting for three hours or more on subjects as diverse as intermediate nuclear forces, cable systems and services, Hong Kong, Northern Ireland, regional policy, the sinking of the Belgrano, shops' opening, airports policy, social security reform, the European community, immigration rules, the Anglo-Irish agreement, the Channel tunnel, nuclear energy, the ship-building industry, the tin industry, employment and training, the motor vehicles industry and the arts.

Adjournment motions

On other occasions it is convenient to have a general debate which leads to no formal expression of opinion or decision. This can be achieved by the use of adjournment motions which preclude the moving of amendments but enable the Opposition, if dissatisfied, to divide the House. Adjournment motions on substantive issues in Government time show some recurring subjects and a large number of others.

In the Parliament of 1983–87, debates on the Army, the Navy and the Royal Air Force took place in most sessions, those on the Army totalling 19 hours and 54 minutes, on the Navy 21 hours and 19 minutes, on the Royal Air Force 20 hours and 17 minutes. Foreign affairs were debated each session for a total of 33 hours and 42 minutes with one wide-ranging debate each year. Welsh affairs were also debated each session for a total of 22 hours and 40 minutes. Small businesses were debated in three sessions for 12 hours and 31 minutes. Policing in London was debated in three sessions for 13 hours and four minutes. The arts were debated in two sessions for 11 hours and 18 minutes.

Other topics, mostly debated for more than four hours, included youth training, the civil service, the Maze prison breakout, GCHQ, CAP and EEC, the Griffiths report on the National Health Service, Hong Kong, civil aviation, the disabled, drug misuse, investor protection, higher education, acid rain, airport inquiries, financial services, immigration, policy for science, road traffic, children in care, prisons, financing the BBC, AIDS, and Sizewell nuclear power station.

Money resolutions and Ways and Means resolutions

Every bill that involves significant expenditure by central Government must be accompanied by a money resolution, usually approved immediately after second reading. No amendment to a bill may be debated that is outside the scope of the resolution (see pages 251–252). Governments therefore sometimes seek to limit this scope. In 1978 the Government excluded private ship repairing concerns from its proposals in the Shipbuilding (Redundancy Payments) Bill. Opposition attempts to move their inclusion failed because of the wording of the money resolution. In the House of Lords, amendments were made for this inclusion but the Government refused to amend the money resolution and the Speaker ruled that the Lords' Amendments could therefore not be entertained by the House.[43]

Money resolutions are rarely debated at length and Standing Order No. 14(1)(d) normally limits debate to 45 minutes. In 1983–84 four resolutions were debated for a total of one hour and 44 minutes; in 1984–85 five resolutions took three hours and 52 minutes; in 1985–86, six resolutions took one hour 37 minutes; in 1986–87 one resolution took 12 minutes. Many other resolutions were agreed without debate. Members who are not called in a second reading debate are often able to make their points during the debate on the money resolution.

Nowadays money resolutions are often widely drawn. But problems may still arise. The Firearms (Amendment) Bill 1987–88 made illegal the possession of or dealings in certain weapons. The bill as presented contained no provisions for compensation for those affected but during the second reading the Minister indicated that a scheme might be introduced. On the motion to approve the money resolution,[44] the question was raised whether the resolution was wide enough to cover a compensation scheme. The resolution authorised the payment out of money provided by Parliament of any administrative expenses incurred by the Secretary of State in consequence of the Act. Some suggestion was made that the compensation might be covered by "administrative expenses" and the Minister thought it might be done by an *ex gratia* payment. Otherwise no amendment could be moved to introduce the scheme. Eventually the Government introduced a further money resolution to facilitate such an amendment and the consideration of alternatives.[45]

Ways and Means resolutions (entitled "Amendment of the Law") provide the occasion for general debates following Budget statements. During the 1983–87 Parliament, these general debates absorbed 84 hours 18 minutes of the 90 hours 42 minutes attributed to Ways and Means resolutions generally. The remaining detailed Ways and Means resolutions moved at the end of the Budget debate are not debatable. Specific Ways and Means resolutions are also frequently required to authorise fees, levies and other revenue provisions in bills other than Finance Bills. These are usually agreed without debate. Occasionally a bill has to be founded on a Ways and Means resolution, which may be debated at length (see page 229).

Affirmative Resolutions

The procedure on statutory instruments has been described on page 246. An instrument requiring affirmative resolution may be debated on the floor of the House on a ministerial motion in Government time unless Opposition Members agree that it should go for debate to one of the standing committees on statutory instruments in which case the resolution is put forthwith

---

[43] H.C.Deb., Vol. 948, cols. 1801–1802 (April 27, 1978).
[44] H.C.Deb., Vol. 125, cols. 1191–1200 (January 21, 1988).
[45] H.C.Deb., Vol. 128, cols. 939–947 (March 1, 1988).

under Standing Order No. 101(5) when it comes before the House and is almost always agreed to without division. The figures for the 1983–87 Parliament were:

Instruments (including draft instruments) requiring affirmative resolution

	Considered by the House other than under S.O. No.101(5)	Question put forthwith under S.O. No.101(5) after being considered by Standing Committee on Statutory Instruments
1983–84	112	73
1984–85	91	72
1985–86	69	86
1986–87	68	51
Total	340	282

All resolutions were approved by the House.

For those instruments debated by the House, the debate, if started after 10 p.m. is brought to a close after 1½ hours under Standing Order No. 14. In 1983–84, 89 per cent. of affirmative resolutions were debated for 1½ hours or less; in 1984–85 the figure was 70 per cent.; in 1985–86, 78 per cent.; in 1986–87, 85 per cent. But extra time may be provided or debate may start earlier in the day, and many motions result in lengthy debate and in divisions.

Instruments (including draft instruments) requiring affirmative resolution

Number approved on a division after debate
Length of debate before division

	1½ hours or less	1½ to 3 hours	more than 3 hours	Total
1983–84	20	8	12	40
1984–85	15	6	12	33
1985–86	15	3	3	21
1986–87	5	2	2	9
Total	55	19	29	103

A further 237 instruments that had not been in standing committee were approved without division.

Of the 29 instruments debated for more than three hours before a division, 14 concerned local government finance: 10 on rate support grant,[46] three on ratecapping[47] and one on housing.[48] A further nine concerned northern Ireland; five on the Appropriation Order which permits a wide-

[46] H.C.Deb., Vol. 47, cols. 935–974 (November 2, 1983), H.C.Deb., Vol. 52, cols. 637–742 (January 23, 1984), H.C.Deb., Vol. 53, cols. 905–957 (February 8, 1984), H.C.Deb., Vol. 64, cols. 355–414 (July 18, 1984), H.C.Deb., Vol. 65, cols. 574–645 (October 23, 1984), H.C.Deb., Vol. 71, cols. 337–424, 1166–1231 (January 16 and 24, 1985), H.C.Deb., Vol. 83, cols. 195–266 (July 16, 1985), H.C.Deb., Vol. 90, cols. 115–135 (January 20, 1986), H.C.Deb., Vol. 113, cols. 434–522 (March 25, 1987).
[47] H.C.Deb., Vol. 72, cols. 976–1026 (February 6, 1985), H.C.Deb., Vol. 74, cols. 23–126 (February 25, 1985), H.C.Deb., Vol. 92, cols. 833–908 (February 25, 1986).
[48] H.C.Deb., Vol. 71, cols. 1038–1095 (January 23, 1985).

ranging debate,[49] and four on public order or emergency provisions.[50] The remainder were three debates on social security[51] and one each on civil defence, local government reform and unfair dismissal.[52]

In all 103 divisions, the Government carried the vote and on only one significant occasion was it run close. This was on a motion to approve the increase of the Lord Chancellor's salary in 1985 which was carried by 249 votes to 232.[53] The opposition was to a large increase in a large number of salaries recommended by the Top Salaries Review Body for judges, senior civil servants and senior members of the armed forces.

The dominance of questions relating to local government finance and Northern Ireland is fortuitous. Rate support grant reports and orders determining the level of general Government financial support for local authorities must be reconsidered regularly, being a significant part of Budget strategy. The tradition has developed that such financial provisions should be subject to affirmative rather than negative proceedings, and, in recent years, with rate-capping, the financing of local authorities has become of the most controversial issues between the parties. It is therefore in no way surprising that Opposition parties should take full advantage of the available procedures in Government time to criticise policy. Over the four sessions of the 1983–87 Parliament, rate support grant reports and orders were debated for 75 hours and 9 minutes—over 17 per cent. of the total time spent on these debates.

The Northern Ireland orders, especially the thrice-sessional Appropriation Orders, are the result of the special procedures flowing from the Northern Ireland Act 1974. The debates on these orders give regular opportunities for Members to debate many aspects of policy and administration. The Appropriation Orders were, in all, debated for 35 hours and 48 minutes in the 1983–87 Parliament. As a single topic this was second only to rate support grant. Many other Northern Ireland orders are debated. For example, in 1984–85, 13 orders on matters ranging from road traffic to historic churches, from wild life to nursing homes, were debated for an average one hour five minutes.[54]

The remaining occasions for shorter debates were diverse in subject. For example, in 1984–85, the subjects included coal industry grants, commencement orders for the Local Government (Interim Provisions) Act, industrial training levy, food safety regulations, London regional transport levy, unfair dismissal, Royal Ordnance Factories trading, and the borrowing powers of the British Steel Corporation. In 1985–86, the subjects included supplementary benefit board and lodging, the National Film Finance Corporation, orders under the Police and Criminal Evidence Act 1984, seat

[49] H.C.Deb., Vol. 45, cols. 440–502 (July 7, 1983), H.C.Deb., Vol. 55, cols. 418–501 (March 1, 1984), H.C.Deb., Vol. 61, cols. 649–734 (June 11, 1094), H.C.Deb., Vol. 112, cols. 219–267 (March 10, 1987), H.C.Deb., Vol. 70, cols. 85–127 (December 17, 1984), H.C.Deb., Vol. 74, cols. 1235–1279 (March 7, 1985).
[50] H.C.Deb., Vol. 50, cols. 517–571 (December 8, 1983), H.C.Deb., Vol. 70, cols. 651–672 (December 20, 1984), H.C.Deb., Vol. 81, cols. 1028–1049 (June 26, 1985).
[51] H.C.Deb., Vol. 46, cols. 1226–1284 (July 27, 1983), H.C.Deb., Vol. 54, cols. 149–232 (February 14, 1984), H.C.Deb., Vol. 99, cols. 331–379 (June 11, 1986).
[52] H.C.Deb., Vol. 47, cols. 336–397 (October 26, 1983), H.C.Deb., Vol. 69, cols. 841–881 (December 10, 1984), H.C.Deb., Vol. 79, cols. 423–464 (May 15, 1985).
[53] H.C.Deb., Vol. 83, cols. 990–1012 (July 23, 1985).
[54] H.C.Deb., Vol. 101, cols. 483–484 (July 15, 1986).

belts regulations, passenger transport authorities, the employment subsidies scheme, extinguishment of liabilities of new towns and protection of food.

Instruments requiring affirmative resolution which are debated in standing committee are usually uncontroversial (otherwise the Opposition would insist that they were debated on the floor) and so divisions are unusual. During the 1983–87 Parliament there were divisions in committee on only four occasions. One was on a draft order of 1984 to make grants to the Redundant Churches Fund. Viscount Cranborne was against the "iconoclastic or Savonarolan tradition of the Church of England by which all things of beauty must be sacrificed to what it regards as the living Church," although he voted for the order which was opposed by one Member on a procedural point and by another as a Presbyterian.[55] Also in that session the Education (Mandatory Awards) Regulation 1983—a matter on which the Government had been defeated a year previously—was opposed.[56] In 1984–85 the draft Town and Country Planning Regulations 1985 relating to fees for applications were divided against[57] as was (by one Member) a Definition of Capital Expenses (Scotland) Order in 1986–87.[58]

As the standing order permits the committee to debate only a motion "That the committee has considered the instrument (or draft instrument)" and to do so for only 1½ hours (or 2½ hours for Northern Ireland instruments) the scope is limited. Nevertheless, the proceedings require the presence of a Minister to propose the consideration of the instrument and to answer the debate.

It is in the nature of regulations requiring affirmative (or negative) resolutions that they should be diverse in subject matter. All subordinate legislation flows from decisions by Government departments that certain matters are best dealt with by orders or regulations rather than embodied in statutes. The reasons for such decisions may be those of administrative convenience, political advantage, or the need for flexibility. Such benefits are to be derived across the board of governmental activity.

Affirmative resolutions require Ministers to take action and to use parliamentary time. Frequently in committee on bills, Opposition amendments seek to replace negative with affirmative resolutions so as to require Ministers to take the initiative in bringing statutory instruments into operation. Frequently also, Ministers resist such attempts. There have emerged over the years certain conventions which help to determine when affirmative resolutions are to be used. These include the approval of instruments of a financial kind as well as other broadly constitutional matters. But otherwise the choice between negative and affirmative resolutions often depends on what departments think they can get Members of committees on bills to accept.

Statements

Ministerial statements in the House of Commons, with subsequent responses and questions, vary in length but seldom exceed one hour.

---

[55] Fifth Standing Committee on Statutory Instruments 1983–84.
[56] Sixth Standing Committee on Statutory Instruments 1983–84.
[57] Fifth Standing Committee on Statutory Instruments 1984–85.
[58] First Standing Committee on Statutory Instruments 1986–87.

Ministerial statements in the House of Commons

	No. of policy statements	Total time hours : minutes	Average time hours : minutes
1983–84	132	76 : 34	00 : 35
1984–85	105	67 : 29	00 : 38
1985–86	109	70 : 51	00 : 39
1986–87	57	35 : 36	00 : 37
	403		

In earlier years, than those shown above, Speakers allowed considerably less time for statements; in 1975–76, for example, the average time was 24 minutes.

The Speaker attempts to call as many Members as possible who wish to respond to a ministerial statement. He often promises to give priority on some later occasion to those who do not catch his eye.

During the 1983–87 Parliament, there were 27 statements on which the proceedings lasted for an hour or more. Four of these were by the Prime Minister on the European Council meetings in Athens and Fontainebleau, on the Anglo-Irish agreement, and on a visit to the Soviet Union.[59] Six were by the Chancellor of the Exchequer, four being the Budget Statements (which inaugurate full debates)[60] and two the Autumn Statements.[61] The Secretary of State for the Environment made six statements of which four were on rate support grant[62] and two on other aspects of local government finance.[63] The Foreign Secretary made one statement on diplomatic relations with Libya.[64] The Home Secretary spoke on inner city disorders and on visas.[65] The Secretary of State for Transport spoke on airports policy and the Channel tunnel.[66] There were other ministerial statements on regional industrial policy, student awards, the safety of football grounds, the review of social security, the Agriculture Council, and training and employment.[67]

That there were a further 376 statements each with less than one hour discussion shows the great utility of this form of proceeding. Certain topics

[59] H.C.Deb., Vol. 50, cols. 216–236 (December 7, 1983); H.C.Deb., Vol. 62, cols. 993–1009 (June 27, 1984); H.C.Deb., Vol. 87, cols. 19–35 (November 18, 1985); H.C.Deb., Vol. 113, cols. 1223–1236 (April 2, 1987).

[60] H.C.Deb., Vol. 56, cols. 286–305 (March 13, 1984); H.C.Deb., Vol. 75, cols. 783–800 (March 19, 1985); H.C.Deb., Vol. 94, cols. 166–184 (March 18, 1986); H.C.Deb., Vol. 112, cols. 815–828 (March 17, 1987).

[61] H.C.Deb., Vol. 67, cols. 415–428 (November 12, 1984); H.C.Deb., Vol. 103, cols. 1083–1098 (November 6, 1986); H.C.Deb., Vol. 107, cols. 1233–1306 (December 17, 1986).

[62] H.C.Deb., Vol. 64, cols. 828–850 (July 24, 1984); H.C.Deb., Vol. 83, cols. 1319–1338 (July 25, 1985); H.C.Deb., Vol. 89, cols. 310–330 (December 18, 1985); H.C.Deb., Vol. 102, cols. 181–199 (July 22, 1986).

[63] H.C.Deb., Vol. 70, cols. 164–179 (December 18, 1984); H.C.Deb., Vol. 90, cols. 797–813 (January 28, 1986).

[64] H.C.Deb., Vol. 59, cols. 209–225 (May 1, 1984).

[65] H.C.Deb., Vol. 84, cols. 30–46 (October 21, 1985); H.C.Deb., Vol. 102, cols. 948–964 (October 21, 1986).

[66] H.C.Deb., Vol. 80, cols. 307–329 (June 5, 1985); H.C.Deb., Vol. 90, cols. 19–34 (January 20, 1986).

[67] H.C.Deb., Vol. 68, cols. 936–954 (November 28, 1984); H.C.Deb., Vol. 69, cols. 360–381 (December 5, 1984); H.C.Deb., Vol. 79, cols. 19–39 (May 13, 1985); H.C.Deb., Vol. 80, cols. 34–51 (June 3, 1985); H.C.Deb., Vol. 107, cols. 1213–1228 (December 17, 1986); H.C.Deb., Vol. 109, cols. 337–354 (January 28, 1987).

continually recur. The Foreign Secretary speaks on visits he proposes to make or has made to other countries and on emergencies that have arisen. Ministerial meetings within the European Community are reported. Public expenditure generally and social security payments in particular are common subjects. So are industrial disputes and closures. Reports of investigations are commented on. Ministers report on the outcome of natural disasters or tragic accidents. Sometimes the statements are immediate responses to events and are followed by full-scale debates initiated by the Government.

Many statements are made because a convention has emerged that certain events (for example, the Autumn Statement) will be so dealt with. Others are made because the Government wishes to put its activities or its reactions on the record. Others are made under pressure from the Opposition which the Government finds politic to respond to in this way, at least in the first instance. Ministers frequently announce decisions, sometimes on policy, by means of written answers to inspired Questions. Sometimes Opposition Members object on the ground that an oral statement, open to questioning, should have been given.

Governments frequently publish statements of policy in the form of white papers. Bills may be subsequently drafted to put these proposals in legislative form. During the Parliament of 1983–87, 85 such statements were issued. Some subjects are dealt with in most sessions, such as defence estimates, developments in the European Community, the Government's expenditure plans. But others range over the wide field of Government activity reflecting the particular concerns of the session and the Government's legislative programme either for that session or the next. In addition, some hundreds of other papers are published by Government departments in the form of green papers or consultation documents. These are designed to sound out public opinion and the reaction of interest groups. They may re-appear, revised, as white papers. None of this precludes Ministers from informal private soundings. By these means, departments become better informed about the possible difficulties they may face in implementing their policies and enable them to buy off or placate opposition well in advance of parliamentary debate.

OTHER GOVERNMENT INITIATIVES

Many procedures in the House may, under standing orders, be initiated only by Ministers. Amongst these are the referrals of various forms of business to several standing committees. As we have seen, most of these referrals can be blocked by the objection of 10 or 20 Members. So most referrals are uncontroversial between the parties.

During the 1983–87 Parliament, seven bills, (out of 29 bills certified by the Speaker to relate exclusively to Scotland), were referred to the Scottish Grand Committee for second reading.[68] A similar provision relates to Welsh bills and the Welsh Grand Committee but no bill was so referred in that Parliament. The Scottish Grand Committee has Scottish estimates referred to it. The Scottish and Welsh Grand Committees and the Northern Ireland Committees have referred to them specified matters relating exclusively to those countries. As the choice of matters to be debated is for the Opposition these proceedings are considered in Chapter 9.

---

[68] S.O. No. 93; see above page 312.

The Standing Committees on European Community Documents may have specified documents referred to them. The choice lies primarily with back-benchers and is considered in Chapter 10.

In addition, a large number of initiatives fall to the Government to be taken in relation to the business of the House. It makes business statements and answers business questions; it moves "business of the House" motions giving extra time or restricting time for debate or arranging for several matters to be debated together; it proposes guillotines on bills; it moves motions for the appointment and nomination of members of select committees or to refer matters (for example on privilege or procedure) to such committees. All this absorbs a fair amount of time. For example, in 1984–85, 17 hours 26 minutes were taken on business statements; business of the House motions of various kinds took 4 hours 3 minutes; and debates on guillotine motions took 8 hours 9 minutes. Finally, the Government responds to Opposition initiatives by tabling amendments to Opposition motions.

CHAPTER 9

OPPOSITION INITIATIVES

THE FUNCTIONS OF THE OPPOSITION

"The duty of Her Majesty's official Opposition is to oppose Her Majesty's Government." This favourite definition, while containing the kernel of the truth, serves also to confuse by over-simplification. It is the Opposition's policy to oppose; certainly. But to what end? The ultimate aim must surely be to persuade the electorate to throw out the Government of the day and to put the Opposition party in power so that it may then pursue the policies it believes are best for the nation—or for those sectional interests it would wish to benefit. To this end the Opposition will wish to explore, highlight and publicly oppose those aspects of the Government's policies and administration which it believes to be damaging to the nation, or to the favoured sectional interests, and particularly those policies which are proving, or likely to prove, unpopular with the electorate, or more especially with moderate opinion (the floating vote) and with supporters of the party in opposition. It will not wish to draw attention to, or to oppose, elements of Government policy which are popular with the electorate at large. It may even, as with Peel who "caught the Whigs bathing and walked away with their clothes"[1] in 1845, wish to annexe some of those policies itself. Opposition, therefore, must be selective.

Opposition must also be constructive. If it is not, the party in power will have the easy riposte to any criticism of asking "well, what would you do if you were in our place?" The electorate will wish the Opposition to set out its own stall, and to be prepared and able to defend its own policies and remedies for the nation's ills. The Opposition will seek, at every level, to pursue its opposition to the Government in these ways, and, up and down the country, to seek to catch the ear of the electorate and to sway public opinion to its support.

In carrying out these functions, the Opposition must seek information about the conduct and working of Government at all levels and will use and publicise this information as it thinks fit. The first task of the Opposition in Parliament is to minimise secrecy in Government.

The Opposition must also look critically at all policies and proposals brought before the House by the Government and then oppose and, if possible, delay or even prevent the implementation of those proposals it considers undesirable. It will also take the initiative in seeking to bring to the public's attention aspects of the Government's policies and administration which would not otherwise be brought before Parliament. And it will present its own alternative policies and proposals in the most favourable light. It will either make promises about what it would do if it came to power, or will seek to avoid making such promises in areas where it feels less secure or where its popularity might suffer.

In this Chapter we examine the opportunities available to the Opposition (and sometimes to the smaller parties) to take the initiative in exercising these various and interrelated functions.

---

[1] According to Disraeli, Parl.Deb., Vol. 78, cols. 154–155 (February 28, 1845).

It should not be thought, however, that these opportunities for the Opposition are all precisely or formally defined. In varying degrees, as will be
shown, the Opposition has to fight to secure and preserve its opportunities.
It has to compete, especially with the Government, for time on the floor of
the House; within the time so secured there may be further competition
between Opposition parties for its use. How these competing claims are
reconciled—by formal procedures and by informal deals "through the usual
channels" has already been described in Chapter 7. The Chair also has an
important role to play, especially in dividing time in debate between the
various Opposition parties.

THE OPPORTUNITIES FOR THE OPPOSITION

The time spent by the House on various types of business initiated by the
Opposition was summarised in the Table on page 12. Here we look in
greater detail at how that time was used in two recent normal length
sessions.

Time Spent on Business Initiated by the Opposition Parties

Nature of business	1984–85		1985–86	
	hours	mins	hours	mins
Amendments to the Address	12	45	11	20
Opposition days	117	33	105	21
Opposition motions in Government time	6	44		–
Prayers against statutory instruments	28	36	18	47
SO No. 20 (Emergency adjournment) debates	3	15	3	12
Applications for SO No. 20 debates	1	18	0	32
Private notice Questions	2	59	7	22
Total	173	10	146	34

Debate on the Address

The Queen's Speech from the Throne sets out the Government's business
for the session, and so is properly classified under the heading of Government initiative (see pages 308–310), but in practice the topics in the debate
on the Address in reply to the Speech, after the first day, are, as a Leader of
the House has recognised[1a] largely chosen by the official Opposition.[2]

The main opportunity for the Opposition on the first day of the debate is
clearly defined. After the opening speeches by two Government back-
benchers, the Leader of the Opposition (having first congratulated the
mover and seconder) summarises the response of his party to the policies of
the Government as set out in the Speech, outlining the main lines of attack
that his party intends to deploy throughout the session. A brief summary of
two recent examples serve to show the pattern.

The first example is Mr. Kinnock's speech at the beginning of the 1986–87
session, when a general election was clearly drawing near. He spoke for 25
minutes. Proposals for combatting international terrorism and drug traffick-
ing, and for improving safety at sports grounds were welcomed; and Labour

---

[1a] H.C.Deb., Vol. 142, col. 886 (December 1, 1988).

[2] For the purpose of the analyses in the Tables on page 12 and above, only the debates on
Opposition amendments have been counted as Opposition initiated.

party support for the Anglo-Irish agreement was re-iterated. The proposed poll-tax for Scotland and the repeal of the Remuneration of Teachers Act 1965 were strongly criticised. But the main subject of the attack was the Government's economic and industrial policy and the effect this had on the standards of living of the poorer people in the country. Mr Kinnock concluded "whenever the Prime Minister gathers the courage to face the country, she will be called to account and soundly beaten."[3]

His forecast was mistaken. On June 25, 1987, he was still Leader of the Opposition when he opened Labour's attack on the third Thatcher administration. He enjoyed himself with some banter about the new cabinet, but most of his 26 minute speech was devoted to criticism of Government policies for privatisation, the poll-tax, education changes and further reduction (as he saw it) in the powers and responsibilities of local authorities. It was a broad condemnation of the general political philosophy of the Prime Minister, rather than a detailed criticism of specific proposals in the Queen's Speech.[4]

For the next two or three days of the debate on the Address, the Opposition is able to choose the topics by agreement through the usual channels. On the last two days, Opposition amendments are called, so the Opposition can precisely determine the subject of debate by the wording of its amendments.

At the end of the last day an amendment is also moved by the second largest Opposition party for division only (no separate debate). These amendments need not relate to the topic chosen for that day by the official Opposition, but have frequently done so. The smaller parties have usually taken the opportunity to summarise the main themes that distinguish them from the other parties.

An analysis of the topics chosen in the 1983–87 Parliament shows how the debates on the Address have been used in recent years. Each debate lasted five days. In the 20 debates in those four years (some covering more than one topic), the economy and foreign affairs and industrial policy were debated four times each; the welfare state, especially health and social security, came up three times, as did local government and education; and home affairs was twice specifically listed. Other topics that were once mentioned as subjects for debate by arrangement included defence, privatisation, and Scottish affairs. In each of these years the Labour party chose to concentrate their attack on the Government's policies on industry, the economy and unemployment by tabling amendments on these subjects. The Liberal amendments on the last day also mainly related to these issues. Neither law and order nor environment questions were specifically chosen in these years, in contrast with the period between 1974 and 1979 when the Conservative Opposition twice chose these topics.

It is perhaps dangerous to draw general conclusions from this fairly small sample, though the pattern is typical, and on the whole similar topics were chosen by the Conservative Opposition between 1974 and 1979. It also moved most of its amendments on the subject of the state of the economy. A few trends are apparent. First, there is little attempt to relate the topics to outstanding legislative and other policy proposals contained in the Queen's Speech. Nor, except in the case of a Liberal amendment on the National

---

[3] H.C.Deb., Vol. 105, cols. 11–16 (November 12, 1986).
[4] H.C.Deb., Vol. 118, cols. 46–51 (June 25, 1987).

Dock Labour Scheme in 1975 and a two-day debate initiated by the Conservatives on Rhodesia in 1978, has the opportunity been taken, even when an amendment has been moved, to focus attention on some specific matter of current political interest. The preference has rather been for broad brush attacks on major sectors of government policy. And these have been largely on the home front. Perhaps Oppositions of both parties since 1974 have accurately reflected the concerns of the wider public in choosing the best subject on which to attack the Government of the day. For earlier generations other issues have been to the fore.[5]

The very last day of the debate is usually a major parliamentary occasion. Prominent Members including former Prime Ministers take part, and the debate is wound up with a wider-ranging speech by the Leader of the House. After the amendments have been disposed of, the main question, thanking Her Majesty for her Speech, is put. In the past this has usually been agreed to without a vote, but in recent years the Labour Opposition has voted against the Speech as a whole as a mark of general protest against the Government.

Opposition Days

The most frequent occasions, throughout the session, when the Opposition has the opportunity to debate matters of its own choosing occur on allotted Opposition days when business chosen by Opposition parties has priority over Government business. Since 1985 there have been 17 days each session for the official Opposition and three for the second largest Opposition party; in the 1983–87 Parliament this was the Liberal Party. By informal agreement the larger Opposition parties occasionally allow one of their allotted days to be used by other smaller parties, such as the Scottish and Welsh nationalists or the Ulster Unionists. Some of the allotted days can be taken in the form of half-days, either up till 7 p.m., or from 7 to 10 p.m., in accordance with Standing Order No. 13(2). The Opposition parties may choose to have two shorter debates on any of their days, with two separate motions, instead of one long debate. This is becoming increasingly popular: in 1975–76 there were six half-day debates, but in 1985–86 there were 24. These debates are now spread fairly evenly throughout the session, and in most weeks there is an allotted Opposition day or half-day.

Opposition days are a relatively new development which has grown from the old "Supply days," which were mainly used for debating matters of the Opposition's choosing (see page 11). The formal sub-division of days between the Opposition parties dates only from 1985. These changes make comparisons between periods slightly difficult.

Prior to 1982, when this new system was introduced, while the Opposition frequently tabled substantive motions, some debates took place on motions for the adjournment and occasionally on formal motions to reduce a Minister's salary by a notional amount. These procedures permitted a wide debate without coming to any precise decision.

Since 1982, however, these debates have almost entirely been held on substantive motions tabled by the Opposition condemning or criticising the Government in some respect, to which the Government usually tables an amendment to leave out all the critical words and substitute others express-

---

[5] In 1937 and 1938, for example, amendments were moved relating to foreign affairs, re-armament and defence, as well as (again) unemployment.

ing a more favourable view of ministerial policy. There can be two divisions at the end of each debate; the Opposition words are always negatived; a Government amendment is always agreed to; and the House resolves the wording proposed by the Government. Resolutions are recorded in Hansard and the Journal, but otherwise little attention appears to be paid to them by the media or anyone else. It is the debate which counts, and the general approach and commitment of the main speakers.

A complete alphabetical list of the topics chosen by the Opposition in the most recent normal length session (1985–86) may serve to indicate the way this procedure is used—

Opposition Days, 1985–86
Topics chosen by Opposition parties for debate

Big City Hospitals – (half-day)
British Leyland – (half-day)
Cancer Screening for Women at Risk – (half-day)
Caring for the Carers
City of London – (half-day)
Crime – (half-day)
Economic Policy and the Level of Unemployment – (twice)
Economic Strategy
The Elderly
Education – (Liberal choice) (half-day)
Exchange Rate Policy and Interest Rates – (SDP choice) (half-day)
Gartcosh Steel Mill (Threatened Closure)—(half-day)
Higher and Continuing Education – (half-day)
High Technology Industries – (Liberal choice) (half-day)
Housing – (half-day)
Housing Crisis and Urban Deprivation
Northern Region – (half-day)
Private Tenants – (half-day)
Privatisation of Water Authorities – (Liberal choice) (half-day)
Poverty amongst the Elderly – (half-day)
Regional Strategy – (Scottish National and Plaid Cymru choice) (half-day)
Rural Areas – (Liberal choice) (half-day)
Schools (Effects of Government Policy)—(half-day)
Silentnight plc – (half-day)
South Africa
South Africa – (half-day)
Strategic Defence Initiative – (half-day)
Students in Further and Higher Education (Support) – (half-day)
Transport – (half-day)
Unemployed (Withdrawal of Mortgage Interest Payments Protection) – (half-day)
Westland plc

A broader analysis, covering periods with two different Oppositions, reveals the balance of topics chosen.

Analysis of Subjects chosen by Opposition for debate

	Whole day equivalents	
	(a)	(b)
Foreign and Commonwealth affairs	9	3½
Economic affairs	9	4
Home Office matters	2½	1
Industry, Energy and Trade	4½	6
Defence and Armed Forces	1½	½
Scotland, Wales and other regional matters	4	2
Health and Social Services	4	7½
Agriculture, Fisheries and Food	3½	½
Local Government, Housing and Environment	3	4
Employment and Labour Relations	5½	5½
Education	0	4
Transport	½	½

(a) Subjects chosen by Conservatives, Liberals and others, sessions 1975–76 and 1977–78.
(b) Subjects chosen by Labour, Liberals and others, sessions 1984–85 and 1985–86.

This analysis reveals, with few exceptions, a fairly even distribution of chosen topics, across the whole field of government, and the pattern was broadly similar whichever Opposition party was making the choice.

Both major parties gave economic affairs, industry and employment a high priority, but the Conservatives put more emphasis on purely economic matters like pay and prices policy (a major issue in 1975–76) and taxation, while Labour spent more time on industry. Labour also focused their attack on health and social services and education (the latter surprisingly neglected by the Conservatives in the selected sessions when they were in Opposition). The Alliance parties sometimes chose topics on which they had policies clearly different from those of the two larger parties (for example the S.D.P. chose to debate trade union ballots in 1984–85 and exchange rates policy in 1985–86; this was to urge the Government to join the European Monetary System). The Welsh and Scottish nationalist parties naturally put down motions regarding the affairs of their countries.

As with debates on the Queen's Speech, many of the topics chosen were broad departmental or policy areas—unemployment and industrial policies, the welfare state, housing and foreign affairs, for example. But, unlike the Queen's Speech debates, a fair number related to much more specific, topical issues. Examples from the sessions analysed in the Table include investment in the motor industry (1975–76), sale of council houses (1975–76), elections to the European Assembly (1975–76), pay in the armed forces (1977–78), the Official Secrets Acts (1977–78), famine in developing countries (1984–85), post office closures (1984–85), South Africa (1985–86), British Leyland (1985–86), the closure of Gartcosh steel works (1985–86), and privatisation of water authorities (1985–86). Occasionally the Opposition has used Opposition days for a major debate on a matter of great, immediate, political controversy: the debates in February 1985 on the coal strike, and in January 1986 on the Westland affair fall into this category.

Motions of Censure

By convention—there are no formal rules on this—if the official Opposition tables a motion of censure on the Government, the Government provides time for it to be debated. There is, again, no formal definition of a "motion of censure." Many motions tabled on Opposition days censure the Government in highly critical terms, but do not count as censure motions. Traditionally a censure motion is in the form "That this House has no confidence in Her Majesty's Government," which the Government seeks to defeat without amendment. More recently, however, words have been included to indicate the particular matter on which the Opposition wishes to censure the Government. For example, on July 29, 1980, Mr. Callaghan moved—

"That this House has no confidence in Her Majesty's Government whose economic and social policies are spreading mass unemployment, undermining British industry and demoralising the country."

This was negatived without amendment. A motion in identical terms was moved by the Opposition on July 27, 1981. A motion censuring the Government for its "gross mismanagement of the British economy" was also moved by the Leader of the Opposition on January 31, 1985, but this time an amendment was moved by the Prime Minister and carried. On November 14, 1988, the Leader of the Opposition tabled a motion for the appointment of a select committee to investigate the personal conduct of the Chancellor of the Exchequer regarding the account he had given to the House of a meeting he had had with Lobby journalists[5a]. This was akin to a motion of censure but no time was provided for its debate (the session was nearly ended).

The incidence of specific censure motions since the 1974 election is shown below.

Motions of Censure on the Government

Session	Date	Nature of Motion	Result of Division
Labour Government			
1974–75	–	–	–
1975–76	9 June 1976	No confidence	Negatived: 290–309
1976–77	23 March 1977	No confidence	Negatived: 298–322
1977–78	–	–	–
1978–79	28 March 1979	No confidence	Agreed to: 311–310
Conservative Government			
1979–80	29 July 1980	No confidence in economic and social policies	Negatived: 274–333
1980–81	27 July 1981	No confidence in economic and social policies	Negatived: 262–334
1981–82	–	–	–
1982–83	–	–	–
1983–84	–	–	–
1984–85	31 January 1985	Censuring Government's management of the economy	Govt amendment agreed to: 395–222 Motion, as amended agreed to: 392–221

Censure motions are fairly rare, particularly when Governments have large majorities and their tenure of office is secure. They are always major

---

[5a] EDM 1598 on p. 9487 of Notices of Motions, 1987–88.

parliamentary occasions; the debate is normally opened by the Leader of the Opposition, the Prime Minister speaks for the Government, and the numbers who obey the summons whip (pairs are allowed only in the most limited circumstances) are large.[6] On occasions, as on March 28, 1979, the result is of major political importance.

Opposition Motions in Government Time

Occasionally the official Opposition has moved motions, other than censure motions and motions related to statutory instruments (see below), in Government time. Under the former Supply days system, the Government occasionally used a Supply day for its own business, and returned the favour by letting the Opposition use Government time. This does not happen now that Opposition days are clearly and precisely provided by standing order. Occasionally however, the Government has agreed to provide opportunity in its own time for fairly short Opposition initiated debates on relatively minor matters. Unusual procedures have also been debated in this way, as happened on June 29, 1976 and December 7, 1976 in relation to the Aircraft and Shipbuilding Industries Bill. Overall, in the 13 sessions from 1974–75 to 1986–87, the Government allowed time for debating such Opposition business on 10 occasions, but there were no such debates in the 1983–87 Parliament.

Prayers against Statutory Instruments

A fairly important opportunity for the Opposition is created by the negative procedure for scrutiny of delegated legislation. Official Opposition "prayers" against statutory instruments may be taken on the floor of the House, by agreement with the Government, or, with the same agreement, upstairs in a standing committee (see pages 246–247 and 275).

In theory there could—and perhaps should—be many such debates, as numerous Acts provide that ministerial orders or regulations shall come into force unless annulled by a resolution of either House of Parliament. But motions for such annulment cannot be made unless time is provided, and in practice the right to move prayers is limited by the control of the Government over the time of the House and over the reference of matters to committees. Thus the Government is able to prevent criticism of its delegated legislation despite the fact that statutes provide formally for such criticism. This, and in particular the increasing percentage of prayers which are not debated at all (see Table below), has troubled many people and several procedure committees.[7] However, as far as the official Opposition is concerned (and to a lesser extent the smaller parties), some opportunity is provided, though doubtless less than they would like, to raise matters that concern them which are the subject of delegated legislation.

But not all prayers are actually debated, and the percentage of undebated prayers is growing as the following Table shows—

---

[6] Allowing for the four Tellers, 600 or more Members have taken part in every censure division since 1974 and to these figures should also be added the four occupants of the Chair who do not vote. In the 1979 division only one Member was absent; two abstained although present; there were three outstanding by-elections.

[7] For a discussion of this problem and for the background to the creation of standing committees on statutory instruments, see Report of the Joint Committee on Delegated Legislation, H.L. 184, H.C. 475 of 1971–72, paras. 93–128; and see Second Report of the Procedure Committee, H.C. 350 of 1986–87, paras. 11–36.

Extent of Debate on Instruments subject to the Negative Procedure

Session	Number of instruments subject to negative procedure	Number of prayers tabled	Number of instruments subject to negative procedure referred to standing committee	Number of prayers placed by Government for debate in the House	Number of prayers on which a decision was reached (c)	Number of prayers on which no action was taken	Prayers on which no action was taken as percentage of total number of prayers tabled
1978–79(a)	517	46	29	4	3	13	28.3%
1983–84(b)	947	113	22	51	35	40	35.4%
1984–85	682	91	27	22	14	42	46.2%
1985–86	861	111	9	25	14	77	69.4%

(a) Unusually short session.
(b) Unusually long session.
(c) In several cases several prayers were debated jointly or a prayer was taken together with motions on one or more instruments subject to the affirmative procedure. In such cases the prayer may not be formally moved.

Source: H.C. 350 of 1986–87, para. 12.

It is impossible to measure how far the occasions for debate fall short of demand. It may be that if there were more opportunities, more prayers would be tabled and would then be debated. But it may well be that, with all the conflicting pressures on time and manpower, the Opposition would not expand significantly the number of debates even if this were possible.[7a]

A number of prayers are also tabled by the smaller Opposition parties. In 1983–84, out of a total of 113 tabled prayers, 21 were tabled by these parties (mostly by those then acting together as the Alliance), and in 1984–85 there were again 21 smaller party prayers, out of a total of 91. Some of these are debated in standing committees (see below) but rarely on the floor of the House.[7b]

Turning to those which are debated, we first look at debates on the floor of the House. In the 1974–79 Parliament, the Conservative Opposition was able to secure debates, on average, seven times a session (a total of 35 times). In the 1983–87 Parliament, the Labour Opposition did significantly better: it had an average of 13 debates a session (a total of 53). The great majority of these debates were brought on after 10 p.m. The greater use of prayers by the Labour Opposition may partly reflect increased competition from the Alliance parties, who tabled a number of prayers. But it may equally have been that the Conservative Government has, for some reason, been more willing to allow time for such business; it is difficult to prove either way. For whatever reason the number of debates on prayers has increased recently and that there has also been a small, but consistent, growth in the number debated as part of the main business of the day. The opportunity for Opposition initiative has thus expanded.

Prayers on the floor of the House cover a wide range of topics and typically reflect the political concerns of the party in Opposition. In the 1983–87 Parliament the matters most frequently chosen by the Labour party were housing (eight prayers), agriculture and water (seven), local government and rating (six), social security (six), industrial matters (six), education (five), the N.H.S. (five) and immigration (four). To some extent prayers also highlight the issues of the day: prevention of terrorism, with a Northern Ireland emphasis, was among the prayers tabled by the Conservatives in 1976, and local government reorganisation was a theme of Labour prayers in 1986. In most cases the issues chosen are relatively narrow, and sometimes technical, although made of interest by wider political implications. Specific topics may sometimes lead to wider policy debates, but on the whole debates are fairly well confined (sometimes by frequent reminders by the Chair) to the matter of the statutory instrument which has been selected by the Opposition for debate.

An Opposition front-bench spokesman (frequently one of the more junior) opens the debate, explaining why they have tabled the prayer. A junior Minister normally speaks next explaining and defending the Government's position and the proposals embodied in the instrument. After a few short speeches from either side, the Minister comments briefly in reply to the points raised in the debate. The prayer will then be negatived or it may

---

[7a] On November 30, 1988, the Leader of the House claimed that "the present arrangements are reasonably satisfactory, and those prayers which there is a widespread desire to debate are debated". This was not challenged by the official Opposition (H.C.Deb., Vol.142, col. 769).

[7b] The Leader of the House conceded that the Democrats party "does not get as many prayers as it would like," because of its limited numbers in the House (*ibid*).

be withdrawn; some prayers are tabled simply to probe the Government's intentions and are not necessarily pressed to a division. In 1984–85 and in 1985–86 there were 13 (out of 22) and eight (out of 25) divisions, respectively, on prayers in the House.

Occasionally the Government provides time for a debate on a prayer to start earlier in the day so that there may be a fuller discussion; in 1984–85 there were five-hour debates on water authorities, local government expenditure and the N.H.S. and in 1985–86 immigration rules were debated for four and a half hours. More exceptionally, as happened with a debate on disposal of radio-active waste in 1986, the rule may be suspended to allow a longer debate after 10 p.m. Normally, however, prayers are not debated for more than an hour and a half. The main value of these short debates from the Opposition's point of view would appear to be to highlight areas of governmental action which have caused public anxiety and to show the Opposition's own concern about these matters. The debates also provide a useful parliamentary outlet for junior front-bench spokesmen on both sides who do not speak in more important debates.

Since 1973, the Opposition has also had the opportunity of choosing statutory instruments which are subject to the negative procedure for short debates in standing committees. Again this is dependent on the Government's agreement to refer the matter to a committee (see page 246). As the Table on page 346 demonstrates, not all prayers are debated either upstairs or down, but the Table on page 349 shows the use that has been made of these opportunities by the Opposition parties. (For convenience and comparison, statistics of back-bench prayers and of debates on instruments subject to the affirmative procedure have also been included.) It will be noted that the use by the official Opposition has varied considerably but there has been a clear growth in debates on matters chosen by the smaller Opposition parties. The use of these procedures by back-benchers is discussed on pages 406–407.

An analysis of the standing committee debates on statutory instruments subject to the negative procedure in the 1983–87 Parliament indicates a tendency to concentrate in one or two areas of government. Classifying the subjects according to the Government department (or Scottish equivalent) primarily responsible, we see that the Labour Opposition chose to debate nine statutory instruments relating to agriculture, fisheries or food; seven concerning health or social services; and four in the field of environment, housing or local government. The smaller parties (almost entirely the Liberals) secured debates on seven instruments in the environmental field, including local government; six on health or social services; and five relating to agriculture, fisheries or food. Both the official Opposition and the Liberals chose to debate a number of statutory instruments applying to Scotland. A few other prayers referred to education, transport, trade or energy matters. But the range was wide—from the Scented Erasers (Safety) Order, 1984, to the Inshore Fishing (Prohibition of Carriage of Monofilament Gill Nets) (Scotland) Order, 1986; and from the prohibition of the use of hormone growth promoters, to regulations regarding the dipping of car headlights.

The choice of prayers for debate upstairs is of course conditioned by the matters on which statutory instruments are made subject to the negative procedure, but it apparently also reflects a desire to debate matters, often highly specific, and often related to the less politically central issues such as fisheries or food and drug regulations, that are not generally debated on the floor of the House.

Statutory Instruments Considered by Standing Committees

| Session | Instruments subject to negative procedure | | | | Instruments requiring affirmation |
| | *(Mover of prayer)* | | | | |
	Official Opposition	*Smaller Opposition Parties*	*Government back-bench*	*Opposition back-bench*	*Government*
Labour Government					
1974–75	5	1	6	1	88
1975–76	3	–	17	2	73
1976–77	16	2	14	11	83
1977–78	22	–	14	5	97
Conservative Government					
1980–81	1	1	4	1	55
1981–82	11	1	9	–	59
1982–83	4	3	6	–	57
1983–84	8	8	5	1	74
1984–85	16	10	–	1	72
1985–86	5	4	–	–	88
1986–87	5	4	4	1	51

NOTES
1. These figures have been prepared on the basis of the Member who moved the relevant motion in the committee. In some cases it was not clear whether an Opposition Member was acting on behalf of the official Opposition or as an independent back-bencher. The balance between the first and fourth columns may therefore not be wholly correct.
2. It should be emphasised that the figures relate to the number of instruments formally considered, and not to the number of debates. In several debates on instruments subject to the negative procedure more than one instrument was considered together. This happened frequently with instruments requiring affirmation.

Other factors may at other times influence the choice of topics for these debates. For example, a heavy emphasis shown by the Conservatives when in Opposition before 1979 on fisheries probably reflected concern by certain Members, particularly from Scotland, for this industry. The increasing use of these debates in committee by the Alliance parties shows how they found a way of compensating for the severely restricted opportunities they had to initiate debate on the floor of the House. Many of the topics they chose closely matched the constituency or personal interests of the individual Liberal or S.D.P. Members who spoke on the statutory instruments in the committees.

It should not be thought that the Opposition is necessarily opposed to all the instruments on which it secures debates in standing committee. Many of the debates in committee are narrow or technical and often the topic has been chosen simply to enable the Opposition to probe the Government's intentions and seek explanations. Sometimes it even welcomes the orders or regulations concerned. On the other hand some debates end in a division, although as there is no substantive motion before the committee (see page 275) this is of little significance.

There being no possibility of significant divisions the attendance at statutory instruments committees when considering instruments subject to negative procedure tends to be low—about 10 on average in recent years—and occasionally a quorum cannot be kept. But a few keen specialists usually ensure a reasonably full debate. In general, it may be thought that debates on statutory instruments subject to the negative procedure provide a useful outlet for the Opposition to ventilate matters that would otherwise not be brought before the House.

Emergency Adjournment Debates

The procedure under Standing Order No. 20 for claiming, and if successful opening, an emergency adjournment debate provides a double opportunity for its users to bring issues of their choosing before the House. Although, as the Procedure Committee reminded the House in 1985, "the procedure exists primarily to allow back-bench Members . . . to have the opportunity of obtaining time on the floor of the House for matters they judge to be of great importance,"[8] it is also available to the Opposition front-bench or the Leaders of the smaller parties. This is sometimes criticised on the grounds that the Opposition parties have their own opportunities to initiate debate on Opposition days, and it has been suggested that they should use some of their "half-days" for such urgent matters.[9] The fact remains that this procedure is regularly used by the Opposition. (The use by back-benchers is discussed on pages 377–379).

The double opportunity arises because there is first a short application; and, if this is successful there is, later and separately, a three-hour debate. Both opportunities occur immediately after Questions and statements which is considered prime time and ideal for catching the evening news bulletins on radio and television.

The following Table throws some light on how these opportunities have been used since 1974—

Applications for Standing Order No 20 Emergency Adjournment Debates

Session	Number of Applications (c)	No. of Applications by Opposition front-bench and Leaders of smaller parties	Number granted	Number granted to front-bench
1974–75	33	–	1	–
1975–76	58	1	3	1
1976–77	44	–	3	–
1977–78	38	–	2	–
1978–79(a)	66	–	3	–
1979–80(b)	89	4	2	–
1980–81	48	3	1	1
1981–82	61	9	2	1
1982–83(a)	50	5	2	2
1983–84(b)	84	11	3	2
1984–85	61	13	1	1
1985–86	87	10	1	1
1986–87(a)	48	8	2	2
1987–88(b)	88	16	1	1

(a) unusually short session.
(b) unusually long session.
(c) including some multiple applications on the same matter.

[8] First Report, H.C. 42 of 1985–86, para. 5.
[9] See Memorandum by the Clerk of the House, *ibid.* p. x–x1.

These figures show how the Labour party, since it became the official Opposition in 1979, has increasingly used these opportunities to apply for an emergency adjournment debate, even when there is little probability of this being granted, so as to draw attention to a matter of contemporary concern.

Applications may also sometimes be made by back-benchers on the Opposition side with the connivance or encouragement of their front-bench. For example, in the winter of 1984 there was a considerable period during which the official Labour Opposition did not itself think it advantageous, for political reasons, to press for a debate on the miners' strike, although a number of back-benchers from mining constituencies had done so. Equally, for corresponding reasons, Ministers did not choose to allow a debate on this highly controversial matter on a Government motion. On April 9, 1984, however, Mr. Allen McKay, an Opposition Whip, but also a mining Member, rose from the Opposition back-benches, and asked leave to move the adjournment of the House for the purpose of discussing a specific and important matter that should have urgent consideration, namely "the implications for civil liberties and the rule of law of policing operations connected with the current mining dispute."[10] It was clear that, expressed in these terms, which focussed on the actions of the police rather than the miners' pickets, the official Opposition would not be unsympathetic to the application; indeed a Conservative back-bencher suggested that the Opposition front-bench had intimated such support to the Speaker.[11] Equally, Government back-benchers, and perhaps front-benchers as well, welcomed an opportunity to debate the issues of the strike itself, which had not been formally debated by the House. Whatever the reasoning, the application was granted, and the next day there was a short, but major debate (27 Members wished to take part,[12] but only 15 Members, including four front-bench spokesmen and the Leader of the S.D.P. were able to be called) which canvassed the actions both of the strikers and the police.

Examination of 63 topics chosen by Opposition front-bench spokesmen when applying for emergency debates from 1979 to 1987 reveals a wide spectrum, ranging from sale of *The Times* newspaper (January 26, 1981) to sale of Associated British Ports (February 16, 1983); from Sunday trading (December 10, 1984) to the trial of Clive Ponting (February 11, 1985); from the arts (June 6, 1985) to top salaries (July 22, 1985). Industrial problems including industrial disputes (32), were by far the most prominent but local authority matters (nine), home and legal (eight) and defence issues (seven) were also raised fairly frequently. There were fewer applications by the front-bench on education (four), international affairs (three) or the N.H.S. (three). Although some Members grasped at these opportunities more eagerly than others (one Member who shadowed various departments at different times made nine applications), many of the Labour Party's front-bench team used them at one time or another, as did the Leader of the S.D.P. on seven occasions.

The topics selected have usually been quite specific (as indeed the standing order requires) and indeed sometimes apparently narrow. Their main common characteristic is that they reflected the hot issues of the day—that morning's headlines. It may well be that the main purpose in making

---

[10] H.C.Deb., Vol. 68, col. 24 (April 9, 1984).
[11] *Ibid.*, col. 25.
[12] H.C.Deb., Vol. 68, col. 203 (April 10, 1984).

applications for these debates, which are unlikely to be granted, and for which not more than three minutes is allowed on the floor of the House, is to create publicity for the Opposition's criticism of the Government. It has been the opportunity to raise a topical matter which has counted, not the opportunity for debate.

The few debates that have been granted to the official Opposition (none have been granted in recent years to Leaders of the smaller parties), have nevertheless formed a high proportion of the total number granted (see Table on page 350). Between 1979 and 1987 these debates were—

Debates under Standing Order No. 20

Successful applications by Opposition front-bench

Date of debate	Topic	Member moving
January 27, 1981	Proposed purchase of *The Times*	John Smith
December 22, 1981	The GLC	Albert Booth
December 15, 1982	NATO Council meeting	Denis Healey
February 14, 1983	Dispute in the water industry	Gerald Kaufmann
October 26, 1983	Invasion of Grenada by USA	Denis Healy
May 24, 1984	Closures at British Leyland	Peter Shore
December 19, 1984	Local Authorities Capital Expenditure (England and Wales)	John Cunningham
January 27, 1986	Westland plc	Neil Kinnock
December 18, 1986	Airborne Early Warning System	Denzil Davies
February 3, 1987	Official Secrets Act: Activities of Special Branch	Gerald Kaufmann

No general conclusions regarding their subject-matter can be deduced from such a small base. All that they have in common is that at the time they were of such major, immediate concern that the Opposition thought they should be debated and the Speaker agreed. This is a sufficient definition.

What was important about these 10 occasions was that the Government was required, at the initiative of the Opposition and probably contrary to the wishes of Ministers, to explain and defend its policies on matters of current concern at a peak hour for catching media attention. Such debates are always well attended—with Members heavily whipped for the expected vote (eight of the 10 debates ended with divisions)—and are big House of Commons occasions.

Oral Questions

Although Opposition front-bench spokesmen do occasionally table Questions for oral answer, the great majority are tabled by back-benchers (see pages 262 and 366–372). However, front-benchers are frequently called to ask supplementaries, usually after one or two back-benchers on either side, and thus have an opportunity to put the Opposition's point of view on the record or to challenge the Minister.

A concerted effort is also made on some days to concentrate the Opposition's fire against the Minister who is "up for Questions" that day by pursuing a specific theme, and it is to be expected that the official Opposition spokesman would be influential in the selection of such themes.

We have analysed the extent of intervention by leading Opposition spokesmen,[13] during Questions to Ministers other than the Prime Minister by

---

[13] Identified by membership of the shadow Cabinet, and so excluding junior Opposition spokesmen who may also have asked Questions from the dispatch box.

counting the number of supplementary Questions they asked on 24 randomly selected days (with different departments up for questioning) in three sessions when the Conservatives were in Opposition before 1979 and in three sessions when Labour were the official Opposition since then. The pattern is remarkably consistent. On those occasions there were 61 leading front-bench interventions (an average of 2.5 per day) when the Conservatives were in Opposition and 49 (an average of two per day) when Labour had that role. The largest number of leading front-bench supplementaries was five, on two days; on three days there were no such supplementaries. During each selected Question period, some 15 to 20 original Questions would be asked by back-benchers.

The leading Opposition spokesmen are thus seen to be abstemious on these occasions. They tend to keep a relatively low profile during Question time, leaving their own back-benchers and more junior front-bench colleagues, to make the running. The latter are increasingly well to the fore, especially from the teams shadowing the larger departments, such as the Treasury, when a number of ambitious younger men or women may be anxious to show their paces. This has sometimes caused problems for the Speaker, who has to balance the claims of junior front-bench spokesmen against those of back-benchers on either side[13a]

In one way or other, therefore, the Opposition front-bench does take the chance to focus attention on certain issues at Question time, and once it leads the hunt down a chosen avenue the back-bench pack can follow.

By far the most important opportunity for the Opposition to take the initiative during Question hour arises on Questions to the Prime Minister, from 3.15 to 3.30 every Tuesday and Thursday. By convention, the Leader of the Opposition does not table Questions for oral answer (he occasionally puts down, by arrangement, a Question to the Prime Minister for written answer on such matters as a report by the Security Commission), nor ask supplementaries to other Ministers. On the other hand, by convention he (or in his absence his Deputy) is called to put one or more supplementary Questions to the Prime Minister. The extent to which this has been done in selected sessions in recent years is shown by the following Table:

Number of Questions asked by the Leader of the Opposition
(or by his Deputy, in his absence)

Session	Number of Questions asked on each occasion						Total Number of Questions asked
	One	Two	Three	Four	Five	Six	
1971–72	11	11	8	2	0	0	65
1975–76	19	41	1	0	0	0	104
1980–81	3	26	20	8	0	2	159
1983–84(a)	8	38	27	2	0	0	173
1984–85	1	21	28	1	0	0	132
1985–86	3	24	32	0	0	0	147
1986–87(b)	0	14	30	1	0	0	122

(a) Unusually long session.
(b) Unusually short session.

[13a] See, for example, H.C.Deb., Vol. 147, cols. 995, 998 (February 22, 1989), when the Speaker refused to call a junior spokesman to ask a second supplementary.

It will be seen that the extent to which Leaders of the Opposition have used these opportunities has increased significantly in recent sessions. In particular, the Leader has sought to ask (and if he rises the Speaker always calls him) two or three questions much more frequently than used to be the case. This has sometimes been the cause of protest by Government back-benchers, but two or three supplementaries is now fairly standard.

One of the reasons for the increased number of Questions asked by Leaders of the Opposition has been the almost total adoption of "open" Questions to the Prime Minister[14] (see page 259). These permit supplementaries on almost any subject of the questioners choosing. The Leader of the Opposition is thus able to bring before the House and the public (Question hour is prime media time, and these occasions are often broadcast live on the radio) the issues of the day he thinks most relevant. Obviously these often include events where the Government looks as if it may be in trouble, or an area of policy where the Government appears to be doing badly. When the Leader of the Opposition in earlier years had to confine his supplementaries to matters relevant to the specific Question asked, he clearly was unable to pick his own topic in this way. Indeed on numerous occasions between 1970 and 1974, Mr. Harold Wilson, as Leader of the Opposition, did not ask any Questions at all.

The Table on pages 355–356 seeks to give the flavour of these occasions by illustrating the topics chosen by Mrs. Thatcher when Leader of the Opposition before 1979 and by Mr. Kinnock since 1984.

It would be dangerous to draw too precise conclusions from a limited sample, but close observation of Prime Minister's Question time over the years suggests one or two significant developments. First, Leaders of the Opposition now make significantly more use of these opportunities than ever before. Second, the occasion has become much more heated politically (and also more noisy); this is no doubt a reflection of the widened political gap between the major parties, but Mrs. Thatcher and Mr. Kinnock, particularly, have used these occasions largely to make political points or advance broad arguments rather than to ask Questions on specific matters. Third, Mr. Kinnock in particular has developed the technique of concentrating on one pre-determined area with a series of prepared questions sometimes extending over several days.[15] The "open question" has made this possible.

Whatever the causes—and personalities cannot be ignored—Prime Minister's Question time has become increasingly important politically and as a parliamentary occasion. Here is experienced the direct confrontation of the Prime Minister and the Leader of the Opposition in its most concentrated and highly-charged form. It is an opportunity no Leader of the Opposition can afford to neglect. It is also the occasion when the Prime Minister can be most critically tested, and various commentators or experienced observers have testified to how carefully the Prime Minister has to

---

[14] Before 1970 nearly all the Questions tabled to the Prime Minister were on specific subjects. In session 1971–72 only about 10 per cent. of such Questions were "open" (Fifth Report of Select Comittee on Procedure, H.C. 320 of 1976–77, paras. 18–19). By the 1986–87 session only one or two Questions out of the 150–200 appearing on the Order Paper each Tuesday and Thursday were specific.

[15] This was clearly illustrated by Prime Minister's Question time in February 1988, when on four occasions out of eight Mr. Kinnock (or his deputy) pressed home an attack on the failure, as the Opposition saw it, of Government to fund the N.H.S. adequately.

Topics chosen by Leader of Opposition for Questions to Prime Minister

(Randomly selected days in April or May in selection Sessions)

	Day 1	Day 2	Day 3	Day 4	Day 5	Day 6	Day 7	Day 8
Session 1975–76 (Mrs Thatcher)	Value of pound and economic strategy (1)	Composition of standing committee when Government did not have a majority in the House (2)	Value of pound and incomes policy (1) Economic policy (1) Need for another general election (1)	Sale of council houses (2) Pay differentials and productivity (2)	Sale of council houses (1)	Position of British citizens in Rhodesia (1)	Value of pound and inflation (1)	Proposed suspension of hybridity rule in respect of Aircraft and Shipbuilding Industries Bill (2)
Session 1977–78 (Mrs Thatcher)	Armed forces pay (2)	Pay policy, pay differentials and reward for skills (2)	–	Numbers of people paying income tax (2)	Speech made in China by Chief of Defence Staff, referring to relations with USSR (2)	Marxism in the Labour Party (2)	Basic rate of income tax (following defeat in Committee on the Finance Bill) (1)	Expression of consolences following murder of Signor Aldo Moro (1)

Topics chosen by Leader of Opposition for Questions to Prime Minister (*cont.*)

(Randomly selected days in April or May in selection Sessions)

	Day 1	Day 2	Day 3	Day 4	Day 5	Day 6	Day 7	Day 8
Session 1984–85 (Mr Kinnock)	Manufacturing trends and industrial investment (2)	Levels of rate support grant (3)	Nurses pay (2)	Alleged delay in review of social security benefits before local elections (2)	Review of state earnings-related pensions and other benefits (3)	State-earnings related pensions (1) Child benefits (1)	Numbers of unemployed and recipients of supplementary benefits and family income supplement (2)	Scottish rates (3)
Session 1986–87 (Mr Kinnock)	Need for Government action to protect trade with Japan (3)	Suggestions that payment of unemployment benefit should be made conditional on undertaking compulsory work or training (3)	Government proposals for VAT (2)	Effects of a poll tax (3)	Level of tax-burden since 1979, and earned tax policy (3)	Health etc. of children in poverty (3)	Challenge to PM to face-to-face TV debate (2)	National Health Service (3)

Notes

The numbers in brackets show the number of Questions asked on each topic.
The examples include Questions asked by the Deputy Leader when Leader was absent.

prepare for this ordeal.[16] Success or failure on these occasions can greatly strengthen or seriously weaken the political standing of the two protagonists.

Mention must also be made of the use of oral Questions by the other party leaders. In the 1983–87 Parliament the Leaders of the Alliance parties did not table many Questions to Ministers for oral answer (although they tabled numerous Questions for written answer), but by convention they were usually called to put one supplementary Question to the Prime Minister. In practice the Speaker called Mr. Steel as Leader of the Liberal Party and Dr. Owen as Leader of the S.D.P. (or occasionally their deputies) to ask a Question on alternate Tuesdays and Thursdays, but not both on the same day. Again they used these occasions to bring matters of their choosing before the House. Other Leaders of smaller parties were called from time to time.

Private Notice Questions

Private notice Questions (PNQs) (see pages 260–261) are a special form of oral Question, and although they are mainly applied for by back-benchers (see pages 374–376), they are also frequently applied for by Opposition front-bench spokesmen and quite frequently allowed by the Speaker. They thus provide another opportunity for the Opposition to bring issues before the House that might not otherwise be raised (the Government may not wish to make a statement), and to do so at short notice. The following Table shows the extensive use made of this procedure by Oppositions in recent session.

Private Notice Questions asked by principal Opposition front-bench Spokesmen and Party Leaders

Session	Total No of PNQs	PNQs asked by front-bench and party Leaders
1977–78	21	4
1978–79(a)	29	12
1979–80(b)	45	17
1980–81	8	2
1981–82	9	1
1982–83(a)	7	2
1983–84(b)	48	18
1984–85	26	9
1985–86	43	20
1986–87(a)	19	7
1987–88(b)	39	22

(a) Unusually short session.
(b) Unusually long session.

In looking at this Table it should be noted that only PNQs asked by the principal Opposition spokesman—the "shadow Cabinet"—have been recorded. Numerous other PNQs were asked by more junior Opposition spokesmen, usually from the front-bench. Taking this into account it may be roughly estimated that about half the PNQs allowed by the Speaker, in most

---

[16] For example, Mr. Michael Alison, M.P. (formerly Mrs. Thatcher's Parliamentary Private Secretary) interviewed on Week in Westminster (B.B.C. Radio 4) on March 9, 1988.

sessions, have been front-bench Opposition Questions. This has enabled them to raise a matter of their choosing almost once a week, on average. It is clearly an important opportunity for Opposition initiative.

One striking feature of the statistics is worth a comment. The number of PNQs asked by the Opposition is a product of two factors: the desire of Opposition spokesmen to ask such Questions and the willingness of the Speaker (who has to consider "urgency" and "public importance") to allow them. It is not possible to separate precisely the contribution of these factors, but assuming that the Opposition desire has remained roughly constant, the unusually low figures of PNQs allowed in Sessions 1980–81 to 1982–83 would appear to result from a deliberate policy on the part of the then Speaker. During those years Speaker Thomas continued in office, although the party in power was no longer his original party (which in itself was an unusual arrangement see page 149). It was seemingly his personal decision not only to reduce significantly the total number of PNQs allowed but almost to suppress the use of PNQs on policy matters by the official Opposition. This reduced the extent to which the Government of the day was held to account on the floor of the House. In 1983, Speaker Weatherill reverted immediately to the well established practice of allowing about one PNQ per week, with a significant number for the Opposition front-bench.

As far as substance is concerned, detailed analysis since 1977 shows that Oppositions have naturally concentrated on those matters on which the Government appears vulnerable: industrial disputes and break-down of services in the "winter of discontent" in 1978–79, and troubles in the education profession in 1984–85, for example. Otherwise Oppositions have picked up newly disclosed specific matters (the urgency required to justify a PNQ usually means the matter must be specific and not general) which have political significance, such as leaks of nuclear waste at Sellafield (1983–84)[16a] and the content of the log-books of H.M.S. Conqueror (which sank the "General Belgrano" during the Falklands conflict) (1984–85)[16b]. There are also a number of PNQs relating to accidents or disasters which are major news events at the time, for example, a bomb in Wakefield Prison (1979–80)[16c] and the Abbeyfield Pumping Station disaster (1983–84)[16d], which appear to demand attention in the House but on which, for some reason, a Minister has not volunteered a statement. Finally there are matters of public concern on which it is desired to elicit a government response, for example the situation in Rhodesia (1977–78)[16e], Vietnamese refugees (1979–80)[16f] and the future of *The Observer* newspaper (1983–84)[16g].

Overall, the major use of this procedure has related to domestic matters: only 19, out of a total of 92 front-bench Opposition PNQs between 1977 and 1987, related specifically to foreign affairs or events outside the United Kingdom. The major, continuing, themes have been strikes or other industrial disputes (some 23 cases), economic industrial and trade affairs (some 16 cases) and health and social services (some nine cases), although these figures involve some overlapping classifications. About once a session a

---

[16a] H.C.Deb., Vol.49, cols. 19–22 (November 21, 1983)
[16b] H.C.Deb., Vol.67, cols. 106–111 (November 7, 1984)
[16c] H.C.Deb., Vol.969, cols. 437–438 (June 27, 1979)
[16d] H.C.Deb., Vol.60, cols. 1249–1253 (May 24, 1984)
[16e] H.C.Deb., Vol.945, cols. 973–981 (March 6, 1978)
[16f] H.C.Deb., Vol.968, cols. 908–917 (June 18, 1979)
[16g] H.C.Deb., Vol.58, cols. 883–886 (April 26, 1984)

PNQ is asked by the Leader of one of the smaller parties, sometimes on matters which for some reason the official Opposition did not wish to raise, such as the coal industry dispute in 1983–84[16h].

Sometimes an Opposition PNQ may act as a catalyst and set in train influences that may force a change of policy on the part of Ministers. For example on February 3, 1986, the Opposition asked a PNQ about the future of British Leyland Vehicles and possible disposals, in reply to which the Secretary of State for Trade and Industry confirmed that discussions were in progress between B.L. and General Motors.[17] This was followed by a debate on an Opposition day on February 5, 1986, which also dealt with a possible sale of the Austin Rover Group to Ford.[18] In the course of this debate concern was expressed by a number of Members on both sides, led by Mr. Heath who said he would resist in every possible way a sell out of the British motor industry to American firms.[19] On February 6, 1986, the Minister made a statement, "to end the uncertainty," that the possibility of the sale of Austin Rover to Ford "will not be pursued."[20] Several Members welcomed the fact that the proceedings in the House had revealed the proposals and, as the Leader of the Liberal Party put it, that "the House of Commons has been able to change the Government's mind."[21]

Debates on National or Regional Matters in Standing Committees

Formally, the responsibility for referring various matters to the Scottish and Welsh Grand Committees, and to the Northern Ireland and Regional Affairs Committees lies with the Government, but as most such references can be blocked by the Opposition if it is not happy with what is proposed, the Government's powers in this matter are strictly curtailed (see pages 274–275). Furthermore, as these committee debates do not involve any legislative or other significant decisions (see Standing Orders Nos. 96–100) the Government is content to leave the choice of business to the Opposition.[22] In the case of the Northern Ireland Committee this means, of course, that the Government has sought the agreement of the various groups of Ulster Members.

The extent of use by the Opposition of its opportunities under these procedures has varied over the years. Debates in June and July in the Scottish Grand Committee on the Scottish Estimates have long been well

---

[16h] H.C.Deb., Vol.62, cols. 141–152 (June 19, 1984)

[17] H.C.Deb., Vol. 91, col. 21.

[18] *Ibid* cols. 310–353.

[19] *Ibid.*, col. 328.

[20] *Ibid.*, col. 460.

[21] *Ibid.*, cols. 461–462, 466.

[22] For example, see the following exchanges in the Welsh Grand Committee:

Mr. Gwylim Jones (Cardiff North): "in accord with the usual traditions for setting the subjects for discussions by the Welsh Grand Committee, today's subject was the Opposition's choice"

The Secretary of State for Wales (Mr. Nicholas Edwards) . . . "I confirm that the Opposition asked for this debate on the elderly, and the Government responded to that request." (Official Report of Welsh Grand Committee, December 11, 1985, col. 3).

See also H.C.Deb., Vol. 94, col. *304*W (March 21, 1986) when the Leader of the House stated that debates in the Welsh Grand Committee were arranged following discussions through the usual channels.

established.[23] But until 1981 little use was permitted, and even less made by the Conservative Opposition prior to 1979, of the procedure for debating other exclusively Scottish matters of the Opposition's choice. However in that year, following talks on the consideration of Scottish business in the House (which was a product of the failure of devolution proposals), the Government agreed to increase the maximum number of days allowed each session for such debates from two to six (Standing Order No. 97). The Labour Opposition has subsequently used these occasions regularly. It has mainly chosen debates on specific matters which concern the Scottish people. For example, in 1985–86, it initiated debates on the N.H.S. in Scotland, higher education, a green paper on paying for local government, and the oil industry.[23a] The committee attracts particular attention in Scotland when it meets in Edinburgh, as it does two or three times each session. The Minister (often the Secretary of State) opens all these debates and is required to explain and defend his policies. The meetings are often broadcast on Scottish radio.

The Scottish Estimates debates have tended to be more general, enabling the Opposition, which opens these debates, to range widely over the field of its choice. No attempt is made on these occasions to consider the actual estimates in any detail. They are merely the peg on which to hang policy debates on the various areas of responsibility of Scottish Ministers (much as Supply day debates used to be in the House itself). By convention, one of the smaller parties—the S.N.P. or the Liberals—has from time to time had a debate on estimates of its choosing. In 1985–86, the debates were on estimates for Scottish Office Administration ("the government of Scotland"), education, housing, and health (chosen by the official Opposition), and on industry (chosen by the Liberals).[23b]

The use made by the Opposition of debates in the Welsh Grand Committee has become well established. Standing Order No. 98 is silent on the number of days for these debates, but after a somewhat varied practice in earlier years, the Opposition now regularly chooses each session three, four or five topics for debate upstairs, usually starting in the morning, breaking for lunch and Question time, and resuming again in the afternoon. The debates are opened by a Minister (again the Secretary of State is expected to attend and often speaks) and have almost always ranged fairly wide. Members can take up matters of their choosing within the chosen subject, but little attempt is made to have closely focussed debates on specific events or decisions. Matters chosen for debate in 1985–86 were the elderly in Wales, the roads programme and transport infrastructure in Wales, and the Welsh Development Agency[23c]. Occasionally a vote is forced at the end of a debate. This registers the Opposition's protest against the policies of the Government but is of no practical and little political effect. The committee has no power to express opinions as such; it simply "considers" the matters referred

---

[23] The fact that only two days were devoted to such debates in 1974–75 appears to be an aberration; in most years of the previous decade five or six sittings were spent considering Scottish estimates, and since 1981 Standing Order No. 96 has required that the estimates be considered on at least six days each session.

[23a] Minutes of Proceedings of the Scottish Grand Committee, H.C. 102, 166, 366 and 487 of 1985–86.

[23b] *Ibid*, H.C. 545 of 1985–86.

[23c] Minutes of Proceedings of the Welsh Grand Committee, H.C. 132, 321 and 424 of 1985–86.

to it. Traditionally there is also an annual debate on Welsh matters on the floor of the House, and Welsh affairs may be raised in a number of other ways.[24]

The procedure for a Standing Committee on Regional Affairs was adopted in 1975, and for two years significant use was made of it. This enabled attention to be paid to the problems of various regions (in 1975–76, for example, there were debates on East Anglia, the North West, the South East, and Yorkshire and Humberside economic planning[24a]) and gave Members from those parts outlets for expression of their concern without taking up time on the floor of the House or requiring the attendance, in case of a division, of Members from all other parts of the United Kingdom. Again there were sometimes divisions in the committee which, although largely meaningless, could be embarrassing for the Government. As any English Member could attend, the task of the Whips on either side was not easy. It may be that this was one of the reasons that these debates, although they appear to have been popular with the back-bench Members who took part, did not flourish. A debate on plans for the South-East in 1977–78 was the last use of the procedure[24b], although Standing Order No. 100 is still available.

The Northern Ireland Committee also provided a useful opportunity for the Opposition parties from that part of the United Kingdom to debate matters of their own choosing. Now that all specifically Northern Ireland legislation is enacted by statutory instrument, Members could secure debates at Westminster on draft orders, and although these could not be amended, Members could ask the Minister to take account of their criticisms in preparing his final orders. Wider matters could also be discussed. However, this procedure has also fallen into disuse. The committee only sat on five occasions during the 1983–87 Parliament, and no matters have been referred to the Committee since 1985, when proposals for a draft gas order were debated[24c].

In general, these debates in committee have provided for the Opposition parties useful opportunities—especially for discussion of Scottish and Welsh matters—for which time could not be found on the floor of the House. No significant decisions may be taken, but the two Secretaries of State, and their junior Ministers, are required to defend their policies in areas, and in a degree of detail, that would otherwise not be possible. To that extent their accountability to Parliament is enhanced.

Response to Government Initiatives

This Chapter has examined how the Opposition has used its opportunities to initiate business in the House and committees. But much of parliamentary proceedings resembles a tennis match, with the political issues volleying back and forward between the conflicting sides. When the Government serves, the Opposition returns service, and can sometimes win the point with a powerful passing shot. Major opportunities for the Opposition to make its own points, therefore, arise in response to Government initiatives, and a brief mention must be made of these.

First, the official Opposition can put on record its own point of view by

---

[24] For details see H.C.Deb., Vol. 94, cols. 303–304 (March 21, 1986).
[24a] H.C. 129, 165, 277, 317, 366 and 726 of 1975–76.
[24b] H.C. 584 and 614 of 1977–78.
[24c] H.C. 419 of 1984–85.

tabling amendments to Government motions; these are normally selected by the Speaker and ensure an opportunity for the Opposition to bring the matter to a vote. Similarly the smaller parties can publicise their arguments by tabling amendments to Government motions, although these are not usually selected for debate or vote (except at the end of the debate on the Address (see page 190)).

Occasionally, the Government wishes to avoid a vote on a particular matter and, instead of tabling a motion to approve some aspect of Government policy or even simply to take note of a White Paper or report, to which amendments could be moved, it decides to hold a debate on a motion for the adjournment of the House, to which no amendment can be moved. Even then the Opposition can register its protest against the Government by forcing a division.

Whether or not it tables an amendment, the official Opposition always has the chance of replying to the Minister who moves a motion. An Opposition front-bench spokesman is called first after the mover, and at the end of the debate, unless it is very short, another Member from the Opposition front-bench is called to speak before the Minister winds up. Representatives of smaller Opposition parties are called in the course of the debate.

Major opportunities for the Opposition to record formally its position—apart from speeches in the House or committee—occur during the process of legislation. First, reasoned amendments may be tabled setting out why the Opposition is opposed to giving a bill a second reading, and these are often selected by the Chair. This procedure appears to be becoming more fashionable. Whereas only five reasoned amendments on second reading were tabled and selected in session 1975–76, three in 1977–78, and none in 1980–81, there were eight in 1984–85 and 14 in 1985–86. To some extent this increase appears to have been stimulated by the Alliance parties, who discovered the value of this procedure in enabling them to secure, as would otherwise not be possible, a debate and vote on wording of their choice (provided the official Opposition did not choose to table a reasoned amendment itself); five of the 14 amendments voted on in 1985–86 were moved by Members of the Alliance.

Reasoned amendments on second readings of Government bills are always negatived when it comes to the vote. Even on the Shops Bill, on April 14, 1986, the reasoned amendment tabled by the official Opposition was defeated by 279 votes to 227, but the question on the actual second reading was defeated by 296 votes to 282. Clearly a number of Conservative back-benchers who were opposed to the bill were not prepared to vote for the Labour Party's reasoned amendment.

Reasoned amendments may also be tabled on the third reading of bills, but the rules of admissibility are very restrictive and this procedure is now little used.[25]

Throughout the committee and report stages of Government bills, Opposition parties take the opportunity, in responding to the Government proposals, to indicate their opposition, reservations, unease, or expectations respecting those proposals by tabling detailed amendments, either to leave provisions out or to insert alternatives, or both. Alternatively—and this appears to be becoming increasingly the practice—the Opposition will not

---

[25] There have been two cases in the last 20 years of such amendments being voted on: May 22, 1968, on the Town and Country Planning Bill; July 24, 1980, on the Coal Industry Bill.

prepare detailed amendments but will launch its attacks on matters of political principle by either broad amendments or by debating and voting on whole clauses. To some extent the butcher's cleaver seems to have replaced the surgeon's scalpel as the chosen tool of the official Opposition when scrutinising Government legislation. Some indication of the influence of the Opposition on Government bills was given in Chapter 8.

Two other responsive opportunities should be mentioned. First, whenever a Minister makes a statement, an Opposition front-bench Member is called first and is allowed an extended chance of replying and commenting (see page 262), and the Speaker has recognised the right of the front-bench to ask a final question at the end of the exchanges.[26] Thus, the Opposition's point of view is publicly stated and will usually be referred to in media coverage of the Minister's statement.

Second, when the Leader of the House announces each Thursday the business for the following week (see page 167) the Leader of the Opposition or the shadow Leader of the House (the latter has been usual since the 1987 election) has the opportunity to indicate what other matters the Opposition would wish to see debated. In recent sessions he has customarily indicated some three, four or five such topics each week. He often presses for ministerial statements on some issues. He also presses for longer debates on certain matters than the Government proposes, or for debate at an earlier hour; from time to time Leaders of the House agree to such requests. Thus, the Opposition can also use Government occasions to bring up matters that concern it.

THE OPPOSITION'S SOURCES OF INFORMATION

As was argued in Chapter 1, access to relevant information is essential for effective criticism. If the Opposition is to be able to offer effective and influential criticism of Government proposals and, even more important, if it is to advance well thought out and credible alternative policies and programmes, then it must have reliable and speedy means of obtaining relevant information. Some of the resources available for this purpose within the party organisations have been referred to in Chapter 4, and the information services officially provided by the House of Commons were described on pages 156–157. Much has been written on this subject, and several detailed studies have been undertaken.[27] Here it may suffice to outline the main sources of information available to the Opposition.

First there are the party research services. In varying degrees they are able to brief front-bench spokesmen when in Opposition. In addition an increasingly important process for undertaking research and obtaining information is the use of individually appointed research assistants (see pages 75–76). Most front-bench spokesmen employ one or more such assistants but the use they make of these staff cannot be readily measured. Staff are also employed in the office of the Leader of the Opposition, and by a number of shadow Ministers, paid for out of the House of Commons Vote (the so-called "Short

[26] H.C.Deb., Vol. 123, col. 274 (November 25, 1987).
[27] See particularly: Barker and Rush, *The Member of Parliament and his Information* (Allen and Unwin, for P.E.P. and the Study of Parliament Group, 1970); Rush and Shaw (eds.), *The House of Commons: Services and Facilities* (*Ibid.*, 1974): Janet Morgan, *Reinforcing Parliament* (P.E.P. 1976); and Michael Rush (ed.) and Members of the Study of Parliament Group *The House of Commons: Services and Facilities, 1972–1982* (P.S.I. 1983).

money," see pages 117–118). Such help is also available to smaller Opposition parties on a lesser scale.

Growing use is made by all Members of the research and information services of the House of Commons Library. Although no statistical breakdown is available either by party or between front- and back-benchers, it is clear that extensive use is made of these services by some of the present Opposition shadow Ministers.

A continuing source of information is the press, both national and local, including particularly specialist and technical journals, and radio and television. Other external sources include a great variety of personal contacts, pressure and other special interest groups, especially, in the case of a Labour Opposition, its close contacts with the trade unions and the T.U.C. There are a wide range of local sources—the local party organisations, local authorities, experience in the constituencies, etc., which Opposition spokesmen may draw on.[28]

Within Parliament, the Opposition can obtain information from three sources apart from the Library. First, answers to parliamentary Questions, especially those for written answer, are extensively used by back-benchers, shadow Ministers and spokesmen for the smaller parties. Typical examples (taken from one day) were Questions asked by the Labour front-bench spokesman on transport matters concerning road taxation revenue and road costs in 1987–88, by vehicle class[29]; information regarding the average daily number of available beds in each area health authority in England in 1979, sought by a front-bench spokesman on the health service[30]; a reply to the shadow Home Secretary showing the clear-up rate for all crimes and for various specified crimes for each police force area in Scotland in 1979 and 1986[31]; and the answer to a Question by the Opposition's Trade and Industry spokesman asking for the expenditure on regional development grant in each region of England, Scotland and Wales for each year from 1978–79 to 1986–87 and planned expenditure for this purpose for 1987–88 to 1989–90.[32] Many other examples could be cited.

Second, the official Opposition are able to draw increasingly on the reports of select committees. Much new information is available in these volumes, especially in the minutes of evidence. In recent years such material has often been referred to in debates in the House.

Lastly, the House is a village. Information and advice, ideas and suggestions, comments and criticisms flow freely round the building—mostly, though not exclusively, within the parties. One of the most important sources of information drawn on by the Opposition front-bench is simply the experience of their own supporters gathered in party meetings, party committees or over a cup of tea in the Members' Tea Room.

Thus armed, the official Opposition, and the smaller Opposition parties, can use the opportunities provided for them by the procedures of the House to call to account the Government of the day.

---

[28] For a discussion of the significance of these sources for all non-ministerial M.P.s in 1970, see Barker and Rush, *op. cit.*, Chap. IV.
[29] H.C.Deb., Vol. 116, cols. 211–214 (May 13, 1987).
[30] *Ibid.*, cols. 233–235.
[31] *Ibid.*, cols. 271–272.
[32] *Ibid.*, cols. 281–282.

CHAPTER 10

BACK-BENCH INITIATIVES

As we argued in Chapter 1, in addition to the confrontation between the Government and the Opposition there is an equally important confrontation between the executive and the legislature as a whole. Back-bench Members, on either side of the House, look critically at the policies and decisions of Ministers and of civil servants—on behalf of their constituents, or of some pressure or interest group, or simply reflecting their own private interests, experience or beliefs. In particular Members of Parliament, irrespective of party, wish to raise certain policy issues which do not interest the parties as such, including questions on which opinion within the parties may be divided or which for other reasons are normally considered non-party matters such as abortion and animal rights. Here, the front-benches largely leave the initiative for raising such matters to the back-bench Members on either side. In this Chapter we describe how they have exercised such initiative in recent years.

The following Table gives the time spent on the floor of the House in two recent normal length sessions on various types of business mainly initiated by back-benchers (some miscellaneous business, such as points of order, was partly initiated by the Opposition front-bench, but this has not been separately classified for these statistics).

Time spent on Business Initiated by Back-benchers
(hours and minutes)

	1984-85	1985-86
Private Members' Bills		
Second Reading	31:33	29:03
Consideration	16:02	
Third Reading	7:37	28:12
Lords Amendments	3:49	
Private Members' motions		
Ballotted substantive motions	49:14	57:42
Motions for 10 minutes rule bills	12:57	11:15
Private business	18:56	42:16
European Community documents	22:00	42:18
Adjournment		
Recess motions under SO No 22	12:14	12:06
Last day before recesses	18:42	18:05
After Consolidated Fund Bills	35:49	37:26
Daily adjournment debates	84:40	81:08
Estimates debates	21:14	17:33
Questions for oral answer	124:07	127:16
Private notice Questions	3:45	4:51
SO No 20 applications	4:38	4:47
Points of order, Speakers rulings	14:12	14:21
Privilege motions	5:05	1:17
Public petitions	4:19	2:21
Miscellaneous	5:29	4:21
Totals	497:22	536:18

Two general distinctions are worth noting. First, as shown on pages

291–293, many back-bench opportunities are largely free of control by the Whips. Second, some of the opportunities occur at peak hours for media attention, as well as attention within the House—the daily Question hour is the prime example—but others, such as adjournment debates and debates on Fridays, tend to come at off-peak times, when there will be less media coverage or when few Members are present. This distinction has a major effect on how Members use the opportunities available to them.

OPPORTUNITIES OTHER THAN DEBATE

Back-benchers have a number of opportunities to bring matters to the attention of the House, or to scrutinise the policies and acts of Ministers, without engaging in the full process of debate.

Parliamentary Questions

Questions to Ministers for oral or written answer provide one of the most important opportunities for back-bench initiative. They are used daily by more Members than any of the other opportunities here considered.

The Table on page 262 showed the growth of Questions since the war. Here we show the use of Questions in a recent session to scrutinise the activities and policies of different Departments.

Parliamentary Questions to each Department
(excluding Private Notice Questions)

Session 1985-86

Department	Oral[a]	Written[b]
Agriculture, Fisheries and Food	369	1426
Attorney-General	114	384
Church Commissioners	61	35
Defence	441	2096
Duchy of Lancaster	16	9
Education and Science	381	2185
Employment	315	2261
Energy	426	1008
Health and Social Security	381	5675
Environment	415	3624
Foreign and Commonwealth Office	607	2271
Home Office	325	3466
House of Commons Commission	6	27
Leader of the House of Commons	92	162
Minister for the Civil Service	99	51
Northern Ireland Office	332	1089
Office of Arts and Libraries	111	247
Prime Minister	968	1307
Public Accounts Commission	2	-
Scottish Office	391	2014
Solicitor-General for Scotland	80	83
Trade and Industry	531	1979
Transport	400	2196
Treasury	381	1680
Welsh Office	358	1211

(a) Including supplementaries by Members other than the original Questioner.

(b) Including written answers to Questions tabled for oral answer but not reached.

Oral Questions

The types of oral Questions that Members ask have changed markedly in the last 30 years. In May 1957 a typical oral Transport Question was—

"Mr. Ellis Smith asked the Minister of Transport and Civil Aviation what action he proposes to take to minimise as soon as possible the dangers on the main road between Trentham and Trent Vale, Stoke-on-Trent; and if he will make an order to establish a maximum speed of 15 mph between the hours of 8 a.m. and 8 p.m. within the limits of the road where the greatest number of accidents have happened"[1]

and similar Questions were frequently tabled to other Ministers. Questions for oral answer were usually on specific matters, were detailed and fairly long, and often set out the argument in the questioner's mind. They were often local. Of the 13 oral Questions put to the Minister of Transport and Civil Aviation on May 15, 1957 (a day chosen at random), seven mentioned specific local matters.

Ten years later oral Questions were still specific but shorter, less detailed, and with less supporting argument. A typical Transport Question was—

"Mr. Ronald Atkins asked the Secretary of State for Transport if she will introduce legislation to restore to users, as under the 1947 Act, the right of appeal to transport users consultative committees against the suspension of freight services."[2]

Somewhat fewer Questions appear to have been asked which specifically related to local matters however. Of the 42 oral Questions put to the Transport Minister on July 12, 1967 (another random day), 14 were local (mostly about road schemes).

By 1977 the basic type of Question had changed little, except that the less specific form of simply asking for a statement had become more common and other forms of more general Questions were often used. Local Questions were still used occasionally. Various forms of more "open" questioning had also become fashionable by the end of the seventies, in particular Questions about visiting particular countries (in the case of the Foreign Office) or particular places or constituencies. Another technique that was commonly employed was to ask about meetings with specified persons or organisations, or to ask about representations received on particular matters.

Such Questions are described as "open" because they provide an opening for a wide range of supplementaries on any matter relevant to the place to be visited, the persons met or the subject of the representations. Thus, Members can raise topical issues on their supplementaries without the restriction of relevance to a specific original Question.

Current practice is best shown by reproducing the first five Questions to three selected departments on randomly selected days in 1987.

---

[1] H.C.Deb., Vol. 570, col. 396 (May 15, 1957).
[2] H.C.Deb., Vol. 750, col. 799 (July 12, 1967).

Questions for Oral Answer by the Secretary of State for Foreign and Commonwealth Affairs
(Order Paper of July 1st 1987)

If he will make a statement on relations with Fiji. (Labour)

If he will make a statement on his policy on cultural diplomacy. (Conservative)

If he will make a statement on Her Majesty's Government's response to Iran's failure to respect diplomatic immunity (Conservative)

If he will make a statement on the outcome of the North Atlantic Council meeting at Reykjavik on 11th June. (Conservative)

If he will make a statement on Her Majesty's Government's position on arms control negotiations. (Conservative)

Questions for Oral Answer by the Secretary of State for Transport
(Order Paper of July 20th 1987)

What are his future plans for road safety publicity. (Conservative)

If he will make a statement on the representations he has received on the current campaign against drinking and driving. (Conservative)

If he is satisfied with progress on the construction of the North Devon link road; and if he will make a statement. (Conservative)

Whether his Department has assessed the impact of the Transport Act 1985 on children's fares; and if he will make a statement. (Labour)

What are the estimates respectively of: (a) British rail and (b) Eurotunnel of the additional number of passengers in the peak summer period who will be using Waterloo station as a terminus for channel fixed link traffic in 1993 and 2003. (Labour)

Questions for Oral Answer by the Secretary of State for Scotland
(Order Paper of July 22nd 1987)

What steps he is taking to improve health care in Scotland. (Labour)

If he has any plans to bring forward modifications to the community charge scheme in Scotland, in the proposed legislation introducing a similar tax in England and Wales; and if he will make a statement. (Labour)

If he will hold discussions with a view to setting up a Scottish Assembly with legislative powers. (Labour)

By how much percentage level of youth unemployment in Scotland increased between May 1979 and the most recent date for which figures are available. (Labour)

If he will list the sectors of the Scottish economy which have experienced improvements since 1979. (Conservative)

These are typical Questions, and a few generalisations can safely be made. Oral Questions are significantly shorter than they were 20 or 30 years ago; they are less detailed or specific; very little supporting argument is now used (or indeed permitted by current Table Office practice); fewer Questions are specifically related in their terms to constituency or other purely local issues;

and there is increasing use of standardised forms such as "if he will make a statement on ... " (without defining precisely the information asked for), "what representations he has received on ... ," and "when he next intends to meet ... " specified persons to discuss a stated matter. "Visits" Questions appear, however, to have fallen out of favour again. One other change is worth noting. Far fewer Questions are now tabled about the nationalised industries (see page 256).

The changed nature of oral Questions may, in part, be a matter of fashion or style, but the main reasons for the changes are tactical, and partly in response to changes in the rules of procedure for Questions.

As stated in Erskine May, "the purpose of a Question is to obtain information or press for action,"[4] and all Questions are drawn up in that way. However, the true purpose of Members today when tabling oral Questions is to secure an opportunity to make a political point—to criticise or to praise a Minister; to urge action here or to discourage action there; to draw attention to a politically damaging situation or to highlight governmental successes; or simply to publicise, especially to fellow Members or constituents, the questioners own skills, activities or beliefs in regard to an issue of his own choosing. There may be many variations on this theme.

A Question for oral answer gives a Member the chance to ask a supplementary Question in his own way at a prime time for media coverage and the attention of other Members. The tabled Question has thus become simply the peg on which to hang the supplementary, and the actual terms of the original Question therefore become less important. This move towards the simple, more general, Question has been stimulated by the restriction in the number of oral Questions allowed per Member to one per day to any one Minister. That one question must therefore be broad enough to cover all the points the Member may wish to raise.

The growing number of Questions tabled means that a back-bencher must put down his Question as early as the rules permit if he is to have a chance of being reached on the day (see pages 254–255). A very specific Question tabled two weeks previously may well be irrelevant when the time comes to ask it, but a more general Question will nearly always permit a relevant supplementary on an issue of the day. A Question to the Chancellor of the Exchequer, for example, on what discussions he has had with the C.B.I. or T.U.C. on the state of the economy gives full scope for a supplementary on any aspect of economic policy on the day when the Question is asked. Such open Questions are also readily drafted within the rules of order—and the Table Office are experts on this—while more specific Questions may fall foul of rules regarding Ministerial responsibility.

The use of Questions for oral answer has also been affected by the policies of different Speakers at Question time. Earlier Speakers sought to call as many original Questions as possible but recent practice has been different. For example, in 1956–57 the average number of oral Questions reached during Question time was 42; in session 1986–87 the figure was 18. Until 1961 the Prime Minister's Questions started at No. 45 on Tuesdays and Thursdays, and these were nearly always reached; today some 10 to 15 departmental Questions will normally be called before the first Prime Minister's Question is called at 3.15; the average on ten randomly selected Tuesdays and Thursdays in 1987 was 11.8 (including grouped Questions).

---

[4] May, p. 337.

The higher figures in earlier years were achieved because far fewer supplementary Questions were asked. Quite frequently an answer was accepted without any supplementary. Today, as we described on pages 258–259, it is very different. The author of the original Question always rises for a supplementary and a number of other Members are often called, from both sides. If several Questions are grouped that will involve still more supplementaries. Given this pressure to ask supplementaries, the present Speaker has adopted a policy of selecting from those Questions on the paper one or two topics of greater current interest, and calling as many Members as possible on those topics. Other topics are given less time.

The effect of these practices is reflected in the statistics. Taking six days in January and July 1987, ignoring Prime Minister's Questions, a total of 71 Questions gave rise to 278 supplementaries—an average of 3.9 supplementaries per Question. On ten Questions there was only one supplementary, but on a Question on the Government's decision regarding Sizewell nuclear power station the Speaker allowed eleven supplementaries, and Questions about rating reform in Scotland, defence procurement, and assistance to industry in the North of England each prompted eight supplementaries.

Questions come from both sides of the House, although which Questions are reached is a matter of luck as priority is decided by "the shuffle" (see pages 254–255). The random effect is illustrated by the Questions on three days in July 1987. Of the first 20 Foreign Office Questions, 13 were tabled by Conservatives and seven by Labour Members; 20 Transport Questions divided 12 Conservative, seven Labour and one Liberal; and the 20 Questions to the Secretary of State for Scotland were five Conservatives, 14 Labour and one Liberal.

Although to some extent the outcome is pure luck—individual Members tabling single Questions of their own choosing may come high or low on the list—the overall effect can be influenced by systematic reliance on the laws of probabilities. Those in opposition wishing to maximise the chances of their party having a high proportion of Questions high on the list—and correspondingly reducing the chances from the other parties—will encourage as many Members of their own side as possible to table Questions so as to press the Minister as effectively as possible. But such orchestrated questioning will often prompt the defensive tactic of Government supporters tabling numerous Questions to their own Ministers so as to protect them for much of Question time from the critical barbs of the Opposition. Such tactics are undoubtedly one of the causes of the growth in the total number of Questions tabled.

Tactics of this type are not spontaneous; someone has to organise the operation, and often one or two Members—perhaps through a party committee—collect and table a number of Questions on behalf of their colleagues. This has been called "syndicating," and it has become increasingly prevalant in recent years. Another variant on this theme is the "campaign' where a number of Members agree to table Questions on the same topic. For example on July 22, 1987, six similar Questions about a Scottish Assembly were on the Order Paper.

One of the purposes of such campaigns is to give as much publicity as possible to an issue—and to the point of view of the questioners on that issue—in order to influence the Minister concerned or to impress various opinions or persons outside the House (including constituents). To this end campaigns by groups of Members, or indeed by individual Members, may continue for weeks and will often involve numerous Questions for written answer and the use of other parliamentary opportunities. Some campaigns of this kind are ultimately successful, at least in placing an issue higher on the political agenda and attracting media and public concern, which in its turn may influence the Government. In the winter of 1987–88, for example, many Questions about the N.H.S. helped to highlight this political issue.

Another motive for multiplication of similar Questions is purely tactical. A lone Question may well come too low on the list to be called, but the chances of a topic being reached are clearly increased if a number of similar Questions are tabled. Once one such Question is reached, others may be grouped for answer with it or Members with lower Questions may well be called by the Speaker to ask supplementaries, so riding on the back of the successful Member in their "syndicate."

In general, although there is much demand for supplementary Questions, over a period everyone is given his or her chance. The Speaker keeps a careful list of who is and is not called, so that he can ensure that everyone is treated fairly.[5] He may also give priority, as when calling Questions on statements, to those who have not been fortunate enough to be called in a recent relevant debate.[6]

Prime Minister's Questions afford a particular opportunity for back-benchers on either side to raise almost any matter of their own choosing, by asking supplementaries on the open Question that, since about 1977, has become standard and gives no indication of the matter to be raised (see page 259). Opposition Members naturally try to trip the Prime Minister by raising some awkward issue, and the Prime Minister has to be particularly well briefed to anticipate which issues may be raised. Government back-benchers, however, frequently give advance notice to the Prime Minister's Office of the Question they will ask, or indeed suitable Questions may be suggested to them.[7]

The activists on both sides have become particularly energetic in syndicating as many Questions to the Prime Minister as possible, so as to maximise the chances of their Members coming high on the list. More than 200 Questions are often tabled. However, because the Speaker calls Members alternately from the Government and Opposition sides and further supplementaries need not relate to the first supplementary by the Member whose tabled Question was called, a Member has not lost all chances if he fails to secure a high place. Those lower on the list, or not on the list at all that day, may still be called and may raise whatever they want, provided there is some semblance of Ministerial responsibility. Exceptionally, on March 15, 1988 (which happened to be Budget day), 12 Conservative Members acted as a syndicate in tabling specific Questions to the Prime Minister about war widows' pensions. Sadly for them the first of those drawn in the shuffle came at No. 72 so the ploy failed and the subject was not reached.

Even allowing for the time taken up by supplementaries by the Leader of the Opposition and sometimes by other party leaders (see pages 353–357),

---

[5] H.C.Deb., Vol. 127, col. 523 (February 11, 1988).

[6] *Ibid.* col. 358 (February 10, 1988).

[7] See Mr Michael Alison, formerly Parliamentary Private Secretary to Mrs Thatcher, interviewed on BBC's "Week in Westminster," March 19, 1988.

back-benchers thus have substantial opportunities on Prime Minister's Questions to raise matters of their own choosing and the Speaker takes great care to ensure that as many Members as possible can benefit. Taking 14 days in June and July 1988, 10 back-bench Members were called, on average, each Tuesday and Thursday. Over the whole of Session 1985–86 (a normal length session) 366 Members from both sides of the House (including party leaders) had the opportunity of asking at least one supplementary of the Prime Minister. Of these, 108 Members asked two supplementaries; 67 were called three times; 35 were allowed four supplementaries; 16 achieved five; and 10 Members (excluding party leaders) were lucky enough to catch the Speaker's eye six times or more.

Taking oral Questions as a whole we can see a widespread interest in using this procedure. In 1985–86, 508 Members asked at least one oral Question (including supplementaries); many were more active; and some were persistent questioners. 24 Members (10 Conservative, 11 Labour and three Liberals) asked 40 or more Questions; the most active was Mr. Dale Campbell-Savours (Labour) who asked 95 Questions.[8] This volume of questioning, together with increased specialisation and the use of the tactics described above, has significantly changed the nature of the Question hour. There are, of course, still many individual Members who table their own individual Questions to various Ministers because they wish to pursue specific points of constituency, interest group, or personal concern. But increasingly the Question period concentrates attention each day on one or two current political issues. Opposition Members seek to cause maximum damage, while Government back-benchers generally—but not always— seek to bring the departments successes to the fore or to direct the questioning into calmer waters.

Questions for Written Answer

Questions for written answer are very different. In the first place there is no ration and, as the table on page 262 shows they are used more and more. In session 1985–86, 557 Members were given at least one written answer to a Question (including those originally tabled for oral answer) and many Members received many more; 20 Members (13 Labour, two Conservative, two Liberal, two Plaid Cymru and one S.D.P.) each had more than 300 written answers); and the busiest questioner (Mr. Tony Banks, Labour) tabled as many as 992.[9] Again these Questions come from both sides of the House. For example, of the 548 Questions given written answers by 22 different Ministers on July 24, 1986, 178 were tabled by Conservatives, 292 by Labour Members, and 78 by Members of other parties.

The great majority of Questions for written answer are primarily seeking for information, although occasionally they may simply be urging action to which a "yes" or "no" answer could be given. Frequently they are in batches from one or two Members asking for a lot of details about a specific situation or problem. They are usually far more detailed and specific than oral Questions. The range of topics is as wide as the responsibilities, or potential responsibilities of Government. Many are of local import.

We analysed the first eight columns of written answers on April 20, 1988. The Secretary of State for Wales answered three Questions on cancer

---

[8] House of Commons Library "Polis."
[9] *Ibid.*

screening and on linking the Channel Tunnel to Wales. Ministers in the Department of Energy answered five Questions from the same Member on various aspects of nuclear power and on alternative sources of energy. There were two Questions to the Prime Minister by the same Member who was interested in nuclear power, this time on her visit to Turkey. The Attorney General answered on Greenham Common prosecutions and criteria of eligibility for legal aid. The Trade and Industry Ministers answered 13 Questions, from 11 different Members, on a wide range of matters, including export of Land Rovers to South Africa, expenditure on business improvement schemes, industrial support in Blyth valley, balance of trade with New Zealand, child care for employees of D.T.I., prosecutions against companies for failing to register accounts and expenditure on official hospitality.[10] We list these topics to give the flavour of these proceedings, but this is only a small selection. Answers were also given by Ministers from 14 other departments to 272 further Questions (56 of which were answers to Questions put down for oral answer that day but not reached). Questions and written answers covered 74 columns of Hansard that day.

Some Questions are broad or simple, for example asking a Minister if he will make a statement on a recent official meeting.[11] Others are very specific. One Member asked the Secretary of State for the Home Department:

"what was the number of unopened letters on 21 March at Lunar House, Croydon; and of those how many were (a) applications for citizenship and (b) applications for variation of leave."

(Surprisingly, the Minister was able to give a statistical reply).[12] Members often require tables of figures, for example, the answer to a Question regarding the number and proportion of primary and secondary pupils in classes of over 30 pupils in each local education authority covered nearly four columns in Hansard.[13] Even longer answers are frequently given regarding such matters as rate-support grants for each local authority, or hospital statistics for all health districts.

Some Questions are local and specific, for example:

"how many death grants were claimed in Blyth Valley last year; and how many were awarded."[14]

That one was short and readily answered. Others were more complicated. One Member asked the Secretary of State for Transport:

"if he would name the main roads in urban areas which have all of the following, (a) a higher traffic count than on the A50 at Meir, Stoke on Trent, (b) a percentage of heavy lorries of over 19 per cent., and (c) within five miles of the point where the traffic count is taken have only one main lane in each direction and have private housing bordering on the road".

There were four other similar Questions. Not surprisingly the Minister replied that the requested information was not readily available.[15]

---

[10] H.C.Deb., Vol. 131, cols. *433–440.*
[11] *Ibid.* col. *453.*
[12] *Ibid.* col. *452.*
[13] *Ibid.* cols. *454–458.*
[14] *Ibid.* col. *467.*
[15] *Ibid.* cols. *441–442.*

Some Members ask many Questions on the same topic. On April 20, 1988, one Member asked 39 very detailed Questions relating to the Hungerford shooting tragedy, and another Member asked 15 Questions about London museums and art galleries.

Some Questions for written answer, usually tabled the day before, are "inspired," to enable a Minister to make a statement of a policy change or to give information (see page 336).

Answers to Questions for written answer give a vast amount of information. Occasionally, however, a Minister denies responsibility or refuses to answer. The latter response is given either on matters which the Government wishes to keep secret for security, defence, commercial, personal confidentiality or no doubt occasionally political, reasons, or when it is estimated that the cost of obtaining the information would exceed £200, although this is not a rigid limit and may be waived at the Minister's discretion.[16] Such denials are however, fairly infrequent; on April 20, 1988, answers were not given to nine Questions, out of 298, because the information was not readily available. In several other cases the Minister did not set out his answer fully in Hansard, but promised to write to the Member who asked the Question. In such cases it is normal for the answer to be placed in the Library where it can be seen by other Members (though not by the public); but this is not invariably done.[17]

Obviously, Members are not always satisfied with the answers they receive, and it is often alleged that Ministers are less than fully frank. Clearly on some matters, on either security or political grounds, Ministers may give no more information than the precise terms of the Question require, and often considerably less. It is impossible to compel a Minister to tell everything he knows on every topic. However, if a Question is clearly and specifically drafted, and if the questioner is sufficiently persistent, it is difficult for a Minister to avoid giving even politically embarrassing information, unless he is willing specifically to refuse it. This is rare, as the act of public refusal can itself be politically damaging. On the great majority of matters Ministers reply helpfully and in detail. Written Questions, as a procedure for enabling back-bench Members to discover and publish facts about the actions of the executive, are therefore of considerable value. The back pages of Hansard are a mine of information for many purposes and many people.

However, there is a cost; effective scrutiny of the executive cannot be achieved on the cheap. The average cost of answering a Question for oral answer in December 1987 was estimated to be £75, and for written answer £45.[18]

Private Notice Questions

The opportunity for individual back-benchers to raise matters of current concern, at short notice, is clearly of great value. Private notice Questions (PNQs) which any Member may ask on any sitting day, subject only to the approval of the Speaker, provide these opportunities. We showed on pages

---

[16] H.C.Deb., Vol. 128, col. *393* (February 29, 1988).
[17] *e.g.* answers by Attorney General re Stalker-Sampson investigation, (H.C.Deb., Vol. 131, col. *225* (February 10, 1988)).
[18] H.C.Deb., Vol. 124, col. *208* (December 9, 1987).

357–359 how this procedure is also used by the Opposition front-bench and other party leaders, but its main use remains with back-benchers from both sides.

Private Notice Questions asked by Back-bench Members

Session	Total Number of PNQs	PNQs asked by Government back-benchers	PNQs asked by Opposition back-benchers[c]
1983-84[a]	48	15	15
1984-85	26	5	12
1985-86	43	6	17
1986-87[b]	19	3	9
1987-88[a]	39	4	13

a - unusually long session
b - unusually short session
c - including some junior front-bench spokesmen

PNQs usually come on at about 3.30 p.m. which is prime time for media attention and for attendance of Members in the House. Many applications are rejected privately by the Speaker as the matter is not sufficiently urgent or of enough interest, but—save in the exceptional years of 1980–83 (see page 358)—Speakers have given back-benchers regular opportunities to raise topical issues. As a result the relevant Ministers have had to withstand persistent grilling on such matters at short notice.

The duration of questioning, following a PNQ, depends on the extent of interest, the mood of the House, and the pressure of business yet to come, all of which have to be judged by the Speaker when deciding how many supplementaries, coming from all parties, he can call. In Sessions 1984–85 and 1985–86 (the most recent normal length sessions) the shortest time taken by a PNQ was five minutes (on three occasions) and the longest 40 minutes.[19] The average time allowed was 17 minutes. This is significantly longer than is allowed for ordinary Questions, but shorter than is normally allowed for Questions following Ministerial statements (see pages 334–335).

Whereas Ministers make statements when they wish to inform the House—or at least feel they cannot avoid saying something—and whereas official Opposition PNQs often fasten on to controversial political issues, many back-bench PNQs relate to matters of more local or limited concern. Often these will arise from some major accident or disaster. In 1984–85, for example, Government back-benchers asked PNQs about poisoning of confectionary; an accident on the M25; a gas explosion in some flats in Putney (the constituency Member being a Minister, the matter was raised by one of his colleagues); violence at a Luton football match; and another motorway accident on the M6. Opposition Members tended to raise more political or controversial issues, such as interest rates; the coal industry dispute; cervical screening; shootings in South Africa; and the need for famine relief in the Sudan.

---

[19] On a Friday, on the report of the Top Salaries Review Body in 1985; the matter was raised by the official Opposition (H.C.Deb., Vol. 83, cols. 649–659 (July 19, 1985)).

A similar pattern is demonstrated by the back-bench PNQs in 1985–86. In both sessions most PNQs related to domestic issues (13 of the 17 back-bench PNQs in 1984–85 and 19 out of 23 in 1985–86). In both sessions Members from the smaller Opposition parties also asked PNQs (four in 1984–85 and four in 1985–86).

Business Questions

A weekly opportunity for back-benchers to draw attention to matters which they consider important—and again at prime time—occurs each Thursday when the Leader of the House announces the business for the following week. In earlier times this would be followed by a few questions relating specifically to the business announced. Today, Members have discovered the chance this gives them to raise almost any matter, and many of them seek to catch the Speaker's eye. The Speaker sees the value of these occasions in enabling as many Members as possible to make a brief point. He is reluctant to curtail their questions.[20] Questioning continued, on average, for 28 minutes in session 1984–85. This enabled some 30 to 40 back-benchers to be called each week, usually with roughly equal numbers from each side of the House. For example on Thursday April 21, 1988, business questions lasted from 3.30 p.m. to 4.07 p.m. After the statement, the Leader of the Opposition raised the desirability of debating six further matters. 14 Conservative Members, 17 Labour and four from other parties were then called.[21]

As the Speaker frequently reminds the House, questions should be brief. They should relate to the business of the House and usually consist of requests for a debate or statement on a political or public issue, or raise domestic matters such as appointment of select committees, or the timing and duration of announced business. But Members also use the chance to indicate their own views on the merits of a matter, and sometimes press the Leader of the House to reveal his or the Government's thinking. Frequently the Leader responds, but often he contents himself with agreeing to pass on the point to the Minister concerned. A question which in no way relates to the business of the House will normally be stamped on by the Speaker.

One technique often used by back-benchers is to table an early day motion (see page 268) and then to give it further publicity by asking for time to debate it (in such cases the motion is also printed, in italics, in Hansard). The Leader of the House does not agree to arrange such debates, but frequently draws attention to other occasions when the matter might be raised. On other matters the Leader may agree that a debate may be provided before too long, although a more common reply is "not next week."

The subjects raised range as widely as the responsibilities of government—or even wider. On Thursday April 21, 1988, for example, Government back-benchers asked about the procedures of the House and particularly the priority for Privy Councillors in debate; terrorism; parliamentary behaviour; sport, with reference to an EDM supporting Miss Zola Budd (another senior Conservative Member immediately took the chance to express a contrary view[22]); the need for a motorway to the North East; Summer time; copyright of proceedings of the House; paupers graves; and industrial development in the North of England.

---

[20] e.g. H.C.Deb., Vol. 121, col. 1071 (November 5, 1987).
[21] H.C.Deb., Vol. 131, cols. 983–997.
[22] Ibid. cols. 988, 989.

On the same day Opposition back-benchers raised, among other things, the need for emphysema, bronchitis and associated diseases to be made prescribed diseases; ship building; the health needs of London; the Rover Group; the Settle-Carlisle railway; the need to nominate the Scottish Affairs Committee (see page 415); the Gleneagles agreement; salmon net fishing; use of coal in Scottish power stations; problems of medical research charities; secrecy of documents relating to war crimes; prosecution of war criminals; conduct of the Prime Minister's office and investigation of leaks (the Member drew attention to 7 EDMs in his name[23]); meeting of N.A.T.O Nuclear Planning Group; and the arts.

In general, these weekly occasions lead to a wide-ranging run over the political agenda, with the Leader of the House showing as little of his hand as possible; precise promises have sometimes proved hard to fulfil. It should be noted that when occasional additional business statements are made to announce a change of business, the same wide-ranging exchanges are not permitted; on such occasions questions should relate to the actual business to be taken.

Points of Order

Although points of order are meant to relate to the proceedings or procedures of the House and to raise matters within the competence of the Speaker (see pages 195–197) they are frequently also used by back-benchers to draw attention to political or public issues that concern them, or to complain about the business proposed by the Government. For example, in March 1988, 56 different points of order, so called, were raised after Questions on 15 days out of 20. Only 30 of these referred in any way to a proper point of order for the Speaker's attention. Frustration at the limited legitimate opportunities for back-benchers to raise in a systematic way the current issues of the day appears to have caused this mis-use of points of order. However, there is normally no opportunity for Ministers to comment, so the argument is presented in a lop-sided way. It is a somewhat unsatisfactory use of the time of the House.

Applications for Emergency Adjournment Debates

We emphasised on page 352 how the opportunity for the Opposition parties to apply for an emergency debate under Standing Order No. 20 might be more important than the occasional debates that are actually allowed. This is even truer for back-benchers, on either side of the House, for the number of emergency debates successfully claimed by private Members is very limited, as the following Table shows.

---

[23] *Ibid.* cols. 994–995.

**Emergency Adjournment Debates under Standing Order No. 20
Applied for by Back-bench Members**

Session	Number of Applications by —		Number granted to —	
	Government back-benchers	Opposition back-benchers	Government back-benchers	Opposition back-benchers
1979-80[b]	12	73	-	2
1980-81	4	41	-	-
1981-82	3	49	-	1
1982-83[a]	5	40	-	-
1983-84[b]	1	72	-	1
1984-85	1	47	-	-
1985-86	19	58	-	-
1986-87[a]	9	31	-	-
1987-88[b]	3	69	-	-

a   unusually short session
b   unusually long session

   This is an opportunity largely used by Opposition back-benchers, including those in the smaller parties (a number of applications in recent years have been made by Ulster Members). However, but although applications by Government supporters might sometimes be embarrassing for Ministers, Conservative back-benchers appear, especially since 1985, to have discovered the value of using this way of raising their issues, and have not left all the running to the Opposition side. Since 1986 the application has been limited to three minutes, but it still provides a useful opportunity, at prime time, to draw attention to something specific that has happened very recently. There must be some ministerial responsibility for the matter raised, but the Minister is not able to reply.
   The topics raised also vary enormously, as shown by these samples from recent sessions. In 1984–85 they included shipbuilders redundancies; an immigration case; teachers pay; funding of the arts; closures of or redundancies in local industries (seven separate cases); the coal industry dispute (11 separate applications); severe weather payments; a law centre; the Open University; a school children's strike (raised by a Government back-bencher); ratecapping; board and lodging allowance; the police training manual; and the renovation of the QE2. Only two matters—UNESCO membership and events at the British Embassy, Oslo—fell outside the domestic sphere. Apart from the understandable emphasis on the coal dispute there was no overall theme or evidence of a co-ordinated attack. Members of the smaller parties played their part: three back-bench Members of the Alliance parties were applicants.
   A similar picture emerges from 1985–86. There were 16 applications relating to individual factories or local industries. The changing political issues were reflected in three applications relating to the Westland affair, (one, by the Leader of the Opposition, being granted); six on British Leyland; nine relating to disposal of nuclear radioactive waste (especially after the Chernobyl disaster); and three arising from the News International dispute at Wapping. International concerns were more to the fore, with applications for debates relating to the Anglo-Irish agreement; the draft Single European Act; relations with Libya and the United States attack; the

Chernobyl disaster; N.A.T.O. and chemical weapons; South Africa; agricultural spending by the E.C.; the Commonwealth Games; and the Channel Tunnel. Occasionally Opposition Members appear to organise a series of applications on a common theme, as part of a systematic attack on some aspect of Government policy. This happened in the winter of 1987–88, when there were 10 applications relating to problems in the N.H.S. When turning down one such application, the Speaker reminded the House that the Opposition was able to use its Opposition days for raising such matters.[24]

Many Members make no use of this procedure and others only occasionally. A few Members, however, have been keen to exploit it. In the two sessions 1984–85 and 1985–86, one back-bencher made six applications, another five and another four, and a further 14 back-benchers (all but one on the Opposition side) made two or three bids.

The use of the procedure to enable a back-bencher actually to open a three-hour debate on an urgent matter of his choosing is greatly restricted. The only emergency debates granted to a back-bencher between the 1979 and 1987 elections were two in 1979–80 (closure of a steelworks[25] and British policy towards Iran[26]), one in 1981–82 (N.H.S. pay dispute[27]) and one in 1983–84 (police operations in the mining dispute[28]). For opportunities to initiate an actual debate, the back-bencher must usually look elsewhere.

Early Day Motions

A procedural opportunity of some importance to many back-benchers is provided, off the floor of the House, by their almost unlimited right to table motions. Subject only to a few specific or procedural restrictions (see pages 203–205 and 268) this enables any Member to draw attention to any matter—not even confined by ministerial responsibility—and to set out his views with the full protection of parliamentary privilege. These motions mainly take the form of early day motions (EDMs). This procedure has become ever more popular in recent years as the following Table shows.

---

[24] H.C.Deb., Vol. 127, cols. 519–521 (February 11, 1988).
[25] H.C.Deb., Vol. 970, cols. 1027–1028, 1327–1390, (July 16 and 17, 1979).
[26] H.C.Deb., Vol. 985, cols. 44–48, 254–263 (May 19 and 20, 1980).
[27] H.C.Deb., Vol. 28, cols. 33, 225–269 (July 19 and 20, 1982).
[28] H.C.Deb., Vol. 58, cols. 24, 203–247 (April 9 and 10, 1984); but see p. 350.

Number of Early Day Motions Tabled Each Session

1945-46	71	1966-67[b]	640
1946-47	37	1967-68	446
1947-48	79	1968-69	443
1948[a]	3	1969-70[a]	300
1948-49	77	1970-71[b]	717
1949-50[a]	55	1971-72	474
1950-51[b]	97	1972-73	448
1951-52	106	1973-74[a]	174
1952-53	135	1974[a]	245
1953-54	102	1974-75	759
1954-55[a]	52	1975-76	701
1955-56[b]	116	1976-77	475
1956-57	96	1977-78	611
1957-58	105	1978-79[a]	368
1958-59	99	1979-80[b]	907
1959-60	111	1980-81	631
1960-61	169	1981-82	716
1961-62	154	1982-83[a]	502
1962-63	175	1983-84[b]	1058
1963-64	180	1984-85	979
1964-65	356	1985-86	1262
1965-66[a]	164	1986-87[a]	1000
		1987–88[b]	1601

a   unusually short session
b   unusually long session

Note

The numbers include "prayers" against statutory instruments, frequently in the name of the Leader of the Opposition or other party leaders, which are tabled as EDMs. To indicate their effect on the statistics (including those given below), in 1986-87, out of 1000 EDMs, 80 were "prayers" of this kind.

From this it can be seen that after a long period of moderate increase, there has been a tendency towards surges in growth occurring roughly every 10 years—in the mid-sixties, the mid-seventies and now the mid-eighties. The numbers continue to grow: in 1985–86 an average of 7.4 motions were tabled each sitting day, but in the following session that rose by a further 25 per cent.[29]

About a quarter to a third of EDMs provoke amendments, usually expressing a contrary view to that of the original motion. The figures in recent years were:

Amendments to EDMs

Session	Percentage of motions with one or more amendments
1984-85	34.0
1985-86	29.9
1986-87	24.5
1987-88	26.5

---

[29] This analysis was given by the Principal Clerk of the Table Office to the Procedure Committee in 1987 (H.C. 254 of 1986–87, pp. 1–2 and para. 4).

Many Members add their names to both EDMs and amendments to indicate their support. As shown by the following Table the total number of signatures has risen with the number of motions, but the "propensity to sign" has not increased.[30]

Members signing EDMs

Session	Sig-natures to Motions	Sig-natures to Amndts.	Total	% of total relat-ing to Amndts.	Average No. of Sig-natures per sitting day	Average No. of Sig-natures per Motion (including Amendments)
1974-75	23,815	1,495	25,310	5.9	128.5	34.1
1979-80	33,322	2,670	33,992	7.4	148.1	40.8
1984-85	39,491	4,115	43,606	9.4	255.0	45.1
1985-86	46,044	3,960	50,004	8.8	290.7	39.6

The number of signatures per motion varies greatly. A few motions have only one signature; some attract hundreds. The highest number since the beginning of session 1986–87 up till April 21, 1988 was 317 (support for a campaign against drug abuse); out of 2,000 EDMs in that period, 122 attracted the support of more than 100 Members, and 16 of these were signed by more than 200.

Many motions are "all-party" but the majority are party oriented. Of the 103 motions printed in the notices published on July 13, 1988, analysis based on the first six names on each motion indicates that three motions were official Opposition prayers, 33 were bi-party or all-party (but some of these were only supported by Members of different Opposition parties), seven were Conservative, 56 were Labour and four were tabled by Members of one or other of the smaller parties.

There is a wide range of subject and style. All-party motions usually deal with issues that cut across party lines such as animal rights, problems of the aged, road safety, or abortion, and are usually drafted in undramatic terms. More partisan motions may attack the Government or Opposition Members in as vigorous a way as the rules of parliamentary language will permit. Some motions may convey strong criticism of the personal conduct of individuals outside Parliament and may be in terms that would lead to libel actions if they were not protected by parliamentary privilege. A significant number of motions contain personal criticism of individual ·Ministers or other Members.

Motions critical of individuals' conduct became particularly prevalent in 1986–87, when 143 out of 1,000 Motions appear (by their titles) to have been of this type (many of them arising from the Peter Wright case). The Speaker, from time to time, has deprecated the use of the notice paper for personal attacks by one Member upon another, and has particularly urged restraint in using freedom of speech in Parliament to criticise the motives or honour of

[30] *Ibid.* p. 2.

people outside the House who have no right of reply.[31] This view was echoed by the Procedure Committee in 1986–87,[32] but it was not prepared to recommend any change in the rules which would restrict the essential freedom of Members to draw attention to any wrong-doing on the part of any person, in or out of Parliament, that they believe should be publicised. As the Speaker put it "I realise that we do get some pretty poor motions on the paper from time to time. But this is something I am prepared to live with in the interests of freedom of expression."[33]

On the other hand many motions are hardly political at all. Some deal with local problems; some are about matters outside the responsibilities of central government, including the conduct of local authorities; some, combining both these features, publicise the sporting successes of local teams or individual athletes. Many EDMs deal with domestic policy, but some highlight controversies across the seas. The range, as shown in the following illustrative table, is enormous (although analysis is inevitably somewhat imprecise, as some topics fall into more than one category).

Subject Matter of Early Day Motions

(Analysis of first 100 Motions Tabled in Sessions 1986-87 and 1987-88 (excluding "Prayers")

Topic	Numbers	
	1986-87	*1987-88*
Parliamentary	3	9
Government in general	4	2
eg lack of mandate in Scotland and Wales		
Agriculture	3	1
Trade, Industry and Energy (including press and broadcasting)	13	13
Education	2	2
Health and Social Security	18	14
Law and Order, Crime, etc.,	9	7
Defence	2	4
Environment, Housing and Land Use	3	2
Education, Arts and Science	5	1
Employment and Industrial Relations	5	6
Transport	2	2
Finance and Economy	2	2
Foreign Policy	3	4
Events or conditions in other countries	9	15
Local Government	3	2
Sports policy and sporting events	3	1
Moral issues, animals, etc.,	5	6
e.g. hare coursing		
vivesection		
gambling		
embryo research		
Other local events or individual cases (U.K.)	2	1
Conduct of individuals (praise or blame)	8	4

---

[31] H.C.Deb., Vol. 110, col. 1084 (February 19, 1987).

[32] Third Report H.C. 254, paragraphs 14–16. It may be that the appeals to self-restraint have had some effect, Only 36 out of the first 1,000 Motions in 1987–88 appear to have related to the conduct of individuals.

[33] *Ibid.* p. 19.

Many Members are active in tabling and signing EDMs because they provide quick and readily accessible publicity for policies, causes and beliefs, and for the Member's own attitudes and personality. The press, especially local press, may pay some attention to them and so do pressure groups both nationally and in the constituencies. EDMs are also an easy way for Members to respond to requests from such quarters without too great a political commitment. The Whips allow Members a reasonably free run in tabling and signing such motions, although they expect to be consulted before they are first tabled, especially if they are politically significant.

Many EDMs are, however, of limited political or parliamentary importance. Some, in the name of a single Member, may simply reflect some individual idiosyncracy; others on ephemeral issues may soon be forgotten; many are of no more than local interest. Some EDMs, although signed by many Members, indicate nothing that is not already well appreciated, the Labour Party's desire for more spending on the N.H.S., for example, or Conservative opposition to trade union closed shop agreements. Such motions may have value in reinforcing party cohesion or underlining political loyalties, but their impact is limited.

Three kinds of EDM are more significant, and both the number of supporters and who they are will be closely studied by Government, party leaders, pressure groups and political observers. First there are motions with large numbers of supporters, often all-party, urging Government support for some particular group, say disabled ex-servicemen; if more than 200 Members sign such an EDM, Governments have often responded to such concerted demand. Second, there are EDMs, and amendments, which reveal the strength of support for rival policies within one party; the numbers of pro- and anti-Marketeers on European issues among Conservative back-benchers was, for example, revealed by an EDM and an amendment thereto on the United Kingdom contribution to the budget of the European Communities.[34]

The most significant EDMs, however, are those which show such extensive support on the part of Government back-benchers for a particular policy or attitude that Ministers feel obliged to pay heed to it. Such motions may even play a part in persuading a Government to change its policy. A noteworthy recent example was on January 28, 1988 when two former senior Ministers, supported by 120 other Conservative back-benchers, tabled an EDM calling on the Secretary of State for Education to revise his previously declared policy and to announce an early date for the abolition of the Inner London Education Authority.[35] A few days later he did just that, and the necessary amendments were moved, by the Government, to the Education Reform Bill of that session.

Public Petitions

Most public petitions are presented by Members at the request of their constituents, even if they do not agree with the purpose of the petition (in such cases the petitions are presented privately by depositing them "in the bag," and nothing is said in the House (see page 267)). Only to a limited

---

[34] EDM 312 of session 1983–84. 71 Members signed a motion opposed to any increase in the Community's own resources; 110 supported some such increase if improved budgetary processes could be agreed.

[35] EDM 563; Notices of Motions, 1987–88, p. 3519.

extent can they count as back-benchers' initiative. However, so far as Members choose to present them in the House, which takes up a little time, they do provide an opportunity for back-benchers to bring before the House, in the most direct way possible, the concerns of those they represent. Sometimes this coincides with wider political objectives, and in such cases the Member, when presenting the petition publicly, will make his support apparent.

Members from both sides use this procedure. Of 54 petitions presented publicly in 1984–85, eight were presented by Conservative Members, 42 by Labour and four by Members from other parties; the figures in 1985–86, were 29, 38, and six, respectively, totalling 73.

The change in the proportions reflects the change in topics that concerned petitioners and Members. Many petitions are on local topics—closure of a school, for example. Others concern individuals—prisoners often petition for a review of their case or against their treatment, often asking to be moved to another prison—but such petitions are usually presented privately. The majority of petitions presented publicly relate to current political issues. In 1984–85, 22 petitions against the Government's Transport Bill were publicly presented and there were 16 petitions relating to experiments on human embryos or, more specifically, the contentious Unborn Children (Protection) Bill. In 1985–86 the main issues were Sunday trading and the Shops Bill (11 petitions), disposal of nuclear waste (eight petitions) and the detention of the Soviet dissident poetess Irina Ratushinskaya (four publicly presented, but many more put in the bag); she was eventually released.

Although there is little publicity for petitions presented late at night, and not much more for those presented at the beginning of business on a Friday, sometimes a number of petitions on a similar theme are presented on the same day to make a political point. On April 2, 1985, for example, 10 Labour Members presented petitions against the Transport Bill,[36] and on January 19, 1988, 15 Labour Members and one Conservative presented similar petitions for additional and improved resources for the Birmingham Children's Hospital.[37] Occasionally, on a Friday, petitions have been presented for tactical reasons to delay debate on a private Member's bill or motion (see page 396).

Petitions are published in full as appendices to the Votes and Proceedings. Some are very specific, some more general. The Greenford Residential Group for the Environment complained on November 17, 1986, that their environment was "polluted considerably by aircraft noises, commuters parking and heavy lorries; and it has become very unpleasant because of burglaries and Sunday-trading," and they petitioned the House to urge the Secretary of State to "do something" about it. Some have few signatures, some very many; it was claimed that the petitions presented in 1984–85 for the protection of the human embryo were signed by some two million people.

Ministers frequently reply to petitions, and their replies are similarly published (the incidence of replies was shown in the Table on page 268). Typical replies have included responses to petitions on planning applications; the Government's support for the United States bombing of Libya; investigation of nuclear waste disposal sites by N.I.R.E.X.; proposed

---

[36] H.C.Deb., Vol. 76, cols. 1188–1193.
[37] H.C.Deb., Vol. 125, cols. 936–941.

changes in social security legislation; the Soviet poetess; the reading of an individual prisoner's letter; the siting of a motorway service area; an individual's assessment for invalidity benefit; abortion clinics; and alleged plans to use plastic cards instead of pension books ("the story had no foundation").

BACK-BENCHERS' DEBATES

We turn now to a range of procedures which provide opportunity for back-benchers to initiate debates on matters of their choosing.

Private Members' Bills

Under Standing Order No. 13(4), as amended by sessional order in recent years, 12 Fridays are allotted each session for debate on the floor of the House of various stages of private Members' bills. The procedure for these is essentially the same as the legislative procedures described in Chapter 6, but there are some peculiar features.

Presentation of Bills

Under Standing Order No. 58 any Member may, having given notice, present a bill, have it put down for second reading on a day of his choice and have it printed. Subject to one important qualification, this can be done on any day, and without any restriction on numbers. The exception is that, under Standing Order No. 13(10) no private Member may present a bill under Standing Order No. 58 until after the fifth Wednesday of the session. The significance of that day is that it is then that Members who have been fortunate in the ballot present their bills. The bills brought in by the ballot winners are thus given a start over all other bills. Bringing in a ballotted bill is therefore the first and most important opportunity for a back-bencher to initiate legislation and must be described first.

The ballot for private Members' bills is held on the second Thursday of each session (Standing Order No. 13(6)). Members have been able to sign the ballot book during sitting hours on the two previous days. The ballot is keenly supported, partly because, for a Member who really wishes to introduce his own bill, a high place in the ballot is the only way of ensuring that the bill will be debated in the House; and partly because the Whips on both sides encourage maximum participation by their Members so as to maximise the chances of their coming out winners and to diminish the chances of their opponents. Ministers and Government Whips do not enter the ballot, nor, by convention, do the main party leaders or the main spokesmen for the Opposition. This leaves some 540 back-benchers. In 1983–84, 475 Members entered; in 1984–85, 456; in 1985–86, 426; in 1986–87, 412; and in 1987–88, 432.

The ballot for private Members' bills is a popular annual ceremony, conducted in a crowded committee room (lobby correspondents and representatives of various interest groups are keen to attend, as well as many Members) by the Chairman of Ways and Means assisted by the Clerk Assistant. 20 names are drawn. Of these, much the most significant are the first six, for these Members are guaranteed a top place—and therefore a debate—on one of the first six Fridays allotted for private Members' bills. These are the only days on which second readings have precedence; on the other six Fridays bills that have reached later stages have precedence (see below). The next six names drawn in the ballot can ensure a second place; and the last eight get a third or fourth place.

The actual order of bills each Friday is not, however, decided at this stage. The winning Members must first decide what their bills should be. They have three weeks to do so. As soon as the list of the ballot winners is issued, a successful Member—especially one of the first six—receives advice, requests, pressure and offers from many different sources. One Member said he was "inundated with letters from various organisations seeking his support for what they consider to be important issues"; he had had 35 such approaches (he had come fifth in the ballot).[38] Apart from unsolicited suggestions from many outside bodies, a Member may seek advice—or be offered it without asking—from colleagues in the House, from organisations such as trades unions or private industry with which he is connected, or from his party Whips. In particular there are always other Members anxious to further some particular cause who will ask a Member more fortunate in the ballot than they to take on a draft bill.

How a Member responds to these pursuasions depends on what he wants to achieve. An Opposition Member may wish to bring forward a bill directly in conflict with some aspect of Government policy, which is simply designed to give publicity to a political issue. The left-wing Labour Member from Liverpool (whom we quoted above) chose to introduce in 1985 a Surcharge and Disqualification of Councillors (Abolition) Bill; he added "the Bill is an attempt to show the Conservative Party that we in the Labour Party will continue to use the time accorded to us in the House to raise questions about the liberty, freedom and rights of people which the Government are taking away."[39] Clearly he could not expect his bill to be given a second reading in a House with a large Conservative majority (a closure motion was defeated by 50 to nil).[40] His purpose was to secure a debate rather than to amend the law. Such political bills may have the support of the Opposition front-bench, but often they are backed by distinct elements within the party, rather than the leadership. There are no straight "Opposition bills."

Other Members, from either side of the House may bring in bills to further a case dear to their hearts, even if the cause is unpopular and the bill has little chance of being passed. Mr. Fenner Brockway introduced many bills to make racial discrimination illegal before the Labour Government legislated in 1965 and 1968; Mr. Laurie Pavitt introduced many anti-smoking bills when he was a Member; and Sir Brandon Rhys Williams tried several times to get a Companies (Audit Committees) Bill on to the statute book.[41]

Another popular type of bill is one which deals with some social or moral question which lies outside the normal range of Government legislation. These issues usually cut across party lines and the bills have all-party support (and often all-party opposition). Some of these bills are relatively uncontentious—there have been numerous bills on various aspects of animal welfare—and may well be passed. Others may be highly controversial. In earlier years there were private Members' bills to abolish capital punishment, to legalise adult homosexuality, to legalise abortion, and to abolish theatre censorship.[42] More recently bills have been introduced by private Members

---

[38] H.C.Deb., Vol. 91, col. 1195 (February 14, 1986).

[39] *Ibid.* col. 1196.

[40] *Ibid.* col. 1254.

[41] This story had a sad ending. He succeeded in getting his bill passed by the Commons just before he died in 1988. He was not to know that it would fail in the Lords.

[42] For a full discussion of the nature and significance of private Members' legislation up till 1970, see Peter G. Richards, *Parliament and Conscience* (1971).

to restrict experiments on human embryos and to introduce more restrictions on the practice of abortion. All these issues arouse strong feelings and offer little political advantage; Governments are very reluctant to legislate on such topics, and the field is open for the back-bencher. Here, however, the Member who takes up such a bill is far from sure of success—certainly not at the first attempt (although, as some of our examples show, perseverance may be rewarded).

If a Member actually wants to improve the law by getting his bill passed by Parliament—rather than just securing a debate or advancing a cause—he will probably adopt a less controversial measure which seeks to amend current legislation in some specific way. Sometimes this may be of considerable significance and, with all-party support may make progress; more often it will be a detailed proposal for tidying up the statute book, which derives from experience with the working of earlier legislation, and which an interested outside group or the Government themselves may offer to a Member who wins a ballot place. An example of such a bill was the Copyright (Computer Software) Bill of 1985. Bills of this kind naturally appeal to Members who wish to do something useful without stirring up too much controversy and with less personal inconvenience (the promoter of a highly controversial bill soon finds himself almost overwhelmed by correspondence and demands on his time while the bill is before the House).

The role of the Government in respect of private Members' bills is well understood but less easily described with precision. At one extreme there are numerous bills to which the Government is opposed and on which Ministers will offer no help. Then there are some bills, chosen by Members without Government encouragement, on which the Government may agree eventually to give drafting help if it appears that the bill has enough support from its own back-benchers for it to pass. The Disabled Persons (Services, Consultation and Representation) Bill of 1985–86—which the Government only consented to help at the last moment, on the report stage—is a good example of this category; another was the Wildlife and Countryside (Amendment) Bill of 1984–85. Next there may be bills which Ministers and their supporters are positively keen on, and here Government drafting assistance may be offered at an early stage.

At the other end of the scale there are minor bills which departments are anxious to get on the statute book but which cannot be fitted in to the Governments own legislative programme (perhaps the department concerned already has two or three bills that session). In such cases the Government Whips will suggest such a bill to a Member (usually, but not necessarily, from their own side) who has won a place in the ballot and will assure him that they will draft the bill and give technical and drafting help at all stages. There is little more the Member need do. Such private Members' bills are really Government bills in disguise. This is not always openly stated, but generally it is recognised and often the responsibility of the department is publicly acknowledged and the Minister is thanked.[43] Ministers have sometimes, in advance, indicated their readiness to support a private Mem-

---

[43] *e.g.* see Third Reading of Motor Cycle Noise Bill, H.C.Deb., Vol. 114, cols. 910–911 (April 24, 1987).

ber's bill if it were to be introduced in lieu of a measure of their own for which there was not time.[44]

One theme is common to the Government's response to all private Members' legislation: whatever may be the Government's initial attitude, Parliamentary Counsel (the Government's own draftsmen) will seek to ensure that nothing goes on to the statute book without their approval; if necessary they will draft amendments which completely re-write a bill, in order to achieve this end.[45]

The following Table seeks to analyse private Members' bills presented after the ballot in the 1983–87 Parliament according to the above classifications.

Types of Private Members Ballot Bills
1983-87 Parliament

		Number	Percentage
A	Controversial party-political bills	7	9
B	Campaigning bills, often controversial across party lines	25	31
C	Moral issue bills on which Governments do not normally legislate	6	8
D	Individual Members' less controversial reforming proposals	17	21
E	Government drafted, departmental, bills	25	31
		80	

After the Members who win places in the ballot have decided on their bills they give notice to the Public Bill Office of the short and long title of their bills (they do not need a completed text as this stage). All the balloted bills are then presented by the fortunate Members (or by other Members on their behalf) on the fifth Wednesday of the session in the order of their ballot places. Now tactical considerations begin to be relevant.

Tactics play a major part at every stage in the organisation of business on private Members' bills. In contrast with Government bills, where the time available for their consideration is almost unlimited and is controlled by Ministers through their majority in the House, time for private Members' bills is strictly limited. Bills on each available day are, subject to certain rules (see page 396), considered in the order in which they are set down. Therefore, whereas Ministers can decide their business from day to day, backbenchers put down their bills weeks or months ahead so as to get the most favourable days or to be as high as possible on the list for any given day.

After the presentation of their bills, when days are named for second reading, the first six Members in the ballot put their bills down in the first places for the first six Fridays, so ensuring that their bills will be debated. This is particularly important for controversial bills. It is also important for

---

[44] *e.g.* H.C.Deb., Vol. 107, cols. *85–86* (December 8, 1986) regarding repeal of s.10 of the Crown Proceedings Act 1947. The Crown Proceedings (Armed Forces) Bill was later introduced by a Conservative back-bencher and enacted.

[45] For example, in 1987 all the substantive clauses of the Safety at Sea Bill were negatived in committee and were replaced by 11 new clauses drafted by the Government. The bill then passed without difficulty.

controversial bills to secure as early a Friday as possible so that, if the bill is given a second reading, it gets into committee as soon as possible and is not blocked by other bills being placed ahead of it in the committee queue (see pages 393 and 395).

For bills numbers seven to twelve, a different choice has to be made. They can secure second places on any second reading Friday, but it is usually desirable, especially if the bill is fairly controversial and is likely to need a full debate at second reading, for it to be put down to follow an uncontroversial bill; on the other hand an early Friday may prove more attractive.

For bills numbers 13 to 20, the tactics are less important. If they are controversial they are unlikely to pass second reading (see pages 392–393); for the unopposed bill which is expected to be read a second time, an early Friday, even in third or fourth place, is probably preferable.

The first private Members' bill Friday is usually immediately after Christmas (assuming the session started in the Autumn) so another factor for the Member in charge is by when his bill can be drafted and published. Again the preparation of private Members' bills varies greatly. Some are literally scribbled on a single side of paper and, so long as it sets out clearly the purpose of the bill and falls within the terms of the long title, such a text, although doubtless legally defective, can still serve as an adequate vehicle for debate. Bills are not ruled out of order just because they are not perfectly drafted (although there are other rules, especially regarding provisions involving expenditure or taxation, with which they must comply (see page 229)). Other Members with, perhaps, greater expectations of their bills reaching the statute book, may seek the advice of colleagues who are lawyers or of the clerks in the Public Bill Office who, although not qualified draftsmen, are able to draw up a bill in clear and intelligible parliamentary form, which is sufficient for the immediate purpose of publicity and debate; any technical deficiencies—failure to make consequential amendments to earlier statutes, for example—can readily be cured, if the bill makes good progress, by Government drafted amendments at a later stage.

Many Members choose to introduce a bill urged by some pressure or interest group, in which case that body will produce a suggested text of the bill (with varying degrees of drafting skill). Other Members may wish to receive professional advice and seek help from parliamentary agents (lawyers who specialise in private bill and other parliamentary work) or other experts. Members winning one of the first ten places in the ballot may claim up to £200 in respect of cost incurred in having their bills drafted. The only persons to whom a back-bencher cannot turn for help directly are those who are best qualified. Parliamentary counsel only take instructions from Ministers although, as already described, they may, on occasions, be instructed to draft a bill or parts of a private Member's bill.

One other decision has to be taken when a bill is presented and before it gocs to the printer. A Member may name up to eleven supporters, and a number of names normally appear on the back of bills. This is a simple way of indicating the nature of the political backing for the bill and it is especially significant when names from more than one party are included.

The next stage is the printing of the bill. This is done by H.M.S.O. on the instructions of the Public Bill Office, as ordered by the House. No charge is made for printing, and a private Member is entitled to up 115 free copies of his bill. A Member who presents a bill is not obliged to have it printed, but the great majority of ballotted bills are. Bills introduced under other procedures are often not printed; for example out of 98 private Members' bills introduced in 1984–85, 24 were not printed; and in 1985–86, 26 of the 114 bills were not printed. Unprinted bills are not able, however, to make further progress, as the Chair does not propose the question on their second reading.

There are three other ways private Members' bills may be introduced into the House of Commons. First, as already stated, once the ballot bills have been presented, Members can present other bills. This method enables them to have their bill published, but the presentation procedure does not include any debate or explanation of the purpose of the bill and the chances of debate on later days are slight; thus the proceedings have little publicity value. Bills introduced in this way are usually either formal expressions of an individual point of view (in recent sessions, for example, Mr Tony Benn has introduced a Miners' Amnesty (General Pardon) Bill, a Reform Bill, a Chesterfield Borough Council (General Powers) Bill, a Common Owner-ship of Land Bill, a Representation of the Work People Bill and a Religious Prosecutions (Abolition) Bill) or they are minor, uncontroversial, bills which Members hope to get through without debate. In session 1983–84, 20 bills were presented in this way, of which two received Royal Assent; in 1984–85 the figures were 29 and four, respectively; in 1985–86 they were 33 and four; and in 1986–87, 29 and four.

Ten Minute Rule Bills

A more popular and more important opportunity for a back-bencher wishing to introduce a private Member's bill is offered by what is commonly called the "ten minute rule." Under Standing Order No. 19, each Tuesday and Wednesday after the ballot bills have been presented, a back-bench Member may move that leave be given to bring in a bill for a stated purpose (if leave is given this becomes the long title of the bill).[46] Only one such motion is allowed each day and notice must be given not less than five sittings days (usually one week) and not more than 15 sittings days (usually three weeks) in advance. A Member may give only one such notice on any day and not more than one such notice may stand on the paper in the name of any one Member for a day within any period of 15 sitting days. This prevents a few active Members from hogging these occasions. This procedure has now become so much in demand that Members regularly wait outside the Public Bill Office all night on Mondays and Tuesdays so that the next day they can hand in a notice of a ten-minute rule bill for three weeks ahead, and so that they can deny their political opponents these opportunities.

Ten minute rule motions come on after Questions and statements and so at a peak time for publicity purposes. The Member moving the motion is not permitted to make a full speech, but is allowed a "brief explanatory state-ment" (interpreted as about ten minutes) regarding the desirability and purposes of his proposed bill. If the motion is opposed, another Member may make a statement of similar length arguing the case against the pro-posed bill. By convention and the rulings of the Chair, interventions are not allowed when Members are moving for leave or opposing such motions.

After the motion, and any opposing statement, the question is put "That leave be given to bring in the bill" (unless the Speaker puts the question for

---

[46] This procedure survives from the time, prior to the passage of S.O. No. 58 (ordinary presentation of bills) in 1902, when most bills were introduced on motions for leave.

the adjournment of the debate, which he has not done for many years[47]), and on this there may be a division. The following Table shows the incidence of divisions in the 1983–87 Parliament.

Motions for leave to bring in Bills under Standing Order No. 19

Session	Agreed to			Negatived		
	On Division	No Division	Total	On Division	No Division	Total
1983-84[a]	6	61	67	6	-	6
1984-85	2	40	42	13	-	13
1985-86	7	48	55	2	-	2
1986-87[b]	2	28	30	2	-	2

a   unusually long session
b   unusually short session

The nature of the matters proposed to be dealt with by ten-minute rule bills reflects the combination of relatively high publicity and very poor prospects of much further progress. Motions for these bills tend to make political points or to draw attention to some situation or circumstances that the mover considers needs reform, rather than holding out prospect for legislation on the statute book. However a non-contentious bill is occasionally introduced in this manner. As there will be little or no opportunity to debate it at a later stage, Members may find it helpful to give some indication of its purpose at this first occasion. From time to time ten-minute rule bills are eventually enacted; there were two in 1984–85, but none in 1983–84, 1985–86, or 1986–87.

As shown in the Table, however, other motions for leave to bring in bills are defeated. Many of these are motions by Opposition Members proposing some politically controversial measure that the Government and its supporters are opposed to. Quite frequently a motion by a Government back-bencher is defeated. This can happen when a Member proposes a bill which is clearly unacceptable to the Opposition but which the Government are not prepared to support, so Ministers and all the "pay-roll vote" abstain. For example, on January 12, 1988, a Conservative Member moved for leave to bring in a bill "to extinguish the Post Office's exclusive privilege of conveying letters"; it was opposed by a Labour back-bencher and on a division it was negatived 118 votes to 202.[48] Similarly on May 11, 1988 another Conservative back-bencher sought to bring in a bill to amend and limit the Dock Labour Employment Scheme; it was defeated by 120 to 167.[49]

On the other hand it must not be assumed that the absence of a division means that the bill is not contentious. There are many bills introduced under this procedure by Opposition back-benchers which the Government and their supporters could not possibly accept but which, for various reasons, they do not wish to vote against at this stage. It may not be desirable to be seen publicly to oppose some measures; or opponents may feel that a

[47] See May, pp. 516–517.
[48] H.C.Deb., Vol. 125, cols. 173–179.
[49] H.C.Deb., Vol. 133, cols. 321–326.

division will only give the proposal greater publicity; or the opponents may not wish to reveal possible divisions in their own ranks. The Government Whips may also be anxious not to delay other business in the House by another ten minute speech and a division. In any case opponents of a controversial measure know that there is no need to seek to kill it by voting against it at this stage; there will be ample opportunity to end its life quietly at later stages.

Lords Bills

The last method by which private Members' bills are introduced into the Commons is by a back-bench Member taking up a bill which has passed the House of Lords. He names a day for second reading and the bill is printed. The number of Lords bills taken up by private Members in recent sessions have been: 1983–84, 11; 1984–85, seven; 1985–86, six; and 1986–87, six.

Most private Members' bills received from the Lords are relatively uncontroversial, for it is unlikely that they would have passed in that House if it was otherwise. However that does not mean that they will pass easily through the Commons. Lords bills receive no priority in the Commons; they have to queue up behind other bills introduced before them for debate on Fridays. This means that the chances of a second reading debate are almost nil. Therefore only totally uncontroversial Lords bills will normally be given a second reading[50] and relatively few reach the statute book: two in 1983–84; four in 1984–85; four in 1985–86 and four in 1986–87.

Passage of Bills

The second reading is the Beechers Brook of the private Members' bills race. Many bills fall at this point, but those which are given second readings are likely—though not certain—to complete the course and reach the statute book. The procedures at this and subsequent stages are much the same as for all public bills but the tactics are essentially different.

Those who have a first bill on a second reading Friday can be sure of a full debate and the chance to put the matter to a vote. This means that a controversial bill can be given a second reading if the majority of those present so agree, provided that the supporters are able to muster 102 Members (including two tellers) to secure a closure if the opponents seek to talk a bill out at 2.30 p.m. (sometimes the opponents do not seek to talk a bill out and there is a vote without a closure).

The prospects for second or later placed bills are less certain. If the first bill is controversial there will be little or no debate on later bills and they will only obtain a second reading if unopposed. If however, the first bill is uncontroversial there may be time for a debate on other bills. However this depends on the nature of these bills; if the second bill is controversial there may be extended debate on an uncontroversial first bill simply to limit the debating time on the second bill. Although the closure may be claimed even if there has been less than a whole day's debate, not many bills can benefit in this way. The shortest second reading debate on which a closure has been allowed by the Chair since 1950 was after one hour, 42 minutes on the Road

---

[50] Exceptionally the Sunday Theatre Bill [*Lords*] was discharged from a standing committee and slipped through committee of the whole House and all remaining stages without debate or opposition on April 21, 1972 (H.C.Deb., Vol. 835, col. 1015). It must be assumed that its Sabbatarian opponents were nodding.

Traffic (Driving of Motor Cycles and Mopeds) Bill 1960,[51] but this was very exceptional and closures are not usually granted after less than four hours debate.

The fate of many bills turns on what happens at 2.30 p.m. On every private Members Friday (including the days when motions have priority), after the business under discussion has been disposed of, the Clerk reads the short titles of all other private Members' bills set down for that day. Some bills have not been printed so no question can be proposed, others are not moved because the Member in charge is not present and no one else has been authorised to act for him. But most orders for bills are moved. If a single Member objects the bill cannot be proceeded with (no opposed business can be taken after the moment of interruption) but may be put down again for a later day. Frustration at 2.30 p.m. on Fridays at numerous bills being talked out or blocked in this way often leads to points of order when Members complain about the action of the Government Whips, who are usually those who have signified objection, and about the procedures which permit bills to be blocked unless everyone is agreed to pass a bill without debate.[52] These complaints have been considered several times by Procedure Committees,[52a] but they have always recommended that the procedures be retained.

Members with uncontroversial bills are more fortunate (unless some frustrated Member vents his anger by objecting to all bills regardless of their merits). Such bills are often given a second reading at 2.30 p.m. "on the nod." It is also possible for further stages to be taken. After second reading the bill can be committed to a committee of the whole House; the committee can sit forthwith; the clauses can all be agreed to in committee; and the bill can be reported and read the third time. This happened on 10 occasions on private Members' bills in the 1983–87 Parliament.[53]

The overall fate in recent sessions of private Members' bills on second reading is shown in the Table on page 394. For convenience we also give the statistics for later stages.

The nature of debate on second readings of private Members' bills is much the same as on Government bills, except that the motion for second reading is moved by the Member in charge and the Minister and the Opposition front-bench usually speak to give their views and guidance to their supporters somewhere in the middle of the debate. Obviously the attitude of the Government is of crucial importance; a bill is unlikely to succeed against the wishes of the Government. Sometimes bills about which Ministers are unhappy eventually pass in a somewhat emasculated form.[53a]

When a private Member's bill is read a second time it stands, like any other bill, committed to a standing committee unless the House otherwise orders. Under Standing Order Nos. 84(3) and 95, private Members' bills have precedence in two of these committees. The Committee of Selection regularly designate Standing Committee C for private Members' bills other than those relating exclusively to Scotland, which have precedence in the Second Scottish Standing Committee. Thus, after second reading, private

---

[51] This was a second placed bill for second reading. The closure did not succeed as only 38 Members voted in the majority (H.C.Deb., Vol. 618, cols. 1632–1668 (March 4, 1960)).

[52] See, for example, H.C.Deb., Vol. 131, cols. 1160–1163 (April 22, 1988).

[52a] Most recently in 1987 (H.C. 350 of 1986–87, paras. 69–71).

[53] For example Licensing (Restaurant Meals) Bill [Lords] 1987 (H.C.Deb., Vol. 111, col. 562 (February 27, 1987)).

[53a] e.g. Chronically Sick and Disabled Persons Act 1970.

Progress of Private Members' Bills in Commons

Session	Introduced (including Lords bills)	Read 2° (on division in brackets)	2° Neg on Division	Reported from CWH	Reported from Stg Ctee	Report stage concluded[a]	Read 3°	Lords Amdts	Royal Assent
1983-84[b]	118	14 (1)	1	2	12	13	13	3	13
1984-85	98	22	0	6	16	21	21	4	21
1985-86	114	23 (1)	0	9	13	21	21	3	21
1986-87[c]	85	19 (1)	1	4[d]	14	16[e]	16	1	15

a Or no report stage when bills reported from committee of the whole House without amendment
b Unusually long session
c Unusually short session
d Consideration in committee of one bill not completed
e One bill withdrawn after committee; consideration of another bill not completed

Member's bills form queues for consideration in these two committees. Occasionally, if there are no Government bills awaiting consideration in another standing committee, the Speaker will, at the request of the Member in charge and with the agreement of the Government Whips, transfer a private Member's bill from a lower place in the Standing Committee C queue to that other committee where it can be considered without delay.[54]

Standing Committee C normally comprises 18 Members drawn from both sides of the House, proportionate to the party strength. The Committee of Selection, guided by the names of supporters on the back of the bill and by speeches (if any) on second reading, also seeks to ensure that supporters comprise the majority of the committee while opponents are also fairly represented. Whips are not put on these committees.

Tactics again play a big part in committee. The earlier a bill is reported back to the House, the better its chances of getting through the later stages. Opponents may therefore deliberately prolong debate to delay the report of the bill. Alternatively, there may be extended debate on less controversial bills which happen to be ahead of a contentious bill in the committee queue, so as to delay the start of its consideration.[55]

Standing Committee C normally meets only on Wednesday mornings, for two-and-a-half hours. To counter possible delaying tactics, the Member in charge of the bill may propose additional sittings. The committee on the Abortion (Amendment) Bill in 1988 agreed by a vote of nine to eight to meet on Tuesdays, Wednesdays and Thursdays, morning and afternoon—its supporters were very determined—and eventually, after seven sittings succeeded in reporting the bill in time for the House to consider it.

Despite the tactics on a few highly contentious bills, most private Members' bills that reach standing committee are not particularly controversial and may be disposed of fairly speedily. Normally all bills committed to Standing Committee C and the Second Scottish Standing Committee are disposed of before the last day for the later stages of these bills in the House. The numbers of private Members' bills considered each session by standing committees is shown in the Table on page 394.

A few bills (mainly those drafted by the Government) go through committee without amendment. Many are amended to some degree, and some heavily. The Member in charge may have to make substantial concessions to secure the necessary concensus for a bill's passage at later stages. Ministers, who are nominated to all committees on private Members' bills, may make their continued support for a bill conditional on certain amendments. Improvements are frequently made as a result of debate in the House or in committee, or following representations by outside affected bodies. Many bills, to which the Government is not opposed in principle, are heavily amended to make the drafting acceptable to the experts. Very occasionally a committee is unable to agree to the main provisions of a bill and has disagreed to the effective, or even all, clauses of a bill and made a special report to the House.[56] On other occasions, on a motion of the Member in

---

[54] In 1984–85, the very controversial Unborn Children (Protection) Bill and the Wildlife and Countryside (Amendment) Bill were able to avoid possible delay in Standing Committee C by this manoeuvre.

[55] There were allegations of such tactics when two uncontentious bills were debated at some length in committee in 1988. The next bill in the queue was the Abortion (Amendment) Bill.

[56] See May, pp. 678–679. The last time this happened on a private Member's bill was on the Transport (Amendment) Bill in 1950–51 (Stg. Co. Deb., Co. B, c. 875–878).

charge, a committee has decided not to proceed further with a bill, and has reported accordingly.[57]

One other complication may arise in standing committee. Private Members may not, under Standing Order No. 48, introduce bills whose "main object" is the creation of a public charge (see page 248), but a private Member's bill, as introduced, may include provisions which would involve expenditure and are printed in italics. Such expenditures are usually minor and administrative charges consequential on the main provisions of the bill, but occasionally they are more substantial, involving the payment of grants for example. Once a private Member's bill has been read a second time, the Government normally moves the necessary money resolution to cover the expenditure provisions. The bill can then go ahead and the italicised provisions can be agreed like all other clauses. Very occasionally, however, the Government is not prepared to move a money resolution,[58] or more likely will move a resolution which covers some, but not all, of the italicised provisions.[59] Under these circumstances the committee cannot agree the provisions involving expenditure which are not covered by a money resolution, and must report the bill with those provisions omitted.[60]

The remaining stages of private Members' bills offer further opportunities for tactical manoeuvring. Precedence of bills on the seventh to twelfth bill Fridays, inclusive (and on motion Fridays after the sixth bill Friday) is laid down by Standing Order No. 13(5) as follows: consideration of Lords Amendments, third readings, new report stages, adjourned report stages, adjourned committee proceedings, bills appointed for committee of the whole House, and second readings. This affects the conduct of private Members' bills in a number of ways. For example, if a bill is controversial it is desirable to take its report stage as soon as possible, so that if not completed at the first attempt there may be a later opportunity. However on later Fridays it will come after other bills beginning their report stages, so its chances are diminished.[61]

Indeed this may prompt opponents of the contentious bill in question deliberately to put down non-contentious report stages or third readings of other bills for these later days as a means of blocking the first bill's progress. On the other hand, for a less controversial bill, a second place on the first available Friday may be less favourable than a second or even third place on a later Friday if, on the first day, a highly controversial bill is placed first which will take up the whole day. Choosing a day for report stage after standing committee may involve quite subtle calculations and deals with other Members.

Further amendments may be moved at report stage subject to the Speaker's selection, which is quite stringently exercised to prevent minorities from preventing the passage of bills which a majority must be assumed to support

---

[57] See May, p. 678.

[58] For examples, see May, p. 676, note 19 and p. 678, note 14.

[59] *Ibid.* pp. 676–677, notes 19 and 20.

[60] See, for example, Chronically Sick and Disabled Persons Bill 1970, Stg. Co. Deb. (1969–70) Co. C, c. 178–179).

[61] Exceptionally, the Tobacco and Snuff (Health Hazards) Bill 1971 (which the Government originally encouraged but later did not wish to see passed) was considered at report stage on three Fridays. Its passage was only prevented by a Government inspired filibuster. (H.C.Deb., Vol. 815, cols. 1553–1594; H.C.Deb., Vol. 816, cols. 883–969 and 1877–1913 (April 23 and 30 and May 7, 1971).

(the bill having got this far). For example, on the highly contentious Abortion (Amendment) Bill 1988, four new clauses and 47 amendments were tabled for the report stage on May 6, 1988; only two groups were selected by the Speaker.[62] On this occasion another tactical move by the opponents of the bill was revealed. Certain important amendments were deliberately not moved in the standing committee; this meant that on report they were new points and almost certain to be selected (as they were); if they had been debated in committee they might well not have been chosen for further debate on report. Opponents of bills do not fire off all their ammunition at the first encounter.

Report stages of highly controversial bills are bitterly fought occasions, when feelings run high. It is much easier for a vigorous minority to prevent the passage of a bill at this stage than at second reading or in committee. Apart from the tactics already described, other procedures may be used to delay discussion of the bill itself. On May 6, 1988, 11 petitions were presented which, together with points of order, took up 40 minutes before the report stage of the Abortion (Amendment) Bill could be started, and further long speeches and delaying tactics, with two closures being required, meant that the report stage of the bill could not be completed that day.[63]

Similar delays made it impossible for the Unborn Children Protection Bill to complete its report stage on May 3, 1985.[64] In that case an attempt was made to secure extra time for the bill when a private Member's motion day was used for this purpose, but again that was thwarted by various procedures (see pages 402–403) although the majority of those present were presumed to be in favour of the motion and certainly supported the original bill, which was given a second reading by 238 votes to 66.[65]

However, not all report stages are as contentious. Many useful debates are held on amendments tidying up bills after committee or implementing committee undertakings. On many bills there are no amendments at all on report stage. Most bills that reach report stage pass successfully to third reading. In the 1983–87 Parliament, only two bills that reached this stage failed to obtain Royal Assent.[66]

The third reading is usually formal or fairly brief, unless for tactical reasons it is prolonged to delay some later bill. In recent years no bills have fallen at this stage, and divisions are very few. So on the bills go to the Lords.

The last day allotted for private Members' bills is primarily designed for consideration of Lords Amendments. These normally go through fairly smoothly, as the outstanding points are usually details rather than fundamental. Of course many bills are not amended by the Lords. In the 1983–87 Parliament, no private Member's bill was lost because of failure by either House to agree amendments made by the other.

A noticeable feature of private Members' bill proceedings since 1979 has been the insistence on the part of Government that the battle for and against contentious bills must be fought wholly within the specific time made avail-

---

[62] H.C.Deb., Vol. 132, cols. 1143–1148, 1149, 1179–1181.

[63] *Ibid.* cols. 1139–1209.

[64] H.C.Deb., Vol. 78, cols. 535–592.

[65] H.C.Deb., Vol. 73, cols. 700–702.

[66] The Community Health Councils (Access to Information) Bill 1987 was passed by the Commons, but did not get through the Lords before Parliament was dissolved for the general election; in the same year the Licensing (Amendment) Bill did not complete its consideration stage (and see Table on page 394).

able for such business. As the Leader of the House categorically stated after
the failure of the Abortion (Amendment) Bill to pass on May 6, 1988, "The
Government position is already clear. It is not our practice to provide extra
time for consideration of individual private Members' bills."[67] The only
departure from this policy, since 1979, had been on May 11, 1983, when
Government time had been provided to enable two bills which it favoured
(the Road Traffic (Driving Licences) Bill and the National Audit Bill) and a
third which had all party support (the Broadcasting of Parliament (Annual
Review) Bill) to go through their remaining stages (without debate) before
the impending general election[68]; all three had previously been read a
second time. The first two were given Royal Assent; the third was not passed
by the Lords. The circumstances were however somewhat exceptional, and
it could be argued that the Government was not providing extra time but
simply replacing some of the time that would be taken away from private
Members by the dissolution of Parliament.

The practice of previous Governments, however, had not been so restricted. Between 1954 and 1979, extra Government time had been made
available for 76 different private Members' bills; all but three of these were
eventually enacted.[69] Apart from occasions when time was provided for
generally acceptable bills before general elections, nearly all of these were
Commons bills which had been amended by the Lords after the last private
Members' bill Friday in the Commons; if a little extra time had not been
given these almost totally agreed bills would have been lost. Since 1970,
however, the last private Members' bill Friday has not been taken till
sometime in July, and the need to find this little extra time has been far less;
between 1970 and 1979, extra time was needed for Lords Amendments on
only three occasions.

There were, however, in earlier years a number of controversial bills,
which had ministerial support, which could not have passed the Commons
without the Government providing extra time. In these cases time was given
as a deliberate policy. They included the Death Penalty (Abolition) Bill
1956,[70] the Obscene Publications Bill 1959, the Matrimonial Causes Bill
1963, the Murder (Abolition of the Death Penalty) Bill 1965, the Live Hare
Coursing (Abolition) Bill 1967, the Sexual Offences (No. 2) Bill 1967, the
Abortion Bill 1967, the Divorce (Reform) Bill 1968–69 and the Sexual
Offences (Amendment) Bill 1976. As the Leader of the House made plain
on May 6, 1988 it would not now be the policy of the Government to support
private Members' bills in this way. This has been a significant change in
recent years.

Achievement of Private Members' Bills

Finally we must consider the achievement of private Members' legislation
and how valuable these opportunities are for back-benchers. We must
emphasise that the measure of achievement lies not only in the extent of
legislative success. Members have a variety of purposes when bringing

---

[67] H.C.Deb., Vol. 132, col. 1209.

[68] H.C.Deb., Vol. 42, cols. 888–889.

[69] See, H.C.Deb., Vol. 109, cols. 106–118 (January 26, 1987). The exceptions were the
Death Penalty (Abolition) Bill 1956, the Licensing of Bulls and Boars Bill [Lords] 1958, and the
Live Hare Coursing (Abolition) Bill 1967.

[70] In this case time was provided for second reading as well as later stages.

forward a bill. A political point may be made; or a failure of Government may be demonstrated. Alternatively a cause may be advanced and public awareness of the need for some change in the law may be aroused. In some cases Ministers may only be able to avoid legislation they are unhappy about by promising to bring in their own legislation.[71] On other occasions, even if the matter does not come to debate, proposals that concern a number of Members and people outside Parliament have been given an airing. In all these cases Ministers have been required to prepare their response. It is all part of the role of the House in securing public debate of all issues.

One test of the efficacy of the procedures, however, must be their ability to secure amendment of the law. The figures for recent sessions show that a significant number of private Members' bills reach the statute book.

Enactment of Private Members Bills

Session	No. of Bills introduced into Commons (including Bills from the Lords)	No. of Bills given Royal Assent
1974-75	86	10
1975-76	85	16
1976-77	89	11
1977-78	89	11
1978-79[a]	58	3
1979-80	125	10
1980-81	80	14
1981-82	93	10
1982–83[a]	81	10
1983-84	118	13
1984-85	98	21
1985-86	114	21
1986-87[a]	85	15
1987-88	119	13

a   Shortened session (not all private Members' bill days available)

The titles of the Acts originating as private Members' bills in 1984–85 and 1985–86[72] reveal a wide range of topics. Analysed according to the Government departments most directly concerned (although this cannot be precise) we see that the largest single group, 12, fell under the Home Office (five amendments of criminal law, four concerning civil law, and four others); seven Acts were on transport matters; seven concerned the DHSS (five health and two social security); six related to agriculture and the country-side; there were three housing or local government Acts; and three concern-

---

[71] See, e.g. Mr. Austin Mitchell's House Buyers' Bill 1984 which led to the relevant provisions being included in the Administration of Justice Act 1985; and Mr Richard Shepherd's Protection of Official Information Bill 1988 (H.C.Deb., Vol. 125, cols. 563–637 (January 15, 1988)). In this latter case the Government's Official Secrets Bill 1989 was before Parliament at the time of writing, and its main lines had been foreshadowed in a white paper on Reform of Section 2 of the Official Secrets Act 1911 (Cm. 408). In neither case were the back-bench Members concerned happy with the Government's proposals.

[72] For a list of all private Members' bills that received Royal Assent between 1957 and 1987, see H.C.Deb., Vol. 123, cols. 68–76 (November 23, 1987).

ing trade or industry; defence, employment, Scottish and Welsh Acts made up the balance.

The flavour of private Members' legislation is best given by examples. In 1984–85 and 1985–86, Acts were passed relating to Agricultural Training Board; Betting, Gaming and Lotteries; Charities; Controlled Drugs (Penalties); Dangerous Vessels; Hospitals Complaints Procedure; Prohibition of Female Circumcision; Wildlife and Countryside (Service of Notices); Corneal tissue; Drainage Rates (Disabled Persons); Forestry; Incest and Related Offences; Marriage (Wales); Protection of Children (Tobacco); and Protection of Military Remains.

Using the classifications described on page 388, in the 1983–87 Parliament the 70 private Members' bills which became law can be classified as follows:

Class A - none
Class B -   7
Class C -   1
Class D -   29
Class E -   33

Nearly all of these received Government drafting assistance. None would have reached the statute book without Government acquiescence. But it was the initiative of back-bench Members that secured their enactment. Although some of these Acts were of minor significance, many affected a number of citizens in various ways and some were of considerable social importance. Back-bench Members, by using their opportunities, play their part in creating and reforming the law of the land.

Private Members' Motions

The occasions for private Members' motions are broadly the same as for their bills. Under an order made at the beginning of each session, which in part modifies Standing Order No. 13(7), there are usually nine Fridays when private Members' motions and private Members' bills have precedence, in that order, over Government business. These are known as "motions Fridays." Under Standing Order No. 13(8) and the sessional order, four half-Mondays (up till 7 p.m.) are also allotted for private Members' motions.[73] The motions days are much less significant occasions than bill days and attract less parliamentary or public attention. Again the opportunities are decided by ballot, though this time a separate ballot is held for each motion Friday or half-Monday. Three names are drawn and notice of the subject to be raised must be given at least nine days before the day of debate (Standing Order No. 13(9)). The actual text of the motion may be tabled later.

If the first motion moved is controversial or of fairly wide interest, or if the second motion is controversial so that its opponents wish to avoid a debate, debate on the first motion will last the whole, or nearly the whole, of the allotted time. On other days, however, the first motion may be of lesser interest, or Members may be anxious to debate the second motion, in which case the first debate may conclude in good time and a short debate may be held on the second motion until proceedings are brought to an end at 2.30

---

[73] *e.g.* H.C.Deb., Vol. 86, col. 120 (November 7, 1985).

p.m. on a Friday or 7 p.m. on a Monday. Second motions were debated on three occasions in 1984–85 (out of 13) on four occasions in 1985–86 (out of 13) and on four occasions in the shorter session of 1986–87 (out of nine), although one of those second debates only lasted for one minute. Third motions are rarely reached.[74]

The topics chosen vary widely, but are nearly all on some aspect of domestic or social policy. Debates on foreign affairs are rare; in only one case in the three sessions between 1984 and 1987 was a purely overseas matter raised—a Conservative back-bencher moved a motion on March 23, 1985 on famine in Africa[75]—although a debate on European co-operation on high technology industries, on March 21,[76] also looked beyond our shores. Defence is another subject which is rarely raised, perhaps because there are several other opportunities on Government days.

No one is keen on divisions on Fridays, when constituency business calls, least of all the Whips on either side. If a Government supporter wins the ballot he is therefore under considerable pressure to choose a non-controversial topic, or at least to phrase his motion in a way that will be broadly acceptable: not too lavish in its praise of the Government or too condemnatory of the Opposition. The majority of movers of motions are Government back-benchers, perhaps partly because of the efforts of the Whips to encourage Members to enter the ballot.[77] Thirty-five Conservative Members were able to move motions compared to 12 Labour in sessions 1984–85, 1985–86 and 1986–87. The gods did not smile on other parties in this respect during those years, although they did on certain individuals; six Members won the ballot twice, and one Member won on two successive motions days.[78] The majority of motions chosen by Conservative Members in 1985–86 was unprovocative; the subjects included violent crime among young people; Industry year, 1986; basic and applied scientific research; education and training for young people; sponsorship of the arts; management of the N.H.S.; neighbourhood watch schemes; youth training and the reserve forces; housing in the North-West; private investment in inner cities; manufacturing industry; and the rural economy.[79]

Occasionally, however, a Government back-bencher may choose a controversial matter (abortion was the chosen topic on February 11, 1985[80]) or may table a motion which indicates a personal view distinct from that of his party. A Conservative back-bencher moved a long motion on November 13, 1987 on the Commonwealth and South Africa which included regret "that the United Kingdom appears to be out of step with all other members of the Commonwealth on the subject of sanctions against South Africa" and called for further sanctions; this upset several of his colleagues.[81] However such controversial occasions are rare and no motions moved by Government back-benchers were divided on in the three sessions analysed.

Opposition Members are less inhibited from opening up controversial

[74] But there are cases, *e.g.* H.C.Deb., Vol. 94, cols. 579–584 (March 21, 1986).
[75] H.C.Deb., Vol. 75, cols. 1089–1153.
[76] H.C.Deb., Vol. 94, cols. 562–578.
[77] See, *e.g.* H.C.Deb., Vol. 93, col. 1318 (March 14, 1986).
[78] Mr Edward Leigh, on Monday February 11, and Friday March 1, 1985.
[79] For lists of the subjects chosen in each year, see the Sessional Information Digests prepared by the House of Commons Public Information Office.
[80] H.C.Deb., Vol. 73, cols. 40–71.
[81] H.C.Deb., Vol. 122, cols. 682–691. The motion was eventually talked out.

topics. In 1984–85 they raised board and lodging payments; economic, social and housing conditions in the West Midlands; economy and industry in Scotland; and housing; all in terms which were critical of the Government. In 1985–86, their subjects included child abuse, and employment rights. And in 1986–87 Labour topics included the rarely debated subject of the security services; delay and dereliction of inner city areas; and treatment and care of cancer patients. Immediately before the 1987 election, one left-wing Member moved a motion simply entitled "Quality of Life," which entitled him to mount a broad attack on everything the Government had done or not done.[82]

Faced with such critical motions, the Government side have a choice of tactics (although the whip is not normally officially applied on private Members business, the wishes of the Whips are made apparent). If they have enough Members present, they could defeat the motion on a division; however in the three sessions 1984–85, 1985–86 and 1986–87, no motions moved by Opposition back-benchers were so negatived (although one, on the security services, was negatived without a division[83]). If they are less certain of the outcome of a vote, or if for some other reason they wish to avoid a division, the opponents of the motion will talk it out (unless a closure is claimed and granted, which is very rare on a motions day).[84]

Most private Members' motions, however, are not controversial. Many have all-party support and are agreed without division (19 in the three sessions between 1984 and 1987); others are withdrawn by general consent (two cases).

Special mention must be made of two motions in recent sessions. The first was never debated. A prominent Opposition back-bencher, who had been highly critical of the Prime Minister on a number of issues, won first place for private Members' motions for Friday June 6, 1986, and tabled a motion which strongly attacked the personal conduct of the Prime Minister, with particular reference to the Westland affair, the United States bombing of Libya and the Falklands War.[85] A number of Government supporters were clearly determined to prevent a debate on this motion and continued the debate on the business of the previous day (the second reading and committal of the Channel Tunnel Bill) so that the business ran all through the night and past 9.30 a.m. the next day, so "breaking the sitting" (see page 187)[86] Opportunity to debate the motion was therefore denied. The Opposition side were enraged and a number of other Government back-benchers were obviously far from happy with this manoeuvre. Eventually the Government agreed to allow an extra private Members' motion day to replace the lost day, but as another ballot was held (which the originally successful Member did not manage to win) the controversial motion was never debated. It did not lack publicity, however.

The second unusual case was on Friday June 7, 1985. When the Unborn Children (Protection) Bill failed to complete its report stage, a supporter of the bill who had been successful in the motions ballot adopted the highly unusual, but procedurally legitimate tactic of tabling a business of the House

---

[82] H.C.Deb., Vol. 116, cols. 32–74 (May 11, 1987).
[83] H.C.Deb., Vol. 107, cols. 782–828 (December 15, 1986).
[84] But see *ibid*.
[85] Notices of Motions session 1985–86, p. 10177.
[86] H.C.Deb., Vol. 98, cols. 1100–1340 (June 5, 1986).

motion to give unlimited extra time for the consideration of the bill that day and for any Lords Amendments on a future day. This caused great potential difficulty for the Government business managers who could see the possibility of the House sitting throughout the week-end; they were also anxious about the precedent this would create. The tactic also infuriated the opponents of the bill. Various devices were deployed to prevent the motion being debated, including the fairly lengthy presentation of 23 petitions, points of order and (most effectively) a debate on a motion for a by-election writ that happened to be outstanding. In the end the motion was only debated for 15 minutes and was talked out.[87]

As many motions are uncontroversial and there are few votes, the House is usually thinly attended on motions days. These occasions nevertheless have their value. Topics are often debated which would otherwise not come up at all and on these matters Ministers are required to state the Government position. It is important that from time to time back-bench Members should be able to initiate formal debate on matters of their own choosing.

Very occasionally a back-bencher is permitted to move a motion in Government time. This is sometimes done for debates on reports of various select committees,[88] and is the regular practice for debates on the reports of the Public Accounts Committee.[89] Otherwise, since 1979, the only occasions of substance have been on important motions relating to the death penalty[90] and on televising the proceedings of the House.[91] However these should not count as purely back-bench opportunities, as the matters debated are only put down with the agreement or even at the instigation of the Government.

Adjournment Debates

Although Motions for the adjournment of the House are moved by the Government Whips, there are a number of such debates which provide opportunities for back-benchers.

Daily Adjournments

A principal, though little publicised, occasion for back-benchers to initiate short debates on any matter of their choosing (provided there is some ministerial responsibility) arises on the adjournment at the end of each sitting (see pages 202 and 266). In total these debates comprise a significant slice of the time on the floor of the House (see Table on page 365). Although coming on late at night, they are regularly sought; a ballot is held weekly in the Speaker's Office and a Member usually secures a debate within a few weeks of first applying. Members on both sides take advantage of this procedure. In 1984–85 ninety Conservative, 68 Labour and 17 Members of other parties secured daily adjournment debates.

For many Members, the principal value of these occasions is in enabling

---

[87] H.C.Deb., Vol. 80, cols. 545–611 (June 7, 1985). A similar tactic was tried by the Member in charge of the Abortion (Amendment) Bill 1989, who sought to move a motion to gain debating time for her bill, which had won seventh place in the ballot; obstructive tactics prevented her from moving her motion (H.C.Deb. Vol 145 cols. 591–664 (January 20, 1989).
[88] See H.C.Deb., Vol. 91, cols. 206–208 (February 6, 1986).
[89] See, e.g. H.C.Deb., Vol. 56, cols. 916–982 (March 20, 1984).
[90] H.C.Deb., Vol. 970, cols. 2020–2126 (July 19, 1979).
[91] H.C.Deb., Vol. 87, cols. 277–366 (November 20, 1985) and H.C.Deb., Vol. 127, cols. 194–288 (February 9, 1988).

them to raise some constituency point or a personal case which they have pursued by correspondence or by Questions, but on which they consider more public discussion is desirable. The Member explains the problem, other Members sometimes come in briefly, and the Minister is required to reply. This brief public exposure of the problem will be reported in the local press and may help sustain public pressure for a remedy. On other occasions a number of Members may take the chance to air some local grievance, even though the Minister (perhaps because the matter is still under review) can say little in response.[92]

Analysis of the daily adjournment debates in 1984–85 shows that 73 out of 175 were concerned with local or regional matters, but many debates are not on local issues. Anthing for which a Minister is responsible may be raised, ranging from Mrs. Smith's disability allowance to nuclear defence policy.

The general balance of topics (national and local) raised in 1984–85, is shown by the following Table:

Main Subjects of Daily Adjournment Debates, 1984-85

Agriculture	6	Health Services	24
Defence	6	Home Office matters	15
Education and Arts	19	Housing	12
Employment and Industrial Relations	10	Social Security	10
		Trade and Industry	19
Environment, Planning and Local Government	11	Transport	14
		Other	15
Foreign Affairs and Overseas Aid	14		

To give an indication of the type of subjects raised, the following matters were debated in the period 16-23 May 1988 showing the party of the Member concerned.

Labour	-	Housing benefit (Scotland)
Conservative	-	Dumping of industrial and radioactive refuse in the British Channel
Labour	-	Complaints about solicitors: the case of Mr Patrick McManus
Conservative	-	UK relations with Poland
Social Democrat	-	Travellers encampments in the London Borough of Greenwich
Conservative	-	RAF search and rescue operations in central Scotland

Recess Adjournments

Similar opportunities are provided by the adjournment debate, lasting for nearly five hours, that is held on the last day before each recess (see page 267). Members raise topics in the same way as on the daily adjournment, and a Minister replies to each debate. The topics raised are much the same. In

---

[92] See, *e.g.* a debate on education re-organisation in Kingston upon Thames, H.C.Deb., Vol. 113, cols. 137–144 (March 23, 1987).

1984–85, for example, out of 33 subjects, 10 Members raised individual, local or regional matters.

Consolidated Fund Bill Adjournments

The procedures for debating subjects on the all-night adjournment debates that follow the passage of Consolidated Fund Bills (see pages 265–266) are slightly different and consequently the type of subjects raised, for which again there must be ministerial responsibility, varies somewhat. There are three of these debates each session. The Government commonly puts other business down before the Consolidated Fund Bills, normally including the debate on the dates of a forthcoming recess (see below), so the long adjournment debate, which may last until 9 a.m. the next day (8 a.m. on a Friday) does not usually start till late in the evening[92a]. However, as the Table on page 365 shows, these occasions provide a significant amount of debating time for matters initiated by back-benchers.

A ballot is held in the Speaker's Office for the right to open one of these debates, but the time available for each debate is under the control of the Speaker (see page 266). The debates are not at precise times (as those before recesses), and if a debate takes less than its allotted time, the next one can start. How many matters are debated therefore depends on how long each debate lasts, and how many on the list of ballotted topics will be reached also depends on whether every Member used his chance (some are not keen enough to want to open a debate at 4 a.m.). Tactics may be employed to ensure that a potentially embarrassing topic for Ministers which is marginally reachable does not come up for debate; or that it does.

Attempts are sometimes made, often with official Opposition encouragement, to secure an early debate on a current political issue by a fairly large number of Members submitting the same subject for the ballot; assuming one of them comes up fairly high on the list, the others are then able to contribute to the same debate.

The pattern of the debates is straightforward. The Member who gained the place in the ballot opens the debate; others are called from each side in turn; the Opposition front-bench sometimes contributes; and the Minister winds up. There are no votes.

Because the debates are longer than those on the daily and recess adjournments, less use is made of them for raising local or constituency matters. Taking 1984–85 again, of the 29 subjects listed for debate on July 24, 1985, only three appear to have related to local or specific cases. Fewer subjects are reached for debate than those listed. On December 19, 1984, with the debate starting just before 10 p.m., only eight subjects were raised.[93] The Speaker selected two current political issues (the sequestration of the assets of the National Union of Mineworkers during the miners strike, put down by a Labour Member, and the financing of the B.B.C., chosen by a Conservative) for three hour debates. Other topics raised by four Labour Members, one Conservative and one Liberal were: testing of nuclear weapons;

[92a] In December 1988 complaint was made about private Members' motions, in addition to the recess motion, coming before the Consolidated Fund Bill, and so deferring back-benchers' opportunities still further; the debate on that occasion did not start till 10 p.m. The Leader of the House promised to try to avoid doing this again (H.C.Deb., Vol. 143, col. 1098 (December 15, 1988); H.C.Deb., Vol. 144, col. 106 (December 19, 1988.)

[93] H.C.Deb., Vol. 70, cols. 383–524.

regional development; water charges; the murder of Mrs. Hilda Morrell; Maltby Common; and the dairy industry in South West Wales.

On March 26, 1985, the topics debated were: strike action by Scottish teachers; arts funding; rating revaluation in Scotland (three hours); the newspaper industry; wages councils (three hours); the voluntary sector; education; and the radio regulatory regime.[94] The openers were seven Conservatives and one Labour Member.

The third debate that session was held on July 24, 1985, when the subjects raised by three Conservative, two Labour, one Plaid Cymru and one Liberal Member were: tendering for local authority services; Britain's relations with South Africa (three hours); civil defence (three hours); wages councils and low pay; the Welsh language; the motor industry; and Scottish agriculture.[95]

Motions for Recesses

Opportunities for back-benchers arise on the motions, moved four times each session, providing for the dates of each recess. Under Standing Order No. 22, these debates are limited to three hours. They enable Members to refer to all sorts of different matters that concern them, without notice and with little restriction (even the rule about ministerial responsibility does not apply).

On Friday March 25, 1988, before the Easter recess, to take a recent example, Members spoke about government participation in space research; the Settle to Carlisle railway; development of air services in the North West; housing in Northern Ireland; various problems in East Anglia; the health services in inner London; television and violence in Northern Ireland; European community assistance to Cornwall; problems of the Kurdish community in Iraq; sheltered accommodation for the elderly; reform of parliamentary procedure; Fords; trades unions and industry in Dundee; and N.H.S. expenditure in Bloomsbury. The Opposition shadow Leader of the House usually speaks at the end of the debate, commenting on some of the points made, and the Leader of the House winds up. Having had no notice, and with insufficient time to answer such a wide range of issues, he can only take note of the arguments or promise they will be considered by the Ministers concerned.

Prayers against Statutory Instruments

As we explained on page 345 the opportunities for Opposition parties and back-benchers on either side to initiate debate on prayers against Government orders and regulations are limited. Time is controlled by the Government. Opposition back-benchers have been able to make little use of these procedures in recent years. It is almost impossible for them to secure time on the floor of the House, and in the years 1980 to 1987, only four prayers by Opposition back-benchers were referred to standing committees. In the Labour Government period they appear to have done rather better; 19 such prayers were debated in standing committee between 1974 and 1978 (see page 349).

Government Whips may sometimes allow their own supporters an occasional debate, but in 1984–85, of the 14 prayers on the floor of the House, 10

---

[94] H.C.Deb., Vol. 76, cols. 277–451.
[95] H.C.Deb., Vol. 83, cols. 1126–1281.

were moved on behalf of the official Opposition, and four by Members of the Alliance parties; and again in 1985–86 all debated prayers were from the Opposition side.

More prayers in the names of Government back-benchers have sometimes been referred to standing committees. Under the last Labour Government these were quite frequent; for example there were 17 such prayers debated in standing committee in 1975–76, 14 in 1976–77 and 14 in 1977–78. There have been fewer since 1979: in 1980–81 there were four; in 1981–82, nine; in 1982–83, six; in 1983–84, five; and in 1986–87, four. But in 1984–85 and in 1985–86 there were none.

In general, the prayer procedures provide little opportunity for back-bench initiation of debate.

Debates on European Community Documents

Increasingly important are debates on motions on European Community documents that have been laid before the Council of Ministers and will usually fall to be approved (or not) by that body (see page 201). The time spent on the floor of the House is shown in the Table on page 365. Further debates are held in standing committees (see page 276).

Although these debates take place on Government motions, we deal with them in this Chapter because the selection of European Community documents for debate is essentially made by the back-benchers on the European Legislation Committee (see pages 436–439). Although the Government does not always follow the committees precise recommendations it nearly always does so in one form or other, and the initiative certainly lies with back-benchers. A resolution of the House in 1980 confirmed the rights of the committee in this matter (see page 437), although there has been some delay in providing the requisite debates.[95a]

The debates are often held fairly late in the evening (about half the time spent was after 10 p.m.), or upstairs in committee, but are of some influence because they permit a public discussion of the issues before the United Kingdom Minister has to state his Government's attitude in the Council of Ministers. Such expression of opinion by the House (especially if cross-party) may strengthen the Minister's hand in the negotiations. Thus, although Parliament has no power to amend or approve or reject European legislation, it can exercise some indirect control.

Frequently several closely related European Community documents are debated together, on a motion which usually takes note of the relevant documents and then goes on to express a view sympathetic to or critical of the policy concerned, sometimes suggesting some variation in what has been proposed by the European Commission. A typical example was the motion, debated on May 17, 1988:

> That this House takes note of European Community Documents Nos. 9454/87 and 5616/88 on the Joint Research Centre and 10845/86 on EUREKA and Community Science and Technology; and supports the Government's aims of raising the quality and relevance of the work at the Joint Research Centre and of using EUREKA to help British industry become more competitive in world markets.[96]

[95a] On October 31, 1988, some 20 debates were needed to eliminate the back-log of documents recommended for early debate (H.C. Deb. Vol. 139, col. 664).

[96] H.C.Deb., Vol. 133, cols. 896–917.

Amendments are sometimes proposed to these motions by the Opposition, and on several occasions these have been accepted by the Government and agreed to[97]; this may also strengthen a Minister's negotiating position in the Council.

The types of European matters raised on the floor of the House are indicated by the following analysis. In 1984–85, there were 16 debates usually lasting up to an hour and a half.[98] They dealt with Summer time; meat and poultry (health controls); long drivers hours; lead content of petrol; the European Community Budgets (for four-and-a-half hours); heavy lorries; fisheries arrangements (two-and-a-half hours); the milk supplementary levy; the annual report of the Court of Auditors; CAP prices (three hours); frozen foodstuffs; and liability for defective products. In 1985–86 there were 21 debates relating to European Community documents. The topics were similar to those in the previous session. The longer debates were on the European Community Budgets (five hours); fisheries (two hours); general developments in the Community (five hours); the Common Agriculture Policy (six-and-a-half hours); and the Community's shipping policy (three hours).

Since 1980 there have been debates on less important or less controversial Community documents in standing committees, and in recent sessions this procedure has been used quite often although these debates are usually fairly brief. In 1984–85, there were seven debates covering wine; freight transport; examination of animals and fresh meat and the sampling and analysis of foodstuff; air pollution; use of substitute fuels, and petrol and fuel rationing; discharge of dangerous substances into water; and the labelling and advertising of beer and cider.

In 1985–86 there were nine debates in committee on protection of workers; use of sewage sludge on farms; self-propelled industrial trucks; general medical practice; definition of fishing vessels; risks from exposure to benzine; sugar imports from Lomè countries; measures against counterfeit goods; and trade in bovine and pig semen.

Thus, both on the floor and in committee, back-benchers are able to secure debates on aspects of the working of the European Communities, and of its legislation as it affects the United Kingdom, that would not otherwise come before the House. A measure of this scrutiny work was revealed in answer to a Question. Four hundred and thirty Community documents incorporating proposals by the Commission were deposited in Parliament in the calendar year 1985; 283 were draft regulations, 63 were draft directives, and 84 proposals for Council decisions. Forty-three of these documents were debated; they related to 25 regulations, 16 directives and two decisions. Only three proposals were formally adopted by the Council of Ministers before the House debated them.[99]

Estimates Debates

Another area where back benchers are able, in effect, to initiate debate, although the subject-matter is essentially Government business, is in respect of main and supplementary estimates. Three days are allotted each session

---

[97] e.g. H.C.Deb., Vol. 93, cols. 335–402 (March 5, 1986).
[98] Some European documents are listed as relevant to other debates in the House (e.g. the Budget debate) and so are counted as debated on those occasions.
[99] H.C.Deb., Vol. 103, col. 84 (October 28, 1986).

for formal consideration of estimates; this is all that remains of what was, historically, a principal function of the House (see page 250). The selection of the estimates to be debated is decided by the Liaison Committee. As the Liaison Committee is comprised entirely of back-benchers, and reflects the wishes of select committees also manned by back-benchers, the choice of estimates is made by the back-benchers in a collective fashion[99a], and is not controlled by either the Government or Opposition. Indeed there is no evidence that either of these participants have ever attempted to influence the choice of topics for debate on these days.

More than one estimate may be debated on each day. The actual choice of matters to be debated is much influenced by the work of the select committees. If a committee has inquired into and reported on a supplementary or main estimate and has found some interesting points to make, then that estimate is clearly a good candidate for a debate. For example a supplementary estimate for compensation for storm damage (after the October 1987 storm) was examined by the Agriculture Committee which hurried out a short report on the subject in time for a half-day's estimate debate on March 8, 1988.[1] Even if a report has not been specifically directed at an estimates provision, it may be relevant to a debate on an estimate. In respect of every estimate that is put down for debate on an estimates day, the relevant select committee report is noted on the Order Paper. Debates on the estimates thus also become debates on the reports.

How this procedure works out in practice, and what sort of matters are debated, may be illustrated by the use of estimates days in recent sessions. As it is a new procedure which has received little attention in other studies of the working of the House, we set out the full list of debates in the 1983–87 Parliament.

[99a] On three occasions soon after this procedure was adopted, proposals for debates were negatived by the Liaison Committee (H.C. 396 of 1982–83), but normally there is little disagreement in the committee on the choice of estimates.
[1] H.C. 272 of 1987–88 and H.C.Deb., Vol. 129, cols. 207–247.

Topics debated on Estimates days
(Indicating which committee made the relevant report)

Session 1983-84

8 March 1984   Premature retirement in the NHS (Supplementary
                            estimate) — Public Accounts

                            Assistance to coal industry (Supplementary estimate)
                            — Energy

4 July 1984   Prison education — Education, Science and Arts

                            A range of estimates reported on by the Environment
                            Committee — Environment

17 July 1984   UK diplomatic representation in the Commonwealth
                            Caribbean and aid to Grenada — Foreign Affairs

                            Work of the Property Services Agency —
                            Environment

Session 1984-85

18 December 1984   British National Oil Corporation (Supplementary
                            estimate) (half-day) — Energy

14 March 1985   British Natural Oil Corporation (Supplementary
                            estimate) (half-day) — Energy

11 July 1985   A range of estimates reported on by the Environment
                            Committee — Environment

                            Adult mentally-ill and mentally-handicapped people
                            — Social Services

18 July 1985   UK trade with China (half-day) — Trade and Industry

Session 1985-86

17 December 1985   Famine in Africa (Supplementary estimate) (half-day)
                            — Foreign Affairs

24 June 1986   Special employment measure and the long-term
                            unemployed — Employment

                            Housing and environmental services

9 July 1986   Residential care for the elderly — Social Services

                            Tourism — Trade and Industry

10 July 1986   Budget of the European Communities (Supplementary
                            estimate) (half-day)[2] — Treasury and Civil Service

Session 1986-87

11 March 1986   Assistance to the coal industry (Supplementary
                            estimate) (half-day) — Energy

It is perhaps too early to come to firm judgments about the use of
estimates days, but a few generalisations may be advanced on the basis of
experience so far. The debates tend to be on less controversial subjects.
Controversy is usually avoided by the absence, in nearly every case, of

---

[2] An amendment was moved, by the Chairman of Treasury and Civil Service Committee, to
reduce this estimate by £667 mil. It was negatived on a division (H.C.Deb., Vol. 101,
cols. 461–503).

amendments to reduce the estimates (indeed the argument is usually in favour of increased expenditure), and apart from the debate on the European Communities' Budget there have been no divisions. With only a light whip, attendance at these debates has not always been high. Nevertheless there have been some useful debates on matters which might otherwise not have been brought before the House. In the last Parliament certain committees were more successful in securing debates; there were four debates on estimates of the Department of the Environment, and four on energy matters.

Private Bills

For reasons which we explained in the Preface, we have not dealt with private bill procedure in this book.[3] There is one aspect, however, which is relevant to this Chapter, namely the part played by back-benchers in securing debate on the floor of the House on private legislation.

Private bills, having been presented, are set down for formal second readings at the time of private business immediately after Prayers. If no one objects they can be given a second reading "on the nod" without debate. If objected to, or if a blocking motion is put down, the second reading has to be deferred by the Chairman of Ways and Means, who is in charge of private business, to a later day. Many second readings are at first blocked by back-benchers, sometimes on a cross-party basis, for a variety of reasons—broad political dislike of the bill, opposition to particular points or local controversy—and often on behalf of some outside body. On February 25, 1988, for example, the second readings of 10 private bills were on the order paper; there were blocking motions against all of them; five of these were in the names of Members of more than one party.

Eventually a number of these blocks may be lifted. This usually happens when the promoters of the private bill—the local authority, the nationalised industry, the private company or charity, whoever it may be—have, through their parliamentary agents, contacted the objecting Members and perhaps given some undertaking or promised some compromise which satisfies those on behalf of whom the Members were acting. These bills can then be given an unopposed second reading and be sent to a private bill committee for detailed examination. If, however, a settlement cannot be reached and the objecting Members refuse to remove the blocking motion, then the Chairman of Ways and Means has to name a day for a second reading debate, which usually lasts from 7 to 10 p.m.

It is in this way that back-benchers on both sides of the House can secure debates on matters which they, not the Government nor the Opposition as such (though on some matters the Opposition welcome the action of the back-benchers concerned), believe should be debated. Private bills deal with local matters, and some second reading debates are on matters of local controversy, the acquisition of some land, for example, or the imposition of some bye-law, but many debates are on issues of wider principle or political concern that arise on the bill. Other bills are regularly debated as they give Members an opportunity to discuss the conduct of the promoting body concerned. British Railways Bills and London Regional Transport Bills are often debated for this reason.

Later stages of private bills may also be debated in the same way. Indeed if

---

[3] For a detailed description of private legislation procedure, see Part III of Erskine Mays', *Parliamentary Practice.*

opposition is very strong, more than one day may have to be found to enable the bill to be got through. This happened to the Felixstowe Dock and Railway Bill which had seven debates in sessions 1984–85, 1985–86 and 1987–88, before it finally passed the Commons. Again the occasion of debate results from back-bench opposition and initiative.

The private bills debated on second reading or a later stage in 1984–85 and 1985–86 give some idea of the extent these opportunities are used. In 1984–85, seven private bills were debated briefly (between one and 22 minutes) on second reading because of a particular campaign by one Member. This was not typical. More typically, more than three hours (including division time) was spent on the second readings of the Birmingham City Council Bill and the Felixstowe Dock and Railway Bill; two-and-a-half hours were spent on the second reading of the Greater London Council (General Powers) Bill; and half-an-hour on the same stage of the Yorkshire Water Authority Bill. Two further debates, totalling five hours, were required for the consideration stage of the Birmingham City Council Bill. A further debate of over three hours was needed for a motion to suspend further proceedings on the Felixstowe Dock and Railway Bill till the next session. The total time spent on the floor of the House on private business debates is shown in the Table on page 365.

In 1985–86 even more time was spent on the various stages of 10 different bills. Again the Felixstowe Dock and Railway Bill proved particularly controversial, and again failed to get through that session. Other controversial bills included the Peterhead Harbour Order Confirmation Bill, the British Railways (Stansted) Bill and the Channel Tunnel Bill (a public bill which affected private interests and was therefore hybrid; hybrid bills are treated in part like private bills (see page 227)).

Private bills offer back-benchers a valuable opportunity for influencing legislation and public policy. although they do not initiate the matter of debate, they can secure, of their own volition, the occasion of debate. It is an aspect of the work of the House that should not be disregarded.

BACK-BENCH RESPONSE TO GOVERNMENT OR OPPOSITION INITIATIVE

We have described a range of opportunities open to back-benchers to bring matters before the House or to initiate debate. We must remember, however, that much of the time of these Members is spent responding to or playing their part in business initiated by other participants. They speak in debates on Government and Opposition motions; they take part in consideration of Government and private Member's bills; they ask supplementary Questions on other Members' Questions and on Ministers' statements. The responsive opportunities for back-benchers are almost unlimited.

What is limited is time. Debates are not open ended. Members are increasingly anxious to participate and it is not possible for every Member to speak in every debate in which he wishes to. The Speaker has to select with care from among those who seek to catch his eye. It has been estimated that for main debates (second readings and full-day motions) the average back bench Member can only expect to be called about four times a session.[4] Of course many Members are far from average; some, by perseverance and perhaps because of particular qualifications or qualities, may be called many

---

[4] Information supplied by the Speaker's Office.

more times; others hardly speak at all. But many Members are frequently disappointed by not being called.

Ministers and Opposition spokemen do not share these frustrations. They speak when they are chosen to by their leaders or when the business so dictates; the Speaker, here, exercises no choice. His discretion is also fettered by one old convention, namely that Privy Councillors have precedence in speaking in debate. This has often caused considerable annoyance to some back-benchers,[5] and it is true that in some debates where a number of Privy Councillors, including former Prime Ministers, wish to take part, there can be some four to six speeches (of say 20 minutes each) by such senior Members, as well as the opening speeches from the front benches (say 30 minutes each), before the first non-Privy Councillor back-bencher is called. If a debate does not start till 4 p.m. (which is common) and one hour is kept for the wind-up speeches from the Opposition and the Government, this may leave only two hours for a large number of ordinary back-benchers before the vote at 10 p.m.

Members have many other responsive opportunities however. One of the most important is amendments to bills. Opposition back-benchers may table amendments on detailed matters which concern them, on which for some reason their front-bench have not acted, or they may wish to make a point at variance with the policy of their own front-bench, or with a different emphasis. To take a recent case, 156 amendments and five new clauses were tabled to the Education Reform Bill 1987–88 when it first started in standing committee; 70 of these stood in the names of Opposition back-benchers. On the Local Government Bill in the same session, 17 out of 101 amendments and 10 new clauses were tabled by Members on the Opposition back-benches when the bill was first considered in committee.

Amendments tabled by Government back-benchers to Government bills may be more significant. Often they will reflect the concern of some outside interest or pressure group. If supported by influential Members or by a significant number, these are amendments which Ministers must heed. To take the Education Reform Bill again, seven amendments in the names of Government back-benchers were tabled when the bill first went into committee. We considered the influence of such dissent in pages 118–130.

Since 1979, Government back-benches have periodically brought an issue of great importance before the House by moving an amendment to a Government bill. This is the question of the restoration of the death penalty. The most recent occasion was on June 7, 1988, when an amendment of this nature was tabled to the Criminal Justice Bill, debated all day, and defeated by 218 votes to 341.[6]

Back-bench amendments, from either side of the House, or sometimes both, can be influential when the House is considering its own domestic affairs. Party discipline is then at its weakest. Government motions relating to privilege, procedure, Members' facilities and accommodation, or pay and allowances have sometimes been amended by back-benchers.

For example, in the debate on the report of the Committee of Privileges in 1986 relating to the leak of a draft select committee report (see pages 101–102), it was an amendment moved by a Government back-bencher which led to the rejection of the motion moved by the Leader of the

---

[5] See, for example, Early Day Motion No. 774 of Session 1985–86 (p. 8192 of Notices of Questions and Motions).

[6] H.C.Deb., Vol. 134, cols. 735–810.

House[7]; the same had happened in 1958 regarding the Strauss privilege case (see page 89).[8] The penalties recommended by the Committee on the Conduct of Members, following the Poulson case, for Reginald Maudling and Albert Roberts, were not agreed to in 1977 as a result of back-bench amendments (see page 68).[9] Perhaps most significantly, in 1986 Members took a direct decision on their own allowances, against the advice of Ministers, when office and secretarial allowances were increased by an amendment to a Government motion supported by back-bench Members from both sides (see page 77).[10]

The ability of back-benchers to respond to Government initiatives is sometimes as important as their power to initiate their own debates. The opportunities for such response are numerous.

INFORMATION FOR BACK-BENCHERS

Opportunities and procedures are of little value to back-benchers in their parliamentary work if they cannot be well informed. However little need be added here to the description of the sources of information for the Opposition which we summarised at the end of Chapter 9, as the same sources are available for back-benchers, with only a slight variation of emphasis. In particular, party research services cannot be drawn on as readily by back-benchers as they can be by front-bench spokesmen.

There is one particular source of assistance which is welcomed by many back-benchers: the Ombudsman or Parliamentary Commissioner. We do not deal in this book with his work (the role of the committee which considers his reports and responsibilities is described on pages 439–441), but the value of this officer in examining with great care complaints from constituents that are referred to him by back-bench Members must be emphasised.

Finally, the tremendous importance of the constituency for the individual Member must be re-iterated. The relationship was discussed in Chapter 2. Here we simply emphasise that much the most influential source of information and advice for many back-bench Members is that which comes out of his constituency—from his party officers, from his local committee, from party meetings, from local councillors and their officers, from local businessmen or trade unions, from local pressure groups, and from individual citizens, especially those who come to see him in his surgery or who write him letters. This is what keeps him in contact with the world he represents. He ignores them at his peril. Much that he does in the House is based on these sources.

We have now described the role and initiative of the back-bench Member in all areas of his parliamentary work bar one. Select committees are becoming increasingly important in providing an outlet for back-benchers, particularly those who wish to specialise in some field. They provide a forum where they, on their own and without the participation of the front-benches, can raise issues of their choosing and can secure detailed consideration of many matters that might not otherwise come before the House. The work of these committees is the subject of the next Chapter.

---

[7] H.C.Deb., Vol. 98, cols. 293–332 (May 20, 1986).
[8] H.C.Deb., Vol. 591, cols. 208–346 (July 8, 1958).
[9] H.C.Deb., Vol. 936, cols. 438–460 (July 26, 1977).
[10] H.C.Deb., Vol. 101, cols. 1139–1143 (July 16, 1986).

Chapter 11

SELECT COMMITTEES

Certain select committees relating to public matters are regularly appointed.[1] Of these, 14 are appointed under Standing Order No. 130 and known as departmentally-related committees because they are concerned with the expenditure, administration and policy of Government departments and associated bodies. Nine other committees are appointed under Standing Order Nos. 121–129 and are concerned with: privileges, public accounts, consolidation bills,[2] statutory instruments,[3] Commons services, the Parliamentary Commissioner for Administration (P.C.A.), European legislation, Members' interests, and sound broadcasting. A select committee on procedure is appointed from time to time (but not under a standing order). There is also the Committee of Selection. Finally, the Liaison Committee, appointed under Standing Order No. 131, considers general matters relating to the work of select committees and advises the House of Commons Commission (see pages 160–162).

After the general election of 1987, however, one of the departmentally-related committees—that on Scottish Affairs—was not nominated with the others. The Conservative party won only 10 seats in Scotland; of these, five became Ministers and the Government was unable to appoint a majority of Conservative Scottish Members to the committee. Although the Opposition agreed to accept Conservative Members from English constituencies, the committee was not set up.[3a] Nomination of the Committee on Sound Broadcasting was also delayed. And by mid-1989, no Committee of Privileges had been convened. Three ad hoc select committees were set up in 1987–88: on private bill procedure (a joint committee with the House of Lords), on the televising of proceedings in the Commons, and on the Dartford-Thurrock Bill (a hybrid measure).

Select committees consist primarily of back-benchers. The only Ministers who are members are the Leader of the House who chairs, and the Government deputy chief Whip who is usually a member of, the Services Committee; and the Financial Secretary to the Treasury who is an (inactive) member of the Public Accounts Committee.[4] Parliamentary private secretaries are also usually excluded.[5] Except for the Whips who sit on the Services Committee and the Committee of Selection, Opposition front-benchers are not members of select committees.[6]

---

[1] See generally, G. Drewry (ed.) *The New Select Committees* (1985) D. Englefield (ed.) *Commons Select Committees* (1984); Reports from Liaison Committee H.C. 92 of 1982–83, H.C. 363 of 1984–85; the Sessional Information Digests from 1983–84; the Select Committee Returns H.C. 172 of 1986–87 and H.C. 79 of 1987–88.

[2] A joint committee with the House of Lords.

[3] A joint committee with the House of Lords; the Commons members of the Committee on Statutory Instruments also meet separately (see below, pp. 444–446).

[3a] See H.C.Deb. Vol. 144 cols. 336–394 (December 20, 1988).

[4] When a Privileges Committee is convened, the Leader of the House takes the chair and the Attorney General is a member.

[5] In the 1983–87 Parliament, the Conservatives broke this custom in order to achieve a majority on the Scottish Affairs Committee.

[6] Ad hoc committees may provide exceptions, *e.g.* the Leader of the House and the shadow Leader are both members of the Select Committee to consider the televising of the proceedings of the House.

With the exception of the departmentally-related committees, members of select committees are nominated on a motion moved by a Government Whip. The names for the departmentally-related committees are put forward, as recommendations to the House, on behalf of the Committee of Selection by its chairman or another member of that committee under Standing Order No. 104. The standing order under which the Liaison Committee is appointed most unusually makes no provision limiting or prescribing the number of its members. In mid-1989 it consisted of the chairmen of the departmentally-related committees and the chairmen of the committees concerned with the P.C.A., statutory instruments, Members' interests, procedure, public accounts, European legislation; also the chairman of the Committee of Selection; and a member of the SLDP. Its membership was 21.

THE DEPARTMENTALLY-RELATED COMMITTEES

Structure

In 1987–88 the departmentally-related[7] select committees were:

Name of Committee (and political party of chairman)	Principal Government departments concerned	Maximum number of Members	Quorum
1. Agriculture (Conservative)	Ministry of Agriculture, Fisheries & Food	11	3
2. Defence (Conservative)	Ministry of Defence	11	3
3. Education Science & Arts (Conservative)	Department of Education & Science	11	3
4. Employment (Labour)	Department of Employment	11	3
5. Energy (Conservative)	Department of Energy	11	3
6. Environment (Conservative)	Department of the Environment	11	3
7. Foreign Affairs (Conservative)	Foreign & Commonwealth Office	11	3
8. Home Affairs (Conservative)	Home Office	11	3
9. Scottish Affairs	Scottish Office (not nominated)		
10. Social Services (Labour)	Department of Health & Social Security	11	3

[7] Excluded are the Lord Chancellor's Department and the Law Officers: H.C. 92 of 1982–83 para. 24 and H.C. 225 of 1985–86.

Name of Committee (and political party of chairman)	Principal Government departments concerned	Maximum number of Members	Quorum
11. Trade and Industry (Conservative)	Department of Trade & Industry	11	3
12. Transport (Labour)	Department of Transport	11	3
13. Treasury & Civil Service (Conservative)	Treasury, Management & Personnel Office, Board of the Inland Revenue, Board of Customs and Excise	11	3
14. Welsh Affairs (Labour)	Welsh Office	11	3
		143	

The Foreign Affairs Committee, the Home Affairs Committee and the Treasury and Civil Service Committee are each empowered to appoint one sub-committee. These have, at times, been used respectively to cover overseas aid, race relations and immigration, and civil service issues. There may also be a sub-committee, drawn from the membership of two or more of the Energy, Environment, Trade and Industry, Scottish Affairs, Transport, and Treasury and Civil Service Committees to consider any matter affecting two or more nationalised industries,[8] but so far this power has not been used.

In its report at the end of 1982, the Liaison Committee noted that some of the committees had set up informal sub-committees, each acting in the name of the full committee and needing the quorum of the full committee. The chairmen urged strongly on the Government that more formal sub-committees should be authorised. Successive Leaders of the House rejected these pleas on three grounds. They expressed doubt about the House's capacity to service more sub-committees (though some of the committees said they would not need extra permanent staff); they drew attention to the increased load which more sub-committees would place on Ministers and departments; they suggested that it was too early to make changes.[9] In April 1985, the Liaison Committee returned to this matter but without success.[10] The general powers of select committees have been described above (pages 280–286).

Membership

As we have seen, members are nominated for the whole of a Parliament. Although standing orders do not require the Committee of Selection to have regard to the composition of the House in nominating membership of select committees, the committee adopted this principle when recommending

---

[8] S.O. No. 130(4). The scope of select committees may clash and this can lead to confict as happened between the Energy and Environment Committees over nuclear power in 1985–86.
[9] H.C. 92 of 1982–83 paras. 34–39.
[10] H.C. 363 of 1984–85 para. 28; H.C. 225 of 1985–86.

membership of the departmentally-related committees. When these committees were first set up in 1979[11] the chairman of the Committee of Selection (Sir Philip Holland) emphasised that there would be exhaustive
examination before making nominations to the House, with very wide
consultation.[12] On the Government side of the committee, the Whips'
influence in the determination of the memberships appears to have been
resisted, with some success, by the Conservative members of the committee,
led by the chairman. On the Opposition side of the Committee, the direct
influence of the Whips was more obvious[13] and more complete, though they
did not always get their way.

More recently, it seems that the Whips on both sides of the House have
re-established their usual control over nominations,[14] though there may be
heavy lobbying within the principal parties for membership as this is seen to
reflect the influence of different groups within the parties.[15] Competition for
membership of the more prestigious committees is keen and overall there
are many more volunteers than vacancies. The chairman of the Committee
of Selection is drawn from the Government side of the House and represents
that side, with other Government supporters, on the committee. The Opposition has its own principal representative (who has in recent years been an
Opposition Whip) supported similarly. Each side has its own private meetings and, subject to the Whips' influence, nominates its recommended
members of the committees. As a result, meetings of the Committee of
Selection are usually very short and amount to little more than the receiving
of names. The names are then put to the House and objection may be made,
especially by Members from the smaller Opposition parties if they feel they
have not been fairly treated or if they have failed to agree whom to recommend. Ultimately, only a division in the House can resolve such conflicts.[16]

After the general election in May 1983, there was considerable delay in
nominating members to the departmentally-related committees. At first this
was because the Parliamentary Labour Party waited for the result of their
elections to the Parliamentary Committee. And when the House reas-
sembled after the summer recess, dissatisfaction by the smaller Opposition
parties caused further delay. Eventually nominations were finally approved
on December 14, 1983.[17]

The increase in the Conservative majority at the general election of May
1983 was accompanied by an increase in the total number of members of the
14 committees from 148 to 156. This resulted in a total membership of 96

---

[11] When the committees were first approved on June 25, 1979, those on Scottish and Welsh
Affairs were not included. They were added soon after: H.C.Deb. Vol. 969, cols. 359–362
(June 26, 1979) and H.C.Deb., Vol. 972, cols. 1390–1391 (October 31, 1979).

[12] H.C.Deb., Vol. 969, col. 183 (June 25, 1979); H.C.Deb., Vol. 974, cols. 1029–1070
(November 26, 1979).

[13] Exceptionally, in 1979, the Scottish Labour Members balloted amongst themselves for
membership of the Scottish Affairs Committee on which they had six places.

[14] The chairman of the Committee of Selection (Sir Marcus Fox) has said: "it is for each party
to decide which hon. Members it will nominate": H.C.Deb., Vol. 125, col. 398 (January 13,
1988).

[15] In late 1987, some Conservative Members objected to proposed Labour nominations on
the Defence Committee of certain "unilateralists" and some changes were made.

[16] See, for example, H.C.Deb., Vol. 50, cols. 647–648, 1111–1137 (December 9 and 14,
1983) and below.

[17] H.C.Deb., Vol. 50, cols. 1111–1137; for earlier proceedings, see H.C.Deb., Vol. 50,
cols. 647–648 (December 9, 1983).

Conservatives, 49 Labour, six Liberals, three Ulster Unionists, one Ulster Democratic Unionist and one Plaid Cymru member. In 10 of the 14 committees Conservatives had seven out of the 11 places and, in the Scottish Affairs Committee, eight out of the 13 places. Towards the end of 1985, the Ulster Unionists members resigned their membership of the House in protest at the Anglo-Irish agreement and submitted themselves to re-election in January 1986. Their resignation meant that they lost their places on the committees.

A similar delay followed the election of 1987. This was caused in part by the difficulties over the Scottish Affairs Committee. Also, there was a disagreement among the smaller Opposition parties (particularly Ulster Unionists and SDP) over the names to put forward for other committees. Decisions were eventually taken by the House in December 1987.[18]

The proportion of Members in the House if strictly adhered to would have resulted in 90 Conservative, 55 Labour and 11 Members from smaller parties being nominated to the 14 committees. Particular difficulty was caused by the fact that four of the smaller parties (Scottish National Party, Ulster Democratic Unionist Party, Social Democratic, and Labour Party, and Plaid Cymru) each had the same number of seats (three) in the House but arithmetically were entitled only to a total of three seats on the committees. In the event, on the 13 committees that were set up, 82 Conservative and 52 Labour Members were nominated; the Social and Liberal Democrats had three places and the SDP, SDLP, Ulster Unionists, Plaid Cymru, and Scottish Nationalists one place each.

Chairmanship

The number of chairs taken by the Government side of the House and from the Opposition is a matter of bargaining between Government and Opposition. In 1979 the 14 chairs were divided equally between Conservative and Labour but in 1983 and 1987, the Government took a majority of the chairs. In the eventual agreement as to which party shall chair which committees, some traditional preferences can be seen. For example, the Conservative side is likely to chair the Agriculture Committee, and Labour the Social Services Committee. More importantly, the Government side is likely to insist on chairing the most important committees. After the 1983 election, the Government side took nine of the 14 chairs, retaining those of the Agriculture, Defence, Energy, Foreign Affairs, Home Affairs, Trade and Industry, and Treasury and Civil Service Committees; and taking from Labour, the chairs of the Education and Environment Committees. This left Labour with the chairs of the Employment, Scottish Affairs, Social Services, Transport, and Welsh Affairs Committees. This distribution was also adopted after the election of 1987 (though without the Scottish Affairs Committee).

The negotiations between the Chief Whips take account of many factors. After the 1987 election, some Conservatives wished the chair of the Social Services Committee (which had been held by Mrs. Renee Short for Labour since 1979) to be held by a Conservative but there was no agreement on a nominee. This being so the question of which party should chair the committee was re-opened. Also, Labour would wish to know which chair they were being offered in exchange for the loss of the Social Services chair. If they

---

[18] H.C.Deb., Vol. 123, cols. 1039–1076 (December 2, 1987) and see, H.C.Deb., Vol. 125, cols. 397–424 (January 13, 1988).

wanted the chair of an important committee—say, Education or Environment, previously held by Conservatives—the Government Chief Whip would have to face depriving one of his honourable friends of chairmanship, or denying others of his friends the chance of succeeding their colleagues in that position. In the end, Labour retained the chairmanship of Social Services, though the Member elected did not (it is believed) have the positive support of all members of the committee at that time.

The Opposition, if it feels it is being unfairly dealt with, may threaten to resort to various obstructive tactics, even to the extent of refusing to propose members of select committees. On the other hand, the Government is not likely to be particularly concerned if the setting up of the select committees is delayed. In the end some kind of compromise emerges because both sides wish the parliamentary system to continue to work more or less as before.

Once it has been decided which committees shall have chairmen from the Government side, and which from the Opposition side, the selection of the chairman can proceed. The selection is made formally by the members of each committee, but this is subject to substantial influences. The party groups, whether in the majority or the minority, receive clear indications from their Whips Office whom they should elect so as to put into effect the agreement on the distribution of chairs. This view usually prevails. However the Members on the committee may, exceptionally, not follow the Whips' indication; even (on occasion) when it is known to reflect the party Leader's preference.

It has also happened that all members of the committee have participated actively in the election of a chairman. This occurred when two Labour members were nominated for the chair of the Social Services Committee in 1979 and the members crossvoted. The chairman who was eventually elected (Mrs. Renee Short) was not the person originally favoured by the Whips.[19] When the Home Affairs Committee first met in 1979, the Labour members refused to accept the Whips' agreement that this Committee should be chaired by a Conservative and, one Conservative member being absent, produced a tied result which had to be resolved at a subsequent meeting.[20] On other occasions there may be rival candidates within the party which is due to have the chair. Usually the outcome will be decided outside the committee room by the party members, so avoiding a vote in committee in which the other party would participate. It is also recognised that the chairman should, if possible, be acceptable to the members of the other party. Of the 13 committees set up in December 1987, one chairman was elected on a division,[21] the others being unopposed.

Attendance and Turnover

The statistics[22] relating to the working of the departmental committees from 1979–80 to 1986–87 show that the attendance of members averaged over 70 per cent. The average is adversely affected by delays in appointing new members when vacancies occur. Moreover, these figures exclude those of

---

[19] G. Drewry (ed.) *op. cit.* at p. 241. Another example of a chairman believed not to be the Whips' favoured candidate was Sir Richard Body (Agriculture) in the 1983–87 Parliament.

[20] Drewry *op. cit.* p. 184.

[21] The 4 Labour members voted against the appointment of Mr. David Howell as chairman of the Foreign Affairs Committee (H.C. 724 of 1987–88).

[22] For sets of statistics, see, *e.g.* H.C.Deb., Vol. 89, cols. 691–694 (January 16, 1986) and H.C.Deb., Vol. 90, cols. 287–288 (January 23, 1986); see also sessional returns.

official and unofficial sub-committees, and this also tends to pull down the overall average. Towards the end of the 1983–87 Parliament there was a decline. For the session 1985–86, the overall average was 68 per cent., the lowest being the Welsh Affairs Committee at 56 per cent. and Scottish Affairs Committee at 61 per cent., with the highest being the Defence Committee at 85 per cent., almost certainly a reflection of its two investigations and reports on the defence implications and government decision-making in connection with the Westland affair. In 1986–87, the overall average attendance was 69 per cent. with the Scottish Committee managing only 54 per cent., and the Employment and Transport Committees reaching 79 per cent.[23]

The turnover of membership is significant as so much depends on individual members acquiring an understanding of the working of the department to which their committee is related. During the 1979–83 Parliament the average turnover (excluding sub-committees) was 44 per cent., ranging from the Education Committee at 11 per cent. to the Scottish Affairs Committee at 77 per cent. (on which only three members served throughout). Altogether 87 of the 148 members originally appointed ceased to serve during the course of the Parliament. Of these 53 were promoted to ministerial or Opposition front-bench positions.[24] In the session of 1985–86, the average turnover was over 18 per cent. with the Agriculture Committee losing more than half its original members and the Social Services Committee more than one third. For 1986–87, the average, in the shorter session, dropped to just over 10 per cent., with the Energy, Environment, Trade and Industry Committees each losing 18 per cent.[25] When losses are heavy the role of the chairman and two or three other "regulars" becomes crucial.

Witnesses

In 1985–86 and 1986–87 Cabinet Ministers made 35 appearances and other Ministers made 57 appearances before one or other of the 14 departmentally-related committees. Senior civil servants (Under Secretaries and above) in those two sessions made 190 and other civil servants 275 appearances. Many witnesses from outside Government are also heard.

Travel

Frequently committees seek information away from Westminster. Committees which have power "to adjourn from place to place" can go anywhere in the United Kingdom at their own discretion, their expenses being carried on the House of Commons (Administration) Vote. On average, each committee spends about £3,000 each year on United Kingdom visits. Overseas travel is more tightly controlled. The House of Commons Commission has delegated power to the Liaison Committee to authorise expenditure up to a ceiling for all committees, each of which has to make its case to the Liaison Committee. During 1985–86 and 1986–87 the committees made 33 visits overseas and 99 in the United Kingdom.

In the normal length session of 1985–86, the 14 committees spent some

---

[23] H.C. 172 of 1986–87 and H.C. 79 of 1987–88; and see H.C.Deb., Vol. 89, cols. 681–682 (January 16, 1986).

[24] Drewry op. cit. p. 325.

[25] H.C. 172 of 1986–87 and H.C. 79 of 1987–88; and see H.C.Deb., Vol. 89, cols. 681–682 (January 16, 1986).

£220,000 on overseas visits.[25a] Not surprisingly, the Foreign Affairs Committee spent the most—an estimated £39,000—with visits to the Philippines and south-east Asia. The Defence Committee is usually a big spender and although its costs amounted to only £11,435 in 1985–86, the following short session of 1986–87 saw the amount rise to £54,367 with visits to Oman, Diego Garcia, Hong Kong and the United States; Denmark, the Federal Republic of Germany; and Paris. In 1985–86, the Treasury and Civil Service Committee incurred costs of £23,500 on visits to the United States and Mexico in connection with the inquiry into international credit and capital markets. The Transport Committee spent £26,200 on a visit to Canada to look at the financing of rail services. The Home Affairs Committee spent £23,000 visiting the United States to examine prisons; and its race relations and immigration sub-committee £14,769 on visits to Pakistan, India, Bangladesh and European countries. The Employment Committee went to Japan to look at industrial relations at a cost of £26,884. The Agriculture Committee spent nearly £18,000 visiting the United States and Canada in connection with its inquiry into pesticides; the Education Committee over £10,000 visiting the Federal Republic of Germany on primary schools; the Energy Committee nearly £18,000 on visits to the United States and Brussels on the coal industry. The Social Services Committee visited Sweden and Holland to look at prison medical services at a cost of £5,719 and the Welsh Affairs Committee spent nearly £3,000 going to Holland in connection with its inquiry into tourism in Wales.

To reduce costs, it is quite common for less than the full membership of each committee to make these overseas trips.

The nature of proceedings when committees meet away from Westminster again varies greatly. A committee may wish to take formal evidence, usually in public, from people on the spot, such as various local authorities and local interest groups. This applies particularly in the United Kingdom for it is not usual to take formal evidence overseas from foreigners (although formal evidence has been given by United Kingdom persons, such as Ambassadors and High Commissioners and their staff, and officers of the armed services serving overseas). It may wish to hold informal meetings, off-the-record, with experienced people who are willing to help them in understanding the matter under investigation without giving formal evidence, or where the complexity or nature of the matter inhibits the taking of such evidence. Most overseas visits involve informal meetings (although a formal note is sometimes agreed, summarising the principal points emerging from the discussion); occasionally such informal consultations are also arranged at Westminster.[25b] Committees often go away from Westminster to visit establishments such as factories, schools, hospitals, military installations, farms and laboratories to see what work is done there and to meet people at their place of work. Such visits are arranged both at home and overseas.

Staff and Advisers

Each of the departmentally-related committees has a small complement

---

[25a] The sessional return for the unusually long session 1987–88 indicates an estimated total expenditure in that session of some £420,000 (H.C.99–ii of 1988–89).

[25b] In 1987–88 the Foreign Affairs Committee had 29 off-the-record meetings with overseas visitors, foreign ambassadors, heads of U.K. missions returning to the U.K. etc., (H.C.21 of 1988–89).

of staff employed in the department of the Clerk of the House; the committees have no power to engage their own staff. As with all staff in the House departments, clerks work with a designated committee whatever the changes in the party in power, in members or in chairmen. Normal for a committee is, first, a Clerk of the Committee, usually a Deputy Principal or Senior Clerk,[26] who will usually stay with that committee for four to six years. There may be a second, more junior, clerk, especially if the committee is using a sub-committee, who will probably work with that committee for up to three years. All committees also have a committee assistant. And each committee has its own secretary.

In addition to these "generalist" career staff, some committees have specialist assistants (in whose appointment the chairman of the committee participates) who, although employed full-time as staff of the department, are engaged for a maximum of four years. They have been aged about 28–38, and bring relevant outside subject experience to their work. They do detailed background analyses, advise on questions to witnesses and may help draft reports. In mid-1989, the Agriculture, Education, Environment, Social Services, Transport and Treasury and Civil Service Committees had such assistants working with them. The Defence Committee had an experienced officer seconded from the National Audit Office.

The committees themselves are also empowered to appoint specialist advisers "either to supply information which is not readily available or to elucidate matters of complexity."[27] These advisers are outside experts— academics, researchers, retired professionals—often of considerable eminence who act part-time and are paid fees. In 1985–86 session, 86 such advisers were appointed and 84 in 1986–87. The Treasury and Civil Service, Social Services and Defence Committees appointed most, with 10 or more in each session. The Home Affairs Committee appointed none.[28] Some advisers work continuously with a committee; others are engaged for a short period for a particular inquiry.

Reports

During the Parliament of 1979–83, departmentally-related committees made 193 reports (excluding special reports containing Government replies to, or observations on, committee reports) of which six were debated either on specific motions or on the adjournment. Reports are also debated in the course of normal parliamentary proceedings particularly those relating to estimates and expenditure; and material from reports or evidence is sometimes used on other occasions. Particular reports have also been brought to the attention of Members—on some 40 occasions between the beginning of 1980 and April 1985—by attaching "tags" to the relevant entry on the Order Paper.[29] On March 17, 1986, members of the Energy Committee tabled an amendment to the Gas Bill which was moved by the Conservative chairman. But only one Conservative member of the committee (not the chairman) voted for the amendment.[30] Committees may also take evidence (which is

---

[26] The Clerk of the Treasury and Civil Service Committee is also the Principal Clerk of Financial Committees and has additional oversight responsibilities over P.A.C. and other committee staff.

[27] S.O. No. 130(5)(b).

[28] H.C. 172 of 1986–87 and H.C. 79 of 1987–88.

[29] H.C. 363 of 1984–85 para. 17; and see H.C.Deb., Vol. 89, cols. 683–686 (January 16, 1986).

[30] H.C.Deb., Vol. 94, cols. 109–123.

published) without making reports. These sessions are seen as providing useful information to Members, sometimes on unexpected matters of immediate importance.[31]

During the 1983–87 Parliament, the 14 committees made 229 reports (excluding special reports). The most prolific was the Treasury and Civil Service Committee with 34 reports, followed by the Energy Committee and the Defence Committee each with 26 reports.[32]

The subjects

The departmentally-related select committees are empowered by Standing Order No. 130 "to examine the expenditure, administration and policy" of their assigned departments or associated public bodies, and similar matters in Northern Ireland, and to report to the House. They choose for themselves their subjects of inquiry.

Both the differing activities carried out by the departments and the preferences of the individual committees have resulted in various emphases being given to those orders of reference. The Education, Science and Arts Committee chairman reporting in the summer of 1982[33] itemised four different sorts of reports or enquiry:

"1. Major studies, to influence government thinking over a four or five-year period or longer. Our reports on higher education, the secondary school curriculum and the funding of the arts fall into this category.
2. Shorter scale studies, produced comparatively quickly, to influence government policies and spending decisions in a particular financial year—our reports on information storage and biotechnology fell into this category.
3. Very rapid reports to attempt to influence an immediate situation. Our reports on the Promenade Concerts, the International Centre for the Preservation and Restoration of Cultural Properties, Rome, the siting of the British Library, V.A.T. and the Arts, nitrate film, and the Theatre Museum fall into this category.
4. Finally we have not necessarily produced reports demanding government reply, believing that in certain situations a catalytic effect can be produced by taking evidence in public on a subject while it is topical, and issuing a suitable short report. Our calling of Rupert Murdoch to give evidence on the future of the Times Supplements is one example."

With one addition, these four categories embrace most of the kinds of reports made by all the committees. The addition are the reports or hearings directed specifically at expenditure.

During the Parliament of 1979–83, seven committees reported on main or supplementary estimates. The Treasury and Civil Service Committee did so in each session.[34] The Foreign Affairs Committee did so once in 1980–81 and twice in 1981–82.[35] The Agriculture Committee did so on two occasions.[36]

---

[31] For example, the Employment Committee's inquiry into the position of trade unionists at G.C.H.Q. although on this occasion the committee also agreed, unanimously, a report suggesting a possible compromise solution of the dispute (which was not adopted by the Government): H.C. 238 of 1983–84.
[32] Derived from Sessional Information Digests, 1983–87; H.C. 172 of 1986–87 and H.C. 79 of 1987–88.
[33] H.C. 92 of 1982–83 pp. 47–48.
[34] H.C. 503 of 1979–80; H.C. 226 of 1981–82; H.C. 228 of 1982–83.
[35] H.C. 343 of 1980–81; H.C. 330 and 406 of 1981–82.
[36] H.C. 361 of 1980–81; H.C. 525 of 1981–82.

Others did so once: Defence,[37] Energy,[38] Environment,[39] Welsh Affairs.[40] The public expenditure white papers were on various occasions reported on by the Environment Committee,[41] the Social Services Committee,[42] the Transport Committee.[43] The Employment Committee reported in each of three sessions on the Manpower Services Commission's corporate plans.[44] The Trade and Industry Committee reported on nationalised industries finances in 1979–80 and on British Steel Corporation plan in 1980–81.[45] The Treasury and Civil Service Committee made seven reports on Budgets and expenditure plans, and two on the Autumn statements.[46]

During each of the sessions of the 1983–87 Parliament, the Treasury and Civil Service Committee examined the Budget, the Autumn statement, and the Government Expenditure Plans,[47] as well as various aspects of the Estimates. Witnesses included the Chancellor of the Exchequer, Treasury officials headed by the Chief Economic Adviser and representatives of the Bank of England. The Defence Committee reported on the Estimates in each of the first three sessions.[48] So did the Environment Committee, both for the Department and the Property Services Agency.[49] In each of the first three sessions, the Employment Committee reported on the Manpower Services Commission Corporate Plan[50]; so did the Social Services Committee on the public expenditure white paper as it affected their responsibilities.[51] The Energy Committee reported on the supplementary estimates for the Coal Board in 1983–84 and for BNOC in 1984–85, and on the expenditure white paper and main estimates in 1985–86.[52] The Transport Committee reported each session on the public expenditure white paper.[53] The Foreign Affairs Committee looked, in each of the first three sessions, at one or more aspects of expenditure by the Foreign and Commonwealth Office.[54]

The choice of other subjects presents problems for committees which solve them in different ways. If a committee shows itself to be divided over a report, especially if the division is on party lines, its general impact is lessened. Putting that another way, Ministers are most embarrassed when a report is strongly critical of Government and agreed to unanimously, because this means that the members of their own party have joined with the

---

[37] H.C. 302 of 1980–81. The Committee also took evidence on three other occasions without making a report: H.C. 223 of 1980–81; H.C. 428 of 1981–82; H.C. 89 of 1982–83.

[38] H.C. 231 of 1981–82.

[39] H.C. 170 of 1982–83.

[40] H.C. 61 of 1980–81.

[41] H.C. 714 of 1979–80; H.C. 383 of 1980–81.

[42] H.C. 702 of 1979–80; H.C. 324 of 1980–81; H.C. 306 of 1981–82.

[43] H.C. 573 of 1979–80; H.C. 299 of 1980–81; H.C. 301 of 1982–83.

[44] H.C. 444 of 1979–80; H.C. 101 of 1980–81; H.C. 195 of 1981–82.

[45] H.C. 758 of 1979–80; H.C. 336 of 1980–81.

[46] H.C. 584 of 1979–80; H.C. 232 of 1980–81; H.C. 270, 316, 448 of 1981–82; H.C. 204, 286 of 1982–83; H.C. 79 of 1980–81; H.C. 49 of 1982–83.

[47] H.C. 170, 285, 341 of 1983–84; H.C. 44, 213, 306 of 1984–85; H.C. 57, 192, 313 of 1985–86; H.C. 293, 27, 153 of 1986–87.

[48] H.C. 436 of 1983–84; H.C. 37 of 1984–85; H.C. 399 of 1985–86.

[49] H.C. 414, 444 of 1983–84; H.C. 414, 415 of 1984–85; H.C. 341, 356 of 1985–86; and see, H.C. 25 of 1986–87.

[50] H.C. 340 of 1983–84; H.C. 244 of 1984–85; H.C. 265 of 1985–86.

[51] H.C. 395 of 1983–84; H.C. 339 of 1984–85; H.C. 387 of 1985–86.

[52] H.C. 296, 588 of 1983–84; H.C. 126 of 1984–85; H.C. 392 of 1985–86.

[53] H.C. 328 of 1983–84; H.C. 269 of 1984–85; H.C. 373 of 1985–86; H.C. 290 of 1986–87.

[54] H.C. 280, 421 of 1983–84; H.C. 295 of 1984–85; H.C. 123, 255 of 1985–86.

Opposition members. However, the more controversial a subject, the less likely is unanimity and so some committees choose to avoid conflict and seek policy matters on which they can expect to make unanimous reports. This sometimes means that they confine themselves to issues away from the centre of the political stream and so diminish their impact in the House and among the general public.

Major reports during the Parliament 1979–83 included those of the Education Committee on funding higher education,[55] secondary schools curriculum,[56] and arts funding[57]; of the Energy Committee on the Government's nuclear programme[58] and North Sea oil[59]; of the Environment Committee on the sale of the council houses[60] and private rented housing[61] (after 1983 the committee, with a different chairman, chose less controversial subjects). The earlier years of the Foreign Affairs Committee were especially notable for the hearings and reports on the British North American Acts, in response to Canada's discussions on the patriation of the Canadian constitution.[62] The committee travelled extensively overseas and in 1982–83 took evidence in the Falkland Islands for an inquiry which was continued by the new committee in the following Parliament.[63] The Home Affairs Committee made an influential report on race relations and the "Sus" law in 1979–80[64] and other major reports included that on racial disadvantage in 1980–81,[65] police complaints in 1981–82,[66] and the Representation of the People Acts in 1982–83.[67] The Industry and Trade Committee reported on imports and exports[68] and on Concorde.[69] The Scottish Affairs Committee reported on youth employment[70] and rural road transport.[71] The Social Services Committee's major reports during the Parliament of 1979–83 concerned perinatal and neonatal mortality,[72] medical education[73] and age of retirement.[74] The Transport Committee conducted a largescale inquiry into the Channel link in 1980–81,[75] and transport in London in 1981–82.[76] The Treasury and Civil Service Committee is the most general of all the departmentaliy related committees and one of the most important, not least because its chairman also chairs the Liaison Committee. During the Parliament of 1979–83, the committee produced 24 reports. In addition to its regular financial reports it

---

[55] H.C. 787 of 1979–80.
[56] H.C. 116 of 1981–82.
[57] H.C. 49 of 1981–82.
[58] H.C. 114 of 1980–81.
[59] H.C. 337 of 1981–82.
[60] H.C. 366 of 1980–81.
[61] H.C. 40 of 1981–82.
[62] H.C. 42 i and ii and 295 of 1980–81; H.C. 128 of 1981–82.
[63] H.C. 830 of 1982–83; H.C. 268 of 1983–84.
[64] H.C. 559 of 1979–80.
[65] H.C. 424–I of 1980–81.
[66] H.C. 98–I of 1981–82.
[67] H.C. 32–I of 1982–83.
[68] H.C. 109 of 1980–81.
[69] H.C. 265 of 1980–81.
[70] H.C. 96 of 1981–82.
[71] H.C. 178 of 1981–82.
[72] H.C. 663 of 1979–80.
[73] H.C. 31 of 1980–81.
[74] H.C. 26 of 1981–82.
[75] H.C. 155 of 1980–81.
[76] H.C. 127 of 1981–82.

also reported on the form and substance of the Estimates;[77] on monetary control and policy and on nationalised industries;[78] and on civil service pay, manpower reductions, outside appointments of civil servants, the future of the Civil Service Department and the general efficiency and effectiveness of the service.[79] The Welsh Affairs Committee reported on employment opportunities,[80] on broadcasting,[81] and on water supply.[82]

During the 1983–87 Parliament, some of the major reports, other than the financial, were: by the Agriculture Committee on Dairy Quotas[83] and the effect of pesticides[84]; by the Defence Committee, two reports on the Westland affair, two on Falklands and the south Pacific, one on shipping in the Persian Gulf, and one on the limited United Kingdom involvement in the Strategic Defence Initiative[85]; reports on primary education, student awards, prison education and special educational needs by the Education Committee[86]; an inquiry rapidly undertaken by the Employment Committee following the Government decision to ban trade union membership at Government Communications Headquarters in January 1984[87]; from the Energy Committee on electricity and gas prices[88] and on the coal industry[89]; reports from the Environment Committee on acid rain, the Wild Life and the Countryside Act 1981, radioactive waste, planning appeals, historic buildings and river pollution[90]; the Foreign Affairs Committee on Grenada, the Falkland Islands, the sinking of the Belgrano, famine in Africa, United Kingdom Soviet relations, South Africa, bi-lateral aid and cultural diplomacy[91]; the Home Affairs Committee on remands in custody, compensation for victims of crime, the Special Branch, drugs, the immigration and nationality department of the Home Office, racial attacks and harassment and Bangladeshis in Britain[92]; the Scottish Affairs Committee on the proposed closure of BSC Gartcosh and hospital provision[93]; the Social Services Committee on children in care, community care and Social Security reviews, primary healthcare and A.I.D.S.[94]; two reports from the Trade and Industry Committee on the British Steel Corporation and one on the motor components industry[95]; the Transport Committee on the organisation, financing

---

[77] H.C. 503 of 1979–80; H.C. 325 of 1980–81; H.C. 226 of 1981–82; H.C. 448 of 1981–82; H.C. 228 of 1982–83.

[78] H.C. 713 of 1979–80; H.C. 163 and 348 of 1980–81.

[79] H.C. 712 and 730 of 1979–80; H.C. 54, 216 and 423 of 1980–81; H.C. 236 of 1981–82; H.C. 46 of 1982–83.

[80] H.C. 731 of 1979–80.

[81] H.C. 448 of 1980–81.

[82] H.C. 229 of 1982–83.

[83] H.C. 14, 274 of 1984–85.

[84] H.C. 739 of 1986–87.

[85] H.C. 518, 519 of 1985–86; H.C. 345, 408, 409, 130 of 1986–87.

[86] H.C. 40 of 1985–86; H.C. 28, 138, 201 of 1986–87.

[87] H.C. 238 of 1983–84.

[88] H.C. 276 of 1983–84; H.C. 175 of 1986–87.

[89] H.C. 165 of 1986–87.

[90] H.C. 446 of 1983–84; H.C. 6 of 1984–85; H.C. 191 and 181 of 1985–86; H.C. 146 and 183 of 1986–87.

[91] H.C. 226 and 268 of 1983–84; H.C. 56 and 11 of 1984–85; H.C. 28 and 61 of 1985–86; H.C. 32 and 24 of 1986–87.

[92] H.C. 252 of 1983–84; H.C. 43 and 71 of 1984–85; H.C. 66 of 1985–86; H.C. 277 of 1984–85; H.C. 409 of 1985–86; H.C. 96 of 1986–87.

[93] H.C. 154 of 1985–86; H.C. 33 of 1986–87.

[94] H.C. 360 of 1983–84; H.C. 13 and 451 of 1984–85; H.C. 37 and 182 of 1986–87.

[95] H.C. 344 of 1983–84; H.C. 474 of 1984–85; H.C. 407 of 1986–87.

and control of United Kingdom airports, on airport security and on the financing of rail services[96]; the Treasury and Civil Service Committee on international monetary arrangements and international credit[97]; and the Welsh Affairs Committee on public transport, coastal sewage pollution, and tourism in Wales.[98]

The parts played by the Defence and the Treasury and Civil Service Committees in the Westland affair[99] were important. The Defence Committee inquired into the defence implications of the future of the Westland company. It took evidence from Mr. Heseltine both while he was Secretary of State for Defence and after his resignation. The Committee also took evidence from, amongst others, the chairman of Westland, from Mr. Leon Brittan after his resignation as Secretary of State for Trade and Industry, and on two occasions from the Secretary of the Cabinet (Sir Robert Armstrong).[1] The report of the committee on the defence implications was published on July 23, 1986.[2] On the same date, the committee published its report on the Government's decision-making process in the Westland affair.[3] To these two reports, the Government responded in October 1986.[4]

Arising out of the Note of Guidance issued in February 1985 by the Secretary of the Cabinet and Head of the Civil Service (Sir Robert Armstrong) on the duties and responsibilities of civil servants in relation to Ministers,[5] the Treasury and Civil Service Committee appointed a sub-committee to inquire into those duties and responsibilities. In the course of the sub-committee's inquiry, the Westland affair became public. The sub-committee took evidence from Sir Robert Armstrong, amongst others, and its report was published on May 12, 1986.[6] The Government responded in July 1986[7] and there were further exchanges in December 1986[8] and February 1987[9] on the accountability of Ministers and Civil Servants to select committees. To these exchanges the Liaison Committee also contributed[10] (see pages 31–34).

Dissent within Committees

The procedure when going through a draft report was described on page 285. Divisions both in particular paragraphs or on the report as a whole arise either on party lines or because of individual disagreement; and because one member or more either moves an amendment or votes against the motion that the paragraph stand part of the report. An extreme example of individual disagreement was provided by the Environment Committee's consider-

[96] H.C. 319 of 1983–84; H.C. 597 of 1985–86; H.C. 383 of 1986–87.
[97] H.C. 502 of 1983–84; H.C. 84 of 1986–87; to which must be added the annual examinations of the Autumn statements, the expenditure plans and the Budget.
[98] H.C. 35 of 1984–85; H.C. 101 of 1985–86; H.C. 256 of 1986–87.
[99] See pp. 24–25.
[1] H.C. 169 of 1985–86.
[2] H.C. 518 of 1985–86.
[3] H.C. 519 of 1985–86.
[4] Cmnd. 9916.
[5] See above pp. 28–29.
[6] H.C. 92–I, II of 1985–86.
[7] Cmnd. 9841.
[8] H.C. 62 of 1986–87.
[9] Cmnd. 78.
[10] H.C. 100 of 1986–87. See below p. 33.

ations in 1985–86 of planning appeals and of the Sports Council. There were nine divisions on the first of these and three on the second. All 12 were caused by the dissent by one Labour member.[11] Also in 1985–86 the Environment Committee considered Radioactive Waste resulting in 14 divisions brought about by one Liberal member, occasionally supported by one other opposition member.[12] Frequently two members join in repeated dissent, occasionally being supported by one or more other members. In 1983–84, the Transport Committee considered the organisation, financing and control of airports. Over 50 divisions resulted in almost all of which two particular opposition members were in the minority, sometimes being joined by one or two other members.[13] In the next session the same committee tackled the white paper on buses.[14] There were over 40 divisions in which the principal dissentient was a Conservative member, supported on occasions by two other Conservatives and those same two Labour members who brought about the divisions on the airports inquiry. In 1985–86 two Conservative members divided the Transport Committee on six occasions during its consideration of Tolled Crossings.[15] In the same session the committee also considered the Channel Link which incurred eight divisions but here there were no clear patterns of dissent.[16]

The Scottish Affairs Committee in 1983–84 enquired into Scott Lithgow Ltd. and this resulted in over 90 divisions. Effectively these were brought about at the instigation of two Labour members and one Liberal.[17] Divisions frequently take place within the Treasury and Civil Service Committee when it considers financial matters like the Autumn Statement and the Budget. Sometimes these are on party lines but there are also votes where this distinction is not clearly drawn.[18] The Welsh Affairs Committee divided on 12 occasions in its consideration of tourism.[19]

A clear example of dissension on party lines was provided by the Energy Committee on the structure and ownership of the coal industry. Altogether there were over 40 divisions almost all dividing with the same five Conservative members defeating the same four Labour members.[20] The Foreign Affairs Committee also, where it divided, tended to do so on party lines, as in its consideration in 1984–85 of the sinking of the Belgrano, and of United Kingdom-Soviet Relations and the Single European Act in 1985–86,[21] while the same two Labour members usually provided the minority in 21 divisions on Grenada.[22]

During the 1983–87 Parliament there were eight principal occasions on which committees divided on the motion that the draft report (or the draft report as amended) be the report of the committee to the House.

The Employment Committee had three such dissentients to the report on

---

[11] H.C. 181 and 241 of 1985–86.
[12] H.C. 191–I of 1985–86.
[13] H.C. 319–I of 1983–84.
[14] H.C. 38–I of 1984–85.
[15] H.C. 250–I of 1985–86.
[16] H.C. 50–I of 1985–86.
[17] H.C. 297–I of 1983–84.
[18] See for example, on the Autumn Statement, H.C. 57 of 1985–86 and H.C. 27 of 1986–87; on the Budget, H.C. 313 of 1985–86 and H.C. 293 of 1986–87.
[19] H.C. 256–I of 1986–87.
[20] H.C. 165 of 1986–87.
[21] H.C 11 of 1984–85; H.C. 28–I and 442 of 1985–86.
[22] H.C. 226 of 1983–84.

the dismissal of National Coal Board employees.[23] All three were Conserva-tive members. The Foreign Affairs Committee had two dissentients, both Labour, on the Grenada report,[24] and four, all Labour, on the Belgrano report.[25] The Home Affairs Committee had two dissentients, both Labour, on the report on the Special Branch.[26] The Scottish Affairs Committee had three dissentients, two Labour and one Liberal, to the Scott Lithgow report.[27] Three Labour members dissented from the report of the Treasury and Civil Service Committee on the 1987 Budget[28]; and one Conservative member of the same committee dissented from the report on the duties and responsibilities and Ministers.[29] From the report of the Welsh Affairs Com-mittee on Tourism, one Labour and one Plaid Cymru member dissented.[30]

There are several patterns of dissent. The most common is by some (but not all) Opposition members seeking to strengthen criticism of the Govern-ment by amendment, or addition, or deletion of particular paragraphs. Sometimes all Opposition members combine in the same endeavour. Occa-sionally members from the Government side seek to make changes, usually to modify such criticism; and there may be cross voting by both sides. Only rarely, as we have seen, do members push their dissent to the point of voting against the whole report. Compromises are often come to, with Opposition members accepting words less critical of the Government than they would have preferred in order to achieve unanimity. Other committees, for example the Defence Committee, hardly ever divide.

The Impact of the departmentally-related Committees

Select committees have not made a general impact on Government policies. Nor can it be said that departments today are making policy decisions in a distinctly different way from that of 10 years ago because of the existence of the departmentally-related committees or because of any increased pressure from other select committees. Still less has there been any general change in substantive decisions. Ministers in their departments have always taken into account what is likely to be the response from Members and from Peers, as they have taken into account the public response. But there has been no marked difference of a general kind in recent years.

During the period since 1979, on the other hand, several claims have been made that particular select committees have in particular instances affected Government policy significantly.[31] Twice in 1980 the Home Affairs Commit-tee published critical reports on the use of the Vagrancy Act 1824 to arrest persons suspected of loitering with criminal intent—the "sus" law—and its effect on race relations.[32] There was a debate in the House of Commons in

---

[23] H.C. 436 of 1984–85.

[24] H.C. 226 of 1983–84.

[25] H.C. 11 of 1984–85. These 4 members put forward a full and detailed alternative report which was rejected by the majority. Of the 15 divisions, several were on which questions should be put to various witnesses.

[26] H.C. 71 of 1984–85.

[27] H.C. 207–I of 1983–84.

[28] H.C. 293 of 1986–87.

[29] H.C. 92–I of 1985–86.

[30] H.C. 256–I of 1986–87.

[31] For lists of cases where recommendations have been accepted by the Government, see H.C.Deb., Vol. 98, cols. 433–446 (June 3, 1986) and H.C.Deb., Vol. 101, cols. 460–478 (July 15, 1986). But what "accepted" means would need careful consideration in each case.

[32] H.C. 559 and 744 of 1979–80.

which the Conservative chairman of the committee voted with the Opposition.[33] In the following session, the Government introduced the Criminal Attempts Bill which repealed the "sus" law and introduced a new, more specific offence and the Government acknowledged the influence of the select committee. The bill went to a special standing committee, the first three sessions of which were presided over by the chairman of the select committee, which took evidence from witnesses resulting in amendments to the bill.

But even here, it was argued that the reform would have taken place without the intervention of the select committee.[34] Subsequently this argument has been used, more or less strongly, on several occasions. No doubt it is often true that an issue sufficiently important for it to be examined by a select committee is already being considered within the relevant department. What is unknown is how far the select committee inquiry may have influenced the thinking in the department and how far, in particular, it may have hastened the decision-making process within the department. When Ministers depreciate the influence of a select committee, it is impossible for the outsider to assess how far this is a defence against the charge of inaction. It is abundantly clear that particular issues which have lain fallow for many months, even years, within departments have suddenly sprouted, apparently because of outside stimulus.

A different example arose out of the proceedings on the patriation of the Canadian Constitution, which would enable the Constitution to be amended without reference to the United Kingdom. This required legislation in the Parliament of the United Kingdom and was full of possible embarrassment to the Government of the United Kingdom which did not wish to appear to be interfering with the policy of the Canadian Government or any of the Canadian provinces. The Foreign Affairs Committee began to consider the difficulties at an early stage, many months before the bill was introduced into the House of Commons, and is generally believed to have helped to produce a bill which avoided many of the problems and enabled the change to take place with the least damage to the relations between the two Governments.[35] The situation was unusual in that the select committee could express opinion precisely because it was not the Government and yet could be seen as doing so from the United Kingdom Parliament.

Other cases from the earlier years where select committees could claim to have influenced government policy included those by the Transport Committee on the Channel Link,[36] and on the proposed transfer of heavy goods and public service vehicle testing to the private sector.[37] In this latter instance, the select committee took evidence in record time, before the standing committee had begun consideration of the Government bill which was to implement the policy.[38] The Agriculture Committee produced a major report on animal welfare[39] which formed part of a larger debate both in the United Kingdom and in the European Community, though here again

---

[33] H.C.Deb., Vol. 985, cols. 1763–1821 (June 5, 1980).
[34] See Drewry (ed.), *op. cit.* 199. There was a considerable extra-Parliamentary campaign.
[35] H.C. 42, 295 of 1980–81; Cmnd. 8450; H.C. 128 of 1981–82.
[36] H.C. 155 of 1980–81.
[37] H.C. 344 of 1980–81, 203 of 1981–82.
[38] See Drewry (ed.) *op. cit.* 259–260.
[39] H.C. 406 of 1980–81; see Drewry (ed.) *op. cit.* 62–63.

the Government was unwilling to give the committee much credit for its effect on policy.

The chairman of the Education, Science and Arts Committee claimed that they had made "effectiveness" a high priority and reported to the Liaison Committee in 1982–83.[40]

"Our British Library report was immediately followed by a government decision to build it,[41] our higher education report led to the establishment of a National Advisory Board in the public sector,[42] our "Proms" report restored the concerts to the Albert Hall[43] and our ICCROM report re-established the British subscription to that organisation."[44]

The Energy Committee could claim to have influenced government policy on P.W.R.s,[45] North Sea oil taxation,[46] and energy conservation.[47] Other committees made similar modest claims, more in the way of contributions to departmental policy-making than of changing policy. *Post hoc, propter hoc* is not in itself a persuasive argument but, however difficult to prove, not one to be easily dismissed as of no account. The assessment of the importance of select committee work is particularly difficult on the more continuous operations of departments. This applies to the review of estimates and white papers on public spending, The Defence Committee is one of the most important of all select committees and has made major reports on strategic nuclear weapons policy and the procurement policy of the department.[48] Such reports are not likely to produce immediately ascertainable responses from the Government but the impact is likely to be more important.

Most of the matters dealt with in these reports have been concerned with the details of policy, important in themselves though some have been. Moreover, they have often been matters of which the general public have been unaware. They have rarely centred on any of the great issues of the day as portrayed by the media. During the Parliament of 1979–83, there was one large exception to this. In 1982–83, the Defence Committee made two reports arising out of the Falklands conflict. The first was on the handling of press and public information during that conflict[49] and the other was on the future defence of the Falkland islands.[50] These were later followed by a third report on the lessons of the Falklands conflict.[51] None had immediate effect on government policy but the second and third became part of the general debate. Others making a significant impact on political events, if not directly on Government policy, were those on G.C.H.Q. (an investigation mounted by the Employment Committee very quickly after the Government decision

[40] H.C. 92 of 1982–83.

[41] H.C. 607 of 1979–80; Cmnd. 8237.

[42] H.C. 787 of 1979–80; Cmnd. 8139.

[43] H.C. 772 of 1979–80.

[44] International Centre for the Preservation and Restoration of the Cultural Property, Rome; H.C. 274 of 1980–81.

[45] H.C. 114 of 1980–81.

[46] H.C. 337 of 1981–82.

[47] H.C. 401 of 1981–82; Drewry *op. cit.* 139.

[48] H.C. 35 of 1980–81; H.C. 22 of 1981–82; H.C. 584 of 1983–84.

[49] H.C. 17 of 1982–83.

[50] H.C. 154 of 1982–83. The Foreign Affairs Committees also reported on the Falklands: H.C. 268 of 1983–84.

[51] H.C. 345 of 1986–87.

to ban trade union membership at the installation),[52] and another report by the Transport Committee on the Channel Link.[53]

By far the most significant events of the 1983–87 Parliament affecting select committees, was the Westland affair. The reports and minutes of evidence of the Defence Committee,[54] of the Treasury and Civil Service Committee,[55] and of the Liaison Committee[56] have been discussed on pages 31–34. There can be no doubt that the inquiries were a major political factor in the whole affair. The hearings and the reports were awaited with keen interest by the public and the media. Without these inquiries, the Government would have had a much easier task in making its defence. When the matter was before the House, and passions ran high, attempts to discover what had occurred were often not successful. In the hearings before the Defence Committee, what remained unknown did so because of the refusal of witnesses to answer questions or the refusal of the Government to allow witnesses to appear.

To match the list of instances where select committees had made some impact on government policies may be set a list where the Government rejected proposals. In addition to the disputes arising of the Westland affair, examples include the rejection by the Government of the Environment Committee's criticism of the policy on council house sales[57] and of the Treasury and Civil Service Committee's view on the future of the Civil Service Department.[58] A party row developed over the flat rejection of the majority report of the Employment Committee criticising the dismissal of miners following the coal dispute[59] where one Government supporter voted with the Opposition members. The Government proposal for private management of the naval dockyards was criticised by both the Public Accounts[60] and the Defence Committees[61] but the criticism was disregarded. So also was the Foreign Affairs Committee's appeal to the Government not to pull out of UNESCO[62] and the same committee's arguments in favour of cultural diplomacy.[63] The Secretary of State was highly scornful of the Environment Committee's criticism of the management and public image of the nuclear industry, especially of the Sellafield site.[64]

General assessment of the relative success or failure of select committees, as of other parliamentary activities, depends on differing expectations. On one matter, however, opinion is almost unanimous: select committees since 1979 have increased the flow of information coming out of Whitehall and this has resulted to some extent in debates being better informed both inside and outside Parliament.

---

[52] H.C. 238 of 1983–84.

[53] H.C. 50 of 1985–86.

[54] H.C. 169, 518, 519 of 1985–86.

[55] H.C. 92 of 1985–86; H.C. 62 of 1986–87.

[56] H.C. 100 of 1986–87; The Trade and Industry Committee also issued a report: H.C. 176 of 1986–87.

[57] H.C. 366 of 1980–81.

[58] H.C. 54 of 1980–81.

[59] H.C. 416 of 1984–85.

[60] H.C. 440 of 1984–85.

[61] H.C. 453 of 1984–85.

[62] H.C. 461 of 1984–85.

[63] H.C. 24 of 1986–87.

[64] H.C. 191 of 1985–86.

OTHER SELECT COMMITTEES

In 1987–88 and 1988–89 10 of those regularly appointed were:

Name of Committee (and political party of chairman)	Number of Members	Quorum
Consolidation bills (chaired by peer)[65]	11	2
European Legislation (Labour)	14	5
House of Commons (Services) (Conservative)	20	5
Liaison (Conservative)	21	6
Members' Interests (Conservative)	13	5
Parliamentary Commissioner for Administration (Conservative)	9	3
Procedure (Conservative)	14	5
Public Accounts (Labour)	15	4
Selection (Conservative)	9	3
Statutory Instruments (Labour)[66]	7	2
	133	

Of the three ad hoc committees, that concerned with private bill procedure (a joint committee with the House of Lords) had seven Members of the House of Commons, one of whom was the Conservative chairman; that concerned with televising the proceedings of the Commons had 20 Members with the Leader of the House as chairman; the committee on the hybrid Dartford-Thurrock Crossing Bill had seven Members with a Conservative chairman.

The total membership of these 13 committees was 167.

On each of these committees, the Government side of the House has a majority of members with the official Opposition taking most of the other places. The S.L.D.P. had seven Members on a total of eight committees (Members' Interests, P.C.A., Procedure, Public Accounts, Services, Liaison, Televising and Selection); and the S.D.P. had one Member on the Statutory Instruments Committee.

The work of most of these select committees is discussed elsewhere. The Liaison Committee, as a body of chairman, speaks for select committees generally, if necessary defending their powers, particularly those of calling for persons (including Ministers and civil servants), papers and records (see pages 448–449). Since 1979 the Committee has published two general reports, each of which has contained summaries by the chairmen members of the work of their committees. The first report was published in December 1982 and covered the first three years of the existence both of the Liaison Committee and of the 14 departmentally-related committees, together with the previous three years of the work of other select committees.[67] The

---

[65] A joint committee with the House of Lords.

[66] For the examination of statutory instruments, other than those dealing with finance, the Commons Members of this select committee sit with nominated peers in a joint committee. Financial instruments required to be laid before the Commons only are scrutinised by the Commons Members.

[67] H.C. 92 of 1982–83; for the Government response see H.C.Deb., Vol. 42, cols. 442–445 (May 12, 1983).

second report was published in April 1985 and covered the period from 1983.[68] In December 1986, the committee reported on the accountability of Ministers and civil servants' to select committees.[69] Much of the work of the committee consists in authorising expenditure for travel overseas by select committees and by individual committee members; it has also dealt with delays in, and the quality of, departmental replies to committee reports, leaks of committee proceedings, accommodation for committees, the implications of televising proceedings, debating of reports, overlap between committees, and many other matters of common concern to select committees. Under Standing Order 131(2) the Liaison Committee makes recommendations for debates on estimates days.[70]

Membership and chairmen

The Committee of Selection is not responsible for the membership of select committees other than the departmentally-related. In general, the party Whips put forward lists for nomination by the House—for the whole of the Parliament, where the committee is appointed under standing orders. Members will seek appointment to the more important and more interesting committees. Some may have to be drafted against their wish with promises that their preferences will be more favourably considered on some future occasion. The Whips will seek to persuade their party members on these other select committees, as with the departmentally-related committees, to appoint as chairmen those suggested by the Whips after discussion through the usual channels.[71]

As the Table shows, the Government party in mid-1988 chaired all these committees except the Public Accounts Committee which is traditionally chaired by a senior Opposition Member with some former ministerial experience in the Treasury; and the European Legislation and the Statutory Instruments Committees, also traditionally chaired by the Opposition.

These select committees are divisible in two groups: those that scrutinise matters coming before the House or reported to Parliament but without considering policy issues; and those concerned with various domestic aspects of the services, procedures and business of the House.

Scrutiny Committees

All these committees are appointed under standing order for the duration of the whole parliament.

Joint Committee on Consolidation, etc., Bills Standing Order No. 123 provides that there shall be a select committee to join with the committee appointed by the Lords to consider consolidation bills, statute law revision bills, bills prepared pursuant to the Consolidation of Enactments (Procedure) Act 1949, bills to consolidate any enactments with amendments to give effect to recommendations from the Law Commissions, bills to repeal Acts no longer of practical utility, and Orders in Council relating to consolidation or law revision in Northern Ireland.

---

[68] H.C. 363 of 1984–85; for the Government response see H.C. 225 of 1985–86.

[69] H.C. 100 of 1986–87; for the Government reply see Cm. 78.

[70] See, for example, H.C. 618 of 1985–86 and 396 of 1986–87.

[71] Significantly, the Whips failed in 1983 to have their favoured candidate made chairman of the Liaison Committee, and the matter was resolved only after divisions involving three candidates (H.C. 651 of 1983–84 p. iii).

Such bills and orders are referred to this joint committee which, depending on the nature of the bill, has power to make corrections and minor improvements to the provisions it is consolidating. Consolidation bills are introduced in the House of Lords, and the committee is chaired by an independent Peer. When the bill arrives in the Commons, it is committed to a committee of the whole House which is bound by corrections and improvements made by the Joint Committee.

During the 1983–84 session, the Joint Committee issued reports on 11 bills, during 1984–85 on nine bills, during 1985–86 on five bills and one Northern Ireland Order, and during 1986–87 on one bill. Attendance is poor, only two or three Commons members being present at more than half the meetings, the overall attendance in 1985–86 being 28.8 per cent., while in 1986–87 only three Commons members attended the only meeting.

Select Committee on European Legislation The Committee was first set up in 1974 as the Select Committee on European Secondary Legislation, acquiring its present title in December 1976.

Standing Order No. 127(1) provides:

"There shall be a select committee to consider draft proposals by the Commission of the European Communities for legislation and other documents published for submission to the Council of Ministers or to the European Council whether or not such documents originate from the Commission, and to report its opinion as to whether such proposals or other documents raise questions of legal or political importance, to give its reasons for its opinion, to report what matters of principle or policy may be affected thereby, and to what extent they may affect the law of the United Kingdom, and to make recommendations for the further consideration of such proposals and other documents by the House."

The committee is served by three full-time specialist staff in addition to its clerk and other support staff and has power to appoint specialist advisers. It has the usual powers to send for persons, papers and records and may appoint sub-committees. The committee and any of its sub-committees has leave to confer and meet concurrently with any committee of the Lords on the European Communities for the purpose of hearing evidence or deliberating. The committee is advised on legal matters by one of the Speaker's counsel.

The select committee is concerned with draft legislative proposals made by the Commission in Brussels and with other documents (also mostly from the Commission) published for submission to the Council of Ministers or the European Council. Legislation made directly by the Commission does not come before the committee. The Government attaches explanatory memoranda to the Community documents. The committee sometimes seeks further information by taking evidence from Ministers and government departments or other persons or bodies; it also meets officials of the Commission in Brussels, and other experts in Europe.

The committee reports weekly to the House on each proposal or document within the terms of the standing order. The form of words varies slightly. The most usual form of its positive reports is that, in the committee's opinion, the proposed document raises questions of political and/or legal importance and either that it recommends further consideration by the House or that it does not so recommend. A variant is to recommend consideration but to add that the adoption need not be delayed. Sometimes the committee indicates a particular parliamentary occasion when this consideration might be given; debates may be on the floor of the House or in standing committee.

In the words of the chairman of the committee in June 1986[72]:

"Having taken their decision in favour of debate, the Committee then assess whether such a debate should be on the floor of the House or in Standing Committee. In doing so, we have to make a judgment between the greater exposure provided by a debate in the House as against the flexibility and informality of Standing Committees ... The proposal that a particular document should be considered in a Standing Committee is made by the Government who do not always follow the Committee's recommendation. That proposal ... may be blocked under Standing Order No. 102(3) if at least 20 Members stand and object ... The timing of debates, both when they should be held and for how long, also depends on the initiative of the Government."

The majority of the documents coming before the committee do not raise questions of legal or political importance. In 1986–87 the committee reported on 439 documents of which 165 raised, in its view, questions of legal or political importance. It recommended 59 of these for debate. In the longer session of 1987–88, the figures were 1195, 362 and 117 respectively.

A major difficulty met by the Committee is that of timing because there is always the possibility of the Commission's proposals being adopted by the Council of Ministers in Brussels before the House has had an opportunity to comment. On October 30, 1980 the House resolved that no Minister of the Crown should give agreement in the Council to any proposals for European Legislation which had been recommended by the committee for further consideration by the House, before the House had given that consideration unless the committee had indicated that agreement need not be withheld or the Minister concerned decided that for special reasons agreement should not be withheld. In this latter case the Minister should, at the first opportunity thereafter, explain the reasons for his decisions to the House.[73] As the Council until 1988 always worked by unanimity, its proceedings could effectively be held up until the House had considered a proposal. This is no longer true for those proposals which may be decided by the Council on a majority vote.

The resolution covered only documents recommended for debate by the committee and if a document did not reach the committee in time for it to be considered and reported on before agreement was reached in the Council of Ministers, the control over ministerial actions could not be activated.[74]

In 1983–84 the select committee made a special report on some aspects of scrutiny procedure[75] and the Government replied.[76] On the timing of debates in relation to the final stage of negotiations the Government agreed that it should be the rule "always to err on the side of an early debate." On the adoption of documents before scrutiny, the Government stated that

---

[72] Second Report from the Select Committee on Procedure H.C. 350 of 1986–87 Appendix 14.
[73] H.C.Deb., Vol. 991, col. 843.
[74] H.C. 92 of 1982–83 p. 76.
[75] H.C. 527 of 1983–84.
[76] H.C.Deb., Vol. 65, cols. 798–800 (October 29, 1984).

while in principle the resolution of October 30, 1980 did not bear on proposals yet to be scrutinised, the Government considered that its spirit should apply to all proposals. Where a Minister allowed a document to be adopted before a debate in the House, the Government agreed that the Minister should explain to the House the reasons why a debate could not have been held, as well as the advantages of the proposals to the United Kingdom; and should include a reference to the scrutiny position, an explanation of why the Minister had decided not to withhold agreement and an indication of the likely timing of the debate.

In a special report of May 1986,[77] the committee reviewed its past work drawing attention to the supply of European Community documents to the committee, to Accession instruments, to the identification of the meaning of "legal importance" in its terms of reference, to the shared responsibility of departments and the problems arising therefrom, to the scrutiny of negotiating mandates and to the Single European Act. This last was the subject of another special report[78] which was extensively referred to by speakers in the Commons debates and the Government undertook to provide necessary extra information by means of explanatory memoranda.[79]

In the same report the committee considered that its future work should fall broadly into three categories (a) the continuation of the current function of scrutiny (b) reporting to the House on developments in the Community of which the House should be aware (c) more detailed reports on selected documents or matters.[80] The Government rejected any extension of the powers of the committee.[81]

Some statistics of the committee[82] are:

---

[77] H.C. 400 of 1985–86.

[78] H.C. 264 of 1985–86.

[79] H.C.Deb., Vol. 93, cols. 335–418 (March 5, 1986); H.C.Deb., Vol. 96, col. 393 (April 23, 1986); H.C.Deb. col. 7 (January 25, 1988).

[80] H.C. 400 of 1985–86 para. 59.

[81] Cm. 123.

[82] H.C. 400 of 1985–86 Appendix II. Comparable statistics for later sessions are not available.

	1979-80	1980-81	1981-82	1982-83	1983-84	1984-85
Number of meetings	46	32	30	18	35	31
Documents reported on	963	745	723	461	945	663
Documents raising questions of legal or political importance	340	208	163	161	308	191
Documents recommended for debate	138	81	53	59	146	98
Number of oral evidence sessions	5	2	4	1	4	2
Documents debated in the Chamber	102	66	23	33	83	55
Number of debates in the Chamber	27	22	9	12	23	16
Documents debated in standing committee	-	7	12	-	30	17
Number of debates in standing committee	-	5	10	-	10	7
Balance of documents still awaiting debate at the end of session[82a]	61	49	57	77	96	116

Select Committee on the Parliamentary Commissioner for Administration
Standing Order No. 126(1) provides:

"There shall be a select committee to examine the reports of the Parliamentary Commissioner for Administration, of the Health Service Commissioners for England, Scotland and Wales and of the Parliamentary Commissioner for Administration for Northern Ireland, which are laid before this House, and matters in connection therewith; and the committee shall consist of nine Members of whom the quorum shall be three."

The committee has the usual powers to send for persons, papers and records and to appoint specialist advisers.

The Parliamentary Commissioner for Administration (P.C.A.) is appointed by the Crown on the advice of the Prime Minister to investigate complaints by individuals or corporations who claim they have sustained injustice in consequence of maladministration at the hands of Government departments and other listed bodies. Complaints are referred to him by Members. He has wide powers of investigation. The Commissioner is required to lay an annual report before each House of Parliament.[83] He also acts as the Health Service Commissioner under the National Health Service; in this capacity he can consider complaints referred to him directly by members of the public.

The function of the committee is not to act as a court of appeal from the Commissioners but to consider general matters arising from their annual and other reports, and to take evidence and report on individual complaints when this appears desirable.

[82a] Many of these may be documents no longer under active consideration, awaiting amendment or otherwise not yet ripe for debate; in October 1988, 47 out of 88 documents recommended for debate were of this nature (H.C.Deb., Vol. 139, col. 664 (October 31, 1988)).

[83] Parliamentary Commissioner Act 1967, as amended by Parliamentry and Health Service Commissioners Act 1987.

The select committee considers the annual reports of the Parliamentary Commissioner, the Health Service Commissioner and the Northern Ireland Commissioner and takes evidence from the Commissioner and from others, including government departments and health authorities, on matters arising from the reports to ensure that all reasonable efforts are made to tighten up procedures, prevent the repetition of faults and provide the appropriate remedy. The committee also concerns itself with the Commissioners' jurisdiction.

In 1985–86 and 1986–87, the committee met on 28 occasions and the overall attendance was 51 per cent. The Lord Chancellor and one Minister (not in the Cabinet) gave evidence and amongst civil servants there were seven Permanent Secretaries, three Second Permanent Secretaries, five Deputy Secretaries, four Under Secretaries, and six Assistant Secretaries. Other witnesses totalled 77. There were no divisions.

During the 1983–87 Parliament, the committee made 14 reports. Of these, five arose from investigations made by the Health Service Commissioner,[84] four from the Northern Ireland Commissioner,[85] two from the Parliamentary Commissioner;[86] the other three concerned the enforcement of remedies in local government cases,[87] the jurisdiction of the Commissioners in relation to quangos,[88] and the Preece case (see below).[89] In addition there was one special report which concerned the Parliamentary Commissioner's reports generally.[90]

Most of the time of the committee was spent on taking evidence from chairmen and officers of regional and district health authorities and witnesses from the Department of Health and Social Security in relation to particular cases investigated by the Health Service Commissioner. On two occasions it summoned hospital consultants to account for their actions. Its criticisms are frequently strong, as when it expressed itself as "profoundly displeased" with a health authority as much for its attitude towards them as for the original mistakes.[91] From the individual cases the committee draws more general conclusions and seeks to ensure that changes will be made to avoid repetitions of error. Some of the matters to which it drew attention were procedures to be followed after sudden deaths in hospitals; the care of mentally-ill patients who may go missing from their institutions; the particular dangers for old patients when taking baths or contracting bedsores; the procedures for calling ambulances; maladministration arising from the failure of a regional medical officer to institute the "second opinions" procedure into a complaint about clinical judgment; accident and emergency procedures; the failure of hospital authorities to have proper contact with the social services; and the way in which consent to operations was obtained from mothers of mentally handicapped children. The Health Service Commissioner and the select committee appear to have made a considerable impact on the health service.[92]

---

[84] H.C. 318 and 620 of 1983–84; H.C. 597 of 1984–85; H.C. 569 of 1985–86; H.C. 31 of 1986–87.
[85] H.C. 422 and 643 of 1983–84; H.C. 149 of 1985–86; H.C. 250 of 1986–87.
[86] H.C. 312 of 1985–86; H.C. 251 of 1986–87.
[87] H.C. 448 of 1985–86.
[88] H.C. 619 of 1983–84.
[89] H.C. 423 of 1983–84.
[90] H.C. 424 of 1983–84.
[91] H.C. 31 of 1986–87.
[92] See comment by Permanent Secretary of the department in H.C. 620 of 1983–84.

A major investigation by the committee was stimulated by a Member of Parliament putting down an early day motion critical of the length of time taken by the Parliamentary Commissioner to investigate a case. The Member gave evidence to the committee which expressed "most strongly" the view that the delay was unacceptable and called on the Commissioner to consider what he should do to remedy the situation.[93] Following this, in 1987–88, the committee decided to examine the organisation and work of the Office of the Commissioner.

The Preece case already referred to arose out of the suspension of a Home Office forensic scientist and the delay of the Home Office in reviewing the convictions, including that of Mr. Preece who had been found guilty of murder, based on evidence given by the scientist. The Home Secretary and senior officials were heard by the committee and accepted blame.[94]

This committee has chosen to interpret its order of reference in a way that leads it to examine in public many of those whom the Commissioners (especially the Health Service Commissioner) find at fault. The committee shares with the Public Accounts Committee the great advantage of working with a senior statutory officer who himself enjoys considerable powers of investigation. Building on his reports, the select committee is in a strong position, if it chooses, to oversee the working of the public authorities within its jurisdiction.

The chairman of the select committee said in 1982 that it was widely known amongst civil servants and health service administrators that, while being the subject of a P.C.A. report might well result in a request to appear before the committee, failure to accept the report and apply the recommended remedy would certainly do so.[95]

Public Accounts Committee The Committee was first appointed in 1861. Standing Order No. 122 provides:

> "There shall be a select committee to be called the Committee of Public Accounts for the examination of the accounts showing the appropriation of the sums granted by Parliament to meet the public expenditure, and of such other accounts laid before Parliament as the committee may think fit, to consist of not more than 15 Members, of whom four shall be a quorum."

The committee has the usual powers to send for persons, papers and records and to report. In sessions 1987–88 and 1988–89 there were six Labour members (including the chairman) eight Conservatives and one S.L.D.P. member.

The chairman of the committee has written that the committee seeks to achieve proper accountability by asking for clear objectives to be set, for proper monitoring to be established from the outset so that the progress of a particular programme can be adequately supervised and, if necessary, modified in the light of fresh information, and by comparing achievement with expectation.[96] The committee normally operates on the basis of reports from the National Audit Office (N.A.O.) which is headed by the Comptroller and Auditor General (C. and A.G.). Under the National Audit Act 1983 the C.

---

[93] H.C. 312 of 1985–86.
[94] H.C. 423 of 1983–84.
[95] H.C. 92 of 1982–83 p. 91 (Mr. Anthony Buck Q.C., M.P.).
[96] Robert Sheldon in *The House Magazine* of December 8, 1986.

and A.G.'s appointment by Her Majesty is exercisable on an address presented by the House of Commons on a motion by the Prime Minister acting with the agreement of the chairman of the committee. The Act also provides that the C. and A.G. shall be an officer of the House. He has complete discretion in the discharge of his functions and in particular in determining whether to carry out any examinations of accounts and how to do so but he must take into account any proposals made by the committee. The C. and A.G. appoints the staff of the N.A.O. and determines their pay and terms and conditions of service. He prepares an estimate of the expenses of the N.A.O. for each financial year and presents it to the Public Accounts Commission which lays it before the House with such modifications as the Commission thinks fit. This Commission set up under the Act of 1983 consists of the Chairman of the Public Accounts Committee, the Leader of the House, and seven other Members, non-ministerial, one of whom is chosen as chairman.

The functions of the C. and A.G. and the N.A.O. are, first to carry out certification audits of central Government accounts, to confirm the proper presentation of receipts and payments in accounts, that sums voted by Parliament have been spent on the intended purposes, and the propriety and probity of departmental operations. The Act of 1983 also expressly empowers the C. and A.G. to carry out examinations into the economy, efficiency and effectiveness with which any department, authority or other body under his jurisdiction has used its resources in discharging its functions. This is the value for money audit. But he is not entitled to question the merits of the policy objectives of these bodies. With the exception of the nationalised industries, local authorities and a few other bodies, the C. and A.G. has access to the books of any body which receives more than half its income from public funds. In 1987, about 60 per cent. of the N.A.O.'s audit work was on the certification audit and the remainder on the value for money audit. Recently the emphasis of the value for money audit has moved more from its detailed examination of particular items of expenditure to broadly based cyclical reviews of all major spending programmes.[97]

The certification audit is spread over the year with a peak in late summer before the date for certification. It is concerned to ensure that the systems of financial control are operating satisfactorily and then to test them by statistical sampling. The value for money audit is based on five year rolling programmes designed to identify areas which may merit close scrutiny. Major spending departments such as Defence attract most attention.

When a value for money audit has been completed, the draft report is sent to the Accounting Officer of the department who then has the opportunity to draw attention to any errors of fact and to comment on matters of presentation and judgment. In this limited sense, the published report, presented to Parliament, is an agreed report.

The Public Accounts Committee, on the basis of C. and A.G.'s reports, takes oral evidence from the Accounting Officer of the department concerned (who is the Permanent or Second Permanent Secretary) in the presence of the C. and A.G. who attends all meetings when witnesses are called. The committee pursues the same ends as the C. and A.G. Although not obliged to do so, the P.A.C. purports to avoid making criticism of the policy objectives which lie behind the expenditure. Much depends,

---

[97] Sir Gordon Downey on the role of the N.A.O. in *The House Magazine* of March 6, 1987.

however, on its definition of policy and certainly much of the committee's criticism and that of the C. and A.G. raises questions whether the project was properly costed, whether alternative courses of action were considered, whether the project was effectively implemented, whether too much discretion was left to the decision-makers. Many of such questions could reasonably be called matters of policy. Policy and its execution are notoriously difficult to disentangle. For example; Since 1981–82 the capital expenditure of local authorities in England and Wales has been subject to formal statutory control by central Government. In 1985–86 the C. and A.G. reported on the practical operation of this control and the P.A.C. pursued the inquiry. Amongst the criticisms made by the P.A.C. was that the existing arrangements were seriously flawed, both in their effectiveness in achieving the Government's economic objectives and in their adverse effects on local authorities. The P.A.C. found that the statutory arrangements had signally failed to bring the aggregate net capital expenditure by local authorities under effective control. Its main conclusions and recommendations were contained in 18 paragraphs including comment that it failed to understand why the Government should have continued to go to such lengths in the preparation of detailed spending programmes which it did not seek to have implemented.[98]

Other serious criticisms in recent years have concerned the redundancy compensation payments to university staff,[99] the financing arrangements for the provision of meteorological services,[1] the proposed Defence School of Music,[2] the production costs of defence equipment,[3] the Rayner scrutiny programmes,[4] the housing benefits scheme,[5] national health service energy conservation,[6] the profit formula for non-competitive government contracts,[7] premature retirements in the national health service,[8] home improvement grants,[9] the De Lorean affair,[10] the efficiency of nationalised industries,[11] national health service manpower,[12] the Forestry Commission,[13] sponsorship of non-departmental bodies by the Department of the Environment,[14] Government services to exporters overseas,[15] the rising cost of storing E.C. food surplus[16] and the control and management of major equipment by the Ministry of Defence.[17]

---

[98] 51st. Report of Public Accounts Committee: H.C. 444 of 1985–86.
[99] H.C. 179 of 1985–86.
[1] H.C. 405 of 1985–86.
[2] H.C. 107 of 1985–86.
[3] H.C. 56 of 1985–86.
[4] H.C. 365 of 1985–86.
[5] H.C. 78 of 1984–85 and H.C. 254 of 1985–86.
[6] H.C. 232 of 1984–85.
[7] H.C. 390 of 1984–85.
[8] H.C. 225 of 1983–84.
[9] H.C. 255 of 1983–84.
[10] H.C. 127 of 1983–84.
[11] H.C. 26 of 1986–87.
[12] H.C. 213 of 1986–87.
[13] H.C. 185 of 1986–87.
[14] H.C. 38 of 1986–87.
[15] H.C. 204 of 1986–87.
[16] H.C. 292 of 1986–87.
[17] H.C. 104 of 1986–87.

The authoritative nature of such criticisms means that Government departments cannot ignore them. The responses from the departments are published in the form of Treasury minutes.

Because the reports by the C. and A.G. and the hearings and reports of the P.A.C. are made public, senior civil servants may directly or indirectly be openly criticised. Permanent Secretaries do not enjoy criticism being made of their departments and dislike being questioned about such criticisms. Even more do they dislike being asked at subsequent hearings why they have not removed the cause of such criticism.

Accurately to measure the impact which the criticisms of C. and A.G. and P.A.C. have on Ministers and departments is impossible. Remedial action may be taken during the course of an inquiry and the department may claim that these and other improvements were in train before the inquiry began or the criticisms made. At the least it can be said that inquiries by the C. and A.G. and the P.A.C. spark off activity within the department. At the most, it can often be legitimately claimed that the inquiries have disclosed defects in the working of departments which would otherwise not have been disclosed at that time.

During a session, the P.A.C. covers a large number of subjects. In 1983–4 the committee made 36 reports, in 1984–85 it made 38 reports, in 1985–86 it made 52 reports and in the shorter session of 1986–87 it made 19 reports.

During the two sessions 1985–86 and 1986–87[18] the civil servants who gave evidence comprised 30 Permanent Secretaries on 56 occasions between them, 11 Second Permanent Secretaries on 13 occasions, 10 Deputy Secretaries on 10 occasions, 32 Under-Secretaries on 34 occasions, and 31 others on 31 occasions. The C. and A.G. or his Deputy attended 74 of the total of the committee's 77 meetings; the C. and A.G. of Northern Ireland attended six meetings; the Treasury Officer of Accounts attended 61 meetings; the Treasury Officer of Accounts of Northern Ireland attended two meetings. Evidence was taken at 71 of the 77 meetings. The committee received 336 memoranda of which 175 came from government departments and 78 from associated public bodies. The committee has no power to appoint specialist advisors; nor did it, in these sessions, make visits within or outside the United Kingdom. The overall attendance of members of the committee was 57 per cent. and 54 per cent. in these sessions but this figure was pulled down by delay in making replacements and the fact that the Financial Secretary to the Treasury, nominally a member, by convention hardly ever attends. The turnover during the 1985–86 session was 13 per cent. There was one division and that was on the question of whether to exclude strangers from a sitting on March 17, 1986. There was one parliamentary debate in 1985–86, as is usual. This considered the last 13 reports of the previous session and the first 14 of the current session.[19] In 1986–87, the calling of the general election in June precluded the annual debate.

The Joint and Select Committees on Statutory Instruments Standing Order No. 124 provides that a select committee shall be appointed to join with a committee appointed by the Lords to consider every statutory instrument of general applicability required to be laid before both Houses[20] with a view to

---

[18] See H.C. 172 of 1986–87 pp. 67–71, H.C. 79 of 1987–88 pp. 62–63.

[19] H.C.Deb., Vol. 100, cols. 1198–1263 (July 3, 1986).

[20] The definition of those instruments and other documents which are subject to the select committee is set out in detail in the standing orders.

determining whether the special attention of the House should be drawn to it on any of a number of grounds which may be summarised as follows:

(i) that it imposes a charge on public revenues or requires payments to be made to any public authority;
(ii) that it is made in pursuance of an enactment excluding it from challenge in the courts;
(iii) that it purports to have retrospective effect where the parent statute confers no express authority so to provide;
(iv) that there appears to have been unjustifiable delay in the publication or in the laying of it before Parliament; or
(v) in notifying the Speaker and the Lord Chancellor where an instrument has come into operation before being laid, as required by section 4(1) of the Statutory Instruments Act 1946;
(vi) that there appears to be a doubt whether it is *intra vires* or that it appears to make some unusual or unexpected use of the powers under which it is made;
(vii) that for any special reason its form or purport calls for elucidation;
(viii) that its drafting appears to be defective.

The committee does not have a general power to call for persons, papers and records but it may require any Government department to submit explanatory memoranda to explain particular instruments or to send witnesses. A department must be afforded an opportunity to submit such memoranda or provide such a witness before the committee draws the special attention of the House to an instrument.

The joint committee is advised by Speaker's Counsel and the Counsel to the Lord Chairman of Committees who examine all instruments laid before Parliament and draw the committee's attention to those which appear to merit further consideration. If a statutory instrument is required to be laid before the Commons only, the Commons members of the joint committee exercise the same powers alone.

During the last Parliament the number of instruments drawn to the attention of both Houses by the joint committee and to the Commons by the select committee, under the various heads indicated in the standing order was:

		1983-84		1984-85		1985-86		1986-87	
		Jt.	S.C.	Jt.	S.C.	Jt.	S.C.	Jt.	S.C.
(iii)	Retrospective	-	-	-	-	1	-	-	-
(iv)	Delay in laying	1	-	-	-	-	-	-	-
(vi)	Vires	8	-	3	-	14	1	19	2
	Unexpected etc.	6	-	5	-	6	1	-	-
(vii)	Elucidation	6	2	7	-	14	-	13	1
(viii)	Drafting	13	-	5	1	16	5	16	-
	Miscellaneous	7	-	8	-	4	-	9	-
	Total	41	2	28	1	55	7	57	3
	No. of statutory instruments considered	1475	104	1152	95	1453	88	770	64
	No. of reports	39[21]	10[22]	32[23]	3[24]	34[25]	7[26]	20[27]	3[28]

In the sessions 1985–86 and 1986–87 the joint committee held 54 meetings, with an overall attendance of Commons' members of 41 per cent. and a turnover of 29 per cent. Evidence was taken at 11 of the meetings and the committee received 266 memoranda. The Commons select committee held 41 meetings, with an overall attendance of 39 per cent. and a turnover of 29 per cent. Evidence was taken at two of the meetings and the committee received 43 memoranda.

Domestic committees

Select Committee on House of Commons (Services) The work of this committee was considered on pages 162–164 as part of the organisation of the House.

The full committee makes three or four reports each session. During the 1983–87 Parliament, the accommodation and administration sub-committee met on 104 occasions, the catering sub-committee on 22 occasions, the computer sub-committee on 37 occasions, the library sub-committee on 16 occasions and the new building sub-committee on 39 occasions. In 1985–86 and 1986–87 the attendance varied from 58 per cent. for the accommodation and administration committee to 94 per cent. for the catering sub-committee. The turnover of membership was very low. The accommodation and administration sub-committee is the largest and the most active and in 1985–86 and 1986–87 received 219 memoranda, of which 20 came from Government departments.[29]

---

[21] H.C. 41 of 1983–84.
[22] H.C. 42 of 1983–84.
[23] H.C. 25 of 1984–85.
[24] H.C. 26 of 1984–85.
[25] H.C. 31 of 1985–86.
[26] H.C. 32 of 1985–86.
[27] H.C. 29 of 1986–87.
[28] H.C. 30 of 1986–87.
[29] See H.C. 196 of 1984–85, H.C. 295 of 1985–86, H.C. 172 of 1986–87, H.C. 70 of 1987–88.

Select Committee on Members' Interests The work of this committee has been discussed on pages 58–60.

The committee has made occasional reports on failures to register and declare interests, on its terms of reference, on parliamentary lobbying, and on registers of journalists, secretaries and parliamentary groups. During the Parliament of 1983–87, the committee met on 29 occasions. In 1985–86, the committee had an overall attendance of 70 per cent. and a turnover of 23 per cent.; in 1986–87 those figures were 54 per cent. and nil.[30]

Committee of Privileges This committee is appointed under Standing Order No. 121 without specific orders of reference. It reports on complaints and other questions of privilege referred to it by the House (see pages 97–98).

Select Committee on Procedure This committee is appointed by the House from time to time, not under standing orders. In 1983–84, the committee made a report on short speeches; in 1984–85, on the printing of oral questions to the Prime Minister, on public bill procedure, on Questions lost when a sitting is broken, and on short speeches; in 1985–86, on the operation of Standing Order No. 10 (now No. 20), on the allocation of time to Government bills in standing committee, and on short speeches; in 1986–87, the committee considered proposals for a revised parliamentary calendar, use of time on the floor of the House, and early day motions, and made a report on the work of the committee.[31] During the Parliament of 1983–87, the committee held 67 meetings.

In 1985–86, the committee had an overall attendance of 55.5 per cent. and a turnover of 18.75 per cent.; for 1986–87, the figures were 58.7 per cent. and 21.4 per cent.

Committee of Selection The committee is appointed Standing Order 109 (private business). Its principal functions relating to public business are to nominate members of standing committees under Standing Order No. 86 (see page 271) and to propose members for departmentally-related select committees, under Standing Order 104(2) (see pages 280–281). During the Parliament of 1983–87, the committee held 113 meetings. In 1985–86, the committee had an overall attendance of 64 per cent. and no change in membership; for 1986–87, the figures were 57 per cent. and nil.

Select Committee on Sound Broadcasting Standing Order No. 129 provides that there shall be a select committee to give directions and perform other duties in accordance with the provisions of the resolution of the House of July 26, 1977 in relation to sound broadcasting. The committee has power to appoint specialist advisers and to confer and meet concurrently with a committee of the Lords (see pages 82–83). During the Parliament of 1983–87, the committee held 12 meetings. In 1985–86, the committee had an overall attendance of 87.5 per cent. and no change in membership; for 1986–87, the overall attendance was 73 per cent. while the size of the committee increased by 50 per cent. The committee has not been nominated since the session of 1986–87. Its powers were transferred on May 26, 1989 to the Select Committee on Televising the Proceedings of the House.

---

[30] *Ibid.*
[31] H.C. 520 of 1983–84; H.C. 298, 49, 396, 623 of 1984–85; H.C. 42, 324, 592 of 1985–86; H.C. 157, 350, 254, 373 of 1986–87.

GENERAL POWERS OF SELECT COMMITTEES

Sending for Persons, Papers and Records

The power to send for persons, papers and records is conferred on select committees by standing orders of the House or at the time of their appointment. If an order under this power is made and not complied with, then (subject to what is said below) it can be enforced by an order of the House.

Persons not being Members of either House may be invited or summoned to appear. If such a person when formally summoned refuses or fails to attend, his conduct may be reported to the House as a contempt and he may be ordered to attend at the bar of the House. If he does not obey this order, he may be ordered to be sent for in the custody of the Serjeant at Arms or ordered to be taken into the custody of the Serjeant.[32]

Members of either House, including Ministers, are invited, not summoned. In 1976 the Expenditure Committee tried to secure the attendance of Mr. Harold Lever, then Paymaster General and Chancellor of the Duchy of Lancaster but, on the instruction of the Prime Minister, he declined. The matter concerned the Chrysler Car company and the Prime Minister subsequently justified his decision by saying:

> "What I could not accept was the suggestion that any Minister referred to in press stories as having taken a particular line to Cabinet on the question, having no relevant departmental duties, should automatically be subject to a Committee summons."

He added that to call Ministers with no departmental portfolio would blur existing ministerial responsibilities and impair collective Cabinet responsibility.[33] But Members, including Ministers, may be required by order of the House to attend. (The attendance of Peers is subject to their personal agreement and the consent of the House of Lords.)

On occasion, the law officers have taken the view that they enjoy immunity from select committee scrutiny as they are not answerable to Parliament for the legal advice they give to the Government.[34] But on other occasions, law officers have given evidence on more general matters.

More important in practice is the power to require the attendance of civil servants. The usual course is for select committees to leave to the relevant department the nomination of the appropriate civil servant but a committee is certainly empowered to summon a named civil servant to attend. But if his Minister ordered him not to attend, the committee would not be likely to insist. Early in 1984, the Employment Committee sought to take evidence from the Director of G.C.H.Q. and from the chairman of the union side of the Whitley Council at G.C.H.Q. but the Secretary of State would not authorise their attendance.[35] During the Westland affair the Defence Committee sought the attendance of three civil servants from the Department of Trade and Industry and the Chief Press Secretary to the Prime Minister and a Private Secretary to the Prime Minister. Permission was refused. Instead,

---

[32] May pp. 696–700, 793–743; for a full account see H.C. 588–I of 1977–78 pp. 15–37 (memorandum by the Clerk of the House).

[33] Harold Wilson: *Final Term: the Labour Government 1974–76* (1979) p. 223.

[34] For one example, see H.C. 434 of 1979–80 when Law Officers rejected an invitation to give evidence to the Home Affairs Committee on proposed new immigration rules and the European Convention on Human Rights.

[35] See H.C. 238 of 1983–84 and H.C. 363 of 1984–85 pp. xxiv–v.

the Secretary of the Cabinet and the Permanent Secretary of the department gave evidence.[36]

Giving of Evidence

Ministers may decline to give evidence on the ground that to do so would not be in the public interest.

A Cabinet Office Memorandum of Guidance for officials appearing before select committees states that any withholding of information should be limited to reservations necessary in the interests of good government or to safeguard national security. Committees' requests may also be declined on grounds of the excessive costs involved in obtaining information. Officials are told not to give evidence on advice given to Ministers or Law Officers; or on the private affairs of individuals or institutions on which information has been supplied in confidence; or on questions in the field of political controversy; or sensitive information of a commercial or economic nature; or matters which are or may become the subject of sensitive negotiations with governments or other bodies; or specific cases where the Minister acts in a quadi-judicial or appellate role.[37]

This list is much the same as one given by the Leader of the House (Mr Richard Crossman) in 1967 as matters on which Ministers might decline to give evidence.[38] The Memorandum also reminds civil servants of the need to protect ministerial responsibility and, in effect, not to speak of their own views on policy, and whenever pressed to go beyond such limits to suggest that the question be addressed or referred to Ministers. Any specific instructions about the giving of evidence which they receive from their superiors or from Ministers must of course be obeyed and this includes an instruction not to answer a committee's questions. The right of members of select committees to ask the questions remains.

The Defence Committee in the Westland affair reported that they did not insist on the attendance of the five officials because they would have been under instructions from Ministers not to answer questions and this could have placed them in an intensely embarrassing and unfair position.[39]

Information derived from the papers of previous administrations may also be withheld.

Production of Documents

In general the rules governing the attendance of witnesses apply to the production of documents.

An individual including a Member of either House who refuses to supply information may be reported to the House which could order him to answer the questions or supply the requested papers. In 1986 a witness before the Trade and Industry Committee, which was examining commercial and industrial aspects of the Westland affair, gave evidence in which he made allegations of improper influence being used by two Members of the House of Lords. He refused to give their names. As this information was germane to its inquiry, the committee reported his refusal to supply information to the House. The next day the witness sent a letter giving the names.[40] This

---

[36] H.C. 519 of 1985–86 paras. 225–229.
[37] C.S.D.Gen. 80/38. See revised version of March 1988.
[38] H.C. 588–I of 1977–78 pp. 21, 29.
[39] See above; H.C. 519 of 1985–86 para. 230.
[40] C.J. 1985–86, April 8, (p. 282) and April 9, (p. 281) 1986.

evidence was not published but the committee severely criticised the conduct of the witness.[41]

From time to time, Ministers and other person or bodies resist the request to furnish select committees with particular papers. The Procedure Committee had sought better procedures for bringing such matters before the whole House for debate and in January 1981 the then Leader of the House gave an undertaking that if there was evidence of widespread general concern in the House regarding an alleged ministerial refusal to disclose information to a select committee he would seek to provide time to enable the House to express its view.[42] In 1982 the Ministry of Defence agreed to give to the Public Accounts Committee details of major defence projects costing more than £200m. (later increased to £250m). If the information is highly sensitive on security grounds, it may be given, via the Comptroller and Auditor-General, only to the chairman, not to all members, of the P.A.C. In mid-January 1987, the British Broadcasting Corporation decided on security grounds not to show a planned television programme about the secrecy surrounding the launching of an electronic satellite codenamed Project Zircon. The writer and presenter of the programme (Mr Duncan Campbell) alleged that information concerning this had been withheld from Parliament in breach of the 1982 agreement. The C. and A.G. denied this.[43]

Subsequently the Speaker made an order prohibiting the use of any room under the control of the House for the showing of the film of the withdrawn programme (see pages 103–104). During a debate on January 27, 1987, the question was raised how the Speaker's order affected the work of select committees. The Leader of the House said that if a select committee wished to see the film within the precincts of the House the Government would provide time for the House to debate such a request.[44] This was consistent with the undertaking given in January 1981. The Speaker made clear that his order did not apply to the proceedings of select committees because their powers to send for persons, papers and records were given directly by the House and he had no power to interfere with their use. So his order related only to Members acting on their own responsibility.[45]

In January 1986 the Defence Committee sought the disclosure of minutes of Ministerial meetings which discussed policy towards the Westland company. After exerting considerable pressure, the committee received summaries of these minutes.[46]

On October 24, 1985 the Buffer Stock Manager of the International Tin Council (ITC) informed the London Metal Exchange that he could not pay his debts. Tin trading was immediately suspended. The Trade and Industry Committee decided to inquire into the crisis. The ITC refused to attend the Committee to give evidence and to release any information. The committee was unable to summon the ITC because of a treaty conferring diplomatic immunity on the ITC. The Government decided it could not provide information because of international treaty obligations, because certain

---

[41] H.C. 176 of 1986–87 para. 22.

[42] H.C.Deb., Vol. 996, col. 1312 (January 16, 1981).

[43] In April 1987, the Defence Committee said there were "no grounds for supposing that the Zircon project should have been included in the Major Projects Statement as submitted to us, given the present rules for the compilation of that Statement": H.C. 340 of 1986–87 para. 34.

[44] H.C.Deb., Vol. 109, col. 217.

[45] H.C.Deb., Vol. 109, col. 336 (January 28, 1987).

[46] H.C. 519 of 1985–86 paras. 217–224.

legal proceedings prevented comment on *sub judice* matters and because of the normal constraints set out in the Memorandum of Guidance on advice given to Ministers. The committee protested[47] but the Government insisted and refused to modify its ruling on the memorandum.[48] The House debated the matter on July 7, 1986 and, in a division, supported the Government.[49] In December 1986 the committee issued a supplementary report on the role of the Bank of England. The committee served an order on the Bank for the production of certain documents which were withheld by the Bank on instructions from the Government on the ground that the documents were held in the Bank's capacity as professional advisers to Ministers.[50]

In the last resort the House may make such orders as it thinks fit requiring the attendance of witnesses (including Ministers), the giving of evidence, and the production of documents. If such orders were not complied with by Ministers, a constitutional crisis might arise in which the powers of the House and the prerogative of the Crown were in conflict. However the Government's majority in the House almost inevitably ensures that no such order would be given.

The real power of select committees to secure the evidence they require from Ministers and civil servants lies in publicity. Ministers do not wish to be seen to be refusing to comply with requests. So committees almost always get what they want. But the Westland enquiries show that some information may be refused, even when the reason for the refusal seems to be to save Ministers from embarrassment.

---

[47] H.C. 305–I of 1985–86.
[48] H.C. 457 of 1985–86.
[49] H.C. Deb., Vol. 101, col. 72–118.
[50] H.C. 71 and 275 of 1986–87.

PART IV

THE LORDS

CHAPTER 12

THE HOUSE OF LORDS

INTRODUCTION

Despite many apparent similarities, there are essential differences between the two Houses of Parliament, which require that the House of Lords be considered separately. Writing over a century ago, Bagehot said that:

"with a perfect Lower House it is certain that an Upper House would be scarcely of any value. But ... beside the actual House [of Commons] a revising and leisured legislature is extremely useful."[1]

If true in 1867, this is all the more valid today. Great changes have taken place in the activity and tempo of the Lords since 1945, particularly in the increased flow of public legislation.[2] As the weight of legislation has increased, neither Government nor the House of Commons have been able to prevent the onus of revision shifting increasingly onto the Lords.

The differences between the Houses derive from the source of political authority of the Lords—based on prescription and immemorial antiquity rather than popular election; the retention of its old procedures, which have not as yet been forced into radical change (as were those of the Commons in the late nineteenth century by the Irish Nationalists); the lack of a Speakership with effective powers; a continuing tendency towards one party, because of the hereditary peerage; an absence of priority for Government business; the maintenance of freedoms for the individual member, resulting from the comparative lack of pressures on the time of the House; the lack of power on financial matters; the presence of bishops, law lords and life Peers and the consequent specialist experience of many members; and the distinctive and idiosyncratic contribution of the hereditary peerage. These factors contribute to the peculiar, indeed unique, quality of the House of Lords.

Since the passage of the Parliament Act 1911, whose preamble stated that reform of the composition of the House "cannot be immediately brought into operation," two serious attempts have been made to reform the Lords. Both were at the instance of a government of the left; the first in 1948 and the second in 1968. Both failed, but before doing so they left behind some agreed objectives[3] which had crystallised at the Inter-Party Conferences which accompanied each attempt. To a considerable extent, these objectives have been achieved piecemeal as the years have passed.

The attempt at reform in 1948 was followed by the introduction of Life Peerages in 1958, the payment of daily expenses (first authorised in 1957), and the introduction of women. The 1968 attempt was followed by developments foreshadowed in the White Paper, especially increased select committee activity and new procedures for the consideration of subordinate

---

[1] W. Bagehot, *The English Constitution* with introduction by R. H. S. Crossman (1964 edition) pp. 133–134.
[2] See D. Shell, *The House of Lords* (1988), the most recent academic work, which fills a void in considering the work of the present day House and brings up to date earlier text books.
[3] See Parliament Bill 1947, Agreed Statement on conclusion of Conference of Party Leaders Cmd. 7380 (1948) and White Paper on House of Lords Reform, Cmnd. 3799 (1968).

legislation. More significantly, in the face of the evident unwillingness of the Commons to allow reform of the Lords, the House of Lords has shown greater willingness to test its powers to the full. To this has been added the new confidence which flowed from the creation of life Peers, and perhaps waning respect for the system described by Lord Hailsham in his lecture on "Elective Dictatorship."[4]

Thus twice the waves of reform have swept up to the old House, and in each case failed to make a breach—though the reasons lay largely outside the House of Lords itself. The causes of failure were political expediency and, on the second occasion, an unwillingness by the elected House to permit reform of the unelected House, which, by rendering the Lords more publicly acceptable, might give it greater political authority. A recognition of this has led the leadership in the Lords to attempt to reform the House by its own efforts, in which they have achieved some success.

The House of Lords is not a static institution, indeed in some ways it shows great willingness to embrace change, for example in allowing the televising of its proceedings. It is impossible to catch the bird on the wing and give a definitive account of the House as its practice is subject to continuous change. Nevertheless, this Chapter attempts with brevity to describe the House as it has been in the 1980s in a factual manner.

The House of Lords at present performs the following main functions[5]:

(a) the provision of a forum for debate on matters of public interest;

(b) the revision of public bills brought from the House of Commons;

(c) the initiation of public legislation, including some Government bills, usually less controversial in party political terms, and private members' bills;

(d) the consideration of delegated legislation;

(e) the scrutiny of the activities of the executive;

(f) the scrutiny of private legislation;

(g) select committee work, such as on the European Communities and Science and Technology; and

(h) the supreme court of appeal.

Before considering these functions in the later part of this Chapter, we consider composition, including officers, the political parties, their strength and organisation, the cross benches, and Peers' expenses. There follows a description of the system of self-regulation peculiar to the Lords, the categories and organisation of business, and the different procedures including select committees. Finally we examine the powers and role of the House; especially legislation and subordinate legislation, the existing conventions in the use of powers, debate and scrutiny of the executive, and relations with the public, lobbying and broadcasting. The privileges of the House are broadly the same as in the House of Commons (see Chapter 3), and are accordingly not separately covered but the Lords no longer have cases of privilege as happens in the Commons.

---

[4] See Lord Hailsham's Richard Dimbleby Lecture on "The Elective Dictatorship" (1976) and *The Dilemma of Democracy* (1978).

[5] See Cmnd. 3799 para. 8: since 1968 select committee work has been added. Controversial bills introduced into the Lords have included Football Spectators 1989 and Shops 1986.

Composition of the House of Lords at the End of each Session

	Sessions											
	1957-58	1965-66	1970-71	1975-76	1980-81	1981-82	1982-83	1983-84	1984-85	1985-86	1986-87	1987-88
Archbishops and Bishops	26	26	26	26	26	26	26	26	26	26	26	26
Peers by succession	654	733	764	760	769	765	769	763	760	760	763	759
Hereditary Peers of first creation	161	141	86	58	35	34	30	30	29	30	29	25
Life Peers	27	120	202	295	349	349	356	364	359	355	367	375
(a) created under the Appellate Jurisdiction Act 1876 (as amended)	12				19	21	19	19	19	21	21	22
(b) created under the Life Peerages Act 1958	15				330	328	335	345	340	334	346	353
Scottish Representative Peers	16	N/A	N/A	N/A	N/A	N/A	N/A	N/A	N/A	N/A	N/A	N/A
Irish Representative Peers	1	N/A	N/A	N/A	N/A	N/A	N/A	N/A	N/A	N/A	N/A	N/A
Total	885	1,020	1,078	1,139	1,179	1,174	1,181	1,183	1,174	1,171	1,185	1,185
Of whom: Peers without writs	66	94	101	95	87	91	97	99	95	89	89	84
(of whom are minors)	14	8			6	6	6	6	5	4	3	2
Peers with leave of absence	N/A	195	171	143	160	150	143	153	142	135	133	169
In addition: Persons who had inherited Peerages and who have disclaimed them for Life	N/A	9			15	15	15	14	13	13	12	12

Note: This Table and subsequent tables are based on H.L. 9 of 1987–88 updated with the help of Journal Office, House of Lords, unless an alternative source is quoted.

COMPOSITION

The total composition of the House of Lords over the last thirty years has been as shown on page 457.

In 1988, 168 Peers were on leave of absence; that is, Peers who had applied for leave of absence because they would be unable, or were unwilling, to attend the House. Peers can end leave of absence on one month's notice. Many members not on leave of absence attend rarely, and some never.

Hereditary Peers by succession

The holders by succession of an hereditary peerage of England (granted pre-1707), Scotland (up to 1707), Great Britain (1707–1800), and the United Kingdom (1801 to date) are the Peers by succession, entitled as such to a writ of summons to Parliament from the Crown. The writ of summons cannot be withheld from any rightful claimant over 21 years of age, as long as he or she is not disqualified as an alien; as bankrupt; or as convicted of treason. In practice there are at any one time a number of Peers by succession not in receipt of a writ of summons, and some never go to the trouble of establishing their claim. In 1988 there were 86 such Peers by succession without writs, including two minors. Since 1963, it has been possible to disclaim an hereditary peerage for life, and at the end of 1988 there were twelve Peers who had done so.

Peers by succession are still in the majority in the House. However, a greater proportion of regular attenders are life peers, so the domination of Peers by succession is, in practice, reduced (see page 466). Although some hereditary Peers hold titles of great antiquity, the majority are of relatively recent creation, with only some 30 per cent dating from before 1800, 30 per cent dating from the nineteenth century, and the remaining 40 per cent created this century.

The presence of the hereditary Peers has certain consequences for the House. First, in the event of a conflict with the elected Commons, the argument on the issue in question is often obscured by that of "Peers versus people," and by criticism of the composition of the House. For example, Mr. Harold Wilson as Prime Minister voiced such criticism in 1968: "There is no precedent for the voting down [of the Southern Rhodesia (United Nations Sanctions) Order 1968] by the non-elected Chamber in which, in present circumstances, most of its Members sit, not by the right of creation, but by the right of succession from some new or distant ancestor."[6] The fact that one party, the Conservative party, is supported by a majority of the hereditary peerage lends added force to such criticism.

Secondly, while many life Peers are of advanced age, the accidental incidence of succession to an hereditary peerage means that there are always a number of young and middle-aged Peers in the Lords. Peers by succession also provide an extraordinary variety of occupation and character, in contrast to the Commons, where the majority are, at least for the period of their membership, professional politicians.

Hereditary Peers of first creation

Until the passage of the Life Peerages Act 1958, all new members of the

---

[6] H.C.Deb., Vol. 766, col. 1315 (June 20, 1968).

House were hereditary, except the law lords and bishops. A steady flow of new hereditary creations meant that the lay membership of the House increased from 270 in 1801 to 591 in 1901 and to 908 in 1960. From 1958 to 1964 Prime Ministers continued to recommend the creation of both life and hereditary Peers but, after the 1964 election, Mr. Wilson let it be known that he would recommend no more hereditary peerages (except for the Royal Family). This practice was followed by his three successors, and it had become accepted that the creation of hereditary Peers was a thing of the past. However, in 1983, Mrs. Thatcher surprised commentators by recommending the creation of two hereditary viscountcies "in exceptional circumstances," and a year later an hereditary earldom was also conferred.[7]

But the vast majority of hereditary Peers of first creation date back to before 1965, and this group is therefore declining in both numbers and significance.

Bishops: the Lords Spiritual

Twenty-six bishops of the Church of England have seats in the House of Lords: the Archbishops of Canterbury and York and the Bishops of London, Durham and Winchester, *ex officio*, together with 21 other diocesan bishops by seniority of appointment. They hold their seats during the tenure of their sees, and retire at the age of 70. Historically, the House of Lords has consisted of the Lords Spiritual and Temporal.

Indeed, until the dissolution of the monasteries, the majority of members of the House were spiritual (though many did not attend). Episcopal representation in the Lords has always been associated with the existence of an established church, and when the Irish and Welsh Churches were disestablished in 1869 and 1919 they lost their episcopal representation in the Lords.

Bishops are now appointed by the Crown on the advice of the Prime Minister, who makes the recommendation from candidates selected by the Church itself[8]: they are no longer appointed on political grounds, and certainly feel no obligation to support the party under whom they were appointed. They speak and vote on many different subjects,[9] especially those involving moral or social welfare, housing and education. The lay secretary to the Archbishop of Canterbury provides some organisation, so that there is a Church spokesman to take part in all debates on which a Church view is thought appropriate. But the bishops also speak in a personal capacity on social or moral questions of particular concern, and on local issues of concern to their sees. Although they used to refrain from speaking or voting on straight political issues, in recent years they have shown less readiness to regard themselves as political neuters, and have increasingly ranged themselves against conservative opinions; for example, on television and broadcasting, capital punishment, homosexuality, immigration and inner-city housing problems. However, on Sunday trading, their Christian and sabbatarian views inclined them against change. These standpoints have led to attacks on them by Ministers.[10] The bishops also have the duty of

---

[7] Viscounts Whitelaw and Tonypandy, and the Earl of Stockton.

[8] For each vacancy, the Standing Commission on diocesan vacancies, consisting of the two archbishops, three clergymen and three laymen, and four representatives of the diocese concerned, submit a first and second choice to the Prime Minister, who can choose either for submission to the Queen, or ask for further names to be submitted.

[9] P. A. Bromhead, *The House of Lords and Contemporary Politics, 1911–57* pp. 53–67.

[10] H.L.Deb. vol. 445, cols. 943–950 (December 5, 1983).

reading Prayers in the House at the start of business and each bishop, except those sitting *ex officio*, performs these duties in turn. They may also undertake Church business, such as the moving for the approval of a Measure under the Church of England Assembly (Powers) Act 1919.

Law Lords

The House of Lords is the final Court of Appeal for the United Kingdom in civil cases, and for England, Wales and Northern Ireland in criminal cases. The appellate jurisdiction of the House is largely exercised by the serving Lords of Appeal in Ordinary. By convention, lay Lords take no part in appeals. Up to 11[11] Lords of Appeal in Ordinary may be created for life under the Appellate Jurisdiction Act 1876 (as amended) for the purpose of assisting the House of Lords in the hearing and determining of appeals. At present, the number of judicially qualified Lords, commonly called the "Law Lords," is 33, including retired Lords of Appeal in Ordinary and other Lords who are (or have been) holders of high judicial office.

Lords of Appeal in Ordinary now retire by statute[12] at 75, but, unlike bishops, they retain their membership of the House for life and may be employed part-time to "sit judicially."

The serving Lords of Appeal in Ordinary are governed by a convention that they do not participate in debates on public party political controversy. This crystallised after the controversy over the public pronouncements of Lord Carson on the Irish Treaty in 1922. The convention is less clear in relation to retired Law Lords, and does not apply to Lord Chancellors and former Lord Chancellors.

Although in the years 1911–57 there was a decline[13] in the intervention of Law Lords in general debates, this tendency has recently been reversed,[14] while the increasingly full-time and professional role of M.P.s has seen some decline in the number of practising lawyers in the Commons. In recent years, the Law Lords have taken an active part in the House, speaking on legislation especially where points of law arise, and in debate, especially on law reform and on reports of royal commissions or other enquiries with which they have been connected. They also serve on committees, as Chairmen of the Consolidation Bills Joint Committee, Ecclesiastical Committee, and of the Law and Institutions Sub-Committee of the European Communities Committee; and as members of the Committee for Privileges on peerage cases and of *ad hoc* enquiries.

The Law Lords (like the bishops) are members of the House of Lords by virtue of their function, as judges of the supreme court. The Law Lords and the Anglican episcopate are in the unusual position that they are leading their profession at the time they can speak in the Lords: many other members of the House have retired from their professions. Thus, the judiciary has a privileged position in the body politic.

---

[11] The 1876 Act permitted up to four Lords of Appeal in Ordinary, two at once and a further two on the retirement of certain judges then in post. They were to leave the Lords on retirement. Subsequent Acts raised the limits to six in 1913, seven in 1929, nine in 1947 and 11 in 1968 (with provision for the numbers to be revised by Orders in Council).

[12] Judicial Pensions Act 1959.

[13] P. A. Bromhead, *op. cit.*, pp. 67–72.

[14] L. Blom-Cooper and G. Drewry, *Final Appeal: A Study of the House of Lords in its Judicial Capacity* (1972), Chapter X on Law Lords as legislators.

Life Peers

The idea of life peerages is not new. In 1856 an attempt was made by the Whig administration to confer a life peerage on a distinguished judge, Sir James Parke. The House of Lords twice referred the matter to the Committee for Privileges, and eventually voted that it was beyond the competence of the Crown to grant a life peerage with a seat in parliament. An opportunity for reform was thus lost.[15] This decision was eventually undone by the Macmillan administration, when they passed the Life Peerages Act 1958, which gave the Crown power to create men and women Peers for life. It was decided to treat the newly created Peers so far as possible like hereditary Peers, with the intention that the new breed of Peers should not be second class members of the House. This has helped to ensure that the traditions and courtesies of the House have been maintained.

But if 1958 was no watershed in the history of the House, it was nevertheless one of the major elements in, and a necessary precondition of, the changes witnessed since then. It allowed men and women to accept a peerage without burdening their heirs with a title and for more peerages to be created without permanently and constantly enlarging the size of the House. Life Peers have transformed the House. Instead of a House consisting predominantly of landowners and retired politicians (with a sprinkling of lawyers and bishops), the range of occupations and interests has been vastly increased. The numbers of life Peers created has been large (see Table page 462), and the variety of persons selected for life peerages has been extensive. The largest category is of politicians, whether ex-Ministers, ex-M.P.s or others active elsewhere in party politics, especially in local government. But the many other occupations honoured include businessmen, trade unionists, academics, civil servants and other public servants, diplomats, senior servicemen, industrialists, scientists, economists, journalists, newspaper proprietors, doctors, lawyers, farmers, technologists, actors and artists, clerics, accountants, nurses, social workers, and a composer. Those appointed are not representative in the sense that they are appointed to speak for their colleagues, but they do provide a wide spectrum of expertise. As Peers, they are free to attend the House as and when they wish, although those still working tend to restrict attendance to debates of personal interest.

---

[15] See Pike, *Constitutional History of the House of Lords*, pp. 376–379. Bagehot *op. cit.* pp. 144–146. The Appellate Jurisdiction Act 1876 made limited provision for Law Lords without hereditary peerages with seats in the Lords.

Creation of Life Peerages, 1958–1988[16] (Excluding Law Lords)

Prime Minister	Cons	Lab	Lib/SDP	Crossbench	Total	Average per 12 months
Macmillan/Home	17	29	1	18	65	17
1958–64	(25)		(1)	(22)	(48)	
Wilson	11	78	6	46	141	25
1964–70						
Heath	23	5	3	15	46	13
1970–4						
Wilson/Callaghan	17	82	6	34	139	27
1974–9						
Thatcher	77	39	9	37	162	17
1979–88	(2)			(2)	(4)	
Total	145	233	25	150	553	

Notes: a) Resignation honours attributed to outgoing Prime Ministers.
b) Political affiliation is that of a Lord upon creation.
c) Figures in parentheses give the number of hereditary peerages awarded (excluding advancements).

Expenses

The 1948 Inter-Party Conference on Lords Reform[17] agreed that "in order that persons without private means should not be excluded, some remuneration should be payable to members of the second chamber." In 1957, Resolutions of the two Houses of Parliament enabled Peers to recover, within limits, expenses incurred for the purpose of attending the House of Lords: these Resolutions have since been amended, and the sums permitted increased, largely in accordance with the recommendations of the Top Salaries Review Body.[18]

Lords' Ministers, the Leader of the Opposition, the Opposition Chief Whip, the Chairman of Committees and his Principal Deputy, and the Lords of Appeal in Ordinary all receive salaries. Other Lords, although unpaid, may recover expenses incurred for the purpose of attendance at the sittings of the House or its Committees within the following daily limits[19]:

(a) overnight accommodation £60.00;

(b) day's subsistence and incidental travel cost £23.00;

(c) general office expenses or secretarial or research assistance £23.00.

These allowances are uprated annually, and are subject to periodic review. Lords may also recover travelling expenses incurred within the United Kingdom on parliamentary business. Disabled Members may recover additional expenses of attending the House incurred by them on account of their disablement.

Thus Lords, unlike MPs, have no salary. But they can recover up to £106.00 per day for expenses which are not subject to tax, in respect of any day in which they have actually attended the House: expenses (except secretarial expenses within strict limits) incurred during recesses or on non-sitting days are not recoverable.

---

[16] D. Shell: *The House of Lords* (1988) and Journal Office, House of Lords.
[17] Cmd. 7830.
[18] Cm. 131–I and II is the latest of a line of reports.
[19] October 1988.

Officers and Office-Holders

Lord Chancellor

The Lord Chancellor is *ex officio* the Speaker of the House of Lords, but his role is quite unlike that of other Speakers. He has no effective and controlling powers, and the standing orders of the House deny him power to maintain order. His role is "ornamental and symbolic";[20] the responsibility for maintaining order rests with the House as a whole. It is his duty to attend the House,[21] to sit on the Woolsack, to preside over proceedings and to put the question, save when the House is in committee. These restricted powers are of long standing. A standing order of 1621, the first existing text, states that he "is always to speak uncovered and is not to adjourn the House or do anything else as mouth of the House without the consent of the Lords first had, excepting the ordinary things about Bills, which are of course. Wherein the lords may likewise overrule, as for preferring one Bill before another, and such like. ... " By 1621, the post was normally held by a successful lawyer or bishop, who was the King's Minister. The magnates of the Realm as Peers were equal and there were no "great Lords"; they would not suffer any one to instruct them, as Lord Chancellor Ellesmere said in 1614 on a matter of procedure, "My Lords, you may do, what you will therefore determine as you please".[21a]

The Lord Chancellor is always a member of the Government with a seat in the Cabinet, and has responsibility for a department with recently enlarged duties for the administration of justice. It has increasingly proved difficult for him to obey the standing order which enjoins that "it is the duty of the Lord Chancellor ordinarily to attend the Lords House."[22] When in the House, unlike the Speaker in the Commons, he may take part in debate and vote. There is no convention inhibiting him from party political controversy, and he does not have a casting vote.

When the Lord Chancellor is not present, other Lords may sit as Speaker, by virtue of a Royal Commission; in their absence and that of any Deputy Chairman, the House may, on motion, appoint its own Speaker.

Chairman of Committees

The first Deputy Speaker is the Chairman of Committees, or "Lord Chairman," appointed by the House at the beginning of each session, or whenever a vacancy occurs.[23] He takes the Chair when the House is in committee of the whole House, and is also *ex officio* Chairman of all select committees, unless the House orders otherwise.[24] He is responsible for the supervision of private bills, provisional order confirmation bills and certain delegated legislation.

---

[20] H.L. 9 of 1987–88, para. 13: Report by the Group on the Working of the House.

[21] H.L. S.O. No. 15; he receives in recompense for his Speaker's duties 14 per cent. (£12,810) out of his total £91,500 salary (1989 figure).

[21a] E. R. Foster, *The House of Lords 1603–1649* (1983), p. 31.

[22] Lord Chancellor Gardiner (1964–70) was the last holder of the Office to do so at length. See R. F. V. Heuston, *Lives of the Lord Chancellors, 1940–70*, p. 219. Recent Lord Chancellors have also found it difficult to sit judicially.

[23] Recent holders of the Office have been: 1911–31 E. Donoughmore, 1931–44 E. Onslow, 1944–46 L. Stanmore, 1946–57 E. Drogheda, 1957–65 L. Merthyr, 1965–76 E. Listowel, 1976—L. Aberdare.

[24] H.L. S.O. Nos. 59 and 60.

The Chairman of Committees holds office for a number of years. Once appointed, he adopts a non-party position and does not speak or vote on matters of political controversy. The neutral position of the Lord Chairman, his chairmanship of domestic committees of the House, and his continuity in office make the holder of the office an influential figure in the House. The Chairman of Committees is paid[25] in accordance with the recommendations of the Top Salaries Review Body[26] (TSRB).

Principal Deputy Chairman of Committees

The holder of this office, appointed sessionally, aids the Chairman of Committees as his deputy, and has special responsibilities as Chairman of the European Communities Committee. The Principal Deputy Chairman is also paid in accordance with TSRB recommendations. Unlike the Chairman of Committees, he is appointed for only a few years.

Leader of the House and the Government Chief Whip

The Leader of the House is appointed by the Prime Minister, is a member of the Cabinet, and is responsible for the conduct of government business in the Lords. With the Speaker lacking effective powers of order, it is the Leader who advises the House on matters of procedure and order. He has a special part to play in expressing the "sense of the House" and in drawing attention to transgressions or abuse of the rules. Essentially, therefore, he has to play two roles: the first as the Leader of the Government in the Lords, and secondly as the shepherd of the House, the chief protector of its rights and privileges. These two functions can come into conflict, but there is an obvious advantage to the House in having a Government Minister as its champion. Occasional attempts to question the impartiality of the Leader or his independent role have been unsuccessful.

A Report expressed the position thus:

> "While the Leader of the House has a responsibility for reminding the House of the rules, the exercise of his Office demands great tact lest he should overstep the mark and act as something more than the first among equals. The fact that the Leader is a Cabinet Minister and a member of the governing Party means that his role is obviously a delicate one, especially when matters of party-political controversy are under discussion. We would therefore stress that it is for all members of the House to see that its procedures are followed. . . . "[27]

The Leader frequently acts as the voice of the House, not only in matters of order but also in expressing the sense of the House on formal occasions, on motions of thanks or congratulation, or in tributes to a deceased member. It is an acknowledged convention that he and his private office are available to assist and advise all Peers irrespective of party.

The Government Chief Whip is responsible for the detailed arrangement of government business, and for consultations with the other political parties on the business of the House. He also sends out a weekly "whip," with underlinings, to members of his own party inviting their presence when divisions are expected; the other parties' whips do likewise.

---

[25] Ministerial and Other Salaries Act 1975.
[26] £37,047 in 1989.
[27] H.L. 227 of 1970–71, para. 4.

Party Politics in the House of Lords

Party Allegiance

In 1988 the party allegiance of Peers who attended the House was; Conservative 416, cross-bench or Independent 244 (excluding the Law Lords and bishops, numbering 60), Labour 119, Liberal 43, and SDP 43. These figures represent a significant change in the political complexion of the House. By the end of the nineteenth century, there existed a large Conservative or Unionist majority in the Lords, and this permanent majority continued well into the twentieth century. The 1968 White Paper on House of Lords Reform stated that "the Conservatives have always in modern times been able to command a majority,"[28] and indeed one of the objectives of the reform then proposed was that "no one party should possess a permanent majority."

But, as recently said by the Government Chief Whip "in almost every case and almost every way . . . the Government do not have an overall majority in this House."[29] The following table shows that the Conservatives, although the largest party in the House, have not had an absolute majority in recent years.

Party Composition of whole House (Excluding Peers without Writs or on Leave of Absence)

	1968 (July)	1974 (July)	1983 (May)	1986 (Nov.)	1989 (May)[29a]
Conservative	351	370	448	412	412
Labour	116	134	132	118	111
Liberal	41	37	41	43	-
S.D.P.	-	-	-	43	23
Independent	281	291	315	331	284
Democrats	-	-	-	-	56
	789	832	936	947	885

Nonetheless, the party composition of the Lords normally gives the present Conservative Government a majority,[30] unless the cross-benchers vote overwhelmingly with the Opposition parties. This majority is in doubt only if a significant number of Conservatives either vote with the Opposition, or abstain; either by failing to vote, or by staying away.

The following table shows that there is a difference between the party political composition of the whole House, and of those who attend regularly (here and elsewhere taken as those who attend more than a third of the sittings of the House). 168 Conservative Peers attended over a third of the sittings in session 1985–86, 88 Labour, 27 Liberal and 24 S.D.P., and a further 73 Independent or Crossbench make up the total of 380.

---

[28] Cmnd. 3799, para. 18.

[29] H.L.Deb., Vol. 471, cols. 1506–1509 (May 17, 1984).

[29a] These figures exclude those who had not taken the Oath; the total numbers are therefore likely to increase as each Parliament progresses.

[30] H.L.Deb., Vol. 451, col. 149 (April 26, 1984).

COMPOSITION OF THE HOUSE
WORKING HOUSE : BREAKDOWN BY PARTY

Party	1967-68[30a]	1983-84	1984-85	1985-86	1986-87	1987-88
Conservative	125	167	170	168	173	184
By Succession	87	100	106	101	110	114
Created	38	67	64	67	63	70
Labour	95	98	91	88	82	91
By Succession	14	7	8	7	7	7
Created	81	91	83	81	75	84
Liberal or SLD	19	25	26	27	36	38
By Succession	11	9	12	12	14	15
Created	8	16	14	15	22	23
SDP	N/A	21	23	24	15	13
By Succession		5	6	7	5	4
Created		16	17	17	10	9
Independent	52	76	74	73	73	73
By Succession	26	33	34	36	36	37
Created	26	43	40	37	37	36
Total	291	387	384	380	379	399
By Succession	138	154	166	163	172	177
Created	153	233	218	217	207	222

The Table also distinguishes between Peers by succession and created Peers. Of the 177 Peers by succession who attended regularly in 1987–88, 114 were Conservatives, seven Labour, 15 Democrats, four SDP and 37 Independents. Of the 222 created Peers who attend regularly, 70 are Conservative, 84 Labour, 23 Democrat, 9 SDP and 36 Independent. At the time of the White Paper in 1968 there was a rough equality amongst those who attended regularly between Peers by succession and created Peers. Now a majority of regular attenders are created Peers.

Government

Although the majority of Ministers sit in the Commons, some Cabinet Ministers do sit in the Lords and every department is represented by a junior Minister or spokesman. The whips, who regularly act as spokesmen, hold posts in the Royal Household. At the beginning of 1989, the Government was represented in the Lords by 22 Ministers as follows:

Cabinet Ministers	3	(Lord Privy Seal and Leader of the House, Lord Chancellor and Secretary of State for Trade and Industry)
Lord Advocate	1	
Ministers of State	5	
Parliamentary Under Secretaries	6	
Royal Household	7	

The Ministers meet weekly to discuss forthcoming business for the coming week.

[30a] These periods are all sessions except for 1967–68 which is October to August.

Party Organisation

The Conservative Party has a back bench organisation known as the Association of Conservative Peers (ACP), with an elected Chairman, and a Secretary from Central Office. Until recently, it was called the Association of Independent Unionist Peers. Its organisation was modelled on the 1922 Committee in the Commons. It meets weekly, attended by the Government Chief Whip. Ministers also attend and speak on issues of current importance to muster support for their measures, as well as discussing details of policy with party members in private. The ACP meetings choose the subjects for debate on the days reserved for Conservative debates.

Labour Peers in receipt of the Whip meet every Thursday, and are also entitled to attend the Parliamentary Labour Party meetings in the Commons. The Labour Peers' meeting is preceded by a front-bench meeting at which there is discussion of future business. The Leader and Opposition Chief Whip are *ex officio* members of the Shadow Cabinet, as is one elected representative of the Labour Peers. The Leader, Deputy Leader and Chief Whip are each elected annually. In 1981, the then Leader failed to secure re-election.

Similar meetings are organised by the Social and Liberal Democrats and the SDP. The Opposition parties in the Lords as in the Commons now receive specific subventions of public money ("Short money") to help them to oppose effectively, especially by employing research assistants (see pages 117–8).

Cross Bench or Independent Peers

The cross benches owe their existence to two factors: the architectural arrangement of the House and its composition. Cross benches in the Lords have existed from the seventeenth century and then accommodated the Viscounts (when the House sat according to precedence). When the House stopped sitting by rank, the existence of cross benches was convenient to an assembly in which not all members have belonged to a political party. In 1884 there was pressure for more cross bench seating. One Peer complained that: "the accommodation was so limited on fighting nights that there was scarcely any possibility of getting a seat." The ministerial reply was: "I have no great sympathy with the cross bench mind. While I prefer a good Liberal, I am afraid I prefer a good Tory to those who are neither fish, flesh, nor good red herring."[31]

Despite such jibes, the numbers and significance of the cross benchers has grown, from about 50 in 1945, to about 100 in 1965, and about 221 in 1989; these figures ignore the Law Lords, bishops and those Peers who, although not in receipt of a party Whip, have also chosen to remain outside the cross bench organisation. This informal organisation is of recent origin. It was only in 1965 that a weekly meeting of cross benchers was organised, which sent out a "no line whip," a statement of future business with no "whipping." In that year, under a Labour administration, a "co-ordinator [or convenor] of the cross benches" was chosen and given official recognition. The convenor is now a regular member of domestic committees; is a member of the

---

[31] H.L.Deb., Vol. 284 cols. 849–850 (February 14, 1884). Note also Mr. Michael Foot on the Parliament (No. 2) Bill where he said that "a falsetto chorus from these political *castrati*" would be "the final arbiters of our destiny" (H.C.Deb., Vol. 777, cols. 88–89 (February 3, 1969)).

informal Leaders' and Whips' meetings; and speaks after the party leaders on formal occasions such as tributes.

Days are allocated each session for debates of the cross benchers' own choosing, usually on non-party political subjects: similarly they are given proportionate representation on House committees, and make a large contribution to select committees. Cross bench meetings are held weekly at 2.30 p.m. on Thursdays, when future business is discussed. Occasionally, special meetings addressed by a visitor are arranged on matters of current interest.

"Usual Channels"

The House of Lords gives no formal preference to Government business in its standing orders, and maintains an ancient tradition of equality. However, the conduct of business must be arranged in advance, by informal but effective means. This is supplied by the "usual channels;" that is to say, the Leaders and Chief Whips of the political parties, together with the Convenor of the cross benches. Through them, a wide-ranging process of consultation with members of the House takes place, in an attempt to ensure orderly proceedings on the Floor of the House, without points of order (unknown in the Lords) and with minimum discussion of business arrangements in the Chamber.

The Government "business managers" are the Leader and the Chief Whip. They have to deal on a daily basis with the Leaders and Chief Whips of the other political parties, and also *ad hoc* with any Peers with a particular interest in any forthcoming piece of business. In turn, the Leaders and Chief Whips of the other parties will have discussed future business with their own party members. Prior contact and consultation is the essence of the "usual channels."

The Leader of the House and the Government Chief Whip share a private secretary, who since 1960 has been a clerk seconded from the Parliament Office to the Cabinet Office. He attends ministerial meetings, and, with the help of an Assistant Private Secretary and a private office, assists the Leader and Chief Whip to arrange the business of the House. Nevertheless, there is an understanding that he is available to assist and advise all Peers, irrespective of party.

The lack of priority for government business does not inhibit Governments of either party from arranging the business of the House, provided that they are perceived to do so in the best interests of the House, and discuss the arrangements with those concerned in advance. A written weekly statement of forthcoming business is prepared and circulated by the Government Whips' Office. It gives details of expected business for the coming week (including the time that each business is expected to take, and the names of all known participants in debates), and gives provisional details of the business for a further two weeks: hence members of the House are consulted and informed on the future programme of business to a very marked degree.

But the restrictions on the power of the Government in the Lords and the need for constant consultation with all sides of the House is balanced by the convention that the Government of the day, whether or not it is in a majority in the Lords, has the right to have its business considered. This is important in a House where governments of the left are in a minority position.

PROCEDURE

The House of Lords remains a self-regulatory body. In procedural terms, it has not followed the path adopted by the Commons in the nineteenth century: that of increasing regulation, much of it originally introduced as a result of the unwillingness of a substantial minority of that House—the Irish Nationalists—to abide by the spirit of the old procedures. The House of Lords did not possess an Irish Nationalist minority—and indeed has never been faced with a determined effort by a minority to subvert its procedures. So the House has continued without radical change and the private member still retains great freedom, as well as the opportunity to exercise it.

In 1971, the Leader of the House (Lord Jellicoe) set up a small informal group to examine the working of the House. In its report,[32] the group provided a summary of how the House runs:

"a unique institution in that all its members are equal and that there exist no powers of control by the Speaker. There are few standing orders and the House runs its affairs according to good sense rather than by the rule book. The House is a self-regulatory body which is accustomed to agree on its day-to-day proceedings. . . . We agree that it is desirable that this state of affairs should continue, but this must depend on the vigilance of all members of the House. Peers should therefore be aware that the democratic and flexible way of managing our affairs depends on the responsibility and restraint of each member; abuse by even a handful must certainly entail in due course, the creation of a multiplicity of procedural rules and the importation of a Speaker with powers to enforce them, on the pattern of the House of Commons."

The 1971 group also recommended against the introduction of a Speakership with controlling powers:

"within the terms of standing orders, we have great flexibility in our procedure and are therefore able to conduct our business expeditiously, politely and sensibly. We are not troubled by points of order, nor by the exploitation of time-wasting procedural devices which are often to be observed in other legislative assemblies. The 'sense of the House' is the decisive factor in the conduct of our business, and in the main this works well."

The 1971 group's conclusions were debated in the House,[33] and overwhelmingly supported.

There is no evidence that views have changed since 1971. In 1986 another informal group of Peers was set up by the Leader (Lord Whitelaw) to examine the working of the House. They also considered whether there was a case for a Speakership with effective powers, but again recommended against:

"the reasons against such a change are positive: Peers have pride in our system of self-regulation and the 'liberal spirit' it embodies. The introduction of a Speakership with powers would encourage time-wasting points of order, worsen conduct and curtail the ancient liberties of the House."

In short, the majority view in the House is against radical change, and supports retention of the ancient freedoms which characterise Lords' procedure.

---

[32] Tenth Report of the Procedure Committee: H.L. 227 of 1970–71.
[33] H.L. Deb. Vol. 325, cols. 906–989 (November 23, 1971) and Vol. 326, cols. 1271–1306 (December 16, 1971).

Despite the practice that the House is self-governing, that its members are equal, and that procedural questions relating to the conduct of its business are decided by the "sense of the House," there are rules. The *Standing Orders relating to Public Business* (1984 edition) is a slim volume of some 38 small pages. It originated in a series of "Remembrances for order and decency to be kept in the Upper House of Parliament," first compiled in 1621, and has gradually been extended to cover the main procedures of the House. There are also separate volumes covering *Standing Orders relating to Private Bills, etc.*, and *Forms of Appeal, Method of Procedure and Standing Orders (Judicial)*. Since 1862 the standing orders have been supplemented and explained by the *Companion to the Standing Orders*. From 1862 to 1909 the volumes were circulated privately; from 1909 onwards they have been laid on the Table. The *Companion* is now issued with the authority of the Procedure Committee. Since 1975, the committee has also authorised a *Brief Guide to the Procedure and Practice of the House of Lords*, drawn up on the recommendation of the 1971 group to "set forth simply and shortly the most elementary practices and procedures of the House, the usages in debate and those Standing Orders which all Peers should know." The 1975 *Brief Guide* was considerably revised by the 1986 group, which considered that its emphasis needed to be put more directly on the keeping of order and procedure. Members of the House had described the standard procedural guide, the *Companion*, as "long, legalistic and tedious." Certainly, the *Companion* has expanded in response to the increased membership and business of the House, from 30 pages in 1955 to 211 pages in 1984.

Procedure Committee

Changes in procedure are made at the suggestion of the Procedure Committee which, spasmodic before the second World War, is now appointed sessionally and includes the Leader of the House and the other "usual channels."

In circumstances where there is a clear desire by the House to see a procedure adopted, the Government of the day, if defeated in the committee, has little option but to concede in the House. An example was the battle fought over the terms of reference of the European Communities Committee in 1974.[34] In other words, the House of Lords remains master of its own procedures, and Government whipping is not used to overturn the recommendations of the Procedure Committee.

The Groups on the Working of the House

The Procedure Committee considers specific proposals to reform the House's procedures; but it does not have the time to stand back and examine the working of the House as a whole. As has been noted, informal groups have been set up on two occasions, in 1971 and 1986, for exactly this purpose.

The 1971 group saw that although the House had expected to be radically reformed in the late 1960s, no change in its powers or composition was likely in 1971. Thus responsibility for improving the functions and procedures of the House remained with the House itself.[35]

---

[34] H.L. 58 of 1973–74—1st Report, Procedure Committee 1973–74.

[35] See, H.L. 227 of 1970–71—10th Report Procedure Committee, and H.L. 18 of 1971–72—1st Report Procedure Committee.

The group's two reports were debated on November 23, 1971, and the Procedure Committee, in the light of the reports and debate, made recommendations for limited changes. But the main thrust of the reports was against any revolutionary changes; the House did not want to become more like the Commons, but preferred to continue self-regulation.

The 1986 group once again supported stricter application of current procedures, rather than radical reform.

Thus the reports of both groups had a dual function. In part, they were educative, exposing the fragile basis on which the system works and making clear that its continuance depended on the restraint and responsibility of all its members. But they also made specific, albeit limited, suggestions in an attempt to overcome particular problems.

Practice and Procedure Committee

The House of Commons set up a Procedure Committee in 1976 to consider public business. About a month later, a similar Committee was appointed by the Lords with wider terms of reference, allowing consideration of private legislation. The Commons and Lords Committees were given power to meet concurrently, but they met together only once, possibly because of "political differences between the main parties about the future of the House of Lords,"[36] and partly because each committee concentrated on matters relating to their respective House.

The Lords committee recommended reforms of the legislative procedure of the House, whereby permanent subject committees akin to the Commons special standing committees would take evidence on bills, beginning work while the bills were still in the Commons. But 1977, when the Report was produced, was a time when difficulties between the Lords and the then Government were at their height, and in the light of an equivocal response in the debate, and the understandable lack of enthusiasm by the civil service, no action was taken. Later, one committee, the Science and Technology Committee (see pages 492–493) was established which reflected the Practice and Procedure Committee's proposals for specialist subject committees, but this was not concerned with the passage of legislation.

Business of the House

Activity

In recent years the House has seen an increase in attendance, the number of sitting days, the average length of each sitting, Monday and Friday sittings, and late sittings:

---

[36] *The Table* Vol. XLVII, p. 17.

Sittings of the House
(By Calendar Year)

	1979	1980	1981	1982	1983	1984	1985	1986	1987	1988
Sitting days	101	159	151	151	123	149	152	159	116	158
Hours	572	1,019	960	973	798	1,084	1,038	1,160	793	1,113
Average Length of Sitting (hrs./mins.)	5.40	6.25	6.21	6.27	6.29	7.16	6.50	7.18	6.50	7.03
Average Daily Attendance	289	290	289	286	303	323	318	317	332	329
Monday Sittings	14	31	28	32	25	31	33	32	26	34
Friday Sittings	1	13	11	9	6	11	11	15	2	13
Late Sittings (after 10.00 pm)	17	60	52	46	45	83	57	84	66	53

The increase is yet more marked in a comparison of sessions since the 1940s:

	1945 /46	1950 /51	1955 /56	1960 /61	1964 /65	1970 /71	1975 /76	1980 /81	1985 /86
Sitting days	157	96	136	125	124	153	155	143	165
Hours	450	292	484	599	593	966	969	920	1,213
Average Length of Sitting (hrs./mins.)	2.52	3.03	3.34	4.48	4.47	6.19	6.15	6.43	7.21
Attendance	N/A	86	104	142	194	265	275	296	317

A generation ago the House sat three days a week and 6 p.m. was referred to as "this late hour." Today it sits four or five days a week, with an average rising time late each evening, except on Fridays. The Lords at present sit longer than any other European legislative Chamber except the Commons.

On what does the House spend this increased time? The table on the next page provides the figures.

From this it appears that about half of the time of the House is spent on legislation, a fifth on debates and a twentieth on starred questions and unstarred questions. Other business which occupies a significant amount of time includes debates on select committee reports, statements and delegated legislation (mostly on affirmative instruments).

The figures disclose no large variance between Labour and Conservative administrations; the general pattern is only disturbed in the election year of 1979, when in the first part of the year the Government was preparing for an election, and in the second part the new administration had not prepared its legislation. Nevertheless, there exists a trend towards spending more time on legislation. On average in 1979–83, the House devoted 30 per cent. of its time to debates and unstarred questions. This figure fell to 23 per cent. in 1984–88. The proportion of time devoted to legislation rose from 47 per cent. in 1979–83 to 55 per cent. in 1984–88.

Questions

A main function of the House of Lords is to scrutinise the activities of the

Time Spent on Business of the House by Percentage

	1979	1980	1981	1982	1983	1984	1985	1986	1987	1988
					Calendar Year					
Starred questions	5.7	5.5	5.3	5.8	6.0	5.8	5.7	5.7	5.6	5.7
General debates	32.1	16.3	17.2	19.8	25.0	16.2	20.7	14.6	20.8	14.7
Debates on EC reports	5.6	2.6	4.7	2.7	3.8	3.3	2.2	2.8	1.5	1.7
Debates on S&T reports	0.0	0.2	1.0	0.3	0.8	0.6	0.4	0.5	1.1	0.8
Ministerial Statements	4.4	3.0	2.0	2.9	3.8	3.5	4.2	3.9	2.9	1.9
Public bills	28.8	56.8	55.6	51.5	42.0	55.8	52.1	58.3	51.4	60.9
i) Lords bills	15.1	8.9	24.6	19.5	25.5	13.0	16.5	17.8	27.6	9.9
Commons bills	13.7	47.9	31.0	32.0	16.5	42.8	35.6	40.5	23.8	51.0
ii) Government bills	21.2	53.0	48.7	43.9	36.6	48.9	45.7	54.6	47.6	59.2
Private members' bills	7.6	3.8	6.8	7.6	5.4	6.9	6.3	3.7	3.8	1.7
Private legislation	0.9	0.6	0.2	1.1	0.5	0.2	0.2	0.8	1.2	0.4
Delegated legislation	5.2	4.3	4.2	4.6	5.7	3.8	5.3	3.5	5.8	3.7
Measures	0.0	0.1	0.0	0.0	0.0	0.0	0.0	0.1	0.0	0.1
Unstarred questions	12.6	5.4	6.2	7.7	8.5	7.0	5.4	5.4	5.1	5.3
Other (including formal and adjournments)	4.7	5.2	4.3	3.6	3.9	3.6	3.9	4.4	4.6	4.8

Note: These percentages are rounded.

executive. In practice, this forms part of all the functions of the House; when a bill is being considered, Ministers are questioned on the content and implementation of their policies. But there is one set of procedures specifically intended to allow for the scrutiny of the executive, namely questions; starred, unstarred, by written answer, and by private notice.

Starred Questions

Starred questions are so called because they are asterisked on the Order Paper. They are taken as the first business. They were first introduced in 1919, and were intended "for the purpose of information only," to distinguish them from questions giving rise to debate. At first they did not enjoy priority on the Order Paper, and as a consequence were not a success. They were revived in 1947, when it was agreed that three would be given priority after private business on Tuesdays and Wednesdays. In 1954 this was extended to any sitting day, and in 1959 the maximum was raised to four, with each Lord limited to two per day. The increase was justified on the ground that the previous arrangement sometimes prevented questions being tabled "of immediate interest but not of sufficient importance to justify a private notice question . . . while they are still topical."[37] In the same year they were given priority over private business.

Starred questions are addressed to the Government, not to specific Ministers as in the Commons: their purpose, as laid down by Standing Order 32, is to obtain information rather than to provide an opportunity for the expression of opinions, and they should not lead to debate. Any Peer can ask a supplementary question, beginning with the original questioner, but by convention they are taken in turn from different sides of the House. Such supplementaries are supposed to be short, not to be read, and to be phrased as questions not statements. All questions should be on matters within the Government's responsibility, but questions on matters domestic to the House can be tabled to the Leader of the House and the Chairman of Committees.

Starred questions "are a lively and popular part of the day's proceedings which draws a wide audience . . . [but cause] . . . more procedural disorder than any other business, and repeated but unavailing efforts have been made by the House and the Procedure Committee to remedy the situation."[38] They take longer than they used to; in 1959–60, the average length of Question Time was 10 minutes, with each question taking four minutes, and the percentage of the total sitting time devoted to starred questions was 3.8 per cent. By 1985–86 this had risen to 25 minutes, with each question taking 6.6 minutes, and 5.7 per cent. of the total sitting time. Some Peers ask many more questions that others. A few usually have their maximum down at any one time, and in a recent session, eight members asked over 30 per cent. of the total. To remedy this, the 1986 Group suggested that the number of questions any member can have tabled at any one time be reduced from three to two; this was agreed to.

Unstarred Questions (UQs)

Unstarred questions are questions with debate. They are always taken as

[37] H.L. 36 of 1958–59, para. 1.
[38] H.L. 9 of 1987–88, paras. 43–44.

the last business of the day, and are comparable with adjournment debates in the Commons, with the major difference that they have no time limit. The member asks the question in the form of a speech, but he has no right of reply: a debate follows and the ministerial reply is given at the end. UQs originated in a device called "Their Lordships' conversations" whereby there could be debate without a motion being formally moved. Since 1919, the term "unstarred question" has developed to distinguish them from starred questions. In 1966 it was agreed that they come last; in 1969, that no second UQ should be taken after eight o'clock; and in 1970, that no-one should speak after the ministerial reply.

There has been a great increase in the use of unstarred questions since the advent of life Peers. In 1959–60, the first session after the passage of the Life Peerage Act 1958, there were only 12 unstarred questions, of which five were asked by what was no more than a handful of life Peers; in 1985–86, there were 44, of which 24 were asked by life Peers.

Today they are a popular procedure, in part because they provide a means whereby any back-bencher can initiate a debate:

Unstarred Questions

	76-7	77-8	78-9	79-80	80-1	81-2	82-3	83-4	84-5	85-6	86-7	87-8
No. of UQs	36	46	23	68	31	50	36	60	45	44	24	51
Percentage of time	9.0	8.9	9.4	8.0	4.7	7.8	9.0	7.1	6.5	5.1	4.8	5.3

Thus the proportion of time of the House given to UQs has been reduced in recent years. This results from the legislative demands made on the House rather than from any lack of popularity. The usual channels sometimes try to discourage UQs, especially towards the end of a busy session, but the UQs debated in the second-half of the exceptionally hard-pressed 1985–86 session show that they are not always successful: (see next page).

The list also shows the wide diversity of subject-matter, from issues of prime importance—such as South Africa, or full United Kingdom participation in the EMS—to more esoteric matters such as the use of gallium arsenide in electronic components. Such diversity dictates the differences in the number of participants, duration and number of interventions. Although logic might suggest that some of these issues would have been more appropriately debated on motions, the fact that the procedure is available for anyone to use accounts for its continuing popularity.

Questions for Written Answer (QWAs)

Questions for written answer are placed on the Order Paper. The ministerial replies, normally given within a fortnight, are sent to the questioner and printed in Hansard. There is no limit on the number of such questions which may be tabled.

Unstarred Questions — Second half of Session 1985-86

Date	Topic	Mover	Length of Debate hrs mins	Start Time	Finish Time	No. of Speakers	No. of Interventions
26 Mar 1986	The Multi-Handicapped: Welfare Provisions	L. Stallard	2 00	6.54	8.54	9	1
7 Apr 1986	Licensing Laws in England and Wales	V. Montgomery of Alamein	1 36	5.43	7.19	11	2
9 Apr 1986	The Media & The Law	L. Paget of Northampton	1 40	8.38	10.18	5	3
10 Apr 1986	Prisoners: Aftercare	E. Longford	1 41	8.18	9.59	7	—
16 Apr 1986	Sizewell Power Stations	E. Halsbury	1 07	7.31	8.38	7	1
23 Apr 1986	Forestry Commission	L. Taylor of Gryfe	2 19	8.24	10.43	12	2
30 Apr 1986	South Africa	L. St John of Bletso	2 28	9.00	11.28	12	2
2 May 1986	Gallium Arsenide	L. Birdwood	0 42	3.09	3.51	4	2
6 May 1986	Gliding: Control of Air Space	E. Kinnoull	0 46	9.24	10.10	3	5
12 May 1986	Copyright Material: Protection	V. Blakenham	1 27	5.55	7.22	8	—
14 May 1986	Hong Kong: Vietnamese Refugees	L. Chitnis	0 44	10.55	11.39	4	—
16 May 1986	Helsinki Agreement: East-West Contacts	L. Bethell	0 49	2.53	3.42	4	—
21 May 1986	Bed & Breakfast payments: 1985 Regulations	L. Banks	0 48	7.55	8.43	6	—
6 Jun 1986	European Monetary System: U.K. Participation	L. Soames	1 54	2.23	4.17	8	6
11 Jun 1986	Royal Observatory, Herstmonceux	E. De La Warr	0 45	11.00	11.45	4	1
25 Jun 1986	Marine Pilotage	L. Shackleton	2 11	9.31	11.42	9	6
11 Jly 1986	N. Ireland: Internal Problems	M. Salisbury	0 47	4.40	5.27	3	—
30 Jly 1986	Commonwealth Eminent Persons Group	L. Hatch of Lusby	2 02	10.25	12.27am	10	4
29 Oct 1986	Developing Countries: Health	B. Lockwood	1 43	5.40	7.23	8	4
4 Nov 1986	Parole	E. Longford	2 41	5.24	8.05	8	7
5 Nov 1986	Domestic Heating Standards	L. Ezra	1 21	6.10	7.31	5	2
6 Nov 1986	European Court: Nationalisation Judgment	L. Harris of High Cross	1 49	3.31	6.03	8	5
6 Nov 1986	Personal Information: Access	B. Ewart-Biggs	1 22	6.03	7.25	6	—

The number of QWAs has risen in recent years:

Session	No.
1970-71	283
1971-72	315
1972-73	281
1973-74	92
1974	171
1974-75	350
1975-76	517
1976-77	380
1977-78	544
1978-79	432
1979-80	1,277
1980-81	857
1981-82	1,098
1982-83	619
1983-84	1,350
1984-85	1,142
1985-86	1,182
1986-87	622
1987-88	1,405

Thus the average has risen from 448 in the 1975–78 sessions of normal length to 1,227 in the last three normal sessions. Certain members ask many more QWAs than average; for example, on February 16, 1987 there were 58 QWAs tabled, of which 16 were by one member, and nine by another. QWAs are also used as "planted questions," a means whereby the Government can give information to Parliament and the public without recourse to a ministerial statement. On matters where it is judged that the Lords as well as the Commons would be interested, a planted question is arranged for both Houses.

Private Notice Questions (PNQs)

Oral questions asked by a Lord on a matter of urgency without being on the order paper are known as private notice questions. They have to be submitted to the Leader of the House by noon: the decision whether the question is of such urgency to justify immediate reply rests, in the first place, with the Leader, and ultimately with the general sense of the House. In practice, the House has consistently upheld the Leader's preliminary decision.[39] They have always been a relatively rare proceeding, and have become more so since the decision in November 1983 to discontinue the practice of repeating Commons PNQs in the Lords by an arranged PNQ, and instead to give the reply in the form of a statement.

As a result, the numbers of PNQs have dwindled to a trickle:

1977-8	1978-9	1979-80	1980-1	1981-2	1982-3	1983-4	1984-5	1985-6	1986-7	1987-8
5	7	16	2	6	2	1	0	2	1	3

[39] H.L.Deb. Vol. 481, col. 263 (October 21, 1986), and Vol. 272, col. 1148 (February 17, 1966).

There is no record kept of the proportion of PNQs refused, but in session 1985–86, 14 PNQs were submitted, and only two were allowed.[40]

Statements

Ministerial statements are not of primary importance in the Lords, as most Ministers sit in the Commons, and the majority of statements made in the Lords repeat what has already been said in the Commons.

In their modern form of explanations made by Ministers on behalf of the Government regarding their domestic and foreign policy, they originated in the First World War, as a useful procedure to inform Parliament about the state of the war and Government policy.

There was some increase in the number of statements during the 1980s (see page 479).

The decision whether a Commons statement is repeated is taken after consultation through the "usual channels." The Government Whips' Office asks the Opposition Whips, who in turn ask the relevant Opposition spokesman, whether or not a statement should be repeated. Given this procedure, it is not surprising that statements are frequently repeated. In the 1986 questionnaire, Lords expressed "deep dissatisfaction" about the "present arrangements for statements, on the grounds that they interrupt the main business; cause unforeseen delays in the daily timetable; are rarely reported in the Press, and despite the wording of the standing order, often degenerate into mini-debates, without adequate preparation."[41]

The result of such criticism was that the Procedure Committee recommended that the decision whether to repeat a statement should depend on a specific criterion: statements would be repeated only if, after consultation with the usual channels, the Leader considered that they were on a matter of national importance. It was stressed that this should be strictly interpreted.[42] The evidence of session 1987–88 suggests that the recommendation of the Procedure Committee has had a significant effect on the number of statements.

There is also a procedure, of recent invention, whereby statements can be printed in Hansard, by leave, without oral delivery.[43]

Debates

In principle, one day a week, usually a Wednesday, is reserved for general debate. Motions can be, and are, debated on other days, but they do not take precedence. In the period up to the Whitsun recess, one Wednesday a month is set aside for two short debates initiated by back-benchers and chosen by ballot, each of two-and-a-half hours' duration. At the start of each debate, the Chief Whip gives guidelines for the length of each speech in the debate. The success of the two-and-a-half-hour balloted debates has led to other debates being limited voluntarily to two-and-a-half or five hours.

Debates usually take place on a "motion for papers," a procedure whereby the Government is asked to lay before the House papers on the subject under discussion. This gives the mover the right of reply at the end of the

---

[40] H.L.Deb. Vol. 480, cols. 1093–1094 (October 17, 1986).
[41] H.L. 9 of 1986–87, paras. 72–77.
[42] 1st Report, Procedure Committee 1987–88.
[43] Three in 1983–84, three in 1984–85, seven in 1985–86 and six in 1986–87.

Statements

	1980-81	1981-82	1982-83	1983-84	1984-85	1985-86	1986-87	1987-88
Sitting days	143	147	94	178	151	165	84	192
No. of statements	51	59	49	142	107	112	41	62
No. of statements in Commons	78	107	60	132	105	109	53	98
No. of PNQs in Commons	8	9	7	48	26	43	19	39
Time on statements	c.21h	24h 10m	20h 02m	51h 43m	43h 23m	47h 28m	16h 56m	29h 28m
% of time of House on statements	2.5%	2.3%	3.2%	4.0%	4.2%	3.9%	2.9%	1.9%
Average per day	0.3	0.4	0.5	0.8	0.7	0.6	0.5	0.3

debate, when he asks leave of the House to withdraw his motion. The wording of motions for papers ought not to express an opinion, and should introduce the subject of the debate without provocative or tendentious language. A recent attempt was made to allow members to table motions worded in a controversial or politically charged fashion, in order to advertise the thrust of the debate and to attract greater interest and participation. But the House rejected the proposal.[44] Debates also take place on a motion to "take note," which is the appropriate procedure when the Government invites the House to debate a White or Green Paper, or for debates on select committee reports. There were six such examples in 1987–88:

Take Note Motions

			Hrs.	Mins.
4.11.87	Report on Working of the House	V. Whitelaw	4	40
17.2.88	Report of Nature Conservancy Council	E. Cranbrook	5	07
25.3.88	Report of Committee on Infant Life (Preservation) Bill	L. Brightman	3	52
20.5.88	Electricity Privatisation	V. Davidson	3	11
12.7.88	Defence Estimates	L. Trefgarne	4	40
29.7.88	Reform of Official Secrets Act	E. Ferrers	4	55

Unlike the practice in the House of Commons, the opinion of the House on the subject of a debate is usually expressed in the content of the speeches, rather than by a division. However, if a Lord wishes to invite the House to take a substantive decision, he can put down his motion in the form of a resolution. This is also sometimes done by the Government in seeking approval for a policy. Examples of this in 1985–86 were a debate on a motion by the Leader of the House to approve the Anglo-Irish agreement, which lasted six-and-a-half hours, and one tabled by the Leader of the Opposition calling on the Government to withdraw and amend an affirmative instrument on citizenship rights for Hong Kong ethnic minorities.[44a]

Legislation

Public Bills

Public bills may be introduced and proceeded with in the Lords without any restriction. Unlike the procedure in the Commons, this applies both to Government and private members. Although public bills may be initiated in either House, in practice the majority of Government bills begin in the Commons. This is partly because it is in that House that the responsible departmental Minister sits, and partly because the Government usually decides to start in the Commons bills which will arouse party political controversy. Furthermore, supply bills and bills which will be either certified as money bills, or have a large financial content, also start in the Commons (see pages 227 and 247). Nevertheless, recently it has been customary to introduce a few substantial bills into the Lords as first House, in order to make good use of parliamentary time and to avoid over-burdening the Lords late in the session.

---

[44] H.L.Deb. Vol. 471, cols. 410–417 (February 17, 1986).
[44a] H.L.Deb. Vol. 468, cols. 797–887, (November 26, 1985); H.L.Deb, Vol. 474, cols. 1392–438 (May 16, 1986).

Amendments to Bills introduced into the Lords

Session		Amendments made
1984-85	Administration of Justice	50
	Food and Environment Protection	131
	Insolvency	355
	Prosecution of Offences	73
1985-86	Animals (Scientific Procedures)	26
	Education	80
	Legal Aid (Scotland)	33
	Sex Discrimination	16
	Shops (failed in Commons on Second Reading)	6
	Salmon	81
1986-87 (short session)	Consumer Protection	66
	Criminal Justice (Scotland)	90
	Family Law Reform	31
	Fire Safety and Safety of Places of Sport	26
	Pilotage	103
	Debtors (Scotland)	72
1987-88 (long session)	Copyright Designs and Patents	561
	Criminal Justice	261
	Legal Aid	85
	Merchant Shipping	93

All public bills introduced into the Lords—whether from the Commons or as Lords bills—follow the same procedure. They are read a first time and ordered to be printed. The subsequent stages are normally all taken on the Floor of the House; second reading, committee, report and third reading. Unless Standing Order No. 44 is suspended, which happens at times of great time pressure, they are separated by stated minimum intervals unless special notice is given on the order paper:

(a) two weekends between introduction and second reading;

(b) fourteen days between second reading and the start of the committee stage;

(c) on all bills of considerable length and complexity, fourteen days between the end of the committee stage and report;

(d) three sitting days between the end of the report stage and third reading; and

(e) where possible, reasonable notice is given for the consideration of Commons amendments.

Over the last 20 years there has not been a significant increase in the number of bills considered. The table on page 482 below shows that the exception is Lords' private members' bills, which rose from an average in 1965–66 of 11 to over 20 in the early 1980s. But there has been a distinct decline in the late 1980s (see page 482).

However, the number of amendments made has increased from an average per session of 511 under the 1964–65 Labour administration to 788 per session from 1970–74, 645 per session from 1974–79, and 1,061 per session in 1979–86.[45] It is easy to pin too much on such statistics (some amendments are

---

[45] These averages ignore the three short sessions 1973–74, 1974 and 1982–83.

Public Bills in the House of Lords

Sessions

	1970-71	1971-72	1972-73	1973-74	1974	1974-75	1975-76	1976-77	1977-78	1978-79	1979-80	1980-81	1981-82	1982-83	1983-84	1984-85	1985-86	1986-87	1987-88
Introduced into Lords																			
Government	11	15	13	7	13	20	27	11	22	9	11	12	10	11	14	12	16	14	9
Consolidation	12	9	7	5	5	17	13	8	12	16	17	13	7	8	14	11	5	2	5
Private Members'																			
Introduced	14	16	12	10	13	12	11	21	8	13	22	23	25	21	19	17	13	10	7
Receiving R.A.	3	5	2	0	2	0	2	1	3	1	2	5	2	2	2	4	4	4	2
From the Commons																			
Government	38	24	17	11	15	30	23	15	29	23	46	31	29	28	32	31	29	22	35
Money/Supply	15	12	10	4	6	10	12	11	5	6	9	8	7	5	8	8	7	6	9
Private Members	10	11	13	0	6	9	14	10	8	3	10	10	8	10	11	17	17	12	12
From both Houses																			
Royal Assent	89	76	72	15	42	83	88	53	50	47	81	71	56	51	73	73	71	55	70

important, others are minor), but the trends they disclose are supported by the views of members of the House[46] and by academic research[47] that the House has more impact on legislation and that the Government uses the House to amend legislation more than in the past.

There is also the evidence of an increase in the amount of time spent on legislation, both absolutely and in proportion to debate:

Various Types of Business
(by percentages)

	1976 -77	1977 -78	1978 -79	1979 -80	1980 -81	1981 -82	1982 -83	1983 -84	1984 -85	1985 -86	1986 -87	1987 -88
General debates	30.5	19.4	32.6	19.3	16.3	20.1	23.4	17.6	20.0	15.9	24.3	14.0
Debates on committee reports	4.5	4.1	3.7	4.0	4.3	3.4	3.7	4.2	2.8	2.9	3.5	2.4
Unstarred questions	9.0	8.9	9.4	8.0	4.7	7.8	9.0	7.1	6.5	5.1	4.8	5.3
Public bills	39.7	49.5	30.5	49.2	58.1	50.9	46.2	52.9	50.8	57.9	48.2	60.3
Private bills	0.2	0.4	1.6	0.6	0.1	1.0	0.7	0.2	0.3	0.5	1.4	0.8

Of this time, approximately a fifth is taken up with second reading, nearly a half on the committee stage, 22.5 per cent. on report, 7 per cent. on third reading, and a further 3 per cent. on proceedings after third reading, especially consideration of Commons amendments or reasons (see page 484).

The increase in time spent on legislation is very striking, when compared with ten years ago. So, too, is the very large proportion of the time of the House spent in committee of the whole House, with the second reading and report stages taking together less than half of the time spent in committee.

No mention is made of first reading, as normally it is taken formally; debates or divisions on first reading are so rare as to be negligible. Second reading gives the House the opportunity to debate the main principles of the bill. The Lords do not have the guillotine, and there is no procedural method of curtailing debate. But in practice, much legislation is discussed very briefly, where it is thought to be uncontentious or routine. The second reading debate provides a good indication of the level of interest[48] in, and the time required for discussion of the bill. It is an established convention that the Lords do not divide on the second reading of a Government bill, especially if it was first introduced in the Commons or is mandated. This unwritten rule does not extend to private members' bills.

---

[46] See H.L. 9 of 1987–88, para. 2 end.

[47] J. A. G. Griffith, *Parliamentary Scrutiny of Government Bills* (1974), and articles by G. Drewry and I. Burton in *Parliamentary Affairs* 1974–86.

[48] Examples of second readings of bills which have taken more than one day:

1963 Apr 23/24	2a	London Government
1965 Jly 19/20	2a	Murder (Abol. of Death Penalty) [HL]
1971 Apr 5/6	2a	Industrial Relations
1972 Jly 25/26	2a	European Communities
1972 Jly 31 Aug 1/2	2a	Local Government
1974 Jly 16/17	2a	Trade Unions and Labour Relations
1978 Mar 14/15	2a	Scotland
1988 Apr 18/19	2a	Education Reform

The Third Reading of the Education Reform Bill 1988 also took two days (July 7/8)

Time spent on Stages of public bills in the House of Lords: session 1984-5 & 1985-6

	2a Time hrs mins	%	C.W.H. Time hrs mins	%	REPORT Time hrs mins	%	3a Time hrs mins	%	POST 3a Time hrs mins	%	Total time taken on all stages in H.L. hrs mins
SESSION 1984-5											
All Public bills	118 00	23	231 52	45	115 19	22	37 32	7	17 41	3	520 24
Govt bills	84 54	18½	216 01	47	107 43	23½	33 27	7	17 41	4	459 46
PM bills	33 06	54½	15 51	26	7 36	12½	4 05	7	0 00	-	60 38
HC bills	77 51	21½	167 45	46	84 11	23	26 54	7½	6 26	2	363 07
HL bills	40 09	25	64 07	41	31 08	20	10 38	7	11 15	7	157 17
SESSION 1985-6											
All Public bills	124 20	18	349 12	50	164 44	23	47 33	7	16 49	2	702 38
Govt bills	97 08	15	333 10	51	162 28	25	44 58	7	16 44	2	654 28
PM bills	27 12	57	16 02	33	2 16	5	2 35	5	0 05	-	48 10
HC bills	69 38	15	244 15	51	124 14	26	32 06	7	6 34	1	476 47
HL bills	54 21	24	104 57	46	40 30	18	15 27	7	10 15	5	225 51

Notes: 2a = second reading.

C.W.H. = Committee of Whole House.

3a = third reading, including amendments and on 'bill do now pass'.

POST 3a = consideration of Commons' reasons and amendments.

% = time taken at particular stage as percentage of total time on all stages in the Lords.

The Committee stage is also uncurtailed. There is no selection of amendments and all amendments tabled may be debated. In an attempt to avoid the repetition of arguments on different amendments, there are informal and non-binding groupings of amendments, which is carried out by the Government Whips' Office, acting on the suggestions of the Government department. These groupings are normally discussed with the Opposition spokesmen and if possible with other members concerned. However, as the proposed groupings are based on the marshalled list of amendments, which is usually printed only on the morning of the debate, there is little time for effective consultation with all concerned. Amendments to each clause or schedule are moved, and then each clause or schedule is agreed to on question by the House; this provides an opportunity for discussion of each provision. Manuscript amendments, that is amendments which have not been printed and circulated beforehand, are in order at the committee and report stages, but not on third reading. It is usual for public bills to be considered in committee of the whole House, rather than in standing committees as in the Commons. As shown in the Table, this occupies half of the total time taken on legislation, and is therefore the single procedure on which the House spends most time. Despite this, public bill committees, which take place off the floor of the House, are only used very exceptionally.[49]

The report stage takes place if amendments have been made in committee and otherwise by agreement when desired. Unlike in committee where members can speak as often as they like, at this stage only one speech is allowed on each amendment, except for the mover. At this stage, the Government often comes forward with amendments to meet points made in committee.

Third reading is sometimes a formality, but debate may take place on the form of the bill as it leaves the House. But this is not an opportunity to repeat the second reading debate or discuss changes which have already been defeated. Amendments are frequently moved at this stage to clarify uncertainties, improve drafting, and allow the Government to fulfil undertakings. Issues already debated and decided upon should not be reopened. Despite these limitations, amendments at third reading are common, and attempts to curtail or abolish them have not succeeded. Where amendments are tabled at third reading, the general debate takes place on the motion "That the bill do now pass".

Amendments on third Reading to Government Bills 1983-86

	1983-84	*1984-85*	*1985-86*
Government bills from H.C.	328 (13)	111 (8)	175 (9)
Government bills in H.L.	35 (5)	71 (10)	32 (9)

(Figures in brackets give the number of amendments agreed to which were not inspired by the Government.)

[49] 1967–68 Gaming Bill
1968–69 Development of Tourism Bill
1970–71 Highways Bill
1970–71 Civil Aviation Bill
1974–75 Lotteries Bill
1986–87 Pilotage Bill

Select Committees on Public Bills

Proceedings on the Abortion and Sexual Offences Bills in the 1960s suggested that a committee of the whole House was not the best procedure for producing a workable legislative draft on sensitive issues. Instead, bills have been committed to select committees, which have been able to hear expert evidence, and to have the assistance of specialist advisers and parliamentary draftsmen. If the bill proceeds, it will be re-committed to a committee of the whole House and then follow the usual course of a public bill. The list from 1970 to 1989 is as follows:

Year	Bill	Chairman	Outcome
1972-73	Anti-discrimination (No. 2)	B. Seear	Taken up by Commons committee and by Government: eventually the Government-sponsored Sexual Discrimination Act 1975 was the outcome.
1974-75	Lotteries		
1975-76	Licensing (Scotland)		
1976	Hare Coursing	L. Trevelyan	Killed the bill.
1977-78	Bill of Rights	L. Allen of Abbeydale	Divided report: bill reported as amended which has subsequently three times passed the Lords, but not the Commons.
1978	Foreign Boycotts	L. Redcliffe-Maud	Killed the bill.
1979-80	Laboratory Animals Protection	L. Ashby	Produced amended bill: subsequently passed into law.
1983-84	Parochial and Small Charities	L. Brightman	Produced revised bills and report: subsequently passed into law as Commons private members' bill.
1986-87	Infant Life (Preservation)	L. Brightman	See below.

The above list suggests that this procedure has become a recognised procedure, in particular for private members' bills.

The only Government bill to have been committed to a select committee was the Hare Coursing Bill. This bill was a mandated Government bill which first reached the Lords in session 1974–75, but failed to progress after second reading. In the subsequent session, it was committed to a select committee proposed by the Opposition, which was instructed to report the bill within four months. In their report, the committee concluded that "the bill was not a suitable instrument for reducing the suffering of hares" and that the "bill should not proceed, but that action should be taken by those concerned to examine further current coursing practice and legislation for the protection of wild animals."[50] No further action was taken on the bill, which was not reintroduced in the following session.

The select committee procedure is often resorted to where continued proceedings on the floor of the House would meet with intractable opposition. The Infant Life (Preservation) Bill was introduced by the Bishop of Birmingham in session 1986–87. Proceedings on this bill were unusual in a number of ways. First, it was introduced by a bishop. Secondly, the House divided on second reading, for the only time in that session. Thirdly, because of the complex and controversial nature of the subject, the bill was committed to a select committee. The committee had not reached a conclusion when the session ended, so the bill was lost. However, the bill was reintroduced in session 1987–88, not by the bishop, who had retired, but by Lord Houghton of Sowerby, known to be hostile to the bill but a member of the committee who wished to see its work finished. The new bill was committed to a new select committee, which carried on where the committee of the previous session had left off. The committee reported, in February 1988, against allowing the bill to proceed, and instead made its own recommendations about the maximum gestational age for abortion.

Private Members' Bills

Members of the Lords have an unrestricted right to introduce private members' bills, and provided they begin in the earlier part of the session, time is always found for their consideration. Time is thus more readily available than in the Commons. The table on page 482 shows that the average number of such bills has risen considerably in recent years, although the number receiving Royal Assent has remained low.

In the last decade an average of 18 bills were introduced each year, but only two or three a year received Royal Assent. Many of those introduced in the Lords passed that House but failed to pass the Commons, for reasons of time[51] or policy. But the figures alone do not tell the whole story. The lack of constituency pressures makes it easier for Lords to raise controversial subjects. They can thus raise public discussion of social issues in such a way that the Commons and the Government may take an interest and successful legislation may follow. This was true of abortion and homosexuality in the 1960s,[52] and of sexual discrimination in the 1970s. In the two former cases, bills were introduced in successive sessions in the Lords, and long hours were spent in deliberation on the requisite provisions. Finally, the bills were sent to the Commons where, in a succeeding session, a private member successful in the ballot began them anew after further revision. The select committee considering the Anti-Discrimination (No. 2) Bill in 1972–73 gave rise to sufficient public interest to ensure that first back-benchers in the

---

[50] L.J. 209, p. 369.

[51] The effect of Commons S.O. No. 13 is such that no Lords' private members' bill can achieve Royal Assent, unless it is given a second reading on the nod. The Lords have no comparable restrictive rules, and consequently Commons' Private Members' Bills received late in the session can be agreed and proceed to Royal Assent.

[52] See *Parliamentary Affairs* XIX (1966), J. R. Vincent "The House of Lords."

Commons and subsequently the Government took up the issue—the Sex Discrimination Act 1975 was the result.

In the short session 1986–87, 10 private members' bills were introduced into the Lords. One of these received no more than a first reading, and a further two were debated on second reading, but proceeded no further: they were introduced by Opposition Peers as occasions for debate, but had no prospect of becoming law.

Two bills were passed by the Lords, but lost in the Commons. The first was the Local Government Act 1986 (Amendment) Bill introduced by Lord Halsbury, a cross-bencher, which aimed to prevent local authorities from promoting homosexuality. Neither the Government nor the Opposition in the Lords supported it, but it had considerable support in the House, and in the succeeding session a Government public bill—Local Government—was amended in the Commons by a private Member to include a clause with a similar objective, which was passed into law. The Patents (Amendment) Bill was introduced by a Labour back-bencher, Lord Northfield, to improve patent protection for pharmaceutical products. The bill was supported by the Government, and opposed by the Opposition front bench, passed the Lords but failed in the Commons.

Four bills were passed by both Houses and received Royal Assent in 1986–87. Three had all party support: the Animals (Scotland) Bill, introduced by Lord Selkirk, Conservative implemented recommendations of the Scottish Law Commission; the Billiards (Abolition of Restrictions) Bill, introduced by a cross-bencher Lord Allen of Abbeydale, abolished the licensing of billiards halls.

The Gaming (Amendment) Bill, introduced by Lord Harris of Greenwich, SDP extended casino opening hours; the Licensing (Restaurant Meals) Bill, introduced by the Conservative Lord Montgomery of Alamein, permitted restaurants to serve drinks with meals outside licensing hours. The Government was initially against it, but was satisfied by amendments made in committee.

Delegated Legislation

The powers of the House of Lords over delegated legislation were not curtailed by the Parliament Acts. In 1911 the importance of delegated legislation was very much less than it is today and there is no evidence that consideration was given to the matter. In 1947–49, when the amending Parliament Bill was under consideration, although the matter was considered, it was not thought necessary to extend the ambit of the 1911 Act. In theory, the increase in the importance of subordinate legislation has therefore broadened the capacity of the Lords to obstruct the wishes of the Government majority in the Commons. But conflict between the Houses on this subject has been exceptional, the reason being that the Lords have used their powers with circumspection. As (save for a few antique exceptions) delegated legislation cannot be amended in Parliament, rejection by the Lords is a weapon of last resort, which they have been most unwilling to use. In the period 1950–68, nine affirmative instruments[53] were debated and voted upon, but in no case was a motion to reject carried. In 1968, the Lords rejected the Southern Rhodesia (United Nations Sanctions) Order 1968, but

---

[53] An instrument which cannot come into force (or remain in force) unless approved by resolution of each House.

they subsequently agreed to a No. 2 Order.[54] Since then there have been 22 divisions on motions to approve affirmative instruments, but on no occasion has such a motion been carried. But on two occasions, points raised in debate resulted in a decision by the Government to withdraw and amend an order.[55] In the same period, 16 negative instruments[55a] were prayed against, but none of the prayers was carried on division.

In recent years, other methods of opposing delegated legislation have been used, including motions deprecating certain provisions of an instrument, which if carried do not annul.[56] More effectively motions calling on the Government to amend an order in specific ways may be moved, which if carried have had the effect of forcing the Government to withdraw the order and amend it.[57] Another method of opposition has been a dilatory motion, which if carried has prevented the Government from proceeding with the order.[58] Negative instruments have been subject to a motion to amend, instead of the full annulment motion. In these ways the House has used its powers of annulment as a backstop to force the Government of the day to pay attention to views expressed on subordinate legislation.

Private Bills

Private bills are promoted by bodies outside Parliament and are concerned with private interests. It is "legislation of a special kind for conferring particular powers or benefits on any person or body of persons . . . in excess of or in conflict with the general law."[59] They are not to be confused with private members' bills, which are public bills introduced by private Members of either House, and which, if enacted, are of general application. The promoters are often local authorities seeking special powers not available in the general law of the land. The powers of the House of Lords in relation to private legislation are not limited by the Parliament Acts and are identical with those of the Commons.

The numbers of private bills allocated to each House are equal, but bills of largely financial character and bills promoted by nationalised industries are usually introduced into the Commons. In session 1986–87, a total of 22 private bills and two marriage enabling personal bills (which always start in the Lords) were introduced into Parliament, and into the Lords as first House came 12 bills.

The procedure for considering private bills in the two Houses is similar. In the Lords, the stages which are taken on the floor of the House, namely second and third reading, are taken immediately after starred questions, unless they are to be debated. When debate is expected they are usually taken at the end of business. They are subject to careful scrutiny by the Chairman of Committees and his Counsel in unopposed bill committees.

---

[54] See J. P. Morgan, *The House of Lords and the Labour Government 1964–1970* (1975) Chap. 5.

[55] International Organisation (Immunities and Privileges of Universal Postal Union) Order in Council 1950, and the Food Hygiene (Market Sales and Delivery Vehicles) Order 1966.

[55a] An instrument which may be annulled by resolution of either House.

[56] *e.g.* December 5, 1983, on Equal Pay (Amendment) Regulations 1983.

[57] *e.g.* Town and Country Planning General Development (Amendment) Order 1977; Conservation of Wild Creatures and Wild Plants (Others) Order 1977; Income Support (General) Amendment No. 4 Regulations 1988.

[58] Road Traffic (Seat Belts) (Northern Ireland) Order 1978.

[59] *May* p. 891.

Objectors to a private bill's provision may petition the House for relief. If these objections remain unresolved, the bill is referred to a select committee which exercises a quasi-judicial function. Unlike public bills, the giving of a second reading to a private bill does not imply approval of the principle of the bill, and its effect is simply to refer the bill to an appropriate committee; debate on merit takes place on the floor of the House at second or third reading, and bills are occasionally defeated at those stages.[60] In 1988, discussion of private bills on the floor of the House accounted for only 0.4 per cent. of its time.

A Joint Committee on Private Bill Procedure completed a two-year enquiry into the processes of private legislation in July 1988, and made numerous recommendations which have been debated in both Houses.[60a] No decisions have been taken on their recommendations at the date of writing. In evidence to the committee, the Chairman of Committees said "private bill procedure in the Lords works smoothly and expeditiously."[61]

Select Committees

The select committee activity in the Lords from 1945 until 1972 was mainly concerned with the administration and procedure of the House. Since then, select committees[62] have been set up in response to particular needs, in particular the United Kingdom's accession to the European Communities. But unlike the Commons, the Lords' committees were all established *ad hoc* rather than being the product of a systematic reform. Underlying their development has been the belief, expressed in the White Paper on Lords Reform of 1968, that "there may be scope for involving the Lords in specialist or Select Committees."

Select committees fall into three main categories. First, sessional subject committees, of which there are two: the European Communities, and Science and Technology, which are permanent, choose their own subjects, co-opt members to sub-committees, and produce reports which are debated on a regular basis. Secondly, *ad hoc* committees, on specialised subjects which require careful enquiry, on a matter of general public interest, or on a bill. Finally there are the traditional committees on domestic matters, which have continued to be set up since 1972 as required.

Sessional Committees

European Communities Committee

The entry of the United Kingdom into the European Economic Community on 1 January 1973 posed problems for the leadership in the Lords. The House voted by an overwhelming 451 to 58[63] to approve the Government White Paper on Accession to the EEC (later EC), but the bill made no mention of parliamentary scrutiny of European legislation.

---

[60] *e.g.* Swanage Yacht Haven Bill [H.L.], defeated on Third Reading H.L.Deb., Vol. 491, cols. 650–694 (December 15, 1987).

[60a] H.L.Deb., Vol. 507, cols. 1180–1212 (May 17, 1989); H.C.Deb., Vol. 151, cols. 474–548 (April 20, 1989).

[61] Report H.L. 97 of 1987–88, p. 185; H.C. 625.

[62] See G. Drewry (ed.) *The New Select Committees 1985* (1985), Chap. 2 by St. J. N. Bates on "Select Committees in the House of Lords."

[63] October 28, 1971, the largest division ever recorded in the Lords. The previous record had been in 1894.

The Government had conceded from the outset that there was a need to organise parliamentary scrutiny of EC legislation and indeed had suggested on second reading in the Commons that there should be a joint select committee to make recommendations on the required procedures. But it was only after the European Communities Bill had become law that each House appointed separate select committees to consider the requisite procedures. The Lords committee, under the Chairmanship of Lord Maybray-King, reported in July 1973 and described the operation of the European Community institutions, and the means adopted by other national parliaments to scrutinise draft European legislation. The committee's recommendations included the setting up of a select committee with wide terms of reference—including consideration of the merits of legislation (in contrast to the Commons), and the power to appoint sub-committees and co-opt other members. Two factors, one practical and the other political, caused a divergence in the work of the two Houses: the first was the ability of the Lords to devote time to take evidence and produce considered reports which examined merits; the second was the general acceptance of British membership of the Community in the Lords, which made it "easier for committees of Peers to reach dispassionate conclusions."[64] An attempt by the Government to narrow the terms of reference failed, and the committee was set up in 1974.[64a]

National parliaments, traditionally the place where laws are made, are not given a part in the Community legislative process. Legislation is initiated by the Commission, the European Parliament is consulted, and the final decision is made by the Council.[64b] There is, however, nothing in the EC Treaties to prevent a national parliament from taking steps to restore the balance, and both Houses of Parliament decided to enter the Community legislative process by adopting procedures to enable them to influence the Government before legislation was discussed in the Council. In so doing, they were less radical than the Danish Parliament, which decided immediately after accession to give the Market Relations Committee of the Folketing (the Danish Parliament) the power to mandate in advance Danish Ministers in their negotiations at the Council of Ministers. The Lords' system is one of specialist committee enquiry, directed to the Community initiatives proposed by the Commission. It is thus essentially pre-legislative. The Government has given an undertaking that, except in exceptional circumstances, it will not agree to a proposal in the Council before the scrutiny committees of the two Houses have completed their inquiries and, where appropriate, their reports have been debated. From the beginning the European Communities committee has sometimes made common cause with Whitehall against Brussels. Hence the Government can be in a position to use the reports during negotiations in the Council. Equally the committee's reports can support Commission proposals opposed by the Government.

The Committee's powers to appoint sub-committees and co-opt members give it great procedural flexibility: it can also work concurrently with the equivalent Commons committee but in practice there is little formal collab-

---

[64] See Procedure Committee Report H.C. 588 II of (1977–78), pp. 193–194.
[64a] First Report of the Procedure Committee; H.L. 58 of 1973–74.
[64b] See The House of Lords and the European Communities (1988), House of Lords Information Office.

oration. With its salaried chairman, total membership of 24 on the committee, and some 50 other members co-opted to sub-committees (often experts in the subjects under consideration), it has considerable manpower. It is aided by a staff of five clerks, two legal advisers, a specialist assistant and five secretaries, and it also has expert specialist advisers appointed *ad hoc*—part-timers who are experts in the subjects under enquiry. This permits a publication rate of over 20 reports a year, produced from between 100–200 meetings. Evidence is heard from Ministers and departmental officials, lobby groups such as the trade unions and the CBI, trade associations, Commission or Council officials, MEPs, academics, and other experts from home and abroad. Each report[65] is prepared by one of the sub-committees, but the final version is the report as approved by the select committee.

All the Lords' select committees have, in practice, the satisfaction of seeing that their reports are debated—unlike in the Commons. Some of the E.C. Committee's reports are for information only, but the majority are now made for debate, and its debates take a small but appreciable amount of time on the floor of the House. In practice, time is usually found for debate on the reports to suit the convenience of those concerned. A significant proportion (sometimes over half) of those taking part in the debates are members of the committees in question, which sometimes leads to the criticism that the debates are somewhat incestuous. Some committees have made efforts to broaden the scope of debate on their reports and have discouraged the participation of members, consequently enhancing the variety of contributions.

Government responses to the reports have been varied: most are complimentary; but some are opaque, either for fear of giving away the Government's negotiating position, or because the Government disagrees with the report. On exceptionally long and important reports, the Government sometimes issues White Papers in response, in addition to the oral reply in debate by the Minister.[66] The media often give more coverage to debates on reports than to the reports themselves: the growth in select committee activity in the two Houses and in the number of reports has meant that reports cannot rely on good press coverage.

Science and Technology Committee

The origins of the Science and Technology Committee lay in the report of the Practice and Procedure Committee in 1977, which suggested that there should be a number of select committees linked to specific policy areas, which would scrutinise bills and other proposals within the relevant areas.

When the proposal was debated, it met with a lukewarm reception, and the suggestion was made of an experiment with a single committee on one policy area. A final decision was delayed pending decisions in the Commons about the establishment of the departmentally-related select committees

---

[65] Recently the Committee has tended to produce subject reports on matters of broad concern rather than concentrate on the strict scrutiny of EC draft instruments. For example, Reports on European Union H.L. 226 of 1984–85; EC External Competence H.L. 236 of 1984–85; Ozone Layer—Implementing the Montreal Protocol H.L. 94 of 1987–88; Single European Act and Parliamentary Scrutiny in the House of Lords H.L. 149 of 1985–86. Indirect Taxation and the Internal Market, H.L. 127 of 1985–86; Social Security in the EC, H.L. 12 of 1987–88 and Fraud against the Community, H.L. 27 of 1988–89.

[66] Lord Carrington as Foreign Secretary and Government White Paper reply to the Report on Community Aid.

(hereafter called "departmental"). When this was settled in 1979, the Procedure Committee once again considered the matter,[67] and recommended that a sessional select committee on Science and Technology should be established, instead of the proposed experiments in a policy select committee on public bills. One reason for the choice of subject matter was that, with no department devoted uniquely to Science and Technology, duplication with the departmental select committees of the Commons could be avoided. The Lords' Procedure Committee reported that "the establishment of a Lords Committee on Science and Technology had attracted widespread support, both within the House and outside."

The committee was set up in January 1980 with broad terms of reference "to consider science and technology." Like the EC committee, although the committee is sessional, it is in practice reappointed every session, and has become permanent. It has 15 members and three sub-committees. Its membership includes prominent scientists and engineers as well as those with less specialised knowledge; many members have had practical experience of science-based industry, relevant ministerial experience, or were academic research scientists. The members are divided between sub-committees I and II, which each take on a subject for a year and then are reconstituted to do a different subject: the third is a general purposes sub-committee, whose main function is to recommend subjects for enquiry by the two "main" sub-committees, and to follow up past enquiries. The committee has power to co-opt members to the sub-committees and it is usual to co-opt two or three to each of the main sub-committees for the duration of the enquiry. These are usually experts in the field under consideration, but it is the practice that such specialists are never in a majority.

Given the wide terms of reference, the committee is free to make its own choice of subject. In practice, however, it has concentrated on:

(a)   areas where Parliament can help and stimulate either the advancement or the application of science and technology in the United Kingdom;

(b)   aspects of science and technology in which the Government is, or should be, involved;

(c)   the work of statutory bodies involved in science and technology;

(d)   areas where the interests of the public and those of science and technology may be in conflict; or

(e)   areas where there is public concern over issues of science and technology.

In its choice of subjects, it regularly selects issues which cross departmental boundaries.

As with the European Communities Committee, enquiries are conducted by the sub-committees, one or more specialist advisers are appointed for each enquiry, and written and oral evidence is taken. The sub-committees' draft reports are considered by the select committee, and agreed reports are published in the name of the committee. But there is an important distinction, in that the enquiries are normally longer and in greater depth than those conducted by the European Communities Committee—on average

---

[67] H.L. 97 of 1979–80. Second Report, Procedure Committee.

they last a year each, and all reports are debated. In addition, a written Government response is made to each report, because the detailed and specific quality of the report's recommendations means that a ministerial reply in debate would be insufficient.

For the most part, recommendations are directed at the Government or the relevant research council, but some have asked for reaction elsewhere—such as from industry. The readership for the report and the supporting evidence will inevitably include scientists and technologists concerned in the particular subject: and the committee has been concerned to ensure that its reports are not easily faulted on scientific or technological grounds.[68]

The committee has a practice of following up each enquiry: the main purposes are to ensure that the Government has responded adequately to the committee's recommendations, to pursue those matters where the response has been unsatisfactory, and to identify developments since the report. The form of follow-up varies, and may be by question for written answer or unstarred question, or involve taking further evidence—including from Ministers—leading to a further published report.

The committee may be said to support the non-party political voice of the scientific community and its procedures ensure that the Government is reminded of what that voice is saying.

Ad Hoc Select Committees

On December 9, 1971, a select committee was set up on Sport and Leisure. Earl Jellicoe, the Leader of the House in moving the motion, hoped that it would be the first of "quite a long line of select committees of this House on various subjects"[69]; a prophecy which has proved correct. Thus, a procedure largely dormant in the Lords since 1945 was revived, and a new function undertaken.[70] It has been used in two major ways; first, for select committees looking at public bills (see pages 486–487); secondly, for *ad hoc* committees on major subjects of public interest.

Since 1972, *ad hoc* Select Committees on subjects have become an established feature of the work of the House, as follows:

Ad Hoc Select Committees

	Subject	Chairman	Final Report	Debate
1971-73	Sport and Leisure	V. Cobham	25.7.73	13.6.74
1975-77	Commodity Prices	L. Roberthall	18.5.77	26.7.77
1979-82	Unemployment	B. Seear	10.5.82	16.11.82
1984-85	Overseas Trade	L. Aldington	30.7.85	3.12.85
1988-	Murder and Life Imprisonment	L. Nathan	-	-

[68] Year long inquiries into subjects in depth have resulted in such reports as Reports on Hazardous Waste Disposal H.L. 273 of 1980–81; Civil Research and Development H.L. 20 of 1986–87; United Kingdom Space Policy H.L. 41 of 1987–88; Priorities in Medical Research H.L. 54 of 1987–88.

[69] H.L.Deb. Vol. 326, col. 894 (December 9, 1971).

[70] In 1966–67 there was a Joint Committee on Censorship of the Theatre, which led to the abolition of the Lord Chamberlain's responsibilities for theatre censorship.

The genesis of these committees varied: Sport and Leisure was set up on the initiative of the Government; Commodity Prices was suggested in debate in the House; the Unemployment inquiry was suggested by a sub-committee of the European Communities Committee, subsequently supported in debate; and Overseas Trade was again suggested in debate. In all cases the Government's support, or at least acquiescence, was required for these initiatives by back-benchers or Opposition front-benchers to succeed. A contrast can be drawn between, on the one hand, Sport and Leisure and Commodity Prices, relatively uncontentious subject matters, and, on the other, Unemployment, where the party political implications of the subject under inquiry made progress more difficult. The Unemployment Committee spent two years on the enquiry, and the minutes of proceedings make clear that the committee had difficulty in agreeing their report. Under Lords' procedure there is no provision for a minority report, and dissent is shown by moving amendments to the Chairman's draft report. In most cases there is a large degree of agreement, or at least members with minority views tend to bow to the majority view; divisions on purely party political grounds are almost unknown. The reports of the Unemployment and Overseas Trade Committees, in particular, caused some embarrassment to the Government. It is therefore not surprising that the latest *ad hoc* committee, on Murder and Life Imprisonment, has reversed the trend towards subjects of great party political controversy.

Domestic Select Committees

There are numerous other committees, dealing with House matters such as procedure, privileges, and the judicial responsibilities of the House. The Offices Committee and its sub-committees consider the domestic affairs of the House such as finance, the library, staff and works of art. The Committee of Selection proposes the membership of all select committees except itself and that on consolidation bills. There are Joint Committees on Consolidation Bills and Statutory Instruments (see Chapter 11), as well as the Ecclesiastical Committee. There are also the committees set up to consider private bills. In addition, there have been *ad hoc* select committees on the following issues:

Ad hoc "Domestic" Select Committees

1966-67	Televising the Proceedings of the House
1967-68	Broadcasting the Proceedings of the House
1969-70	Publication of Proceedings in Parliament
1975-77	Practice and Procedure
1984-86	Broadcasting (later Televising the Proceedings of the House)
1986-88	Joint Committee on Private Legislation

Additionally, and increasingly, informal working groups have been established:

Informal Working Groups

Year	Subject	Source	Convenor
1971	Working of the House	Leader	L. Aberdare
1976	Library	Leader	V. Eccles
1977	Computers	Leader	L. Darling of Hillsborough
1984-85	Library and Record Office Storage Accommodation	Leader	L.Trend
1986-87	Working of the House	Leader	L. Aberdare

Conclusion

The value of these committees is a matter for academic inquiry and eval-uation. Certain tentative conclusions may, however, be suggested on the increase of select committee work in the Lords in the last 15 years. Most committee activity has evolved to meet specific needs as they arose, and there has been no grand design to mirror the Commons' departmental committees. Indeed, there has been a conscious desire not to duplicate the House of Commons; the Lords have tried to fill the gaps left by the Com-mons' committee system. The European Communities Committee has wider terms of reference—covering the merits of European Community proposals—than the equivalent Commons committee, which acts primarily as a filter to choose debates on the floor of the Commons. The Science and Technology Committee replaced a Commons committee which had been disbanded, and *ad hoc* committees frequently deal with matters which escape the Commons departmental committees by crossing departmental boundaries.

They use the specialist expertise of the membership of the Lords, both in ordinary committee membership and when members are co-opted for a particular inquiry. They thus tap the resources of the membership of the House, including those who would otherwise be unlikely to play an active role in the House; this is particularly true of cross-benchers previously in Crown service (civil servants, diplomats or members of the armed services). Such Peers can be used because most committee work in the Lords is not party-political: and indeed subjects removed from the heat of party politics often produce the most useful reports.

THE POWERS AND ROLE OF THE HOUSE OF LORDS

It remains to consider the functions of the House not so far considered; especially its judicial functions, in debate, and, above all, its rule in formu-lating legislation.

Judicial

The House of Lords as successor to the early medieval King's Council has the important subsidiary function of being the ultimate court of appeal in the United Kingdom. This appellate function was preserved by the Appellate Jurisdiction Act 1876. This Act reversed the situation which would have existed under the Jurisdiction Act 1873 whereby the judicial functions of the House would have been abolished. A Conservative Government retained the appellate jurisdiction of the Lords by a compromise intended to bolster the hereditary branch of the legislature, and thereby kept the name of the

House of Lords for the supreme court, but in such a way that it became a court of professional appeal judges, whose judicial work is carried out alongside but separate from that of the legislative body.[71]

The judicial functions of the House have been recently studied[72] and, although significant, are not intrinsic to the work of the House as a legislative and deliberative assembly. Nevertheless, the polite fiction has been preserved. The Appellate Committees which hear most appeals, consisting of five Law Lords, normally meet in Lords' committee rooms, and the reports of the Appellate Committee are considered, and judgment delivered, in the Chamber at judicial sittings. These are usually brief, because the "opinions," as the Law Lords' judgments are called, are delivered in writing. Exceptionally, appeals are held in the House itself, when it sits judicially, but since 1944, such hearings have been infrequent, only taking place on days when the House is not sitting for public business.

Trial by Peerage was abolished in 1947. Peerage cases are still considered by the Committee for Privileges, on which four Lords of Appeal must take part. The last impeachment took place in 1806.

Debate

Of the main functions of the Lords, the White Paper on Reform listed first "the provision of a forum for full and free debate on matters of public interest." Indeed, a generation ago, it could be claimed that "the functions of the House of Lords as a legislative assembly are far less important"[73] than those of debate. In spite of the increasing proportion of time taken up by legislation, debate remains an essential activity of the House; and the House of Lords provides a forum particularly well suited to debating issues of interest where a straight political division is not paramount. Hansard has long provided a verbatim report, and to this facility has recently been added radio broadcasts (in 1978) and television (in 1985).

As shown above, members of the Lords have every opportunity to raise matters in debate: they also have the time, as about a quarter of the lengthy sitting time of the House is still spent on debate.

A contrast is often drawn between the alleged high quality of debate in the Lords, and those of "another place" or of other assemblies; but such subjective judgments are impossible either to prove or to refute. What can be suggested is that the quality and purpose of debate in the two Houses are often different.

The first difference is that the Government's life does not depend on avoidance of a motion of censure. Never in the Lords is there the high tension of an important censure debate, like that held in the Commons in 1979 which led to the resignation of the Callaghan administration. Hence the histrionic and exciting quality of a major Commons debate is missing. But there also tends to be less of the party political point scoring which often incites criticism of the Commons.

Lords debates concentrate less on party politics than on subject-matter; as

---

[71] See R. Stevens "The Final Appeal: Reform of the House of Lords and Privy Council 1867–1876." *Law Quarterly Review*, 80, July 1964, p. 343.

[72] L. Blom-Cooper and G. Drewry, *Final Appeal: A Study of the House of Lords in its Judicial Capacity* (1972) and Alan Paterson, *The Law Lords* (1982).

[73] I. Jennings, *Parliament* (2nd ed.) (1969) p. 446. Originally written in the 1930s, it gives a good picture of the old leisured House.

a general rule those which are on straight party political issues are the least successful, as are those which are mostly closely modelled on the Commons. Certainly such debates tend to receive little media coverage. By contrast, those Lords' debates which concentrate on subjects of specialist or expert concern are often those which attract a full Chamber, are well reported by the media, and of which the Hansard reports go out of print.

Debates, whether on motions for papers, resolutions, or unstarred questions, are organised to the extent that there is a list of speakers drawn up by the Leader's Private Secretary, taking account of the wishes of the Chief Whips of the various parties. Speakers' lists are prepared in advance, so that everybody knows the order of speaking, and usually on the following lines:

Mover of the motion;
Opposition front bench spokesman;
Democrat front bench spokesman;
Minister (if a long debate);
Cross-bencher/Bishop;
Speakers for the parties in order (depending on the party of the mover or the nature of the debate), and cross-benchers arranged so as to provide contrasting views;
Wind-up speeches—Democrat, Opposition, Government Minister and a brief reply from the mover.

Debates can get wide or minimal coverage, depending on the level and content of the debate in question and on external competition. The usual absence of a Minister with direct responsibility in the Lords results in less immediacy in the governmental reaction. To that extent, ministerial speeches are of less importance. In the House, there is a convention that those taking part in debate are expected to attend the greater part of it, but in practice this is taken by many to mean attendance at the opening and winding-up speeches.

Many speeches are either read or made from extensive notes, despite the procedural convention which ordains that "the reading of speeches is alien to the custom of the House and is an obstacle to good debate."[74] Thus some Lords' debates may lack spontaneity and there are fewer interventions than in the Commons; despite the Lords' practice whereby there is an obligation to give way. Some speeches sound more like contributions to a learned colloquy rather than to debate.

The debating role of the Lords is helped by four factors. The first is its own membership, nearly all of whom possess a seat for life, and most of whom have nothing to fear or gain from public or governmental reaction to what they say. This encourages independence of mind and independent criticism in debate. Secondly, the presence of the life Peers since 1958 has added many men and women of ability and authority, and greatly extended the specialist element in the House. Thirdly, the fact that the Government is present and must provide an answer serves to provide an edge, a focus to debates. Finally, the absence of procedural warfare, lack of formal time restriction and the principle of equality throughout the House mean that private members can still raise subjects for debate without much difficulty and in a less hurried and pressurised atmosphere than in the Commons.

The Standing Orders provide that on one day a week, Wednesdays, debates take precedence over legislation. Thus, as for most of the session the House sits on four days a week, about a quarter of the time of the House is taken up by debate. However, of late, there has been a tendency for this proportion to be diminished in response to the continuing demands for more

---

[74] *Companion*, p. 38.

Motions Leading to Debate

	1978-79	1979-80	1980-81	1981-82	1982-83	1983-84	1984-85	1985-86	1986-87	1987-88
Unstarred questions	23	68	31	50	36	60	45	44	24	51
Motions for papers	17	31	17	18	11	22	13	7	5	8
Timed Debates										
Short	10	19	12	18	12	16	14	14	10	16
S.D. rules applied	N/A	N/A	N/A	N/A	1	13	10	12	13	16
Five hour	N/A	N/A	N/A	N/A	N/A	1	3	7	4	8
Take Note Motions										
General	1	7	2	6	7	5	4	7	3	6
EC committee reports	3	13	15	12	9	15	9	8	5	10
S&T committee reports	-	-	-	1	1	2	2	2	1	3
Other	2	4	1	5	6	11	11	9	2	6
Total	56	142	78	110	83	145	111	110	67	124

General Debates—Session 1985-86

Date	Topic	Mover	Type of Motion	Length of Debate hrs	mins
14 Nov 1985	New Technologies	E. Stockton	Papers	6	32
20 Nov 1985	National Health Service & Reform of the Social Security System	L. Ennals	Papers	6	21
26 Nov 1985	Anglo-Irish Agreement	V. Whitelaw	Resolution	6	30
3 Dec 1985	Overseas Trade Committee Report	L. Aldington	Take Note	7	54
4 Dec 1985	Care of the Mentally Ill	L. Mottistone	Papers	4	56
13 Dec 1985	Channels: Fixed Link Proposals	E. Caithness	Take Note	3	52
20 Jan 1986	Hong Kong Act 1985: Nationality Provisions	L. Glenarthur	Take Note	2	28
29 Jan 1986	Inquiry into British Housing: Report	L. Seebohm	Papers	5	47
5 Feb 1985	Education: Avoidance of Politicisation	B. Cox	Papers	6	50
10 Feb 1985	Fraud Trials Committee Report (Roskill Report)	L. Hailsham of Saint Marylebone	Take Note	4	58
26 Mar 1986	Rates Reform	L. Marshall of Leeds	Papers	3	52
23 Apr 1986	Violent Crime: Protection of Public	B. Faithfull	Papers	4	59
12 May 1986	Televising of Proceedings of the House: Report of the Select Committee	L. Boyd-Carpenter	Take Note	2	49
16 May 1986	Hong Kong Ethnic Minorities: Citizenship	L. Cledwyn of Penrhos	Resolution	3	26
25 Jun 1985	The Defence Estimates 1986	L. Trefgarne	Take Note	6	34
4 Jly 1986	South Africa	B. Young	Take Note	6	22

Timed Debates: Five Hour Debates—Session 1985-86

Date	Topic	Mover	Length of Debate (hrs mins)	No. of Speakers	No. of Interventions	Time Allowance (mins)
19 Feb 1986	The Economic Situation	L. Barnett	3 48	15	15	15
19 Mar 1986	Voluntary Organisations	L. Bottomley	4 10	19	3	15
9 Apr 1986	Economic Recovery: Co-operation with Industry	L. Bruce of Donington	4 41	18	9	17
18 Apr 1986	Libya: U.S. Action	V. Whitelaw	4 50	31	14	7-8
30 Apr 1986	Government Policies: Social Effects	L. Wells-Pestell	4 55	21	10	14
7 May 1986	Schools: Investment in Education & Science	B. Seear	4 43	24	3	11
21 May 1986	The Water Industry	B. Nicol	4 15	16	7	18

Timed Short Debates—Session 1985-86

Date	Topic	Mover	Length of Debate (hrs mins)	No. of Speakers	No. of Interventions	Time Allowance (mins)
27 Nov 1985	Denationalised Industries	L. Taylor of Gryfe	2 11	12	5	12
27 Nov 1985	Money Supply & The Private Banking System	L. Beswick	1 33	7	4	15
11 Dec 1985	Liverpool City Council	L. Harris of Greenwich	2 25	11	7	14
11 Dec 1985	Higher Education	B. Seear	2 32	13	4	11
18 Dec 1985	Community Education & Employment	L. Stewart of Fulham	2 08	10	1	15
18 Dec 1985	Aid to African Agriculture	L. Walston	2 21	10	1	15
15 Jan 1986	Codes of Practice & Legislation	L. Campbell of Alloway	2 17	11	4	14min
15 Jan 1986	Employment Policy	L. Jacques	2 28	11	2	14

Timed Short Debates—Session 1985-86—continued

Date	Topic	Mover	Length of Debate hrs mins	No. of Speakers	No. of Interventions	Time Allowance (mins)
22 Jan 1986	Schools & Their Problems	L. Irving of Dartford	2 31	13	7	10
22 Jan 1986	Monopolies & Mergers Policy	L. Gallacher	2 15	11	4	12
12 Feb 1986	China: Economic Change & Trade Openings	L. Rhodes	2 28	15	1	9
12 Feb 1986	Parliamentary & Democratic System in the U.K.	V. Hanworth	2 20	9	6	9
26 Feb 1986	Crime in London: Preventative Measures	L. Harris of Greenwich	2 29	14	2	10
26 Feb 1986	Government, Parliament & The Civil Service	L. Hooson	2 27	10	5	10
5 Mar 1986	Charity Law	L. Allen of Abbeydale	2 22	16	8	8
5 Mar 1986	Higher Education: Institutional Framework	L. Annan	2 25	14	2	10
12 Mar 1986	Legal Status of Nuclear War	L. Jenkins of Putney	1 22	6	5	15
12 Mar 1986	World Disarmament	L. Molloy	1 40	6	8	15
16 Apr 1986	Grendon Prison Kingsbridge	L. Donaldson of	1 55	8	4	15
16 Apr 1986	The Tourist Industry	L. Campbell of Croy	2 26	15	1	12
14 May 1986	Disability: Prevention Brompton	L. Henderson of	2 31	13	2	11
14 May 1986	Agricultural Research & Development	B. Nicol	2 11	12	1	12
4 Jun 1986	Criminal Legal Aid	L. Benson	2 21	15	2	9
4 Jun 1986	Pharmacy: Nuffield Foundation Report	L. Hunter of Newington	2 04	10	5	15
18 Jun 1986	Housing: Public Investment	L. Dean of Beswick	2 28	11	1	14
18 Jun 1986	The Environment: Protection	L. Ardwick	2 23	13	2	10

time for legislation. It will be seen that, even if debates on select committee reports and on unstarred questions are added—with the exception of election years—there has been a decline in the proportion of time taken by debates. But this is not true of the total number of debates: (see page 500).

Wednesday debate days (other than one Wednesday a month reserved for balloted debates) are shared out by agreement between the parties by the "usual channels": in session 1985–86 there were eight Labour, six Conservative, three Alliance and three cross-bench days; previously the allocation was more heavily weighted to the Opposition, who used to get a half of the Wednesdays, while the Government, the Liberals and cross-benches together accounted for only a quarter. The subjects for debate are chosen by the party concerned, and are discussed in the weekly party meetings: no longer are they chosen by the party leadership. In addition, until Whitsun, there is the one Wednesday a month allocated to the ballotted short debates. Increasingly, all Wednesday debates are being subjected to time limits by agreement, whether for two-and-a-half hours or five hours, but a number remains unlimited.

In one session, the subjects debated by various categories were as shown on pages 501–503).

Ministers and ministerial accountability

A major difference between the two Houses lies in the degree of ministerial accountability. In the eighteenth and nineteenth centuries, the division of Ministers between the two Houses was different: there were far fewer Ministers, and the number in each House was approximately equal. For instance, in Mr. Gladstone's great ministry of 1868, six out of a total of 15 in the Cabinet were Peers, and in Mr. Disraeli's administration of 1874 there were six Lords to six Commoners. The twentieth century has seen a great change, and with increased governmental activity administrations have grown greatly. The increase in ministerial numbers has taken place overwhelmingly in the Commons, and has not been mirrored in the Lords, where in 1989 there were three Cabinet Ministers, 12 junior departmental Ministers and seven Whips. Thus most responsible Ministers answer for their actions in the Commons, and only a minority can speak for their own departments in the Lords; with the majority of Government business being taken either by Ministers without direct departmental responsibility or by a Government Whip, acting as a Government spokesman. For this reason, questions and motions are addressed in the Lords to "Her Majesty's Government" generally. There is less direct accountability of Ministers to the House than in the Commons.

Legislation

The House of Lords has essentially the same right to initiate and revise legislation as the House of Commons, subject to the Commons' financial privilege (see pages 238–9 and 247) and the limits on the powers of the House of Lords imposed by the Parliament Acts 1911 and 1949 (see pages 240–242).

Parliament Acts

The Parliament Act 1911[75] was meant to be a temporary expedient, as the preamble made clear:

"and whereas it is intended to substitute for the House of Lords as it at

---

[75] On the passing of the Parliament Act 1911 see articles reprinted in *The House of Lords 1603–1911* ed. C and D.L. Jones, 1986, pp. 460–539.

present exists a second chamber constituted on a popular instead of an hereditary basis, but such substitution cannot immediately be brought into operation."

But the political troubles of the time, especially with regard to Ireland, coupled with the outbreak of the First World War, prevented further action. Indeed, although the Attlee administration came to power in 1945 pledged to "not tolerate obstruction of the people's will by the House of Lords," their 1949 Parliament Act did no more than change the timetable in the 1911 Act.

In practice the provisions of the Parliament Acts mean that a bill to which the Lords are opposed cannot be passed in less than 13 months from the original second reading of the bill in the Commons, and in some circumstances the period may be substantially longer. The effective delay which the Lords can cause is less, since the 13 month period includes the time needed for the bill to pass through its stages in the Commons after second reading. But if a bill is introduced towards the end of a Parliament it may be lost altogether.

Subordinate legislation, private bills, provisional order confirmation bills and those under the Private Legislation Procedure (Scotland) Act 1936 are not subject to the Parliament Acts.

The use made of the powers under the Parliament Acts has been very sparing.[76] Governments, in practice, are anxious to get their legislation on the statute book early and to this end are willing to accept compromise amendments rather than waiting for the procedures and time allowed by the Parliament Acts to take their course in order to secure the bill in the original form.

Conventions on the Use of Powers

It has been the attitude of the Opposition in the Lords which has moulded the conventions governing the use of the Lords' powers. These conventions in modern times were firmly established by the then Conservative Opposition during the period of Labour government immediately after the Second World War though the Labour party before the war had observed similar restraints.[76a] In 1964, Lord Salisbury, who had been Leader of the Opposition in the Lords between 1945 and 1951, described the position in the Lords under the post-war Labour administration:

"our broad guiding rule [was] that what had been on the Labour Party programme at the preceding General Election should be regarded as having been approved by the British people. Therefore we passed all the nationalisation bills, although we cordially disliked them, on the second reading and did our best to improve them and make them more workable on Committee stage. When however measures were introduced which had not been in the Labour Party manifesto at the preceding election, we reserved full liberty of action."[77]

Lord Salisbury added that the rule was more difficult to apply when a Government had a small majority in the Commons and there had been a

---

[76] The provisions of the Parliament Acts, the Commons' procedures for their application and the rare occasions of their use are described in Chapter 6, pages 240–242.

[76a] See Lord Ponsonby of Shulbrede then Opposition Leader on the second reading of the Ottowa Agreements Bill, H.L.Deb. Vol. 85, col. 1239 (November 10, 1932).

[77] H.L.Deb. Vol. 261, col. 66 (November 4, 1964).

substantial vote in the general election for minor opposition parties, as was the case in 1964. But in general, this "doctrine of the mandate" has been given as a reason by both Conservative and Labour Oppositions for refraining from voting against the second reading of mandated government bills.

The doctrine has not, however, prevented Conservative Oppositions from voting to insist on amendments disagreed to by the Commons, even if this has resulted in killing a bill. For example, they insisted on amendments to the House of Commons (Redistribution of Seats) (No. 2) Bill in 1968–69; to the Trade Union and Labour Relations (Amendment) Bill in 1974–75–76; and to the Aircraft and Shipbuilding Industries Bill in 1975–76–77. This effectively killed all three bills in the sessions concerned, though the last two became law in the following session after amendments had been agreed between both Houses.

In the debate on whether to insist on their amendments to the Trade Union and Labour Relations (Amendment) Bill 1974–75, Lord Carrington dealt with the question how far it was right for the House to use its powers of delay under the Parliament Acts:

"In our system we have hitherto taken the view that the will of the elected House must in the end prevail, but that there should be a second House which has the opportunity—in rare cases, perhaps—to enforce a delay in which there can be reassessment by Government, by parties and by the people of this country of the rights or wrongs of an issue. If now we decide to use that very limited power, we are not thwarting the will of the people for, in so far as it is represented by the House of Commons, it will and must prevail in a comparatively short time. We shall be using those powers for the purpose for which they were given to us—that is, as an opportunity for further consultation, for second thoughts before this legislation inevitably reaches the Statute Book and because we did not want the Second Chamber to be associated with what the Government are doing."[78]

Labour Opposition have neglected the doctrine of the mandate on two occasions: by a reasoned amendment directly negativing a mandated Commons Government bill—the London Government Bill in 1963—and by a motion to adjourn the second reading of the Industrial Relations Bill 1971 to allow negotiations with both sides in industry to take place. On both occasions, the motions were voted on and disagreed to.[79] The conventions governing the official Opposition have not always been observed by back-benchers.[80]

Other procedures have been devised to enable the House to vote on second and third readings without directly negativing the motions. The first is by giving the bill a second reading, but with a reasoned amendment, which without seeking to negative the second reading, invites the House to put on record reasons for disliking it. This procedure was adopted on the European Communities Bill 1972 on third reading, the Southern Rhodesia Bill 1979, the British Nationality Bill 1981, the Companies (No. 2) Bill 1981, the Rates Bill 1984 and the Local Government (Interim Provisions) Bill 1984, although none of these motions were carried. A second procedure for

---

[78] H.L.Deb. Vol. 365, col. 1742 (November 11, 1975).

[79] H.L.Deb. Vol. 251, col. 1205 (July 8, 1963); H.L.Deb. Vol. 317, col. 22 (April 5, 1971).

[80] British Standard Time Bill November 23, 1967, Industrial Relations Bill April 6, 1971, Immigration Bill June 24, 1971, European Communities Bill July 26, 1972.

expressing dislike of a bill without refusing it a second reading is to move a resolution on the same day as second reading, deploring certain provisions of the bill. Such a motion has to take account of the rule against offering the same question to the House as one on which its judgment has already been expressed that session. This was done on the Immigration Bill 1971 and the British Nationality Bill 1981.

The Revising Process

A majority of Government bills are introduced into the House of Commons, and the efforts to reduce the imbalance have been only partly successful. An average of 16 bills (excluding consolidation bills) per session in the last ten years were introduced in the Lords, compared with 13 in the previous decade. This is no surprise; the elected Commons expects major bills, the subject of party political differences, to be discussed there in the first instance. Moreover, the responsible Minister usually sits in that House, and he usually wishes to promote his own bill. Finally, while supply and financial bills subsequently certified must be introduced in the Commons, many other bills with significant financial implications are of prime interest to the taxpayers' representatives.

If, then, most Government legislation has already passed the Commons, it follows that the main legislative role of the Lords is that of revision. The idea that the Lords can be left the chore of tidying up legislation is not new.[81] An analysis of the two Houses in 1968–69 and 1970–71 showed that in the Commons, 6.0 per cent. of amendments were accepted in committee and 5.1 on report; compared with 12.3 and 19.3 per cent. in the Lords.[82] But this also, even allowing for the vagaries and uncertainties of statistical comparisons, confirmed the impression gained from reading the debates that Ministers in the Lords were more willing to accept amendments than their counterparts were in the Commons, possibly because of the less contentious and less partisan atmosphere in the Lords.

The idea that most revision can be left to the Lords has recently gained greater currency in the Commons. On a timetable motion in the Commons on the Local Government Finance Bill 1987, the Leader of the House said "The main motivation and desire has been to get the bill to another place where it will be undoubtedly very fully considered."[83]

The Weight of Legislation

If the primary function of the Lords is to revise legislation, there have been recent complaints that it is increasingly difficult to fulfil this responsibility. Members replied to a questionnaire from the 1986 Group on the Working of the House with the following reasons why the House had been placed under strain:

"(a) More public legislation, especially from the Government, has provided a greatly increased workload for the House, with longer hours, taking over 52 per cent. of the total time last Session.
(b) Government legislation has been more heavily amended in the Lords than in previous Sessions, and there has been a tendency to 'legislate as

---

[81] See 2nd Report, Commons Procedure Committee (1970–71), QQ.773–776.
[82] J. A. G. Griffith, *Parliamentary Scrutiny of Government Bills (1974)*.
[83] H.C.Deb., Vol. 109, col. 39, (January 26, 1987).

you go' (the majority of the amendments made originated from the Government, which suggests that legislation may have been introduced without adequate consideration).

(c) Another external cause of increased pressure on the Lords is that, with a large Government majority in the Commons, there has been greater lobbying in the Lords. Also, when a bill is guillotined in the Commons, more time is usually needed for subsequent discussion, as parts of bills reach the Lords without previous consideration.

(d) The number of Life Peers (about 200 at the time of the 1971 Group) has now increased to 346, and many suggested that the House cannot continue effectively with its present procedures and facilities if the number of Life Peers, particularly those able to attend regularly, continues to increase. . . .

(e) Increasing democracy within the political parties, the emergence of another Opposition party (with inevitable complication in inter-party negotiations), and the rise in numbers and impact of the Cross-benchers (who cannot be bound by inter-party negotiations) have made the arrangement of business through the 'usual channels' more difficult.

(f) The result of these pressures is that the established procedures of the House have been subjected to increased strains, and many Peers believed that these strains have hampered the ability of the House to carry out its function as a revising chamber."[84]

Hence a combination of internal factors concerned with composition and party organisation of the Lords, and the external factor of the management of the legislative programme, has placed a strain on the Chamber.

The Importance of the Lords as a Revising Chamber

It is difficult to judge with truth or academic rigour the impact of the House of Lords on legislation. Government papers are normally not available for 30 years; the perceptions of protagonists are naturally coloured (even if unwittingly) as there is an understandable wish in those who have laboured for a cause to magnify their achievement. Ministers and civil servants may wish to dignify, as well as to conceal, the process of Government; while oppositions need to magnify their achievements to keep up their morale. An example of the difficulty of apportioning responsibility for a change of policy to some extent caused by the House of Lords occurred over the decision in 1967 not to proceed with Stansted as a third London airport, and instead to set up the Buchanan enquiry. The stated cause for the change of policy was a report of the Council on Tribunals; unstated causes were the appointment of a new Minister, and the Lords' hostility to the proposal, expressed in a debate in December 1967. The fear was that they would vote down the special procedure order required to give effect to the proposal. The Crossman diaries suggest that the two unstated reasons were the major factors: a fuller picture will only emerge after 1996.[85] If such obscurity is evident on a major policy change, where the Commons had already approved the siting of the Third London Airport at Stansted on a three line whip, it is hardly surprising that on lesser changes, with less publicity, the apportioning of responsibility for changes is difficult.

---

[84] H.L. 9 of 1987–88, para. 2.
[85] See J. Morgan, *The House of Lords and the Labour Government 1964–70,* pp. 96–97; and Crossman, *Diaries* (1976) Vol. 2 pages 562–3, 684.

Level of Government Amendments

The revising function of the Lords includes the opportunity first, to force amendment of the bill, or force the Government to make changes; secondly, to allow the Government to make its own changes to the bill. It is invariably the case that the great majority of amendments agreed to are Government amendments in form: they are often proposed to meet minor drafting points suggested by the department, but also to meet points made in debate, or in response to outside representations. It has been suggested that what is new is that the Government rewrites substantial sections of its own bills during passage through Parliament. In particular, enormous changes can be made to Commons bills in the House of Lords, and Ministers have been accused "collectively and individually" of failing to take "the necessary care with regard to the substance and detail of bills before they are presented."[86] The Leader of the Opposition complained in 1986–87 of "legislation as you go," with huge batches of Government amendments being tabled at very short notice, and went on to give a number of examples to show "that Government bills have not been properly thought out."[87] In reply, the Leader of the House said that he had "to accept what the noble Lord says."

A list of the numbers of Government amendments in 1985–86 explains the unanimity on this point: Education Bill, 77; Airports Bill, 107; Building Societies Bill, 206; Social Security Bill, 114; Financial Services Bill, 582. The Housing and Planning Bill was brought from the Commons on May 1, 1986, but did not receive a second reading until July 30, after a delay of three months. The Lords' proceedings from committee to third reading were taken in the "spillover" between October 7 and 28; 17 clauses and two schedules were added, 354 amendments discussed at committee (of which 80 per cent. were Government), 100 amendments made on report, and 24 on third reading. The Education Reform Bill 1988 provides evidence of the Lords legislative influence.[88]

Drafting Amendments

A considerable proportion of the amendments discussed and agreed to are drafting amendments. As such they do not take much time: the Minister often merely says "drafting," or gives a very brief explanation. On the Channel Tunnel Bill 1987, out of the 204 amendments made in the Lords, some 54 were drafting; while on the Pilotage Bill 1986 there were 31 drafting amendments out of a total of 102 agreed. The proportion of drafting amendments made varies with the draftsmen, the speed at which the legislation is prepared, and the related legislation which is under consideration before Parliament: but on many bills the prime importance of consideration in the second House is to provide opportunities for improved drafting.

Allied to drafting amendments are technical amendments, where the department has second thoughts on the exact method to be used to achieve an agreed objective, but makes no policy change. On the two bills referred to, the numbers of such technical amendments have been calculated at 65 in

[86] H.L.Deb., Vol. 480, cols. 1024–1029 (October 17, 1986).
[87] H.L.Deb., Vol. 478, col. 171 (July 8, 1986).
[88] 569 amendments were made, many technical but some 70 were substantive, including many government concessions as on religious education and collective worship; protection of academic freedom; definition of redundancy for academics; protecting universities' and colleges' private funds; and on grant maintained school ballots.

the case of the Channel Tunnel Bill and 28 in the case of the Pilotage Bill. Thus drafting and technical amendments together accounted for over half of the total agreed to. Another allied category of amendment which is reasonably frequent is where mistakes are noticed during the passage of legislation.

Fulfilment of Pledges made in the Commons

Many amendments are moved in the Lords to implement undertakings given in the Commons; especially when the business managers wish to expedite the passage of the bill through the Commons, or where the point at issue requires extensive consultation with outside interests before the appropriate amendment can be drafted.

Examples of this are common. On the Banking Bill 1986, there were 11 amendments arising from Commons undertakings. The Agriculture Bill 1986 required 15 amendments in the Lords to ensure that Scottish provisions would be introduced at the same time as the English and Welsh provisions.

Policy Amendments from Departmental or External Sources

Second thoughts on policy matters by the Ministers and departments themselves provide an important and frequent source of amendments in the Lords. This can hardly be a matter of surprise or criticism—on many issues the arguments are finely balanced. It may be rather a matter for congratulation that departments are capable of refining their proposals in the light of arguments advanced either in Parliament, or externally, or indeed within the department itself. This is the more praiseworthy as it is a natural wish of those working on the bill to see it passed into law as quickly as possible. There is much evidence that such changes do frequently take place.[89]

Policy Amendments due to Pressure in Parliament

Many policy changes are made as a result of parliamentary pressure, and a great many made in the Lords result from pressure in both Houses. A classic example would be that a point is raised in standing committee in the Commons, often at the instigation of outside lobbyists or pressure groups, but resisted; nevertheless, the case is made and is on the record. This is taken up when the bill reaches the Lords, is mentioned in second reading speeches, and eventually, at one of the consideration stages the Government agrees to look at it, and returns at the next stage with an amendment to meet the point. Often this is a compromise which has been worked out in private between the department, the interests concerned, and the Lords who have spoken on the point. There is a tendency for points which have been raised by Government supporters in the Commons to be followed in the Lords by a Conservative back-bencher, and if raised by the Opposition members in the Commons, for the case to be taken up again in the Lords by the Opposition. But this is not invariably the case. Again, it is not unusual for there to be all-party pressure in the Commons, which is then followed in the Lords.

Cases of such policy changes as a result of pressure in both Houses are common; more so than the much publicised "Government defeats" in the Lords.

Policy Changes as a Result of Lords Pressure

A variant of the above class is where the pressure is applied only in the

---

[89] *e.g.* Legal Aid (Scotland) Act 1986. Amendment extending the provision for loss of office or employment for Scottish Legal Aid Board to staff of the board.

Lords. In the simplest case, this occurs when a member of the House raises a point which has previously escaped notice. Alternatively, it may occur when a pressure group is late in noticing a point, perhaps because the implications of a provision are not immediately obvious. Of course, bills introduced in the Lords can attract the interest of pressure groups straight away, and the concerns of the Lords can be met by an amendment in the Commons.

Government Defeats on Policy Issues

Finally, there is a class of policy amendments carried by the House against the Government of the day, to which a good deal of academic and media attention has recently been given.[90]

Governments have, for many years, suffered occasional defeats[91] in the Lords. In the past, defeats were rare under Conservative administrations, but recently such defeats have become both more frequent and much more significant, in that in the majority of cases the defeats are accepted at least in part by the Government and, in consequence, the Commons have acquiesced. This is the reverse of the situation under recent Labour administrations where, although the Lords have inflicted frequent defeats, most of these have been overturned in the Commons, and the Lords have not insisted.

Several reasons have been suggested[92] to explain why, despite the large numbers of Conservative Peers in the House, the present Government has been defeated so often in the Lords. First, there is the composition of the House. The "floating vote" of the cross benches has been steadily growing, both in numbers and impact on debates, to provide an element of uncertainty. Secondly, those within the party structure are more loosely held than in the Commons. It is difficult to discipline Peers holding a tenure for life, and with so many Peers either retired or happily involved with careers outside politics, the bait of ministerial office dangled so effectively in the Commons is missing. There are far fewer jobs to fill, with the result that the

---

[90] See D. R. Shell in "The House of Lords and the Thatcher Government," *Parliamentary Affairs* XXXVIII pp. 16–32; also P. Norton, ed. *Parliament in the 1980s* (1985).

[91] Recent examples over a six-month period include the following:

1988 16 Feb	Local Government Bill	Report	Contractors to follow with code of practice for disabled employees (17)	128-119
1988 3 Mar	Social Security Bill	Report	Annual review of Child benefit (new after 4)	97-84
1988 19 May	Education Reform Bill	CWH	The University Commissioners (173)	152-126
1988 28 Jun	Education Reform Bill	Report	Universities Funding Council (123)	78-69
1988 30 Jun	Local Government Finance Bill	Report	Relief for students (13)	85-65
1988 19 Jly	Health & Medicines Bill	CWH	Charges for dental appliances (11)	118-97
1988 19 Jly	Health & Medicines Bill	CWH	General ophthalmic services & optical appliances (13)	120-94
1988 28 Jly	Housing Bill	CWH	Housing action trust areas (60)	102-95

[92] See works cited by Shell and Norton, and P. Silk with R. H. Walters *How Parliament Works*, pp. 141–145.

"payroll vote" in the Lords is only 22, compared with nearly 100 in the Commons. With no direct role in the election of the party leadership, less obligation is felt to follow every word of the party manifestos; and indeed less rests on a Government defeat, since it is not taken as a matter of no confidence. Finally, there are political differences between the two Houses. One academic has pointed out that "in the elected House, the moderates of *both* sides have been driven out—if not out of the House, then at least out of the key positions of power. In the Lords, the unelected House, the moderates of both sides remain."[92a] Certainly deference to the elected House has waned, perhaps because of greater confidence born of the higher profile of a televised house and greater scepticism of the Commons' majority produced by the electoral system.

Lobbying

Lobbying in the House of Lords is comparatively recent; but in the last 20 years it has become significant. One reason recently suggested for increased pressure on the Lords is the large Government majority in the Commons.[93] On bills which have been guillotined, the only place where lobbyists may be able to act effectively is in the second House, but more usually it is a device for a second attempt. Looser party discipline and less governmental control of time on the floor of the House combine to make lobbying action in the Lords attractive.[94]

The success of certain longer term social reforms in the 1960s and 1970s, especially abortion, is remembered and copied; much time and energy was then given to the Lords by those conducting the campaign. While some lobbyists are indiscriminate, others are selective, and cultivate links with selected Lords interested in, and expert in, particular subjects; apart from written briefs, they organise meetings and lectures, visits, or oral briefings. Select committees are the recipients of much lobbying. What is comparatively new is that lobbyists now apparently think it worth their while to spend considerable time and energy on the Lords; their labours contribute to the increased workload of the House.

Broadcasting and Televising the House

The first move towards broadcasting the proceedings of the House was taken in June 1966, when it was agreed: "That this House would welcome the televising of some of its proceedings for an experimental period as an additional means of demonstrating its usefulness in giving a lead to public opinion." A select committee was accordingly set up, which recommended a three-day closed circuit experiment.[95]

The experiment took place in February 1968, and the closed circuit transmission of the Lords' proceedings was made available to the House of Commons and the Press Gallery. Programmes of "highlights" were authorised, both on television and on the radio. The committee then recommended a one-year experiment, during which the broadcasters could record events in

---

[92a] D. R. Shell, *Parliamentary Affairs*, XXXVIII, The House of Lords and the Thatcher Government.

[93] H.L. 9 of 1986–87, para. 2(c).

[94] See forthcoming Study of Parliament Group publication *Parliament and Lobbying*, and especially Chap. 8 by N. Baldwin "The House of Lords and Pressure Politics."

[95] H.L. 190 and 284 of 1966–67.

the chamber, for television or radio, as and when they wished. The broadcasting authorities would have had to pay for the privilege, but would have been allowed editorial control.[96] These recommendations were debated in 1969, but no action was taken. One reason was technical: the available technology was cumbersome, and an expensive risk to take for what remained an experiment. Another was that the House wished to remain in line with the Commons.[97] The Commons had recently rejected the recommendation of their own Select Committee on Broadcasting that their proceedings be recorded.

In the following decade, television cameras were allowed into the precincts of the Palace for the purpose of documentaries. The conditions imposed on these filmmakers in the early 1980s were less stringent than in 1971; but access to the Houses' proceedings was still refused.

More progress was made in the field of sound broadcasting. In 1974, the Queen's Speech promised that both Houses should have an opportunity to decide whether their proceedings should be broadcast. In 1975, the Commons conducted an experiment, and the following year both Houses agreed to the permanent sound broadcasting of their proceedings. Broadcasting of the proceedings of both Houses began in April 1978.

On December 8, 1983,[98] the Lords agreed to a motion by Lord Soames, a former Leader of the House, that the House endorse its decision of 1966 in favour of televising its proceedings, and take steps to implement it.[99] Lord Soames gave two reasons for re-opening the issue. First, that if the Lords had to wait for the Commons to support televising, "we might be waiting for an endlessly long time." But his main reason for urging the House to take action was that an unelected chamber in a democratic country needed to prove itself, and that "the public would like to see us at work, warts and all."

The Sound Broadcasting Committee recommended a six-month television experiment during which the broadcasting authorities would be permitted to come to the House on a "drive-in" basis, as and when they chose.[1] Editorial control was left to the broadcasters, although Commons' ministerial statements repeated in the Lords were not to be televised. In return, the broadcasters were to bear the costs. The galleries of the House were out of bounds to the cameras. The committee also recommended that public meetings of select committees could be televised.

These recommendations were approved, and the experiment took place. Towards the end of the experiment it was agreed that broadcasting could continue until a final decision was taken. That decision came in 1986: a few months after the Commons had once again rejected the cameras. The Lords were satisfied that the experiment had been a success. During the debate on the decision, the broadcasting authorities were praised for producing "responsible programmes that reflect well on the work of the House." Fears that technical difficulties would cause serious inconvenience or that the behaviour of members in debate might change in front of the cameras proved unfounded. A final and commonly-held argument was provided by Lord Boyd-Carpenter: "At one time there was a proposal for the abolition of

---

[96] H.L. 159 of 1967–68.
[97] H.L.Deb., Vol. 300, cols. 1118 and 1093 (March 20, 1969).
[98] See H.L. 9 of 1987–88 and *Table* LIII, pp. 17–28 and LIV, pp. 28–43.
[99] H.L.Deb., Vol. 445, col. 1191 (December 8, 1983).
[1] H.L. 299, of 1983–84.

Your Lordship's House. I should be very surprised indeed if it had that support today."[2]

A study by the Hansard Society[3] suggested that daily and weekly summaries of the Lords' proceedings had worked well, although the use of recordings in news programmes was less successful. They also praised the coverage of policy debates, especially on economic issues. The confidence of the Lords that televising the chamber would work was illustrated by the large majorities supporting the cameras every time the House was consulted, in contrast to the successive defeats suffered by pro-television M.P.s until 1988. The Hansard Society concluded that: "It would be unfortunate if, for the second time in twenty years, the learning which has clearly taken place in an experimental period of Parliamentary broadcasting should be wasted." With cameras now an accepted part of the furniture of the Chamber and the Commons preparing for their introduction, it seems unlikely that the Lords will wish to leave the screen.

Conclusion

The description given above of the House of Lords as it is today is one of a legislative chamber in flux; great changes have taken place in the last two decades, and the House is now so changing and enlarging its functions, largely as a result of external pressures, that it may appear fanciful to think that it can continue with the same procedures, powers and composition for much longer. But talk of reform has so often been unfulfilled in the past, that once again no drastic changes may occur, despite rumblings of discontent. Up to now it has proved impossible to get opinion to converge to produce specific reform proposals which would command majority support. What are the changes which could be made?

The first was the official policy of the Labour party in the 1970s—though not reflected in recent manifestos—of abolition. This policy has recently been modified in favour of a reformed second chamber. The case made for abolition was twofold: democracy as a principle, and the failure to agree on any alternative. Against this can be set the view that this might be unpopular, as it would strengthen the elective dictatorship of a government, which may, under our electoral system, be in a minority in the country; that it would inevitably strengthen the Government and the executive against Parliament; and that minority interests would suffer. In addition, as the Labour party has found in recent years, much of the work of opposing a Government with a big majority in the Commons has fallen to the Lords, not only on big political issues like the abolition of the GLC and the metropolitan county councils, but also in the painstaking legislative grind seen in recent sessions.

The second possibility would be to reform its composition. The case for doing this is, in brief, public doubt about the logic or fairness of giving individuals legislative power by the accident of inheritance. The inbuilt preponderance of one party also helps to diminish the political authority of the Chamber. The reasons against it are the fact that reform would increase that authority and strengthen the Lords, as was feared in 1968, *vis-à-vis* the Commons. The easiest change would be to take away the right to a seat or vote of newly-succeeding hereditary Peers. Such a change, because of the

---

[2] H.L. Deb., Vol. 474, cols. 963–1005 (May 12, 1986).
[3] *Televising the House of Lords* by R. Stradling and E. Bennett (May 1986).

demographic state of the House, would quickly lead to a waning of the hereditary Peers' presence. Another possibility would be to institutionalise the checks which informally govern the creation of peerages, by strengthening the Political Honours Scrutiny Committee. A further step would be to add an elective element—as proposed by the Conservative Committee of 1978 chaired by Lord Home, and by the Alliance parties: this could be based on proportional representation and might have a regional basis, and an intended regional function. Most radical of all would be to sweep away the present House, and replace it by an elected senate.

A further possibility would be to alter the powers of the House. This seems to command least support, except possibly in relation to subordinate legislation. The 1968 White Paper proposed little real change on public bills, but it did give the Commons the right to override a Lords veto on delegated legislation. At present, although the Lords have unrestricted powers on subordinate legislation (except financial), they are restrained by convention from using them. On ordinary public legislation, the present position is that the Lords have a delaying power of at least 13 months and a day after second reading in the Commons, but less from the time they receive the bill. But because of the complications of the Parliament Acts, and the fact that all Governments want their legislation on the statute book as soon as possible, no bill has been enacted by the use of the Parliament Acts since 1914, except the 1949 Parliament Act itself. On other measures, a compromise has been reached. It is, in practice, the use of these limited powers which is the issue, and the conventions which govern their use, not their extent.

In the absence of a real likelihood of changes in powers or composition, there is the final possibility of procedural change within the House, to seek to redress the considerable increase in the workload of the House, without, up to now, matching procedural change, or any improvement in the administrative infrastructure of the House or facilities for its members. This would be change from within. The greatest single problem is the burden imposed by the weight of legislation requiring consideration and revision, which is at present done on the floor of the House. One possibility would be legislative select committees for consideration of public bills off the floor of the House, saving the House the time taken at present by committee of the whole House, the procedure which takes much the biggest amount of the House's time. Other possibilities would be a restriction of rights to move similar amendments a second time round on the report stage, or the selection of amendments. Both these later proposals would be difficult to inject into Lords' procedures without having a Speaker with effective powers.

The House of Lords, in its procedurally innocent state of Utopian freedom and voluntary regulation, works on the basis of self-restraint. It is increasingly being tested. Its ancient procedures were not designed for the huge task of the revision of Government legislation with which it is now faced. Procedurally, will the Lords go the way of the Commons in the late nineteenth century, when the determined misuse of the ancient freedoms forced the majority to invent the guillotine and the closure, and the paraphernalia of standing orders which give the Government of the day almost complete control? Or will the Lords find a way to change in directions which will continue their ancient traditions?

PART V

EVALUATIONS

CHAPTER 13

IS PARLIAMENT EFFECTIVE?

In Chapter 1 we described the main task of Parliament in Amery's words as being "to secure full discussion and ventilation of all matters" and to hold Government to account. This was meant to indicate not only the width of the parliamentary function but also its limits. For Parliament is not directly involved in the process of governing, although it has the secondary task of sustaining in office the Government of the day. Members of the House of Commons and Peers, other than Ministers, respond and react to Government proposals and actions, and so influence Governments. But governing the country is not their responsibility.

The crucial parliamentary task can too easily be taken for granted. Governments are by nature secretive and must be forced into the open. And Governments prefer to conceal actions which in the event do not reflect credit on their administration. The more that is known of what Governments intend, the greater is the scope for criticism.

Debates in Parliament should not be regarded as isolated events. They are often only the part that surfaces of a considerable discussion with affected interests bringing pressure to bear on Ministers, civil servants and Parliamentarians. And that discussion is further carried on in the press, on television, in books, articles and public speeches, as well as in Parliament itself. All this is well known but the success of a democracy is to be judged by the extent to which it can ensure that Government is publicly accountable. To do so is a continuing struggle, secrecy and censorship being the principal enemies, freedom of speech in Parliament being the vital privilege.

Under many systems of government, secrecy and concealment are commonplace. Dictatorial regimes do not admit of elected assemblies which do more than record their assent. Challenges even to the most unlawful of official acts will, at best, go unanswered. Arrest and imprisonment without trial, widespread searches of private property, torture and murder may all be carried out in the name of such regimes, without redress.

That western democracies are relatively free of these injustices is not due solely to the existence of representative assemblies. An independent judiciary and a free press are also essential. These institutions are established and are the foundations on which we can discuss their merits and demerits. We may question how "free" are the press and the broadcasting authorities, we may consider what is the price we pay for a judiciary that is irremovable, and we may examine in some detail how effective are the powers of Parliament in the face of strong Government.

Parliament is an ancient institution but in modern terms the Commons as a representative assembly dates from no earlier than 1884 when adult male franchise was largely provided for; and full adult franchise is a mere 60 years old. Since the middle of the last century, Government activity has greatly increased and is still increasing. In absolute terms, Parliament may well be more active, more lively than it was fifty or twenty years ago. But it may still be asked whether, in relative terms, Parliament is managing to keep pace with the expanding powers of Government.

In the House of Commons, there are three forums, each presenting different opportunities for discussion, ventilation and accountability: the Chamber, standing committees, and select committees.

THE CHAMBER

The major set-piece debates in the Commons provide opportunities for Ministers to inform the House of their intentions and to defend their actions, and for the Opposition and back-benchers on either side to criticise, to question, to seek more information, whether the occasion is a Government or an Opposition motion, part of the legislative process, or more generally.

It is on the floor of the House that the great events take place, where Ministers should ultimately be brought to account, where their political lives may be threatened, where they will be supported or abandoned by their colleagues and held to blame, fairly or unfairly. The reputations of Ministers, and of shadow Ministers, are enhanced or diminished by their performances in the Chamber. It is on the floor of the House that the crucial issues are finally decided, even the continuance in office of Governments.

But although the floor of the House is an effective place for debating the large issues on great occasions and may be a severe test for Ministers, even for Governments, debates on most occasions put Ministers under little pressure. They are protected by the traditional style of debate, by procedural rules that limit interruption and questioning, by departmental briefing which covers the points likely to be raised, by the majority of Government supporters available for vocal assistance and for divisions, and by the agreements made through the usual channels which minimise unexpected developments in the course of debate. So long as Ministers carry their back-benchers with them, although they can not evade accountability, they can avoid the fullest penalties for failure.

The physical characteristics of the Chamber, the rules of procedure, and the traditions combine to produce a pattern of proceedings where, for most of the time, set speeches are made from both sides. It is expected that Ministers will reply to points made in the debate but they cannot be obliged to do so and, save during Question time, the debate is not one of cut and thrust. A Member who is addressing the House is under no obligation to give way to a questioner (it is otherwise in the Lords) and if he does so the answer he gives is unlikely to be informative. From time to time Members become angry and obstructive and orderly practice collapses until the Speaker or chairman is able to restore an atmosphere in which Members can be heard.

Opinions are expressed and disagreements registered. Discussion certainly takes place but accountability is achieved only at this most general level. The positions of the two sides, their divergencies and convergencies on policy, are set down both for the present and as the bases for more detailed discussion in the future. The set pieces on the floor of the House are conducted as adversarial encounters and most resemble election campaigns carried on by other means.

The result is that many words are spoken, few of which are intended to persuade the other side and virtually none of which succeeds in doing so. The hope is that some of the words will reach the public outside through the press, television and radio. Each political party, in or out of office, seeks to create a climate of opinion favourable to its policies and unfavourable to those of the other parties. Each party is heavily dependent on the media for conveying its messages, which are variously publicised. Something of what is said on the floor of both Houses by the principal speakers is likely to be reported in some form or another. This is what gives Parliament its ultimate influence.

One of the advantages for the general public of the committee stage of controversial bills being debated in committee of the whole House of Commons is that the proceedings are likely to receive more press coverage. A recent example is that the Official Secrets Bill 1988–89. Lengthy debates in the Commons on such matters as the demand for a public interest defence were widely reported. (No doubt another reason for the coverage was the special interest of the press in the subject). Many of those who took part had wide experience, some as former Ministers. They included several Privy Councillors and some Government back-benchers, as critics of the bill. The function of the House of Commons as a debating chamber was fulfilled. But attendance was thin and only those few amendments moved by Ministers were adopted. The arguments and the criticisms were recorded and became part of the continuing history of the conflict between the demands of national security and of access to information.

Proposals for reform of proceedings on the floor of the House of Commons have been few. There are complaints that the shortness of debate on specific matters, such as the second reading of a bill, sometimes means that not all Members who wish to speak have an opportunity to do so.[1] The precedence given to Ministers, Opposition spokesmen and Privy Councillors means that opportunities for other Members to participate in debates on the floor of the Commons are restricted. The Speaker has said that if he is entirely fair "the average Member will be called four times a year." He added that during the 1983–87 Parliament he had witnessed 19 speeches when back-benchers had swung Commons debate by the force of their argument.[2] Given the nature and purpose of these debates it is not surprising that the number of these occasions is no greater.

Other opportunities for back-benchers arise at Question time, on adjournment debates and private Members' bills and motions, but some of these have to be ballotted for.

The position of back-benchers is a reflection of the central political realities that the House of Commons is dominated by the party conflict and by the Government majority. Although as much as a third of the time on the floor of the House is devoted to business initiated by back-benchers, the party conflict ensures that the rest of the time is taken by the principal gladiators on the two sides of the House. The Government majority ensures that the outcome of the debate is, on almost every occasion, known in advance; and this, inevitably, shapes the contents of the speeches. These realities in their turn determine the extent to which the role of Parliament is fulfilled.

STANDING COMMITTEES

The principal criticisms of proceedings in standing committee on Government bills stem from the style of debate. The process by way of debates on

---

[1] Some 73 Members applied to the Speaker to take part in the second reading on the Shops Bill 1985–86; see Second Report from the Select Committee on Procedure H.C. 350 of 1986–87 para. 6.

[2] See analysis by Anthony Bevins in *The Independent* newspaper of May 16, 1988, drawing in part on an interview with the Speaker on London Weekend Television during the previous week.

numerous amendments or on the clauses of the bill is undoubtedly time-consuming. As we have seen, on controversial bills the likelihood of an Opposition amendment being immediately successful is remote. But assurances from Ministers that particular provisions will not be used in particular ways may be obtained (though the value of such assurances is uncertain) or Ministers may be persuaded to re-consider the provisions. Sometimes, even on controversial bills, the detailed examination in standing committee produces significant amendments under pressure from the Opposition, supported by opinions expressed by extra-parliamentary bodies. Other major Government bills may be pushed through without any Opposition or back-bench amendments being successfully moved.

Much of the recent discussion has centred on the timetabling of bills and on the modification of procedure so as to permit witnesses to be called. We have discussed these matters on pages 306–307 and 318.

One undeniable effect of the procedure in standing committees on controversial Government bills is that Ministers are forced to defend the provisions in detail and, out of this, additional information about the Government's intentions may be obtained and the ability of Ministers to withstand criticism is tested.

SELECT COMMITTEES

In Chapter 11 we discussed some of the matters considered by the departmentally-related select committees and the extent to which their reports had influenced Governments. On their overall effectiveness there is disagreement which flows from different views of their purpose and their potential.

If we compare these committees with their predecessors there is little doubt that the new committees present a more formidable critical presence to Ministers and departments. With the exception of the Scottish Affairs Committees, all are now in their third Parliament with nearly 10 years almost continuous existence. Despite considerable turnover of membership, the committees have acquired much historical knowledge of how their departments operate. The departments are aware that the committees are most likely to continue to investigate departmental matters for the foreseeable future. There is much evidence to suggest that Ministers and civil servants are influenced in policy-making by the knowledge that what they propose may well come under the scrutiny of these committees and by the very process of committee inquiries. This great gain has not been without price. The nationalised industries (now diminishing in number) have not been subjected to the close scrutiny they had before 1979. And complaints have been made that, in the Commons though not in the Lords, science and technology have not received sufficiently close examination. Also, the Lord Chancellor's Department and the Law Officers remain outside the structure of committees.

To their credit as parliamentary bodies, the committees have managed to achieve a high degree of unanimity in their findings and recommendations. Inevitably this has been more apparent on issues which are not highly controversial between the parties. This has meant that some committees and some chairmen have chosen to avoid some of the big issues of the day or to deal with them in a low key. But even where committees divide sharply, much information has been revealed which would otherwise have been likely to remain hidden. The Foreign Affairs Committee's investigation in 1984–85 into the events surrounding the week-end of May 1–2, 1982 in the

Falkland Islands (the sinking of the Belgrano) is an example of this.[3] Four Opposition Members regularly divided the committee, unsuccessfully moved their own detailed draft report and voted against the report that was finally the report of the committee to the House. Here, the party political factors were too strong for agreement. On the other hand there was unanimity even on some highly charged issues such as those examined by the Defence Committee arising out of the Westland affair.[4]

The Public Accounts Committee, backed by the Comptroller and Auditor General and the National Audit Office, has a high reputation as a financial watchdog. Apart from its numerous reports on separate matters, it has also considered financial reporting to Parliament generally[5] and brought about improvements as a result of its pressure. The Defence Committee has similarly obtained better information on defence projects.[6]

The PAC is sometimes criticised for being insufficiently adventurous, with the suggestion that it should concern itself more with the impact of policies lying behind expenditure. This would bring the C and AG close to questioning the merits of policy objectives which he (though not the PAC) is expressly debarred by statute from doing. It would also bring the PAC into conflict with other select committees, especially the Defence Committee. It has also been suggested that the PAC should consider whether provision of particular public services meets the need for those services.

These and other criticisms may apply to select committees generally. One criticism has been that these committees are not concerned to inquire into objectives, measures of output and performance, impact and results and that this is because Members do not think in management terms, in systems, but focus on events, on happenings, because these are politically the most interesting.[7] The Efficiency Unit reported: "Pressure from Parliament, the Public Accounts Committee, and the media tends to concentrate on alleged impropriety or incompetence, and making political points, rather than on demanding evidence of steadily improving efficiency and effectiveness."[8] But the Treasury and Civil Service Committee said that this comment was "ill-informed" and the committee did not recognise the Unit's view of the work of Parliament and its committees.[9] Others argue that parliamentarians should concentrate on policy issues, not managerial matters.

Many proposals have been made, in the House and outside, to improve the performance of departmentally-related committees. They include the strengthening of their staff so that more hard information can be obtained from sources other than the departments; the right to appoint more sub-committees; and the opportunity for regular debates in the Chamber of committee reports.

The inquiry and the report of the Agriculture Committee into the egg salmonella affair in the spring of 1989 exemplified several of the conflicts within which select committees operate. The committee met with commen-

---

[3] H.C. 11 of 1984–85.

[4] H.C. 518, 519 of 1985–86.

[5] H.C. 98 of 1986–87.

[6] Expenditure on Major Defence Projects: Accountability to the House of Commons: H.C. 340 of 1986–87.

[7] See John Garrett M.P. "Developing state audit in Britain" in 64 Public Administration (Winter 1986) pp. 421–435.

[8] Improving Management in Government: The Next Steps (1988) para. 9.

[9] H.C. 494–I paras. 5, 40.

dable speed after the Parliamentary Under-Secretary of State (Mrs E. Currie) made the statement which led to her resignation. When she declined the committee's invitation to give evidence, the chairman at first appeared to accept this but later, under pressure from the members of the committee, repeated the invitation. When this was declined, the members resolved to put down a motion in the House ordering her attendance, whereupon Mrs. Currie agreed to appear. When she did so, she refused to add to certain statements she had made earlier and the chairman discouraged the committee from pressing her. In the event, opinion was divided whether the committee had shown its strength or she had shown its weakness. The report of the committee was highly critical of Ministers.[10] They rejected the criticism.

Over the period since 1979 when the departmentally-related committees were created, some of them have tested the reactions of Ministers by the way they conducted their inquiries. The Defence Committee tried and failed to call certain civil servants to give evidence in the Westland affair. The Foreign Affairs Committee did not uncover all the facts about the sinking of the Belgrano during the Falklands war. By one means and another, Ministers from time to time successfully block inquiries. But, as we have said, new facts and information which Ministers have sought to conceal do emerge.

Two recent events, which had different outcomes, illustrate the tension that may be created and the co-operation that may be achieved. In late 1988 and early 1989 the Defence Committee began to investigate the future of the Brigade of Gurkhas as a time when the Ministry of Defence was considering its policy. This led to civil servants refusing to answer questions.[11] On the other hand, the Treasury and Civil Service Committee became involved at a very early stage in the discussions on the future of the civil service deriving from the Efficiency Unit's report on The Next Steps. And both Ministers and members of the committee welcomed this.

Party remains the dominant factor in the House of Commons. But as Mr. Biffen said in the debate on the egg industry on March 7, 1989: "in the past decade or more we have seen a situation in which increasingly the power of the Prime Minister dominates the Cabinet and the Executive dominates the House. The traditional means whereby this House has sought to balance the Executive by debates and the normal forms of processing legislation are becoming less and less effective. I do not yet assert that Select Committees can tangibly help to restore that balance but the process is well started and I offer congratulations to my hon. friend and to the members of the Select Committee [on Agriculture]."[12]

CONCLUSION

There can be no clear answer to the question of Parliament's effectiveness. We can say that Parliament does at considerable length discuss a vast range of public and individual constituency matters and seeks constantly to reduce the area that Governments wish to keep secret. And to that extent, it holds Government to account, though imperfectly.

One experienced Member has said: "If we consider what are normally regarded as the proper functions of a Parliament, we are not too bad at the

---

[10] H.C. 108 of 1988–89.
[11] H.C. 68 of 1988–89.
[12] H.C.Deb., Vol. 148, col. 790.

redress of individual grievances; but everyone has to accept that we are not too smart at scrutinising the activities of the Executive, we are absolutely deplorable at controlling Government expenditure, and we have not been too good at producing understandable, workable laws."[13] Some argue that the scrutiny of the Executive has been much enlarged by the operations of the departmentally-related select committees. Others are concerned that the committees have diminished the importance of the Chamber of the House of Commons, that Members are less independent and more "ministerially minded" than formerly, and that this has been fostered by the great increase in the number of parliamentary private secretaries.[14] Others, including some on the Government side of the House, deplore the reluctance of the Government, as they see it, seriously to consider the merits of amendments to Government bills or to respond to criticism.[15] Others observe that parliamentary criticism is still able to force Ministerial resignations.

Much of what we have said in this chapter is as applicable to the House of Lords as it is to the House of Commons. In some specialised areas, such as science and technology and legislative proposals from the European Communities, the Lords scrutinise Government action and inaction more closely than do the Commons. But the outstanding contribution of the Lords in recent years has been the extent to which they have been willing to threaten the Government with the possibility of defeat in divisions and, from time to time, to make that possibility a reality, especially when this has reflected or been matched by similar dissent by Government back-benchers in the Commons. But the Lords lack the political authority, in the great majority of cases, to reject any Government policy firmly insisted on.

The traditions of both Houses are strong and Members and Peers are not particularly interested in major institutional reform.[16] Front-benchers are primarily concerned with policy and political manoeuvrings. Ministers have no wish to improve parliamentary procedure if to do so will make them more accountable. Shadow ministers look forward to the day when they will hold office on the same terms. Most back-benchers try to cultivate particular areas on which they can become expert, rather than seek to assume the heavy mantle of constitutionalists.

The confrontation between Ministers and other Members and Peers is shaped by the politics of party and by the Government's majority in the House of Commons. But although party is the strongest determinant, it is not the sole factor for Members and Peers do not always do as the Whips tell them. Beyond the Whips lie the electorate who will, within a few years or months, decide the immediate political future of Members and of the Government itself. At the heart of the "unwritten" constitution is the requirement in the Bill of Rights for the holding of free and frequent elections which puts the Government under sentence of death from the day of its election. To postpone the operation of that sentence, the Government must persuade the electorate that it is acting in their best interests. And to do that it must publicly process legislative proposals through Parliament, and

[13] H.C.Deb., Vol. 142, col. 801 (November 30, 1988) (Mr. Frank Dobson).
[14] See survey in *The Independent* newspaper March 1, 1989.
[15] See, for example, H.C.Deb., Vol. 147, col. 86 (February 13, 1989) (Mr. E. Heath and Mr. H. Dykes).
[16] For attempts to change this attitude see H.C.Deb., Vol. 144, cols. 647–52 (December 22, 1988) (Mr. Graham Allen).

adequately account in Parliament for its actions. Neither of these two great institutions is complete without the other.

The three main participants in the processes of Parliament—Government, Opposition and back-benchers—have opportunities to initiate debate and to bring forward proposals and issues of their own choosing. These processes also enable the Government to be held to account and the procedures of the two Houses provide formal channels for this purpose. Whether the balance is properly struck between the participants and whether they use their opportunities to the best advantage are major questions for judgment. Our aim in this book has been to provide the facts and the analysis on which others can make their own decisions.

BIBLIOGRAPHY
(revised November 4, 1988)

G. ALDERMAN	British Elections: Myth and Reality (1978)
-do-	Pressure Groups and Government in Great Britain (1984)
A. BARKER & M. RUSH	The Member of Parliament and his Information (1970)
R. L. BORTHWICK & J. E. SPENCER (ed.)	British Politics in Perspective (1984)
L. BLOM-COOPER & G. DREWRY	Final Appeal (1972)
K. A. BRADSHAW & D.A.M. PRING	Parliament and Congress (1982)
P.A. BROMHEAD	The House of Lords and Contemporary Politics 1911–57 (1958)
D. BUTLER (ed.)	Coalitions in British Politics (1978)
D. BUTLER	Governing without a Majority (1983)
D. BUTLER & G. BUTLER	British Political Facts 1900–1985 (1986)
D. BUTLER & D. KAVANAGH	The British General Election of 1979 (1980) The British General Election of 1983 (1984) The British General Election of 1987 (1988)
B. CASTLE	The Castle Diaries 1964–70 (1984) and 1974–76 (1980)
R.H.S. CROSSMAN	The Diaries of a Cabinet Minister, Vol. 1 (1975), Vol. 2 (1976), Vol. 3 (1977)
-do-	Inside View (1972)
-do-	Introduction to W. Bagehot *The English Constitution* (1964)
M. DAVIES	Politics of Pressure: The Art of Lobbying (1985)

DOD'S PARLIAMENTARY COMPANION

B. DONOGHUE	Prime Minister (1987)
G. DREWRY (ed.)	The New Select Committees (1988)
G. DREWRY & J. BROCK	The Impact of Women on the House of Lords (1983)
D.J.T. ENGLEFIELD	Commons Select Committee (1984)
-do-	Parliament and Information (1981)
-do-	Whitehall and Westminster (1985)
N. FISHER	The Tory Leaders (1977)
V. FLEGMAN	Called to Account (1980)
-do-	Public Expenditure and the Select Committees of the Commons (1986)

P. GOODHART & U. BRANSTON	The 1922 (1973)
J.A.G. GRIFFITH	Parliamentary Scrutiny of Government Bills (1974)
A. HEATH, R. JOWELL & J. CURTICE	How Britain Votes (1985)
P. HENNESSY	Cabinet (1986)
R.F.V. HEUSTON	Lives of the Lord Chancellors 1940–70 (1987)
C. & D.L. JONES (ed.)	Peers, Politics and Power: The House of Lords 1603–1911 (1986)
D. JUDGE	Backbench Specialisation in the House of Commons (1981)
D. JUDGE (ed.)	The Politics of Parliamentary Reform (1983)
A. KING (ed.)	The British Prime Minister (1985)
P. LAUNDY	The Office of Speaker in Parliaments of the Commonwealth (1984)
LORD LONGFORD	A History of the House of Lords (1988)
P. LOWE and T. GOYDER	Environmental Groups in Politics (1983)
D. MARSH (ed.)	Pressure Politics (1983)
G. MARSHALL	Constitutional Conventions (1984)
T. ERSKINE MAY	Parliamentary Practice (20 edn. 1983)
C.H. McILWAIN	The High Court of Parliament and its Supremacy (1910)
C. MELLORS	The British M.P. (1978)
D.R. MIERS & A.C. PAGE	Legislation (1982)
C. MILLER	Lobbying Government (1987)
J. MORGAN	The House of Lords and the Labour Government 1964–70 (1975)
F. MORRELL	From the Electors of Bristol (1977)
P. NORTON	The Commons in Perspective (1981)
-do-	Conservative Dissidents (1978)
-do-	The Constitution in Flux (1982)
-do-	Dissension in the House of Commons 1945–74 (1975)
-do-	Dissension in the House of Commons 1974–79 (1980)
P. NORTON (ed.)	Parliament in the 1980s (1985)
P. NORTON & A. AUGHEY	Conservatives and Conservatism (1981)
M. PHILLIPS	The Divided House: Women and Westminster (1980)

L.O. PIKE	Constitutional History of the House of Lords (1984)
C. PONTING	The Right to Know (1985)
M.H. PORT	The Houses of Parliament (1976)
E.J. POWELL and K. WALLIS	The House of Lords in the Middle Ages (1968)
T. PROSSER	Nationalised Industry and Policy Control (1986)
L. RADICE, E. VALLANCE & V. WILLIS	Member of Parliament (1987)
P.G. RICHARDS	Honourable Members (1959)
J.J. RICHARDSON & A.G. JORDAN	Government Under Pressure (1985)
M. RUSH & M. SHAW	The House of Commons Services and Facilities (1974)
M. RUSH (ed.)	The House of Commons Services and Facilities 1972–1982 (1983)
M. RUSH	Parliament and the Public (1978)
M. RYLE & P.G. RICHARDS (eds.)	The Commons Under Scrutiny (1988)
B. SEDGEMORE	The Secret Constitution (1980)
D.R. SHELL	The House of Lords (1988)
P. SILK & R.H. WALTERS	How Parliament Works (1987)
C. TURPIN	British Government and the Constitution (1985)

VACHER'S PARLIAMENTARY COMPANION

LORD WADE	Behind the Speaker's Chair (1978)
S.A. WALKLAND (ed)	The House of Commons in the Twentieth Century (1979)
S. WILLIAMS	Conflict of Interest: The Ethical Dilemma in Politics (1985)
A. YOUNG	The Re-selection of MPs (1983)

INDEX